MW01014964

LOST TOWNS
of
TIDEWATER
MARYLAND

To my dear friend
Dave Fogle
Best wishes,
Don Shomette

Other Books by the Author

Ghost Fleet of Mallows Bay and Other Tales of the Lost Chesapeake

Tidewater Time Capsule: History Beneath the Patuxent

The Hunt for H.M.S. De Braak: *Legend and Legacy*

Raid on America: The Dutch Naval Campaign of 1672–1674

Pirates on the Chesapeake

The Othello Affair

Shipwrecks on the Chesapeake

Flotilla: Battle for the Patuxent

London Town: A Brief History

Shipwrecks of the Civil War:
The Encyclopedia of Union and Confederate Naval Losses

LOST TOWNS
of
TIDEWATER
MARYLAND

DONALD G. SHOMETTE

TIDEWATER PUBLISHERS
CENTREVILLE, MARYLAND

Copyright © 2000 by Tidewater Publishers

All rights reserved. No part of this book may be used or reproduced in any manner whatsoever without written permission except in the case of brief quotations embodied in critical articles and reviews. For information, address Tidewater Publishers, Centreville, Maryland 21617.

Library of Congress Cataloging-in-Publication Data

Shomette, Donald.
    Lost towns of Tidewater Maryland / Donald G. Shomette. — 1st ed.
        p. cm.
    Includes bibliographical references and index.
    ISBN 0-87033-527-8 (hc)
    1. Maryland—Politics and government—To 1775. 2. Maryland—History—Colonial period, ca. 1600–1775. 3. Maryland—History, Local. 4. City planning—Maryland—History—17th century. 5. City planning—Maryland—History—18th century. 6. Cities and towns—Maryland—History—17th century. 7. Cities and towns—Maryland—History—18th century. I. Title.

F184 .S56 2000
975.2'02—dc21
                                                                                        00-058957

Page v: The Roman Catholic chapel, erected ca. 1695 by Henrietta Marie Bennett Lloyd on Chapel Cove at the site of old Wye Town (later Doncaster), as it appears on an early plat. Courtesy Delaware State Museums, Dover, Delaware.
Page viii: St. Ignatius Church, Chapel Point, Maryland, 1997.

Illustrative material not otherwise credited was drawn or photographed by Donald G. Shomette.

Manufactured in the United States of America
First edition, 2000

For Lanie, Julian, and Tristan

There is a community of spirit.
Join it, and feel the delight
of walking in the noisy street,
and being the noise.
—*Rumi*

CONTENTS

⚜ PREFACE

The late afternoon shadow cast over the landscape by the steeple of St. Ignatius Church was thin but well defined on that frigid December day when I paid my first visit to Chapel Point, Maryland. I had discovered the church majestically ensconced upon the crest of a precipitous hill overlooking the entrance to one of the state's most historic waterways, the Port Tobacco River. As the sun eased below the horizon, from my perch on the slope I could plainly see the headwaters of the little rill below being slowly swallowed by the mist of oncoming evening. It was a scene of utter tranquillity.

At the entrance to the church I found a weathered historical marker, grayed and all but indecipherable after years of exposure, yet still capable of informing the accidental tourist of the historical significance of the site. The plaque's almost imperceptibly raised letters told me that the present St. Ignatius was built in 1798, the third successive house of God to occupy this same site since the 1642 foundation of St. Thomas Parish, of which it was the heart and soul. The parish itself had been established by one of Maryland's first pioneers, Father Andrew White, a Jesuit priest of inordinate faith and, thankfully for history, an inveterate chronicler of events. It was a modest marker, for it understated the importance of the church and the hillside graveyard nearby, both of which have over the centuries borne witness to the passage of innumerable momentous events and the actions of countless notable personages. Through the church's hallowed portals had strolled the bearers of many conspicuous southern Maryland family names—Semmes, Posey, and Hamilton—as well as those of Everyman. In its crypts and beneath its monuments rest the bones of hundreds more ancient pedigrees, often divided in loyalties and torn asunder in life by the tumultuous events that shaped Maryland's stormy past. Many fought in colonial battles and rebellions, in the War of Independence, the War of 1812, the Civil War, the War to End All Wars, World War II, and the other conflicts of the nation. Others had tended the fields, shops, and home fires for those away at the front. They had given their allegiances variously to England, the proprietary of the Lords Baltimore, the Confederate States of America, and to the republic. On any given day, scattered throughout this venerable marble orchard and adorning its countless lichen-covered monuments and tombstones, can be seen recently planted flags bearing the stars and bars of the Confederate States of America, nestled beside those bearing the stars and stripes of the Union.

But for all of its rustic, historic patina, there is little left to note that Chapel Point was also one of nearly sevenscore tidewater sites authorized for development as towns and ports in the early days of the Maryland colony. Like most, it had simply slipped into obscurity well before experiencing its full day in the sun. Some among this number had been given birth through proclamations, declarations, and ordinances. Many more had been legislated into all-too-brief existences as ports of entry to facilitate the tobacco or wheat trade. A few were founded first as judicial and governmental centers or as tobacco inspection stations. Apart from the authorized towns, a handful of communities managed to evolve from crossroads settlements, trading hamlets or, like Chapel Point, religious centers. Regardless of their beginnings, some of Maryland's early towns achieved notoriety far beyond their diminutive sizes. Yet, most shared a common end: an early demise and dark oblivion.

The legislative chronicle of seventeenth- and eighteenth-century town and port development in tidewater Maryland is both complex and, at times, perplexing. It is a history laced with proclamations, politics, laws, and acts which, as time and experience eventually proved, often flowed against the grain of rural plantation society in colonial Maryland. The trials and tribulations, experimentation, and speculations concerning the use of controlled urban development as a tool for government and taxation did not begin until a full thirty-four years after Governor Leonard Calvert and his intrepid band of settlers had planted roots on the banks of the St. Mary's River. The effort to erect centralized communities amidst a landscape only recently extracted from a howling wilderness, however, could not long be delayed, for it was also a psychological need of a transplanted European civilization that had no frontiers of its own to create them. It is not surprising that the founding fathers sought to fill the vastness of tidewater Maryland with centers of order to bring a sense of mastery, community, and belonging to the New World as much as to establish an economic base. Peopled by émigrés who were often unskilled and disposable in the Old World and who had come willing to work while searching for roots, opportunity, or religious freedom, the colony was from the beginning a place that endorsed diffusion and independence rather than centralization and dependence. Though the colony was increasingly reliant upon slaves for labor to fuel a single-crop economy, the framers of the early towns and ports legislation were unwilling to accept a sense of place in the tidewater as it developed on its own. Instead, they sought to change the order of rural plantation society to suit their concepts of a world as it should be. In laying out the mundane grids they called towns (often placed on the map more because of political pull than simple logic), they struggled to cling to essentially old ways and concepts. The realities demanded by the tobacco-based economy that dominated the lives and fortunes of every Maryland colonist were largely ignored.

In the numerous edicts and laws decreeing that towns and ports be erected almost overnight can be discerned a recital of flawed concepts founded in tradition rather than reason, in manifestos rather than geography, and in a stubborn belief in the supremacy of man over the forces of nature. Colonial officials, bound by models of the mother society of England as well as late feudal and Renaissance Europe, repeatedly attempted to swim against the tide. They doggedly persevered in their endeavors to erect towns despite natural, economic, social, and topographic realities that doomed most to short lives and ultimate collapse as urban centers. Many of these unpretentious towns died aborning, some in precise syncopation with the silting up of the protected waterways upon which they had been erected. Some succumbed to pressures that were governed by frequently fickle legislative attempts to improve upon the foundations of a one-crop economy. A few survived only to fall victim to the ravages of war, most notably during the periods of the American Revolution and the War of 1812. A handful managed to achieve maturity, only to die of political chicanery, the realignment of regional road systems, or from the redirection and centralization of trade to the great port of Baltimore. A scant few lived long enough to witness the arrival of the industrial age, steamboats, the great inland canal systems, and the railroad before gasping their last. The amazing thing is that in the weaning-out process, some survived, and a few achieved metropolitan status.

Although the new town programs were not considered an experiment at the time of their inception, between 1668 and 1751, an experiment they were indeed. With no less than 130 towns and ports established by legislative fiat or authorized by the Lord Proprietor to be erected, the colony of Maryland was subjected to an urban development program unrivaled in scope by any other colony except Virginia. It was, unfortunately, an endeavor which sought to impose the structure of European community on a wholly unwelcoming environment and which engaged a frequently hostile plantation society that resisted the most arduous efforts of both the proprietary and royal governments. Today, only fourteen of the original towns established by decree or acts of legislation survive as cities or towns of any note—Annapolis, Baltimore, Oxford, Bladensburg, Charlestown, Prince Frederick, Leonardtown, Salisbury, Princess Anne, Upper Marlboro, Chestertown, Snow Hill, Vienna, and Benedict. The roll call of those that failed or were later reincarnated into urban centers under the same or another name are legion: Aire, Battle Town, Beckwiths Island, Bennet's Land, Breton Bay, Bridgetown, Bristol, Broad Creek, Bush, Canterbury Town, Cecil Town, Chaptico, Charlestown, Dangyes Point, Dorchester Town, Elk Ridge Landing, Fredericktown, Georgetown, Gloucester Town, Green Hill, Gunpowder, Hallowing Point, Hunting Town, Islington, John Wests, Joppa, Kilkenny, Kings Town, Little Yarmouth, London Town, Lower Marlboro, Magothy, Milford Town, Nanjemoy, New Yarmouth, Newport, Newtown, Nottingham, Ogletown, Pig Point, Piles Fresh, Piscataway Town, Plymouth, Pooles Island, Port Tobacco, Prices Neck, Pukewaxen, Queen Anne's Town, St. Clement's Town, St. George's Town, St. Jerome's Town, St. Leonards Town, St. Mary's City, Sassafras Town, Shrewsbury, Spesutie, Stumpneck Town, Swetenham's, Talbot Town, West River Town, Westwood, Worton, Wye Town, York, and many, many more.

Within the pages of a single book, it would be impossible to present the histories of every lost tidewater town or port, either those that were created in the many new town programs or those that developed on their own during the early colonial period. Thus, I have sought to provide an overview of the complex legislative sequence that gave birth to scores of towns and ports in tidewater Maryland and to present the histories of ten that I believe form a representative cross-section of all: nine are from the town development group and one, Frenchtown, evolved from a crossroads settlement. Each was also unique in the manner in which it was given birth, matured, and finally expired. All of the towns I have addressed ultimately failed for a variety of reasons, but unlike some towns founded by mindless legislation, each had flickered into existence against all odds and actually flourished before disappearing into the twilight of antiquity or being reborn as an entirely different urban entity. As a consequence of their eventful but often truncated lives, the fortunes and future of tidewater Maryland society were molded.

In researching this book, I have been fortunate to follow in the wake of some remarkable pioneers. I have been influenced and guided by the works of a few intrepid researchers, historians, and archaeologists who, though generally unheralded, long ago delved into the history of the lesser-known but no less important sites, towns, and ports in Maryland. Fortunately, the histories of many forgotten Maryland sites have been more than adequately told in a handful of county histories and in individual form; they have stood the test of time and are not likely to be eclipsed soon. They have proved to be both inspirational and educational for me, and I am deeply indebted to those authors and historians who have led the way. I am particularly grateful to John W. Reps, whose pioneering work, *Tidewater Towns,* has set the standard by which all subsequent works on urban development in the colonial era will be judged. Clayton Torrence's classic history *Old Somerset* documents the stories of Annemessex Town, Somerset Town, Chips Landing, Tipquin, Ballards, Mudford, Oyster Neck, Rehoboth Town, and Snow Hill in an analytical fashion that must serve as the archetype for any historian of colonial town development to emulate. Oswald Tilghman's *History of Talbot County,* George Johnston's *History of Cecil County,* Louise Joyner Hienton's *Prince George's Heritage,* and C. Milton Wright's *Our Harford Heritage* have also addressed in admirable fashion the new town programs in their own counties and have been more than useful in helping this author to understand the tortured road that each new town act was obliged to follow. Individual town histories have also proved to be exemplary models: "New Yarmouth, a Town of a Vanished Era, 1675–1697," by Robert L. Swain, Jr.; "Port Tobacco, Lost Town of Maryland," by Ethel Roby Hayden; the history of Elk Ridge Landing in *The Patapsco: Baltimore's River of History,* by Paul J. Travers; the accounts of Kingston, Doncaster, Dover, and York in *Ghost Towns of Talbot County,* by James C. Mullikan; and the study of Piscataway Town in *Piscataway Park, Maryland,* by Anna Coxe Toogood.

   The written history of urban planning is, of course, not the only means for developing a greater understanding of tidewater Maryland's colonial development. Within the last thirty-five years major strides have been taken in examining the archaeological record of early town and port sites throughout the state. In 1966 the Maryland General Assembly authorized the formation of the St. Mary's City Commission to "preserve, develop, and maintain . . . historic St. Mary's City and environs." As a result, the excellent ongoing historical and archaeological research program, rediscovering the hitherto lost and forgotten site of Lord Baltimore's first capital, continues to measurably increase our knowledge of early town planning in colonial America. Another exceptional program of significant importance is the Annapolis Archaeology Project, sponsored by the University of Maryland and Historic Annapolis Foundation, Inc., which systematically examines important components of that city's unwritten heritage. This landmark project has produced not only a wonderful slice-of-life view of a colonial municipality and seaport, but a greater understanding of class and race, in the seventeenth- and eighteenth-century capital of the Maryland colony. The Lost Towns of Anne Arundel County Project, spawned by the discovery of early seventeenth-century artifacts in Burle's Field on the Severn River in 1991, has generated extensive research into the vanished towns of Providence, London Town, and Herring Town. And the superlative ongoing archaeological investigation by the Maryland National Capital Park and Planning Commission at Mount Calvert in Prince George's County has continued to yield exciting new data on the extinct riverport of Charlestown, the county's first seat of government. Less-publicized but no less important investigations have also been carried out to locate and assess the archaeological importance of the lost towns of Warrington, Harvey Town, St. Leonards Town, and Old Baltimore. I am indebted to all of these programs and to the gifted men and women who work on them, wrenching from the soils the physical fragments of the past to enhance the historic record.

   It would be impossible to thank the many individuals at the major institutions who lent assistance to me during the years that have been consumed in the research and writing of this work, which began in 1986. I would at least like to acknowledge a conspicuous few. Among this number are counted the superb staffs of the Maryland State Archives in Annapolis, the Maryland Historical Society in Baltimore, the Local History and Genealogy Section and the Manuscript Division of the Library of Congress in Washington, D.C., and the Cecil County Historical Society. I am also indebted to Paul Berry, Librarian of the Calvert Marine Museum; Linda Collins and Anne F. Whisman, Archivists for the Calvert County Historical Society; and Susan Pearl of the Maryland National Capital Park and Planning Commission. Without their invaluable assistance, this book would have been substantially deficient.

   I would also like to thank Louise and Terry Van Gilder, proprietors of the Kitty Knight House in Georgetown, Maryland, for permitting me access to the Kitty Knight Collection. Susan Hance Wells deserves a note of appreciation for permitting access to one of the most wonderful and historic properties in Maryland, the Taney House estate on Battle Creek.

An archaeologist digs into history at the site of colonial Charles Town, the first—and largely forgotten—county seat of Prince George's County. Courtesy *Bay Weekly,* Deale, Maryland.

Fred Tutman provided important assistance in my research on Queen Anne's Town. I am indebted to my friend and colleague Bern Waterman for providing me with important information on the history of railroading in the tidewater. And a special acknowledgment must be extended to Harry Brooke Watkins for so freely sharing with a complete stranger his wonderful life story, which has so enriched this book.

In an effort to investigate firsthand in the field as many of the tidewater Maryland town sites as possible, I have been accompanied and ably assisted by a number of intrepid colleagues who have helped me bridge the gap between the archival and the archaeological records. Dr. Ralph E. Eshelman, Dr. Fred W. Hopkins, Jr., Bill Clark, Carl Sheffel, Pete Ferguson, my brother Dale E. Shomette, and my wife Carol Shomette deserve special thanks for helping me hack through the brush of overgrown sites or dive beneath the muddy waters of rivers and Bay to touch the past.

I would like to thank my friend and mentor, Dr. Arthur Pierce Middleton, for his critical reading of sections of the manuscript while in progress. His work and dedication to a better understanding of history have long served as an inspiration and beacon for me, for which I am deeply grateful.

Finally, a word about the text and illustrative matter. As the prevalence of archaic spellings, random capitalizations, irregular abbreviations, and lack of formal punctuation in many early letters, documents, and publications cited herein can make reading a chore rather than a pleasure, I have attempted to ease the burden: I have modified spelling, capitalization, abbreviation, and punctuation to reflect more current usage. Excerpts from seventeenth-, eighteenth-, and nineteenth-century documents that normally would be presented in their original form, errors and all, have been made more readable without losing the flavor that such materials can add to the story. Several salient exceptions remain, in order to prevent loss of context. Those who wish to examine the original source material will find bibliographic reference notes to guide them. Owing to the fragility and frequent illegibility of most original plats of town sites discussed herein, traits that do not lend themselves to adequate reproduction in many cases, I have provided accurate redrafts taken from several original plans to help the reader navigate. I trust you will find the voyage worthwhile. I certainly have.

LOST TOWNS
of
TIDEWATER
MARYLAND

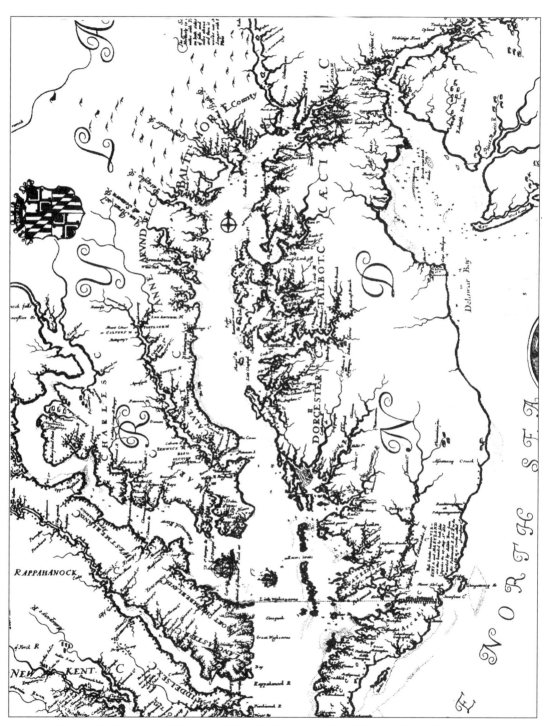

Augustine Herrman's famous map *Virginia and Maryland*, completed in 1670 but published in 1673, was commissioned by Lord Baltimore to encourage immigration to Maryland. This map is one of the earliest to indicate the new towns and plantations of tidewater Maryland and Virginia with reasonable accuracy. Courtesy Library of Congress, Washington, D.C.

INTRODUCTION

"A fit place . . . to seat a town"

On the bleak morning of St. Cecilia's Day, November 22, 1633, twenty-five-year-old Leonard Calvert, filled with anxiety and hope, stood nervously at the rail of the good ship *Ark.* His eyes scanned the snug little English harbor of Cowes on the Isle of Wight, perhaps for the last time in his life. He then turned to his ship's tiny companion, the forty-ton pinnace *Dove,* and he must have wondered about the sanity of the great odyssey he and nearly two hundred fellow adventurers were about to begin. The safe crossing of the great Atlantic Ocean aboard the two diminutive vessels was just the start, for it was to be followed by the settling of an untamed wilderness frontier inhabited by pagans and wild beasts. The settlers hoped to establish an entirely new society, the likes of which had never been seen in the New World: a community of religious toleration where all people would enjoy the right to freely worship as they pleased. The colony was to take the form of an individual proprietorship under the management and total command of Leonard's elder brother, Cecil Calvert, the second Lord Baltimore, and it was to be called Maryland after the Catholic consort of King Charles I, Queen Henrietta Marie.

From the beginning, Maryland's fortunes, like those of its neighboring colony of Virginia, were inextricably linked to the water. Yet, unlike Virginia, which was begun as a corporate endeavor and had come perilously close to failure as a consequence, Lord Baltimore's colony was to be established along entirely centralized governmental lines. Cecil had benefited from the efforts of his late father, George Calvert, the first Lord Baltimore, who had secured a patent granted by Charles I to a vast territory lying along the Chesapeake Bay between the Potomac River on the south and the fortieth parallel on the north. The Calverts had learned from a generation of harsh reality—George's own failed colonizing attempts at Avalon in Newfoundland and the brutal experiences of the Virginia Company, which had nearly abandoned its own American venture altogether. Thus, the Maryland colonists, ably led by Leonard (who was to serve as governor), came well-outfitted with the necessities of civilization: weapons to use for hunting and fighting, tools to clear and cultivate the land and to build homes, and Bibles to tend to their spiritual needs and to help tame the natives. And they had a plan.

The Calverts were a Catholic family, members of a minority religion in a hostile Protestant nation. Yet, in faithful keeping with Cecil's policy of toleration, their efforts to enroll potential colonists did not arbitrate against Protestants. Now, outfitted with a set of instructions drawn up by the Lord Proprietor himself, *Ark* and *Dove* raised anchor and finally set sail upon a gentle east wind. The great adventure had begun.

Lord Baltimore's instructions on just how the settlement of Maryland was to proceed were comprehensive in scope. Among the first objectives upon arrival in the new land were the selection of a fit place "to settle the plantation" and the establishment of an appropriate site for a fort, within which was to be built a "convenient house, and a church or a chapel" for the "seat of his Lordship or his Governor or other Commissioners." A plat of the buildings and their situation (or if not completed, that which was intended) was to be sent to him at the earliest opportunity. He also ordered that "they likewise make choice of a fit place near unto it to seat a town."[1]

The instructions specifically defined the manner in which the town was to be erected:

> That they cause all the planters to build their houses in as decent and uniform a manner as their abilities and the place will afford, and near adjoining one to the other, and for that purpose to cause streets to be marked out where they intend to place the town and to oblige every man to build one by another according to that rule and that they cause divisions of land to be made adjoining on the back sides of their houses and to be assigned unto them for gardens and such uses according to the proportion of everyones building and adventure and as the conveniency of the place will afford which his Lordship referreth to their discretion, but is desirous to have a particular account from them what they do in it, that his Lordship may be satisfied that every man hath justice done unto him.[2]

On February 27, 1634, after a most trying and eventful voyage, *Ark* and *Dove* finally came to anchor off Point Comfort, Virginia. Less than a week later, they pressed northward and soon encountered a great river. "The Thames," recorded Father Andrew White, a Jesuit priest accompanying the expedition, "seems a mere rivulet in comparison with it." The majestic stream was not disfigured with any swamps, "but had firm lands on both sides. Fine groves of trees appear, unchoked by briers or bushes and undergrowth, but growing at intervals as if planted by the hand of man, so that you can drive a four-horse carriage, wherever you choose, through the midst of trees."[3] The river, of course, was the Potomac, and the land along its northern shore was to be the new colony of Maryland.

The company soon put ashore at a small islet which was dubbed Heron Island because of the great number of birds upon it. On this cedar- and sassafras-covered rise (later renamed St. Clement's Island) on the day of the Annunciation, 1634, the first Catholic Mass in English America was celebrated. Afterward, the company ceremoniously took upon their shoulders a great cross hewn from a tree, and "advancing in order to the appointed place, with the assistance of the governor and his associates and the other Catholics, we erected a trophy to Christ the Saviour, humbly reciting, on our bended knees, the Litanies of the Sacred Cross, with great emotion."[4]

Then, Governor Calvert proceeded to explore another eighteen leagues of the Potomac as far as the seat of the Piscataway Indians, taking Captain Henry Fleet, a grizzled Virginia fur trader intimately familiar with the great river, as his guide aboard *Dove*. Upon their return, Fleet guided the colonists into a tributary river on the north side of the Potomac. "At its mouth," reported Father White, "are two harbors, capable of containing three hundred ships of the largest size." One was consecrated to St. George and the other to the Virgin Mary. Upon the west bank of the St. Mary's River dwelled the king of the peaceful Yaocomaco Indians. To avoid consternation among the natives, the company landed upon the east bank. Soon, negotiations were opened between the two peoples culminating in the purchase of thirty miles of land from the natives in exchange for axes, hatchets, rakes, and cloth.[5]

Well aware that spring was coming and the planting season was at hand, Calvert moved quickly to pick a site on the eastern shore of the St. Mary's, one that was fertile, level, substantially elevated above the water, and generally suitable for a town. So far, Lord Baltimore's instructions regarding settlement had been well followed. But as for his directive to "send a plat of what they intend to do," Leonard Calvert either failed to follow through or the plat was later destroyed or lost. Thus, few descriptions of the early settlement survive, aside from Calvert's own reports. The colonists, who had managed to land without native opposition, were diligent in following Baltimore's instructions. Soon, they were seated less than half a mile from the river within a palisaded fort of 120 square yards in extent, with four flanks. A single piece of ordnance and six small antipersonnel weapons, called "murthers" or murderers, were mounted at "convenient" locations along its walls. Nearby, probably on Mill Creek, a watermill was built to grind corn.[6] Dwellings were built on the lands surrounding the fort, and a loosely knit village of sorts slowly began to take shape.

It was the first glimmer of urban development in Lord Baltimore's colony and the beginnings of a process destined to be long, complicated, and troublesome. Maryland would eventually have its towns and villages as Cecil Calvert had desired, but it would have to weather years of turmoil and growth, economic development, and population expansion before it was ready. Not for the next thirty-four years would the colony be ready to even consider the establishment of formal towns and ports. When it finally did, it would embark upon nearly a century of experimentation and testing in the cauldron of urban evolution perhaps without equal in colonial America. In the process, many towns would fall by the wayside and die.

Summer 1668. The first colonywide "new towns" program, as the legislative efforts came to be known in the Maryland proprietary, had lain dormant for decades, alive only in the fertile imagination of Cecil Calvert, who patiently awaited the seasoning of his colony. As the years passed, Maryland would suffer from revolts and invasions, pirates and pests. Tobacco would become its staple crop, indeed, its only crop. The manorial plantation system that would develop to sustain it would prove to be the blessing and affliction of the colony—and the repeated efforts at new town development within it—until the onset of the American Revolution. The tobacco planters scattered throughout the tidewater, usually along the banks of its waterways, were a self-reliant, independent lot who rapidly became accustomed to doing business directly with shipmasters at their own wharves and landings, making it impossible for the government to effectively monitor or regulate trade, prohibit smuggling, or even begin to manage the commerce of the colony. But the time had come, and the means for breaking the back of planter intransigence toward proprietary controls lay in the establishment of formal port towns, checkpoints through which all commerce would be required to pass. When Lord Baltimore issued instructions to his son Charles (who had become governor of the young colony following the death of Leonard Calvert) to establish formal ports for the importation of goods, he could not have foreseen the years of trial and error that lay ahead before his vision would finally be realized.

The actual beginning of the new towns program seemed modest enough. On June 5, 1668, in accordance with his father's directive and after consultation with his own council, Charles Calvert delivered a proclamation regarding the designation of specific places for the unloading and selling of all goods and merchandise imported into the province. The move was not taken without serious forethought, for it was the first intentional effort since 1634 to establish formal urban centers throughout adolescent Maryland, and it would influence the manner in which commerce and trade would be carried out ever after. Or so it was hoped.

For all of its importance, the actual directive was surprisingly brief and to the point. Baltimore's instructions to Calvert called for him

To make, erect & constitute within this province such & so many sea ports, harbors, creeks & other places for discharge & unlading of such goods & merchandises out of ships, boats and other vessels in such and so many places & with such rights, jurisdictions, liberties & privileges unto the said ports belonging as some shall seem most expedient.[7]

The proclamation was clear in its intent: eleven locations throughout the colony were designated as places for the off-loading of merchandise and other trade into the province; this would provide an adequate means for taxation on imports. After August 20, masters of all vessels bringing goods and merchandise into Maryland would be prohibited from unloading any cargo, or selling, bartering, or trading with any inhabitants except at the appointed ports or places. Violators would be strictly punished, usually by imprisonment for a year without bail. Moreover, as a deterrent to traders seeking to avoid detection by surreptitiously conducting their business with planters, the decree also stated that any inhabitant purchasing goods from ships that had not unloaded in the designated ports was not to be legally liable to pay for them.[8]

The edict appears to have fallen upon deaf ears, for on April 20, 1669, it was replaced by "An Ordinance of the Right Honble the Lord Proprietary of this Province of Maryland for the erecting of several Ports within the same." The intention of the new directive was much the same as that of 1668, albeit with the expansion from controlling only the off-loading of merchandise to including the on-loading of cargoes for export. The new order provided the proprietary government, for the first time, with a mechanism to maintain adequate records regarding trade and to manage and tax exports and imports as necessary. There were to be no exceptions, unless expressly authorized by Lord Baltimore or his heirs, their lieutenants, or the governors of the province. This time, a total of twelve sites were designated as "the sole and only seaports, havens, stations, creeks and places" authorized for loading and unloading, five of which were the same as cited in the 1668 proclamation. Each site was to be considered an "overt" mart, where public markets were to be established and where the sale of imported goods could be conducted. The ordinance was to go into effect on July 20.[9] Interestingly, at least six of the designated sites were mentioned for the first time in conjunction with "town land," indicating that as a consequence of the 1668 proclamation, or possibly even before it, several counties had already taken up property to be used for development.

The 1669 instruction was no more successful than the 1668 proclamation, for two years later the basic provisions of both ordinances were again repeated in a declaration issued on June 30. Acting under the impression that more was better, the proprietor this time named a total of fifteen sites. Six were among the original places designated in the 1668 proclamation, and five more were repeated from new sites mentioned in the 1669 ordinance.[10]

It is uncertain just how many of these early "new towns," twenty-two locations in all, were actually laid out, although by 1671, the groundwork for at least several infant communities, if not towns per se, was certainly extant if not formally established. Only one town site appears to have been formally planned—Calverton (also referred to as Battle Town), which was first designated in the 1669 ordinance to be built on William Berry's lands on Battle Creek in Calvert County. Although the original survey plat has never been located, a later resurvey indicates that it was laid out prior to 1671 with a street sixty feet wide and gridded lots statically placed on a twenty-acre tract. Interestingly, the precise pattern for the capital of the colony at St. Mary's City, established soon after the arrival of the *Ark* and *Dove* in 1634, appears to have followed existing Indian paths and trails, at least until 1672, when the first formal street was laid down. A third town site, this one on the Port Tobacco River, most likely located at or near Chandler's Hope and the Indian village of Potobaco, already possessed a church and a rudimentary settlement but no formal plan.[11]

Documentation regarding the early layouts for other proposed town sites is sparse, but the publications of mapmaker Augustine Herrman and author John Ogilby indicate that at least some survey work had been carried out. With the pledge of a large land grant and the rights and privileges of a manor lord offered by Lord Baltimore as compensation for his services, Herrman had been lured to Maryland specifically to map the Chesapeake. He may have completed his first draft as early as 1661, but it was 1670 when the final version was given to the engraver, William Faithorne, and 1673 when the first edition appeared.[12] The map, entitled *Virginia and Maryland,* showed thirteen town sites, ten of which were named; at least six of them—St. Mary's City, Herrington, Calverton, Arundelton, Baltemore Town [*sic*] (on Bush River), and Somerset Town—were sites designated under the same names or by land names cited in the 1668 and 1689 ordinances. The town of Oxford was not noted as a town by symbol but in name only. It has been suggested by some historians that many of the sites indicated may not have actually existed at the time, and that Herrman merely incorporated locations specified in the various edicts issued by the colony executive.[13] Yet, sites not established in the new town initiatives were also significantly in evidence, which would argue to the contrary. These included the towns of Warrington, Bristol (Charles Town Church?), Harvington, Darrington, and Cecilton. Two sites designated by town symbols but unnamed were noted on the Sassafras River. One may have been the town of Sassafrax, authorized in the 1669 ordinance and located in Cecil County, approximately in the area of modern Ordinary Point; the other was on the south shore of Worton Creek in Kent County, on or near present-day Handy Point. The first of the two unnamed sites might also correspond to a site designated in the 1671 declaration as "Hatton's land" on the Sassafras River; the second might be Jonathan Sibrey's land in Kent County.

In 1671, a year after the completion of Herrman's map but two years before its publication, John Ogilby published a remarkably popular work entitled *America: Being the Latest, and Most Accurate Description of the New World.* Although it has been suggested that Ogilby may have drawn upon information from Herrman's final draft, the author's variations regarding towns indicate otherwise. "There are," he wrote, "foundations laid of towns, more or less in each county, according to his Lordships proclamation, to that effect issu'd forth in the year 1668. In Calvert County, about the River of Patuxent, and in the adjacent Cliffs, are bounds of three towns laid out, one over against Point Patience, call'd Harvington, another in Battle-Creek, call'd Calverton, and a third upon the Cliffs, call'd Herrington, and houses, already built in them, all uniform, and pleasant with streets, and keys on the waterside."[14]

Of the three towns mentioned, only one, Calverton, was created by the 1668 proclamation. Harvington (also later referred to as Harvey Town and Harrington) was indicated as lying in St. Mary's County, opposite Point Patience (not in Calvert County). Herrington, which lay in Anne Arundel County, was almost certainly the site designated in the 1669 and 1671 ordinances as lying on Herring Creek. The town of Warrington, on the cliffs of Calvert, probably in the vicinity of Parker's Creek, was never mentioned in any of the three edicts.

It is unlikely that much actual construction had begun by this date in any of the towns noted in the various ordinances, with the exception of Calverton and possibly St. Mary's City. Yet, it is not surprising that Ogilby's work, errors and all, were replicated almost immediately by European copyists (John Speed for one) who were far from the scene. In

Top: Detail from Augustine Herrman's draft for his map *Virginia and Maryland,* showing the sites of Darinton (Darington) and the first Baltimore Town on the shores of Bush River. Courtesy Library of Congress, Washington, D.C.

Bottom: Detail from John Ogilby's famous map *Noua Terrae-Mariae tabula,* 1671, showing the towns of St. Mary's, Harrington (Harvington), Calverton, and Herrington. Courtesy Library of Congress, Washington, D.C.

1676 Speed reported almost verbatim the same minor errors that Ogilby had, adding only that "There were also some years since in all the rest of the counties the foundations of towns laid, which no doubt by this time are very near, if not altogether completed, particularly in Calvert County near the River Patuxent."[15]

When John Thornton and Robert Greene published *A Mapp of Virginia, Maryland, New-Jersey, New-York & New-England* in 1678, unlike many other copyists, they updated the Herrman map and included new information that was suggestive of the status of town development. Some sites included on the Herrman map had been removed, while others had either diminished or increased in stature as suggested by the presence or absence of town symbols, type size, and the like. For the first time, Oxford was displayed with a town symbol. Other sites indicated by town symbols included Cecilton, Baltemore Town [*sic*], Arundelton, Herrington, Warrington, St. Mary's City, and Bristol. Somerset Town, Darrington, Calverton, and Port Tobacco were indicated only by a name. No other towns were noted, suggesting that some may have progressed in development faster than others and many not at all.[16]

Little forward motion regarding new town development was discernible for the next decade. The early initiative had been generated entirely by the proprietary in an effort to create urban centers almost overnight through decree. No thought was given to the requisites of community life or to societal needs other than those of bettering the upper class's economic viability while providing the tools for governmental controls over trade and commerce. For many reasons these efforts met with minimal success. Population densities remained low throughout the seventeenth century, and settlement patterns were diffuse. Moreover, the innate desire of Lord Baltimore to emulate the "peaceable kingdoms" on the model of the New England townships was simply not suitable for the tobacco-based plantation economy of the Maryland tidewater because the manner of doing business was inimical to the centralization of community life.

Most trade was organized around direct transactions between English shipmasters, planters, and, later on, merchant factors who saw to the importation of goods and servants to the colony in return for the exportation of tobacco. The normal routine required that the ships stop at landings, usually on riverways or naturally protected harbors and embayments. Sloops, flats, or canoes would be used to deliver goods and merchandise where the merchantmen themselves could not go. The small boats could collect tobacco directly from a planter's own landing since overland transportation of the heavy, leaf-filled hogsheads was arduous in the extreme, and roads, other than the narrow rolling roads, were often nonexistent.

The geographic realities of the Maryland colony dictated the developing settlement patterns as much as the tobacco culture around which tidewater civilization was centered. An extremely complex drainage system, the inordinate length and convoluted nature of the navigable waterways, and over four thousand miles of coastline permitted nearly limitless access to fast and cheap water transportation and severely deterred the concentration of storage and loading facilities. The very nature of the colonial staple upon which planters thrived—a low-bulk, easily preserved crop—would continue to discourage centralization throughout the colonial period. Finally, the production of the crop itself rapidly depleted the soil in a given area and required ever-increasing amounts of land. This, combined with the eagerness of planters to remain independent and trade from their own wharves, deterred the early evolution of a merchant class, which was a necessity for successful town development.[17]

As the golden age of the tobacco culture arrived and overall population and commerce increased, the proprietor was painfully aware of the need for better regulation of trade, both for economic and practical reasons. Still, aside from a few notable exceptions, the 1668,

1669, and 1671 initiatives had failed to generate widespread support for town development among the plantation society of Maryland because they required a major alteration in the acceptable patterns of doing business. Although only a handful of sites designated in these early ordinances had taken root, the lessons wrought seemed not to have been fully understood by the government. The failure of the ordinances must have fostered certain misgivings, for more than a decade would pass before the next initiative at general town and port development would be launched. The concept of legislated towns had not died, only gone into hibernation.

In 1675 Cecil Calvert expired, and Charles Calvert became the third Lord Baltimore, the new master of Maryland. The new proprietor decided to replace the earlier weak efforts of his brother with a more comprehensive legislative agenda to create ports and towns throughout the colony. Thus, during the fall session of 1682, when the Assembly began to consider a proposed bill tentatively entitled "Bill for Advancing the Trade of Tobacco," the proprietor commenced the most sweeping efforts to that date to legislate urban centers into existence.[18] Unlike the earlier proclamation, ordinance, and declaration, the bill was far more detailed and expansive in its scope. Consequently, the legislative battles that it generated before its passage were heated, often bitterly contested, and occasionally tessellated in their complexity.

One of the first modifications was the title of the bill itself, which a committee from the Upper House recommended be changed to "An Act for the Advancement of Trade," since the incorporation of the word tobacco was considered too particular and provided no leeway for other commodities that might be exported. Disagreements arose over specifications limiting the time ships would be allowed to off-load cargo. The manner in which the new town and port sites were selected and approved also required finessing. For the first time, the direct input of the inhabitants themselves—the most affected people—would be heard regarding actual choices of site locations. It was recommended early on that the proprietor consult with the county delegates in the Lower House, or at the very least, with commissioners representing their respective counties, before any ports were designated officially, in order that "there may be such and so many ports and places convenient in each county as may suit with the conveniency of the inhabitants of each respective county." Rules and regulations were necessary regarding how property at each site was to be purchased, who was to be permitted to acquire and hold property, in whose name it was to be held or for whose use it was to be acquired, how many acres per town or port site would be necessary and how it was to be subdivided, how much it would cost, and how surveyor's fees would be paid for laying out each site and dividing it into lots.[19]

There were also questions regarding the way planters would deliver their tobacco to ports appointed in each county. Until the introduction of the first new town programs in the late 1660s, the rivers and creeks of Maryland, which were generally accessible to many planters right at their doorsteps, had served as veritable highways for shipping. Generally, the best tobacco lands were situated along waterways rather than in the hinterland, and settlement patterns had reflected this simple reality. Now, with the centralization of shipping points, planters would be required to alter their transportation habits to reflect the new system. The legislators, most being planters themselves, were equally concerned about how they and their neighbors might secure their products safely in ports while awaiting shipment and how much it would cost for storage. How, they asked (with an eye on their own pocketbooks), would public levies, rents, port collector fees, and other debts be collected?[20]

The context of the bill was filled with many knotty issues that had to be smoothed out and agreed to by both houses before a final rendering could be submitted to the governor for approval. Amendments were proposed concerning the effective date of the act, the Assembly's authority to designate specific locations for new towns and ports (rather than permit the proprietor to exercise the function), methods of acquiring land, and payment of surveyors, as well as other issues. On November 3, Colonels Vincent Lowe and William Burgess of the Upper House agreed to convene in a joint committee session with members of the Lower House to hammer out their differences.[21] The spirit of cooperation between the aristocracy of the Upper House, appointed by the proprietor, and the delegates of the Lower House, elected by the inhabitants, started off well enough, but degenerated rapidly.

The Upper House again approved the proposed law with the suggested amendments offered by the joint committee, but the Lower House, having twice read the revised bill, raised the objection that nothing in the act prohibited the taking of any existing dwelling of a property owner for town land. There was also disagreement about dividing the proposed town sites, each being fifty acres, into one hundred lots. To do so, the burgesses feared, would not permit the incorporation of any streets in a town, and if streets were laid out, the lots would probably be too small for use. The flaws, the delegates claimed, were enough "to sett the inhabitants together by the ears." It is likely that the real, though unstated, opposition was also driven by discomfort among the burgesses with the overall move towards the centralization of trade and the necessity for transshipment of commodities to and from designated ports rather than direct to the shipping itself. Let the matter lie until the next session of the Assembly, they proposed. Undoubtedly spurred by the governor, the Upper House refused to acquiesce and insisted that a special joint conference of both houses be convened to mitigate the issues. The Speaker of the Lower House, in his opening of the current session, obfuscated by replying that the proprietor had stated that the purpose of the 1682 Assembly had been to consider other matters not related to the new town proposals and that it was improper to introduce such legislation.[22]

The objections were successful enough to delay further action on the bill until the following year. It was enough time for the discontent of the burgesses, which had grown considerably during the 1682 session, to blossom into spirited opposition over the objectives of the Upper House. At the onset of the new fall Assembly in October, which convened at Thomas Larkin's "Ridge" plantation in Anne Arundel County, the Lower House sought to employ the new town bill as leverage to achieve its own ends. A bill governing the methods of electing burgesses, which was vigorously introduced by the burgesses but was not popular with the proprietor and his council, was one of the bargaining chips employed in the contest. On October 9, a trade-off was hinted at by the Upper House. In a message to the Upper House complaining of stonewall tactics employed on the elections bill, the burgess noted that it appeared the bill was being held up "with intent to exact compliance from this house to the bill for towns thereby rendering it suspicious to this house that the Upper House doth not intend that fair correspondence with this house as the present affairs require and this house earnestly desire."[23]

One of the principal subjects of debate, of course, centered on which places should be appointed for the new towns and how much of a voice the Lower House should have in the final choice of sites. The selection of commissioners "for the managing the business of the towns" was yet another issue to be decided upon. Finally, the first list of sites nominated by the Lower House was presented to the proprietor and his council and included twenty-nine locations.

Many of the sites nominated were the same as or near to those designated by the 1668, 1669, and 1671 proclamations and ordinances, while many more were newly introduced. As before, a number of sites were designated because of the influence of certain large plantation owners, who sought to profit from commercial traffic and the sale of lots when their lands were selected for town development, as well as from their own convenient proximity to inspection and shipping points.[24]

After further massaging of the proposed legislation, including some minor revisions, the Lower House made a last-ditch attempt to wed passage of an elections bill as well as another bill dealing with military duties to that of the towns bill. Calvert was intensely irate over the tactic and summoned the burgesses before him to personally demand immediate passage of his cherished port and new town program. Finally, the deadlock was broken, probably owing to the Lord Proprietor's direct intervention. No doubt with enmity on both sides, the Lower House finally approved the bill, formally entitled "An Act for the Advancement of Trade," and it was signed into law on November 6, 1683.[25]

At first glance, the act appeared to be far-reaching in its magnitude and specific in its actions. After the last day of August 1685, all vessels trading in Maryland were to unload imported goods and take on commodities for export only at one of the specified locations designated by the act. An incredible total of thirty-two sites, each to be one hundred acres in extent, were chosen. Commissioners were nominated for every county and were to be held responsible "for the surveying & laying out of the said ports, towns & places aforesaid, & making & staking out the several lots to be laid out in the said towns to the end the length, breadth & extent of every town & the several lots in every town, port & place may be the better known & observed."[26]

The commissioners were to meet before March 25, 1684, on the respective sites chosen for towns, or at a convenient location nearby, to negotiate the purchase of the property from the owners and thereby acquire the necessary land for each site designated. Upon purchase, they were to have the sites surveyed by the surveyor general or his deputy in each county, staked out and divided "into convenient streets, lanes & alleys, with open space places to be left on which may be erected church or chapel, & market house, or other public buildings."[27] Each town tract was to be equally divided into one hundred lots, marked by posts and stakes, oriented toward the streets or lanes and numbered one through one hundred. The original owner of the tract was to have the first choice of one lot. To prohibit speculation or landgrabs, no individual purchasing property in the town was to be permitted more than one lot during the first four months of availability after March 25, and sales during this period were to be limited to county residents only and payable to the original owner of the tract. In the event that no inhabitants of the county had taken up any lots within the four-month time limit, or if any tract owners refused to sell or there were other impediments to sales, the commissioners for each county were authorized to issue warrants to the county sheriff empowering him to impanel and return a jury of freeholders in the county to determine the value of the land, payable in tobacco, and to adjudicate "such damages and recompence as they shall think fit to be awarded to the owners & all persons interested according to their several & respective interests."[28]

Anyone purchasing a lot in any town was obligated to build "one sufficient twenty foot square house at the least" before August 1, 1685, and to pay the Lord Proprietor, his heirs, and successors a yearly rent of one penny per lot. If construction of the prescribed building was not completed by that date, the title was to be forfeited and might be taken up by someone else provided "the second taker up or purchaser begin to build within one month after such his entry." Upon meeting all of the criteria, each lot owner was to be ascribed full title and rights to perpetual ownership of the property, which could be transmitted to his heirs or assignees, and could not be challenged by anyone, even the proprietor himself (unless the yearly tax was not paid). Surveyors were to receive payment of thirty pounds of tobacco for each lot surveyed, payable by the purchaser of the lot.[29] At the end of five years, if any lots remained unsold, ownership was to revert to the original tract owners.

Beginning on August 31, 1685, violators of the trading provisions of the law were to suffer severe penalties, including forfeiture of all goods and merchandise imported or exported at places other than ports designated in the act. One third of all forfeited goods was to be awarded to the proprietor, one third to the justices of the county court in which the goods were landed (to be used for the benefit of the nearest town in the county in which the offense was committed), and one third to the informer or individuals whose reports led to the seizure. For the protection of planters who were unable to maintain tobacco warehouses in the towns, owners with warehouses were required to accept for storage any tobacco sent into the town for that end, with the proviso that storage capacity was available. A cap fee of ten pounds of tobacco was established for each hogshead of tobacco stored annually. Warehouse owners who willfully refused to take in tobacco were to be held liable for damages sustained by the planter.[30]

The legislators who forged the act were cognizant that to persuade inhabitants to purchase lots, certain incentives would be necessary. Thus, one of the salient advantages outlined in the act was that all rents due the proprietor, as well as all public levies and officer's fees payable in tobacco, were to be shipped to one of the towns, thereby creating another important role for urban centers as revenue collection sites. To reduce the expense to the residents in the initial stages of town development, the act provided that no burgesses were to be chosen to represent the area in the Assembly until as many families "as the said town . . . shall be actually inhabited by . . . such delegates" who were to be elected by the freemen of each town.[31]

In an effort to ensure that goods and merchandise imported into a given town benefited that town's trade and hastened the growth of stores and trading houses, the act permitted any citizen who had erected a building and dwelled within a town or port to barter or purchase any quantity of goods desired for resale. All goods and merchandise purchased from imports in a given town could be sold at any other town in Maryland. Persons who were not inhabitants or taxable in the colony were to be strictly prohibited from loading tobacco or other goods for export aboard any vessel from any plantation or places other than at designated town sites. Those who chose to violate the law would suffer not only the loss of the tobacco or goods, but also that of the vessel being employed or the value thereof.[32]

For the encouragement of trade and the prompt dispatch of vessels trading in Maryland, the following places were authorized for entering and clearing ships and other vessels trading in the province: the Wicomico River in St. Mary's County, the Patuxent River and other principal rivers of Anne Arundel County on the western shore, and Talbot and Somerset Counties on the Eastern Shore.[33]

To pass an act was one thing. To successfully implement it and enforce its provisions was another. Many tobacco planters, who had simply ignored the earlier proclamations by the proprietor, viewed the new act with alarm, owing to the punitive measures included. Even some of the commissioners appointed to address the nuts and bolts of instituting the new legislation were less than impassioned with their assignment. There were many difficulties to be overcome, not the least of which was that tobacco merchants had grown accustomed to dealing directly with the planters. There was a dearth of marine support facilities; services and infrastructure would have to be established from scratch. A lack of the most basic building supplies in the colony, such as nails, compounded the problem further. The inconvenience and expense of having to transport the heavy hogsheads to specified sites (rather than ship them directly from one's own wharf) was roundly despised. Moreover, the specter of widespread smuggling and the impossibility of contending with it along the thousands of miles of shoreline around the Chesapeake was, no doubt, paramount in the minds of many in the administration.

By the cutoff date of March 25, 1684, for the acquisition of designated sites, only a few of the town tracts had been purchased, "and very few or none laid out into lots and staked out as by the said Act as directed."[34] At a council meeting convened at St. Mary's City on February 27, a month before the cutoff date, the proprietor was informed that the reason for the delay had been that commissioners in several counties had simply "been very remiss and negligent" in promoting the act. Irate over the lack of progress, the proprietor sought to buttress the legislation with yet another proclamation. He commanded in no uncertain terms that the commissioners appointed for each county immediately put the act, "that so laudable a design," into execution by having them survey the "ports, towns and places of trade" which were then to be "forthwith laid out." Those who failed to follow his instructions would "answer the contrary at their peril."[35]

Opposition to implementation of the act remained visible even at the highest levels. Resistance continued as punishment for violations was anything but severe. From time to time the council berated "some evil minded persons" who were chastised for seeking only personal gain and caring little for the public good, but fearing that enforcement might touch off widespread hostility, it did little more.[36] The situation was further electrified by an atmosphere already charged by political and religious differences that threatened the survival of the proprietorship itself.

By ignoring the recalcitrance of the population to embrace the initiative and by adopting the more-is-better concept that added new town sites to the already swollen and improbable 1683 list, the government appears to have felt there would be a greater likelihood of success. In the spring of 1684, the Assembly passed legislation supplementing the 1683 act. By creating even more "paper" towns, the government evidently hoped to counter the charges that the act caused inconveniences and expenses for the planters. By authorizing more ports, it was felt, planters would have less distance to travel. On April 26, citing petitions that had been submitted by the inhabitants of several counties requesting "more and other towns, ports and places for the ease and benefit of the inhabitants . . . & conveniency of trade," the burgesses passed "An Additional & Supplementary Act to the Act for the Advancement of Trade." Thirteen new sites were added and two previously designated towns were moved to other locations in the same general vicinity.[37]

The failure of the 1683 act was all but acknowledged by passage of the new supplementary act, which sought to correct the weaknesses of the original. Even though a handful of sites in several counties had been surveyed, there was still no stampede to purchase lots in any one of them, despite the revisions. The commissioners were given wide latitude to adopt any rules and regulations of their own that would forward the work of town development and remove any obstructions to progress in that direction. Deputy surveyors were to "make a true draught of the towns, streets and lots therein, and deliver the same to the Comissioners to be recorded for the fee of thirty pounds of tobacco per lot." The commissioners were empowered "to compel workmen, laborers and others to help to carry the chain, to cut stakes and assist in the measuring and staking out of the ground of the several hundred acres of land at the towns, ports and places" prescribed. Those who refused to undertake this work were to be fined two hundred pounds of tobacco.[38] A strict new deadline date of September 29, 1684, was given for completion of all works designated in both the 1683 and 1684 acts.[39]

In spite of the deadlines, fines, and improvements in the means for implementation and control, as well as the inclusion of thirteen additional town sites for greater convenience, the supplementary act was no more successful than the 1683 act. Only very limited progress was made in new town building. Town sites were surveyed and laid out and lots were sold, yet actual development lagged far behind the proprietor's hopes. An extension of the deadline was set at December 31, 1685.[40]

Other amendments would also be necessary owing to the paucity of roads and small craft in the colony. Before the acts, tobacco to be shipped was transferred directly from the various plantations. Now, planters were faced with the necessity of transporting their tobacco to authorized port sites by overland means or, for those fortunate enough to have property on waterways (or neighbors willing to provide access), by watercraft. Unfortunately, the new town and port legislation failed to consider the shortage of small watercraft in the colony. An analysis of the inventory of small craft available to planters in one typical Maryland district, All Hallows Parish in Anne Arundel County, is perhaps suggestive of the situation colonywide. During the period from 1660 to 1769, inventories indicated that an average of only 13.6 percent of all estates in the parish possessed watercraft suitable for tobacco transport. Boats were expensive to build and maintain, and small planters could ill afford such luxuries. Nevertheless, during the 1680s, owing to the town and port legislation, planters were forced to add small vessels to their holdings to transport their tobacco, and the average increased briefly to 22.6 percent. With less than one in every four estates possessing suitable watercraft and only a primitive road system available, many planters were in a quandary. Thus, on November 25, 1685, the council adopted a conciliatory attitude and allowed ships to again call first at plantations to transport tobacco to ports.[41]

The risks in such measures were obvious. There was nothing to prevent ships from calling at plantations and then sailing for Europe without making the required visit to a designated port or paying the necessary duties and fees. The error in judgment was soon evident, and on September 14, 1686, by proclamation, the council rescinded its conciliatory actions and re-instituted the trading provisions of the 1683 and 1684 acts, ordering that they be rigidly enforced. Furthermore, in an effort to squelch the increasing undercurrent of criticism in the countryside concerning the acts, anyone who dared to publish or otherwise report or declare that the building of towns and ports in Maryland was *not* for the advancement of trade "shall be deemed as persons ill affected to the government and to be accordingly severely punished."[42] In a dismal sign of government frustration, criticism of the acts was thus elevated to a near par with outright sedition or treason.

The council, nevertheless, moved vigorously to prepare and adopt instructions needed to enforce the trade provisions of the new town acts. Copies of the 1683 act, the 1684 supplementary act, and the proclamation of September 14, 1686, were to be provided to each county inspection officer, who was instructed to make note of anyone failing to conform to them. Each officer was also directed to "take a strict account of all tobaccos and other commodities of this province that shall be brought to the said town," and loaded on ships of the port. Careful records were to be kept of all vessels that came to anchor at towns, including the names of their masters, the locations from whence they came and whither they were bound, as well as all goods, wares, and merchandise landed ashore. The officers were to issue certificates to the masters of ships for the quantity of tobacco legally taken aboard for clearance with the customs collector. They were to submit data on any and all suspected violations of the acts, including the illicit shipment of tobacco from nearby plantations. Finally, to prohibit frauds carried out by port officials themselves, *all* officers were instructed to take note of any violations of the acts, not only in their own jurisdiction but anywhere else in the colony.[43]

The initiatives at new town and port development proved lacking in success. Thus, in late October 1686, the Assembly passed a second supplementary act encumbered by the long and awkward title "A Further Additional Act to the act for Advancement of Trade and to the Supplementary Act to the same." No fewer than thirteen new port sites were added to the long list already established, while five were removed, bringing the total count of towns and ports included in the combined acts to fifty-two.[44]

The new act was virtually the same as the last, and it produced similar results.

Although the archival record is generally lacking in documentation on the actual reaction of planters to the myriad enactments and proclamations concerning town and port development and the regulation of trade, it would appear from the sheer number of laws passed that resistance was strong, and compliance was minimal. Moreover, outright opposition toward the proprietary government itself was growing in Maryland, as the population became dominantly Protestant and revolutionary upheavals in England were in the offing. The poor showing of the new town and trade acts were, in that regard, only symptomatic of a greater willingness of Maryland's planter population to resist such efforts. In the mid-1680s, Calvert returned to England to mend fences and placate the tide of discontented Protestantism threatening to engulf his dominion. Thus, in an effort to mollify the planters during his absence, while in London on July 23, 1688, he suspended the trading provisions of the various town acts. But it was still geography that was the final arbiter in governing public sentiment. The infinite complexity—and convenience—of Maryland's waterways, which allowed planters direct access to shipping from their own wharves, remained the deciding factor against centralized town development. "The number of rivers," wrote one observer of the situation in 1688, "is one of the chief reasons why they have no towns."[45]

Strangely enough, the Assembly itself now refused to let the project die, and in early December 1688, it proceeded to institute yet a fourth town and port act, entitled "An Act for Erecting some new necessary Towns." This time, it would appear that pressure had been brought to bear by certain elements in St. Mary's, Kent, Calvert, Dorchester, and Talbot Counties who were simply unsatisfied with the location of sites designated in earlier acts. Unlike the previous acts, the 1688 law offered no commands, rules, or regulations regarding trade in the newly designated towns.[46]

It was the 1688 Glorious Revolution in England that prompted the end of the proprietorship and religious toleration in Maryland and also shut down for the next seventeen years the new towns and ports programs favored by the Lords Baltimore.

When Maryland was drastically altered from palatinate to royal colony, the once awesome authority of Lord Baltimore was reduced from that of potentate (whose laws in accordance with the Maryland Charter could not be altered by the king himself) to mere landlord. Lionel Copley, an ineffective, corrupt executive, arrived in 1691 to assume the duties of the colony's first royally appointed chief executive. During the next two decades, sweeping changes in the manner of policy making and legislation would ensue under the administrations of Governors Sir Edmund Andros (1693–1694), Francis Nicholson (1694–1698), and Nathaniel Blakiston (1698–1702), as well as Thomas Tench, president of the council (1702–1704), Governor John Seymour (1704–1709), Edward Lloyd, president of the council (1709–1714), and Governor John Hart (1714–1715). Nicholson, Blakiston, and Seymour were notably more liberal in permitting the Assembly a voice in decision making than the Baltimores had ever been. As a result, the Assembly, exercising its newfound authority, instituted major reforms that included changing the court, establishing the Anglican Church as the state religion, and revising the legal code. For many, particularly religious minorities, the changes were for the worse. Quakers lost the right to sit in the Assembly, and Roman Catholics were forbidden from holding Mass except in privately owned chapels. Yet, some acts proved quite progressive. In 1694, Governor Nicholson, cognizant of the dramatic shift of population from south to north (and its incumbent importance to the political powerbase) moved the capital from St. Mary's City in the center of Catholic Maryland to the Severn River, heartland of Protestant Maryland.[47] One of the glaring omissions of the early days of royal government was the temporary abandonment of town development programs. As one of the failed legacies of the palatinate era, it was an omission that was most certainly intentional, as royal, Anglican Maryland attempted to divest itself of its former trappings. One of the most important acts initiated during the early days of the Copley administration was the passage on June 7, 1692, of "An Act of Repeal of all Laws heretofore made in this Province & confirming all Laws made this General Assembly." The repeal law had the effect of nullifying all of the general port and town acts of the previous quarter-century, thereby producing a snakepit full of problems regarding ownership, boundaries, and taxes for those who had settled in new towns.[48]

By the early days of the administration of Governor John Seymour, the town and port initiatives, which had been first consigned to the legislative scrap pile and then repealed in full, provided some large landholders with the excuse to reclaim property already sold out as lots. Lot owners protested, and not without justification, that they had legally paid for, taken up, entered, and built upon and improved their lots as required by the former laws of the colony. "Yet," it was claimed, "they [the lot owners] are now threatened disquieted and disturbed by the persons claiming rights to the said lands upon pretence that because . . . the said Acts are since repealed. The titles of such takers up builders and improvers are destroy'd and die with the said Acts of Trade contrary to the true sense and rational construction of the same laws or any other of like Nature."

To prevent the seizures of such property, on October 3, 1704, the governor, with the advice and consent of his council and the Assembly, signed into law a bill declaring that lot holders were authorized to "have hold and enjoy a good sure indefeasible estate of inheritance in fee or in and to every such lot and lots of land so taken up and built on."[49]

The damage, fortunately, was less than it might have been. At the time the 1688 act was passed, the success rate of the nearly sixty towns that had been proclaimed or legislated into existence was far from stunning. With only twenty-five thousand inhabitants in the colony, both white and black, the sheer quantity of sites competing against each other for the commerce of the lightly populated tidewater colony all but doomed many if not most to miscarriage.[50] Some progress, however, had been made. A number of towns had actually been surveyed; lots were sold, and development finally had begun despite all of the handicaps.

By the end of the first decade of royal administration, the evolution of a new mindset regarding urban development had slowly taken hold in Maryland. Now, new town initiatives were authorized based upon the growing population's needs as much as upon the administrative requirements of government. Communities were created at sites believed to be more favorably situated to address the prerequisites of the inhabitants, not simply as a means to effectively enforce the regulatory measures of trade. Town and port legislation was now usually generated by the General Assembly, in response to public petitions from local inhabitants or on its own, rather than through executive directives. New towns were no longer laid out by individuals who sought sanctions of the government afterward, but at the direct order of the legislature.[51]

Seymour was cognizant of the failures of the early urban development efforts, but he was equally aware of the consequences of abandoning the idea of a port system as a means for managing regulatory controls over customs and trade. On July 3, 1705, in a letter to the board of trade, he complained vigorously that there was simply too much illegal commerce in Maryland. He suggested that only five ports (or harbors) in the colony—Annapolis, Oxford, Somerset, Patuxent, and St. Mary's—should be permitted to ship tobacco or receive imports. Pointing out that each planter still had his own wharf, he noted that it would be hopeless for "all ye officers in ye world to know what was shipped or unshipped." In fact, it had been impossible to even have a survey made of the extant ports and harbors in the colony because the Assembly (still comprised largely of planters) refused to pay for it as they considered it "a great step to hinder their private trade." There were, of course, other motivating factors that encouraged the governor to condemn the shipping practices of the planters and to see trade laws respected. Most prominent among them was that his own salary was dependent upon receipts from taxes realized from tobacco exports. Centralization of shipping through the aforementioned five ports, he concluded, was the only answer to the smuggling problem.[52]

The ascension of Queen Anne to the throne of England would see a revival of interest in town development in Maryland. Some colonial officials in court hoped to emulate the successful townships established in Massachusetts, Connecticut, Rhode Island, and New York, and all but ignored the differences in the social and economic foundations between the colonies to the north and those of the Chesapeake. A renewal of new port initiatives provided Governor Seymour with the ammunition needed to institute his own port concepts.

When the crown issued instructions to Maryland's chief executive to motivate the Assembly "to pass an act for the building of towns, warehouses, wharves and keys" on the Potomac and Patuxent Rivers and on the Eastern Shore, the objectives were again sweepingly expansive—and entirely out of touch with reality. The number of towns to be created were not to exceed a total of three on the Potomac and the Patuxent, and two on the Eastern Shore. The governor was also instructed to correspond with the Governor of Virginia to coordinate with a like effort that was to be carried out in that colony.[53]

True to its historic form, in 1706 the Assembly enacted legislation entitled "An Act for advancement of trade and erecting Ports & Towns in the province of Maryland" establishing not the maximum number of five towns as instructed by the crown, but forty-two. Seymour got not only the five "reputed and appointed ports" he requested, but an additional one on the Chester River to boot. Many of the town sites designated were the same or nearly the same as others nominated in earlier acts. The 1706 act was in most ways little more than a rehash of the failed legislative measures of the 1680s.[54]

A few new provisions were added as incentives to settlement in towns. Tradesmen, artisans, and laborers who took up residence were to be exempted from paying public levies for themselves or for their journeymen and servants during their first four years of occupancy. Foreign tradesmen, merchants, and laborers who took up residency for a period of four years in any port or town designated in the act were to be granted citizenship. All male orphans under the jurisdiction of the county courts were to be put out as apprentices to tradesmen and other inhabitants of the towns and ports.[55]

After January 1, 1707, all imports and exports were to be shipped only through the six appointed ports. Anyone trading at any but the prescribed ports would be subject to forfeiture of all goods and merchandise sold or bartered. Any persons "that shall dwell and inhabit" in any of the designated ports or towns were to be allowed to contract for purchase or barter any goods provided they only sell the goods at one of the authorized towns or ports within the province of Maryland. To ensure that visible official presence was maintained, "all sheriffs, clerks of the county courts, naval officers and collectors, the Lord Baltimore's Collectors and Receivers of his Lordships Revenues," or their official deputies, were required to dwell or inhabit in some of the ports and towns "for the necessary and quick dispatch of all business." Deputy county commissioners were also obliged to live in ports and towns "for the ease and conveniency of the inhabitants thereof."[56] Stiff fines were to be levied against violations of the act.[57]

It seemed, noted one chronicler of the Seymour administration, that the act creating an astounding forty-eight towns and ports "made practically every important exporter's wharf a port, and contained provisions for the establishment of towns that could never exist except on paper." Many of the towns were not even laid out. Some individuals who had purchased lots in towns claimed, as with earlier acts, they had been unable to build upon them as required by law "for want of nails," an item which had to be imported. The consequences of the delay, however, were entirely unexpected. Although many of the towns that had already been named in earlier acts were struggling to survive, a flood of petitions from the inhabitants of numerous counties calling for even more towns to be erected practically inundated the Assembly during the spring of 1707. Many of the petitioners were concerned, given the tardiness of survey work, that the towns designated in the 1706 act either might never be established or were too inconvenient for them to use. The inhabitants of some counties, including Somerset, Prince George's, Anne Arundel, and Charles, requested alternative new sites or enlargements of existing sites![58]

The Assembly responded by passing yet another "Supplementary Act to the Act for the advancement of Trade and Erecting Ports and Towns." By now, the format was predictable, with only minor variations from earlier laws.[59] The 1707 act varied from its predecessor in that all towns were divided into six groups. Each town in a given group was required to direct its trade through one of the six ports designated for its use. After September 10, 1708, all tobacco and other merchandise produced in the colony for export (with the exception of timber, pipe staves, billets, and wooden wares) were first to be brought to the nearest town and then to the appropriate port. All towns on rivers, creeks, and coves on Kent Island in Talbot County and on the Great Choptank and Little Choptank Rivers in Dorchester County were to be processed through the port of Oxford. Products passing through all towns on the waterways of the remaining part of Dorchester County and all of Cecil, Queen Anne's (with the exception of Kent Island), and Somerset Counties were to be taken to the port of Green Hill on the Wicomico River. The outlet for all towns on the Patuxent was to be Port St. George on Beckwith's Island. Annapolis, a town barely off the drawing boards, was to serve as the port for all towns in Baltimore and Anne Arundel Counties (with the exception of sites on the Patuxent River). St. Mary's, though having fallen into general decline, was to serve as the port for all towns on the Potomac.[60] Commanders of all ships trading in the colony were required, upon arrival, to enter their ships with the naval officers and collectors of the district wherein they chose to anchor and unload.[61]

No longer able to ignore the difficulties endured by planters in moving their tobacco to designated towns and ports, the commissioners in each county were instructed to appoint and purchase convenient public landing sites on rivers and creeks to which planters might deliver their tobacco for transport by water to the nearest outport. The landing sites were to be a half-acre in extent. Rolling houses, no more than two furlongs distance from the water, were to be built upon land convenient to each landing for the storage of tobacco awaiting shipment. Each site was to be surveyed by the county surveyor and records kept the same as town surveys.[62]

The shipment of tobacco and merchandise from one town to another was also authorized, but to curb illegal exports, some safety measures were enacted. If transport was carried out in an open boat of less than eighteen feet keel length, no permit was necessary from a collector or naval district officer. If it was conducted "in any open boat, sloop, shallop boat or other vessel being above eighteen foot by the keel," a yearly fee of two shillings and six pence for a license was necessary, payable to the naval officer. To transport tobacco and goods between towns and ports in the colony on the larger vessel required the owner or master to post a security of £40 to the naval officer.[63]

Only a few plats from the 1706 or 1707 acts have survived. Typical of these conservative plans is the plat for Upper Marlborough, which was laid out and surveyed in 1706 by Thomas Truman Greenfield. In it, the town was shown as a rectangular gridiron affair, with three streets running generally east and west intersected by two more running at right angles. Four lanes formed the boundaries of the town. A total of 102 numbered lots are defined, two of which were public spaces to be used as a market place, located where two main streets intersect in the upper portion of the town. Another was reserved for the Presbyterian Meeting House.[64]

On the Eastern Shore, an unusual variation of the almost standard grid plan of the period appears in the plat for the town of Green Hill in Wicomico County (then part of Somerset), which was one of the six ports of entry authorized by Governor Seymour. As urban historian John Reps suggested, it was quite apparent from the design that legislators and planners had great expectations for the success of the chief town and port of the region. Although the town was generally designed along a formal grid pattern, the plat's most unique feature was the inclusion of three twin-turreted town gates topped by staffs and flags or pennants, reminiscent of the gates of feudal English towns of an earlier time. The layout was simple, with two main streets running almost parallel with the Wicomico River intersected by two more that ran at right angles leading to the boundary of the upper town. For lots not situated on an avenue front, access was provided by several small lanes. One lot, situated at the crossing of two main streets, was provided for a market place. A triangular plot was designated for a commons. A third lot was located near Green Hill Creek, a tributary feeding into the main river. On this spot, a church was eventually constructed in 1723, but it was replaced ten years later by a brick edifice that remains today as the sole surviving structure in the town.[65]

The unique portals of Green Hill Town notwithstanding (if they were ever built), no one could accuse the planners who produced the designs for the 1706 and 1707 crop of new towns of being innovators. For the most part, their town designs were boring gridded schemes laid down with very little concern for the topography of the land upon which they were situated or the waters adjacent to them. A lot might be either a long rectangular shape, to allow for a house space fronting on a street and a garden and outbuildings space in the back, or it might be square, sometimes shortened or cut diagonally along one side by the water's edge or a town boundary line. It would be almost impossible to find more static plans than those of the riverport towns such as Vienna (originally Emperours Landing), Oxford, or Wye Town (also known as Doncaster), which were typical of the lot. Those that would follow were little better. Economy may have been one of the factors influencing their design, for they were relatively simple to survey and lay out, hence less expensive. And given the frequent rows over payment to surveyors, cost was certainly a most important factor in such undertakings.

That the 1706 and 1707 acts were less than striking practical successes is perhaps confirmed by the protests of a certain Captain Darcott, master of the ship *Susannah* of Barnstable, Massachusetts, who arrived in Maryland to trade in February 1708. The captain had dropped anchor in the Chester River, and like any honest trader, he was required to adhere to the tenets of the various acts, which obliged him to sell his goods in towns that still didn't exist and to store his wares in warehouses and storehouses that still hadn't been built. His displeasure, which was expressed in a public letter of protest, perhaps typified the weakness of the acts on the Eastern Shore as throughout all of Maryland. The inhabitants of some counties were not mollified by the 1707 act; in St. Mary's County, residents repeatedly petitioned for even more towns as if it were a contagion. The Assembly reacted in a most predictable manner. It instituted still another supplementary measure with the cumbersome title "An Additional Act to the Supplementary Act for advancement of Trade and Erecting Ports and Towns in this Province and for Sale of some public Lands and buildings in the Town of St. Mary's in St. Mary's County."[66]

The following year, additional legislation added to the stew. The 1708 act incorporated all the mandates of the 1706 and 1707 legislation and designated four town sites into existence in Somerset, Queen Anne's, Kent, and St. Mary's Counties. The act also authorized the move of the St. Mary's county seat from St. Mary's City to a site at the head of Breton Bay called Shepherds (or Sheppard's) Old Fields.[67]

In 1709 the administration of Governor John Seymour came to an end, and for more than a decade, further initiatives in new town and port development were abandoned. The causes were many. The period of royal government during the administrations of Nicholson, Blackiston, and Seymour had been clouded by almost perpetual warfare between Protestant England and Catholic France, with the economy of the colony demonstrably suffering as a consequence. Tobacco prices had remained low, with resultant hardships and economic stagnation imposing hard times upon colony planters. The economic and political stamina required to plant and sustain urban centers simply did not exist. But in 1713, the long War of Spanish Succession was finally concluded with the signing of the Treaty of Utrecht, and a new era of commercial investment by the English and Scottish mercantile communities commenced. The year 1714 brought the death of Queen Anne and the accession of George I; Charles Calvert, the last of the Catholic proprietors, died the following year, and the Maryland scene began to change radically. Benedict Leonard Calvert, who had taken Communion and become a loyal Protestant, was entrusted with the government, but he soon died and was succeeded by his son Charles, the fifth Lord Baltimore. The period of direct royal administration over the colony was thus ended and a proprietary government of sorts was once more installed. In 1714 John Hart, last of the royal governors, continued on under the new proprietary regime. Six years later, Charles Calvert, cousin of Lord Baltimore, assumed the governorship. A resurgence in new town development began, assuming an even more ambitious range not unlike that of the early 1680s.

Fortunately, the experiences of efforts made in the seventeenth and early eighteenth centuries, when many sites were designated in scattershot fashion, had at last been seen for the failures that they were. A new order had arisen, and a more methodical and logical manner of new town creation was soon adopted, and none too soon. Towns were to be authorized on

Top: By the onset of the nineteenth century, the town of Green Hill had all but vanished. In this detail from the 1795 Dennis Griffith *Map of the State of Maryland,* the site was noted only for its church. Like many of the legislated towns, it was no longer on a major overland road. Courtesy Library of Congress, Washington, D.C.

Bottom: Green Hill Church, built in 1733 on the Wicomico River, is all that remains of the town designated by Governor Seymour in 1707 as one of six Maryland ports that were to serve as outports for all commerce in the colony.

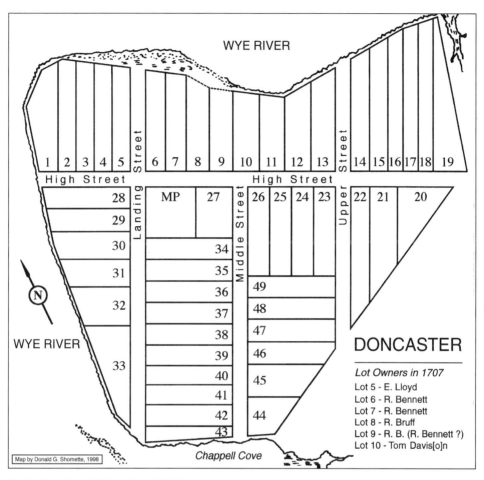

WYE RIVER

Landing Street

1 | 2 | 3 | 4 | 5 | 6 | 7 | 8 | 9 | 10 | 11 | 12 | 13 | 14 | 15 | 16 | 17 | 18 | 19

High Street

Upper Street

High Street

28

MP | 27

26 | 25 | 24 | 23

22 | 21 | 20

29

30

34

31

35

N

36

49

32

37

48

38

47

WYE RIVER

39

46

33

40

45

41

42 | 44

43

Middle Street

DONCASTER

Lot Owners in 1707

Lot 5 - E. Lloyd
Lot 6 - R. Bennett
Lot 7 - R. Bennett
Lot 8 - R. Bruff
Lot 9 - R. B. (R. Bennett ?)
Lot 10 - Tom Davis[o]n

Chappell Cove

Map by Donald G. Shomette, 1998

Above: Plan of Doncaster, Maryland, ca. 1707. From a plan by Philemon Hemsley in the Wye House Collection, Wye, Maryland. The division of the town into long lots was somewhat unusual and may reflect a desire to incorporate space for small herb gardens, warehouses, or other uses for the lots by property owners.

Left: As late as 1877 the site of old Doncaster was well known in the lore of Talbot County, as attested to by its inclusion as the "Ancient Town" on a map entitled "Easton Dist. No. 1 Talbot Co." by G. M. Hopkins in the *Atlas of Dorchester & Talbot Maryland* (Philadelphia, 1877). Courtesy Library of Congress, Washington, D.C.

a site-by-site basis rather than wholesale, and usually by popular demand. Unlike the earlier initiatives, there would be a commonality in form and content to each individual act. Most would result from the petitions of inhabitants living near a proposed site. The majority would be situated convenient to the water.

The actual methodology required by the government for laying out a town and the lots therein has been recorded in only one instance—in the 1745 resurvey of Princess Anne Town, a site that had originally been laid out thirteen years earlier. In the instructions outlined in the 1745 act, it was written that the commissioners

> shall cause to be set up good substantial and durable posts, or such other boundaries as to them shall seem to settle and distinguish the same survey for ever; always having regard as near as may be to the original survey thereof, and the lots already improved and built upon, as aforesaid. And that the surveyor so to be chosen, as is before directed, shall at his own proper cost and charge, find and provide good substantial and durable posts, sufficient and necessary for each respective lot, street, lane, or alley, in the said town; and fix the said posts in their proper places, with the mark or number of the lot, which post is to ascertain the beginning of said lot; and likewise shall make out fair and exact plats of the town aforesaid, and survey thereof, whereby each lot, street, lane, and alley, therein may appear to be well distinguished by their respective numbers, and names, and the same plats, with full and plain certificate said thereof.[68]

Lot owners were required to build a house of four hundred square feet in size. In several of the general acts, the construction of houses with wooden chimneys was forbidden. Only brick or stone chimneys were allowed, for obvious reasons. In the case of the re-creation of Upper Marlborough in 1744, a supplementary act had to be passed directing that all wooden chimneys in houses already erected in the town must be replaced within a year or the lot owners would face a stiff fine.[69]

Although its roots had been laid eighteen years earlier, the first site to receive attention during the proprietorship of the fifth Lord Baltimore in 1724 was in Baltimore County (upon a site now in Harford County) on the Gunpowder River. By the 1706 "Act for the Advancement of Trade and Erecting Ports and Towns," one of the forty-two locations that had been selected for a town was on a tract called Foster's Neck. The following year, having been found to be inadequate, the site was ordered deserted. Despite protests from some inhabitants, a new fifty-acre tract located northeast of the Gunpowder town site and belonging to Ann Felks (called Taylors Choice) was chosen in lieu of the earlier selection. This locale, named Joppa, was deemed suitable enough to serve as the county seat, and a courthouse was ordered built upon it to replace the earlier but less centrally situated county seat called Baltimore Town on the Bush River.[70] Unfortunately, the 1707 act made no provisions for actually building the courthouse, so the county commissioners proceeded at their own expense. Colonel James Maxwell, a county justice and son-in-law of Ann Felks, built the courthouse and prison in 1709 at a cost of six hundred pounds of tobacco for the purchase of the lot and forty-five hundred pounds of tobacco for the construction of the 25-×-24-foot two-story structure.[71]

The court building project at Joppa, however, had been completed before the queen had approved the site as a town. Such approval was a necessity during the era of royal administration of the colony, and Queen Anne failed to give it. The colony government scurried to pass a new law in 1712 to officially implement and approve of the use of the existing courthouse and to ensure that the lots already laid out for public use could be employed as intended. Although the courthouse and a prison were completed and county governmental and judicial activities were soon be to conducted, not a single dwelling had been built. In 1719, Maxwell and his wife Ann acquired Taylors Choice through the will of Ann Felks "during their natural lives." Upon their demise, the land was to fall to their eldest son Asaele Maxwell. Five years later, it was discovered that the land upon which the courthouse and prison had been constructed belonged to Colonel Maxwell's son, still a minor under twenty-one years of age and not legally able to convey a title. The government responded, legalizing the conveyance by the passage of a special bill which also reauthorized the erection of the town, though it reduced the overall area to twenty-one acres. On November 4, 1724, Lord Baltimore signed into law bill number 16, "An Act for Erecting a Town at Joppa in Baltimore County; and for Securing the Land whereon the Court-House and Prisons are built, to the Use of the said County." The specific reason given for the law was that there was a lack of accommodations and "convenient places of entertainment" for those obliged to travel great distances to court or on other county business, causing great inconvenience. A town, it was believed, was absolutely necessary.[72] Commissioners were duly appointed and instructed to lay off the land in streets and half-acre lots, with a one-acre tract for St. John's Parish Church.

A surviving survey plat of Joppa, a nineteenth-century redraft from the original, indicates the town was drawn up with two avenues named Court and Church running on an east-west axis. These streets were joined by another avenue called Sharping Lane on the west side of the courthouse lot. High Street and Low Street ran north to the town's boundary. Despite the legislature's directives, individual lots varied in size from slightly less than a half-acre to a bit over a third of an acre. One acre, in the center of town and adjoining the courthouse lot, was dedicated to the use of St. John's Church. Negotiations with Colonel Maxwell for sale of the property did not go smoothly. The colonel was offered £3 per acre but declined until a warrant requiring condemnation was prepared for execution by the sheriff. Thereupon the colonel agreed and the deal was consummated without further problems. When the lots were finally offered up for sale by the commissioners on April 20, 1725, to all those who would build, a total of thirty of the forty lots were quickly snapped up for £1.70 each. The town, most thought, was well on its way to becoming a major port and court center. Before long, besides the courthouse, two prisons, and the church, there were forty to fifty dwellings, as well as warehouses, wharves, ordinaries and inns, stores, and tradesmen's shops.[73]

The enthusiasm demonstrated by the citizens on the Gunpowder for the first new town in nearly two decades was well founded, for commerce and trade prospered; for a time, Joppa thrived as a bustling tobacco port that seemed to be on the rise. Ironically, the seeds of its early demise were planted only four years after its birth, in 1729, when another new town, called Jonestown, was ordered erected on the banks of the Patapsco River. Then, three years later, the government passed "An Act for erecting a Town on a Creek, divided on the East, from the Town lately laid out in Baltimore County, called Baltimore Town, on the Land whereon Edward Fell keeps Store."[74] The two new towns would eventually combine and become the great American city of Baltimore. The new port on the Patapsco, with its commodious harbor, quickly became a magnet to business and shipping that all but doomed Joppa.

Joppa suffered from the same ills that contributed to the demise of many other tidewater towns that had somehow managed to get off the drawing boards. Sediment from the hinterland, which had been denuded of its forests and ground cover for agricultural purposes, had

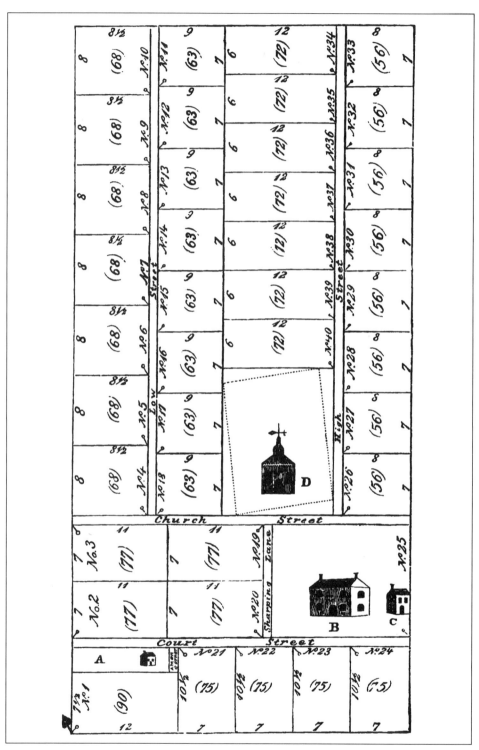

Plan of Joppa, Baltimore County (now in Harford County), Maryland, in 1725, as redrawn by J. Thomas Scharf, 1879. Courtesy Library of Congress, Washington, D.C.

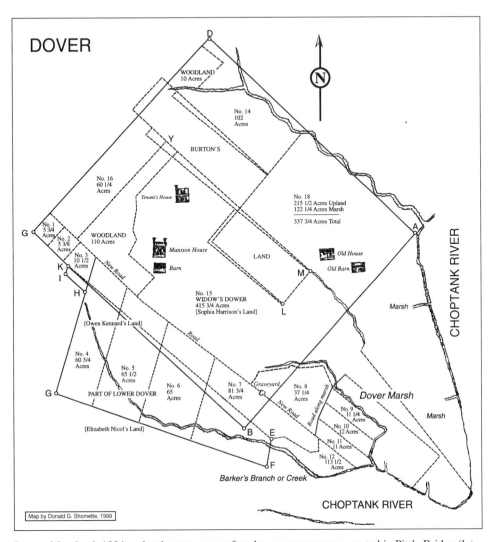

Dover, Maryland, 1804, only nineteen years after the county seat was erected in Pitt's Bridge (later Easton). Drawn from two plans in the Burton Papers Collection, Historical Society of Talbot County, Easton, Maryland.

begun to fill the harbor, intensifying the difficulty of navigating to the port. A smallpox epidemic, brought aboard a ship entering the harbor in 1731, had also hindered the growth of the town. There was political and economic pressure from influential citizens and merchants of the city on the Patapsco, who declared their port to be a more dynamic and progressive center for trade. In 1768, no longer capable of competing, Joppa relinquished its role as county seat, and within a few years had entirely vanished, save for the home of a single merchant, Benjamin Rumsey. There is some irony in that the town that had replaced the first court town named after Lord Baltimore on Bush River—thereby dooming it to extinction—was itself replaced as county seat by a second town named Baltimore, this one on the Patapsco River.

With Joppa, a trend of sorts had begun. By the mid-1720s, the shifting demographics of tidewater Maryland would influence changes in the locations of county seats not only in

Baltimore County, but in others as well, such as Calvert, St. Mary's, and Charles Counties. Ironically, following these new alterations, a spate of individual new town creations would come, many of which, unlike their antecedents, would endure, grow, and thrive to the present time.

In 1725, owing to pressure from many inhabitants seeking a more centralized location for their county government, the citizens of Calvert County succeeded in having their court moved from Battle Town (Calverton) on Battle Creek to a new site in midcounty, a place called Williams Old Fields. The new court site, the first to be erected without being directly adjacent to a navigable body of water, soon became the town of Prince Frederick. Then, in 1728, the government passed an act for erecting a town in St. Mary's County on fifty acres of land adjoining the courthouse on Breton Bay, "at a place formerly called Seymour Town." This site was divided into eighty equal lots, with the methodology and regulations for survey, laying out lots, sales, and building being the same as those followed in the more recent acts. The town was named Leonardtown, and it has faithfully served as the county seat of St. Mary's County, the oldest county in Maryland, to the present. In Charles County, the court was moved to a site at the head of the Port Tobacco River called Chandlers Town, which was formally established as Charlestown in 1729 and later reestablished nearby as Port Tobacco.[75]

The genie was again out of the bottle, not on the scope of the heyday of new town ordinances and acts experienced between 1667 and 1707, but with substantial force nevertheless. No fewer than thirty acts and supplementary acts would be passed between 1729 and 1751, calling for the erection, enlargement, reduction, or enhancement of no less than eighteen new towns, and the rededication or enlargement of four more—Chestertown, Benedict-Leonard, Upper Marlborough (or Marlborough Town), and Snow Hill—enumerated in the acts of 1706 and 1707 or earlier. Of the new towns to be erected in nine different counties, more than half would disappear before reaching maturity. But with a survival rate of approximately 50 percent for the remainder, a unique page in tidewater urban history had been turned.

Occasionally new town acts were passed authorizing the re-creation and resurveys of towns laid out in earlier acts: Snow Hill in 1742; Upper Marlborough in 1744; Baltimore and Jonestown in 1747 (the combining of two towns that were rapidly growing as one); the reduction in size of an earlier town site such as Benedict-Leonard Town on the Patuxent in 1732; or the enlargement of a town, such as when Baltimore sought to add twenty-five acres to its borders in 1750.[76]

The concept of competing sister towns had failed when Queen Anne's Town and Kilkenny Town were founded on opposite sides of the Patuxent River in Prince George's and Anne Arundel Counties in 1706 and 1707, but this had not dissuaded certain inhabitants of the Eastern Shore counties from attempting the same experiment. In 1730, Chestertown was among several sites to be laid out anew in Kent County, and the town became the county seat. Two years later, Kings Town was ordered erected on thirty acres of land on the Chester River directly opposite the county seat and was thus doomed from the outset. The concept was again tested in 1736, this time with moderate success, when Fredericktown was laid out on the Sassafras River in Cecil County, and a rival port named Georgetown was established on the opposite shore in Kent County. The only intentional attempt to erect a single town bifurcated in two counties came in 1732 when the government ordered commissioners in Queen Anne's and Dorchester Counties to survey and lay out a town at the head of the Choptank River, comprised of twenty acres of land in each county and joined together by a bridge over the river. The Queen Anne's County surveyor was authorized to conduct the survey for both counties. The town was to be named, of course, Bridgetown.[77]

In 1751 the General Assembly enacted the last significant piece of new town and port leg-islation in colonial Maryland history when it authorized the creation of another George-town, this one to be situated above the mouth of Rock Creek on the Potomac River.[78] The move was perhaps symbolic in a way, for the site was to be laid out on sixty acres of land just below the fall line, thus becoming the westernmost tidewater town in the colony, lo-cated at the head of deepwater navigation on the Potomac. No longer was the frontier at the edge of the coastal zone; it was pushing westward. Soon, following the close of the Seven Years War, more counties would be created, and Maryland emigrants in increasing numbers would press toward the Allegheny Mountains, the Ohio River, and beyond. The port of Bal-timore would continue to grow and, after independence, eventually dominate all trade in the state. Denuded soils, no longer fertile thanks to decades of nonstop tobacco farming, would erode into the streams, rivers, and Bay, silting them up and reducing access to the innumera-ble towns and ports erected upon their banks, killing off those that had managed to thrive against all odds. The War of 1812 would see the destruction of many others. The steam age would arrive with its wonderful boats and trains, and an improving system of overland high-ways would bypass the few remaining towns and landings of the colonial era, causing them to expire.

Today, all that remains of more than 130 towns proclaimed, ordered, or legislated into ex-istence during the great colonial experiment in urban development are a handful of commu-nities and a city or two worthy of note. Unfortunately, the contributions of many of Maryland's now extinct ports and towns are little known and less appreciated for their role in the greater scheme of tidewater history. Suffice it to say their very existence was instru-mental in shaping the course of Maryland's early history. Theirs are the stories not only of the illusions of what might have been, but of times and places that did exist, a vanished era patiently awaiting rediscovery.

1 BATTLE TOWN

"In Battle Blood, and fractious Clamour"

November 26, 1997. It was a leaden, windy, bitterly cold morning on the lower Patuxent River shoreline, not suited for either comfortable explorations or photography. However, the fields were devoid of the ground cover that normally masks features in the earth, such as the soil stains, scars, depressions, and surficial artifact scatters which often indicate archaeological sites—the discovery of which was the principal reason for our coming. The harvest was in and the winter snow and ice had not yet obscured the landscape; it was the optimum time to conduct such investigations, chilly winds and gray skies notwithstanding. Our objective was to examine a shoreline terrace shouldered by the river on one side and a diminutive waterway called Battle Creek on the other, on which had once stood one of tidewater Maryland's premier ports and the first county seat of Calvert County—a vanished town once known as Battle.

I had come to Battle Creek accompanied by Bill Clark, the gregarious head of the Calvert County Soil Conservation District Office. He had orchestrated a meeting with Susan Hance-Wells, whose family had for generations held a sizable chunk of the land we were about to examine and who was to provide access to the site. Except for one short spell, the Hances, one of the most prominent and respected old-line families in the county, had maintained ownership of much of the tract for nearly two centuries, ever since Young Dorsey Hance had acquired it from the Taney family back about 1835. The Taneys had owned the better part of that since 1681.

The scenic peninsula of the Hance farm slopes gently toward the confluence of the Patuxent River on the west and Battle Creek on the southeast. Its 325 acres are ensconced on some of the most fertile land in all of southern Maryland. They are also among the most majestic in the entire tidewater. The farm's moderate- to well-drained soils, according to my friend and guide from the Soil Conservation Office, are technically referred to as the Othello-Keyport-Elkton Association and range from a dominantly silty clay loam to a sandy clay-loam substrate. Susan and her husband, Walter Wells, have served as capable stewards of the land, raising tobacco, corn and small grain, cattle, and sheep, while managing a small horse-boarding business. From the elevation to the east, a grand view of the peninsula, which contains only a few small farm buildings erected in modern times, can be seen from the Hance homestead, a large, rectangular, colonial brick manse known as Taney Place. Surrounded by aged cedar trees, this famous manor house, though rarely opened for any "house and garden" tours, is steeped in history. Architecturally, it is a sturdy, Georgian structure with solid brick ends more than two feet thick and clapboard sides that were added in the nineteenth century. An unusual carved wall is in the living room, and a dumbwaiter (a luxury seldom seen in manorial estates of the pre-Revolutionary era) rises to the dining room from the kitchen, which in the eighteenth century was in the basement.[1] Down through the centuries, the many tenants of the building provided the grist from which Maryland history was molded. "I knew," Susan confessed, "the house was special, but I never knew how historic it really was. There are no ghosts here, but there are a lot of memories. If these walls could only speak."

After our cordial meeting with Susan and a tour of the Taney Place grounds and stables, Bill and I set off in his truck for the Battle Town peninsula a half mile below, specifically for its rivermost projection known as Prison Point. As we approached our destination, we could readily discern an enormous scatter of oyster shells on the littoral ahead, a prehistoric shell midden many acres in extent and sprinkled throughout the plow zone. Even beneath overcast skies, each gray-white shell reflected the daylight like a dull pewter star that had dropped to earth, and before us was an entire galaxy.

For the archaeologist, the prospect exhibited was truly awesome, for here was the physical testimony of extensive prehistoric activity right below our feet, turned up by several hundred years of tillage but potentially untouched and even more ample beneath the plow zone. Buried beneath us was a wealth of evidence that Native Americans had settled, lived out their lives, and probably died in this very spot. The middens were also the most prominent reminders that the natives had also supped frequently and well off the bounty of the river and Bay, discarding their refuse in massive heaps spread literally over acres of land. As we began to walk the fields, we observed a slight depression running the length of the midden area; on either side were concentrations of tiny brick fragments. We moved along the depression toward the Patuxent shore, and small flecks of pottery, both prehistoric and historic, could be seen among the shells on both sides of the line, also turned up by years of tilling. Even as Bill picked up a stone projectile point, I noted a conglomerate of badly corroded iron peeking from the lip of a small and recently dug pit nearby. I had seen such excavations many times before at other sites where relic hunters, often wielding metal detectors, had despoiled the archaeological record in search of artifacts for their personal collections.

To help us interpret the surface of the site and to identify the probable locations of important feature areas when we arrived on the plain, we came well armed with an arsenal of aerial infrared photographs as well as historic and geologic maps, including a copy of an original seventeenth-century survey of the early town that had once stood here. Interpretation was not, unhappily, as easy at it might seem. In the last few years, alterations of the shores were carried out to facilitate local development beyond but close to the peninsula, and the hydrodynamics of the nearshore waters had been subtly changed. Now, as we reached the beach and walked along it toward Prison Point, we discovered large clods of earth, freckled with shell, eroding into the water along the entire reach. The ancient terrace upon which the town had been erected, hitherto stable for centuries, stood only about six feet above the waterline. The shoreline, which had seemingly remained unchanged for well over three hundred years, had suddenly begun to mutate. Thanks to the hand of modern man with his so-called beach stabilization programs, harbor moles, and jetties that changed the flow of water and influenced sedimentation, the old peninsular coastline was rapidly disappearing. Yet, there were unexpected benefits. The dramatic knifelike erosional process also presented us with a perfect cutaway profile, thousands of feet in extent, of perhaps four thousand years or more of the archaeological record.

As we walked along the edge of the shore, we could plainly see that shells liberally mixed with brick extended from the surface to a depth of about nine inches, indicating that the area had been well plowed, mixing the upper historic strata with the earlier prehistoric record. At one location, which coincided with the terminus of the long depression encountered earlier, we detected a sharp dip in the shell line, which suggested an undisturbed trash or fire pit, or possibly even a burial site. Upon closer investigation, we discovered a thin stratum of ash about fifteen inches below the surface, indicating a fire had been burned in the hollow perhaps a thousand years ago or longer, topped by another stratum of shells two inches above.

Top: The historic Taney House, birthplace of Supreme Court Justice Roger Brooke Taney and scene of the infamous Taney-Magruder duel, as it appears today overlooking the site of old Battle Town. *Bottom:* The author investigates an eroding prehistoric shell midden near Prison Point at the site of Battle Town, Maryland. Photograph by William Clark, 1997.

Large bones and small flakes of pottery, exposed by the incessant pounding of waves during periods of storm, protruded seaward from the cavity. As we continued westward, the shell concentrations became sparse but remained visible until we arrived at the edge of a former wetland, now largely filled in. At the remote tip of Prison Point, further evidence of midden materials was encountered, exposed by the upturned soils at the bases of small trees growing from the embankment. Along the entire reach, it was apparent that we were likely to be the last to observe these exact features owing to the intense and ongoing erosion, as much as four feet a year, that was claiming one of the most important, unexcavated prehistoric and historic archaeological sites in the entire Chesapeake tidewater.

Battle Town, formally established in 1669, witness to innumerable pivotal moments of history, erected on a site that had been occupied for nearly twenty-three hundred years before the coming of the white man, was ultimately doomed, it would appear, to the unrelenting depredations of nature itself—coastal erosion.

Precisely when the first human occupation occurred along the shores of Battle Creek is uncertain. Archaeological evidence, however, indicates that Native Americans had been active in the area since the beginning of an era referred to as the Early Woodland Period (about 2100 B.C.), and activity progressed through several distinct phases thereafter. The onset of the Early Woodland was a time of climactic change in the Maryland tidewater, from warm, dry, sub-Boreal conditions to a substantially milder but wetter age known as the sub-Atlantic episode, comparable to today's weather. It was also an era of dramatic environmental change when vegetation patterns that exist today were first established, and animal species achieved their present distributions. About 1000 B.C., natural sea level rise, which had been underway for many millennia following the retreat of the glacial age, slowly began to stabilize in many estuarine zones, such as the Chesapeake tidewater and its innumerable tributaries, including the Patuxent River. Although hydrostatic change did not entirely halt (it continued to drive estuarine habitats of many life forms further upstream), some archaeologists believe the event itself may have triggered an expansion of the populations of certain species along the Patuxent drainage, setting the stage for increased human habitation in many areas.[2]

The earliest positive evidence of continued human activity along the shores to the north of Battle Creek appeared during a 350-year period referred to by archaeologists as the Accokeek Phase (750–400 B.C.). The areas about Duke's Wharf and Battle Creek are believed to be the southernmost extent of this phase encountered to date on the eastern shores of the Patuxent, as evidenced by extensive shell middens adjacent to the estuarine zone. The presence of such middens has been attributed by most archaeologists to a shift from the hunter-gatherer lifestyle among the native population of the Late Archaic Period to the subsistence-based economy of the Early Woodland, one made possible by the introduction of suitable ceramic vessels in which oysters and other foods were boiled for consumption. The type of pottery prevalent during this era in the Duke's Wharf–Battle Creek area is called Accokeek Cord, named by archaeologists after the patterns of cord impressions that decorated its surface.[3]

The second known occupation occurred during the period of A.D. 200 to 800 and is called the Selby Bay Phase. During this period, sites selected for settlement by the natives were dependent upon the location, the productivity of the area, and the behavioral characteristics of the available resources. Small groups of people gathered the bounty of the river for food and other uses, and returned repeatedly to productive and proven areas such as Battle Creek. Larger groups of natives focused their subsistence upon fishing for anadromous fish. A subsequent period known as the Little Round Bay Phase (A.D. 800–1250) bore many similar patterns to that of the Selby Bay Phase but was supplanted by the fourth and last period, known as the Sullivan's Cove Phase (A.D. 1250–1600). During this concluding period, wild food played an important role in native subsistence along the Battle Creek shoreline, particularly fish, oysters, clams, and certain plants, as well as deer and small mammals.[4]

In 1608, when Captain John Smith visited the river, he recorded the presence of the Indian village of Onantuck somewhere on or above the north shore of the creek, possibly as far upriver as present Duke's Wharf. On the south shore, most likely in the vicinity of Parkers Creek, he noted the town of Pawtuxunt, namesake of the river and the Indian tribe that inhabited its banks. Unlike native groups elsewhere in the tidewater, the peoples living all along the Patuxent welcomed the white explorer with friendship. Although Smith perceived their greatest strength at no more than two hundred warriors, he recorded: "These of all we found most civil to give entertainment."[5]

Soon after his arrival in Maryland in 1634, Father Andrew White quickly became as knowledgeable about the Patuxent Indians as anyone. He described them as "very proper and tall men, by nature swarthy, but much more by art, painting themselves with colors in oil a dark red, especially about the head, which they do to keep away the gnats." Their faces were occasionally decorated in other colors as well, often in blue from the nose downward and red upward, "and sometimes contrary wise with great variety, and in ghastly manner." Only the very old men had beards, and most young men drew long lines with colors from the sides of their mouths to their ears. They wore their hair in many fashions, some having it cut short on one half of the head and left long on the opposite side, while others wore it all long. Almost all of them wore "a lock at the left ear, and sometimes at both ears which they fold up with a string of wampampeake or roanoke [shell] about it." Some of their great men or advisers, known as Caweawaassough, wore copper ornaments in the form of fish on their foreheads, and both men and women wore bead necklaces. A few adorned themselves with hawk bills, eagle talons, the teeth of animals, and sometimes a pair of great eagle wings linked together. Their garments were generally made of deerskins and other pelts and were loosely worn like mantles or as girdles.[6]

Their weapons consisted of spears, stone axes, and bows with arrows about forty-five inches in length, feathered with turkey feathers and tipped with points of deer horn or flint. The arrow shafts were fashioned from small cane or sticks; they could be fired with accuracy up to twenty yards to kill birds as small as sparrows. The Patuxents' daily subsistence of game meat included deer, partridge, turkey, squirrels, and the like. Their diet also included pone made of wheat and hominy, eaten with peas and beans, fish, fowl, and venison. Houses in the village were constructed in a half-oval form, twenty feet long and nine or ten feet high, with an opening in the ceiling half a yard wide to admit light and to let out smoke from the fire built in the middle of the dwelling. At night they slept upon mats spread on a low scaffold about eighteen inches above the ground to protect them from the cold and damp.[7]

The Patuxent Indians, members of the Piscataway peoples and of Algonquian linguistic stock, were governed by an emperor called a tayac, who possessed absolute power over life and death among his minions. The tayac alone possessed certain prerogatives of honor and wealth not enjoyed by others, but in personal appearance he was almost indistinguishable from the multitude. The local tribe was administered by a chief, or king as the English called him, who differed little in outward appearance from his people. The only peculiarity by which a chief might be distinguished was a badge, either "a collar made of a rude jewel, or a belt, or a cloak, oftentimes ornamented with shells in circular rows." His fiefdom, however, was "generally circumscribed by the narrow confines of a single village and the adjacent country," although the tayac's dominion, which was based on the Potomac River at Piscataway, stretched approximately 130 miles.[8]

Father White was delighted to observe the natural wit of the natives, their excellent senses of smell and taste, and their keen eyesight. They were a polygamous people, but their women were noted as "modest and grave." Father White was impressed by these peaceful natives who he described "as generally so noble, as you can do them no favor, but they will return it." As for their religious inclinations, he observed: "They acknowledge one god of heaven, whom they call our god, and cry a 1000 shames on those that so lightly offend so good a god, but give no external honor to him but use all their might to please an Okee which signifies a frantic spirit, for fear of harm from him."

The priest reported that they also worshipped wheat and fire as gods beneficial to mankind. In the Matchcomaco, or temple of the Patuxents, this ceremony had been witnessed by English traders. The ritual began at an appointed day and location when the participants built a great fire. Standing about the fire, they lifted up their hands to heaven crying "Taho Taho." Then a bag of tobacco (which they called "Poate" or "Potu") and a great tobacco pipe were carried around the fire. A young man followed, dancing after the pipe carrier and crying as before, "Taho Taho." This being done, all smoked the pipe "which they breathed out on all parts of their bodies, as if it were to sanctify them to the service of their god."[9]

The Patuxent Indians, a peaceful tribe, were delighted by some of the possessions of their visitors from across the great sea, especially their strange garb. So great was the attraction that within a short time of the first contact with European settlers on the nearby St. Mary's River, the werowance, or priest, of the Patuxents had adopted the white man's fashions and taken to wearing English attire.[10] Unfortunately, the Indians' adoption of the clothing of the white man would not prevent the latter from occupying, and then completely usurping, the lands of these gentle, hospitable people.

Though the Patuxents who lived on and near the creek did not yet know it, their lands would prove to be among the most desirable of any along the entire watershed for settlement by the white colonists. In June 1650, when Robert Brooke arrived in Maryland with his wife, children, and servants, the native population along both shores of the lower Patuxent had already receded from the scene. Brooke was understandably drawn to the wonderful lands that they had abandoned. He first settled on a two-thousand-acre tract on the south side of the river some twenty miles from its mouth and named the patent "de la Brooke Manor."[11] Two years later, he acquired another twenty-one hundred acres on the north shore of the river where it joined a large creek. Nearby, the native villages of Onantuck and Pawtuxunt had flourished less than half a century earlier. He named the beautiful little waterway Battle Creek, in memory of his late first wife, Mary Baker, who had been born in the town of Battle in Sussex, England, site of the famous 1066 Battle of Hastings. On the south side of the creek he erected his new plantation and called it Brooke Place Manor.[12]

Until 1658, the north shore of Battle Creek was without European settlement. In that year, as part of a grant of six hundred acres, James Berry, a Puritan who had emigrated from Virginia, obtained title to lands on the shores of the creek opposite Brooke Place Manor, and he promptly named the new tract "Berry." A man of substantial importance, Berry had been a leader of the Puritans in Virginia after landing there in 1632. Upon his arrival in Maryland with his son William and other family members in 1652, he had served as a county commissioner and judge when the county was briefly called Patuxent County. His son William settled in nearby Hunting Creek Hundred and married Rhoda Preston, the daughter of Richard Preston, Sr., the acknowledged leader of the Puritan element in the colony.[13]

Berry's selection of property could not have been better. Battle Creek was a splendid waterway. Tucked into the Calvert County shoreline, it ran only two miles in length in a northeastern direction. On the lip of its southeastern shore, a small, uninhabitable marshy peninsula and shoal projected into the river. On the northwestern lip, standing several feet above the water, the terrace was flat, fertile, and featureless. Both shores of the creek were wrinkled with numerous indentations and coves, each a miniharbor suitable for sheltering small vessels of light draft. The first cove provided deep water directly adjacent to the shore, suitable for service as a full-sized merchant-ship anchorage. Although the water depth at this point is today little over eight feet, in Berry's time it was far greater.

The commodious north shore peninsula was delightful to behold. Brooke had been charged by Lord Baltimore, his friend and master, with no less a task than to bring organized settlement and government to this sector of his frontier empire, and he saw substantial possibilities for the land. As he gazed across the broad creek toward the Berry patent, he may have been the first to envision the spacious terrace as a town suitable to serve as a seaport and possibly even a municipal center. But actual promulgation of the concept would be years in coming.[14]

In 1666, James Berry died, and his son William inherited the Berry tract on Battle Creek.[15] Two years later, on June 5, 1668, Governor Charles Calvert, acting under instructions sent by Lord Baltimore, issued a proclamation designating eleven sites in the colony as "sea ports, harbors, creeks, and places for the discharging and unloading of goods and merchandise out of ships, boats, and other vessels." The Battle Creek site was not included. The following year, when Calvert's proclamation was replaced by an ordinance of the Lord Proprietary, it was ordered that all imports for every county in the province be channeled through twelve designated and convenient ports. This time, the Battle Creek site was officially designated and even given a formal name: Calverton. It was also the first time some sites were specifically referred to as "town land." Apparently, resistance by planters to the 1669 ordinance convinced the governor that it was not expedient to require exports to pass through these ports and harbors, for in 1671 he repeated the 1669 provisions in a third declaration but removed the offending section on exportations. This time he listed fifteen sites and revived the Calverton site, which was now identified as "at William Berries land in Battle Creek in Patuxent River."[16]

Although the declarations met with limited success elsewhere, the 1669 government edict had the effect of stimulating the first positive move to create an actual town on the shores of Battle Creek. William Berry, who apparently had converted to Quakerism, was of the same mind as the visionary Brooke on the concept of a town site at the entrance to the creek, and he agreed to donate acreage for the purpose. Under the tenets of the ordinance of 1669, Berry "did apply himself to your Lordship & humbly besought Your Lordship that twenty acres of land, part of a tract of land belonging to him the said William at Battle Creek aforesaid, might be appointed for town land for that part of the said County."[17]

It seems likely that Berry's donation was probably in the works almost as soon as the ink was dry on the proprietor's 1668 proclamation, even though the site wasn't named. On August 27, 1668, a warrant to survey Berry's donated land was issued to Charles Boteler, deputy surveyor of Calvert County, the timing of which suggests that the offering may have been stimulated by the first edict. Boteler was instructed to lay out "so many lots that convenient streets [to] be left of sixty foot in breadth . . . leaving by the water side a street one hundred foot wide." Upon completion of the survey and laying out of the town lands, any inhabitants who were willing to "build out of hand," were to be assigned the "greatest lots," suggesting that, unlike later towns with standard gridded plots of equal size, those of the new town on Battle Creek varied in proportions. Upon certification by Boteler, the property owners were then to be granted patents by the proprietor "to those that build, to them and their heirs forever." The surveyor was also instructed to keep a register and record of the survey and patents. Boteler seemed qualified for the task, having already served as deputy surveyor under the first county surveyor, Colonel Baker Brooke in 1675.[18]

The prospect of a town and port in the heart of Calvert County was well received. The Calvert County commissioners, "finding the said town land to be in the center of the said county, and the most convenient place for holding the courts for the said county" quickly ordered that a courthouse and prison be erected on the site, thereby officially recognizing it as the site of the county seat, even though that status had not been formally declared. Two hundred thousand pounds of tobacco were appropriated to pay for the construction, suggesting that the building was to be both substantial and commodious. Plans were rapidly laid out for the future town to include not only a courthouse and jail, but a chapel, residential buildings, a cistern, and docks.[19]

The beginnings of Calverton were significant in that the town was destined to become one of the few early planned urban centers to actually survive during the Maryland colony's first century. Yet, as with the beginnings of many such towns, memories are clouded by the passage of time, and records are lost, destroyed, or rendered unreliable due to the occasionally inaccurate machinations of professional and amateur historians alike. The town's origin and even its correct name remain grist for scholarly contention. Archaeologist Dennis Pogue, a nationally reputed authority on early tidewater urban and manor sites, has observed that the names Battle Town and Calverton were often used interchangeably. The former was the most commonly employed throughout history, most notably after the Revolution of 1689 when the name Calvert was, for a time, shunned. Charles Francis Stein, a historian well known for his *History of Calvert County, Maryland*, suggested that Battle Town was actually laid out by Commander Brooke well before 1654. The contention was supported by Annie L. Sioussat in *Old Manors in the Colony of Maryland*, but neither writer supported the claims with evidence. In fact, no documentation has been located to date to suggest that the town was actually laid out prior to 1668, although it was probably considered by Calvert, Brooke, and others.[20]

The early years of Battle Town, or Calverton as it was at first officially called, are shrouded in mystery, with only an occasional detail or record exposed here and there for analysis. The dedication of land and the survey carried out upon it had a most positive affect in stimulating a number of inhabitants to "build and erect several dwelling houses and store houses upon the said twenty acres of land," and to take up residence. That the site was significant enough to be recorded in Europe only a few years after its founding testifies to its early importance. In 1671, when John Ogilby published his famous work *America: Being the Latest, and Most Accurate Description of the New World,* he reported that the three towns in Calvert County—Harvington, Herrington, and "another in Battel-Creek call'd Calverton"—already had houses built upon them "all uniform, and pleasant with streets, and keys [quays] on the water side." Two years later, Calverton first appeared on a published map when Augustine Herrman presented his celebrated chart of Virginia and Maryland.[21]

Despite Ogilby's contentions, called promotional by some historians, it is questionable if much development had actually taken place at the site on Battle Creek by the time that his and Herrman's works first appeared, although the courthouse had almost certainly been erected early on and a few inhabitants had taken up private occupancy and opened businesses. One of the first settlers known to take up residence was Thomas Cosden, who emigrated to Maryland in 1668 with his wife Sarah and two daughters. For a brief period, Cosden made his home in St. Mary's City and became one of the original aldermen of that town after it was chartered. Following the death of his wife in 1670, he married Elizabeth Thompson Brooke, the widow of Robert Brooke, Jr.[22] About this time, Cosden operated an inn at New Town on the Potomac River, but he soon found the location not quite to his liking. Five years later, he was a wealthy "innholder of Calverton" who was contributing an annual levy of two thousand pounds of tobacco, second highest in the county and exceeded only by the governor himself who paid ten thousand pounds.[23]

Cosden's inn was called Punch, and it was often employed by the government as well as the occasional wayfarer. When the industrious innkeeper first arrived in Battle Town, the county courthouse and the diminutive prison were already in poor condition. The courthouse, which had been constructed at great expense, had to be repaired with clapboards because holes in the roof had become so large one could peer through them. Though only twelve feet square, the county jail, or "cage," required a new stairway, described as "half pac'd large stairs," with easy treads or half steps. It is thus not surprising that the court and government business was obliged to be conducted at an alternative site from time to time, and Cosden's inn fit the bill. Between 1675 and 1679, Chancery Court meetings were often convened there, and the innkeeper received two thousand pounds of tobacco in payment "for quartering men raised for public service," undoubtedly persons involved in court business such as jurors and court personnel. Cosden would remain in Battle Town managing his inn until his death in 1683.[24]

On occasion, the governor's council itself found it convenient to meet in Battle Town to conduct business critical to the management of the colony, thereby making the town the temporary *pro forma* executive seat of colonial government, at least for the duration of the council sessions. On June 1, 1680, the council convened in town at the home of Michael Taney (or Tawny) to confer on important matters relating to the Mattawoman Indians and their war against the Susquehannocks.[25]

The Taney house in which the council met belonged to the founder of one of the earliest Puritan families to settle in Calvert County. The name Taney was of French origin and had been derived from the ancient name de Tani, a family of Huguenots who had been among the refugees seeking sanctuary in England from the Catholic reign of terror in France. Michael Taney and his brother John had been among a number of Puritans who had been brought to Maryland by Thomas Letchworth before 1655. Letchworth received a grant, known as Letchworth's Chance, at Plum Point on Chesapeake Bay as a consideration for having borne much of the expense for bringing the refugees and others to Maryland, as was the proprietor's policy.[26] The new immigrants were employed as soon as they touched the sandy shores of the tidewater.

Both Michael and John Taney were apprenticed to men of some property, Michael to Thomas Letchworth and John to Major Thomas Truman. Of the two brothers, Michael's star showed the brightest. After serving his time as an indentured apprentice, he was able to prosper considerably as a merchant. He married twice, first to Mary Phillips, daughter of a Puritan ship captain, named Samuel Phillips, whose ships plied between Calvert County and London, and later to Margaret Beckwith. From his lowly beginnings, he eventually rose to become the high sheriff of Calvert County, a position of enormous prestige, power, and influence. In 1663, he acquired his first major land grant, which he purchased from John Lawrence and dubbed Taney's Right. Michael Taney was not slow to capitalize on his rights. Two years later, he demanded a land grant promised him for helping to transport himself and his brother to the colony.[27] There were to be many grants in the future, all situated within Hunting Creek Hundred, including Taney's Desire, Littleworth, Wooden Point, Long Point, Blind Tom, Taney's Ease, Taney's Addition, and Taney's Delight. About 1680, Taney acquired part of the Berry tract from William Berry and the following year, a 125-acre tract adjoining Berry and the Calverton lands. The new tract overlooked the confluence of the Patuxent River and Battle Creek and the infant village between.[28]

It has been suggested that by acquiring the 125 acres of land adjacent to the town, Taney may have been speculating on Calverton's growth.[29] In 1682 it was reported that "Several inhabitants . . . did build and erect several dwelling houses and store houses upon the said twenty acres of land and from that time have continually resided there and did order and appoint the courthouse and prison to be built."[30] It appeared that the little village was finally about to take hold and grow a bit, albeit not on the scale originally hoped for.

Unfortunately, as was frequently the case in the dedication of lands for municipal development, a property dispute arose over town and lot boundaries. In this case, the argument concerned those lands belonging to Berry and Taney. In May 1682, a petition to the Assembly was submitted by a number of inhabitants led by Taney. It charged that Berry, having found that the land was "much improved" and the creek had grown to become "a considerable place of Trade" thanks to the labors of the inhabitants, had become covetous of said improvements. As a consequence, he denied that any title or assurances of ownership had been given at all. The petitioners, having spent their fortunes in settling, claimed that they would be ruined and their loss would be "to the manifest damage of the whole County."[31]

The petitioners requested the proprietor and the Assembly to settle the disagreement to ensure title to their property. Taney was one of the principal complainants, charging that Berry had failed to live up to his agreement in ceding the town lands. The controversy over the precise boundaries of the Taney, Berry, and town properties served only to compound the problem.[32]

In an effort to resolve the situation, the Upper House ordered Taney, Berry, and the surveyor to personally appear on May 6, 1682, and to produce the certificates of ownership and the plots taken for Berry by the surveyor in 1668 as well as the certification and plots for Taney's land. Two days later, Taney and Boteler appeared before the council as ordered. The surveyor testified first, stating that the town land had always been the property of William Berry and that the 1668 survey and laying out of the new town had been carried out in his presence. The people who had been encouraged to build and establish themselves in the new county seat, he stated, had "well hoped" the survey would be sufficient enough to ensure that no future surveys would be necessary.[33] Taney spoke next, offering to relinquish his claim to property he had taken up within the bounds of the town, though it lay outside of the lines of Berry's land. He was willing "to take a certificate if any without Berry's lines and not within the town land" if it would resolve the issue.[34] William Berry, who had also been summoned, failed to appear before the legislators, and by default, may have forsaken his own interest in the contested land. With Boteler simply stating history and Taney presenting his willingness towards accommodation (even as far as a land exchange) to end the dispute, the legislators agreed to address the petitioners' requests.

On May 8, the Upper House of the General Assembly ordered a resurvey "to lay out the lines of William Berry's land according to the due courses and distances mentioned in his patent, thereby to discover what land is lost betwixt that and the creek." A true plot was to be laid out in the presence of the inhabitants and certified to the governor and council "with all convenient speed." Berry was specifically ordered to be present during the survey.[35]

Three months later, on August 3, a survey of the Berry tract by Charles Boteler and his assistant Robert Jones was carried out for William Berry, although it appears that he again failed to appear. The surveyors' task was carried out in the presence of Cosden and Taney and included a supplemental survey of the Calverton site and its boundaries and also the production of a drawing showing the disposition of actual structures in the town.[36] Upon completion of their work, Boteler and Jones, in their report on the Berry tract survey, officially certified "that there is within the expressed lines five hundred fifty four acres of land and water, but of land without water no more than four hundred eighty five acres. We also certify that between the north-northeast line of the said land and Battle Creek there is upon several points extending themselves into the creek the quantity of sixty three acres, whereof ten acres of town land formerly given by Wm. Berry is part, as by a plot of the survey here unto annexed more plainly appeareth."[37]

The survey description of the town land was also quite definitive. "Beginning at the mouth of Battle Creek upon the point and running as the bank of the creek runs to the head of a bight or cove called and known by the name of Cosden's Landing, and from thence running south sixty-three degrees westerly for the length of nine chains seventy-five links to a mulberry tree on the back side of Thomas Cosden's houses, and of Patuxent River without Battle Creek's mouth and from thence with said river to the point where it first began, containing twenty acres."[38]

Two plats are known to have been produced from the August 3 survey, one of which is the earliest known plan of a seventeenth-century Maryland town. The first plan was of an area lying between the Battle Town tract and the Berry Plantation, and the second presented a detailed but smaller-scale rendering of the quite compact community of Battle Town.[39] The buildings represented in the plan of Battle Town were identified as the courthouse, a prison, a chapel, the residences of Michael Taney (indicated by the label "Tawny"), and a residence belonging to William Berry. Another building, probably a residence belonging to an occupant named Banks, was located near the courthouse. There were also five other buildings, possibly slave or servant quarters, tobacco barns, warehouses, stores, or kitchens. A structure identified as belonging to Cosden was most likely used as an inn (probably Punch) and lay at the northwest boundary of the town. Along the shores of a small cove on the creek abutting the town lands were two wharves, or quays, one identified as Tawny's Landing (directly opposite the Taney and Berry homes) and a second identified as Cosden's Landing.[40] Though certainly not what most people today would consider a proper town, here was a community that was an organized hub with political, social, and economic consequence, and with structures representative of governmental, judicial, religious, commercial, domestic, and maritime activities.

Recent analysis of the plats by Pogue provide considerable insight into the actual makeup of seventeenth-century Battle Town. The town, he notes, was somewhat less organized than suggested in the contemporary description provided by Ogilby. Yet, the site was obviously laid out in an orderly manner and with considerable forethought, with the line of structures running parallel with Battle Creek and public buildings intentionally grouped together. The public buildings—prison, chapel, and courthouse—were indicated without chimneys on the plan, undoubtedly as a safety precaution against fire. Another building without a chimney, identified as Banks, was located near the courthouse. Pogue hypothesized that the structure may have been a clerk's office or associated with some court related function, since the absence of a chimney in a building without an apparent public or government purpose and labeled as if a private residence could be quite misleading. It was, in fact, not unusual for such a building to be built without a hearth as an intentional safeguard against the possible devastation of the clerk's records by fire.[41]

The Taney and Berry homes were relatively close together, with a smaller structure, possibly a kitchen or quarter, adjacent to the former. An additional pair of buildings were situated to the east and, as suggested by the presence of chimneys, were most likely servant quarters rather than warehouses or barns. It is also possible that they may have been storehouses as Michael Taney was, among many other things, a merchant. The Cosden building, with its single dormer being its most prominent feature, probably served as both a residence and an inn, as was common practice. Situated a short distance away was a smaller structure, possibly a kitchen or quarter, and another chimneyless building somewhat inland, believed to be a warehouse or barn.[42]

Pogue's analysis of the plat was almost microscopic and resulted in perhaps one of the better descriptions recorded of a midseventeenth-century town in the Chesapeake tidewater. He noted that all twelve structures pictured on the plan had been rendered in great detail. While admitting that some aspects may have been artistic conventions rather than actual duplications, the representations of the architectural characteristics of each building, such as relative size, windows, door placements, chimneys, and roofing and building material, proved invaluable. "This evidence from Calverton," he observed, "adds support for many archaeologically-derived ideas pertaining to seventeenth-century housing types and spatial layouts of home lots." Since pictorial representations of seventeenth-century Maryland buildings of any kind are uncommon, and actual standing structures from the period are rarer still, such data as found on the Boteler plat was priceless and contributed significantly to a greater understanding of the architectural realities of the era in tidewater Maryland.[43]

It was apparent that each of the buildings was constructed of wood, with exterior clapboards and steep gabled roofs that may also have been clapboarded. It was impossible to discern whether chimneys were made of brick or of mud and stud construction, which uses dried mud and mud bricks over wooden frames. All four public buildings and the Cosden warehouse/barn were without chimneys, but the remainder, except for the Taney home, had single chimneys. Michael Taney's residence, probably the grandest of all in the little town and one befitting a man of his standing and influence, had two chimneys, one in a gable and the other serving a fireplace in the interior of the house. The Berry house also had an interior chimney. Each of the buildings except the Cosden warehouse/barn featured a single doorway on its long axis, flanked by windows. There were also windows in the gables.[44]

Pogue observed that the two most commodious structures in town were the courthouse and the Taney residence. In both buildings, a single dormer window was positioned above the entrance, undoubtedly to provide light to a half-story or sleeping loft. "Such a loft in the courthouse," he wrote, "would have been used by visitors to the court." But there were a number of unexpected features as well, including a series of floor-to-ceiling windows in the front facade of the courthouse. Unlike all the rest of the single-story structures, the Taney home appeared to be a two-story building as two rows of windows were pictured in addition to the loft.[45]

Surveying and laying out a new town was one thing, but getting paid by a stingy government for the work was another, as Robert Jones, who apparently conducted the actual field survey work on Battle Creek on August 3, 1682, soon discovered. On November 3, Jones, by then deputy surveyor of Calvert County, was obliged to petition the General Assembly for payment of sixteen hundred pounds of tobacco "for three resurveys by him made in Battle

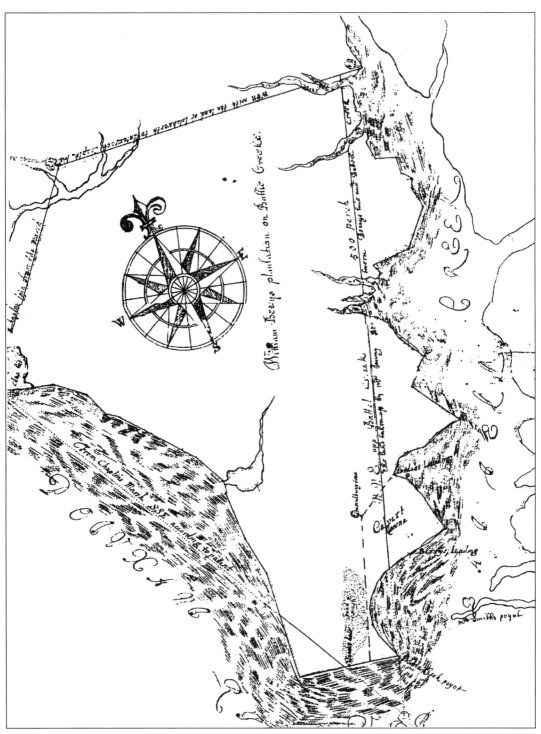

Charles Boteler's plan of the Battle Creek peninsula was one of three known plats produced from the August 2, 1682, survey of the Berry plantation, Calverton, and environs. Courtesy Calvert Marine Museum, Solomons, Maryland.

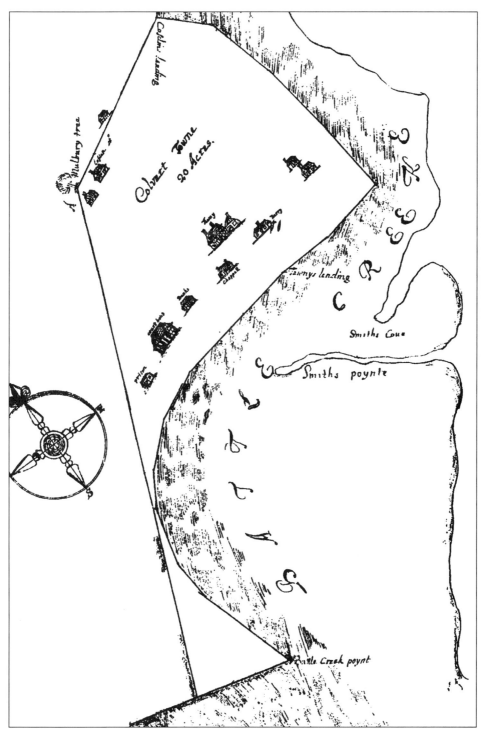

"Calvert Towne," the second of three plats by Charles Boteler. A superb descriptive visual index of a seventeenth-century governmental center and port, this is the earliest town plan produced in colonial Maryland discovered to date. Courtesy Calvert Marine Museum, Solomons, Maryland.

Creek," indicating that a third plat, as yet undiscovered, had also been produced. The following day, the Upper House shifted the request from its own lap into another and instructed the petitioner to "make his demands of the county for whose benefit the resurveys have been made."[46] It is unknown whether Jones received any more satisfaction from the county than he did from the General Assembly that had ordered the work done in the first place.

It is also uncertain how William Berry reacted to the final product of the resurvey. It appears that soon afterwards, he sold his plantation to Michael Taney, probably after 1682 but certainly before 1691 when he died. The transition may not have been too bitter a pill to swallow, for at the time of his death, Berry was still the owner of almost two thousand acres of land on the Eastern Shore and in Pennsylvania.[47]

In October 1683, when the government of Maryland again immersed itself in debate over sites to be designated as new towns, four locations were recommended for Calvert County: in or near Coxes Creek off the Patuxent River, at or near Warrington upon the Cliffs of Calvert, at Harvey Town, and in Battle Creek. All four sites were approved, but the status of Battle Town was set, for it was already a town in existence and one with a courthouse to boot.[48]

The presence of the courthouse was significant, not only to county justice and administration, but on occasion, to that of the whole colony, for from time to time the Provincial Council was also to convene there. On February 13–15, 1684, a session of the council attended by the Lord Proprietor, Colonels Taylor, Darnall, and Burgess, and Major Nicholas Sewell met in Calverton Court House. During the meeting, various petitions were heard; items considered included a dispute over the ownership of a servant and relief for an inhabitant unable to pay taxes. A debate established the proper fee to pay the doorkeeper of the council, a spousal abuse case was settled, and trials were held regarding a case of sedition and also a felony committed by an Eastern Shore Indian.[49]

On April 18, 1684, the Upper House again convened in the county building to address a supplement to the Act of Trade regarding new town legislation. Present were Colonels Henry Coursey, Thomas Taylor, Vincent Lowe, Henry Darnall, William Stevens, William Burgess, Major Nicholas Sewall, and John Darnall. The first orders of business were the small number of inhabitants in Battle Town, the consequent revision of the proprietors's new towns program, and a troublesome petition from Michael Taney. It was then moved that, under the tenets of the 1683 Act of Trade, the land given by Berry to the inhabitants of Battle Town "in consideration that the same should be constituted a town...revert to the donor, the consideration being taken away" unless remedied by the supplementary act.[50]

The Upper House promptly voted that the site was indeed a convenient location and should be settled upon as a town or port of trade and requested the Lower House to insert a provision in the supplementary act "it being the humble request of all the inhabitants there and diverse others in that county [that] the courthouse be thereon built at the great charge of the county." The same day, the Lower House complied and ordered (as if paper were a substitute for building materials, people, and sweat) "that there be a town at Battle Creek." On Saturday, April 19, the Upper House voted its consent. There were problems with the act that were not as easily addressed, nor were they amenable to the few property owners in the town such as Michael Taney. On April 21, only two days after the Upper House vote, Taney submitted a petition "for a town in Battle Creek upon his land; and that the same may be so laid out as to reserve his houses thereon built to himself." Taney's request carried enough weight that a clause was proposed for insertion into the act "reserving to every person his house or houses already built upon [in] any the ports or places of trade in the said act." The following day, however, the Upper House read and rejected the petition. There were to be no exceptions to the act as it regarded Battle Town.[51]

The enactment of "An Additional & Supplementary Act to the Act for Advancement of Trade" that was soon passed stated that "all tobaccos, goods, wares & merchandizes of the growth, production, and manufacture of this province intended to be sold here or transported out of this province shall be for that end & intent brought to the said ports and places" and included the site "in the County of Calvert at Calvert Town in Battle Creek."[52] On September 15, 1686, the government issued orders and instructions to officers appointed for each port in the colony to ensure that the acts for the advancement of trade were strictly observed. It came as no surprise that Michael Taney was selected as the officer for Calverton. He was sworn in by Robert Brooke and Captain Richard Ladd.[53]

From its recertification as a town and port by the 1683–1684 acts to the onset of the Protestant Revolution in 1689, the record of Calverton, like that of much of civil Maryland history of the period, is wrapped in darkness. The activities of Sheriff Michael Taney—Calverton's most visible citizen and one of the more politically and socially prominent men in the county—are known. Taney and his wife Mary, though Protestants, were vigorous supporters of the proprietor, under whose dominion they had fared exceedingly well. Although there was a chapel in the town, it apparently suffered for lack of clergy. Taney repeatedly sought to address the deficiency by submitting petitions to both King James II and to the Archbishop of Canterbury for help in maintaining "an orthodox divine at Calvert Town" lest neglect be "the utter ruin of many poor souls." The request, made as political and religious upheavals were sweeping across England and Maryland, went unanswered, and the chapel went unministered.[54]

In 1689, with the Glorious Revolution having brushed the old Catholic order out and a new Protestant one into power in England and Maryland, the citizens of tiny Calverton were undoubtedly torn in their loyalties during the ensuing revolt against the proprietary government. One town resident, John Broome, had heard rumors concerning Colonel Henry Darnall, a Catholic member of the council since 1679 and a cousin of the third Lord Baltimore by marriage, which said he was raising soldiers to support the proprietor. Broome was summoned to provide a deposition to that effect by Colonel Henry Jowles, one of the leaders of the anti-Baltimore faction. Broome's testimony is unknown, but it was likely the intent was to employ it as damaging testimony against Darnall. Such pressure had little effect upon Taney, who was outspoken in his opposition to the change of government. Unhappily, Taney, still high sheriff of Calvert County by a commission derived from Lord Baltimore, would pay dearly for his loyalty. Following the overthrow of Lord Baltimore's administration, Captain John Coode ordered him to hold an immediate election. "I endeavored," Taney later stated in describing his rebellion against the order, "with what arguments I could use to persuade all people . . . to lie still and keep the peace of the country . . . and I and many more of the better sort of the people set our hands to a paper writing that expressed modestly and loyally some reasons why we were not willing to choose any representatives to sit in that intended Assembly."[55]

In spirited support of the proprietary, Taney circulated the petition among many Calvert County planters. Sixty-seven other residents sided with him as he voiced his opposition by questioning both the necessity and the right of Protestants to overthrow the colonial government and also by refusing to elect representatives to the Protestant Assembly. For his troubles, he was ordered arrested by Coode and was seized at his house in Calverton on August

25, 1689, by James Bigger and six armed men. Taney remained a prisoner at Mattapany for at least five months. His health and political career were destroyed. After his release, he had only a short time remaining to him, for in 1692, undoubtedly broken by imprisonment, he died, leaving his plantation to his son Michael II.[56]

An examination of the elder Taney's inventory suggests that if speculation in land (at Calverton and elsewhere) had been his goal, he had succeeded far beyond the wildest dreams of the young indentured apprentice who had come to America with his master, Thomas Letchworth, many years before. His personal estate was worth more than £800 sterling. Unpaid debts owed him by nearly two hundred inhabitants of the surrounding area, totaling 162,875 pounds of tobacco, made him indeed a very prosperous man for his times. His inventory accounts also included a healthy variety of farming equipment and substantial livestock holdings, as well as large quantities of trade goods such as axes, hoes, knives, nails, fishhooks, bushels of salt, casks of sugar, tapes, thread, ribbons, stockings, bolts of a wide variety of cloths and silks, and more, indicating that he served as both merchant and planter as well as speculator.[57]

Following the Revolution of 1689, the name Calverton continued to be used interchangeably with Battle Town, though not as often. The conflict had imposed little if any damage to the tiny county seat. But the alteration of government itself would have a far more dramatic impact. From time to time, the governor's council had continued to meet at the courthouse in Battle Town, principally during the period of February 1693 to June 1694. The reasons for holding these sessions away from the acknowledged capital may have been connected to the efforts of some in the colony to have the government moved from St. Mary's to Anne Arundel County. In late 1693, when Sir Lionel Copley, the first royal governor of Maryland, died, he left the colony without an acting chief executive. It is possible that the council, without a governor at the helm and finding itself in the middle of contention between the pro- and anti-movement forces, had thought it more politically appropriate to assume the middle ground and await the arrival of the next duly authorized governor. During the council sessions that were convened in Calverton in the 1693–1694 period, numerous affairs of state were addressed, including protests against the "plunder" of the colony moneys by the former governor, the issuance of certificates for land surveys, matters concerning the Great Seal of Maryland, conflicts regarding port collectors, the administration of oaths of allegiance, defense issues and other military affairs, border problems with the natives, condemnation proceedings regarding various vessels, the appointment of county sheriffs, and the management of Indian affairs.[58] In the summer of 1694, a new chief executive, Francis Nicholson, arrived in Maryland and found himself immediately immersed in the power struggle regarding the proposed move. On October 18, 1694, two days after the Assembly passed "An Act for settling Assemblies & Provincial Courts & Erecting a Court house at Ann Arundel Town in Ann Arundel County," Nicholson gave his approval to the deed.[59]

The first meeting of the General Assembly in Annapolis was convened on February 28, 1695. But Nicholson's council would pay one last official visit to Calverton before his term was through. The move to Annapolis had been heavily objected to by the counties in southern Maryland, especially in the Catholic stronghold of St. Mary's; although the new capital was more geographically central to the colony as a whole on both shores, it obliged residents in the south to travel a considerable distance. Nicholson, a master of tactical compromise, could do little about the Assembly, but he resolved to make one last demonstrable effort to meet the grudging southerners halfway. In late December 1697, with the "happy and joyful news" that a peace had been achieved between England and France, ending the most recent round of hostilities known as King William's War, the governor saw his opportunity. He decided to order the council to assemble in special session but determined that "for the better convenience of the gentlemen of the council's meeting that live in the lower counties," the conference would be held at Calverton. The conference was to be convened on January 11, 1698, and was to include not only council members, but all of His Majesty's receivers, collectors, and naval district officers from the western shore, as well as other military and civilian leaders. The council members from the Eastern Shore were excused from attending on the grounds that it would be "altogether inconvenient and almost impossible" for them to come. Colonel John Addison was exempted owing to his garrison duty on the Potomac frontier. Persons required to testify before the council for various reasons, including John Shanks, Richard Cloud, Philip Clarke, William Taylard, Samuel Cooksey, William Husbands, Notley Maddox, Mary Vanswaringhen, Captain John Bayne, Major William Dent, George Lingan, and James Cranford, were instructed not to fail to appear "at their peril." To ferry the residents of St. Mary's and Charles Counties across the Patuxent, the governor instructed the high sheriff of St. Mary's, Robert Mason, to ensure that two "good substantial boats" and enough hands to man them be ready at Charles Ashcombe's plantation on the river to meet all those attending the session. Apparently, the session came off without a hitch. On January 11, from Calverton, Maryland, Governor Francis Nicholson issued the first public statement regarding the end of King William's War, announcing peace between England and France and calling for a day of public thanksgiving. The proclamation also called for a special election to permit the Assembly to meet in special session at Annapolis to address demobilization of military forces along the colony frontier.[60]

Although Calverton (or Battle Town), with deep water access right at its doorstep, had the capacity to serve as a port, its principal utility appears to have been as a court town. The courthouse standing in 1697–1698 was apparently a substantial building, and its fame was well known throughout the colony. As with most wooden buildings, fire was an ever-present danger, and the planners who designed and built the structure were not ignorant of the hazard. "The records of Calvert County are kept in a very good court house and distance enough from any other houses in which no ordinaries are kept nor is there any chimney" to prevent the danger of burning cinders falling upon the roof.[61] The wisdom of the builders of the Calverton Courthouse was, unfortunately, ignored by those charged with the erection of later halls of justice. In 1748 and 1882, two county courthouses in Prince Frederick were destroyed along with the records therein by accidental fire, and in 1814, another was burned by the torch of invaders.

In 1702 the justices of Calvert County, pursuant to an act of the Assembly, ordered Calvert County surveyor (and former clerk of the court) Edward Batson to resurvey "a parcel of land not exceeding three acres . . . upon which the courthouse of the said county now stands." He carried out his assignment with promptness on August 19 of the same year, and his survey was reported as follows: "Beginning at a locust now [marked] with four notches and running North fourteen perches [231 feet] to a stake, then East fourteen perches to another stake, then South ten perches [165 feet] to the creek side, then down the creek as the creek runneth to the first locust." The courthouse lot contained a total of "one acre and eight square perches of land."[62]

❖

The year after Batson's resurvey, Battle Town emerged briefly at the center of a most infamous admiralty case. By 1703, armed conflict between England and France had again erupted, this time in a contest known as Queen Anne's War, which would provide the backdrop for the scandal.

HMS *Oxford* was a substantial fourth-rate warship of 54 guns, 675 tons cargo capacity, 127 feet long and 34 feet abeam. Originally constructed at Bristol, England, in 1674, she had been rebuilt in 1702 at Deptford and by most accounts was not a vessel to be trifled with. In early 1703, *Oxford* was serving under the command of Captain Josiah Moore as a convoy ship for the Virginia tobacco fleet and had the good fortune to encounter a French ship named *St. Paul*, which was heavily loaded with a valuable cargo of sugar from the West Indies. As the war was by that time in full swing, Captain Moore suffered few pangs of conscience in taking the rich sugar ship as a prize.[63]

Oxford escorted her enormously valuable captive into the Chesapeake about mid-August and brought her safely to anchor in the Patuxent. Upon his arrival, Captain Moore immediately informed Her Majesty's receiver and naval officer for the Patuxent Naval District, George Plater, that he wished for *St. Paul* to be condemned as a prize by Her Majesty's Vice Admiralty Court in Maryland. Unfortunately, the Prize Office in England had not appointed anyone in the colony to administer to the queen's share of any prize money resulting from the capture of enemy shipping. Plater promptly informed Colonel John Hammond, chief judge of the vice admiralty, and William Bladen, register of the court in Anne Arundel County, of the recent seizure. As Moore "was much indisposed and his stay very short in this Province," and as it was unlikely that neither Hammond or Bladen would be able to conveniently make the long trip down to the lower Patuxent to condemn the prize, Plater requested the president of the governor's council, Thomas Tench, to appoint a special commission to designate a person on the river to handle the case in the captain's behalf.[64]

Sometime before August 24, Tench met with Hammond on the matter. The colonel was apparently incensed by the request that he designate someone to act in behalf of a chief judge of the vice admiralty court simply because the captain was unable or unwilling to come to Annapolis. He responded that Moore or a procurator acting in his stead, as soon as he wished, should present his libel to the court in Annapolis to ensure that the condemnation process be expedited. As no direct application had been made to him, Hammond stated bluntly, and in the absence of any sufficient reason offered to persuade him that he should be the one to make the trip rather than the captain, the judge did not believe that he should be obliged to go down to the Patuxent.[65]

Moreover, Tench emphasized, in accordance with the Act of 4 & 5 of William and Mary, which governed such prize cases, Moore must first deliver up the prize to the government in the person of naval district officer Plater. Plater was mildly rebuked for his purported ignorance of the admiralty codes, noting that the law was written "in plain English words which you must need know." Finally, he informed Moore that only if he placed the ship in Plater's hands would the court hear the case in Annapolis. "Otherwise, in regard to your indisposition of health and the shortness of your stay here considered, the judge of the Court of Admiralty, who is always ready in his duty, will meet you and all concerned at the Court House in Battle Town in Calvert County upon your intimation and a reasonable time prefixed," as long as Her Majesty's interests in the prize were protected. The proceedings against *St. Paul* at Battle Town, unfortunately, have not been found, but the prize was soon condemned and ordered to be sold, with half of the income from the sale to go to the queen. The ship was valued at £6,000 sterling.[66]

The affair would continue to create reverberations for some time to come. On October 13, 1704, George Morely of the Prize Office in Annapolis complained to the Privy Council that Captain Moore had failed to give a satisfactory report on the capture of *St. Paul*. The prize officer would eventually have cause to regret his displeasure with the captain. A year afterwards, the Privy Council replied to Morely's complaints by noting coldly that the estimable Plater had, in fact, already sent over the charges of the condemnation of *St. Paul*. The Privy Council, whose attention had been drawn to the case by Morley's complaint in the first place, was shocked, not at Moore's actions, but at the discovery of a clutch of outrageous fees, totaling £593.15, taken in behalf of the Maryland Court of Vice Admiralty—fees that were inimical to the interests of Her Majesty and those of the *Oxford*'s officers and crew, who had taken the prize. The Privy Council informed Morely that the court of admiralty fees for a like case in England amounted to only £12.10. With egg on its face resulting from its own scandalous efforts at enrichment from the proceedings at Battle Town at the queen's expense, the Prize Office had no choice but to agree with the Privy Council and order the return of all but £12.10 to the crown prize agents in Maryland.[67]

Battle Town's real reason for being, despite its wonderful location and accessibility to the maritime trade of the lower Patuxent, continued to be its role as county seat. It was the purpose for which it had been specifically created and one which it would be obliged to cling to if it were to survive. As a court town, it had a certain stability, as regular and reliable as the change of seasons, based upon the necessity for the governance of county affairs and justice. As such, Battle Town could count upon a steady flow of visitors and on court days, an influx of many more who provided support for the local inns and ordinaries, livery operations, and the like. Its status was viewed with keen envy by other towns not so fortunately endowed, and its supporters were obliged to occasionally contend with efforts to remove the court to another site.

In 1707, one such effort was mounted by a number of county petitioners who were unhappy with the location of Battle Town. The geographic and demographic fulcrum of Calvert County had changed, and the town and its court were no longer considered by some to be as conveniently or as centrally located for many inhabitants as it had once been. On Friday, March 28, a petition was formally presented to the Upper House, "praying that the court house of that County may be for the future appointed at Hunting Town," on Hunting Creek, some miles to the north. The proposed bill was read and readily approved by the governor and council and sent to the House of Delegates. The bill was carried from the council to the Lower House by Colonel Francis Jenkins and James Saunders, where it was read and ordered to be acted upon the following day. The next morning, undoubtedly after being heavily endorsed by the citizens of Hunting Town, who stood to gain considerably from its passage, the bill was again read and debated upon. The Lower House decided against the bill and resolved that the county court would remain in Battle Town.[68] But the message was clear. Although the challenge failed, for many inhabitants ensconced along Battle Creek it must have appeared an ill omen for the future.

The somber tones of the official proceedings of the county courts of Maryland, filled with legal jargon that pertained to disputes, adjudications, and resolutions to ensure justice in the frontier-like environs of the era, cannot begin to relate to the modern reader the social importance of the courts and court days in the colony. In 1708, however, Ebenezer Cooke, a satirist of colonial America, published a book-length poem entitled *The Sot Weed Factor,* a burlesque account of life in Maryland at the onset of the eighteenth century. In his work, Cooke sought for the first time to characterize, through the eyes of a fictional traveling tobacco factor, the uniquely evolving identity of tidewater Maryland society. A singular address of his sometimes ribald narrative included the judicial proceedings of the colony as epitomized by the factor's visit to the county court at Battle Town.

In the story, the Sot Weed Factor and his trusty guide set off astride "a skittish Colt, and an aged Roan" for "a Place In Mary-land of high renown, Known by the Name of Battle-Town." His avowed reason for going was

> to view the Crowds did there resort
> Which Justice made, and Law their sport,
> In that sagacious County Court

After a brief encounter with Indians (who were in fact long departed from the area by 1708), the factor and his accomplice soon arrived at their destination. The first thing the two travelers spied upon their arrival in town were

> roaring Planters on the ground
> Drinking of Healths in Circle round.

Cooke then provided what was undoubtedly the most cutting and extensive passage of the entire poem, an introduction to the legal process at Battle Town satirically suggestive of that employed throughout colonial Maryland and reflective of the social stage upon which justice was actually meted out.

> We sat like others on the ground
> Carousing Punch in open Air
> Till Cryer did the Court declare;
> The planting Rabble being met,
> Their Drunken Worships likewise set:
> Cryer proclaims that Noise shou'd cease,
> And streight the Lawyers broke the Peace:
> Wrangling for Plaintiff and Defendant,
> I thought they ne'er wou'd make an end on't:
> With nonsence, stuff, and false quotations,
> With brazen Lyes and Allegations;
> And in the splitting of the Cause,
> They us'd such Motions with their Paws,
> As shew'd their Zeal was strongly bent,
> In Blows to end the Argument.
> A reverend Judge, who to the shame
> Of all the Bench, cou'd write his Name;
> At Petty-fogger took offence,

And wonder'd at his Impudence.
My Neighbour Dash with scorn replies,
And in the Face of Justice flies:
The Bench in fury Streight divide,
And Scribles take, or Judge side;
The Jury, Lawyers, and their Clyents,
Contending, fight like earth-born Gyants:
But Sheriff wily lay perdue,
Hoping Indictments wou'd ensue,
And when -
A Hat or Wig fell in the way,
He seiz'd them for the Queen as stray:
The Court adjourn'd in usual manner,
In Battle Blood, and fractious Clamour.[69]

Although presented as a satire, the poem had a direct relevance to the court system throughout the colony, where magistrates were frequently illiterate and shamed by those who could read and write. Lawyers were pictured as often disreputable brawlers, an allegory not without considerable historical precedent.[70] The sessions of the court, which were usually convened three times a year and lasted for three to four days each, were viewed much like entertainment by colonists whose hard, dull lives were provided with precious few other amusements. Indeed, comparing the crowd of drunken judges, lawyers, sheriffs, plaintiffs, defendants, jurors, and spectators to a circle of actors who were shouting, drinking, and fighting on a stage as orchestrated by an invisible director was a parallel not lost on the reader of the day.[71]

Despite its importance as a judicial center, Battle Town appears to have fared poorly as a commercial urban community, perhaps as a result of competition from more geographically advantaged towns created on the river by the 1683–1684 and 1706 acts. It is uncertain when the sparse population of inhabitants began to migrate from the town. By the first decade of the eighteenth century, however, as the first challenge was being presented by Hunting Town for the privilege of being called county seat, it is likely decline was well underway. The Taney family had already moved out and installed itself in a new manor house at Taney Place, overlooking the town site. Continued lobbying efforts by some for a more centralized county seat were gaining a growing number of supporters, and finally the campaign to relocate the county court was met with warm affirmation by the colony government. In 1725, the Assembly finally passed an act for "Removing the Court-House from [Battle Town] in Calvert County, and for building a Court-House for the said County." The pretext given for the transfer was that the "courthouse already built on Battle-Creek, is very old, decayed, and inconvenient to the greatest part of the inhabitants of the said county." The new county seat was to be located at "William's Old Field," a location centrally positioned on the spine of the Calvert County peninsula at the intersection of the north-south road leading to St. Leonards Town and the east-west road running from Battle Town to the Cliffs of Calvert. William's Old Field would eventually be renamed Prince Frederick and would remain ever after as the county seat.[72] The transfer appears to have been made with barely an audible complaint from the few remaining inhabitants in the little village on Battle Creek.

With the removal of the courthouse, some historians suggest, Battle Town soon died out as a community, but there is other evidence indicating that it survived, at least in skeletal form for nearly ninety years. It was considered important enough to serve as a target for a British naval attack in 1814, indicating that something must have remained. But not much.

As Battle Town withered, its degeneration was probably watched with interest from Taney Place on the hills overlooking the village. Here, generations of Taneys were born, married, managed their plantation, prospered, and died. Owing to the singular national importance of one of its members in later years, the genealogy of the family and the history of the marvelous old estate the Taneys created bears some examination, particularly since its origins were so intimately linked with the short but important life of Battle Town.

Unlike the founder of the dynasty, the first three generations following Michael Taney lived out their lives in quiet solitude as simple planters, unencumbered by high public office or much social prominence. Michael Taney II married well, taking as his wife Dorothy Brooke, daughter of Roger Brooke, but he died in 1702 at an early age. The Taney Place plantation then devolved to his son, Michael III, born in 1695. In an act that no doubt would have incurred the displeasure of his grandfather, Michael III married Mary Neale, a Roman Catholic from St. Mary's County. The children resulting from this marriage were the first Taneys in Maryland to be raised as Catholics. Upon the death of Michael III in 1743, his eldest son, Michael IV, inherited Taney Place and married Jane Doyne of Charles County. Only one member of the many Taneys born during these generations, Augustine Taney, founder of Taneytown in western Maryland, achieved any renown.[73]

Michael V, born in 1749, was to become the exception, for he was indomitable and more obstreperous than even his great-great-grandfather. Educated at the Jesuit College at St. Omer in France, where well-to-do Catholic planters sent their sons, he received enough instruction to enable him to carry on the business of planter and to keep his accounts. Upon his return to America, he married Monica Brooke, daughter of Roger Brooke IV of Brooke Place Manor, right across the creek. If the Taney-Brooke relationships over time seemed a bit incestuous, they produced few negative side effects, for Michael and Monica had a number of sons, including Michael Taney VI, who was expected to inherit the family plantation; Octavius Taney, who became a noted physician; and Roger Brooke Taney, born on March 17, 1777, who became one of the most notable and controversial chief justices of the Supreme Court in the history of the United States.[74]

Upon conclusion of the Revolutionary War, when Catholics were permitted to hold public office for the first time since the early eighteenth century, Michael Taney V, an ambitious man, entered politics and was elected to the Lower House of the Assembly in 1782. In 1795, 1799, and again in 1812 he was reelected to the same office.[75]

Michael Taney VI, to whom Taney Place was supposed to eventually devolve, carried on the family name with less than spectacular results. With the onset of the War of 1812, he served in a prominent military role, first as major, and then as lieutenant colonel of the Thirty-first Regiment, Calvert County Militia. In June 1814, when the United States Chesapeake Flotilla became locked within the shallows of nearby St. Leonard's Creek, the county militia was called up, but in the eyes of the flotilla's commander, Commodore Joshua Barney, Taney proved next to useless. Barney personally despised Taney for his inaction and complained of his failings, for the major seemed to be everywhere the enemy was not. In early July, when British raiders penetrated into the middle Patuxent region, Taney was at the upriver port of Nottingham to defend the town beside the flotilla, which had escaped to that point in late June. He then decided to march down to St. Leonards Town, which had already been destroyed. In frustration, Barney informed the secretary of the navy that Taney "has never done anything, nor do I believe would, if in his power."[76]

The war was being conducted at the very doorstep of Taney Place and old Calverton, and Taney, like many in the county, was ill-disposed towards calling British attention to the family estate. Unfortunately, the Battle Creek area was not destined to long escape the enemy's fire and sword. In mid-July, the Royal Navy commander then in charge of the Patuxent blockade, Captain Joseph Nourse of HMS *Severn*, received an order from Admiral Sir George Cockburn, commander of all British forces on the upper Chesapeake, to proceed up the Patuxent "for the purpose of endeavoring to surprise and get possession of a store called Wilkinson's Store above Benedict where articles of considerable value are supposed to be deposited." Nourse was instructed to bring off the articles of value and destroy the rest, and then "cause any other arrogance" which he found practicable. He was to proceed with the frigates *Severn* and *Brune*, the bomb ship *Aetna*, and the sloop-of-war brigantine *Manly*. Battle Creek was to be one of the first targets to suffer from his British "arrogance."[77]

The record of the British descent upon Battle Creek is only cursory, but on July 16, 1814, the invaders landed on the shores of the little waterway and totally destroyed whatever remained of old Calverton. Considering their general *modus operandi* over the next few days, when they moved north to land first at Sheridan's Point and then at Taney's headquarters at God's Grace, destroying everything in their path, as many as three hundred men may have landed at the confluence of the creek and the river following a brief bombardment. Their work was swift and total. All remnants of Battle Town, nee Calverton, were erased from the face of the earth. The first truly planned town in Maryland was no more.[78]

Incredibly, Taney Place, overlooking the town site, was not touched. The precise reason is unknown and can only be surmised. The British were often selective in their predatory foraging expeditions and raids, and they frequently paid for provisions or livestock sold them by local inhabitants who sought to preserve their plantations from destruction. One Royal Navy officer recorded the method in which such transfers of goods, especially cattle, were carried out, even by members of militia units. "The plan agreed on was this," he wrote. " They were to drive them down to a certain point, when we were to land and take possession—for the inhabitants being all militiamen, and having too much patriotism to sell food to 'King George's men'—they used to say 'put the money under such a stone or tree,' pointing to it and then we can pick it up and say we found it."[79]

Taney was accused of participating in the nefarious commerce when Barney charged that "Old Major Taney" was one of those engaged in the practice when he supplied a British shore party with horses.[80] Whether or not the colonel was guilty of trucking with the enemy will never be known. Yet, the physical record is indisputable; however it was managed, Taney Place, unlike nearby Calverton at the foot of the hill, somehow survived.

❖

Whatever his son's failings might have been, Michael Taney V was still a man of great physical energy and passion at the end of the War of 1812, unsinged by the enemy or his son's apparent lack of leadership. By the age of seventy, he had finally retired from politics and resumed the life of a country gentleman, riding frequently with his hounds and entertaining extravagantly. He would soon cap his life with one of the most notorious events in southern Maryland history.

The story of the so-called duel between old Taney and John Magruder is oft told and with as many variations as there are indentations in the Patuxent River shoreline. One of the better-known versions has it that in 1819, with his wife deceased, his lawyer son Roger Brooke ensconced at Frederick in western Maryland since 1801, and his heir, Colonel Taney, having run off to the western frontier, the elder Taney had hired a widow, a certain Mrs. Dorsey, as a housekeeper for Taney Place. Dorsey brought with her a beautiful young daughter named Barbara. Michael was by now an irascible and opinionated old man, unhappy with life and ready to vent his spleen at a moment's notice. It was a dangerous mix.

During one of the many sumptuous fox-hunt dinners held at the plantation, so the tale goes, the guests were enjoying a feast of terrapin, oysters, and duck while heavily imbibing great quantities of eggnog, wine, and other liquid refreshments. At the dinner table, John Magruder, a young planter who lived on an adjoining estate, made an off-handed bantering remark about the elder Taney having two women in his house. Some say the two men engaged in an argument concerning the favors of belle Barbara. Taney took immediate offense. The disagreement caused Magruder to become enraged "and as the blood rushed to his face, he slapped Taney in the face." Another version, perhaps a smidge more acceptable to the Taneys, "is that young Magruder offered a toast insulting to the young woman, an orphan and relative of the Taneys, and he [Taney] being always a gentleman where a woman's honor was involved, challenged Magruder to a duel." Either way, "satisfaction" was to be achieved only by a contest of "honor."

Although dueling was illegal in Maryland, the antagonists retired to the front lawn of the house overlooking the river, and beneath a majestic old cedar tree, they selected pistols as their weapons of choice. In an effort to avoid a fatal conclusion to the affair of passing passions, the other guests, close friends of both men, secretly removed the bullets from the pistols, replacing the lead with paper wads before handing them to the two duelists. When the paces were stepped off and the guns fired, the scheme was instantly revealed; the guests erupted in laughter and the duelists in red-faced embarrassment. The affair might have ended there had not Magruder, perhaps stung by the trick, taunted his elder host with cowardice. There is much disagreement about the events that then ensued. Some say that Taney became enraged anew over the charge and resumed the duel, this time with swords, and quickly ran his antagonist through. Others suggest that he simply stabbed Magruder through the heart with a pocket knife. The young guest instantly collapsed and, bleeding profusely, was carried into the house with Taney's assistance.

The wound, obvious to all, was fatal. In those few moments of excitement, as young Magruder lay dying, Taney retreated in panic into a "secret passage" in the house, most likely into the dumbwaiter to the basement kitchen. Moments later he was at the riverside; that night, with the help of slaves, he reached Sheridan's Point, a bit upriver, and from there fled across the Patuxent into St. Mary's County. The following day, he crossed the Potomac into Loudon County and the sanctuary of Virginia.

Magruder's relatives were outraged at the death of their young scion and sought legal action to have Taney extradited. The laws of Virginia, however, did not include enforcement against dueling, and Taney remained free in that state until his own death a few years later, the result of a fall from a horse. The Taneys, believing that harsh feelings had subsided with the old man's demise, brought Michael's body back to Taney Place for interment amidst his ancestors. At the funeral, one of Magruder's siblings insisted that the casket be opened to see if the burial was being faked. Upon seeing the body, he was so overcome with rage that he battered a stone down upon the face of the corpse.[81]

❖

Taney Place did not devolve to Michael Taney VI as his late father had once hoped. Instead, the militia colonel who had allegedly failed to oppose the British invaders during the late war dropped from sight entirely and headed west to seek his fortune in St. Louis, Missouri, where he had resettled by 1830. The property was held in trust by his two brothers, Roger and Octavius. Octavius remained in the county managing the estate for the rest of his life while attempting to live down the disgrace of the Magruder incident, even as his brother rose to become one of the most famous men of his age.[82]

Upon the death of Octavius Taney, Taney Place, which had for nearly two centuries remained in the Taney family, was sold to Young Dorsey Hance, a grandson of Benjamin Hance of Overton. Young Hance was the heir of an ancient and wealthy Calvert County family, descended from John Hans Tilman, who had arrived in Maryland in 1659. It is likely that it was after Young Dorsey's acquisition of the estate in 1835 that the architecture of Taney Place was substantially altered to its present appearance. The manor known today started as a modest plantation house, the skeleton of which dates from the early colonial period. It was enlarged at a later date by the construction of a full second story. The architectural style of Taney Place in its present state would indicate that the reconstruction took place in the nineteenth century, undoubtedly after it had been acquired by the Hance family. With its unencumbered panoramic view of the Battle Town peninsula and the waterway beyond, it is today one of the finest and best preserved plantation houses in Calvert County. The estate would remain in the Hance family for more than a century and a half, with but a brief interruption when the property was sold and then reacquired.[83]

Life on the Taney Place farm and on the site of the onetime county seat of Calverton was entirely that of a large, rural, southern Maryland tobacco plantation, and it remained virtually unchanged until the Civil War. With the onset of those bloody hostilities and with Calvert County lying so close to the nation's capital but almost entirely prosecessionist in its sympathies, Union occupation of the region was deemed imperative. The period was to see the last true flirtation with history to be visited upon the Battle Town peninsula.

In his monumental history of Calvert County, Charles Francis Stein reported succinctly on the Union Army's utilization of the peninsula as an arsenal as well as a place of confinement for Confederate prisoners of war. The site of the prison camp on the narrow point of land where Battle Creek joins the Patuxent was given the name "Prison Point," although the appellation may have originated much earlier, deriving from the jail that had been erected at Battle Town. Brooke Place Manor, located directly across the creek from the Union camp, was reputed to be the site of counterespionage activities by Southern sympathizers. On dark nights, it was said, boats departed from the old Brooke estate bound for Virginia with medicines and supplies for the armies of General Lee. Such vessels were frequently intercepted by the Union men-of-war and naval skirmishes between blockade runners and blockaders were said to have been common. "This is a story whose full details have never been known," wrote Stein, "but it is among the traditions of Brooke Place Manor."[84]

The lore and legends of Calvert County are heavily laden with tales of old Battle Town, both true and mythical. From time to time on Battle Creek, watermen have caught cannonballs while tonging for oysters. Some say they date from the destruction of the town itself during the War of 1812. On the majestic crest of the hill a half mile away, with its brilliant view of the Patuxent Valley below, the legend of Taney Place lives on. For years, the stump of the cedar tree where John Magruder's murder allegedly took place was known as a local landmark. The secret passage, actually the dumbwaiter, through which Taney escaped is still shown to the few visitors fortunate enough to view the old manse, as is the stain in the hallway said to be from the blood of that most unfortunate victim of passion and rage, young John Magruder.[85]

Today, Prison Point Farm and Taney Place are all that stand on and adjacent to one of the most historic and significant archaeological sites in Calvert County and the State of Maryland. The farm occupies a substantial portion of the Battle Town peninsula, and Taney Place, still in the possession of the Hance family, is situated just outside its entrance.[86]

As I walked the fields, I reflected on the history lying buried beneath my feet. Battle Town had been one of nearly sevenscore towns and ports legislated into being over the course of seventeenth- and eighteenth-century Maryland history, few of which were ever actually laid out, and fewer still having achieved any size or importance. Yet, this site was somehow different, albeit as short lived as most. It had achieved an eminence as a judicial and governmental center that far overshadowed the sparse population that inhabited it, or the far greater trade enjoyed by other sites. As one of the half dozen seventeenth-century town sites to be designated in Calvert County, its importance could not be ignored. And as the first true planned community in Maryland its relevance to history was undeniable.

On Tuesday, June 23, 1998, the southern Maryland news media published a stunning announcement. Maryland Governor Parris Glendening had stood on a beautiful grassy sward on the grounds of another historic town site called Mount Calvert, overlooking the Patuxent River in Prince George's County, and announced that $1,500,000 had been awarded to Calvert County under the new and innovative Rural Legacy Program. The grant was to ensure the preservation of areas surrounding the town of Prince Frederick as well as a greenway link from Patuxent River to Chesapeake Bay. The designated areas totaled 2,643 undeveloped acres of farmland, forests, and wetlands. The largest and most important section of acreage to be preserved lay along the Battle Creek watershed and included Battle Creek Cypress Swamp and, even more significantly, the site of Calvert County's first county seat.

As I read the article with delight, I thought back to that cold November day months before when we walked along the water's edge, viewing fragments of pottery, bone, brick, iron, ash, and shell. These physical remnants showed not only the seat of ancient peoples, but also, for a few brief moments, an executive fulcrum of colonial Maryland. It was all quite overwhelming. Here, beneath the fertile soil, with its surface being turned by the plow and its substance being lost to time, was the handwriting of the archaeological record—who we were, how we lived, and how we governed ourselves in an age when we first became Marylanders.

2 LONDON TOWN

"Fetch it . . . carry it . . . roll it"

August 18, 1976. There in front of me lay the coin. I could barely see it in the coffee-brown waters of the South River, even though I was only three feet down and my dive mask was just two inches from the mud and pebble bottom. As I paddled slowly less than fifteen feet from the shore, guided by one of several cables set up for the divers along preset survey lanes, I could not help but recall what one of my colleagues had called our underwater investigation of the waters off the London Town peninsula: archaeology by Braille. Nevertheless, I gingerly marked the coin site with a wire and flag and pressed on, careful not to disturb the area with my fins as I pulled myself along the line looking for the next feature or artifact. Later, we would mark the coordinates and retrieve the artifact for analysis and conservation, thus helping to fill in the archaeological site map we were developing of the transect.

My nonprofit research group, Nautical Archaeological Associates, had been methodically investigating the nearshore waters off the peninsula for several days. We had been requested to conduct the exploration, the first systematic underwater archaeological survey ever carried out in Maryland, by the London Town Publik House Commission. The purpose of the survey was to locate and identify any drowned cultural resources relating to a long-extinct colonial-era riverport situated along ten acres of waterfront maintained by the Anne Arundel County Recreation Department. The port had been called London Town. The sole surviving remnant of the town, known as the London Town Publik House, was a national historic landmark and was being well maintained by the commission. Yet as we had learned early on, little was known about the town itself.

A valiant but entirely underfunded research effort had been carried out by volunteers, and an extensive title and probate research program had been undertaken by Gladys Nelker, administrator of the Publik House. But aside from a contracted architectural study and restoration of the Publik House, no comprehensive historical or archaeological investigations of the town inself had been promulgated. Even less attention had been given to the waters surrounding the eroding peninsula upon which the old town once stood. Our business was to discover just what lay there—the physical evidence of the past, the flesh on the historical bone.[1]

Months later, as I completed my final report, I was amazed at what we had discovered from the seemingly random assemblage of detritus from three hundred years of human activity. For here, beneath the lands and waters of the London Town peninsula, lay a marvelous history that had never been fully told.

❖

1648. The party of religious dissenters led by the Puritan Richard Bennett had emigrated from the Virginia tidewater northward to the new colony of Maryland. They came as many did, seeking religious freedom in Lord Baltimore's colony of toleration and, it was hoped, a new and prosperous life. After firmly entrenching themselves on the gently sloping banks of the Severn River at a site appropriately named Providence, these newcomers flourished as never before and rapidly began to spread throughout the adjacent countryside. They quickly occupied wilderness areas along the Severn, West, and South Rivers in what is now Anne Arundel County, Maryland, finding the spacious and fruitful expanses much to their liking.[2]

Two years after the Puritans' arrival, Captain William Burgess, a twenty-eight-year-old seafarer, and his brother-in-law Richard Beard settled on the south bank of the South River, having heard glowing accounts of fertile lands and bountiful waters. Burgess, a native of Truro, Wales, was destined to become a leading figure in the early history of the central Maryland tidewater and especially of the South River region of Anne Arundel County. Arriving in the province with two fellow adventurers, Anthony Holland and Thomas Hilliard, Burgess staked out a remarkably fine parcel of land on an easily defended peninsula jutting into the South River just three miles from its mouth. He also busied himself with establishing a small fleet of merchant ships and opening a profitable trade between Maryland and Bristol, England. In this same year, he resolutely populated his new settlement by bringing in 150 European immigrants.[3]

On February 15, 1658, from a patent granted by Lord Baltimore (Cecil Calvert), William Burgess purchased full rights and title to "all that parcel of land (called the Burgh) lying on the West side [of] Chesapeake Bay and on the South side of a River in said Bay called South River, next adjoining the lands lately laid out for George Westill and Thomas Besson, in said county, planters."[4]

The property was officially surveyed on December 15, 1658. A description of the surveyed area read: "Beginning at the said Westernmost bounded tree in said Besson's East and by North line West and by South in said line 40 perches to a marked oak and West by South from said oak 110 perches to a marked poplar by a run bounded on the West by a line drawn Northwest from said poplar 320 perches to marked oak in a valley on the North by a line drawn East and by North for breadth from said oak 150 perches unto land of said Westill on the East by said land on South by said Besson land and the West and by South line. Containing and now laid out for 300 acres more or less."[5]

According to a deed later written by Burgess's son Benjamin, Lord Baltimore had granted to George Westill on May 2, 1659, by a letter "under his seal of arms," an adjoining eight-hundred-acre tract of land called Scorton. On March 10, 1673, William Burgess expanded his holdings on the South River by the addition of this land after having acquired title and interest.[6]

Burgess proceeded to superintend the development of his South River plantation and the construction of expanded marine facilities on the adjacent Shipping Creek. He also thrust himself into provincial politics and military affairs with zest, serving not only as a member of His Lordship's deputy governors and as a justice of the high provincial court, but also as a colonel of "a regiment of trained bands," or militia.[7]

The South River region was still sparsely populated, and many settlers were obliged to tame the land as well as defend themselves from Indians. In 1681, the region was directly threatened by a large band of Indians from the north, and Burgess, now a colonel of militia, was summoned to active duty. He immediately raised a detachment of local settlers to form a defense for the region. The plantation of Major Welch, located at the head of the river, was attacked on September 12. The marauders killed a negro, tomahawked two Englishmen, and plunged the South River region into panic. Although the casualties were brought off and the dead buried, the lightly armed militia was hard pressed to patrol the frontier. As the raiders continued to menace the region, the Snowden and Duvall plantations were soon besieged. Colonel Burgess and his men, though short of ammunition, were dispatched to kill or drive off the Indians. The expedition almost turned into disaster, however, when the unit was nearly cut off and managed to extract itself only when another force under Burgess's friend and neighbor Colonel Nicholas Gassaway came to the rescue.[8] Fortunately, the crisis passed without more serious damage to the river valley.

On June 5, 1668, when Governor Charles Calvert issued a proclamation designating eleven Maryland sites as official ports to be used for importing goods into the province, he set in motion the chain of events that would ultimately influence the history of the South River valley for the next century.[9] Although the region was overlooked in the early ordinances and acts, its day was bound to come, undoubtedly owing to Colonel William Burgess and his influential post on the governor's council.

In 1682, the Maryland Assembly repeatedly attempted to tackle the problem of new town and port legislation. Former Governor Charles Calvert had become the Lord Proprietor and proposed that the proclamations of 1668, 1669, and 1671 be replaced by more comprehensive legislation, and thus the 1683 Act for the Advancement of Trade was born.[10]

The law, as passed, closely resembled legislation passed in Virginia three years earlier, for much the same purpose. Virginia had faced the same problems of decentralization as did Maryland, and the manner in which it handled the new town legislation had been closely watched by the Lord Proprietor. In Maryland, innumerable sites were nominated, and a year of wrangling ensued. One of the more contentious sites debated as suitable for a new port was on Colonel William Burgess's beautifully situated Burgh tract.

The evaluation process for Burgess's Burgh had begun on October 9, 1683, when it was included in a list of prospective port sites submitted by the Lower House to the proprietor for his consideration for nomination. Two days later, having been duly nominated by the proprietor and Upper House (possibly with a bit of prompting from the colonel), the Burgh, noted as "South River Coll. Burgess Land by gift of Coll Burgess," was included in a list sent back to the Lower House unchanged. Some delegates in the Lower House, however, were not comfortable with the decision. Some in the Anne Arundel County delegation believed that a town seated at some more strategic place on West River would be far more convenient to the inhabitants living between Herring Creek and South River than a town at the Burgh. To argue their views, a delegation was dispatched to meet with the Upper House—but in vain.[11]

The Lower House tried to compromise and suggested a location "between West and Road River."[12] The two houses were soon deadlocked. The Upper House requested that the proprietor make the final decision. Lord Baltimore, of course, sided with the Upper House. A total of thirty-two sites were designated throughout the colony, three of which were in Anne Arundel County: "at the town land at Proctors" on Severn River, "at Herring Creek" on Herring Bay, and "at South River on Col. Burgess his land."

At each of the specified sites, as has already been noted, the commissioners were obliged to have the land surveyed and then "marked, staked out, and divided into convenient streets, lanes and alleys, with open space places to be left on which may be erected church or chapel, and market house, or other public buildings, and the remaining part of the said one hundred acres of land as near as may be [divided] into one hundred equal lots."[13]

The designation of a section of William Burgess's Burgh as one of Maryland's official ports of entry was not without logic or practical consideration. The peninsula on which the new port was to be erected was adjacent to several deep anchorages; it allowed easy access to the Chesapeake Bay by water and to the interior of the county by roads. Communication with the north was facilitated by a ferry across the South River and with the south by a series of rolling roads converging near the neck of the peninsula. The South River was another important incentive. This river and its sheltered harbors had already begun to lure more and more ships from anchorage sites elsewhere. Their wooden hulls, honeycombed by the dreaded wood-eating shipworm, would be purged in fresh water while awaiting loading or unloading. There were also available harbor facilities already installed by William Burgess for his own vessels.

On November 6, 1683, the same day the new town bill was being signed, a move was made in the Upper House to nominate a new site for the provincial government. The colony's population center was rapidly shifting northward away from its original stronghold in southern Maryland, and the Lord Proprietor favored a relocation of the government. He saw the South River region as the place most appropriate for the new seat of authority and therefore, "being moved by this house to nominate a place for the courthouse and doth say and declare that when a conveniency shall be provided in South River in Anne Arundell County sufficient for reception of his Lordship and Council and for holding of assemblies and provincial courts and the several and respective offices thereon depending his Lordship will make use thereof for such ends so long as he shall see convenient."[14]

Development of the new town and port systems, however, was almost impossibly slow owing to planter apathy or outright opposition. Whether William Burgess, one of the commissioners selected from the South River region, was among this body of recalcitrants is not known. By the end of February 1684, a proclamation had to be issued directing that the commissioners in each county immediately implement the act and have the ports laid out or face being excluded from any benefits to be derived from it.[15]

Thus, whether the move was voluntary or not, Burgess was obliged to set about laying out a hundred-acre plot of land situated on the peninsula portion of the Burgh fronting on the South River. He was assisted in the project by his brother-in-law Richard Beard, his immediate neighbor Thomas Besson, and Colonel Nicholas Gassaway. More than likely, Beard handled the work of laying out the town and conducting the mapping and surveying. He was, indeed, proficient enough to be selected in 1696 to undertake a similar task for the new capital city of Annapolis. It is almost certain a plat of the port that would soon be called London Town was drawn up at this time, as one is referred to in several title transactions, but the subsequent history of the document is a mystery. Its existence today is highly doubtful. Documents of this importance were maintained rather casually in early Maryland, as illustrated by the fate of Richard Beard's original plat of Annapolis, which in 1697 had been "spoiled in some parts by the rats." It is also possible that the London Town plat was never completed. Beard once complained he was unable to provide the Assembly with some requested plans of Annapolis because he could find no paper large enough on which to draw them. The plat of London Town was probably destroyed long ago and may have burned, along with Beard's original plat of Annapolis and many other precious documents, in a fire in the Maryland Statehouse in 1704.[16] The early destruction of the plat is hinted at by the irregular numbering of the town plots recorded after that date, as evidenced by title transfers and wills. In a normal system such as that encountered on many other gridded town plats of the era, the numbering would have been in regular order, but in the reconstructed town plan the numbers are randomly scattered.

Despite some high hopes in certain circles that the provincial government would be permanently seated on the South River, possibly at London Town, chances for such an event were dashed when Lord Baltimore sailed for England. In his absence the plan was abandoned, though the government did convene temporarily at the estate of John Larkin on South River Ridge. Neither the early settlers in the area of the Burgh nor the commissioners themselves fully realized the importance of Calvert's departure concerning this issue. A courthouse was erected in London Town, or at least a building employed as a courthouse, possibly with some hopes the government would eventually convene there. From a 1699 title transfer in which innkeeper John Larkin sold two unidentified lots in London Town to John Baldwin of Anne Arundel County, it is apparent that the building was little larger than the four hundred square feet dictated by the new town act and was simply referred to as "the twenty-five-foot house wherein the court was formerly held."[17]

On July 26, 1684, the first plot of land in London Town, lot number 33, was sold to Thomas Linthicum (Lynthecombe) of Anne Arundel County. Development of the town was slow, and for some time Linthicum was not only the first property owner but almost the only one. On January 24, 1686, William Burgess died and his position as commissioner and justice devolved, by appointment of the governor's council, to his son Edward.[18]

Despite its slow beginning and the handicap of William Burgess's death, London Town as a community began when a commission of neighboring landowners in the immediate vicinity of the new town, initially under the elder Burgess's command, was appointed to conduct the affairs of London Town and to proceed with the sale of lots. Some forward motion was evident, for soon after the erection of the building that served as a court, the Anne Arundel County government began to convene at the new town site. The trappings of colonial justice, "the cage, whipping post, pillory and stone," were erected and criminal prosecutions initiated. Issues of countywide concern, as well as those pertaining to the town, were taken up and voted upon.[19]

Little is known about the actual proceedings of the Anne Arundel County Court while seated at London Town, though certain incidents have been recorded. In August 1689, for example, a quarrel between Captain Richard Hill and John Hammond concerning the alleged disloyal statements by the latter against the interests of Lord Baltimore culminated in a court case at London Town. Hammond had rejoiced vigorously upon hearing of an unofficial announcement concerning the downfall of the Catholic House of Stuart (Lord Baltimore's patron), and the accession to the throne of the Protestant William of Orange. Word of this event, however, had not officially reached Maryland because of the untimely death of Lord Baltimore's courier while en route. Although the news was common knowledge throughout the English colonies of America and had spread into Maryland, the London Town court refused to accept the fact. Hammond was admonished not to be too sure of himself because there was the possibility that William had not succeeded James Stuart as King of England.[20]

In 1692, during Captain Edward Burgess's term as justice, a trial involving the conspiracy of a Captain Cood was held at London Town. Cood and his associates were alleged to have belonged to "Browns Fleet of Plymouth" and were believed to have deliberately sought to intercept and destroy—for their own reasons—a packet of letters and mail addressed to the governor of Maryland. In January 1694, one of the most important governmental actions pertaining to Anne Arundel County was undertaken by the London Town court. The Assembly was presided over by Colonel Nicholas Greenbury and Thomas Tench, Esq., councilors, and attended by James Saunders, Major Henry Ridgely, Nicholas Gassaway, Henry Constable, Philip Harwood, John Dorsey, and Seth Biggs. The meeting had been convened to consider and act upon the mandatory division of Anne Arundel County into parishes and districts, as ordered by an act of the Assembly in 1691. All Hallow's Parish, as well as the rest of the upper county parishes, was established at this time.[21]

During the last two weeks of the October 1695 session, the court was convened at London Town, possibly for the last time. In early October, George Slacum (Slacombe), a German immigrant awaiting naturalization and possibly working as an indentured servant at the time, was charged by the Maryland Assembly with "bringing the cage, whipping post,

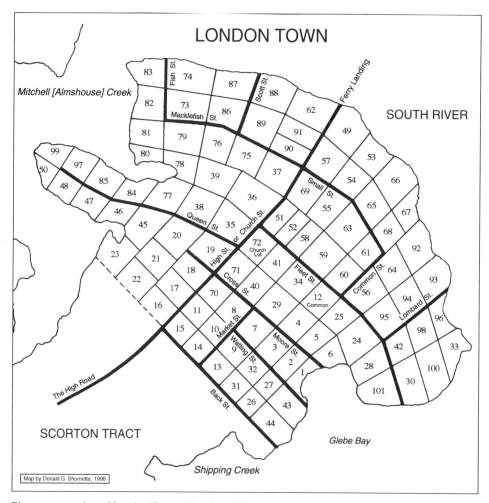

Plat reconstruction of London Town, Maryland. This conjectural plan is based upon title and probate research conducted in the 1970s by Gladys Nelker, first chairperson of the London Town Publik House Commission, and later by independent researcher Charles E. Moylan and by the author.

pillory and stone from London Town to Annapolis." He was referred to the county government for payment and, incidentally, received full citizenship two years later. It was a symbolic transfer of county authority from London Town to the new capital of the colony and soon-to-be county seat of Anne Arundel County. The following year, a town council met in London Town, despite the move and the retarded growth of the settlement. The council consisted of Captain Henry Houslop, John Gresham, William Roper, Edward Burgess, John Watkins, and Walter Phelps. It is of significant note that none of the members resided within the town or owned town land.[22]

It was soon apparent that if London Town was to prosper, it would have to be as a seat of trade, for it was no longer a seat of government.

Few lots in London Town had been sold by the time of William Burgess's death, and by 1703 little in the way of development had been undertaken. A single lot was purchased by Richard Welsh and two others by innkeeper John Larkin. In addition to a house on Larkin's land, a few other buildings had been erected and certain improvements, including a garden, had been made. After restrictions on property acquisitions limiting sales to residents of Anne Arundel County had been lifted, lot number 49 was purchased by Colonel Henry Ridgely of Prince George's County. One undesignated lot, lying on the eastern extremity of the London Town peninsula and abutting Shipping Creek, was purchased by Richard Jones. Upon it he erected "houses, edifices, buildings, gardens and landing ways."[23] The nature of the edifices, one of them possibly a private Catholic chapel, can only be guessed at, but the landing ways were most certainly developed for the use of river flats and tobacco droughers (vessels designed and built to transport tobacco) servicing the ships calling at the South River or Shipping Creek. This property was probably situated at the foot of one of the many shallow ravines perforating the shoreline of the London Town peninsula.

By 1703, several ordinaries had been established in London Town, providing the first commercial income in the township. These establishments thrived from the trade brought in by users of the South River Ferry, which ran from the town to Ferry Point on the opposite shore. Whenever court was in session, both residents and justices alike provided additional revenue. Seamen from visiting ships began to frequent the inns, where liquor was available. Credit was extended to one and all but was charged against the accounts of individual ship captains. Many large bills were lodged by seamen and loudly protested by the visiting sea captains who were required to pay them. The problem eventually became so great that the government was obliged to enact legislation limiting the amount of credit of this sort available to seafarers and extending controls over the ordinaries.[24]

In 1703, the court issued a license to Hester Groce to open one such establishment in the town. Mehitabel Holland was another who was granted a license to keep an ordinary in Anne Arundel County by the June court of 1703. Her husband, Otho Holland, had died in February 1702 and in his will he left some land to their four sons and the rest of the estate to his wife.[25] Mehitabel was one of the daughters of John Larkin who had a house on the Ridge and two houses in London Town. On March 28, 1699, John Larkin sold his land in London Town to John Baldwin, "excepted the 25 foot house wherein the court was formerly held," and enough land between the old courthouse and the water to permit another twenty-five-foot house. These were reserved for the use of Mehitabel for the remainder of her life and thereafter for John Larkin "for his life, and then for Thomas Holland, son of Otho and Mehitabel, and his heirs forever."[26]

In 1703, Mehitabel married John Pierpoint, a carpenter, in whose name the license for the ordinary was renewed in 1704 and 1705. In 1709 and 1711, the license was renewed for Mehitabel Pierpoint, who continued to keep the ordinary after her husband had left her without making any provision of reasonable maintenance for her and her children. She later married a certain Captain Thomas, a vestryman of St. Ann's Parish, Annapolis.[27]

Ten years before Hester Groce applied for her license to open an ordinary in London Town, an enterprising individual named David Macklefresh began to acquire property at a surprising clip. On June 15,1693, he purchased Richard Welsh's lot (probably lot number 57). By a deed dated June 8, 1703, and recorded July 1, 1703, he obtained lot number 49 from Colonel Ridgely. He was soon to relieve the Linthicums of their property for £10 sterling and Colonel Taylor of his property (recently acquired by him from Richard Welsh) for £20 sterling. In 1706, Macklefresh took up yet another property, a lot belonging to John Stroud, and still another from Anne Lambeth. Macklefresh now found himself the largest single landholder in the town. In 1707, he received a license to open an ordinary in the town. He soon expanded his enterprise from merely acquiring land and operating an ordinary to maintaining the South River Ferry as well.[28] Macklefresh was soon styling himself as the Lord High Mayor of London Town.

As a result of this concentration of property ownership and the subsequent dominance over commerce by one man—a situation the government had sought to avoid in its new town planning—London Town seemed doomed to a future without growth. It was the same fate being shared by many other legislated "paper" towns of Maryland. Though David Macklefresh may have possessed a near monopoly over the small quantity of land thus far sold in London Town, he lacked, as one historian noted, enough capital to promote town growth and its development. Macklefresh died in 1712, leaving only £37.80 and all of his town holdings to his heirs.[29]

From the unimpressive numbers of lots sold in London Town, it was obvious that the town's growth would inevitably have to be stimulated by external forces or the effort at new port development on the South River be given up. Ever since the act of 1683, the governor's council had sought to encourage development by means of several legislative acts. These attempts were almost entirely discouraged by the lassitude and hesitancy exhibited by the planters of Maryland. The provisions of the new town acts were obviously running counter to the wishes of most plantation owners and pressure had grown so strong against the provisions that on July 23, 1688, from his estate in England, Lord Baltimore issued a proclamation suspending the acts.[30] Still, the provincial government persisted, and moves toward additional new town and port legislation were initiated.

With the accession of the Protestant King William of Orange to the throne of England, Maryland became a royal colony and the role of Lord Baltimore was reduced to that of caretaker landlord. Eventually, the government of the colony was again urged to pass acts for the establishment and development of towns and ports at key sites in the province—this time with royal backing.[31]

In 1706, 1707, and 1708, the Maryland General Assembly once again undertook the passage of new town legislation. Many sites—including London Town—had been listed and identified in previous acts. The provisions of the 1706 bill were, of course, virtually the same as those of the 1683 Act. In 1707 and 1708, supplemental acts were passed and London Town was given a second chance at survival. More significant events, however, were to contribute to the rebirth of the town.[32]

In 1701, Europe was plunged into a disastrous conflict, the War of the Spanish Succession, and England became one of the chief contestants. After sapping the vitality of all Europe, the war had reached a virtual stalemate by 1711. At last, in January 1712, the belligerent nations convened at Utrecht in the Netherlands to discuss peace. On April 11, 1713, a treaty was signed by Great Britain, Savoy, Prussia, Portugal, and the United Netherlands. On July 13, 1713, Great Britain and Spain signed another agreement and the conflict was finally brought to a long-awaited close.[33]

With the signing of the Treaty of Utrecht many English and Scottish merchant houses and numerous individual speculators as well, reasoning that a lasting peace had finally been achieved, began to search for avenues of commercial expansion in the English-speaking colonies of America. One of the most lucrative fields of investment was the tobacco trade, in particular the Maryland tobacco trade. Many firms, through agents or factors, began to look for ports in the colony offering advantageous geographic locations and potentials for future growth. London Town filled the bill.[34]

One of the first merchant factors drawn to London Town was a Scotsman named Patrick Sympson, agent for the London firm of Higginson and Bird. Sympson acquired a piece of land in the town, lot number 24, in 1715 from Thomas Davis, an innkeeper and resident. Sympson proceeded to lease property adjacent to his own until he felt the time was ripe for expansion, probably when his first consignments of stock had arrived from Europe. Then, he purchased from Otho Holland's heirs the leased plot of land "consisting of 400 square feet of the said [land on which] Sympson's warehouse now stands being opposite to the same lot of land bought by the said Sympson of one Thomas Davis." Three years later he acquired yet another plot, lot number 44, from Oliver and Rebekah Cherry for £30.[35]

Like most Maryland merchants who supplemented their own stocks with goods consigned by English firms, Patrick Sympson sought to conceal his English ties from his customers, wishing them to consider him as an independent dealer, owning his own goods and conducting business autonomously. In 1718, he was obliged to sail for London on urgent business, no doubt pertaining to his London Town operation. Sympson's sponsors in England, Higginson and Bird, also believed that his links to European houses should be kept concealed as much as possible. Before his return to America, he was instructed by his company to send John Belt, a respected resident of All Hallows, up the Chesapeake Bay "in some place where you have not already many debts owing." Goods consigned to Sympson would be committed to Belt as if they belonged to him. "You need not take notice to any person that the affair is wholly under Mr. Belt's care which we desire you will observe & let nothing be said of it but between you & he."[36]

Patrick Sympson was the first of a blossoming community of merchants now beginning to settle in London Town. On October 30, 1716, Samuel Peele, a factor for his brother John Peele of London, acquired from Edward Mitchell lot number 19, bounded by Church, Cross, and Queen Streets in the central section of the new town. Eight months later he acquired lot number 28 and one month after that number 96. In 1719, Peele purchased lots 30 and 91, the former being a piece of land deemed by the reputable merchant as suitable for his habitation. He soon acquired yet another property known simply as Taylor's Lot, bounded by Fleet Street and Shipping Creek. Samuel Peele's second brother William, also a merchant, was enticed to take up residence in London Town and may have entered into partnership with Samuel. In 1715, William purchased his first property in London Town, lots 42, 95, and 98, but apparently did not open up shop until after Samuel had. In later years, William rivaled his brother in town-land ownership by acquiring several more prime pieces of property, including lots numbered 50, 93, and 101. After Samuel's death, William inherited a considerable portion of his property as well.[37] Wisely, the Peele brothers had managed to procure a great deal of the best property in London Town, much of it in the heart of the settlement facing the main thoroughfares.

Samuel Chambers arrived in London Town in 1718, purchased lot number 33, and erected a substantial 40-foot-long house. He was soon occupied with the project of developing his business and competing with the earlier arrivals.[38]

William Chapman, another merchant, also opened up shop in London Town in 1718. From John Baldwin, he purchased lot number 93, a property that was bounded by the South River and Lombard Street and contained 104 perches of land. Chapman soon acquired more property, including lot number 51 "lying and being in the said town on the S.E. side of Church Street that leads out of the country unto the new ferry landing being the next lot in the street on the right hand side down the ferry road [aforesaid] to the lot laid out for a church on the top of the hill or rising in the said road . . . thereon the said William keeps store."[39]

Chapman later acquired several more lots in the town, including numbers 33 and 57, the former from Samuel Chambers. Chapman had come to Maryland from England in 1713 with a letter of attorney from Phillip Smith, merchant of London. He was to remain in London Town until his death in 1762, leaving an estate valued at over £1,400 sterling.[40]

In 1720, William Black established a store in London Town after purchasing lot number 62 and another property with no number. He remained in the town for about six years, extending credit to local planters and increasing his personal wealth considerably. He was not alone in this enviable position, and the merchant population of the entire town enjoyed nearly three decades of economic boom despite occasional periods of depression in the countryside. During these boom periods, many citizens were obliged to live beyond their means, obtaining credit from merchants like those at London Town until better times arrived. One consequence of this was occasional bankruptcy, and merchants such as William Black were often obliged to foreclose. This situation is graphically illustrated by the fate of Henry Darnall, master of an estate in Prince George's County known as the Woodyard. Darnall had inherited the estate, about 13,000 acres in extent from his father, and with it, a considerable stock of Negro slaves, livestock, an elegant home, and more. He had become accustomed to a lavish style of living far beyond his means and soon became indebted to Black and his London partner John Hyde. Unable to meet his commitments when the debts were called in, Darnall lost everything, and the considerable Woodyard estate became the property of Black and Hyde. In 1726, Black returned to London, England, leaving Peter Hume in charge of the lucrative London Town operation.[41]

William Nicholson was a local merchant from Anne Arundel County, drawn to London Town by the success of the earlier arrivals. Though he may have acted as the "attorney in fact" for Peter Paggen and Company of London, Nicholson was his own man. He, too, purchased property in the town and opened a store.[42]

There were a few English merchants known to have purchased land in London Town with the intention of establishing shops and dealing through local agents, but who never did. Sometime before 1721, for example, William Sottle, a mariner, took up a plot of land "for the use of David Poole of Liverpool, merchant." The intention never reached fulfillment and the property was eventually sold.[43]

It was around this nucleus of London-connected merchants that others from nearby began to flock. Richard Moore, originally a Philadelphia-based trader and son of the reputable and wealthy Dr. Mordecai Moore, purchased several lots in London Town, including lots 55 and 63, both fronting on Small Street. It is also likely that he acquired lots numbered 53, 66, 82, 83, 69, and 7, which were passed after his death to his wife Ursula and children Mary, Mordecai, and Samuel Preston Moore.[44]

James Mouat, another local, moved into London Town in 1728 after his marriage to Elenor Sympson, the eligible daughter of Patrick Sympson. He acquired through marriage Sympson's lot number 24, together with all the dwellings and buildings thereon, and opened a store soon afterwards.[45]

Another notable, Turner Wootton, acquired property in London Town, possibly lot number 51, by marriage. In 1728, he was betrothed to Anne Jones, only daughter of Richard Jones. Wootton may have operated not only a store in London Town, but also a private ferry. His property lay at the junction of Church Street and the main road to the ferry landing, but his tenure as a merchant in the town was short despite this enviable location. The property was later sold to William Chapman, who operated a store there.[46]

In 1722, Stephen West, a local innkeeper, purchased a remarkably well-situated piece of property in the town—lot number 74. This plot contained a single acre of land located on the South River beside a convenient road, Fish Street, which led directly to the water's edge. The next year he purchased an adjoining lot, number 87, from Edward Rumney, former ferrymaster of the South River Ferry. This property had considerable improvements, including a dwelling, a landing way, wharves, and a ferry house. West later acquired lots numbered 86, 2, 44, 1, 82, and 83, making him one of the larger landholders in the town.[47]

Shortly afterwards, other merchants such as Thomas Meigan, James McCulloch, James Dick, and Anthony Stewart were attracted to London Town. By the 1730s, the prosperity of such mercantile endeavors was beckoning to many others. Tradesmen and craftsmen drawn to the commerce stimulated by the London Town merchants arrived in a steady stream. Mariners, carpenters, coopers, watermen, shipwrights, tailors, cabinetmakers, tanners, and even physicians found the site much to their liking and settled. By the late 1730s, London Town was more than a simple dot on a map. It was a healthy, prosperous town, with a future seemingly as bright as any in colonial America.[48]

Perhaps one of the most dynamic settlers in the new town and the leader of its energetic merchant community was the Scotsman James Dick. Arriving in America in the 1730s, Dick proceeded to dominate the economic scene in London Town almost from the day of his appearance. In 1737, he purchased his first plot of land in the town, although he may have leased some other properties before that time. This property included lots 2 and 44, as well as two-thirds of an acre in lot number 1, much of which fronted on the water and contained about two and a half acres which Dick sold the next year to his close friend and business associate Stephen West. In 1740, he purchased lot number 7, a plot one acre in extent, bounded by Market, Moore, and Watling Streets. In 1748, he acquired land that was bounded by Mitchell's Creek (now Almshouse Creek) and another lot on the main road leading into London Town. He also purchased lots numbered 9, 10, 11, 13, 14, and 15 in London Town proper. In 1755, he acquired from Joseph Hall, a cooper, lot number 20, "together with all houses, outhouses, [and] improvements."[49] James Dick, however, did not limit himself to local investments. He proceeded to increase his holdings throughout the colony, following an example set by several of his associates and competitors.

Dick became quite active in early land speculation in Frederick County, in the Potomac Valley, and near Rock Creek, Maryland. In 1756, as a result of the Seven Years War between France and England, an outbreak of hostilities between settlers and Indians on the colony's western frontier forced the Maryland General Assembly to action. On March 16, 1756, the Assembly passed an act granting £40,000 to be used to build a fort and blockhouses on the frontier and to man garrisons with a force of several hundred men. Money was also to be applied to engage the aid of friendly Indians and to pay bounties for the scalps of the enemy. James Dick, a heavy investor in much of the land being fought over, and two other reputable merchants, Daniel Wolstenholm of Annapolis and William Murdock of Prince George's County, were named as agents by the government to purchase provisions and arms for the new force.[50]

Fort Frederick, backbone of the western defense system, was eventually erected on the Potomac River about fifteen miles west of Conococheague (present day Hagerstown); Dick and his fellow agents began to advertise for bids to provision the army. Dr. David Ross of Bladensburg was the successful bidder and entered into a contract with the agents to provide the required provisions. Dick and Murdock were required to inform the governor periodically of the conditions of accounts pertaining to the provisioning of the troops. In 1758, they were obliged to inform the governor that the General Assembly was no longer willing to provide assistance and that all funds had been exhausted. This information contributed to a growing rift between the chief executive and the assembly—a rift that would never heal.[51]

During the war, several military units were provided with winter quarters in London Town and other major towns of Maryland. On the South River, their provisions and well-being were attended to unofficially by James Dick and officially by Nicholas Gassaway and Samuel Chapman. Chapman was also a resident of the South River community and had personally led a company of South River militia to defend western Maryland in the early days of the conflict. By the end of the winter of 1756, unfortunately, the troops quar-tered in London Town were practically destitute, near starvation and barely able to survive because of the lack of monetary support from the Maryland Assembly.[52]

James Dick, first and foremost a businessman, was also a citizen of wide repute. He ex-tended credit to several parish planters in financial difficulties, and, judging from the num-ber of debts he was obliged to call in, he was perhaps one of the foremost economic mainstays of the South River area. In the latter days of London Town's history, Dick alone accounted for over twelve percent of all credit extended in All Hallow's Parish. In 1758, he served as one of the original sponsors of the first provincewide lottery in Maryland history. He was deemed trustworthy enough to be named executor of the estates of many prominent citizens of Maryland, including some of the more important planters and merchants of the South River region, such as Thomas Lloyd and William Peele.[53]

As one of the more farsighted merchants in the colony, James Dick was clever enough to forecast the prevailing winds of change, especially when they related to the potential future decline of London Town. In 1746, a year before the town's fortunes began to falter, he sailed for England on important business, leaving Stephen West, Jr., in charge of his Mary-land affairs. Upon his return the following year, he wisely opened a second store in Annapolis, but continued to maintain his first outlet and a private estate in London Town.[54]

In May 1748, Dick entered into another theater of commerce—the slave trade. On a small scale at first, he began to offer slaves for sale in both Annapolis and London Town "for cur-rent money or sterling." Pleased with the results of his initial undertakings, he soon entered into an agreement with a fellow merchant, James Russell, to import slaves on a large-scale basis. In May 1751, he and Russell announced the importation of a parcel "of choice Ne-groes," who were to be exposed to sale onboard the ship *Koulikan* at Nottingham on Patuxent River. Dick returned to Europe in 1751, again leaving his London Town and Annapolis operations in the hands of Stephen West, Jr. Returning to Maryland in April 1752 with a consignment of goods, probably aboard the snow *Russell,* he thrust himself with vigor back into Maryland commerce. In 1753, he invested in another slave-trading expedi-tion to the African coast. Once more he utilized the *Koulikan.* This vessel sailed from the Guinea Coast of Africa with a full cargo of slaves, stopped briefly at St. Kitts in the West In-dies, and finally entered the Patuxent in June 1753. The sale of the slaves was again held at Nottingham, possibly owing to the proximity of one of Russell's stores there.[55]

Employing London Town as a base for his various enterprises, James Dick became an ex-ceptionally wealthy man. His import business permitted him to offer perhaps the widest va-riety of goods of any merchant in the colony, providing an extra drawing card for his shops both in London Town and Annapolis. He imported goods from the West Indies, Europe, and the Far East. He was a strong believer in advertising, and the *Maryland Gazette* was his pri-mary tool. Lists of items gleaned from his ads provide an exceptional insight into the range of commodities available at both of the Dick stores. In a single announcement, he listed nearly one hundred items available, recently imported directly from London aboard the ships *Betsy* and *Charming Nancy*. The items were "to be SOLD by the Subscriber, by Wholesale or Retail, very cheap, for Ready Money or for Credit" and included the following:

> Great Variety of superfine and coarse Broad-Cloths, Forrest Cloths, German Serges, Druggets, Duroys, superfine Sagathies, Fearnaughts, napt Duffels, Bearskins, Half-Thicks, Kerseys, emboss'd Serges, check'd and striped Swan-skins, white Flannels, Hair Plush, Manchester Velvets, strip'd Duffel Blanketing, Rugs, Blankets and Coverlids, Welch Cottons, Irish Linens, and Sheeting, Linen and Cotton Checks, strip'd Cottons and

Hollands, figur'd and strip'd Dimities, Counterpanes, dyed Jeans, Tickets, Bed Bunts and Bed Ticking, Russia Drabs, Cambricks, Clear Lawns, Cottons and Callicoes, strip'd China Taffaties, India Damasks, plain and strip'd India Persians, Cotton Romals, Table Cloths and Napkining, Russia Diaper for Towelling, Tammies, Durants, Starrets, superfine scarlet and other colour'd Camblets, fine 1/2 Ell Callimancoes, superfine black Ruffels, black, scarlet and buff colour'd Everlastings, black, scarlet and buff Amens, Serge Denisme, blue and black Norwich Crapes, Hatband Crape, Variety of figur'd Dresdens, Vellurets, Prussianets, Floramels, Silk, Prussia Grograms and shaded Brolios for Men and Womens Wear, Alamode, Mantua Silk, Lutestring, green Musketo Knitting for Bed Curtains, or Blinds for Windows, great Variety of Millenery and Haberdashery Ware, Writing Paper, Bound Books, and other Stationary, Nails and Iron Ware of all Sorts, Variety of China and Glass Ware, fine Bohea and Hyson and Green Teas, Spicery and other Grocery, WESTON and ARNOLD'S SNUFF, Corks, Gilt Trunks, Mens Saddles and Bridles, Turnery, all Kinds of Ship Chandlery, Brasiery, Pewter, Gunpowder, Shot, Men and Womens Silk, Thread, Cotton, and Worsted Stockings, Gloves, Hats, Womens Shoes, Cutlery, Anchors, Cables, all Sorts of Cordage, &c. &c.

Also available, the notice read, was a large quantity of thirty-penny and two-shilling nails sent from Europe by mistake.[56] There were a great many other items as well to be had periodically at the Dick stores. These included cheap double- and single-refined loaf sugar and good Muscovado sugar from the West Indies, osnaburgs, fringes, bays, fine salt, a variety of "great and small" ship's rigging, British sail duck, anchors from 1 to 500 weight, grapnels, humhums, "best Crown glass 8 by 10," Cheshire and Gloucestershire cheese, bottle beer, rugs and blankets, quart bottles, "best Florence oil," ship's compasses, good West Indian rum, coffee, chocolate, oakum, "best English flour of mustard," Riga hemp, country-made hemp, Carolina, Virginia, and Maryland pork by the barrel, floor carpets "from six to eighteen square yards each, with great variety of gauze, aprons, and handkerchiefs," and many, many more items which he called "too tedious to mention."[57]

James Dick's success closely paralleled that of London Town and the vigorous merchant community therein. He served not only as a representative of that town's economic progress, but also as an indicator of the strength of the town system in Maryland.

Interest in the slave trade among the South River plantation communities and at London Town matured early and quickly, even though slave trading in Maryland was, in the beginning, a costly venture in which only the very well-to-do were capable of engaging. Such undertakings generally required enormous outlays of capital well beyond the means of many London Town citizens and even many of the town merchants. By the second decade of the eighteenth century, a one-eighth share in a venture to the Angola coast might be purchased for about £500. Still, some were interested, among them sponsors like the Higginson and Bird Company of London. In 1718, they urged their factor in London Town, Patrick Sympson, to investigate the potential of such ventures by acting in concert with several reputable Marylanders. Sympson was requested to speak to Richard Snowden and other leading citizens about outfitting a slaving expedition since "we are ambitious of such gentlemen being concerned with us." Little resulted from these talks and slave trading along the South River had to wait another eleven years before other investors became interested.[58]

In April 1729, a ship under the command of Captain Lax arrived in the South River. It was probably aboard this vessel that "about two hundred choice slaves," the first large shipment of blacks to the South River region, were transported to London Town. They were being imported by a triumvirate of investors—Daniel Dulany, Richard Snowden, and Peter Hume, the London Town merchant and factor for William Black and Company. The slaves were to be exposed for sale on May 22 and, like other such transactions, the auction was to continue until all were sold. The sale was not as successful as the three investors had hoped, and they were obliged to continue it through June and July as well. Peter Hume took the opportunity of attaching to notices of the sale advertisements and announcements promoting his own stocks of imported items. "Very good Madeira-Wine," read one advertisement, "to be sold for twelve pounds sterling or three thousand pounds of tobacco per pipe [a cask equal to two hogsheads]."[59] The Dulany-Snowden-Hume venture at slave-trading seems to have been the largest major effort of its type at London Town for the succeeding thirty years, although minor transactions and private sales were quite common.

The presence of slaves in London Town can be taken for granted, for it was graphically illustrated by the public notices, wills, and other documents of London Town residents. Three merchants—James Dick, James Mouat, and James Nicholson—managed almost all of these sales of slaves or public auctions concerning estates of deceased persons in London Town, especially the estates of prominent citizens.

Dr. Carville Earle, in his history of the All Hallow's Parish region, noted that a small, infrequent trade in slaves thrived between the West Indies and the Chesapeake. This trade was tapped by the merchants of London Town. Several of the more prominent planters of the parish, including some early property owners in London Town such as Thomas Taylor and William Burgess, had correspondence concerning the West Indian slave trade as early as the 1680s. Of particular interest was the trade with the island of Barbados.[60]

There seems to have been a preference in London Town for slaves born in the colony over those imported from Africa, since many imported Negroes possessed little immunity to the diseases caused by the climate of the tidewater region. As many as one out of every three slaves died within a year after reaching the Maryland coast. Thus may be explained the paucity of transactions in imported African slaves in the South River area.[61]

One notable exception, however, took place in 1760. The previous year, two of Maryland's leading citizens, Thomas Ringgold and Samuel Galloway, had engaged Captain John Wilkerson, commander of the Liverpool ship *Jenny,* to undertake a voyage to Angola to obtain a cargo of Negroes who were to be brought back to the colony and sold as slaves. Wilkerson reached the African coast without incident, procured a cargo of three hundred unfortunate blacks, and departed by March 4, 1760. On April 29, while still sixty leagues east of Barbados, *Jenny* was attacked by a fourteen-gun French privateer sloop. *Jenny* had a crew of twenty-four men and boys and a few small carriage guns, and was no match for the Frenchman. In desperation, "the Captain arm'd fifty of the slaves, who all behaved well." Twice the enemy was beaten off. A third time the privateer came alongside in order to board, but was again obliged to sheer off and then sailed away. The slaves, who had saved the day, then "laid down their arms as soon as the engagement was over."[62] The ship was finally brought safely to anchor in the South River, and an advertisement was published announcing the sale of the same shackled individuals who had saved the ship. "A parcel of choice healthy slaves, consisting of men, women, boys and girls," was to be held at the South River Ferry beginning July 21, 1760.[63]

Perhaps one of the main reasons for the small interest in the slave trade at London Town was the availability of indentured servants and convict labor. Reference to this manpower pool in the town is sparse since it was generally referred to only in occasional reward notices for runaways, or in notices of sales. "To be sold," read one typical advertisement, "the time of a servant man, who is a very good tanner, and has four years to serve. Enquire of Mr. Brinton at Londontown."[64] From these notices concerning white slavery—indentureship— it seemed that most indentured servants in the town possessed a craft or skill of marketable value. Few were listed as simple laborers. As was common practice, many youths were apprenticed to skilled craftsmen, either by their parents or by the state in return for five to seven years of servitude. They received the minimum legal requirement of room, board, and clothing, but were frequently treated worse than Negro slaves, since their masters were attempting to obtain the maximum of labor from their short-term investments. Many found such servitude unbearable and, like many Negro slaves, ran away. Advertisements for runaways were perhaps among the most prolific notices to appear in the weekly paper. One typical such ad pertaining to a London Town runaway reads as follows:

Four Pistoles Reward

Ran away on the 6th of March last, from the subscriber, living at London-town, a convict servant man, named Edward Merriott, by trade a joyner, he is about 5 feet 4 inches high, much pitted with the smallpox, has a hoarse way of speaking, is a well-set fellow, with large eyebrows, and a full red face, like one that drinks hard, he is about 50 years of age, and has short, black, curl'd hair. Had on when he went away, a blue fearnought jacket, much worn, another light colour'd Jacket, lined with red, a pair of grey halfthick breeches, light yarn ribb'd stockings, much darned, country made shoes, an osnabrigs shirt, and an old worsted cap. He has got a forged pass. Whoever takes up the said servant, and secures him, so as he may be had again, after the date of this advertisement, shall receive four pistoles reward, and reasonable charges paid, if brought home, by

William Brown[65]

The lot of black slaves and the white indentured servants was not a happy one, but they did provide an acceptable labor pool upon which the economy and well-being of the entire colony depended.

Without question, the chief factor in the rise of London Town as a commercial hub of tidewater Maryland was its superb geographic location. The town was situated on the banks of a fine freshwater river, only three-quarters of a mile wide at London Town and, according to one eighteenth-century visitor, deep enough to admit vessels of three hundred tons capacity or more to a distance of ten miles from its mouth.[66]

Overland travel in William Burgess's day—and for a century thereafter—was an exceedingly arduous task, and the wayfarer on horseback had a difficult trip. A journey from a central city such as Philadelphia to another like Williamsburg was a major ordeal. In general, these overland routes avoided watercourses as often as possible, yet at certain places ferries and bridges were obligatory and formed an integral part of the transportation network. It was around many of these early crossings that commercial centers grew.

As early as 1673, a private ferry was in operation on the South River, though the exact location of the crossing is unknown. The average toll for a man and a horse during this period was between twelve and eighteen pounds of tobacco. This charge was later increased, and by the 1860s the toll per man and horse was thirty pounds of tobacco. By the first decade of the following century, a public ferry was in service at London Town.[67]

The operating expenses of the South River ferry were paid from funds drawn from the annual levy of Anne Arundel County taxables. The ferrymaster was licensed by the county court which, it soon became apparent, was careful not to grant the lucrative post to just anyone. The position of ferrymaster was avidly sought by some, primarily because of the extra money to be made by feeding and lodging travelers obliged to use the ferry. Rarely, it seems, were two ferries in operation on the South River at the same time, although several such instances in colonial times are recorded at other locations. In 1734, Stephen West and William Wootton both maintained a ferry at London Town, though the latter was most likely a private operation. In 1747, Richard Maccubin, a wealthy and influential Annapolis merchant, attempted to operate a private toll ferry to a new tobacco inspection station upriver near Beard's Creek. Maccubin placed an advertisement in the *Maryland Gazette* to inform the public: "The subscriber keeps a ferry over South River above London Town, where good attendance is given, and it is a much leveler and nearer road for gentlemen passing and repassing from Queen Anne to Annapolis than to go over the ferry at London Town. The said ferry is passable in any wind."[68]

This venture, it appears, was doomed to failure when the inspection station was eventually removed from the terminus point.

At first, all taxpayers in Anne Arundel County were permitted to use the county-maintained ferry without charge. In 1715, the county court ruled that members of the taxpayer's family were not to be included unless the taxpayer was a nonresident with an established settled plantation in the county. At times, even county taxables were obliged to pay a toll. Free crossings were limited to daylight hours Monday through Saturday. At all other times, a fee of six pence per man and horse was to be charged. Special exemptions were to be given to Sunday churchgoers at specified hours and later to jurymen after sunset. In 1750, free passage was extended to all county residents and to justices, sheriffs, jurymen, and witnesses at any hour of day or night. Initially, some goods and stocks were ferried at no charge, although this practice was later changed. There was no charge for pack horses in 1713 nor, by 1750, for hogs, poultry, geese, turkeys, and "dead meat."[69] This exemption did not include cattle and sheep nor wheeled vehicles, at least not until 1773. Hours of operation varied with the season and were usually extended when court was in session and more travelers were in need of the service.

Operating the ferry, as mentioned earlier, was a lucrative business and competition for licenses was strong. The South River ferrymaster received the highest pay of any of the four Anne Arundel County ferries. In 1741, he received £80 a year, and by 1773 the amount had increased to £140. At the beginning of the eighteenth century, competition among prospective ferrymasters became a costly rivalry. Edward Rumney petitioned four times for the coveted license between 1712 and 1714, citing verbal promises made by the court and an investment of more than £300 in boats, hands, and a place of entertainment for travelers as reasons why he should be awarded the post. Rumney had, in fact, gone into considerable debt to raise the necessary money and was even obliged to mortgage his property in London Town to Charles Carroll—property that included his home and other buildings on lot number 87. Finally, in 1715, he was awarded a license. His tenure was short-lived, however, for it was rescinded by the court only four months later. Rumney was never again to operate the South River ferry.[70]

Most of the South River ferrymasters, it seems, took up residence in London Town, although there were some exceptions in later years. The ferrymaster was required by law to maintain two vessels at all times, and three vessels on county court days, election days, and during the sittings of the General Assembly. A ferry license awarded to William Brown and Jacob Lusby in August 1773 called for two ferrymasters to provide sufficient boats, each of which was to be manned by "two good hands." At least one boat was to be available on each side of the river "from Day light to Day light," and all passage was free.[71]

The ferrymaster was obliged by county law to provide adequate, trained personnel to maintain continuous service. Yearly records were required, showing operations, passengers served, and financial transactions relating to the operation of the ferry itself and also, in the late 1770s, of the London Town Publik House.[72]

By the time of the American Revolution, at least two and possibly three types of vessels were being used as ferry boats, each providing a specific type of service. Utilization of the service by county residents was continuously monitored by the ferrymaster and chargeable accounts for services rendered were kept in a ferrymaster's logbook for the county government.

It is not known for certain what type of vessels were employed in the ferry service, how they were constructed, or what methods of propulsion were used. It seems likely that a combination of oars, poles, and sails may have been used at different times. The two terminal points of the ferry, London Town on the south shore and Ferry Point on the north shore, were less than a mile apart. This distance, and the need to keep the river open for maritime traffic, would have prohibited the use of a ferry "line" or rope along which the vessels could have been pulled, a common practice in narrower rivers like the upper Patuxent at Queen Anne. The vessel was probably flat-bottomed and not very seaworthy in bad weather—nor was it intended to be. Transportation was hindered and often even halted by high winds blowing down the river, especially between London Town and Ferry Point. That the winds were a problem to operations can be assumed by Maccubin's boasts in 1747, when he opened a competing ferry operation further upriver, that his route was "passable in any wind."[73]

At times, the London Town ferry was unable to operate because of foul weather. On one occasion, it became the focal point of high tragedy. On October 26, 1769, a "melancholy" account appeared in the *Maryland Gazette*. "On Tuesday last," the story read, "a number of people impatient to cross South River, in order to see the race [in Annapolis] the wind blowing fresh, one of the ferry boats was overloaded in such a manner, that she sunk within about two hundred yards of the shore, by which unhappy accident, Mr. Samuel Marlow, of Prince George's County, and another man, were drowned. —'Tis said there were eleven horses and near twenty people in the boat, and it was with the utmost difficulty the other passengers were saved."[74]

It was not uncommon for oxen, horses, and other livestock to bolt overboard and drown; their carcasses would be found on the London Town shore days later, stripped of flesh by the crabs.

However, there was a much brighter side to travel on the South River ferry. At the end of a crossing from the Annapolis side of the river, the weary traveler could find entertainment, refreshment, and lodging in London Town. There were several establishments from which to choose, of course, but convenience more often than not dictated that a traveler visit the London Town Publik House, which was maintained right at the ferry landing. The first such public house was probably operated by David Macklefresh and later by Edward Rumney. Its operation was then taken over by Stephen West, Sr., who maintained the ferry and the public house until his death. In 1753, William Brown, a joiner and cabinetmaker, assumed the position of keeper of the public house and ferry. It was advertised that the new ferrymaster "has provided himself with good boats and skillful hands; and also with good beds, liquors, and provender for horses." He noted that "All gentlemen who shall think fit to

Top: Artist Lee Boynton's rendering of colonial London Town in 1750 based upon recent archaeological investigations. The brick building at top center is the London Town Publik House, situated directly on Scott Street and the South River. Courtesy London Town Foundation, Inc.

Bottom: Detail from Joshua Fry and Peter Jefferson's 1775 *Map of the most Inhabited part of Virginia containing the whole Province of Maryland* shows the critical position on the state's road system still occupied by London Town at the end of the eighteenth century. Courtesy Library of Congress, Washington, D.C.

favor him with their custom may depend on a quick passage over the ferry, good entertainment, and civil usage." A night's lodging in 1778 cost two shillings, six pence, and for ten shillings more a visitor could eat three full meals. To quench his thirst, he could buy a gill of whiskey for one shilling, three pence.[75] There is, unfortunately, no record of the type of entertainment a lodger could expect at the London Town Publik House.

The terminal landing point for the South River ferry in London Town was probably at the foot of High Street, between lots 62 and 49. This property undoubtedly had some form of wharf or landing to facilitate the arrival and departure of the vessel as well as the embarkation and debarkation of passengers, animals, and freight.

The ferry service over the South River was long-lived, continuing well into the nineteenth century. However, its utility was gradually compromised by later road and bridge development further upriver, another ferry operation near the head of South River, and a shift in popular travel objectives. With its usefulness long gone, the South River ferry, like the town it nurtured, ultimately slipped into quiet oblivion.

The development and evolution of the All Hallows Parish road system and its important relationship to the South River and London Town were neither planned nor carefully considered by the colonial government. Yet, this haphazard development considerably influenced the rise and fall of London Town as a center of commercial and civic activity.

By the middle 1680s, a complex pattern of public and private roads had begun to crisscross All Hallows Parish, cutting swaths through forests and fields alike. Rolling roads were opened up to service the plantations and to permit the overland transportation of tobacco. Public roads were being developed to permit overland travel and better communications. Though overland travelers generally sought to avoid waterways, at the few places that boasted of ferries or bridges (such as London Town, Queen Anne's, and the head of South River), travel was expedited. Thus, within a few years of its creation, the South River ferry had become an integral part of the north-south road system of the colony and an important segment of the developing system of the middle-Atlantic seaboard.

Because of the ferry, many of the parish roads converged at London Town. In August 1734, the Anne Arundel justices recorded the public roads of Anne Arundel County. Seven of the twenty roads of the county passed through All Hallows Parish, and six of these seven terminated at the intersection leading to the South River ferry in London Town. From London Town, roads radiated to Bell's Mill at the head of South River, to the Queen Anne's ferry on the upper Patuxent, to Anne Arundel Manor due south, to Fishing Creek in St. James Parish, and to the Pig Point ferry near Lyon's Creek on the Patuxent in St. James Parish. London Town became the most accessible point in All Hallows Parish, and the roads leading to it were among the most traversed in the colony. These roads, of course, brought commerce and tobacco to the prosperous port on the South River. Southern Maryland was connected to the north by the vital link of London Town. By the late 1740s, a shift in the colony's traffic and travel patterns was reflected by the decreasing usage of the roads of All Hallows Parish and, consequently, the port of London Town. Commerce began to falter. German settlers were developing western Maryland in the Monocacy Valley, and migrants from the tidewater pushed north and west up the Patuxent and Potomac Valleys. Urbanization of areas like Bladensburg and Baltimore began to siphon off commercial development from Anne Arundel County. By 1764, the city of Baltimore alone had more than five thousand inhabitants—more than double the population of Annapolis.[76]

Such external changes brought a need for road development elsewhere, and the flow of commercial traffic was soon diverted from its older course over the South River. By the 1770s, travelers rarely used the "great road" servicing London Town simply because the more direct routes to the new population centers did not pass through it.[77] Thus, by the time of the American Revolution, London Town was unseated from its once strong position astride the early intercolonial travel routes—a key factor in the town's decline.

A single main road serviced London Town, and from it, routes radiated to the extremities of All Hallows Parish and beyond. This route, known simply as High Street (and after its juncture with another road in the center of town, Church Street) may also have been known in earlier days as Macklefresh or Macklefish Street. (Macklefresh Street is definitely known to have intersected the main artery of London Town, but whether the names became enmeshed, supplemented one another, or were interchangeable, is not known.) The town was serviced by a total of thirteen streets, alleys, and roads which crossed, recrossed, and subdivided the peninsula into convenient sections and lots. The shapes of these lots were not consistently squared off, having been determined instead by the course of the roads. The roads, in turn, were developed not necessarily for convenience, but as a result of the contour of the land. Practically every lot in the town was situated on a street; those that were not seemed to have remained undeveloped entirely, although they may have been serviced by private, unnamed streets.

It is uncertain if there was a strand or street that may have encircled all or much of the peninsula. If encompassing the entire town, this route would have formed strategic junctures with at least eight and possibly nine major roads, believed to be Fish Street, Scott Street, High (or Church) Street, Lombard (or Lumber) Street, Fleet Street, Moore Street, Watling Street, Back Street, and possibly Queen Street. Several of these avenues were laid out to take full advantage of natural depressions and ravines running from the heights of the main peninsula area down to the South River and Glebe Bay (Shipping Creek), thereby facilitating transport to and from shore facilities, harbor installations, and the like. Traces of several of the ravine-located streets may still be seen today, and at least one major street in London Town, once known as High Street, is still in use.

The western border of London Town was marked by the intersection of Back Street and High Street. Church Street (or upper High Street), situated on perhaps the highest elevation of the peninsula, was named after the church that by law was to be erected in the town, although there is no record of any such construction. The town's residents were obliged to obtain spiritual guidance elsewhere, many taking advantage of the services offered at All Hallows Church, only a few miles away. A number of the streets and lots, though identified by name and title transactions, have never been fully situated on reconstructed plats of the town, and their actual existence is, in several cases, open to conjecture.

From its very beginnings, London Town was destined to become a riverport of some note. Shortly after William Burgess settled in the area, the annual tobacco fleet entering the Chesapeake Bay numbered between 30 and 40 vessels, about 20 of which entered Maryland waters. By the middle of the eighteenth century, this number had increased to about 150, occasionally increasing in number to as many as 300. Of these, Maryland could expect to host from 50 to 75 vessels. Most ships chose to fan out to the deeper water estuaries that provided safe anchorage, easy access to tobacco plantations, and a minimum of competition from other vessels vying for the regional tobacco trade. The fleet usually arrived in November and remained until late spring or even summer before departing for Europe. Anne Arundel County estuaries accounted for at least 10 to 15 of these ships a year, or 20 percent of the Maryland tobacco fleet. The South River was by far the most popular of the county waterways and accounted for 42 percent of all ships giving freight rates in the county court records—and this does not include ships loaded by Maryland factors representing English firms (the bulk of London Town's merchant population).[78]

Mariners found the South River a convenient and important place where they could careen their vessels to cleanse their hulls of marine growth and shipworms. The hospitality offered to seamen by the local ordinaries and taverns, particularly at London Town, was attractive, and several stores in the town catered specifically to the maritime trade, selling provisions, ship chandlery, rope, and rigging.

By 1745, London Town was of considerable importance to the local planters, the same body of citizenry that had shunned and delayed the beginnings of the town so ardently in the late seventeenth century. At that time and well into the eighteenth century, it had been necessary for sailors to occasionally travel inland for their cargoes of tobacco, to "fetch it from plantations to carry it aboard their ships, sometimes being forced to roll it by land four or five miles," and sometimes much farther just to get it to their boats. At London Town, however, enterprising merchants had erected warehouses and boat landings to facilitate storage and transport of the tobacco to the flat boats and droughers which carried it to ships lying in the South River and sometimes beyond. One such warehouse, constructed of brick, was erected by James Dick near the water's edge and later deeded to merchant Anthony Stewart, his son-in-law and sometime business partner, for £100 sterling in 1772. This particular building became a noted landmark on the South River. It was general practice, however, to construct warehouses of wood. Pointing up the considerable hazards of this building medium, one such wooden structure belonging to Stephen West caught fire and was totally destroyed, presumably along with its stock, in 1746.[79]

During wartime emergencies the tobacco fleet, gathering at the mouth of the Chesapeake near Yorktown, Virginia, sailed to England under the protection of armed guardships of the Royal Navy. Many tobacco ships were themselves armed in the event of separation from the main fleet, yet often this was not enough. Occasionally, ships sailing from the South River under convoy fell victim to enemy warships or inclement weather. In 1745, nearly an entire flotilla, including several vessels loaded at London Town, was captured by a French squadron from Brest and taken into French ports as prizes.[80]

The return voyage across the Atlantic was just as hazardous. Yet once a vessel put into the Chesapeake she was relatively safe, and when she put into her South River anchorage, she was assured of all the amenities that "southern hospitality" could furnish.

Business was leisurely, and ships calling at London Town often remained at anchor for an extended period. Some captains were even known to have conducted sales on the decks of their ships tied up at the town's wharves. Many prospective customers were rowed out by ships' boats to vessels anchored in the river, but indications suggest that most vessels tied up directly at London Town to conduct their business. In October 1747, Captain John Fearon was reported as "lying at London Town" aboard the ship *Marshal*. Fearon advertised the sale of "Choice olives in casks, fine Florence oil, fine Devonshire kersey, table linen, osnabrigs, earthenwares, and sundry sorts of goods, at reasonable rates, for paper money or sterling."[81]

Once a vessel had disposed of her stocks, another cargo was taken aboard, usually consisting entirely of tobacco. In wartime, it was not unusual to see heavily armed ships docked at London Town or lying in the river directly offshore from the town. In October 1748, it was advertised that Captain Stephen Hooper's Ship *Ranger,* "lying in South River at

London Town, carrying 16 guns and 32 men . . . takes in tobacco consigned to Mr. John Hanbury, merchant in London, at eight pounds sterling per ton." *Ranger,* which was finally ready to sail by May 1749, sprang a leak while at sea and foundered. Her crew was fortunately taken up by a French brigantine and carried into France. The unhappy incident received scant attention in the press and was simply chalked up as another misfortune to be endured in the trade.[82]

That London Town was capable of servicing such vessels points to the utility and physical extent of its harbor and storage facilities. Almost all property fronting the river and creeks was owned by the town merchants, whose source of revenue was dictated by their relationship with the maritime industry of the colony. The maritime character of the town was indicated as much by the employment of its inhabitants as it was by the form of trade on which it thrived. The presence not only of merchants and factors but also of ship captains gave the site much of its seagoing flavor. In 1741, John Spence, a Prince George's County merchant, purchased two lots in London Town formerly owned by William Black. Soon after acquiring these lots, Spence turned directly to the sea, leaving his store in London Town to become the captain of the *Prince Frederick.*[83]

Alexander Scougall was another mariner with roots in London Town and a loving wife awaiting him there. In 1744, he purchased lot number 96, overlooking the South River, from William Peele for £250. In 1765, he acquired lot number 93. Scougall commanded several coasting and seagoing vessels during his time. Among these were the schooner *Bladen,* the sloop *Mary,* the brigantine *Annapolis,* the ship *Elizabeth* (probably named for his wife), the schooner *Nancy,* the snow *Annapolis,* and the ship *Frederick.* Scougall sailed the seven seas and is known to have conducted voyages throughout the Chesapeake and to South Carolina, New York, Barbados, and London, England. He was captured by the French and carried into Quebec as a prisoner of war in 1745, but was eventually freed and was again sailing Maryland waters by 1747. In 1759, he advertised that his schooner *Nancy* was ready to take on freight for Philadelphia, New York, or any ports of the West Indies. Scougall was not only the master but also the owner of *Nancy* and was able to charter his ship independently of outside investors. Unfortunately, in December 1759, he was shipwrecked near New York City and *Nancy* was lost. The captain managed to escape and returned to Maryland where he was soon back in business.[84]

London Town boasted not only of its own resident sea captains, but also of a respected shipbuilder. William Chiffen, an Anne Arundel County master shipwright, is known to have acquired property, lot number 4, in the town as early as 1724. He was still living in the area as late as 1753, as evidenced by an advertisement requesting the return of two runaway indentured servants to London Town ferrymaster, William Brown. The two fugitives reportedly fled to the Eastern Shore "having taken a schooner boat belonging to William Chiffen." Chiffen may have maintained a boatbuilding operation at London Town and for decades was quite active in the South River area. Like many craftsmen, Chiffen was obliged to move away as the town fell into decline, and eventually he took up residence above Disney's Mill near Annapolis.[85]

Other evidence of London Town's maritime character is provided by the presence in the town of waterman John Lewis and resident seinemaker Thomas Mullen. Nothing, though, denoted the town's relationship to the sea better than its first and only major industry, the London Town ropewalk—a facility where rope was manufactured.[86]

In March 1747, Stephen West, Jr., the industrious and ambitious son of Stephen West, Sr., London Town's oldest merchant, placed a singularly important advertisement in the *Maryland Gazette.* "Any persons who are skilled in spinning of hemp for sailcloth etc., or laying of rope may apply to the subscriber and meet with good encouragement, he having all materials in readiness for carrying on the business."[87]

West was about to initiate London Town's ropewalk, soon to become known throughout the colony as the London Town Manufactury. By May 11, 1748, he was ready to announce to Marylanders the grand opening of his newest enterprise.

The subscriber in London Town on South River has erected a ropewalk and makes all sorts of cables, cordage, and rigging for ships and other vessels; as also sail-twine, log-lines, deep-sea lines, houseline and marline, and white rope for country uses. He is provided with an excellent workman from London, well skilled in all parts of the business. Any gentlemen who may have occasion to purchase may be furnished at said ropewalk or at Mr. James Dick's store in Annapolis, and may depend on having what is good and clean, great pains being taken to bring it to the greatest perfection. There is now ready-made all sizes of cordage and running riggings, both at London Town and Annapolis, to be sold by Stephen West, Jr.[88]

It seems quite probable that James Dick was a silent partner to young West in the London Town Manufactury and eventually took over complete control when West moved from London Town in 1750. Both West and Dick continued to advertise the sale of cordages of all types and sizes for several years after the former's departure.[89] Ironically, a week after West opened the London Town works, another ropewalk was opened by B. Hards and Company in Chestertown, Maryland. Competition was assured.[90]

Who actually operated the London Town ropeworks is questionable. Day-to-day operations were probably managed by William Bicknell, a sailmaker who served his time in His Majesty's Yard at Chatham, England, sailed to America, and at West's urging finally took up residence in London Town. Bicknell soon struck out on his own, however, and set up an independent operation in Annapolis at the store of a Mr. Williams, a merchant. Yet Bicknell continued to maintain his residence in London Town and is known to have had in his employ at least one trained indentured servant, John Flack, a sailor and sailmaker.[91]

West was able to sell his product from his own outlets and those of James Dick as well. In 1750, he persuaded another Annapolis merchant, William Roberts, to sell cordage of the "London Town Manufactury," taking up the slack in sales when he was obliged temporarily to close his own shop and sail for the West Indies on business. In West's absence, Dick continued to boost the sales of London Town rope, which he claimed could be procured "near as cheap as can be imported from London." Competition was heavy, especially from Annapolis importers such as Nicholas Maccubbin, who pointedly stocked "good London cordage," and advertised it as being "as cheap as any made in the country."[92]

James Dick's link to the ropemaking operation in London Town is hinted at by a notice in the *Maryland Gazette* concerning the establishment of a ropemaking business by Andrew Thompson, ropemaker, near the Annapolis city gate in 1757. In the ad, Thompson noted that he had once lived with Dick, and by implication may have also worked for him on the South River ropewalk operation.[93]

It is almost certain that by 1760, the ropewalk in London Town was entirely managed by James Dick. Stephen West, Jr., had moved his own store first to Annapolis and then to Prince George's County, abandoning all ties to London Town, including most of his property there. Faced with stiff competition from lower-priced imports, the increase in numbers of other local rope and sail manufacturers, and the general decline of London Town itself, the ropewalk operation was ultimately doomed to failure.

Above: Ropemaking was the principal industry of London Town. It was conducted at one of the first ropewalks in colonial Maryland, the London Town Manufactury. Courtesy Library of Congress, Washington, D.C.

Below: The family crest of the Peele family on the gravestone of Samuel Peele, one of the more successful merchants of London Town at its apex, as it lies in the All Hallows Church cemetery.

The last note concerning the ropewalk was perhaps its saddest. On November 6, 1760, the manufactury was raided by vandals who carried off two giant grindstones, each thirty inches in diameter and four and a half inches thick, and several barrels of Carolina tar—all necessary elements in the ropemaking operation. It was believed the guilty party was a white servant man "who was on board of a small shallop, the master of which, one Caleb Balding, had delivered about six thousand feet of plank at London Town." Dick offered a reward of £20 for the conviction of the offender, but no arrests were made. It was the last public mention concerning the London Town Manufactury ever made.[94]

The actual date the London Town Manufactury ceased operation is uncertain, but it closely paralleled the decline of the town's own fortunes. The actual location of the works is also uncertain, though it was probably situated on one of Dick's properties. In 1765, Stephen West opened another ropewalk near his new home in Upper Marlborough, and it is probable that the London Town Manufactury was defunct by that time.

The decline and fall of London Town from its enviable position as a local economic center was swift, and based upon the very thing that had promoted its rise—tobacco. Maryland suffered from a malaise common to single-crop agrarian economies throughout the colonies and was often on the verge of total economic collapse. In the mid-1740s, that collapse was more than a specter. Tobacco was earning less than half a penny per pound on the European markets. Existing laws aimed at the control of tobacco sales were conceded to be woefully inadequate.[95] The marketplace was glutted, not only with an overabundance of the crop but also with an alarmingly high percentage of inferior-quality trash tobacco. As prices continued to decline, the indebtedness of Maryland planters increased, and the fortunes of dependent tradesmen declined accordingly. London Town merchants, hitherto a major credit factor in All Hallows Parish, seemed immune to such problems, owing in part to their direct ties to European money sources. In 1747, the situation changed radically.

Rarely did the Governor and the Assembly of Maryland work in unison. Yet in 1747, the colony's economic crisis had reached such a critical point that they were obliged to take immediate concerted action. Controlling legislation entitled "An Act for amending the Staple of Tobacco, for preventing Frauds in His Majesty's Customs, and for the Limitation of Officers Fees" was passed and became law. One of the main purposes of the act was to prevent the exportation of trash tobacco and avoid the rampant frauds perpetrated against customs officers in the export of the product, a weak point in previous legislation. The law, as in earlier new town legislation, was modeled after successful Virginia laws and provided for the establishment of fixed stations throughout Maryland where tobacco inspectors would examine all produce for export.[96] They were required to burn all trash tobacco on the spot and issue receipts for quality stock passing inspection.

Obviously, sites chosen for the establishment of these stations were likely to thrive economically, and those that were not would fall by the wayside. Only one station was chosen for the South River, and it was not at London Town. The designated site was curiously situated "at Macclefish's alias Howard's Point, on the South side of South River," upriver near present-day Beard's Creek.[97]

The incredible selection of Howard's Point in lieu of London Town as the site of the tobacco inspection station was the beginning of the end for the town. The net effect of the act had been to shift the focal point of tobacco marketing away from London Town, causing the town to lose its reason for being. Though outright collapse was not a danger, prosperity soon decreased steadily. Despite efforts to keep the civic and commercial flame alive through such ventures as the establishment of the ropewalk, London Town's fortunes began to falter.

The disintegration of the fabric of community life proceeded at a much slower rate than that of the town's commercial decline, and daily activity continued much as always. In November 1758, the town welcomed the opening of its first school, a private affair begun by Daniel M'Kinnon, who gave public notice that he would be teaching grammar at four guineas per annum "and all gentlemen who may be pleased to favor" him with their custom could depend upon being served with ardor and fidelity. M'Kinnon's establishment was as close as London Town would ever come to possessing a regular school. Thirty-four years earlier, in March 1724, the Anne Arundel County regents, authorized by the Maryland General Assembly, convened at London Town "to treat with any person or persons who are inclinable to sell one hundred acres of land" near the center of the county on which a free school could be erected. London Town had not even been considered.[98]

Only one new merchant, Thomas Meigan, took up residence in the town after the passage of the inspection acts, but within a year even he was obliged to close up shop and leave.[99] Older merchants began to die off, and the younger ones, like Stephen West, Jr., moved away. Steadfastly, James Dick remained, but he began to concentrate his attention on his Annapolis operation, choosing to let the London Town store take care of itself.

More and more often, announcements appeared in the *Maryland Gazette* requesting the settling of accounts by London Town merchants and citizens. Property in the town began to fall into the hands of absentee landlords. Mortgages were foreclosed. Vandalism of unoccupied or unprotected property began to occur. The vacant estate of the late William Peele, for instance, was stripped of window sashes, panes of glass, hinges, and even locks. Few tradesmen or craftsmen appeared to replace those who died or those who chose to move away or retire. Auctions of estates and possessions of former London Town citizens, either deceased or bankrupt, became commonplace. One such typical auction, held on October 10, 1752, disposed of the entire stock of furniture, store goods, horses, and slaves belonging to the late Thomas Caton.[100]

Not everyone moved away. Several craftsmen, such as Alexander Ferguson, a London Town tailor, appears to have viewed the town's decline as an opportunity to increase his holdings, possibly expecting a resurgence of prosperity in the near future. Very few craftsmen took up residence in the town after the 1747 act. Two who did were seinemaker Thomas Mullen and cobbler John Sefton.[101]

Nature was as responsible as Maryland's legislative acts for London Town's loss of maritime trade. With the removal of vast stretches of forests along the South River shoreline and beyond plus the application of the plow to thousands of acres of surrounding countryside, tons of soil were washed into the river and its many feeder creeks every year. Erosion, aided and abetted by the hand of man, began to spread into areas never before endangered. At first only the smaller creeks began to fill with silt, but eventually the larger waterways and even the river itself began to suffer. Sandbars and mudbanks formed in Shipping Creek on London Town's eastern perimeter. Large bars began to form at almost every major intersection of nearby creeks and the river. Fewer and fewer captains chose to chance the treacherous trip into the South River. The possibility of running aground on any of the increasing number of shoals was simply too great. Maritime traffic slowly ground to a halt.[102]

There was little left of London Town by the time of the American Revolution, and travelers passing through (and they were but few) failed to even mention the town in their journals or diaries. Those who did noted that the former town was hardly more than a few houses in a quaint setting.[103]

Still, several of London Town's citizens played an important role in the formulation of Maryland's revolutionary attitude in the days immediately preceding the American War of Independence. After the conclusion of the French and Indian Wars, the British government attempted to reassert control over its affairs in colonial America. Leading Marylanders, including several former London Town residents such as Stephen West, Jr., contended with the resurgence of British authority over colonial commerce by engaging in a general boycott of English goods. Others, such as James Dick and Anthony Stewart, refused to become party to such measures. Both Dick and Stewart attempted on at least one occasion to ignore the boycott altogether but were obliged to send their vessel back to Europe fully laden— with her original cargo. This move served only to strengthen opposition to loyalist interest in the province.[104]

The loyalist sentiments maintained by Dick and Stewart were strong. Dick, with practical foresight, began to divest himself of, or disguise his ownership in, much of his property in London Town before outright hostilities began, placing several parcels in the hands of trusted friends and relatives. Stewart refused to be stilled in his loyalist actions. In 1773, England passed the Tea Act, stubbornly insisting on the right to tax the American colonies. In Boston Harbor, the action was met with hostility, and rebellious Bostonians, dressed as Indians, dumped a shipload of tea in the harbor. In Annapolis, actions were a little stronger. When Anthony Stewart's ship *Peggy Stewart* put into Annapolis harbor with a quantity of tea in her holds, a howling mob called for either Stewart's head or the destruction of the ship. Stewart, by then a resident of that city, was obliged to put the torch to his own vessel, destroying it in the harbor.[105]

Following Dick's lead, Stewart was soon carefully divesting himself of lots 33, 57, 90, 59, and 53. His father-in-law had already transferred title to his tracts of Scorton, the Burgh, Mitchell's Chance, and all of his London Town property—totaling more than 350 acres—to his eldest daughter, Mary Dick McCullough.[106] London Town was by then completely devoid of the merchants upon whom the town had depended. Total collapse had finally occurred.

The estate of Anthony Stewart fared terribly despite his protective measures. In accordance with the laws of Maryland pertaining to property owned by inhabitants who proved to be loyal to the King of England, all of his large holdings throughout the state were seized. Among them were many holdings lying on the South River and at London Town. The confiscation process took years, but it was relentless. Finally, on July 9, 1795, Jonathan Gassaway, the state agent, reported to the governor and council that these properties belonging to Stewart had been officially appropriated: a 62½-acre tract called Security and 177½ acres of Scorton and Burgh, all lying on South River; and a 38-acre residential tract near South River Church.[107]

James Dick held on. One property the "old Tory" (as he was referred to locally) did not relinquish in London Town was the double lot (numbers 74 and 87) upon which the London Town Publik House had been erected. These lots had been purchased by William Brown from Stephen West, Jr., shortly after the death of Stephen West, Sr., but were mortgaged by Brown to Dick. Upon Dick's death, the property was sold at public auction to Allen Quynn, Sr., on March 7, 1789. Brown promptly repurchased the property for £606, but again Charles Stewart and James McCullough, executors of James Dick's estate, auctioned the property, and on June 8, 1793, it was bought by Colonel John Hoskins Stone.[108]

Stone was a notable Marylander who had achieved a distinguished reputation during the Revolution and was considered one of the rising stars in state politics. Less than a year after Stone's acquisition of the two lots and the Publik House in London Town, he became the governor of Maryland.[109] Whether the Stone family actually resided in the former Publik House is open to conjecture, but it has been asserted by many aficionados of the old town's history that they did.

On the second Tuesday in May 1803, a lawsuit was filed against Stone by Frederick Green of Baltimore. Green was suing Stone for $150 and 2,192 pounds of tobacco plus damages and costs to the sum of 631 pounds of tobacco. The former governor, however, died on May 21 and the case was tried against his estate. In October 1805, the court ruled in Green's favor and "it was considered that the aforesaid Frederick Green should have execution against Robert Couden Stone, Elizabeth, Anne, and Thomas Stone heirs at law . . . of John H. Stone."[110]

The Stone family had long since rented the former Publik House to various tenants, among them John Craggs and Robert Welsh. Upon a ruling of the court, on March 3, 1806, a writ was handed to Anne Arundel County Sheriff Jasper Edward Tilly. Stone's heirs, unable to pay Green as ordered, were obliged to turn over the London Town property to the county, and the house was promptly exposed "to public sale to the highest bidder." Thus, the property passed to Edward Hall of Anne Arundel County for $326.[111] James and Mary Larrimore bought the property from Hall that same year.

In 1801, James Larrimore, an enterprising individual, began to buy up property in the former town at a steady rate. Larrimore's first acquisition consisted of two lots, numbers 49 and 53, purchased from Henry Sample (Semple) for £46 currency. In June 1806, he acquired an unidentified piece of property that was undoubtedly the former London Town Publik House. This property was described in the deed as "one large brick house and lot situated on the West side of South River at the lower ferry over the same . . . which said house and lot were formerly occupied by John Craggs and lately by Robert Welsh." On December 1, 1807, Larrimore purchased a large parcel of generally unimproved land in the town from Dr. James Steuart of Baltimore for £45 currency. This parcel included lots 21, 22, 23, 45, 46, 47, 48, 84, 85, and 97. He also acquired a third of an unidentified lot from Anne Welsh for £25 currency. Two months later he obtained another property belonging to David Chalmers, including "buildings, improvements, woods, ways, waters, water courses, rights, liberties and privileges" for a consideration of $65.66. In November 1808, he purchased a third of an unidentified lot from Jeremiah Nicholson, Joseph Harwood, and Thomas and John Sparrow for £25 current money. Exactly two weeks later, he purchased fifteen more lots, numbers 54, 55, 56, 58, 59, 60, 61, 62, 63, 64, 65, 68, 69, 92, and 94, from Mary Mann, executor of the estate of her late husband George Mann, an absentee landlord, for $180. On September 9, 1809, he purchased lot number 7 from William Cheney for $20.[112] In all, James Larrimore had purchased thirty-two parcels of land for practically nothing.

Larrimore's land speculation paid off handsomely. On September 13, 1825, he sold practically all of his holdings in London Town, primarily from the Hall, Cheney, Steuart, and Mann properties, to John Stephens of Calvert County, Maryland, for $4,000! There was one exception. Ten acres of land had been set aside by Larrimore for sale to the Anne Arundel County Trustees for the Poor. On May 5, 1828, for $2,500, he conveyed ownership of these ten acres to the board of trustees. This board consisted of Robert Wheeler, Kent Thomas, H. Carroll, Ramsey Waters, William O'Hara, and Joseph Noble Stockett.[113]

The final transaction between Larrimore and the Trustees for the Poor was apparently only a formality, for the former Publik House had been used for some time already (though for exactly how long is unknown) as a county almshouse. The property was legally acquired in "pursuance of an act of the general assembly of the . . . state of December session 1821, Copt. 124, Sec. 11." Though more than seven years were to pass before it actually took title to the property, by this act Anne Arundel County assumed ownership of a large plot described as follows:

Beginning at a stone now planted on the edge of the West side of the South River at the upper landing place of the lower ferry across the said river and at the intersection of the Main Road with as follows to wit N. 80 degrees 15 minutes W. 68 p. [perches] to the mouth of a creek running up and bounding on the said creek as follows to wit S. 8 degrees E. 14 p. S. 13 degrees W. 9 p. to another stone now planted on the edge of the said creek leaving the said creek and running S. 73 degrees 15 minutes E. 60 p. to another stone planted at the N. end of the Main Road leading to the [aforesaid] ferry landing place and running from with and bounding on the N. edge of the Main Road as follows to wit N. 12 degrees 15 minutes E. 6 p. N. 25 degrees 45 minutes E. 12 p. with a straight line to the beginning containing 10 acres.[114]

Anne Arundel County thus took over property that was to be maintained for nearly 150 years as the county almshouse. A superintendent was charged with the actual day-to-day operations of the home and was responsible to an elected board of trustees. A surgeon or physician was employed to make periodic visits to the home and generally serve as an adviser to the board or as a member. Meetings of the board were held monthly at the county almshouse. In later years, these meetings must have adopted a somewhat political flavor since many of the trustees, and even the superintendent, at different periods held other political offices. Monthly meetings often became festive occasions; in fact, they were the only occasions of note in the vicinity.[115]

Trustees attending these meetings at the county home were treated to bountiful dinners of turkey or oysters and a traditional seven-gallon jug of liquor after the proceedings had been completed.

After the Civil War, the county home was operated on an entirely public basis, though at what date the first Negroes were admitted is unknown. Eventually, Negroes were permitted residence, though only on a segregated basis. At first, they were relegated to the basement of the main building and later to a separate facility altogether.

Except for the county home and its immediate outbuildings, the remnants of London Town gradually disappeared. Older buildings fell into decay and were torn down by local farmers. Some, like the original Burgess house, were destroyed by fire, leaving only a brick chimney or two as a reminder of their onetime presence. Yet even these were eventually torn down and carted off to be used as building materials elsewhere. The terraced land fronting the South River soon became the abode of honeysuckle and wild vines. A few local residents attempted to put the land to good use. Berry farming was attempted, and a large section of the peninsula was even turned over to tomato growing.

By the beginning of the twentieth century, the memory of London Town had all but faded. Flat-bottomed steamboats like *Emma Giles,* now decaying in Baltimore harbor, plied the shallow waters of the South River with weekend excursionists.[116] Occasionally, bugeyes from Baltimore would call in adjacent Glebe Creek to take on shellfish and produce, mostly tomatoes.

In 1917, a structure called the Aisquith house, believed by many to be the original William Burgess Manor House, was accidentally burned to the ground. The disaster was watched with interest by local schoolchildren who were unaware of the history of the old house. Only the stubs of two brick chimneys remained after the fire, and these too eventually fell victim to scavengers.

In 1965, with the passage of the Welfare Act, the county home and its services were considered obsolete. The old brick structure—having served as home to London Town's foremost citizens (possibly including a governor of Maryland) then as a Publik House, tavern,

Top: In this 1834 painting by an unknown artist showing South River as viewed from Ferry Point, the London Town shoreline on the opposite side of the river appears practically devoid of habitation. Only the Anne Arundel County Almshouse, upper right, survives today. Note the vessel, possibly one of the ferryboats, in the foreground. Courtesy London Town Foundation, Inc.

Bottom: The Anne Arundel County Almshouse as it appeared in the 1920s. Courtesy London Town Foundation, Inc.

inn, county almshouse, and finally a home for the aged—was all that remained of a once-thriving Maryland town. With its dedication as a twenty-three-acre county-owned national historic landmark, the London Town Publik House and Gardens came into being, a site to be restored and preserved.

In the early 1990s, with the leadership and political support of Anne Arundel County Executive John G. Gary, a challenging archaeological research program called "The Lost Towns of Anne Arundel County Project" was born. It was an ambitious program, with no less a goal than to locate the county's colonial past as manifested in the remains of its vanished towns and settlements and document it for the archaeological record. In 1995, after successfully discovering and excavating the 1649 site of Providence, the earliest organized European community in Anne Arundel County, the project managers turned their attention to the search for ancient London Town.

"It's at least the second oldest town in Anne Arundel County, and the mysteries about the place are numerous," waxed Project Director Al Luckenbach, as he began his monumental journey. "We don't even know how it was founded, or when."[117]

An aerial view of the London Town peninsula in 1938 reveals just how much of the colonial town site had been claimed by nature and the plow, even as modern suburbs had begun to creep in. Courtesy National Archives, Washington, D.C.

3 ST. LEONARDS TOWN

"No matter we will do our duty"

July 2, 1814. In St. Leonard's Creek off the Patuxent River, Sailing Master John Geoghegan lightly fingered the trigger of his U.S. government issue musket as he took a bead on a red-coated marine in one of the lead enemy barges. The Saturday morning sky was cloudy, and the warm air was ruffled with a slight breeze that forced the young officer to compensate for windage, just as he had been obliged to do with the big guns he had commanded only six days earlier during the climactic battle at the mouth of the creek. It seemed an eternity since he and his men, accompanied by a stout band of U.S. Marines under the command of Captain Sam Miller, had manned a battery of big guns on the bluff overlooking the entrance to the creek. They had fought gallantly until their ammunition had been expended, even as a tiny American flotilla struggled to break the shackles of the powerful squadron of British blockade ships below. Since that time, it seemed that neither he nor anyone in his little detachment had slept a wink. Yet, the surprise predawn assault on the enemy frigates blockading the creek had been successful beyond anyone's imagination and had resulted in the escape of most of the American fleet to the upper Patuxent River. The exceptions had been a pair of ancient gunboats, *No. 137* and *No. 138,* which were deemed by Commodore Joshua Barney, commander of the flotilla, to be too cranky to make the fast run upriver.[1]

Barney had placed great faith in Geoghegan and his tiny band of seamen throughout the month-long ordeal on St. Leonards. After the battle, the sailing master had received orders from the commodore's second in command, Lieutenant Solomon Rutter, to stay behind to scuttle the two wretchedly slow gunboats in the harbor of the port of old St. Leonards Town to prevent their capture should the enemy return. Geoghegan knew the vessels well, for he had commanded one of them, *No. 138,* since its induction into the flotilla in 1813. He had been upset when the squadron had found itself blockaded in the creek on June 7 and the tattered old gunboats had been relegated to transport duty behind the American line. He had incessantly badgered the commander for a more active role at the battlefront and finally got it. On June 25, Barney instructed him to build a masked battery of artillery on the bluff overlooking the anchorage of the enemy blockaders and to personally open the land component of the attack while the commodore led the charge by water.[2]

Soon after the battle, when the enemy had retreated and the flotilla had successfully escaped upriver, Rutter and Geoghegan had been dispatched to tiny St. Leonards Town, the American naval base of operations at the head of the creek since the blockade had begun, to bring off whatever materials they could as quickly as possible. They may have eyed the decrepit old village with some disdain, for it seemed to a number of American officers that its inhabitants had been almost as hostile as the British. Though the enemy had departed, his return was expected at any moment, and the town and everything in it, including military supplies, were at risk. Thus, Geoghegan and his weary men had hastily set to loading spars and iron, which had been taken off the flotilla before the battle, onto a schooner at the head of the creek. Then the town was relieved of all miscellaneous military paraphernalia as expeditiously as possible. By June 30, the work had been completed, and the schooner was prepared for departure. Though bone weary, the sailing master, who had been left in official charge of St. Leonards Town, had little time to relax.[3]

While Rutter's men prepared the schooner, Geoghegan dispatched a reconnaissance party down the creek to keep a lookout for the enemy. Within hours, his scouts had returned and informed him that a pair of British warships—HMS *Loire* and *St. Lawrence*—and several armed schooners had come to anchor about 4 P.M. a little above the mouth of the waterway. The return of the foe to St. Leonard's Creek effectively destroyed any chance of the American schooner's escape. Frantically, the little party of sailors began off-loading the spars and iron that had been brought aboard with so much labor and returned them to a safe and hidden storage place ashore.[4]

About the evening of July 1, Geoghegan and Rutter met at the lieutenant's camp near the banks of the creek to discuss what their next move should be. The following morning, it was decided, Geoghegan would march down to St. Leonards Town with a work party and several wagons; the men would remove whatever spars and naval items still remained there and carry them overland to Hunting Town, a small upriver port where the flotilla had briefly sought refuge. With a detachment of eight men, he marched back to the town but had barely completed the loading of a single wagon when a scout breathlessly reported that the enemy was approaching. The sailing master immediately broke off the loading work, sent off the wagons at hand, and ordered those coming up to turn back. Quickly, he pushed into the creek thirteen masts belonging to the flotilla's armed war barges, which had escaped days before under oar power alone, along with the yards belonging to the row galley *Vigilant,* to hide them from the enemy. A gun slide belonging to *No. 138* was also dumped into the water to prevent its discovery by the invaders.[5]

Now the British were approaching once more, eager to avenge their recent defeat. This time they came with a detachment of 150 Royal Marines loaded aboard several barges and a pair of armed schooners. About two miles up from the mouth of the creek, Captain Thomas Brown, commander of HMS *Loire,* and a detachment of marines landed and proceeded overland toward the town, while the boats under the command of Lieutenant William Gammon of HMS *Severn* moved up by water. John Geoghegan and every man in his unit knew that to defend against so great a force with less than a dozen men was utterly hopeless. But they had been determined to provide the invaders with at least a rousing reception.[6]

Slowly, Geoghegan's finger squeezed the trigger as the first enemy boat in the procession neared the town. As his musket fired, the guns from the entire party erupted in a furious fusillade. The firing was instantly answered by a thunderstorm of grape and round shot. With enemy bullets whistling close to his ears but satisfied that he had done his duty, Sailing Master John Geoghegan ordered his men to fall back, leaving only a forward observer, an officer, to watch the motions of the enemy from a safe distance.[7]

The following day, the observer reported on what transpired. The British quickly took possession of the ancient riverport of St. Leonards Town; they destroyed all of the shipping that remained in the harbor, removed whatever tobacco had been found in the warehouses, and set fire to anything they could not carry away, including many buildings in the town. They then turned their attention, albeit with notably less success, to the destruction of the two gunboats, which had been earlier scuttled side by side, with their decks awash. By 8:30 P.M., satisfied with their revenge and satiated with plunder, they returned to their ships, leaving in their wake the charred and smoking remains of what had been one of Calvert County's oldest surviving towns.[8] St. Leonards Town, a diminutive but venerable Maryland seaport for 131 years, had been all but destroyed.

❖

The long and mysterious history of old St. Leonards Town (not to be confused with the modern crossroads village of St. Leonard several miles away) is, like many early urban centers in Calvert County, blurred by the shadows of time, primarily owing to the destruction of county records when the British burned the county courthouse in Prince Frederick on July 19, 1814. The few musty archival records that exist are sketchy at best, but from the fragments that remain, much can be discerned about both the little village and the beautiful waterway it once commanded.

Geographically, St. Leonard's Creek is a major four-mile-long tributary of the Patuxent River, Maryland's longest intrastate waterway. The entrance to the creek is located approximately seven miles northwest of the river mouth at Drum Point. Its own mouth is shouldered on each side by tree-covered bluffs ranging in elevation between forty and fifty feet above the river. Today, the direct water approach to the creek's main channel is shielded by a long, tongue-like bar, at one time land, that swoops southward from the western lip of the entrance now known as Peterson Point, posing a natural hazard that once caused no end of navigational difficulties for the uninitiated.

At the time of the first contact between English explorers and the native population along the Patuxent watershed, the villages of Opanient and Wasameaus were reported by Captain John Smith to be situated on or in the vicinity of both bluffs at the entrance.[9] As elsewhere on the Patuxent, such as at the site of old Battle Town, the lush littoral plains at the crest of the bluffs, particularly on Peterson Point, were covered with innumerable rings of oyster shells, the most visible evidence of centuries of occupation by Native Americans. Both sites were located on excellent, defensible peninsular projections. Just within the southern lip, sheltered by a steep, twenty-million-year-old fossil-bearing matrix of earth, sand, and clay, a wonderful freshwater spring bubbled forth near the shore, making the site doubly suitable for occupation.

St. Leonard's Creek is still a full sixteen to twenty feet in depth at its entrance, but less than a foot or two at its head, owing to siltation during the historic period. The creek was once quite navigable for sailing ships of considerable size clear to its innermost recesses. For the most part, the main channel was narrow but deep, shouldered closely by steep, compressed shores indented by numerous coves and stream outlets. At its headwaters, the creek forked. The western arm, known as Mill Branch, dwindled after a half mile to become a placid valley; the eastern arm, later known as Quaker Swamp Branch, was far narrower in extent and ended in a wetland area fed by a pair of tiny streams. But it was the peninsula between the two branches, with its gently sloping elevations on all sides, that was the dominant geographic feature in the area. Barely a hundred feet from the toe of the peninsula, where the two branches met, water depths up to eighteen or twenty feet may have been enjoyed by early mariners choosing to anchor their vessels there. And a strategically convenient anchorage it was too, for the headwaters of St. Leonard's lay directly astride the spine of the Calvert County peninsula, just a mile and a half from the Chesapeake on the other side of the ridge. Given the criteria of seventeenth-century planners regarding port development, the location at the headwaters of St. Leonard's Creek was most admirably situated (at least when it was first selected for a new town site). With protected, defensible deep water at its feet, its back located on the ridge of the county, freshes running down on either side suitable to purge ship hulls of the wood-eating shipworms, and the ready access to the open Chesapeake, it seemed a site to be reckoned with.

The earliest European settlement on the stream was probably undertaken by Leonard Leonardson, whose will, the first document to mention actual property holdings on St.

Leonard's Creek, was probated in 1640.[10] The first significant occupation of any consequence, however, was undertaken by Henry Bishop, who arrived in America in 1634 along
with fourteen other immigrants under the sponsorship of Father Thomas Copley.[11] Within
four years of his arrival, Bishop had ensconced himself as a planter on the south shore of the
Patuxent in Mattapanient Hundred and had risen to some importance when he was elected in
1638 as a burgess representing the hundred in the Lower House.[12] Though illiterate, his
Catholic religion and ties to the Jesuits at first held him in good stead with the proprietary
government. Sometime between his election and 1642, Bishop moved to the northern shore
of the river, an area that was almost entirely unsettled by the white man and still occupied in
many places by the natives. As a friend and intimate of Leonard Leonardson, he was probably already familiar with the area and was well aware of its virtues.[13]

But for every virtue, there was a contrary aspect. The close proximity between native and
white in the Maryland colony was an uneasy one during the best of times, and ensconced in
his new seat on St. Leonard's, Bishop experienced hostilities from the very start. Within a
short time, his difficulties with the natives culminated in the slaughtering of his swine by a
handful of Indians.[14] In 1642 attacks by the Susquehannock Indians from the north had severely damaged the Jesuit mission at Mattapany, at the mouth of the Patuxent, and settlers in
the remoter regions of the colony, such as on St. Leonard's Creek, were undoubtedly terrified. Bishop was not entirely alone in his concerns for his safety, for about this same time
Francis Posie, a bachelor and former resident of Mattapanient Hundred who had recently
moved to the shores of the waterway, also reported "damage to him in housing and goods at
St. Leonard's Creek" by Indians.[15] The threat of attack was significant enough that at least a
handful of settlers who had taken up residence on the creek in Leonardson's and Bishop's
wake chose to leave almost as soon as they arrived. Walter Cotherell, noted in March 1640
as a resident and planter, was one of those who elected to vacate and take up residency in
Mattapanient Hundred sometime prior to July 1642.[16] Bishop, however, was resolute and
anxious for revenge against the Indians. But more importantly, he looked to his own preservation by constructing a fort on his property, the first defense works to be erected in what
would soon become Calvert County.[17] They would not be the last.

Bishop had ambitions and saw the land he had settled as a political entity not unlike
Mattapanient Hundred, albeit lacking the one critical ingredient: inhabitants. He refused to
let such concerns sway him, for soon after the swine incident, he boldly informed the Assembly that he was a burgess representing a new district, St. Leonard's Hundred, and
"pleaded that it was acknowledged to be a hundred." The Assembly was not about to declare
a wilderness area occupied by a meager handful of settlers as a hundred and refused to acknowledge either St. Leonard's as a legitimate hundred or Bishop as a burgess. The precise
geographic parameters of Bishop's quixotic St. Leonard's Hundred are problematic, although it is almost certain that the location was situated on the west shore of the creek, most
likely contained in the core tract of present-day Jefferson Patterson Park. Bishop would not
live to see the actual institution of the area as a hundred as it would one day become, for by
1644 he was dead.[18] But he had led the way.

As pressure for expansion in the Maryland colony increased, numerous patents for land
along St. Leonard's Creek began to be issued to a slow but steady stream of settlers. After
Bishop, one of the first to arrive and stay had been Cornelius Abrahamson, who received a
patent for fifty acres of land on the west side of the creek in 1651, a parcel that was later gen-
erously expanded to three hundred acres.[19]

In 1652, the employment of the name St. Leonard by Governor William Stone, who patented 350 acres under that title sometime between 1648 and 1652, suggests that the tract he

took up on the creek may have been at least somewhat analogous to Bishop's proposed hundred.[20] It has also been suggested by some historians that Stone, a Protestant who had arrived in Virginia in 1628, upon accepting Lord Baltimore's appointment as governor of Maryland in 1648 and moving to St. Mary's City the same year, may have also been offered the parcel by the proprietor as an enticement to ensure his loyalty. It was, in any event, only a small part of the 8,000 acres of land Stone would ultimately own in Maryland, but certainly a key portion which may have triggered the effect desired by the proprietor. The following year, during Stone's turbulent administration, the colony government passed one of the most momentous pieces of legislation in American history, entitled an "Act Concerning Religion,"[21] which guaranteed freedom of worship to one and all. It was a milestone of the religious toleration that would one day be granted to every American citizen by the Constitution of the United States.

There is no direct evidence that William Stone took up residence on his St. Leonard tract, although there is circumstantial data indicating that some dwellings may have been erected on his property early on. In 1652, Stone's son Thomas repatented 350 acres of the original tract, again formally naming it St. Leonard.[22] In 1658–1659, at least six sessions of the provincial court and two sessions of the council convened at a site designated as St. Leonard, with Stone and other known residents of the area in attendance. As the meetings were held in a building of some sort, it is possible that it may have been an actual residence belonging to the Stone family or perhaps to one of the other important local settlers such as Richard Smith.[23]

A native of England and founder of one of the more significant dynasties in southern Maryland, Richard Smith had been trained as a lawyer at the Inns of Court in London, and he brought to the colony a talent that would see him rise rapidly to a position of authority and wealth. Smith came to Maryland in 1649 and was followed two years later by his wife Eleanor and sons Richard, Jr., and Walter. As a solicitor, he was politically judicious and tactically forthright, and his legal counsel left its imprint on many of the early cases of the provincial court. From 1657 to 1661 he would serve as the first attorney general of Maryland. He served four terms as a burgess for Calvert County between 1658 and 1666, and he was a lieutenant in the provincial militia.[24] In 1659, he purchased his first tract of land on St. Leonard's from William and Anne Dorrington, a 100-acre parcel on the west side of the creek, which he promptly dubbed Smiths Joy. Then, on September 9, 1663, he acquired another 350 acres at the mouth of the creek from Governor Stone. By 1665, he most certainly had taken up actual residence on the tract, for it was recorded in that year that Thomas Wylde, "a doctor and surgeon," was "lying and dying at Richard Smith's house in Leonard's Creek in said county." At the time of his own death in 1689, Richard Smith owned at least 1,690 acres of land throughout the county.[25] But the St. Leonard tract was among his finest holdings and would remain under family ownership for six generations.

Slowly at first, usually with axe and hoe in hand, settlers began to trickle onto the shores of St. Leonard's Creek and take up small parcels of land, building their homes and planting their crops. Among the new arrivals were such men as Thomas Thomas, Cornelius Abrahamson, Robert Blinkhorn, John Covell, William Durand, John Mackdowell, Leonard Gunis, Francis Armstrong, Thomas Manning, Gabriel Goulden, John Norwood, and Thomas Meares. They were a hearty lot of pioneers who gave their lands names such as Dear Bought, Dicks Cabin, Gouldens Folly, Foxes Road, Wolfs Quarter, Norwood, and Blinkhorn, titles that reflected their hopes and dreams, the environment around them, and, often as not, their own egos. Blinkhorn soon erected the first mill in the area on the headwaters of St. Leonard's. By 1673, Augustine Herrman's map indicated no less than six plantations seated directly along the shores of the creek, but there were many more.[26] Even then, the im-

Blinkhorn's Mill was established about 1664 somewhat above the head of the waterway named after it, Mill Branch. The facility, which serviced the citizens of St. Leonards Town and the plantations of the St. Leonard's Hundred region, was still in operation as late as 1800 and probably well afterwards, when known as Gott's Mill. The remains of the mill, a substantial earthen dam and spillway complex, the millhouse foundations, and a primitive road system leading to the site were discovered by Calvert County surveyor Pete Ferguson about 1965. Pictured are *top,* portions of the remaining foundations of the mill house, and *bottom,* grindstone jack lift.

pact of settlement upon the wilderness landscape was expected to be dramatic. "All the low land is very woody, like one continued forest, no part clear but what is cleared by the English," wrote one astute observer. "Indeed in a few years we may expect it otherwise, for the tobacco trade destroys abundance of timber, both for making of hogsheads and building tobacco houses, besides clearing of ground yearly for planting."[27]

Almost perceptibly, the wilderness was pushed aside as frontier civilization set in, bringing with it all the political and religious upheavals that had already begun to disrupt the core of mother England. The oscillation of European politics, especially for Protestant families such as Richard Smith's who were loyal to the Catholic Lord Baltimore, brought with it times that were difficult at best. Yet, of necessity, life followed in much the same pattern as always amidst the tall but receding forests on the frontier waterway for both Catholics and Protestants—birth, marriage, work, and death. Those fortunate enough to have been born into the newly emerging aristocracy would bear the added burdens of civic duty and enjoy the benefits of leadership and government. For the Smith clan, status and position were everything. Sometime prior to 1679, Richard Smith's son, Richard, Jr., married Elizabeth Brooke, the youngest daughter of Robert Brooke of Brooke Place Manor. Richard, Jr., destined to serve as surveyor general of Maryland from 1695 to 1699, maintained a stout loyalty to the Lord Proprietor, planted his tobacco, and lived much the same as his father before him.[28]

As the governments of the Lords Baltimore lurched forward through the numerous efforts to develop urban centers and ports in Maryland, it was evident early on that the Patuxent Valley would receive more than its fair share of site nominations. In 1683, it was finally the right time for St. Leonard's Creek to attract the attention of colony legislators. This may have been due, in some measure, to the appointment of Richard Smith, Jr., to the twenty-four-member county board of commissioners selected to institute the Act for the Advancement of Trade signed into law on November 6. In accordance with the act, one of the three sites selected for Calvert County ports was "at St. Leonard's Creek on Richard Smith's land."[29]

Identifying the precise location of the site is problematic as the archival record is sparse. Calvert County historian Charles Francis Stein has suggested that the town was to be situated at the head of navigation, that is, at the head of St. Leonard's Creek.[30] However, extensive title and probate research by others, most notably historian Ailene Hutchins, indicates that neither Richard Smith, Sr., or Jr., owned land in that vicinity in 1683. The Smith lands on the creek, including Smiths Joy and St. Leonard, were, in fact, situated along the western shore at the confluence of the waterway with the Patuxent. Support for this contention is offered by recent archaeological discoveries of at least eight seventeenth-century settlement sites within the borders of Jefferson Patterson Park, the largest center of such sites identified to date outside of St. Mary's City.[31]

As has already been illustrated, the legislation establishing a town and the actual implementation of such acts frequently proved ineffectual in colonial Maryland. It is thus not surprising that the historic records of the first St. Leonards Town, including an actual survey plat of the site, have yet to be discovered, if they even existed. It seems feasible that if the town ever actually got off to a start, like many legislated centers in early Maryland, it was hobbled from the beginning by planter intransigence rooted in an opposition to Lord Baltimore's efforts to harness the manorial system of commerce and trade. That the government found it necessary to reauthorize the town in subsequent acts suggests that its beginnings in

1683–1685 were inadequate at best. The situation was best summed up by the rector of nearby Christ Church (1696–1702), the Reverend Hugh Jones, who wrote in 1696: "We have not yet found the way of associating ourselves in towns . . . There are indeed several places allotted for towns, but hitherto they are only titular ones."[32]

There were, of course, other factors that undoubtedly came into consideration. Although the probable location of the first town site was on the west shore of the creek near its mouth, where deepwater access for shipping was to be had as well as freshwater springs for water, the site was not readily convenient for planters living in the interior of the county. Yet, the Patuxent had rapidly become one of the premier shipping outlets in the colony. Between August 1695 and August 1701, the number of vessels clearing from the river had risen from 12 to 42 a year, with a record 59 clearances in 1699 alone. During this period, a total of 203 ships had sailed, usually laden with tobacco bound for London and other English ports. But free waterfront access for the smaller land-bound planters in the vicinity of St. Leonard's Creek was marginal at best.[33]

The increase in marine traffic was certainly one of the reasons why another bill was passed in 1695 authorizing the establishment of yet one more port on the Patuxent. Two possible locations, St. Leonard's Creek and Bouges Bay, were considered. Significantly, Bouges Bay was finally chosen by the Assembly as the port site.[34] More importantly, the selection of Bouges Bay over St. Leonard's Creek indicates that if the 1683 site was ever developed at all, it had also failed, for if a town had been started, it would most certainly have been selected over an undeveloped site. Development of the selected site, of course, failed miserably.

Whatever the rationale may have been, by 1706 the government again saw fit to reestablish the town of St. Leonards under the "Act for advancement of trade and erecting Ports & Towns in the Province of Maryland." Unlike the 1683 act, the 1706 legislation, far more precise in providing a location for the new town, instructed that the site was to be erected in "Calvert County at the head of Saint Leonard's Creek on both sides of the mill branch at the mouth of the said branch." Again, two of the most prominent landholders on the creek, the brothers Walter and Richard Smith, Jr., were appointed as commissioners and influenced the selection of an "appropriate" site.[35] Unlike the 1683 act, the owner of the land upon which the town was to be erected was not named. Fortunately, at least a portion of its whereabouts were confirmed by a surviving survey plat drawn up soon after the act of designation. This time, there was no question; the location of a major portion of the town was to be on the peninsula at the head of St. Leonard's Creek, between old Mill Branch on the west and Quaker's Swamp Branch on the east.

Part of this site was first patented as a hundred-acre tract in 1665 by Gabriel Goulden (also referred to as Golden or Golding) and named "the Angell" (or Angel or Angle). The patent description defined the property as lying:

> at the head of St. Leonard Creek, beginning at the easternmost bounds of the land of Golding and run[ning] west by north 100 perches to the main swamp or branch of said creek and run[ning] up the swamp north by east 100 perches to land formerly laid out for Golding, bounding on the east with said land 100 perches, on the south with land formerly laid out for Thomas Manning of this province, gentleman, of this province, and the land of Francis Armstrong 160 perches to intersect a parallel from the first bound tree being the easternmost bound of Golding's land, bounding on the west with said land.[36]

Its selection as the most appropriate locale for the establishment of the second St. Leonards Town, it may be speculated, was influenced by several factors. By 1706, there was already some industry in the immediate vicinity. As the nomenclature of the adjacent Mill Branch suggests, a water-powered mill had been in operation on the tributary since 1664 or possibly even earlier, and it would remain in operation until at least 1800. In Richard Smith's will of 1710, the site is identified as "Blinkhorne together with ye mill that is thereon," and is also referred to as "the mill at the head of St. Leonard's Creek." By 1800, the site was known as Gott's Mill, and it may have continued in service well into the nineteenth century.[37] The then-navigable headwaters of the creek ended at the very edge of the central upland spine of the Calvert County peninsula less than a mile and a half from the Chesapeake. Along this spine, the north-south ridge road, a primitive but developing artery, provided the only major overland transportation route in or out of the county.[38] The site was thus more convenient than the earlier locale to a greater number of planters, who were spread over a large interior area and on both shores of the creek. The tip of the town peninsula was a gradual slope that provided an excellent landing area for lighters, flats, and small watercraft.[39]

The extant town plat for the second St. Leonards Town is believed to date from the same year the act was implemented, suggesting that, unlike at other locales, action by the county commissioners was speedy and judicious, perhaps thanks to a bit of prodding from Smith.[40] The design of the plat on a rather standardized grid pattern was typical of most Maryland town plans of the period and was only partially influenced by the topography of the peninsula upon which it was to be erected. Significantly, a total of only sixty-three lots numbered 38 through 100 (rather than the usual "one hundred equal lots") and three public lots for "church, chapel and market house and other public buildings," were divided into fourteen blocks comprising the town. The purpose of beginning the lot numbering with number 38 rather than number 1 is uncertain. It is possible that numbers 1 through 37 were intended for the opposite shore of Mill Branch, as required by the wording of the 1706 act. Later tax records and wills provide some indication that lot numbers other than those noted on the peninsula tract were definitely owned and built upon. The remains of a roadbed snaking down from the elevated littoral to two likely landing sites below the west bluff and directly opposite the peninsula suggest active usage. Moreover, in 1814 and presumably much earlier, the main road that ran along the crest of the Calvert County peninsula terminated on the western shore of Mill Branch, opposite rather than at the plotted peninsula town site. Although one road led from the west shore to the peninsula, and another led from the town to the mouth of the creek at what is today Peterson Point, intersecting the ridge road along the way, it seems odd that the main county road terminated at an unimportant point rather than in the main town. It thus appears likely that the western shore of Mill Branch may have been somewhat developed after all, although no town survey plat for this area has been located to date to verify this hypothesis. A very limited archaeological survey of the area on the western shore of the branch undertaken in the 1980s, prior to development of the sector for a housing tract, failed to identify any artifactual evidence of eighteenth-century domestic sites.[41] It has also been suggested by some that the first thirty-seven lots may have actually been assigned to the 1683 site,[42] although there appears to be no precedent for this in any of the other tidewater Maryland towns where different sites were established by the various acts under the same town name.

The town planners were, if nothing else, generous in their allocation of space for streets and alleys on the site. The central avenue, later identified as the town's "main street," which bisected both the peninsula and the town, was a spacious 5 perches (82.50 feet) wide and extended from the foot of the peninsula 162.5 perches (2,681.25 feet) oriented in a 19-degree west-of-north direction. A parallel street of the same width was laid out 330 feet east of the central thoroughfare. Four parallel avenues intersected these two main boulevards at right angles. The northernmost avenue was 3 perches (49.5 feet) in width, while the three southern avenues were 4 perches (66 feet). Only two years earlier, in 1704, the legislature passed a law providing that "all public roads were to be here after cleared and well grubbed, fit for travelling, twenty foot wide."[43] The boulevards planned for St. Leonards Town were ample. In terms of lot allocation, the town was about equally divided on either side of the main street: a total of thirty-one private lots were situated to the west of the main street and the remainder to the east, including the three public lots.

One of the first inhabitants to purchase property in the new town was Captain Thomas Clagett. An English gentleman and naval officer, Clagett had settled on the banks of St. Leonard's Creek soon after 1670. By 1682 he had established a 376-acre plantation called Clagett's Delight just south of the creek. A man of some substance, he also acquired several larger plantations to the north (in what would one day become Prince George's County) and also on the Eastern Shore. Unfortunately, he did not live long enough to enjoy his new acquisition in St. Leonards Town, for he died the same year the town was established. By his will, we see that Clagett left his town property to his second wife Sarah to dispose of as she saw fit; the remainder of his lands on the creek he left to his son Charles. In 1716, Sarah sold some of the family lands to John Rousby but retained some of the town property for her own use because both she and Captain Clagett are said to be buried in the town. Though their gravesites have never been identified, they would thus have been the first to be so interred.[44] Others also purchased lots, though as elsewhere in Maryland, quite slowly. Among the earliest known families to take up property in town were settlers John and Frances Johnson, who on November 4, 1709, provided St. Leonards Town with another first—the first child born there, Thomas.[45]

Town development, if any at all, was agonizingly slow. By the second decade of the century, the Smith family, who by this time had acquired another 200-acre tract at the head of the creek that included the Angle, was ubiquitously referred to as the "Smiths of St. Leonards."[46] In 1713 Richard Smith repatented 607 acres of his land. The Angle, which was included in the patent, was enlarged to 200 acres, and described as

> now laid out into one tract beginning at the easternmost branch of St. Leonard Creek and run across the neck of land to the great swamp called Mill Swamp and down and with said swamp (several courses), then with a straight line to the first beginning, bounding on the west with said mill branch, on the south with the waters of the head of St. Leonard Creek, on the east with the main run of the east branch of the creek, on the north with the first west by south line.[47]

Between 1723 and 1726, when the tract was again resurveyed, 125 acres of "ye Angel lying and being at ye head of St. Leonard Creek" passed into the hands of John Critchard.[48] By 1733, St. Leonards Town still had apparently failed to attract more than a few occupants, though the land between the north shore of St. Leonard's Creek and Battle Creek had become populated enough to be designated as a hundred. In that year the taxables in the new St. Leonard's Creek Hundred numbered only 121 individuals; they owned 170 slaves, but there was nary a mention of property owned by any of them in St. Leonards Town. Elsewhere on the waterway, plantations belonging to families such as the Smiths, the Johnsons, and the Parrotts flourished. Equipped with their own landings and self-sufficient systems, the large plantation owners appear to have been somewhat ambivalent regarding the survival of the so-called town (which was by this time little more than a handful of dwellings). But others had a different view.

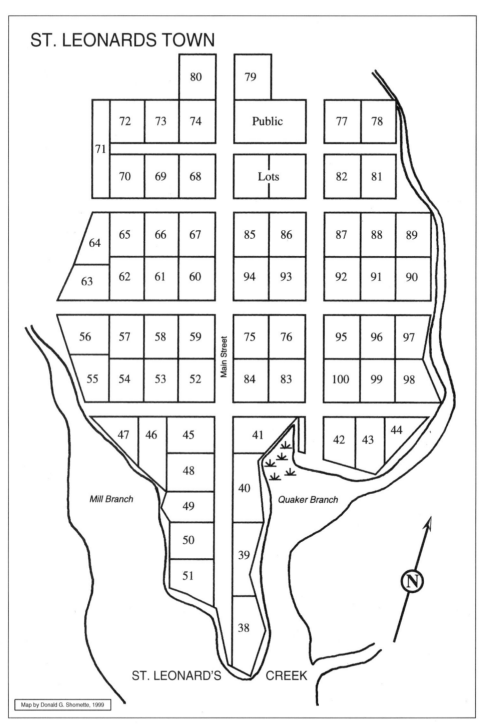

Plan of St. Leonards Town, 1706. Based upon an unsigned manuscript plat in the Maryland Historical Society, Baltimore, Maryland, entitled "St. Leonard Town." As the 1706 town was to have been erected on both sides of Mill Creek and the existing plat begins with lot number 38, it is probable that a second plat indicating lots 1 to 37 was also produced but has yet to be located.

On March 27, 1735, a petition "of sundry the inhabitants of Calvert County" was read in the Lower House, "praying that the land formerly laid out for a town called St. Leonards Town may be laid out a new [and was] referred to the consideration of the next session of Assembly, and ordered that the petitioners give notice to the owner or owners of the said land of their application."[49] It is possible that this petition meant that the town's development necessitated a resurvey to reverify or expand its boundaries, or that a resurvey of its previously established lot boundaries might induce further settlement. Whatever the motivation might have been, the town is not alluded to in existing documents again until the head of the creek was mentioned as the site for a tobacco inspection station. In 1747, as a result of the "Act for amending the Staple of Tobacco," St. Leonards Town found a new reason for being when an inspection station was ordered erected "In Calvert County at the head of St. Leonard's Creek" and the inspector's salary was fixed at £40 worth of tobacco per year. Significantly, though this would most likely have been on the town site, St. Leonards Town was not identified in the act as would have been expected if an actual town of any substance was then extant.[50]

The physical size and appearance of the town at this date is unknown. That it was suitable enough to serve as a very minor military center, however, is indicated by a list of eighty-seven soldiers mustered from St. Leonard's Hundred, Eltonhead Hundred, and the Lower Hundred of the Cliffs and assembled at St. Leonards Town on October 15, 1748, under the command of Captain Robert Sollers. Twenty-three of that number were from St. Leonard's Hundred. If the town was large enough to host such a militia muster, it was still too small to satisfy the needs of the local inhabitants, for in 1749 another petition was presented to the Upper House again requesting that the government "lay out a new St. Leonards Creek Town." It has been suggested by some that the 1749 petition indicated that the town was continuing to expand and required resurvey; it is also possible that the 1734–1735 petition had simply not been acted upon.[51] It is likely that the renewed interest was generated by the location of the new tobacco inspection station on or near town lands and the increased visitation to the area such a facility would probably cause.

The establishment of a tobacco inspection warehouse at the head of the creek had the effect of serving as a small magnet. As with such stations elsewhere, it drew planters from the local area, whose attentions were primarily focused upon the business to be carried out at the warehouse. But these same planters, during their visits, provided additional revenue for local service establishments such as the ordinaries, stables, smiths, and the like that soon sprang up. The hub of this activity, the tobacco inspection warehouse itself, was spartan and the inspection process almost ritualistic. One observer of a typical Maryland inspection station operation some years later wrote:

The warehouse is a square shed open to the inside of the quadrangle in which the planters deposit their tobacco until it is inspected. The quantity here at present was not great, there being only about 200 hogsheads which I am told are valued on the spot at about ten guineas per hogshead. Altho the day was very severely cold we waited to see the ceremony performed which was simply thus. The tobacco being pressed so very hard into the hogshead that when the hoops are started it comes off and leaves the tobacco standing in a hard mass, into which it is with difficulty they can drive a crowbar. This must however be done in three different places so that he may see the center of the hogshead, in presence of the public inspector who is an officer paid for that purpose by the State and who is the judge whether or not it is marketable tobacco. If he finds it is not it is rejected, if it is, it is passed and from that time becomes saleable. This ceremony over, the hogshead is again put over the tobacco and the hoops which had been before started replaced. The hogshead is then turned upon its other end, the tobacco again pressed into it, when it is headed and hooped as before.[52]

The inspection process itself was repeated thousands of times yearly throughout the colony at warehouses in every county, serving in one respect as the equivalent of a banking transfer, with the inspection station as the bank and tobacco as the currency. Wrote the observer:

There is one very singular circumstance relative to the tobacco trade that deserves notice, which is that it answers the purpose of ready cash by the following means. A planter brings down as many hogshead of tobacco as he can make which is inspected and lodged in the warehouse where it remains, the inspector giving a receipt or note that so many hogsheads of tobacco of such a quality are lodged in such a warehouse. This note the planter can pass to any merchant he pleases and it may pass thro several hands like a bank note before it gets into the hands of one of the shippers who purchase them up, and going to the warehouses, on producing the notes receive the quantity of tobacco therein mentioned, at a port ready to be shipped whenever he pleases to demand it. In this country in speaking of any mans estate they do not say he is worth £800 a year but that he makes 80 hogsheads of tobacco.[53]

Not until October 2, 1750, would four tobacco inspectors—William Dawkins, Richard Roberts, John Johnson, Jr., and Isaac Rawlins—be nominated to the post of inspector "at the head of St. Leonard's Creek on the land of John Somervill [sic]." The commission was finally granted to Rawlins. No mention was made of the town per se, only that the station had been erected on land belonging to Somerville.[54]

Though property ownership within the town was stimulated by the nearby inspection station, actual evidence is still subjective. In 1754, the earliest eighteenth-century references to transfers of property in the town were noted in the wills of John Rigby, who bequeathed to his wife Catherine "my lot in St. Leonard Creek Town . . . to be sold at her disposal or redeem," and Joseph Johnson, who had inherited his property from his father John and left his wife Mary two tracts, one "commonly called The Town," and the second "part of The Angle which my father gave me in his will."[55] Another lot owner was Thomas Ireland, son of William Ireland, Constable of Hunting Creek Hundred, who had purchased the property from one of the first landowners in the town, John Johnson, and bequeathed it to his own son Richard in 1761.[56]

Tantalizing tidbits of information about this time began to surface suggesting that at long last, St. Leonards Town was emerging from its cocoon. By 1758 the struggling hamlet was large enough to be formally referred to in the colony press as a town when on February 23, Samuel Gray advertised in the Maryland Gazette various goods for sale at an auction to be held at "St. Leonard's Creek Town."[57] The following year, John James Mackall, at "St. Leonard's Creek Town," advertised that he was taking subscriptions for Abraham Milton, the tobacco inspector at Chestertown, for his recent publication The Farmer's Companion.[58]

In 1763, the locale of the tobacco warehouse noted as "on the land late of John Somerville" was identified in another act concerning tobacco inspection.[59] By this legislation, the inspector's salary was raised to 6,400 pounds of tobacco annually.[60] Unhappily, John Johnson, Jr., a thirty-four-year-old bachelor who had served as inspector for several years following Rawlins's term, would not live to enjoy his rewards. On October 4, the

Maryland Gazette reported that Johnson, "having crossed the creek [from the warehouse] in order to breakfast at his own dwelling . . . was seized with an apoplectic fit, as is supposed, just as he was going into the canoe. He was found dead, with his head at the edge of the water." [61]

That St. Leonards Town (or St. Leonard's Creek Town as it was also called) was by this time fairly well occupied is certain as evidenced by references in the wills and oblique notations found in other sources. Yet, inexplicably, the county debt book for 1767 fails to mention any instances of land ownership in the town, though it enumerates lots owned in other county centers such as Lower Marlborough and Hunting Town. The debt book for 1769, however, refers to 300 acres of land called St. Leonard owned by John Mackall of St. Leonard [Town], the Angle owned by Samuel Dare, 140 acres owned by Colonel William Ireland, 87 acres owned by Mary Ireland, and two plots, one of 350 acres and another of 87 acres (part of the Angle), owned by James John Mackall. [62]

By the onset of the American Revolution, the town was apparently still little more than a lightly occupied landing, unsuitable even for inclusion on contemporary maps. In an era when some plantation complexes were as large as, or larger than, many small towns and frequently appeared on colonial maps while the towns were ignored, it is not surprising. Situated on the shores of a tranquil backwater such as St. Leonard's Creek, bypassed by war and commerce alike, life went on quietly and without much notice. On August 30, 1780, Thomas Johnson of the Cliffs (the first child born in the town) was appointed inspector. Less than two months later, he was replaced by John Manning. [63]

By the end of the War of Independence, county tax lists for Eltonhead Hundred indicate that at least five individuals owned lots in the town. In 1782, Brian Taylor, Edward Hall of Frederick County, and Alexander Somervell were listed as lot owners. The following year, Somervell disappears from the list but Catherine Frazier, Samuel Johnson, and Dorcas Gray were added to the roll, the latter owning two lots. With the exception of Hall, all of the owners possessed additional land holdings in the county, and it is uncertain if any had taken up permanent residence on town lots. By 1782 the surrounding Angle tract was divided among five owners: William Ireland (87 acres), Richard Ireland (54 acres), Margaret Ireland (40 acres), Samuel Dare (140 acres), and Michael Taney (3 acres). [64]

Although skeletal, at least by comparison to other county towns, St. Leonard's Creek Town was by this time significant enough to serve as a meeting place for the vestrymen of Christ Church Parish. The parish had been formally organized in 1692 as one of two such in the county, embracing the hundreds of Hunting Creek, St. Leonard's, Eltonhead, and the Lower Cliffs. [65] At the first meeting, held on February 12, 1781, vestrymen Samuel Dare, Thomas Johnson of the Cliffs, Daniel Rawlins, and Samuel Parran decided to authorize parish lands to be let out to the highest bidder, undoubtedly to raise funds for the church. Three years later the vestrymen again met in the town and agreed that payments of tobacco due from parish members for the support of the church were to be delivered to the warehouses either at St. Leonard's Creek Town or at Hunting Creek. This is the first indication that the inspection warehouse was actually on land in the town. [66]

As the eighteenth century neared its end, activity in the town had accelerated slightly, according to the few surviving land records and court deeds. The town could probably best be described as a sleepy and peaceful southern Maryland backwater, little noticed or troubled by the tumultuous events of the era. From time to time a new tobacco inspector was appointed to superintend at the warehouse. In 1790, for instance, Nathaniel Dare held the post and he was reappointed in 1801 and again in 1802 "to examine all tobacco brought to the St. Leonard Creek warehouse." [67]

Property in St. Leonards Town, of course, occasionally changed hands by bequeathment or direct sale. Besides the earliest known owners of lots in St. Leonards Town—Thomas and Sarah Clagett (1706), John Johnson (1709), and John and Catherine Rigby (1754)—at least nineteen more property owners can be identified by name for the period 1761–1814. Ironically, on the eve of the War of 1812, a conflict in which the village of St. Leonards Town would fleetingly bask in its only prominent moment in history, the town had also achieved its greatest extent.[68]

Though gray clouds still hid the sun, the early morning air on St. Leonard's Creek, purified by a predawn shower, was brisk on June 8, 1814. In St. Leonards Town, the morning began as always. The slaves fed the pigs and began tending to the daily chores, while the few small stores opened for business. At the town landing, a handful of vessels lay at a safe and snug anchorage. Several had retreated into the creek a week earlier as a result of pending naval action between a fleet of American naval gunboats and invading Royal Navy warships.

The engagement that had been fought off the entrance of the Patuxent on June 1, known as the Battle of Cedar Point, had been a spirited, if lopsided, contest and had ended poorly for the Americans. With their tiny squadron of shallow-draft gunboats, armed barges, and miscellaneous other craft, they had been forced to retreat into the river in the face of overwhelming odds. Within a short time, eighteen small vessels belonging to the United States Chesapeake Flotilla, under the command of Commodore Joshua Barney, found themselves under a full blockade by a far superior force of British frigates, schooners, rocket boats, and armed barges. It is uncertain whether the residents of St. Leonards Town and other inhabitants living along the creek had the slightest hint of the tragedy about to envelop them.

As the British blockade of the Patuxent grew stronger with every passing day, it was obvious that American arms would unlikely prompt an escape from the river. It was equally clear that the enemy was massing for a decisive blow, and the only alternative for Barney was further retreat. Thus, at 7:00 A.M., June 8, he made his move, not up the river as most anticipated but into the narrow, forest-canopied fastness of St. Leonard's Creek. His Majesty's brig *Jaseur* and schooner *St. Lawrence,* being the lightest and fastest ships of the British blockading squadron, took up immediate pursuit as the remainder came up to tighten the noose.[69] The consequences would prove pivotal to the survival of the village at the head of the creek.

Barney's choice of St. Leonard's Creek as a refuge was made with considerable forethought. Unknown to the enemy, a substantial sandbar swooped down from the northern lip of the creek. After nearly two centuries of siltation, the waterway's maximum depth of approximately twenty feet extended only a short distance in from the river, thereby prohibiting entry by the great frigates and allowing only the lighter, smaller-draft warships access. The narrow stream, pinched to a maximum width in at least four different locales to approximately 350 yards or less (allowing for concentrated fire by defenders), was buttressed on both sides by steep banks that made landing and envelopment by the enemy difficult. Moreover, the elevated, tree-lined shoreline provided Barney's marines and the local militia with cover and other tactical benefits over their better-equipped foe. Most importantly, at the head of the creek lay the sleepy little port of St. Leonards Town, connected by overland road to Washington itself, which could serve as an admirable base of operations.

Led by Captain Robert Barrie, commander of HMS *Dragon,* the British were eager to eliminate the only serious naval opposition they had encountered in Maryland waters and

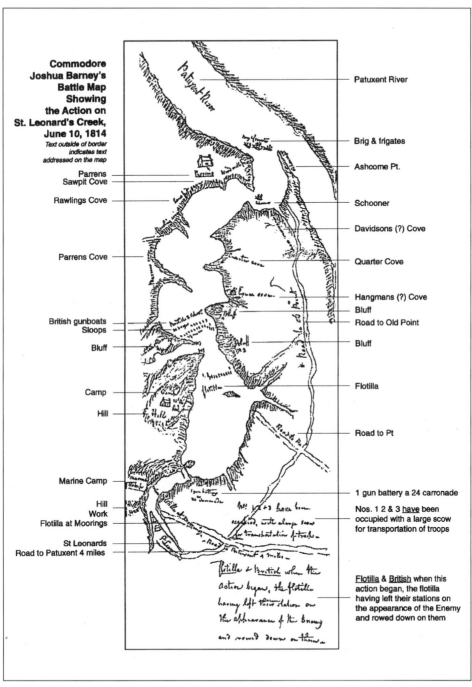

Commodore Joshua Barney's Battle Map Showing the Action on St. Leonard's Creek, June 10, 1814

Text outside of border indicates text addressed on the map

Parrens Sawpit Cove

Rawlings Cove

Parrens Cove

British gunboats Sloops

Bluff

Camp

Hill

Marine Camp

Hill
Work
Flotilla at Moorings

St Leonards
Road to Patuxent 4 miles

Patuxent River

Brig & frigates

Ashcome Pt.

Schooner

Davidsons (?) Cove

Quarter Cove

Hangmans (?) Cove
Bluff
Road to Old Point

Bluff

Flotilla

Road to Pt

1 gun battery a 24 carronade

Nos. 1 2 & 3 <u>have</u> been occupied with a large scow for transportation of troops

<u>Flotilla</u> & <u>British</u> when this action began, the flotilla having left their stations on the appearance of the Enemy and rowed down on them

Commodore Joshua Barney's map of the June 10, 1814, Battle of St. Leonard's Creek indicates two roads, one leading to each side of the Mill Branch. The main road from the north (right), often referred to as the "ridge road," terminates on the north side of the branch at what is believed to have been the smaller section of the town. The road leading from the peninsular component of the town to the entrance of St. Leonard's Creek may have been a secondary road. Courtesy Library of Congress, Washington, D.C.

The Battle of St. Leonard's Creek, June 10, 1814. Watercolor by Irwin J. Beavan, date unknown. Courtesy Naval Historical Center, Washington, D.C.

immediately pressed on with their attack within five hours of Barney's entry into the creek. The first Battle of St. Leonard's Creek, a bloody seesaw naval contest that would continue sporadically for the next three days, ranged from the mouth of the waterway as far north as Johns Creek. Twice each day, the two forces would engage in combat. The British, aboard their schooners and armed barges, increased in numbers and force at every encounter. They entered the fray with gallant huzzahs accompanied by strains of music, firing their dreaded Congreve rockets and seeking to close with the foe or to draw him into the open Patuxent within range of the superior firepower of their blockading frigates. The Americans, having taken their masts down, resolutely entered each contest under oars alone, the boats arranged in a single line thirteen barges wide, stretching from one side of the creek to the other. Of Barney's much-vaunted flotilla, only his war barges, each carrying a carronade in its bow and a long gun in its stern, were sent into combat. His two cranky gunboats (*No. 137* and *No. 138*) the row galley *Vigilant,* a lookout boat, and his flagship sloop *Scorpion* were kept in the rear as reserves, for use as troop transports or as communication and supply vessels.[70]

On June 10, the first Battle of St. Leonard's Creek finally ended in a draw, with the grounding and near destruction of HMS *St. Lawrence*. The British realized that despite the overwhelming superiority of the Royal Navy forces displayed against it, the Chesapeake Flotilla could never be defeated within the confines of the little waterway. Finding that the Americans in the creek "showed no disposition to again venture from its fastness," the British commander reluctantly concluded that "by destroying some of the tobacco stores [along the Patuxent] the inhabitants would be induced to urge Commodore Barney to put out and defend their property."[71]

Thus commenced a veritable reign of terror specifically designed to draw Barney out. It was a terrible expedient that would result in the plundering or near total destruction of practically every farmstead, plantation, hamlet, and town along the entirety of the navigable Patuxent watershed. The scars would last for more than a century.

As the smoke of combat drifted northward each day of battle, St. Leonards Town must have assumed a new visage. A few inhabitants had abandoned their homes early on. At the "common landing," near a "tobacco house" or barn belonging to John Ireland, Barney's men had erected a small tent city "for the purpose of receiving stores and provisions from Baltimore and the city of Washington." The rafters in the tobacco house itself had been readily employed for drying sails and "to keep them from the weather." One of the few town inhabitants who remained offered to fleet surgeon Dr. Thomas Hamilton the use of a small house for the quartering of sick and wounded. A handful of flotillamen such as Hamilton took up residence but, as most of the seamen remained aboard their ships and the marines and land forces were encamped further down the creek, the military occupation of St. Leonards went without a hitch.[72]

Indeed, there were few problems in the tiny village, for soon after his arrival at St. Leonards Town, Barney looked to his strategic defenses, both ashore and on the water further down, and paid little attention to the town itself. For the most part, his five hundred flotillamen remained aboard their crowded vessels, each of which could be covered at night by an awning to ward off the evening dew and rain but still be ready to row into battle at a moment's notice. A contingent of U.S. Marines assigned to the fleet was stationed on a bluff on the eastern shore of the creek and encamped approximately a quarter mile below the town where an earthen fort was thrown up to protect the left flank of the squadron's mooring site. The right flank of the fleet was protected by an earthen-walled battery on the opposite shore, where a single 24-pounder carronade was mounted. A second encampment site, occupied by elements of the Thirty-sixth U.S. Infantry, was also erected on the east shore a mile further down from the Marine camp on an elevation just above Johns Creek, to guard the squadron's left flank when it arrayed for battle. At the narrowest portion of the waterway, a point just north of Planters Wharf Creek less than a mile below the town, a log boom was laid across the passage to hinder any surprise naval assault against either the fleet or the town.[73]

For more than two weeks, St. Leonards Town and the waterway which it dominated would serve as the focal point of state and national attention, as the locale at which the only regular naval fleet engagements in Maryland history were being fought. The War of 1812 on the mid-Atlantic seaboard, for a single fleeting moment, had now concentrated all of its fury on this hitherto tranquil byway. The consequences for the inhabitants, whose homes and hearths were directly in the field of fire, were devastating.

When Barney arrived on the creek, southern Maryland was politically a Federalist-dominated region already in strong opposition to "Mr. Madison's War." That the flotilla had acted as a magnet, drawing enemy attentions to the Patuxent, was a fact roundly despised by local residents who stood to suffer the most. After the first Battle of St. Leonard's Creek, when the British turned their untender attentions to local plantations to draw the flotilla out to fight, local hatred for Barney, his men, and the government knew no bounds. In an effort to spare their property from enemy destruction, a number of residents openly collaborated with the invaders and claimed that Barney had intentionally brought the fight to southern Maryland "to make the federalists feel the pressure of the war they abhor."[74]

Recriminations erupted on both sides. When two brothers named Parran, owners of an estate at the mouth of the creek, paid a visit to one of the American encampments, they mentioned that they both had been taken prisoner by the British and had secured release only upon the stipulation that they urge the local inhabitants to remain at home. Should they flee, one of the Parrans warned, the enemy would consider it a sign of hostility and would destroy all of their property and dwellings. To reinforce this statement, he informed the commodore that the property of the flotilla's own purser, John Skinner, which lay near the entrance of the creek, had been completely ruined after the big battle because its owner was not present. Yet, Parran's inquisitiveness caused Barney to suspect him as a traitor, especially after he let slip that he had just come from the enemy flagship. The commodore, who thought little of the locals or their questionable patriotism, promptly had him placed under arrest. The Calvert County Militia, he complained, was "to be seen everywhere but just where they were wanted—whenever the enemy appeared they disappeared." Likewise, poor relations between the navy and the U.S. Army, specifically a unit of the Thirty-sixth Infantry under Colonel Henry Carberry, a local commander sent to guard the fleet's shoreline flanks, served only to exacerbate the situation.[75]

To prevent further depredations, it was obvious that action had to be taken. Barney was forced to play the enemy's game after all. Finally, assured by Washington that help was on the way, he resolved to fight but by his own rules. He would launch a surprise breakout attempt whatever the odds against success might be. On the night of June 25, with the arrival of army reinforcements (two regiments of infantry from Baltimore and a few batteries of cannon under the overall command of Colonel Decius Wadsworth) as well as a unit of U.S. Marines (from the Washington Navy Yard under Captain Sam Smith), the flotilla mustered for the last time at St. Leonards Town. All of the barge masts were removed and stored in the nearshore waters at the foot of the town landing, even as the senior officers gathered to map out their attack.[76]

It was a simple plan. Just before dawn, a surprise combined land-sea assault would be launched on the enemy ships blockading the creek. Two batteries, commanded by Sailing Master Geoghegan and Captain Miller, were to be silently erected on the north shore bluff directly overlooking the waterway's entrance and the enemy anchorage. The two recently arrived infantry regiments were to take station on the plain behind the batteries and protect their right flank from any enemy landing or envelopment. As the land troops moved into position under the cloak of darkness, Barney's barges were to move quietly down from their defensive battle line below the town, under oars alone, to a position just inside the mouth of the creek. The remainder of the fleet was to remain behind as before. At precisely 4:00 A.M. on June 26, the batteries were to open a surprise bombardment upon the blockading ships, signaling the beginning of the battle. Barney's thirteen barges, manned by some of the most heroic men in U.S. naval history, were then to charge head-on in a desperate but coordinated assault against the giant frigates and awesome British enemy firepower. Surprise was everything if success was to be achieved.[77]

As in any major engagement, especially those begun in the darkness of night, the second Battle of St. Leonard's Creek, once underway, assumed a life of its own. Although outgunned by better than three to one and hindered by miscommunications, delays, logistical problems and, once the fight had begun, sheer panic among many of the U.S. Army troops ashore, Barney and his flotillamen fought with a bravery hitherto unmatched in the tidewater theater of combat. Two badly mauled frigates, HMS *Loire* and *Narcissus,* were sent reeling down the river in sinking condition and were saved from foundering only by beaching them on a sandspit so their hulls could be patched. The rest of the enemy followed helter-skelter, and the United States Chesapeake Flotilla escaped into history.

Jubilation aboard the flotilla was universal. "Thus, we have beat them and their rockets, which they did not spare," wrote one seaman. "You see we improve: first we beat off a few boats, which they thought would make an easy prey of us. Then they increased the number. Then they added schooners. And now behold the two frigates, all, all, have shared the same fate. We next expect ships of the line. No matter we will do our duty."[78]

The atmosphere at St. Leonards Town was anything but heady, for British retribution would most certainly be forthcoming. With no one left to protect the town, given the enemy's penchant for brutishness, the consequence was predictable. When the invaders licked their wounds for more than a week before venturing back into the waterway, it was certainly a testament to the degree of the damages inflicted upon them. Their subsequent depredations would have been devastating with or without Geoghegan's reception. The landing party, it was later reported, burned all of the buildings in town "except that where the doctor had his quarters with the store adjoining, and another immediately opposite." Little, it appeared, was to be spared, and everything, no matter how inoffensive, was considered fair game, including even the slave quarters, hen houses, and pigpens.[79]

When the British officers, standing amidst the blazing village, inquired of the few terrified residents remaining who it was that had fired upon them, they were told it had been the flotillamen. "It was like them," mocked one officer in derision, while conveniently forgetting his own flight only a few days earlier, "that they regrettably had not stayed a little longer."[80] At 6:00 P.M. the incendiaries departed, having loaded a captured schooner with tobacco and proceeded out of St. Leonard's Creek, never to return again. On July 9, Admiral Sir George Cockburn crowed about his revenge, claiming that his frigates had been up St. Leonard's Creek and destroyed the vessels left by Barney and brought off forty hogsheads of tobacco. "Our only difficulty is what to do with it all." It was not even mentioned that the century-old town of St. Leonards lay in utter ruin.[81]

The morning after the raid, Solomon Rutter and John Geoghegan completed reloading their wagons with the spars and rigging that had been hidden from the enemy. Soon afterwards they returned to the waterfront to inspect the two scuttled gunboats and assess the possibility of raising them and placing them back in service. At the landing, Geoghegan was stunned to encounter "a number of inhabitants who had been onto the gunboats, and tore up and plundered every piece of iron and copper etc. they could get at." Enraged at the predators, he immediately seized the plundered goods and reported to Barney that the inhabitants "were more anxious to plunder the property of the U.S. than defend their own, which is certainly the case as there were more men collected for that purpose than has been seen together since we lay in the creek."[82]

Disgust with the federal government ran deep on St. Leonard's Creek, and not a few victims of British vengeance sought to hold the United States accountable under a federal claims law enacted on April 9, 1816. Two citizens of St. Leonards Town, John Ireland and Mary Frazier, filed formal claims for reimbursement for damages, charging that their property had been employed by the U.S. Navy and thereby had become targets for enemy retribution and had been destroyed. Ireland declared that his tobacco house had been burned "on account of having been occupied, etc. by men belonging to the flotilla," while Frazier sought $800 in compensation for the loss of her frame house.[83] The Claims Committee of the U.S. House of Representatives forwarded the claims to Barney for comment. The commodore, with obvious pique, rebutted both.

Ireland's building, he reported, was a tobacco house and was situated at the town's common landing where the tents were erected. True, the rafters had been used for drying some "few small sails" but these were removed before the British arrived and carried to Hunting Town, "nothing being left but some round shot and iron ballast near the said house on the landing." Moreover, the building itself was never occupied by his men.[84]

Mary Frazier's effort to secure a lucrative compensation for the loss of her house, which she charged had been employed as a hospital for the flotillamen, was also rebuffed by the commodore. To back up his rejoinder, he immediately queried Dr. Hamilton on the charge. The doctor replied that another resident of the town told him that the house had not, in fact, been burned. The commodore so informed the Claims Committee. In the event the house *had* been burnt, however, he added a substantial defense. First, he noted, a small house had in fact been occupied by a few sick flotillamen, but it had not been taken over by the commodore's orders. And it was only a short time after the flotilla had departed the creek that the British themselves burnt the tobacco house and several other houses in the town. The commodore added:

I am very confident if Mrs. Frazier's house was burnt, it was not in consequence of the sick men having occupied it for a few days, for the house where Dr. Hamilton lived was not burnt, although several officers, sick and wounded, occupied it. If the house which Mrs. Frazier claims was burnt, and was the one my men occupied, it was a wretched hovel, being deserted and vacant at the time, without windows, and entirely open, being a small one-frame and entirely rotten, and if valued at the very highest, could not be worth more than fifty dollars; and in this opinion I am supported by Dr. Hamilton, who also informs me that he was solicited to occupy the house, and I now believe with a view to make a claim for it in case of accident; but as several other houses were burnt at the same time, I do not think our occupation of it was the cause. . . . But sir, the fact is, that [in] Calvert County, and particularly at St. Leonard's, the inhabitants were more the enemies of the officers and men belonging to the United States service than they were to our enemies the British.[85]

Though not completely destroyed, the venerable village on St. Leonard's Creek had ceased to exist as a riverport, for all intents and purposes. What the British had begun, nature inevitably concluded as the upper reaches of the waterway rapidly silted up, denying access to all but the shallowest draft vessels. Eventually, whatever commercial shipping reached the St. Leonard's was off-loaded at Planters Wharf, three-quarters of a mile below the town. Yet, some remnant of urban life remained, as a few inhabitants returned to rebuild.

When the war had begun, St. Leonards Town had already enjoyed a regular postal service for more than sixteen years. Although service was undoubtedly slow to return—nearly nine years would pass before a new town postmaster, William C. Dawkins, would be assigned to replace the last to hold that office, James M. Sollers—mail delivery to the town would resume. From the beginning of postal delivery to the town in 1796 until 1918, a total of thirty-four postmasters would faithfully serve the town.[86] Property owners such as Hezekiah Coberth and his kin would live out their lives, die, and be interred in family burial plots located on unoccupied lots at the town's outer periphery. From time to time at the foot of the town landing, watermen would build shallow-draft fishing boats to be launched into the silting basin. Small boys would swim out to the still visible wrecks of Barney's old gunboats

Left: The headstone of Hezekiah Coberth, the eleventh postmaster of St. Leonards Town, still stands in the family burial ground. *Right:* The remains of part of the Coberth family burial ground, though subject to the depredations of nature and man alike, mark the site where a town once stood.

and others lying in both Mill Branch and Quaker Swamp Branch to inspect the curious relics of a war most sought to forget.[87]

The basin off the old town site continued to fill with silt, eventually preventing even the lightest of shipping from approaching the landing. Totally cut off from direct river traffic and now well off the beaten path between Prince Frederick, seat of county government, and Solomons Island, seat of most of the county's new shipbuilding and oyster packing industries, St. Leonards' days were numbered. In 1882 a Maryland geographic directory alluded only briefly to the ancient town thus: "Five miles from Port Republic at the head of St. Leonard Creek. Planters Wharf on the Patuxent River is the shipping point. The climate is mild, and not much business is done there. Crops are good; land is valuable in quality at $5.30 per acre, and about one-half of the land is cleared."[88]

By the onset of the twentieth century the town that had barely survived the War of 1812 was little more than a backwater assemblage of modest dwellings. On March 12, 1894, the name of the town was officially changed from St. Leonards to St. Leonard, but such frivolous alterations mattered little. By 1928, there were only six buildings standing along Main Street, four on the west side and two on the east side. Another building stood on the edge of the wetlands shore of Quaker Swamp Branch, and an additional structure lay well up Mill Branch.[89] Within the next decade, even these had been all but abandoned, and little sign of habitation, save for a few cellar holes and dirt road beds, could be found on the peninsula.

Even as the last traces of the ancient town slowly disappeared beneath bracken and brush, two and a half miles further north, at a nondescript crossroads astride the old ridge road, another small hamlet began to stir. A new town named St. Leonard had already been born.

❖

July 17, 1997. The Chesapeake Flotilla Project was not going well. As principal investigator
and project director in charge of the first comprehensive archaeological effort to systematically locate and excavate the remains of Joshua Barney's ill-fated fleet, I was nearing the
height of frustration. A full seventeen years had passed since our group had located and ex-
cavated one of Barney's nearly intact ships not far from Upper Marlboro. Afterwards, it had
taken a decade and a half to convince federal, state, and local agencies to support a search
for the rest of the fleet. Now, we had come back to finish the job—to excavate a site believed
to be a gunboat in St. Leonard's Creek and to locate and investigate the remainder of the
shipwrecks upriver.

    The program, carried out between 1995 and 1997, was the result of a project design which
I had submitted for consideration to both the Maryland Historical Trust, which in 1988 had
become the administrator of all historic shipwrecks in navigable waters of Maryland, and
the U.S. Navy, which owned all navy wrecks no matter where they lay. Amazingly, the project received widespread support and was funded through the Trust by a modest navy grant
of $27,000. The project, a multidisciplined effort, was to be carried out under my direction
but under the auspices of the University of Baltimore's Office of Sponsored Research. Extensive logistical assistance had been provided by East Carolina University, the Maryland
National Capital Park and Planning Commission's Patuxent River Park, the Calvert County
Soil Conservation District Office, the Academy of Natural Sciences, the Maritime Archaeological and Historical Society, and volunteer agencies, organizations, and individuals too
numerous to list. Between twenty and thirty people were in the field at any given time, operating aboard a small fleet of three to five boats. More than a thousand hours of underwater
time had already been logged in. Total value for these in-kind contributions was later stated
in Trust publications as well over $100,000. The true value in sweat and dedication of the
team was priceless—but to date our efforts had been measured in failures, not successes.
And I was exhausted.

    During the course of the 1997 field program, two huge tracts of the Patuxent had been thor-
oughly examined. The primary area, wherein the bulk of the Chesapeake Flotilla wrecks were
believed to lie (referred to in our official reports as the Hills Bridge Transect), began approximately thirty-two miles upriver, between the Western Branch of the Patuxent and Mount
Pleasant Landing, a range about six miles in length near Upper Marlboro. The secondary area,
where we believed the gunboats and merchantmen lost in 1814 lay (the St. Leonard's
Transect), included the entirety of St. Leonard's Creek above Johns Creek to the foot of the
old St. Leonards Town peninsula. In the Hills Bridge Transect, state-of-the-art remote sensing
investigation had been ongoing for a year. Aerial infrared photo surveys, three magnetometer
surveys, two side-scan sonar surveys, an underwater ground-penetrating radar (GPR) survey,
and another GPR survey on the adjacent wetlands were all undertaken to locate and pinpoint
the remains of the fleet. Then, a half million square feet of river bottom had been probed by
hand using ultrahigh-velocity waterjets every ten linear feet to subsoil depths up to
twenty-five feet below the bottom, testing for deeply buried targets indicated by the remote
sensing. It had proved to be a backbreaking and utterly frustrating endeavor for we had
failed to find the main fleet in the very reach where the historic record said it should be.
Now, halfway through the season, one of the sites being test-excavated in St. Leonard's,
which we had located twenty years earlier a mile below the old town site but left for later
survey, turned out to be a late nineteenth-century vessel named *Widgeon* and not a gunboat.
Historically and archaeologically relevant? Yes. But the wreck of my dreams? No.

Top: Marine archaeologists from East Carolina University examine a crudely fashioned breasthook from the remains of a shipwreck located near the foot of the St. Leonards Town Peninsula. The badly worm-eaten piece was discovered beneath four feet of sediment and was the first evidence of historic shipwreck sites found in the immediate vicinity of old St. Leonards Town.

Bottom: Archaeologists examine a timber from one of two of Joshua Barney's gunboats, scuttled on July 2, 1814, and discovered by the author on July 17, 1997. Two more seasons of archaeological investigation by graduate students from East Carolina University would be needed to verify the two wrecks as American gunboats from the War of 1812. Photograph by Eugene Meyer.

The news of our failure to find either the main fleet or the gunboats had not been well received by our funding agency, which was eager for a showy discovery. Both the director of the Maryland Historical Trust and the head of the State Museums Programs recommended to the offices of U.S. Senator Paul Sarbanes and Congressman Steny Hoyer, two key federal representatives whose support had been deemed imperative to secure future funding to continue the search, that their scheduled visits to view field investigation be canceled. Having not been informed of the action, I was extremely agitated.

Ironically, the day after I had been told of the cancellations, a foray into the mouth of Quaker Swamp Branch had turned up a tantalizing clue—a crudely tooled part of a wooden ship's bow section known as a breasthook, which had been found beneath four feet of sediment. Thus, the first evidence of wreck sites was discovered at the foot of the old St. Leonards Town peninsula on July 14 by simply lining people up in the shallows of the branch and having them march along in a line in water too shallow for small boats, systematically probing to a depth of ten feet below the bottom with steel and wood poles to locate buried features. But we had still failed to find anything even resembling an articulated shipwreck.

Now, as I managed the wheel of *Roper,* one of our dive boats, with *Washington Post* reporter Eugene Meyers and Maryland State Underwater Archaeologist Dr. Susan Langley aboard to see our skimpy find, I had a sinking feeling in the pit of my stomach. It looked as if the project was not only in for an early close but was unlikely to be reopened anytime soon.

We approached the foot of the St. Leonards Town peninsula, and I tried to envision the place from the perspective of a Royal Marine approaching the town on that fateful day in 1813, with its beached merchantmen in Mill Branch and Quaker Swamp Branch and the two gunboats lying scuttled, their decks flush with the water. I listened for the staccato reception of American muskets, and I pictured the little town in flames.

Our prop began to stir up mud, and I brought *Roper* about. "Drop the hook," I shouted out to Langley. But try as she might, she could not get the anchor to grab. Perturbed, I cut the engine, grabbed the anchor, and jumped overboard in the shallow water to hand plant it myself. As I trudged shoreward I felt something through the almost porous bottom mud about twenty-five feet from the boat. A wooden log. No, a wooden plank. Then another, and another. Having employed the most sophisticated technology to locate the fleet without success, I had managed to walk, or blunder quite by accident, squarely into a gunboat! The following day, a second wreck, believed to be the other gunboat, was discovered close by. Though the sites would have to await two more archaeological expeditions before their true identities as U.S. Navy gunboats belonging to the Chesapeake Flotilla could be confirmed, a mission finally accomplished by East Carolina University in 1999, I believe John Geoghegan would have been pleased.

4 LOWER MARLBORO

"Really a great town . . . fifty years ago"

November 5, 1965. All day long, the parade of mourners shuffled in and out of the building to pay their final respects. Clarence Plummer temporarily abandoned his tobacco barn and H. S. Jackson left work at the sawmill to visit for the last time. Although Calvert County Commissioner Arthur Jones decided to drive, Bob Spicknall elected to walk with his friend William Reick. Some old-timers, perhaps wishing to ignore the inevitable, simply attempted to forget. Eighty-two-year-old Griffith Armiger, a veteran Patuxent River fisherman, had only just finished stuffing a big old catfish with onions and potatoes and wrapping it in bacon strips when his younger brother, Bernard, dropped by to remind him that they too must make one final call.[1]

All day long visitors converged on the tiny fourth-class post office to present their solemn and sincere condolences to seventy-year-old postmistress Elsie Cox, affectionately known to the locals as "Miss Elsie." Always cheerful but businesslike, Miss Elsie welcomed mourners, even as she lovingly stamped the last of the commemorative postcards sent by philatelists from as far away as Pennsylvania, Oklahoma, and even Washington State. It was indeed a sad and perhaps symbolic occasion, for after this day the tiny Lower Marlboro Post Office, its official duties transferred to another postal jurisdiction, would be no more. Its reason for existence, like the town it had so faithfully served, expired.

Miss Elsie had served as postmistress for a quarter of a century, having stepped into the shoes of her father, Samuel J. Cox, who had completed his own forty-year stint as postmaster in 1940. One can only imagine what memories passed through her mind as she carefully prepared the postage stamps, the money-order machine, and the old weighing scales for transfer. Undoubtedly with some pangs of sentimentality, she looked about the general store in which the post office had been kept, perhaps reminiscing of days long gone. She was definitely getting on in years and had determined to close down the family store as soon as the post office business was out of the way. Nostalgia was the order of the day, and both she and her visitors were awash in memories: the great white steamboats that once came to call, the terrible cyclones, the Sunday School meetings at Largents Chapel, the fields ripe with tobacco and orchards lush with peaches. There was the big muddy Patuxent, which for so long had blessed the town with its spirit and vitality. But that was long ago.

"It's not bad enough that they're closing the post office," mumbled Clarence Plummer as he walked sadly away. "But the general store is going with it. Why there has been a general store in this building for 200 years. It's like the death of Lower Marlboro, that's what I think." Then, as the last of the mourners shuffled out, the door to the old post office was closed and its weathered old American flag was furled for the last time.[2]

Clarence Plummer was right. After nearly three hundred years of existence, a tidewater town had finally passed on. But its life story is still well worth the telling.

❖

Situated on a spacious, alluvial terrace of the Patuxent River shores of Calvert County, approximately twenty-five miles upriver from Drum Point, sits a modest village called Lower Marlboro. Today it is a sleepy bedroom community on the outskirts of urban sprawl, largely occupied by business and government professionals employed in Washington and Annapolis who have accepted their long commute in exchange for the tranquillity of the southern Maryland countryside. Regarding the town's beginnings, most residents know only that the lands they now occupy were once the site of a town that, for a time, served as one of the more important trading ports in the Chesapeake tidewater.

It was not always known as Lower Marlboro. Its life, in many ways, mirrored many of the typical "paper" towns created by acts of the Assembly during the seventeenth and eighteenth centuries. Its first incarnation may be traced back to the fall 1683 session of the Maryland Assembly, when the new town sites proposed for inclusion in the Act for the Advancement of Trade were first being considered. One tract under scrutiny, which lay on the west shore of the Patuxent in what is now Prince George's County, was referred to by the Assembly as "Gaunts Lands," and was part of the estate of Thomas Gantt, a property owner who held 350 acres of land known as Myrtle Range. The description of the site submitted to the Lower House by the governor and the Upper House on October 11 suggested that the specific location should be near Gaunts Landing (later known as White's Landing). After some debate, revisions were adopted, and the proposed town site was moved to another riverfront tract owned by John Bowling.[3]

As with many proposed sites selected during the 1683 session, there was little activity directed toward surveying or laying out the town, and efforts by opponents to annul the proposed Bowling location were soon being pressed upon the Lower House by the Calvert County delegation. On April 18, 1684, armed with a petition signed by fifty-eight inhabitants of the county, the delegates moved that the Bowling site be nullified and that the town be erected instead on Cox's Creek, located somewhat to the south and on the eastern shore of the Patuxent.[4] Cox's Creek ran through a five-hundred-acre tract of land known as Cox's Choice, which had been taken up by Henry Cox (probably a member of one of the original Puritan families that had emigrated to Maryland in 1649) and eventually settled upon by his brother Thomas. To the north and west was a tract known as Patuxent Manor, which had been taken up by Captain John Boague (or Bogue). To the immediate north was another tract on Hall's Creek belonging to Walter Smith, son of Maryland's first attorney general, Richard Smith. To the east, in later years, the great plantations of the Tasker and Chew families would take root and grow.[5]

The Cox Creek site had many positive virtues. Several fertile terraces running for nearly a mile and elevated between twenty and forty feet above the river were situated to the north of the little stream; they offered a fine platform for development. Indeed, before the coming of the white man, it had already been occupied for centuries by Native Americans during the Middle and Late Woodland Periods. During the Contact Period, when the first Europeans appeared upon the scene, the Patuxent Indian village of Tauskus, first noted by John Smith in 1608, probably lay somewhere in the vicinity of the creek.[6] The terraces were perforated by a number of small streams, providing a fine supply of fresh water from the highlands to the east. During the early colonial era, at most points along the shore the river was between a quarter and a half mile in width, and deep enough to host the deepest draft merchantmen of the day. It was, in general, a "better and more commodious place for trade and shipping" than the Bowling site, primarily because the latter was "adjudged to be inconvenient for the inhabitants," the majority of whom lived on the eastern shore of the river. Since little had been done to lay out the Bowling site, the delegates reasoned, it was altogether appropriate that the opportunity be taken to make the move to the better location before it was too late. The Assembly agreed, and on April 22, 1684, in the Supplementary Act for Advancement of Trade, it was enacted "That there be a town appointed at the said Coxes Creek on the land adjacent in the stead and place of John Bowlings land and that the said John Bowlings land be discharged from being a town port or place of trade."[7]

When, or even if, Cox Town (as the site was locally called) was surveyed is open to question. To date, no plat has been discovered, although some sources suggest that in 1815 a record indicated that one had actually been produced but probably did not survive. Many of the early records of Calvert County that were ensconced in the county courthouse went up in smoke during the devastating Prince Frederick fires of 1814 and 1882, and it is probable that they included the town plans.[8]

The early history of Cox Town is unknown, but it seems likely that, as with most of the Assembly's designated towns, it had a painfully slow beginning—if it started at all. Aside from the land owned by Thomas Cox and Captain Richard Smith, who were among the first to engage in any activity in the area then known locally only as Cox Town Quarter, practically nothing is known regarding the first efforts to actually survey the tract, sell lots, or erect buildings.[9] By the onset of the eighteenth century, the designated site was most certainly a town in name only.

As with many of the 1683–1684 sites that had failed to take hold, the Cox Town site (or at least one close to the original locale) was still considered significant enough to be reintroduced in the 1706 Act for the Advancement of Trade and Erecting Ports and Towns. The redesignated location was now more specifically described as situated "in the freshes of Patuxent river at the plantation of George & Thomas Hardesty," on a tract somewhat to the north of the original Cox's Creek site. On April 19, the act was signed into law by Governor John Seymour and the new site was officially designated as a Maryland port of entry, although it is doubtful it could even boast of a wharf.[10] This time, the designation would prompt some action and a true town would actually evolve, not only on the Hardesty land known as Hardesty's Choice, but spreading to adjacent tracts including Archer's Meadows, Strife, and Woolridge situated on the broad terrace lying between streams later known as Graham's and Chew's Creeks. The town would briefly be renamed Marlborough in honor of John Churchill, the first duke of Marlborough, victor of the 1704 Battle of Blenheim.[11] When Belt's Landing, somewhat upriver on the Western Branch of the Patuxent in Prince George's County, was named a port in the same year and was also designated as Marlborough, the different sites were conveniently defined as Upper Marlborough (Belt's Landing) and Lower Marlborough (Hardesty's) to avoid confusion.

By the third decade of the eighteenth century, several grand residences had sprung up in the vicinity of Lower Marlborough, and a few commercial trappings began to appear of a village that would briefly become one of the principal seaports on the middle Patuxent and the primary outlet for Lyons Creek Hundred, the richest tobacco growing region in the county. By 1720 Richard Smith had become one of the more prominent merchants in the community. He had purchased the part of Hardesty's Choice that was nearest the river from the heirs of George Hardesty—lands originally surveyed for the Hardestys and George Berkley in 1663—[12] and set about to build himself a substantial brick dwelling conveniently near the infant town.

Smith's familial relations were, to say the least, somewhat unique. His wife was Eleanor Addison, whose birth on March 20, 1705, was registered at St. John's Church on Broad Creek in Prince George's County. She was the daughter of Colonel Thomas Addison and Elizabeth Tasker. Soon after Eleanor's birth, her mother died and her father remarried, this time to Eleanor Smith of Calvert County, who was coincidentally Richard's elder sister. Thus, when Richard married Thomas's daughter Eleanor, his sister Eleanor became his mother-in-law and his brother-in-law became his father-in-law![13]

Smith's residence was, for the times, a grand place, with its steep gabled roof perforated by dormers, centered gable-ended chimneys, and Flemish bond walls with all glazed headers. The first known inventory of the house, it contents, and surrounding property, compiled on February 12, 1732, after Smith's demise by Joseph Wilkinson and Sabrett Sollers, is perhaps indicative of the epicurean status of its late owner, Lower Marlborough's first and foremost citizen.[14] Every enclosed space in the mansion had a spartan designation: the green room chamber, the parlour chamber, the great parlour, the back room, the children's room chamber, the head of the stairs, the passage below the stairs, the little parlour, the closet, the children's room, and the cellar. Each room was beautifully appointed with the best furniture and accoutrements, and the great parlor was lavishly finished with wood paneling. The outbuildings of the estate were equally substantial. There was a counting house, kitchen (or cookhouse) and kitchen chamber, a house by the river, two storehouses, and several quarters for slaves.[15]

Besides Smith's store, the little port had its own ordinary, possibly a blacksmith's shop, and a cooperage. With the passage of years the village barely grew, though a few merchants, such as John Skinner, John Ireland, and William Hardy, the latter a factor for the firm of John Buchanan and Richard Molineaux, had arrived to set up shop.[16] In 1747, Lower Marlborough received a much-needed boost when it was selected by the Assembly to serve as one of three Calvert County tobacco inspection station sites. The specific location selected for the station was not noted in the 1747 Tobacco Inspection Act, but was probably erected on the property of Major John Smith since this was the site mentioned in a subsequent renewal of the law in 1753 and again ten years later. By the first act, the inspector was to be paid £40 per year for his service, a wage later raised to £55, and finally to eight thousand pounds of tobacco annually.[17] The consequences of the law, which obliged all of the tobacco grown and shipped from the hundred to be channeled through Lower Marlborough, produced a renaissance for the village. Indeed, the three decades between the passage of the Tobacco Inspection Act and the American Revolution would prove to be the town's golden age.

The community began to expand almost exponentially with the arrival of merchants and factors such as David Arnold, John Moffatt, John Dowten, John Wardrop, and Andrew and Alexander Symmer, and also numerous tradesmen, artisans, and shopkeepers. A few of the new citizens were destined for both wealth and position. Charles Grahame was one such man.

Exactly when Charles Grahame, a Scotsman, came to Lower Marlborough is uncertain, but when he arrived, he already had connections. His older brother, David Grahame, had married Charlotte Hyde, niece of Frederick Calvert, the sixth Lord Baltimore. When David died in 1754, Charles was appointed to a pair of lucrative patronage positions, naval officer of the Pocomoke Naval District and surveyor general of the Eastern Shore, so that he might provide support for his sister-in-law befitting her station. Although the appointments lasted only as long as Charlotte's widowhood (she remarried the following year and Grahame was replaced), such temporary status had been worthwhile. Sometime after 1755, Grahame, then in his midthirties, purchased several parcels of land near Lower Marlborough from Christian Smith who, by a previous marriage, was the mother of Thomas Sim Lee, a man fated to become the second elected governor of Maryland (1779–1782) and then elected for a second term (1792–1794). Bloodlines and relations were everything. Grahame's son, John Colin Grahame, married Ann Jennings Johnson, daughter of Thomas Johnson, Maryland's first elected governor and later a U.S. Supreme Court justice, and became Johnson's close associate. The two men would serve together in the Lower House of the General Assembly (1762–1771). As a delegate to the provincial conventions (1774 and 1776), Grahame would help draft Maryland's first constitution. He would serve on the Council of Safety from 1775 to 1777. And his election to the state senate in 1777 brought him in close association with many notables, such as Samuel Chase and William Paca, two signers of the Declaration of Independence.[18]

The first evidence of Charles Grahame's commercial presence in Lower Marlborough appeared in the *Maryland Gazette* on July 17, 1760, when, together with William Fitzhugh, he advertised the sale of a parcel of slaves just arrived in town from Africa aboard Captain John King's *Diamond*. The venture was profitable enough that the following year Grahame and Fitzhugh took in Benjamin Fendall as a partner in another slaving venture. In July 1761 a second parcel of Africans was delivered at the town wharf by the slaving ship *Africa*, a snow commanded by Captain William Penhale.[19] Grahame ensconced himself in the old Smith house then known as Patuxent Manor, which he purchased from Christian Smith in 1762 as part of a 1,000-acre tract of land originally patented under grant and lease by Captain John Boague. Grahame was assiduous in his own land acquisition and eventually assembled an estate incorporating several tracts totaling 521 acres of land. The Patuxent Manor house was given the name of its new owner and was later popularly referred to as Grahame House.[20]

The maritime character of the port now became even more visible, as the tobacco trade drew an increasing number of ships. A small shipbuilding operation was established at the river's edge by Littleton Watters, and by 1750 at least one wharf had been erected along the town's waterfront opposite a store managed by town merchant John Wardrop.[21]

Unlike at many other tidewater river ports, ships arriving at Lower Marlborough could anchor in the deep water off the town or tie up directly at the town wharf to load and unload while their hulls were purged of shipworms by the freshes. The direct communication with the shore and town, of course, had some drawbacks, particularly for the masters of incoming merchantmen. After a long voyage, sailors usually spent their hard-earned wages ashore in local taverns such as the Sign of the Crown, operated by Philemon Young, who also managed the town ferry to Magruder's Landing in Prince George's and rented out fine horses for day-trippers. Young provided sojourners with "a house of good entertainment" which also kept many sailors on leave well-supplied with spirits. But for mariners unhappy with their officers or unwilling to return to duty, such ready access to the land frequently resulted in their jumping ship. Desertion was, indeed, one of the only expedients available for many seamen to avoid possible impressment into the Royal Navy, to escape returning to disease-ridden ports, or to evade the grasp of a brutal master or mate. From the succession of advertisements posted in the *Maryland Gazette* requesting the return of seamen who had run away from their ships while at Lower Marlborough, it would appear that the town was somehow specially suited for such escapes. Despite usually severe punishments meted out for such transgressions, desertions at Lower Marlborough, interestingly, tended not to be carried out by single men or even pairs, but in larger numbers. In the heat of July 1747, what may be the Maryland record for desertions from a single merchantman at one time appears to have occurred when no less than sixteen sailors jumped ship en masse from Captain Hugh McQuaid's *Downes* as she lay at anchor near the town.[22]

The little riverport was also attractive to some mariners inclined to settle, and more than a few colorful sea dogs installed themselves there. One of the most noteworthy was Captain David Carcaud, master of the merchant brigantine *Duke of Marlborough*. Although Carcaud's origins are unknown, he was of such a reputation that Governor Horatio Sharpe saw fit to employ him and his vessel on at least one sensitive and dangerous state mission. On

October 18, 1760, he was appointed by the governor to carry, under a flag of truce, an exchange of French naval prisoners of war. The mission was anything but simple, for it required Carcaud to proceed from Maryland with the prisoners to the French West Indies naval base at Port Louis, Hispaniola. There, he was to negotiate a trade "like for like," that is captain for captain, officer for officer, and sailor for sailor, with the lieutenant general of Hispaniola, Monsieur De Bert. Carcaud's notoriety as a sagacious fighter stemmed from an encounter on March 16, 1761, while en route to the island, with the commander of an unidentified privateer schooner who ordered him to board and show his papers. Carcaud responded to the order tenfold and boarded the schooner with his mate, Middleton Belt, and his entire crew. The contest was brief. After his antagonists were disarmed and left securely tied, he proceeded on with his mission without further challenge.[23] David Carcaud eventually returned to commercial trading and with his substantial profits secured property along both shores of the Patuxent River in Calvert and Prince George's Counties. He would eventually settle in Lower Marlborough and erect a home at the north end of town near one of the more picturesque bends on the waterway.

Lower Marlborough served as a local waypoint on the river, with small service establishments to handle the flow of travelers, maritime traffic, and, of course, the tobacco trade. From time to time, its citizens would indulge in one of Maryland's most esteemed pastimes. In October 1765, the town hosted its first horse races for a subscription purse of £25 in which the best of three heats won the prize. Four times around the half-mile track were required to complete the two-mile heats. Not until September 1779 would another race be run at the town, but this time there were several purses, including one for £300 and another for £200. John Spicknall registered the horses and collected all subscription money, $30 for the first purse and $20 for the second if the prospective racer was a subscriber, and double the amount if he were not.[24] For out-of-towners to attend such a festive occasion was not easy. Like most small, urban centers in the county, Lower Marlborough had little access to any of the well-traveled overland highways of the colony other than the primitive ridge road running along the Calvert County peninsula. The town's main highway, nurtured only by the complex of capillary rolling roads that funneled tobacco to it and the water's edge from surrounding Lyons Creek Hundred, was the Patuxent and the sea beyond. Thus, almost all social activities, including horse racing, gravitated toward the town as the virtual fulcrum of hundred life.

Educational opportunities in the tobacco society of colonial Calvert County were dismal at best. Those of the wealthier class who wished to educate their children in the basics of reading, writing, and arithmetic usually had several options: send them to schools in other colonies or to England, hire or purchase the indentured time of a private tutor, or secure the services of a clergyman to provide private lessons.[25] Those less endowed with estates or funds had no options. There were simply no schools in the county to handle the task. Moreover, by 1754, the General Assembly had abandoned all efforts to support free schools in Maryland, thereby leaving elementary and secondary education to private and community enterprises. In December 1759, for the more financially able in Calvert County, the educational picture would improve markedly when R. Philipson, master of languages, opened the first school in the county at Lower Marlborough. Philipson advertised that under his tutelage, "youth are taught after an entire and most expeditious method, English, French, Latin, Greek, Hebrew, Punt Hand and Italic," and arithmetic.[26] The success of Philipson's school served as the nexus for the subsequent foundation of the first true educational establishment in the county, a private institution overseen by a board of directors and called the Lower Marlborough Academy. At first, it was a very modest endeavor, but at least it was a start.

Among the academy's earliest and most noteworthy alumni was Thomas John Clagett, who had been born across the river at White's Landing on land belonging to his mother's family, the Gantts. In 1776 Clagett would become rector of All Saints Church near Lower Marlborough, the only Protestant Church in the northern part of the county. In 1792 he was elected and consecrated as the first bishop of the Episcopal Church in the United States. In 1800 Bishop Clagett would serve as chaplain of the United States Senate.[27]

Yet, the Academy needed more than a bootstrap operation and good intentions to survive: it needed a permanent home, direction, and supporters. It did not go wanting. On land donated near the town in 1775 by Dr. John Hamilton Smith (one of the largest slave owners and among the wealthiest men in the county), a privately funded schoolhouse was erected. Unfortunately, before the institution could be opened, another event of a more dire consequence was to intercede, namely the American Revolution.[28]

Throughout most of the War of Independence, Lower Marlborough was generally deemed safe from enemy depredations. Rural Calvert County was strategically unimportant to the planners of the main theater operations on both sides of the conflict. Its somewhat remote location, miles up the Patuxent and relatively unconnected by roads to other larger urban areas, shielded it from the tides of battle that swirled about the Chesapeake. Nevertheless, as throughout the Maryland tidewater, the loyalties of some town citizens were often brutally torn asunder. Many answered the patriot's call to arms. Some refused, attempting to remain neutral. And still others struggled to maintain their allegiance to King George and England. One who chose to support the crown was Captain David Carcaud. On May 17, 1776, as the dissension and protests began to emerge into full-blown revolution, Carcaud informed his wife Henrietta that he had determined to go to London and would not return to Maryland until the "civil war," as he termed it, was over. America would not see his face for the next nine years, although he would make at least one commercial voyage to Quebec during the war in July 1778 as commander of the ship *Calvert*.[29]

A number of the town's citizens would serve in the cause of independence. One such individual was Captain John David, or Davy, who had arrived in Lower Marlborough about 1740 to settle down after a considerable career at sea. He purchased a lot in town, built a home and tavern on it, and turned the latter over to the management of his son Joseph, also a sea captain, who later ran the packet boat *Patriarch* between Baltimore and Alexandria. When the Revolution began, John David readily joined the fray. In August 1776, after British aggressions in the Chesapeake had already commenced, he entered into an agreement with his neighbor Charles Grahame, then a member of the Council of Safety, to hire out his schooner to the state. David was anxious to secure a regular naval commission, though there were as yet few vessels available to command. In October 1776, probably through Grahame, he learned that contracts had been awarded to several firms by the Maryland Council of Safety to build a Maryland State Navy, primarily a fleet of shallow-draft row galleys and gondolas (gunboats), to patrol and protect state waters. Wisely, he sought the support of a powerful, well-connected shipbuilder on the West River in Anne Arundel County, Stephen Steward, to secure a commission on one of the new vessels. It was probably no coincidence that Steward and his partner, Samuel Galloway, had only recently signed one of the contracts to build a pair of row galleys for the new Maryland Navy. Thus, Steward's endorsement, undoubtedly supported by the influential Grahame, was bound to carry considerable weight with the Council of Safety as it labored to find officers and sailors to man the fleet.[30]

"This will be handed to you by Mr. John David," opined Steward in a glowing recommendation penned on October 17. "He, I think, is a very fitting man for first lieutenant of one of the galleys. He is a very brisk man. He likewise sailed a long time in one of the French galleys. If you should think well of giving him a commission, he may be recruiting till the galley is ready to ship, which will be in a few days."[31]

On February 13, 1777, the first galley built by the Steward Shipyard, christened *Conqueror,* splashed into the brown waters of the West River. Exactly two weeks later, John David was appointed as her captain. Under his command, *Conqueror* was eventually outfitted with an armament of four 18-pounders, ten 4-pounders, and nine swivel guns and manned by a complement of sixty-nine officers and men and nineteen gunners mates, the largest single crew in the state navy.[32]

The beginning of David's short career in the Maryland Navy was anything but auspicious. Not long after securing his commission, he was stripped of command as a result of a display of public drunkenness. On March 22, he appeared before Governor Thomas Johnson and the Council of Safety with a petition requesting forgiveness for his transgressions and reinstatement in the state navy.[33] Undoubtedly assisted by the influence of allies in high places, he was promptly returned to duty and actively served for more than a year. In the summer of 1777, he and his ship participated in the defense of Baltimore, when the city was menaced by Royal Navy forces. Later he commanded *Conqueror* in interstate operations, including a voyage from Williamsburg to Maryland to ferry French arms and other war materials, an expedition to Tangier Sound to seek out British tenders, and reconnaissance operations on the Potomac. In April 1778, the enemy captured the merchant ship *Lydia,* a privately owned vessel employed in government service that *Conqueror* had been ordered to protect, and John David's career in the state navy was terminated immediately afterward. He and his crew were paid off and command of the ship was turned over to Captain John Gordon.[34]

Throughout the early days of the Revolution, Lower Marlborough mercifully remained a backwater in the conflict. Charles Grahame and Patrick Sim Smith occasionally arranged for the purchase of local cattle, which grazed freely in the luxuriant marshlands adjacent to the town, for the provisioning of the Continental Army.[35] Life proceeded as always, seemingly unaffected by the war. The crops were grown. Children were born. Old men died. Basil Williamson was appointed inspector of tobacco for the town inspection station.[36] From time to time, news trickled in from the front, where Calvert County patriots such as Captain James Somervell and Dr. Thomas Parran of the famous Sixth Maryland Regiment were serving with distinction. The war in which they fought seemed far away indeed.

All of that was soon to change.

During the summer of 1780 British and Loyalist depredations began to strike closer to home. Enemy ships appeared off the cliffs of Calvert, and the county was aroused. By fall, enemy raiders seemed to be everywhere on the Bay, honing to a sharp edge the fine art of plundering and burning. As the towns and plantations of St. Mary's, Somerset, and Wicomico Counties were systematically subjected to devastating attacks, the citizens of southern Maryland and the Eastern Shore repeatedly cried out to the penniless state government for protection. But the Maryland Navy was now but an impotent shell. In November, the first serious enemy attack on the lower Patuxent was carried out. The raiders probed as high as Point Patience, seized the home of John Parran, which was then fortified, and employed it as a temporary headquarters. Numbering approximately one hundred men, the invaders burned homes, destroyed the Rousby Hall estate of Colonel William Fitzhugh, and carried off his slaves. In January 1781, a British frigate drove three Maryland privateers—which had been operating under contract with the Maryland government—aground on the southern lip of the river's entrance at Cedar Point and totally destroyed two of them.[37]

As spring approached, the inhabitants along the Patuxent drainage held their breath in anticipation of the next enemy assaults. The Bay would soon be swarming with Loyalist guerrilla sloops and armed barges, but Lower Marlborough, located well upriver, still seemed secure. In April, new depredations were reported. Colonel William Fitzhugh, already stung once, fretted over the safety of flour stocks produced by his mills in the lower county and consigned to the government, and he queried the Council of Safety as to where they might be more safely stored for "greater Security." On April 6 the council suggested that the flour be removed to Lower Marlborough, a place it deemed "sufficiently safe and convenient." Fitzhugh was promptly instructed to contact Patrick Sim Smith, the government commissary of Calvert County, to begin the move.[38] But it was already too late.

On Saturday, April 7, the Patuxent was covered with a fog so dense that the movement of several armed barges entering the river went entirely unnoticed. The vessels were largely manned by ex-slaves liberated by British and Loyalist "picaroons," or waterborne guerrillas, in raids on Maryland and Virginia plantations. Many had been freed during the plundering of Colonel Fitzhugh's Rousby Hall estate, and most carried with them enmities and desires for revenge in retaliation for their years of slavery. The barges were under the command of Captain Jonathan Robinson, a white man and one of several prominent Tories who had been conducting raids on the Bay for nearly a year. Robinson held a British commission, with authority to grant commissions of his own to others as prize masters. It is possible that he may have been informed of the defenseless state of Lower Marlborough by Fitzhugh's former slaves, some of whom were familiar with the town and its valuable stores and warehouses, several of which were owned by the colonel himself. Proceeding with one vessel and leaving a second behind to protect the rear and pick up any patriot craft that might escape him, Robinson pressed with alacrity up the Patuxent toward the town, intentionally ignoring other potentially richer targets on the lower river. His goal was to strike where least expected, and he accomplished his mission with utter success.[39]

The surprise descent upon Lower Marlborough was carried out without contest. Colonel Peregrine Fitzhugh and William Allein, two of the county's more prominent citizens, were taken hostage before anyone knew what was happening. All of the shipping tied up at the town wharves was captured, including a vessel laden with provisions from Patrick Sim Smith intended for removal to Upper Marlborough. The raiders worked quickly but efficiently, loading as much of the store of tobacco from the town warehouses and inspection station as their captured vessels could hold.[40]

Robinson and his men remained in town until Sunday morning, then departed with a strong northwest wind to help them on their way. But before leaving, perhaps as a message to all patriots, they set Captain John David's home and inn afire, and the flames consumed all, including a hapless traveler who was sleeping soundly within. At the mouth of the river, the raiders rendezvoused with two ships and a brig that had been ravishing the upper Bay regions and then, satiated with booty, they sailed off together. Fitzhugh and Allein, of no further use as hostages, were released. The ripple effects of the raid were soon felt as riverfront homes all the way from Swanson Creek to Upper Marlborough were deserted by a panic-stricken public. The local militia, which had been ordered out as soon as word of the attack reached Annapolis, arrived in time to do little more than pick up the pieces.[41]

The war was building towards its climactic conclusion as the great armies of Washington, Rochambeau, and Cornwallis embarked upon their separate marches towards the York River and the little Virginia port that was destined for immortality. As Washington's tattered veterans began their secret moves southward from New York, many key ports in the tidewater were pressed into action to provide vessels to ferry the troops arriving at Head of Elk down Chesapeake Bay. On August 30, 1781, at Lower Marlborough, Samuel Maynard was one of several state agents empowered by the Maryland government "to impress all the vessels capable of transporting troops or military stores, with their hands, provisions and furniture that are within any of the rivers or harbors of Chesapeake Bay" to carry the army to its rendezvous with history. The record is quiet regarding the shipping then at the town wharf, but it is probable that Lower Marlborough was among the many ports that contributed substantially to the allied triumph at the siege of Yorktown by ensuring the timely carriage of American and French soldiers to the scene of battle.[42]

Victory at Yorktown did not ensure either an immediate end to conflict—it would continue for another fifteen months—or an immediate return to prosperity. Even before the fighting was over, recriminations against Loyalists in the form of outright confiscation of property became the order of the day. One of those in danger of having his property seized was David Carcaud of Lower Marlborough. In May 1781 a grand jury indictment for treason was issued in absentia for Carcaud and twenty other men for leaving the country after April 30, 1775, and "continuing with the enemy." Carcaud was not without his champion. His wife Henrietta, who had remained behind, vigorously petitioned the Maryland Senate and House of Delegates to be permitted to retain the family lands, house, slaves, horses, and cattle. Even as his legal struggle was underway, Carcaud continued his seafaring career as sailing master of *The Alfred Aron'd* (or *Bron'd*). The effort to save his estate proved in vain. All of the captain's property was confiscated, although the indictment on the charge of treason had yet to be ruled upon. Finally, assuming the worst, on February 7, 1784, he submitted a petition to the British government seeking financial reimbursement as a Loyalist for the loss of lands, house, slaves, cattle, and other property. About this time, it appears that the indictment against him either was overturned or was not to be acted upon. By 1785, undismayed by his losses and buoyed by the failure of the indictment, Carcaud felt secure enough to return to America to rejoin his family and attempt to rebuild his shattered estate. On December 3, 1785, he began by purchasing 258 acres of a tract called Hall's Craft, located on Hall's Creek in Calvert County, from Patrick Sim Smith for £800. By the turn of the century, the metamorphosis of David Carcaud had been completed. He owned at least 1,000 acres of land, and in 1798 his son, William Molleson Carcaud, was elected to the House of Delegates for Calvert County.[43]

The last years of the war had been traumatic for Lower Marlborough. Most of the tobacco merchants in town, cut off from their European markets by the hostilities and frequent enemy blockades of the Chesapeake, had been forced to close down their businesses, causing great distress to the planters in the immediate countryside. In October 1782, Dr. Edward Johnson of Lower Marlborough dispatched a letter to Joshua Johnson, a principal in the great Annapolis trading house of Wallace, Johnson, and Muir (WJ&M), citing the distress of the local farmers and begging that the company open a store in town. His letter was not without logic since WJ&M was one of the largest, most successful trading firms in the state. Joshua Johnson, however, lamented that his company, which already had a considerable quantity of tobacco on hand, was itself unable to procure enough shipping to handle it. Lower Marlborough would simply have to wait for the official peace and an improvement in the business environment.[44]

Peace would come, and the town would slowly—very slowly—resume its quiet ways. Its actual size at the end of the Revolution is uncertain, but it is quite probable that its population had been substantially reduced by the war and hard times. In 1782, Lower Marlborough Hundred, which was partitioned that year from Lyons Creek Hundred, was added to the county tax list for the first time. The list, compiled by tax assessor John Spicknall, indicated the new hundred contained only 127 landholders and 557 white inhabitants. The list also indicated that there were only sixteen lots in town, all owned by the following persons: Rebecca Arnold (two), Richard Bishoprick (one), Dammund Camphin (one), Samuel Chew (two), Thomas Contee (two), Henry Cox (two), Captain John David (two), Colonel William Fitzhugh (two), Francis Harwood (one), James Weems (one), and Philemon Young (one).[45]

Fortunately, the town would recover, although not to the scale of its prewar heyday. Its golden age had passed, but, masked by a brief resurgence of commerce, few realized it. By 1785, WJ&M was employing fifteen ships, five of which were owned outright and all of which would usually tie up at one or two landings during their normal three-month layovers in Maryland. At this time, the company adopted Edward Johnson's suggestion and erected a new store at Lower Marlborough. Once again the town began to serve as a magnet not only for local tobacco growers but for planters elsewhere in the state as well, indeed some from as far away as Wicomico County.[46] Waterborne commerce and transportation were still all important to the village's survival since overland traffic was limited to the muddy web of private rolling roads and horse trails, which were often closed off by private gates and fences. In 1794 Lower Marlborough was still connected by formal, private roads leading only to All Hallows Church and to a point near present-day Hunting Town.[47]

Peace also brought a renewed interest in other matters. The Lower Marlborough Academy, which had been closed throughout the Revolution, was soon resuscitated. In April 1791, it was reported, the academy "at length, collected the scattered finances and procured a tutor, Mr. McCormick, recommended by Mr. Davidson of Philadelphia College, not only for his literary acquirement but also for his rectitude of conduct . . . This Academy is within 1 1/4 mile of the Town of Lower Marlboro, situated on a dry and healthy spot."[48] The sons of local planters would again be able to receive a substantial education. And the academy would once more begin to churn out men destined for distinction, men such as Joseph Kent, who would study medicine, establish a practice in town, and eventually enter public service. Kent would go on to serve his state not only as a U.S. Congressman, but also for three terms as its governor.[49]

Unfortunately after the brief postwar resurgence of commerce and optimism, like many other towns in southern Maryland, Lower Marlborough soon began another downward spiral. The Jeffersonian embargo on British and French trade proved devastating. Almost overnight, the great ships that had regularly anchored off the town before and immediately after the Revolution stopped calling. Those that managed to carry on interstate coastal operations began to be routed to more youthful urban centers such as Baltimore and Alexandria. Almost as if the event were a talisman for the future, in 1800 John David's tavern, rebuilt after the last war, burned down again.[50] Somehow, Lower Marlborough dug in and held on, and its warehouse facilities continued to serve the community. But with the outbreak of the War of 1812, they would once again pose a tantalizing temptation to enemy raiders.

In June 1814, when Commodore Joshua Barney's United States Chesapeake Flotilla found itself tightly blockaded within the confines of St. Leonard's Creek by a strong Royal Navy force, a score of miles to the southward of Lower Marlborough, the ports along the Patuxent drainage were again paralyzed with terror. False alarms were commonplace and the citizens of the town were no more immune to panic than their neighbors. When a small schooner that had escaped the blockade was observed making its way up to the town waterfront, the inhabitants instantly fled into the countryside. Some called upon William Contee, the local militia officer in charge of the district, and reported that the enemy had descended upon them with five hundred men. In fact, at that moment, the contest was being savagely fought on St. Leonard's, where the American Navy was successfully repelling the repeated assaults of the enemy. Yet, it was the stout resistance of the flotilla itself that was destined to trigger British actions against many of the towns of the lower Patuxent. Finding the Americans in the creek showed "no disposition to again venture from its fastness," the British commander, Captain Robert Barrie, decided upon a stratagem to draw Barney's forces into the open Patuxent where the Royal Navy might destroy them in short order with its superior firepower. If he carried out a systematic campaign of depredations against the tobacco warehouses, plantations, and towns of the river valley, he correctly reasoned, the inhabitants would urge Commodore Barney to put out and defend their property.[51] One of the primary targets of Barrie's planned campaign of devastation was to be Lower Marlborough. And, as during the American Revolution, the town was totally unprepared to meet the foe.

Barrie's raiding force, outfitted on the afternoon of June 15, 1814, consisted of 160 Royal Marines from the frigates *Loire* and *Narcissus* and a thirty-man contingent of the Black Colonial Corps, mustered from slaves freed by the British during their various forays throughout the tidewater and trained at the Royal Navy base established on Tangier Island in Chesapeake Bay. The raiders were ordered to proceed up the river from St. Leonard's in three divisions. The first division consisted of five vessels led by Captain George Edward Watts, commander of HMS *Jaseur,* the second by Lieutenant Alexander of HMS *Dragon,* and the third by Lieutenant Armstone of HMS *Albion. Dragon's* tender was also sent along to facilitate the removal of plunder. The soldiers embarked aboard their barges at 1 P.M., and soon afterwards carried out a successful descent upon the town of Benedict. Then, leaving the tender behind to transport captured tobacco, they pressed on to Lower Marlborough, five miles to the north, where Barrie was given to understand a large warehouse was bulging with the golden leaf as well as other property. And "as Marlborough is near the Seat of Government I thought an attack on this town would be a sad annoyance to the enemy and oblige the regulars and militia to try their strength with us."[52] The militia was at that moment busily occupied in saving their own skins.

Although the heights to the south of the town commanded a strategic bend in the river and might have provided the militia with a superb defensive choke point at which the enemy advance might have been contested, no resistance was offered. Thus, about 6 P.M. on Thursday evening, June 16, Captain Barrie, joined by the Royal Navy brig-sloop *Jaseur,* was permitted to "take quiet possession" of Lower Marlborough even as the militia and local population fled terror-stricken into the woods.[53]

The British caroused in a bacchanal of willful destruction. One resident documented their ruthlessness. "They opened all the feather beds they could find," reported one eyewitness, "broke the doors and windows out and so tore the houses to pieces inside as to render them of very little value; 4 barges that night came as high as Hall's Creek, and more landed above [Lower] Marlborough. We moved our beds and principal furniture to Caicard's [Carcaud's] and put the rest in the house.[54]

The next morning Barrie's marines began loading tobacco, cattle, and other plunder aboard a small schooner belonging to the unfortunate Captain David, which had been captured along with the town. They then proceeded to set fire to the tobacco-swollen store-houses that hadn't been stripped. At 8 A.M., June 17, the decidedly aromatic smoke from more than 2,500 hogsheads of burning tobacco, valued at more than $125,000, blotted out the morning sun. The invaders, delighted with the morning's work and with a hostage named Reynolds onboard, turned their prows downriver.[55]

The news of the raids on Benedict and Lower Marlborough soon reached Washington, and a plan was quickly produced to send an artillery battery and troops to St. Leonards to help drive the British away once and for all. In the meantime, Lower Marlborough held its communal breath, fearful of a second enemy descent upon the town. It wasn't the Royal Marines, however, who would next pay the little port a visit, but Joshua Barney's battle-worn flotilla.[56] For a very brief moment, the town would serve as the principal United States Navy base on the river. Few of its citizens, though, breathed easier, for most laid the blame for the enemy's presence on the river at the feet of Barney, whose flotilla, they believed, had drawn them into the Patuxent in the first place. That is, until the fleet was ordered to retreat even further upstream to the port of Nottingham, and the town was once more left defenseless. In July, enemy barges once more penetrated upriver, almost as high as Lower Marlborough, and fear of another raid again all but paralyzed the inhabitants.

The town would not have long to wait, but the next time the foe was seen, his focus was fortunately not upon the little riverport. In mid-August, when an English army of invasion arrived on the river and landed at Benedict, a large naval force of barges and light-draft warships ascended the river in tandem with the army's line of march on the western shores of the river. The invader's destination was Washington. The British Army commander, General Robert Ross, was uncomfortable with his mission and required constant reassurance and goading from his naval counterpart, Admiral Sir George Cockburn, who commanded the naval force ascending the river. On August 21 the two officers met for several hours at White's Landing, opposite the town. The admiral, in one of the most fateful conferences of the war, convinced his colleague, whose enthusiasm was dulled by flagging spirits, that the march on Washington must proceed.[57]

There is a charming folktale concerning Cockburn's visit to the region near Lower Marlborough about this time, perhaps true, perhaps not, but one that merits telling. The yarn states that after the British dropped anchor off Lower Marlborough, a number of naval officers went ashore "to see something of the land of the Yankees." While taking a walk through the woods and fields, they came upon a hornet's nest. Not knowing what it was, they summoned a young boy who was playing nearby and asked him. Recognizing the officers to be the enemies of his country, the youth cleverly declared that the hornet's nest was actually the nest of a rare hummingbird. "If you stop up the hole at the bottom and take the nest out to sea, perhaps about ten miles," he told the gullible officers, "you will have a couple of little birds that will stay with the ship as mascots." Soon afterward, the ship weighed anchor and fell down the Patuxent with the tide. The plug must have been withdrawn according to the youth's directions, because about sunset that same day, several of the town's residents, watching through spyglasses, saw Admiral Cockburn and his officers dive overboard into the water, swords and all! The event later inspired a short ditty:

> The hornets surely won the day,
> And made their foes feel shame;
> Those insects were American
> And lived up to their name![58]

The rest is history not so engaging. The American Army defending the capital was soundly drubbed at the Battle of Bladensburg on August 24, and the nation's capital was put to the torch. Several days later, the British Army, flush with victory, again passed Lower Marlborough en route to reembark on the ships at Benedict. It would fortunately be the last time the town would chafe under the oppression of foreign invaders.

The downstream passage of the British Army produced grist for a number of other interesting folk tales which are kept alive to this day by local old-timers. As late as 1900, some say, the graves of several British soldiers, victims of tidewater "swamp fever," were discernible on the hills to the south of town. Others claimed that numerous depressions at the juncture of Graham's Creek and the Patuxent were the gravesites of many more "redcoats," all of which were destroyed by bulldozers during later road construction. In the cove adjoining the old Plummer estate on the river and near the town, yet others believed, lay the remains of a British warship that was burned and sunk after actions upriver.[59]

The War of 1812 was finally over and Lower Marlborough, a little roughed up, again emerged unbowed. Life resumed its slow but measured pace, and despite another postwar recession, thoughts gradually turned to public improvements. Until 1820, the Lower Marlborough Academy had been managed by a board of directors, and operating funds were administered by a board of trustees. In January, the state of Maryland finally moved to make education a public right. The academy fund was soon consolidated with the public school fund in Calvert County, and the school was no longer dependent upon private operating capital.[60]

The following year, Captain George Weems's little steamboat *Eagle* entered the river for the first time, ushering in a new age of commerce. The merchant factors of the colonial era had long since disappeared, and most independent tobacco trading houses of the post-Revolutionary period had fallen into decay. Many Calvert County planters had suffered through embargoes, depression, despair, and finally ruination from the last war. The methodology of commerce itself was assuming a new format. With the advent of the age of steam, Lower Marlborough, like most small waterfront towns in the tidewater, was destined to become totally subservient to the big, brawling port of Baltimore, which served as the main hub for the broad white steamboats that plied a weblike complex of routes and lines connecting it with every river and landing in the region.

For the next half century, Lower Marlborough would lead a quiet, unremarkable existence, little more than a vassal to the dynamic port on the Patapsco. The inroads made by the great Baltimore steamboat lines upon commerce in the Patuxent and its river towns were absolute. On November 26, 1859, James Harrison, owner of the Lower Marlborough wharf, sold the facility to Mason L. Weems, owner of the Weems Line, and the conversion was complete. Weems would thereafter maintain ownership and, in effect, dominate all of the town's maritime affairs.[61] It was, fortunately, a symbiotic relationship, but symptomatic of the total dependence all small Maryland tidewater towns had for Baltimore. Lower Marlborough's days as an international shipping center were over.

Yet, isolated as they were and reduced in circumstance and importance, neither the town nor the county were immune to the discord in national and local politics that was drawing America towards the Civil War. Like most of Southern Maryland, though opposition to slavery had occasionally been voiced, the sentiments of the white inhabitants of Calvert County were strongly allied to the Southern cause, and many of its sons would serve in the Confederate Army.[62]

In the early days of the war, Union forces would be obliged to make numerous forays into the Calvert County countryside to maintain federal control. Typical of these expeditions was one launched in the fall of 1861, ostensibly undertaken to ensure that rebel agents would not intimidate voters in local and state elections. In actuality, the move was a calculated display of brute military force intended to intimidate the local secessionists. Thus, on November 1, Major General John A. Dix issued instructions to the U.S. marshall of Maryland and the provost marshall of Baltimore "to take into custody all such persons in any of the election districts of precincts in which they may appear at polls to effect their criminal attempt to subvert the elective franchise into an engine for the subversion of the Government and for the encouragement and support of its enemies."[63]

To ensure that the orders were carried out, Union infantry units under the overall command of Generals George Syckes and O. O. Howard, marched from Washington, D.C., on November 3, 1861, to occupy polling stations throughout Southern Maryland. The terminal point of their march through Calvert County was Lower Marlborough.[64]

Notwithstanding such events, aside from loss of pride, the town suffered little from the Union presence. For the white population, perhaps the most bitter pill to swallow had been the establishment of a conscription station in town for able-bodied Negroes in October 1862. Not until April 1865, when federal soldiers combed the nearby marshes in a fruitless search for conspirators in the Lincoln assassination, would the last grievous residue of the Civil War be experienced in town.[65]

Fortunately, Calvert County was largely immune to the active conflict itself, and Lower Marlborough had managed to survive on the little steamer traffic afforded it. Despite the postwar depression, a few small businesses had actually begun to emerge and prosper, and the warehouses, with their red roofs and weathered gray planked siding, continued to welcome the tobacco and other produce of the county. A canning factory was opened nearby, specializing in tomatoes, berries, and peaches. There was C. H. Bryan's slaughterhouse, where beef was dressed every Friday, then put on a wagon and carried from home to home to be sold fresh. There was George S. Younger's blacksmith shop and a gristmill where wheat and corn were ground. On Windmill Hill, at the edge of the village, there was a windmill which powered the town sawmill. There were shops for a tailor, a carpenter, a wheelwright, and a cobbler. The town also had a post office, a "Mechanics Hall," and, of course, several taverns. The main street bore the name Varden and intersected with Goose Lane. The southern end of town seemed to be sloppy after every rain, which occasionally caused flooding of both the post office and the blacksmith's shop. The ducks were delighted. In the winter, when the great puddles that formed in the lower sections froze, the townspeople could even skate on them. Among the country folk, the town soon earned the sobriquet "Swampoodle."[66]

Summertimes were highlighted by two major entertainments, sports and politics. By the mid-1870s, baseball fever had struck Calvert County, with hometown teams being fielded by practically every village on the peninsula. Lower Marlborough was no exception, and by 1877 the town's nine were taking to the field to compete against Prince Frederick, Hunting Town, and out-of-county clubs such as Benedict and Upper Marlborough. Politics always provided issues for debate. In 1876, the state legislature enacted a law making it a duty of the office of registration "to sit at some place convenient to the voters of their respective district, for five consecutive days, commencing on the first Monday in September" to discharge their duties and register voters. In Calvert County, four locations were authorized for voter registration centers: Lower Marlborough, Prince Frederick, Solomons Island, and St. Leonards.[67]

As in many rural environs, folk tales, legends, and ghost stories often filled the evenings. For the citizens of Lower Marlborough, especially the children, there were yarns aplenty to tell and retell. There were tales of the Devil's Woodyard, a once impenetrable, thicketed area shouldering the bay where the Devil himself held court and indulged in high revel with witches on Friday nights. There was the story of the murdered peddler who haunted the road at Briscoe's Turn and mischievously rolled his pack between the legs of unwary travelers to trip them up. In the old Grahame house, it was said, a highland chief in full clan regalia walked the rooms whenever disaster befell the family owning the place. There was a mysterious great blue dog, always bathed in an eerie light, that ran through the neighborhood on pitch black nights terrifying the citizenry.[68]

In 1868, Lower Marlborough welcomed the construction of its first Methodist church, built under the leadership of J. J. Largent and named Largent's Chapel after him. On June 14, 1882, the Smithville Methodist Circuit was organized, consisting of the Smithville Church (built in 1840), Mount Harmony (established in 1847), and Lower Marlborough, or Largent's Chapel. A second church, Bethel Church, erected for the Methodist Episcopal Church, South, was built in the village in 1882 but was later moved to another location out of town.[69]

By the 1880s, the maritime commerce of the town was almost entirely dominated by the Weems Line, the Baltimore-based steamboat company that carried the majority of Patuxent exports to the port on the Patapsco. The trade was at first substantial. In 1886 alone, all of the river landings and towns shipped a combined total of twelve thousand hogsheads of tobacco as well as corn, wheat, poultry, fruits, and fish. Incoming cargoes usually consisted of farming implements and agricultural necessities, which were dispersed through the town stores. During the peach harvest season, three Weems steamers made calls at Lower Marlborough each week. On June 21, 1888, the line announced an increased schedule for the coming months. "The fruit season schedule of the Weems Line of Steamers to Patuxent River will go into effect on Sunday, June 29. After that date thirteen trips will be made each week by the steamers *Theodore Weems, Essex, Westmoreland* and *Wenonah*—six to bay landings and seven to points on the Patuxent River." By this time, the town was a small and quiet village consisting of three warehouses, forty-five houses, two stores, several mechanic's shops, and a church. The biggest house in town, of course, belonged to its wealthiest citizen, John S. Hinman. The closely knit community, mostly merchants, mechanics, and farmers, consisted of "quiet, temperate and church going people . . . noted for their hospitality and kind disposition toward each other." By this time, they had even modernized the name of the town from Lower Marlborough to the simpler Lower Marlboro.[70]

Despite its local importance, Lower Marlboro was still not easily accessed by road. The unpaved dirt road running down the spine of the Calvert County peninsula, as well as those radiating from it in the late nineteenth century, were primitive in the extreme, often slick and slippery with mud and pitted with ruts and potholes. But it wasn't the condition of the roads as much as the infernal gates that hindered overland transportation. At nearly every property line along the way, the traveler encountered gates that had to be opened (often only with the express permission of the owner) to allow passage before the journey could be continued. In February 1880, the state legislature finally addressed the problem and called for a referendum in the November county elections with ballots to be marked "For Gates" and "Against Gates." The sheer threat of action was enough to motivate many farmers to remove their gates. On March 27, the *Calvert Journal* reported on the progress in this direction:

> In passing along our public roads it is gratifying to notice the preparations of our farmers for the removal of gates. In some instances this has required fences on either side of the roads. This may be a matter of inconvenience and labor at first, but we doubt any man in the whole county will ever favor restoring any gate on the public road after it has once been removed. While our representatives in the Legislature may not be able to agree upon a new gate law, these nuisances however will likely be removed 'all the same.' Public sentiment is at last against them to such an extent that those farmers who live along the public highways will likely find it to their advantage, and a help to their peace of mind to get rid of these gates on any public road leading through their farms.[71]

In 1886 the venerable Lower Marlboro Academy burned to the ground. One of the town's leading citizens, Dr. John Ireland, was soon afterwards authorized by the Calvert County School Commissioners to advertise for proposals for the construction of a new public schoolhouse either on the same site or adjacent to the one destroyed by the fire. The winning bid was awarded to a pair of town contractors named Spicknall and Boyd, and the school was erected at a cost of $370. Four years later, the new building was moved to a more centrally accessible lot on the north end of town beside the Methodist Church.[72]

By this time, Largent's Chapel was in need of considerable repairs, and efforts were initiated to attend to the necessary maintenance. The church, with its hand-hewn timbers and rigid lines, was closed for the first time to permit refurbishing. Finally, on Sunday, August 25, 1889, it was reopened "in glorious all day meeting" with the assistance of two former pastors, Brothers E. H. Smith and T. E. Peters. In October 1889, when the Smithville Circuit held its quarterly meetings in the chapel, the pastors were able to report that considerable improvements had been made in the church—it was completely repaired, refurbished, and painted, inside and out. It had also been beautifully ornamented by a large memorial window donated by Brother George Spicknall. But best of all, the work had been paid for, and there was still $40 left in the treasury.[73] The church had been restored, and with money to spare!

In June 1899, a building committee met for the purpose of determining a location for a parsonage, the first for the Smithville Circuit. Seventy years later, Suzan Swann, a ninety-seven-year-old native of the town, recalled why the decision was made that Lower Marlboro be the site of the parsonage. "There was a senior pastor, usually married, and a junior pastor that was unmarried," reminisced Swann. "The junior pastor stayed with one family then another. Transportation being slow, and Lower Marlboro being last to have preaching on Sunday (2 'clock youth Sunday School, evening preaching) meant the pastor completed his day's service in Lower Marlboro, often after dark. This made Lower Marlboro the natural place to put the parsonage."[74]

Land north of the church was soon purchased for the parsonage from C. H. Bryan, owner of the town's sawmill and slaughterhouse, for the lordly sum of $165. But the schoolhouse was already ensconced on it, so the building committee agreed upon a trade with the county school board. The school would be moved again to the Bryan lot, this time at the church's expense and labor with the proviso that the schoolhouse and fence be put back in good

order. Funds were raised by a Fourth-of-July steamboat excursion to Bay Ridge in Anne
Arundel County. A steamboat was chartered, and the profits from the proceeds were to be
dedicated to the parsonage fund. A contract was awarded to Charles G. Spicknall, a leading
layman in the church, and the building was soon up at a cost of $855.[75]

In 1901 the church was presented with a new face and painted white with green shutters.
A successful effort was also initiated to procure a bell "8 feet at the base" for installation in a
proposed bell tower. A new tower was eventually completed in 1905 and the bell installed.[76]

With the passage of time and the increasing reliance on the improved county road system
for transportation, dependence upon riverboats diminished. The commerce of the Patuxent
was rapidly decreasing, even though Lower Marlboro's share was by far the largest of all
the river landings. Ironically, by the turn of the century the town was deemed by the federal
government to be the most important on the river. It was a dubious distinction on a waterway that was doomed to closure by siltation. By 1907, the town's river trade produced only
$2,572.67 in revenues, an all-time low. Still, big Baltimore steamboats such as *Three Rivers*
and *Anne Arundel* regularly called at the town wharf to pick up or deposit both passengers
and freight.[77] Many in town benefited directly from employment or indirectly from the commercial spin-offs associated with steamboating. Until 1904 Martha Spicknall served as the
steamboat agent down at the wharf. Upon her death she was succeeded by George W. King,
who would maintain the post for the next thirty-six years until the very end of the steamboat
era. King, who had been employed by the steamer line for a number of years, had joined the
company in 1898 as a waterman, eventually working his way up to first mate before becoming wharf agent. He liked to boast that he was once offered a captain's commission but had
declined in order that he might take on the less stressful post of wharf agent.[78]

By 1916, life in the village proceeded at a slow pace, entirely syncopated to the rhythm of
the steamers, which arrived on Sundays and laid over until Mondays for loading. During the
busier shipping periods at harvest time, runs became more frequent to accommodate shippers. Often, the captain and his crew attended services in Largent's Chapel. The town's
main streets were comfortably spaced with business and civic establishments providing the
local citizenry with their everyday material and social needs. But, where there is life, there is
also a need for a place for those who have completed its rounds. In 1919, the church formally laid out its cemetery grounds, and a price of one dollar per foot was set for each plot.[79]

Modernization was slow to arrive in rural Calvert County and doubly slow in reaching
Lower Marlboro. In April 1912 the telephone company began to cut telephone poles in the
area and then started to install them the following month. By June 13, the first individual
telephone boxes were in use in the town. Streetlights were put up through a community effort. A play, put on by the youngsters of the town under the auspices of Dr. and Mrs.
Ellsworth Hinman, served as the vehicle to raise funds for kerosene streetlights with round
globes. Every home with a lamp placed on its street front had the responsibility of lighting it
each evening and extinguishing it the following morning. The kerosene lamps would remain in service until electricity finally came to town in 1936.[80]

In 1921 the Maryland, Delaware, and Virginia Line, successor to the Weems Line, addressed its fall schedule to accommodate the local trade. In September, to facilitate the
transport of the tobacco harvest to Baltimore, the line formally announced that its Patuxent-
bound steamboats would leave Pier 4 in Baltimore on Tuesdays and Thursdays at 2 P.M.,
weather and tide permitting, and make calls at eighteen landings on the river run, the last of

which would be Lower Marlboro. The steamers would lay over at Lower Marlboro overnight, and on Wednesdays and Fridays they would depart the town wharf at 9:30 A.M., making nineteen stops on the return trip to Baltimore. On Saturdays, the ships would stop at
Lower Marlboro but continue upriver as far as Lyons Creek, where they would lay over until 7 A.M. the following morning, then make numerous calls on the return run, including a 9
A.M. stop at Lower Marlboro.[81]

At the peak of summer and fall, the Lower Marlboro wharf was perhaps the busiest place
in town, with farmers delivering tobacco, crates of peaches and apples, and other produce
for shipment to Baltimore. Although the town was geographically closer to Washington and
Annapolis than to the city on the Patapsco, Baltimore was Lower Marlboro's commercial
link to the outside world—farm equipment was purchased there, produce was sold there,
and farmers and merchants alike depended on the city for all their business needs. Even in
matters of life and death it was the Baltimore steamers that the townspeople relied upon.
This situation was best exemplified when ten-year-old Carroll King, son of the wharf agent,
was stricken with appendicitis. He was carried by stretcher to the landing, then taken aboard
a steamboat to Baltimore for the operation at Mercy Hospital that would save his life.
Though both Annapolis and Washington were much closer, getting to either would have
been a rough overland trip.[82]

With the advent of the automobile, the waterfront of Lower Marlboro briefly increased in
local commercial importance, and a road from upcounty was deemed imperative, not only
for the benefit of the townsfolk, but for all in the county who needed access to the waterfront
facilities. In 1899 there were only 265 miles of roads in all of Calvert County, and none of
them went as far as Lower Marlboro. The main road ran from Smithville to Chaneyville,
Sunderland, Hunting Town, Prince Frederick, Port Republic, St. Leonards, and Drum Point,
with turnoffs to Bowens, Broomes Island, and Wallville. Access to Lower Marlboro was
still possible only by traversing a dismal dirt thoroughfare.[83] The citizens of the county were
eventually obliged to petition the county road commission to make the path, the only avenue
running from Chaneyville to the Lower Marlboro wharf, a usable public artery. The petition
was signed by many leading merchants, farmers, and watermen of the county, including
some of the town's most prominent citizens—W. H. Swann, L. L. Chaney, James W. Gibson, C. B. Plummer, J. E. Plummer, James N. Hinman, H. F. Lane, R. Z. Younger, J. B.
Bourne, and H. C. Ireland. By 1921, with the coming of better roads and the automobiles
that used them, the wharf had also been improved. It was soon large enough to facilitate the
erection of several waiting houses upon it and was even capable of welcoming an automobile or two on its deck of rough-hewn planks.[84] When the road finally came, it was welcomed heartily and not without a bit of humor. R. E. Manely, the Smithville Circuit pastor
who traveled as much as anyone in the county, commented in 1927 on its value by stating
that he "greatly appreciated the increased ease of travel and dares hope that the roads of the
county will remain in good condition at least until the common use of the flying machine in
pastoral visitation renders it necessary to transfer our worry about good roads to worry
about good landing fields."[85]

Even with improved roads and the conveniences of the modern world, the final days of
old Lower Marlboro were rapidly approaching. Reduced in circumstance and significance,
the town had over time become little more than a cluster of buildings far from the beaten
path. Somehow it had survived wars and depressions and still managed to maintain a sense
of community and pride that had thus far countered its diminution. Few could have guessed
that in the decline of the steamboat era the seeds of its demise had already been planted, or
that dissolution would be preceded by a dramatic series of catastrophes. The first serious

calamity occurred in 1913 when a terrible cyclone whipped across the Patuxent Valley and imposed injury to the town. Many buildings suffered damage and several were totally destroyed. Seven years later another cyclone struck, and this time the destruction was more extensive. The winds ripped apart the steam mill, gristmill, and a modest little shipyard at the river's edge. Several homes had their second-story floors torn off, and a stable was devastated, although a horse inside miraculously survived. An icehouse and a barn chock full of tobacco and stacks of wheat straw were blown away. Parts of the wreckage landed in the village of Chaneyville, several miles distant. Lower Marlboro looked like a war zone and the cost to the economically strapped little village was telling.[86]

The arrival of the Great Depression conspired with the demise of steamboat service to put an end to the town. In 1932 the school building was sold to Thomas S. King for $275 and moved to King Fields where it remained.[87] The worst blow, however, was struck on April 13, 1936, when a fire devastated much of the remaining town. The origin of the blaze was traced to a defective flue in the living room of Samuel J. Cox's big eight-room home. Fanned by high winds, the flames gained rapid headway and spread to the adjacent town store, which was jointly owned by Sam and his son Melvin. Before a fire company arrived from the Upper Marlboro fire station many miles away, the blaze had spread. Though the firefighters from Upper Marlboro were eventually joined by units from North Beach, Galesville, and even as far away as Washington, D.C., they were powerless to defeat the flames owing to a lack of water. The town simply had no fire hydrants. Before it was all over, the store (which had also served as the village post office and its social hub), the Cox home, a large tobacco barn in the rear of the store, the icehouse, and the "town hall" were totally destroyed. Nothing was saved from them but a few personal belongings, less than $100 worth of merchandise, the post office receipts, and a small safe. By today's standards, the conflagration would have been considered serious but certainly not fatal. But for tiny Lower Marlboro, already in the throes of decline and depression, it was more than the ailing village could withstand.[88]

When the steamboats finally stopped running, it was all over. On May 11, 1936, barely a month after the fire, James U. Dennis, a trustee for the bankrupt Baltimore and Virginia Steamboat Company, which last owned the Lower Marlboro wharf, sold the historic old facility to Goodman Goldstein. It soon fell into irreversible disrepair. The last arterial connection to Baltimore was closed forever.[89] In a few years, the town would wither and all but vanish as a viable community in both spirit and form, with only a small core of aging residents to recall its livelier days.

Today, there are still a few remnants of the old times, silent witnesses of the heyday of Lower Marlboro. That which remains has suffered the ravages of time, termites, and the often corrosive handiwork of modern society. Grahame House, or Patuxent Manor, once the dwelling of the town's first citizen, was stripped of its wonderful wooden paneling and accoutrements. Shipped en masse to the Du Pont Winterthur Museum in Delaware, they are now displayed in the famous Marlborough Room and can be seen for a fee. The manor house itself, fortunately, still remains. A building now stands upon the site of Philemon Young's Sign of the Crown Inn. Hinman's Store and home (Millennia), the ruins of the early steamboat wharf (now but a few piling stubs underwater), the home of cabinetmaker Eli Gibson, the old Armiger House, the Spicknall House, John Snyder's blacksmith shop, the town stable, the Green Gable House, and the David Carcaud House still endure, although many of the buildings' exteriors have been altered over time. Some details of their colonial interiors have remained intact. In 1954, during the Tercentenary of Calvert County, it was reported that cross doors, high mantels (some intricately carved), and wall cupboards

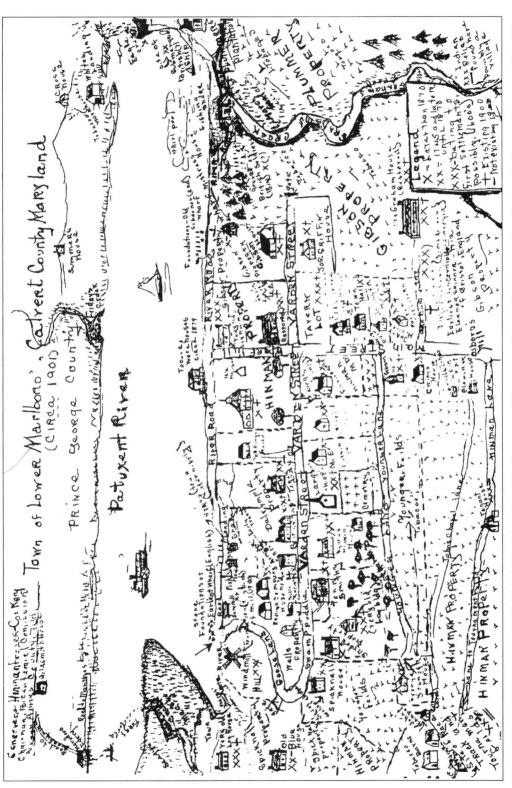

"Town of Lower Marlboro," ca. 1900. This delightful and surprisingly accurate folk art map of Lower Marlboro, unsigned and undated, reveals the continuity of the colonial grid format that governed town design throughout seventeenth- and eighteenth-century Maryland. Courtesy Patricia Lavato, Lower Marlboro, Maryland.

The Grahame House, also known as Patuxent Manor, is believed to be the earliest residence in Lower Marlboro. Significant portions of its interior, including delicate wood paneling, were purchased by the Winterthur Museum in Delaware and may now be viewed for a price. Courtesy Calvert County Historical Society, Wilfong Collection, Prince Frederick, Maryland.

still in use were of the kind people seek in antique shops. A village store was still doing business and had the same counters and the same nail-studded shutters (to prevent robbery) that it had when the ships from London docked at the wharves below the hill. "And still, here and there, about the village bloom the flowers from the lost gardens of long ago—tawny day lilies, Bouncing Bet or 'shimmy tails' as early settlers called it, lush cabbage roses and the Blue Bells of Scotland."[90]

In the early 1970s, Perry B. Van Vleck of Silver Spring, Maryland, began a controversial project to revivify and expand Lower Marlboro in a manner never before conceived. Van Vleck owned a home construction business and in 1938 had entered the field of historic home restoration with a passion. He restored a colonial house called Red Hall in the village of Dunkirk, several miles north of Lower Marlboro. In 1954, he began to consider the feasibility of establishing an entire community of up to twenty-five restored historic homes, which would be moved from various places in the tidewater to a tract of land in and adjacent to Lower Marlboro. About 1971 he embarked upon his ambitious project in earnest. By the spring of 1972, houses from all over the Chesapeake region had begun to arrive, moved overland by truck and over water on barge from as nearby as Upper Marlboro and as far away as Nelsonia and Wills Wharf, Virginia. Each house was to be placed on a three- to five-acre lot and sold for upwards of $150,000. When asked why he had embarked upon such a quest, Van Vleck responded: "Every house has a story to tell. My aim is to try and save a little bit of American history and background . . . I laughingly say I'm building a monument to myself." Before he was through, Perry Van Vleck had moved a dozen or more historic homes to Lower Marlboro on 105 acres adjacent to the Chaneyville Road, and he'd

The Slye House, originally a one-story structure, had second and third stories added in 1729. The building was one of many colonial buildings moved by Perry Van Vleck from various points in the tidewater
to Lower Marlboro. This residence once stood across the Patuxent River at Benedict. It was moved intact by first constructing a board road over three miles of fields, transporting the house along the road,
and then transferring it to a barge. While it was being towed up the Patuxent to be placed at its present location overlooking the tidal marshlands, Hurricane Agnes struck. To preserve the house, the barge had
to be sunk so it would not float away. Courtesy Calvert County Historical Society, Wilfong Collection,
Prince Frederick, Maryland.

purchased several others in town for restoration, including the Cox House and the Armiger
House. "When we're all through," said the builder, "we're going to change the name of the
place to Lower Marlboro Towne, with an E, the way it was originally."[91]

   The great restoration movement was underway. By April 1985, nine houses in the Van
Vleck–created neighborhood had received historic status from Calvert County. But many in
the local community, which had expanded to forty houses and two hundred inhabitants,
were not pleased. As comparisons with a famous colonial site in Virginia kept cropping up,
some residents brimmed with disgust. "They keep mentioning Williamsburg, but that's a
museum, not a living community," declared one irate citizen. In bestowing the historic site
status upon the Van Vleck community, county officials had agreed with the builder that the
homes "could have been" in the town during the eighteenth century. But they weren't.
Old-line families who traced their lineage to the early settlers were clearly unhappy with

"the transplanted homes occupied by transplanted people" who lived in the new bedroom community and commuted to workplaces far away. When one resident, a newcomer, led a movement to have the entire town declared a historic district, she encountered angry opposition from longtime residents and the issue was dropped. The few old-timers were simply disgusted by real estate promoters who were attempting to sell the "ambiance" of their quiet little town and at prices many considered exorbitant.[92]

But two decades after Miss Elsie had closed down the post office and the last store in town, it was a new day and a new era. Few actually remembered the town as it once was, and fewer still recalled the words of Robert Spicknall as he left the old Cox House post office for the last time on that cold November day in 1965. His final eulogy for Lower Marlboro was short and to the point: "Great town. Really a great town . . . fifty years ago."[93]

5 NOTTINGHAM

"Sunk are its bowers in shapeless ruin all"

April 21, 1781. Robert Bowie leaned back in his chair, folded his hands across his stomach, and slowly surveyed the familiar but troubled faces of those assembled for the emergency meeting in the old Patuxent port town of Nottingham. The gathering consisted of some of the most important merchants and property owners from both Prince George's and Calvert Counties. Many of those entering the room were from old-line Maryland families, a few were more recent arrivals, but most had already participated in one manner or another in the defense of liberty.[1] Indeed, ever since 1774 when the tumultuous drift toward revolution had begun, Bowie himself, like many of those convened in the tavern, had devoted his life to the cause of independence.

As the din of voices washed over him, Bowie may have briefly reminisced about the years of personal triumph and national turmoil he had witnessed since his controversial marriage to Priscilla Mackall, the beautiful daughter of General James Mackall of Calvert County. Their union in 1770 had been unconventional to say the least, for Priscilla was then under fifteen years of age and he not yet twenty. Some of his more righteous neighbors had called it a "runaway match." But his father and mother, Captain William Bowie and Margaret Sprigg, having prepared both Robert and his older brother Walter for early adulthood and responsibilities as leaders of the community, had stood by him. The Bowie boys were well-educated men in an era marked by illiteracy. Both had been privileged to receive private tutoring at the school of the Reverend John Eversfield at nearby Croom and later at the home of the Reverend Mr. Craddock's near Baltimore. After Robert's marriage, his father had given him and his young bride the gift of a house and lot in Nottingham as well as a farm adjoining the town.[2]

For a very young couple recently entered into a state of connubial bliss, foreign affairs and local politics must have seemed at the time unimportant indeed. But not for long. On April 12, 1770, when the *Maryland Gazette* reported that several ships were expected daily in the Patuxent with European goods, a fuse was lit that would ensure for the next full decade the destinies of Bowie and all those who, like him, were ensconced along the Patuxent's fertile shores.

It all began for young Bowie that fateful spring when growing disapproval of recently imposed taxes by the British Parliament had tripped off a colonywide protest against the importation of English goods. "The inhabitants of Prince George's County thought it necessary to meet in order to appoint proper committees to support the [nonimportation] association." Although the bone of contention, the hated Townsend Revenue Act, had recently been repealed by the British government, a tax on tea had been left in place as a symbol of Parliament's authority. Many residents of Prince George's considered it as much an infringement upon their rights as the Townsend Act itself. Accordingly, at Nottingham, five of the town's leaders, including Robert's father William, his uncle Allen, John Cooke, Joseph Sim, and Truman Skinner, met to select a delegate to represent Nottingham Hundred at the meeting. Joseph Sim, son of Dr. Patrick Sim and grandson of Thomas Brooke, one of the region's more illustrious landowners, was selected. On June 9, a group of citizens convened at the county seat in Upper Marlborough. Sim was appointed moderator, and the meeting resulted in establishing a countywide adherence to a nonimportation agreement.[3]

The commotion soon died down, at least for a time, and local affairs seemed to return to normal. In 1772 the prosperous little river town of Nottingham, which Robert now called home, was already well over half a century old, and its population had grown to such an extent as to allow it to be named a hundred. Bowie found much to boast about in his home town. It had a grammar school administered by master Edmond Fogery. It had all the trappings of law and order, including its own constable, Richard Groom, to keep the peace.[4] It had a number of fine ordinaries, such as Margaret Gibson's place and John Dorsett's.[5] But what appealed to most true Marylanders such as the Bowie clan were the annual horse races and fairs.

Nottingham had gained a certain notoriety for its horse races, for they were contests which had drawn many of the colony's rich and famous. Robert may have recalled with amusement the two-day fair in mid-May 1773, when the showcase race had pitted the popular governor of Maryland Robert Eden's famous but aging horse Why-Not against Dr. Hamilton's six-year-old bay mare Harmony and Mr. Barnes's fleet gray Regulus. The affair had been publicized throughout the colony and betting was expected to be heavy. Why-Not had run three very hard four-mile heats at Philadelphia only a fortnight earlier and had then traveled in unseasonably scorching weather from Pennsylvania to the Patuxent to compete again. The horse was generally considered the underdog, but amazingly, in the first heat run at Nottingham, the governor's champion had soon distanced the two favorites and easily won. The *Maryland Gazette,* commenting upon the contest several days later, reported gleefully that "the knowing ones were greatly taken in." The following year, Eden returned with Why-Not, raced the horse against four new challengers, including Dr. Hamilton's Primrose and Colonel Barnes's Young Tanner, and again won handily. On the third and final day of racing, the prize was won by another of the governor's horses, a six-year-old chestnut named Slim, which thoroughly trounced Colonel Sim's favored horse Wildair.[6]

The race, Robert knew, had been the royal governor's last excuse to smile, for by fall, England and her American colonies, including Maryland, were again on a collision course from which there would be no turning back. In November, a meeting of freeholders and citizens of Prince George's had convened in Upper Marlborough and a committee was selected to execute the instructions of "The Association of the American Continental Congress" throughout the county. Robert Bowie and his brother Walter, father William, and uncle Allen, all from Nottingham or its nearby environs, had been selected as members. For the next year, young Robert would serve as a novitiate participant and emerge as a local leader in the formulation of plans for resistance against the mightiest power on the globe.[7]

Thereafter, events seemed to escalate uncontrollably. In mid-December, the Maryland Convention met and called for the fielding of county militias. In Prince George's, at a committee meeting in Upper Marlborough held on December 21, it was agreed that funds would be raised to support the effort. Of the ten companies of county militia to be organized, one was to be from Nottingham and its immediate neighborhood. By September 12, 1775, a Committee of Observation had been formed and had instructed Robert, along with Leving Covington and John Hawkins, to enroll a company of "minutemen" from their respective districts for the defense of the country. John Contee, William Turner Wootton, and Captain William Bowie, Robert's father, were directed to select and procure appropriate uniforms for the new force. By January 20, 1776, a company of the Nottingham Militia had formed. Joseph Sim was commissioned colonel of the unit, while Fielder Bowie was elected first lieutenant, William Newman second lieutenant, and Thomas Hoyte ensign.[8]

The Bowie brothers of Nottingham and Mattaponi had been zealous in their support of the American cause. On June 21, 1776, Robert was commissioned as a captain of the Second Battalion, Maryland Flying Artillery. When funds for the unit's support were not forthcoming, he maintained it at his own expense for months. In August, Walter, who had also served on the state Committee of Correspondence, was elected to the state convention to help frame the first state constitution. He would also serve as a lieutenant of the militia and eventually rose to the rank of major.[9] But it was Robert who shined most as the warrior.

In September, the Flying Artillery received orders to proceed to New York to join General Washington and the Continental Army. The march was difficult; the unit arrived too late to participate in the Battle of Long Island but soon acquitted itself with distinction at the Battles of Harlem Heights and White Plains. Robert was in the forefront of the fighting and suffered a painful wound in the knee. As a Bowie genealogist later wrote: "He believed his wound had not been properly treated, and locked himself in a room so as to be undisturbed," then cut the limb with his pocket knife and "removed a splinter of bone, which was causing irritation, and [then] rebandaged the leg." Returning home, though still suffering from his wound, he was commissioned as a captain of a militia company attached to a battalion commanded by Colonel Luke Marbury in September 1777. The unit was soon dispatched to the front and participated in the Battle of Germantown, wherein Robert was again wounded, this time in the shoulder.[10]

Robert Bowie returned to his home in Nottingham to convalesce and was pleased to find that the war had mercifully left the Patuxent River Valley and its myriad little towns in relative peace. The only local event of note had been promulgated by the authority of the new state government, organized under the Maryland Constitution of 1776, when the county court appointed Henry Webb constable of Nottingham Hundred. Soon afterwards, Webb opened an ordinary in town. In 1780 Robert Bowie's uncle Allen had been appointed tobacco inspector, but he soon resigned and was replaced by Robert's old mentor, John Eversfield. For some undisclosed reason, Eversfield also resigned and was replaced two weeks later by Leonard Warring.[11]

Tranquillity was to be short-lived. In 1780, enemy attentions began to focus on the Chesapeake, and alarms along the Bay coast became more frequent. Then, in November, the enemy actually entered the river and raided several estates in the Point Patience vicinity. In early 1781, three privateers, *Cato, Hawk,* and *Nautilus,* sailing on state business, were driven ashore by an enemy warship at Cedar Point near the mouth of the river, and two of the vessels were destroyed. *Nautilus* had been saved, but just barely. Many merchants along the river grew increasingly worried as enemy ships began to patrol off the mouth of the waterway with impunity. Merchant Stephen West expressed the general concern in April when he stated: "Every hour's experience shows the necessity of having some armed vessels in . . . the Patuxent & Potomac." But the tiny Maryland State Navy was nowhere to be seen. Then, on April 7, enemy barges came into the river and sacked the town of Lower Marlborough. Three days later, a plantation at the mouth of the river was destroyed. Things went from bad to worse when in midmonth it was reported that an enemy privateer called *Jack o' the Lanthorn* was lying off the river entrance waiting for any hapless victim that might happen along.[12] Fortunately, the raider was herself soon taken by a pair of Maryland privateers and hauled off to Baltimore for sale at a prize auction. The capture, however, failed to alleviate the anxieties of the citizens along the Patuxent.

The inhabitants of the river valley towns and plantations, farmers and merchants alike, repeatedly appealed to the state for protection. From time to time, watchboats and observers were sent to keep a lookout for enemy ships. A fort was ordered erected at Drum Point at the river entrance, but little in the way of any substantial defense was forthcoming.[13] The young state government was penniless, and its tiny navy, lacking men, money, vessels, and guns, was next to useless. If the Patuxent valley was to be defended, it was up to its own citizens to look to their own devices. Thus, on April 21, twenty-three of the leaders of Prince George's and Calvert Counties convened at Nottingham to form their own defense committee.

As the committee's first meeting was about to commence, young Robert Bowie, gentleman farmer, patriotic activist, battle-scarred soldier and officer, and one of Nottingham Town and Hundred's most prominent young citizens, leaned back and ticked off to himself the names of the men who were charging themselves with the security of the valley and all of its people: Colonel William Fitzhugh, Thomas Contee, William Allein, Patrick Sim Smith, Joseph Wilkinson, David Craufurd, Frank Leckie, Alexander Howard Magruder, John Harrison, Dr. Leonard Hollyday, Leonard Hollyday, Jr., John Read Magruder, John F. A. Priggs, Thomas Gantt, John Warings, Thomas Walker, Thomas Harwood, Nathaniel Weems, Samuel Maynard, and John Brown. The Bowie clan, as always in such important matters, was well represented with Fielder Bowie, Dr. John Bowie, and Robert all present. The order of the day, "to consider of and adopt some plan, for the good and safety of the public in general, and particularly for the defence of the river Patuxent and the inhabitants of the several counties lying on and adjacent thereto," was laid before the committee. Fitzhugh was appointed chairman and John Harrison secretary.[14]

As Robert and his fellow committeemen began to chart a course designed to save the river valley from the enemy's fire and sword, the little port of Nottingham was about to begin a complex new chapter in a life which up to this time was like that of any other tidewater tobacco town. Yet, as one of the most important ports on the Patuxent, it possessed a future potential that seemed well worth defending. And as one of the few legislated urban centers that would actually survive for more than two centuries before disappearing from the landscape, it was perhaps as unique as any of them.

In the 1706 "Act for the advancement of trade and erecting Ports & Towns" it was written: "Be it enacted by the Queen's most excellent Majesty by and with the advice and consent of her Majesty's Governor, Council, and Assembly of this province and the authority of the same that from and after the end of this present session of Assembly the towns, ports and places therein after mentioned shall be the ports and places where all ships and vessels trading into this province shall unlade and put on shore all Negroes, wares, goods, merchandise and commodities whatsoever."[15]

On the Patuxent, seven sites designated by the act, each one hundred acres in size, were chosen for port development, with instructions for lots, streets, and alleys to be laid out. Five of the ports were to be built or reauthorized on the Prince George's County shore. Of all of the sites established in the county on the Patuxent River, the lands upon which the Port of Nottingham was to be erected were among the more strategically situated for the convenience of shippers and shipping. Located fourteen miles south of Queen Anne's Town, the site occupied a central position convenient for farmers in midcounty as well as those along the river banks. A bend in the river forced the current flow to scour the bottom continuously, ensuring a fine anchorage in some places thirty feet deep or more. The designated site was specifically to be fixed "at Mattapany Landing," on a tract owned by Thomas Brooke called the Prospect. Only a few years before, in 1696, the site had been included in part of Mattapany Hundred. On April 17, 1706, the enabling act creating the port was read and assented to by the House of Delegates, and two days later it was signed into law by Governor John Seymour.[16]

Although the official survey plat has not been found, speculation on the lots apparently may have begun right away. At least one property owner, Prince George's County merchant George Harris, had made numerous improvements upon his own estate in anticipation of the new town erection, including the construction of dwellings and storehouses. He was not pleased that the tract failed to include his own property. Thus, the following year, during the spring session of the legislature, Harris petitioned the government, requesting that three acres of his property be incorporated into the new town. The political clout he managed to wield was apparently considerable, for on April 15, 1707, in a supplementary act, the legislature declared that Harris's three acres "be adjudged accepted reputed and taken to be part of Nottingham Town within said county whereunto it adjoins and shall enjoy all benefits, priviledges, and advantages to that said town belonging."[17]

Little is known about the early days of Nottingham. As with other "new" ports, despite land speculation, development appears to have been retarded, for it would take a full decade before the site was deemed substantial enough to warrant stocks and a whipping post—a sure sign of a maturing town.[18] Here and there, however, a rare glimpse of the infant town appears. In 1729, for instance, an advertisement in the colony's only newspaper, the *Maryland Gazette,* reported, "A lot, with a good convenient dwelling house, 2 brick chimneys, sash-windows, &c. and a stable very convenient for an ordinary, in Nottingham, Prince George's County, to be sold by Gunder Erickson."[19]

Slowly but surely, the town grew in importance during the first half of the century. Unlike Queen Anne's, which was situated at the navigable headwaters of the river and was difficult to approach by ship, or St. Leonards Town, which lay at the head of an extremely narrow tributary further downstream, the port of Nottingham benefited from its good, deep harbor, wide approach, and long fetch. Moreover, it found itself situated on the edge of what was developing as the most productive tobacco growing region of the county. Accessibility to shipping and high tobacco yields proved to be an unbeatable combination. As productivity increased, the town's population grew and business blossomed.

In 1747, like many other well-positioned towns and landings throughout the Maryland tidewater, the port of Nottingham was named as the site for an official tobacco inspection station. At that time, inspectors at all county warehouses were nominated and recommended by county vestrymen. Such would be the mode of selecting the inspector for every year through 1775 except 1771 and 1772, when inspection bills failed to pass the legislature. In 1748, a single inspector was nominated to manage both the Nottingham warehouse and the nearby station at Hannah Brown's Landing (later known as Magruder's Landing) further downriver. But not everyone was pleased with the required division of the inspector's labor, which would have obliged him to regularly travel between the two points. In 1750, the "Inhabitants, Freeholders & Traders of Prince Georges and Charles Counties" petitioned that the two warehouses be assigned to separate inspectors. The legislature agreed and approved inspectors for both sites. The inspector at Nottingham warehouse was to receive £45 per annum, while the agent at Hannah Brown's Landing was to be paid only £35, an indication of the marked difference in business expected to be transacted at the sites. In September 1750, the vestrymen and church wardens of St. Paul's Church offered a slate of no less than six candidates for the coveted post of Nottingham inspector: William Beanes, Jr., Jeremiah Berry, Edward Clagett, Allen Bowie, Captain John Smith, and Thomas Hollyday. Three years later, the legislature passed an act amending the 1747 act and, after apparently reassessing the amount of tobacco passing through, reduced the annual salary of the inspector to £38.[20]

Yet, business was booming for the town's merchants. James Russell, owner of a prosperous import-export operation, was perhaps typical of the lot. "Just imported, in the Ship *Ruby,* Capt. Bailey, and to be sold by the subscriber at his store at Nottingham on Patuxent River," read one of Russell's advertisements in the *Maryland Gazette,* "all sorts of East-India, and European Goods, at reasonable rates, for bills of exchange, current money, or heavy tobacco. Also imported in the schooner *Polly,* Capt. Bustell, from Barbadoes, a parcel of rum and sugar."[21] Russell's importation of high quality goods and the large selection of items frequently advertised for sale suggest that there were a number of well-to-do individuals in town. China, silks and other fine cloths, and luxury items of a wide variety were often sold in addition to the more mundane imports intended for Everyman.[22] That Russell himself lived on the high side is suggested by his ownership of three splendid white horses once owned by Governor Thomas Bladen. That he possessed political influence as well is suggested by an act passed in the October 1753 session of the legislature specifying that the town's inspection warehouse be established "on the land of James Russell under one inspection."[23]

When compared with other Patuxent River towns in the county, Nottingham's geographic and deepwater advantages stood the port in increasingly good stead with traders. Situated on the edge of the county's highest tobacco production region, it rapidly outstripped the upriver town of Queen Anne's in size, since the latter was obliged to draw its support from a smaller agricultural hinterland. It would eventually outship even the county seat of Upper Marlborough, which was stuck at the head of the silting Western Branch. Queen Anne's population was small, and the town depended upon those residing in farmsteads around the town for support. Nottingham contained a larger number of residents and a growing infrastructure of tradesmen and services, including blacksmiths, physicians, lawyers, innkeepers, and the like. Surrounded by innumerable large plantations and farms that required a substantial labor force for the upkeep of the estates and the maintenance of tobacco crops, Nottingham briefly became a hub for the slave trade.[24] "Just imported from Africa," read one typical advertisement promoting the commerce, "a parcel of choice Negroes, which will be exposed to sale this day, on board the ship *Koulikan* at Nottingham on Patuxent River, for bills of exchange, current money, or crop tobacco, by James Russell, James Dick." The Russell-Dick slaving venture proved so profitable that a second jointly sponsored expedition was fitted out to the Guinea Coast of Africa almost as soon as the first shipload of unfortunates were sold. On June 21, 1753, the *Maryland Gazette* reported: "Tuesday last [June 19] arrived in Patuxent, from Guiney, but last from St. Kitt's, the ship *Kouli Kan,* Capt. Henry Bonham, with a large cargo of choice slaves, consign'd to Messurs Russell and Dick, merchants, which will be exposed to sale at Nottingham, on the second of July. It is said there was scarcely a healthier and liklier parcel of slaves ever imported." An advertisement placed in the same paper announced the slaves "will be sold on board the said ship, lying at Nottingham."[25]

The sale or auction of locally born slaves was also regularly conducted in the town, often along with an assortment of property and stocks. When William Potts, a farmer living near the town offered to sell "a parcel of slaves, chiefly country born, consisting of men, women and children," he also offered for sale in the same advertisement household furniture and stocks of cattle, hogs, sheep, and horses. When a local slave-owner such as Thomas Hodgkin died without heirs, his estates (470 acres of land in four different tracts in Hodgkin's case) was often disposed of along with "a choice parcel of country born slaves" that had permitted the plantations to be effectively operated.[26]

Although James Russell was the principal merchant in the town during the late 1740s and early 1750s, he was not destined to remain. Perhaps it was the onset of the Seven Years War,

which had a most detrimental effect upon the colony trade, or perhaps it was simply a long-
ing to return to England that induced him to abandon his enterprise in provincial Nottingham. He sailed at least twice for London, the first time on August 10, 1752, aboard the ship
Caesar, Captain Wales commanding, undoubtedly to prepare for his permanent return. He
revisited the colony only briefly, just long enough to close up his affairs, and then sailed
again for London on May 19, 1753, aboard Captain Hutchinson's ship *Diamond*. On August
27, his agents advertised the sale of his house near Nottingham and all of the household furniture, stock, and slaves therein at public auction.[27] It appears that there were many merchants and traders, such as Hancock Lee, Stephen West, James Dick, and George Maxwell,
ready to fill the vacuum created by his departure.

The system of rolling roads that evolved throughout the county to service farmers in the
movement of their tobacco may be described as rugged at best. The ragged hodgepodge of
dirty, rutted routes, almost always leading through the private property of neighboring
farmers, was a source of irritation to many. Each landowner was responsible for the maintenance and repair of the rolling roads that passed through his property. The work was often
costly and time-consuming and, in leaner years, it was frequently delayed or entirely ignored by some, causing unending disputes among neighbors. Complainants often resorted
to the county court. In March 1750, when Allen Bowie alleged that the rolling road from his
house to Nottingham was so bad that he could not move his tobacco or even traverse the
path in a cart, the court referred the complaint to William Beanes and John Orme, Sr., the
property owners, and instructed them to view and repair the road.[28]

Until midcentury, communication and commerce between Nottingham and Calvert
County across the Patuxent were infrequent and circuitous at best. Aside from the ferry operations between White's Landing and Lower Marlborough in Calvert County downriver
and between Mount Pleasant Landing and the Anne Arundel County shore upriver, no
nearby cross-river service was available. Finally, in 1752, with prosperity and demand
on the rise, Abraham Wood and William Mackay, a pair of rival but enterprising tavern
keepers in town, seized the initiative. On February 20, Wood took the lead and advertised the first known ferry operation based at Nottingham. "Abraham Wood," read the
ad, "living at Nottingham, on Patuxent River, hereby gives notice, that he keeps a house
of good entertainment for travelers; and likewise keeps ferry, having a good boat and
hands to cross Patuxent, for horses and carriages; which way from St. Mary's and
Charles County, to Annapolis, is by far the nearest, and the roads a great deal better, than
any other way."

Not to be outdone, three weeks later Mackay advertised: "William MacKay. Living at
Nottingham on Patuxent, hereby gives notice, That he has a good boat and hands to cross
Patuxent, for horses and carriages: And likewise keeps a good entertainment for travelers."[29]
Over time, many operators would come to manage one ferry or another crossing the river
from Nottingham. And all, it appeared, tied up their boats at the town waterfront. On the opposite side of the river, a corduroy road was eventually laid through the marsh lands to the
rising shoreline of Calvert County to facilitate landing.

As Nottingham prospered, a proliferation of ordinaries and taverns in town commenced
operations. William Mackay had petitioned to open his public house in 1750, as had a competitor named Elizabeth Taylor. Abraham Wood opened his own establishment soon afterwards. Within a few years, William Frazier Noble petitioned the county court to open yet a

fourth ordinary, suggesting that visitation in town was substantial enough to support so many establishments.[30]

Although the complexion of Nottingham at midcentury was tinted by the golden glow of well-aged tobacco, there were occasional shades of a different color. Dr. Richard Brooke was born near the town in 1716 at Brookfield, the family estate of his parents, Thomas Brooke and Lucy Smith (daughter of Colonel William Smith). The doctor was a methodical man blessed with the learned abilities of a scientist. What distinguished him from other colony doctors, however, was his most notable claim to fame—his compilation of the first systematic recordation of weather and temperature, observed between September 1, 1753, and August 31, 1754, within the limits of the present states of Maryland and Delaware. His descriptions, though often plain, presented a clear assessment of local weather conditions and their influence on local agriculture. These were otherwise ignored in the commentaries of the day. In 1755, his description of a drought prevailing at and around Nottingham provided a clear record of how weather caused difficulties for the farmers of Prince George's County. In May, for example, he wrote in clinical fashion that it was "extremely dry, seldom any clouds; no rain. Every vegetable almost burnt up; strawberry leaves, green plantain, and others, so crisp as to crumble. In this month many black cattle died for want of food." Brooke's works were considered important enough to be published in the *Philosophical Transactions* of the Royal Society of London for 1759, a most unusual honor for a colonial physician.[31]

But for most of the inhabitants of Nottingham Hundred, the seasonal cycle of life—slavishly tied to the golden leaf, but uncomplicated, honest, and filled with hard work and a few simple entertainments—went on as always. Until revolution came.

The debates held in Nottingham on April 21, 1781, regarding the measures to be taken for the defense of the Patuxent River were tinged with the appetite for immediate action that most men experience when their homes and families are endangered. But the concerned citizens meeting this day were men of intelligent deliberation willing to first explore all proper avenues of relief before taking an independent route. Their first goal was to organize themselves into a formal body, and, according to the truest form of parliamentary procedure, to appoint appropriate subcommittees to address, define, and vocalize the objectives of the group. Thus, it was resolved that Thomas Contee and William Allein be appointed a committee to meet with Governor Thomas Sims Lee and the council to formally request that the state government provide "all necessaries, they conveniently can, and give directions to the lieutenants of the several counties, to afford men from time to time to guard the several posts on Patuxent River, and furnish them with provision." They were also to request that one hundred or more men from Prince George's, Calvert, Charles, and St. Mary's Counties be raised to act on each side of the Patuxent in its defense; that officers be empowered to impress all boats, canoes, and bateaux necessary to transport their troops from place to place; and that provisions be supplied for the force, including four 9- and 6-pounder cannons mounted on traveling carriages, replete with ammunition. They were to inquire about the status of the fort that was to have been erected at Drum Point. To add legitimacy to the authority of the citizens committee, the delegates were also instructed to entreat the governor and council "to invest the gentlemen of this meeting with proper and sufficient powers, to order the men and articles they may think proper to furnish, in such manner as they think most conducive to the public good." And finally, circular letters were ordered to be sent by chairman William Fitzhugh to various leaders in Charles, St. Mary's, and Anne Arundel Counties requesting that they each send deputations from their respective counties to attend the next meeting. In the meantime, the small schooner *Resource,* commanded by Captain Ander, and several cannons owned by Mr. Denistee were ordered employed to serve as a stopgap defense measure on the river until the state government's position was resolved.[32]

Contee and Allein's meeting with the governor and council produced very limited results indeed. Although the chief executive agreed in principle to provide whatever assistance he could, the state treasury was empty. He decided to instruct military commanders in the affected counties to order the militia to defend "the several posts that shou'd be though necessary" and to provide them with the authority to impress vessels necessary to transport troops on the river. Unfortunately, only two 9-pounders, two barrels of powder, and fifty shot could be spared. Worse, the available artillery did not have carriages, so it was up to the citizens committee to provide them if they needed the guns. Moreover, construction of the fort at Drum Point had not yet begun and no funding was available to start the work. Both Contee and Allein were undoubtedly chagrined when the governor suggested that if the committeemen were willing to advance the money to the government, work would begin immediately. The two delegates politely demurred, claiming they lacked the authority. The committee's hopes for assistance were further reduced when the two delegates were informed that all of the meat provisions the government had were already earmarked for the Continental Army. They were taken aback even more when the administration suggested that the committee itself should consider providing meat for the greater cause rather than requesting it for their own local defense needs. For the embassy from Nottingham, it seemed that the only positive response was when the governor and council authorized the committee to "do and execute whatever may be thought proper and best for the security of the inhabitants on Patuxent River and parts adjacent; having a due regard to frugality to avoid every unnecessary expence, and to hand in a charge of the whole which they will reimburse." There was, of course, no reassurance that the government would ever reimburse expenses.[33]

The Nottingham citizens committee, it was clear, was on its own.

Though dismayed at the government's poverty and inability to provide assistance, the committee was not dissuaded from taking action. Meeting again in Nottingham the following week, another subcommittee was formed to offer recommendations about "what ways and means are most advisable and immediately expedient, for the defence of Patuxent River." The defense committee's advice was succinct. The two cannons offered by the government should be accepted and placed in a battery at or near Holland Cliffs immediately below Nottingham at a strategic narrows on the river, but they should be mounted on traveling carriages so as to move about occasionally. Thirty men should be stationed at the post. One 3-pounder cannon on a traveling carriage should be mounted on each side of the river at or near the mouth, each to be manned by twenty-five select militiamen. A row galley or other vessel of force, properly manned and equipped, should be immediately procured and stationed at the mouth of the river. A sixteen-oar barge of forty-foot keel length armed with two swivel guns should be provided to cooperate with the row galley and the land artillery. A whale boat should be employed as a lookout. Alarm beacons should be properly fixed at appropriate stations along the river. Finally, it was recommended "that an Association or agreement be entered into by the gentlemen now present, and such other inhabitants of Saint Mary's, Calvert, Prince George's, Charles and Anne Arundell counties, as think proper to join with them, in this necessary defence, whereby every man shall bind himself each to the other, to carry the above measures into execution."[34]

Assured that "the whole expence of such necessary defence shall hereafter be defrayed out of the Public Treasury of the State," the committee's recommendations were approved with only minor alterations. The board then launched into a flurry of activity. Rules, regulations, procedures, and protocols were established for members and for the conduct of meetings and business. The group formally styled itself the "Board of Patuxent Associators." Thomas Contee was elected chairman. A Committee of Purchases was chosen to establish a budget, open up lines of credit, and begin the procurement process for such items as artillery, flour, and other necessaries. The board placed a limit on procurement of supplies—not to exceed 1,000 pounds of tobacco. Flour was promptly purchased and moved to a safe place for storage. Captain William Bowie, Jr., and Joseph Walker met at Upper Marlborough with the private owners of four cannons to negotiate their purchase. The two 9-pounders offered by the government were secured, properly test-fired, and dispatched to Holland Cliffs to be mounted in the battery being erected there. Then, looking toward the naval defense of the river, the board issued instructions to agents from the Committee of Purchases to proceed to Baltimore and negotiate the acquisition of the recently captured loyalist privateer *Jack o' the Lanthorn.* On May 12, agents Samuel Maynard and Rinaldo Johnson returned to report that unfortunately the privateer "wou'd by no means answer the purpose of this Board together with the price demanded for her." Instead, they had purchased the eighty-five-ton former privateer schooner *Nautilus,* which, while on government business, had recently been driven ashore by HMS *Isis* at Cedar Point. The schooner with its full outfit lay at Fells Point but was to be had from its owners, Dorsey Wheeler and Company and Thomas Worthington, for 375,000 pounds of "Merchantable crop tobacco properly inspected . . . since the 15th Septr. 1780," which was to be paid over a period of three months. Maynard and Johnson seized the opportunity and signed the contract on May 10, 1781.[35]

Captain John David of Lower Marlborough, former commander of the Maryland State Navy row galley *Conqueror,* was selected to command the newly acquired warship, but before accepting, he had "engaged himself to another vessell for the defence of our Bay." The lack of a commander caused a delay in the transfer of the ship to the river. The board then began to have second thoughts about its acquisition and considered selling it off even before delivery, replacing it with a row galley. The board was also concerned about the government's willingness to reimburse the expenses already incurred.[36] As spring leaned toward summer, trepidation about enemy intentions increased. "We know not at what hour the enemy cometh, therefore no time should be lost to meet the implacable foe," wrote Chairman Contee to the governor. By mid-April, the enemy was again raiding on the lower Patuxent and Potomac causing inhabitants on both waterways to flee in abject terror. On the Patuxent, homes as far north as Nottingham were abandoned almost overnight.[37] The historic record is silent regarding the initial effectiveness of the defensive measures set in motion by the Board of Patuxent Associators. By late summer *Nautilus* was finally riding on Patuxent waters, and a naval base for the so-called Patuxent Navy was established at the port of Nottingham. Though no fort was ever erected at Drum Point, and no row galley or lookout boats had been fielded, by fall enemy depredations on and about the river had finally come to a halt, and everyone breathed a sigh of relief. Not a shot had been fired, but the work of the Board of Patuxent Associators, operating from their headquarters at Nottingham, had achieved the desired effect as enemy intentions were deflected elsewhere.

❖

Robert Bowie viewed his many responsibilities, both on the board and in the military, with all seriousness. In June 1781, still suffering from his wounds but with his battlefield experience being too important to ignore, he was appointed by the Council of Maryland as a captain in the county militia. Soon afterwards, the government, then in desperate need of horses for Washington's army, passed a law authorizing the collection of privately owned horses for the emergency and appointed Robert as collector of horses for Prince George's County. In September, in accordance with passage of an "Act to encourage the raising a Volunteer Troop of light horse in Baltimore Town and each county of this State," he was also appointed lieutenant of a Prince George's County troop of light horse.[38]

As Robert moved upwards in importance, the monumental march of the American and French armies toward a decisive clash with the British was also underway. Clothing, arms, and supplies of every kind were ordered seized for the use of the Continental Army. At Nottingham, hats, shoes, and a variety of cloth for clothing were confiscated by the government from the firms of John Smith Brookes and Company and Alexander Contee with a promise that all goods taken would later be paid for. On September 8, Washington himself issued a plea to Maryland "that every exertion may be made for collecting vessels from all parts" to assist in the transfer of troops from the headwaters of the Chesapeake to the fields of Yorktown. Governor Thomas Sims Lee was informed that "The Nautilus lays in Patuxent & would be of service on this occasion," and was presumably soon fielded once more in the cause of liberty.[39]

Following the climactic allied victory at Yorktown, which assured American independence, the war would continue in fits and starts for more than a year. But on the Patuxent, the emergency that had seen the birth of the Board of Patuxent Associators at Nottingham was nearly at an end, and the body dispersed with barely a notice.[40]

Even before the peace treaty was signed, Nottingham appeared ready and eager to resume its prewar vigor. The tobacco trade was reestablished with unvarnished alacrity, and by 1784, the town was second only to Upper Marlborough in tobacco shipments on the river. Between 1785 and 1787, a total of more than a half million pounds of tobacco would be shipped from the little port, more than any other location on the Patuxent.[41] Applications for new licenses to operate ordinaries in town began to trickle in to the county court.[42] In June 1786 Robert and Fielder Bowie were authorized by the court to contract for the erection of a new whipping post and stocks in town. Two years later, Fielder applied to the court to operate a ferry at the town landing, and in September of the same year Edward Griffiths was also authorized to manage a ferry there, ensuring stiff competition. As elsewhere along the Patuxent, the sport of horse racing began again in all earnest.[43]

The importance of Nottingham to both county and state was growing. In 1782, the General Assembly ordered that five commissioners of the tax be appointed in each county. Three years later Prince George's commissioners were instructed to divide their county into ten districts, up from two. The earliest tax assessment lists for the county cover the period of 1793–1794 and indicate that Prince George's was divided into eight discrete districts, with contiguous hundreds in each often joined together. Nottingham Hundred and adjacent Mattapany Hundred were joined together. In 1795, Nottingham-Mattapany was officially to become the First District. Prince George's government was evolving as well. On April 6, 1795, at a meeting of the Levy Court, management of county affairs was officially vested in a board of county commissioners, a form of administration that would continue until 1971.[44]

But for Nottingham, everyday problems and controversies drew most of the local attention. Appointed by the new board of county commissioners, Thomas Ball replaced George Cole as town constable and was obliged to deal with maintaining law and order. Unfortunately, the sale of liquor from such establishments as Ignatius Boone's new tavern had a negative influence upon some of the town's inhabitants and visitors, resulting in public drunkenness and rowdiness. Yet, there were also important public works to attend to, such as the erection of public buildings and the repair of bridges and roads to keep traffic and commerce flowing. In May 1795, Robert and Thomas Bowie were appointed by the court to supervise the purchase of two acres of land in Nottingham and then to erect a warehouse suitable to hold 250 hogsheads of tobacco. The road connecting the town with Magruder's Landing over the head of Spicer's Creek (now Spice Creek) had fallen into a sorry state, and its repair became an issue in the spring of 1795. Upon the petition of a cadre of local inhabitants, the Levy Court appointed Thomas Gantt, Rinaldo Johnson, and Benjamin Mackall to supervise the work and to keep the road maintained for five years. When the bridge over the Mattapony Branch near Nottingham fell into disrepair, the court appointed Richard Cramphin and Richard J. Lowndes to oversee the repair job.[45]

In contrast to the government-maintained roads, the care and tending of roads that ran through private estates but were used by the public produced problems for everyone. At a December 1796 meeting of the Levy Court, a number of inhabitants of nearby Mattapany informed the court that a particular road struck out from the main road leading from Nottingham, ran directly through the plantation of Benjamin Mackall, and passed the plantations of Samuel Townsend, Jr., John Lawson Naylor, and the Widow Wall, intersecting the main road leading to Washington via Piscataway; this "hath been used from time immemorial as a road to Nottingham." Unfortunately, the petitioners noted, they had only recently been told that the road would be stopped up unless it was made a public road "which will be attended with great inconvenience not only to the said petitioners but to numbers who carry their tobacco to Nottingham warehouse and to people who travel from Nottingham towards Piscataway, the way being a nearer than any other and the road level and dry; and we pray that the same be put into the Observer's Warrant and made a public road."[46]

The court agreed and granted the petitioners their wish.

In 1798 and 1799, two pieces of legislation, one state and the other federal, were passed that would directly affect the future of Nottingham politically and economically. By virtue of chapter 115 of the Acts of 1798, which effected an amendment to the state constitution, the method of holding elections in Maryland was modified. The amendment directed that the several counties of the state should be divided into separate districts for the purpose of holding all future elections for delegates, electors of the senate, and sheriffs. Prince George's County was to be divided into five districts, and the Nottingham District was designated number 1.[47]

The following year, the institution of section 10 of the Laws of the United States of America, which pertained to "ports of entry and delivery" throughout the nation, declared that Maryland would henceforth be divided into ten districts, to wit: Baltimore, Chester, Oxford, Vienna, Snow Hill, Annapolis, Nottingham, Nanjemoy, Georgetown, and Havre de Grace. "The district of Nottingham," it was decreed,

shall include all the waters and shores of the west side of Chesapeake Bay, to Drum Point on the river Patuxent, together with the said river, and all the navigable waters emptying into the same, to which Benedict, Lower Marlborough, Town Creek, and Sylvey's Landing, shall be annexed, as ports of delivery only, and a collector for the district shall be appointed, to reside at Nottingham, and a surveyor, at Town Creek; and Nottingham shall be the sole port of entry.[48]

The simple tidewater town on the Patuxent was now not only a tobacco inspection and shipping center, but a national port of entry, replete with its own customs office and officer.

As Nottingham continued to grow in importance, so did the reputation and career of its most prominent resident, Robert Bowie. With the war behind him and his star on the rise, Robert decided to enter politics. On October 15, 1785, at the age of thirty-five, he was elected to the Lower House, where he would serve effectively for five consecutive terms. Not one to neglect his military obligations, for the next decade he would also serve as a major of the county militia. In 1801 and 1803 the warrior-statesman again filled a seat in the Lower House as one of the most influential and upwardly mobile politicians in Maryland. On November 17, 1803, when the General Assembly cast a vote for a successor to Governor John F. Mercer, Bowie was the man named. From 1803 to 1806 he served three terms as his state's first elected Jeffersonian Democratic-Republican Governor. He was, above all else, a nationalist of the first order. When news regarding the accession of Louisiana (which more than trebled the territorial size of the nation) reached Washington, Governor Bowie and his old friend and political ally Thomas Contee presided over a joyous and tumultuous celebration of state which was convened at Boone's tavern in Nottingham in March 1804.[49] In 1807 Bowie returned to Prince George's County to serve as a justice of the peace and a member of the Levy Court. Two years later, he became a presidential elector for James Madison and in 1811 ran for a senate seat only to be defeated by a Federalist in an election held on September 12. On November 11, his influence, power, and party loyalty having stood him in such good stead, the state legislature elected him to a fourth term as governor. Following Madison's lead, Nottingham's first citizen initially opposed military confrontation as a means of resolving the growing differences between England and America. But the drift toward open hostilities was increasingly embraced by Democratic-Republicans, including Bowie, and in June 1812, when Congress formally declared war on England, he "was so rejoiced when he heard the news that he did not wait for his hat, but with a few friends proceeded through the streets [of Annapolis] bare headed to the State House, where he congratulated the leaders upon the welcome news."[50] He would live to regret his exuberance, for in 1813 and 1814, when he again sought the governorship, a Federalist-dominated legislature awarded the prize to Levin Winder, a staunch opponent of the war.

Back home at Nottingham, the new war with England was largely ignored. In May 1813, the Levy Court ordered Henry Waring and Dr. William B. Beanes of Upper Marlborough, a cousin and close associate of Robert Bowie's, to arrange and supervise the construction of a brick or wooden arch to be placed over the branch of the road leading from Nottingham to the county seat at Upper Marlborough.[51] Tobacco continued to be inspected (although little was able to pass through the British blockade of the Chesapeake), business was conducted, and toasts drunk in the town taverns to liberty and victory.

Not until the summer of 1814, when the Chesapeake Flotilla found itself bottled up inside of St. Leonard's Creek, did the citizens of Nottingham actually begin to sense the danger. On June 16, the British commander on the Patuxent sent probes northward on the river, and two days later, the *Washington Daily National Intelligencer* published claims that the enemy had already burned Benedict and Lower Marlborough and was hovering in sight of

Nottingham. The effect of the enemy's probes and the rumors of their depredations were galvanic. On June 18, an early morning express arrived in Washington from Nottingham informing the secretary of war of an enemy ascent and requesting immediate assistance. The War Department responded with alacrity. Major General John P. Van Ness, commander of the District of Columbia militia, was soon issuing instructions to selected unit commanders to assemble immediately. A force of 280 men, consisting of Peter's Georgetown Artillery with six field pieces, Stull's Georgetown Riflemen, the Georgetown Dragoons, Thornton's Alexandria Riflemen, and Caldwell's Washington Riflemen, the whole under the command of Major George Peter, was ready to march by 10:00 A.M. After the group formed, however, another rider reached Washington and reported to the government that the British had retired from Benedict, the only town they had actually assailed. The militiamen were promptly permitted to go home. Then, almost immediately afterwards, a third express arrived informing the government that the enemy had returned.[52]

Early the next morning, June 19, Peter's force formed once more and about 4:00 A.M. began the march to Nottingham. By late evening, a vanguard of the Georgetown Dragoons, approximately 75 strong, arrived at the town after a forced march, fully expecting to find it in ashes. They were immediately joined by 250 county militiamen.[53] In fact, the town may well have been saved by an "unexpected interposition from destruction" by a tiny detachment of the U.S. Army armed with several 18-pounders under the command of Lieutenant Harrison of the Thirty-sixth U.S. Infantry Regiment. Harrison and his men had crossed the river at Nottingham only a short time earlier to reinforce other army units on St. Leonard's Creek in Calvert County. It was later learned that the lieutenant had been persuaded by nervous locals to linger for a while in the neighborhood and while still near the town, he had observed a number of enemy barges near Hall's Creek, barely a mile and a half downriver. He promptly turned his guns on the enemy and quickly drove them off. The invader's presence so near Nottingham produced utter pandemonium in the town and a flood of refugees raced toward Upper Marlborough. Soon afterwards, upon his own arrival at Nottingham with the bulk of his troops, Major Peter ordered the Georgetown Dragoons to press on for the relief of Benedict, which was believed to still be imperiled if not already in enemy hands.[54] A portion of his force would stay to defend Nottingham until the emergency was over.

On June 26, the Chesapeake Flotilla broke out of St. Leonard's Creek and pressed up the Patuxent, stopping for rest at Benedict, which had been sacked only a few days earlier. Five days later, his men having been rested after weeks of continuous action, Barney ordered the fleet northward, first to Hunting Town, then to Lower Marlborough, and finally to Nottingham, which he now determined to employ as his new base of operations. There was much to recommend the site, for it could easily be defended on the water by lining up ships across the wide reach at the town and concentrating fire on the narrows below, through which any enemy vessels would have to pass single file. There were direct overland communications with Washington and port facilities already in place to service his vessels. Yet, when Barney and the flotilla arrived, they discovered the inhabitants who had returned to their homes were in a complete state of alarm and confusion, for the district volunteers had been ordered back to the capital and the residents had taken their departure as a sign of abandonment.

Barney found the local militia useless, especially those from Nottingham. On one occasion, a call had gone out to muster forty men at the tanyard just outside of town. Of the number called, only six appeared. Clement Hollyday, a local farmer and supporter of the war effort, was embarrassed by the poor showing and beseeched relatives to whom he had written not to mention it to anyone. "It would give them a bad opinion of our part of the country." It may have been by way of excuse that he added "Nottingham has been & is now very sickly. The inhabitants has the flux & measles."[55]

A week after his arrival in town, Barney was informed that the Thirty-sixth and Thirty-eighth U.S. Infantry Regiments, having lately been at Benedict, had arrived at the tanyard, ostensibly to protect his landward flank and the main road to Washington. The regiments were now under the personal direction of General William Henry Winder, commander of all defense forces protecting the nation's capital. Barney was not impressed by either the army or its commander. The two regiments, he recalled with disdain, had hightailed it out of St. Leonard's at the opening of the second Battle of St. Leonard's Creek barely two weeks before, leaving him alone to face the entirety of British might during the engagement. Moreover, Winder seemed incapable of making a decision of any kind whatsoever. No sooner had the army arrived than the general received War Department orders to march immediately for the South River. By dusk, the army was lodging in and about Upper Marlborough. When a rumor reached Winder that same evening that an enemy naval force was again ascending the Patuxent just as his own artillery units were arriving in town, he was obliged to dispatch the unit back to Nottingham but was undecided as to what to do with the rest of the army. Barney was anything but amused by the commander's fickleness.

Winder appeared entirely befuddled as he continued to do nothing but loiter uselessly about the area for another week. Finally, on July 15, after confirming news of enemy raids lower down and fearful of a British ascent up the river, he ordered General Stephen West, commander of the Prince George's County Militia, to march his entire force to the defense of Nottingham. Ignoring desperate calls for assistance, most notably from Colonel Michael Taney in Calvert County, West marched a small army consisting of the Prince George's Militia, a battalion of the Montgomery County Militia, and Captain John C. Herbert's Bladensburg Troop of Horse into town. Within a few days more, additional forces, including the district volunteers made up of Davidson's Light Infantry, Burch's Artillery, and Doughty's Rifles, all of which had been called up by the War Department once more, had also come in.[56] Nottingham literally bristled with troops and artillery. Its waterfront was lined with war barges as well as innumerable merchantmen seeking the safety of American firepower.

Fortunately, the alarm had been false. A British raiding force under the command of Captain Joseph Nourse had ascended the river, looting and burning as it went, but it never ascended higher than Hunting Creek. Though seriously ill from exposure, Barney sent a scouting expedition southward from the town on July 21. The expedition soon found the river devoid of enemy ships and men clear to the entrance.[57] The militia was again dispersed.

Nevertheless, Barney was certain that the enemy would eventually make a move against him. He was also satisfied that, given enough troops, the invaders would most certainly march against Washington itself, not by the most obvious route via the Potomac, but from the unexpected backdoor quarter of the Patuxent. The Navy Department disagreed but nevertheless ordered the commodore to explore the feasibility of moving his fleet from Nottingham even higher upriver to Queen Anne's Town. Thus, on July 27, Barney dispatched his son, Major William B. Barney, to take soundings to determine whether such a move was possible.[58]

For the flotillamen, at least, the occupation of Nottingham was a bit more pleasant than their stay at St. Leonards Town, for life was as close to normal there as could be expected despite the frequent alarms, an easily panicked population, and an outbreak of the flu and measles. The town, at this time, was unexceptional but comfortable. As one foreign first-hand observer wrote about this time: "The houses are not such as indicate the existence of much wealth or grandeur among the owners, being in general built of wood, and little superior to cottages; but around the village are others of a far better description, which convey the idea of good substantial farm-houses, a species of mansion very common to the United States." The town itself was erected about four short streets, two running parallel to the river and two crossing at right angles with dwellings, shops, stores, warehouses, and stables perforating both sides of the roadways and several small lanes running off from the main avenues.[59]

Once the panic of mid-July had subsided, civic affairs were once more conducted as usual, as if the lion was at someone else's gate. On August 1, the county court authorized Edward H. Calvert and Dr. William Beanes to contract for the construction of a bridge over the Charles Branch on the main road between Nottingham and Upper Marlborough.[60] Buoyed by a strong naval presence, the citizens of Nottingham went about their daily routines. Unfortunately, the war would not go away.

On August 15, the British sent another reconnaissance expedition upriver to determine if Barney was still at Nottingham. The very same day, a great armada of Royal Navy warships and transports carrying an army of invasion arrived at the Virginia Capes. The enemy objective was the capture of Washington, D.C., and the main route of attack was to be via the Patuxent, as Barney had predicted. The only questions were where he would land, where he would go, and where he would be met on the field of battle. Early on the morning of August 20, the commodore's forward observers informed him that a great landing was being made downriver at the twice-sacked port of Benedict. At 7:00 A.M., he dashed off an urgent express to Secretary of the Navy William Jones informing him that the enemy had finally committed himself.[61] The sweating express rider, after an incredibly swift journey, reached Washington at 11:30 A.M. Secretary Jones, uncertain as to whether the invaders would take the overland road from Benedict to the capital or were simply intent on the destruction of the flotilla, immediately sent back instructions to Barney. "Should the enemy dash for this place," he wrote, "he will probably take this road [from Benedict], unless he should follow the bank of the river to Nottingham with his advance guard to drive back your flotilla and bring off his main body by water." The secretary acknowledged that this, of course, would have already been discovered before the commodore received the letter. Thus, he continued, " you will immediately send the flotilla up to Queen Anne's with as few men as possible and a trusty officer to remain there and in the event of the enemy advancing upon the flotilla in force, to destroy the whole effectually and proceed with his men to this place." As soon as the commodore had issued these instructions, he was then to retire before the enemy towards Washington, "opposing his progress as well by your arms, as by felling trees across the road, removing bridges, and presenting every other possible obstacle to his march."[62]

At 4:00 P.M., General Robert Ross and Admiral Sir George Cockburn, with their twenty-five-hundred-man force and with bugles blaring and loud huzzahs from the ranks, started out on the road to Nottingham and destiny.

As the crow flies, the distance from Benedict to Nottingham was approximately thirteen miles, but by the river road, with its crooked runs and elbow turns, it was more like seventeen. The weather was scorching, and even for seasoned British veterans (dubbed by the press as "Wellington's Invincibles" for their victories in Spain under the Duke of Wellington), it was a difficult trek, especially after weeks at sea. By the end of the first day's march, the troops had barely made half a dozen miles and were utterly exhausted.

At Nottingham, anxiety reigned supreme as the inhabitants watched the flotillamen methodically prepare for their retreat upriver. About midday, August 21, the first of Barney's fleet shoved off under oars, and panic erupted throughout the village. Aware of the destruction that had befallen other towns and villages that had hosted federal troops or naval forces, such as at St. Leonards, many residents assumed the worst for their community and promptly fled with whatever they could handily carry. Within hours, the town was entirely deserted. The first troops to reach Nottingham were not those of the invaders but a detachment of Colonel William Thornton's Alexandria Dragoons, led by a most unlikely officer.

Secretary of State James Monroe had been among the first Cabinet officers in Washington to learn of the British landing, and he'd responded with vigor. He had immediately volunteered to direct a most unstatesmanlike function by personally leading a reconnaissance in force to ascertain the precise disposition of the invaders. Having served as a cavalry officer during the American Revolution, he was not unsuitable for the task in a military sense, and in the excitement of the emergency, President Madison reluctantly approved of the mission. A detachment of Thornton's Dragoons commanded by Captain Trist was pressed into service and was soon on the march to conduct the most unusual mission ever carried out by a sitting secretary of state. Monroe probed as far south as Butler's Mill, four miles from Benedict, and then galloped on to Aquasco Mills where he learned of the presence of enemy pickets a mile away. Then he saw the ships, dozens of them, off-loading troops.[63] Impatient with merely watching the enemy from a distance, he retired to Charlotte Hall to spend the evening, unwittingly permitting the enemy to get between his troops and the capital. The following morning, he returned to monitor the British and counted twenty-three ships at anchor. But where was the army? What, he thought, if the British were marching directly on Washington? Instantly, he wheeled his troops about and raced north, but he found nothing. He then turned east for Nottingham. There he might at least consult with Commodore Barney.[64]

At 5:00 P.M., Monroe and his detachment of dragoons, their horses frothy with sweat from the hard ride in the summer heat, rode into Nottingham, having unintentionally circumvented the entire British line of march along the river banks. The town was entirely deserted and ghostly silent. The fleet was gone. Abandonment had been so rapid that several empty houses still had bread baking in the ovens. It was unclear to Monroe whether he was in front of the enemy or behind him. Then, at 5:30 P.M., three of Cockburn's armed barges were spotted pressing up the river. Excitedly, the secretary of state dashed off a message to General Winder suggesting that he immediately send five to six hundred men to the town. But it was already too late, for at that moment, thirty to forty more barges hove into sight. The dragoons opened a desultory fire upon them from the shore. Just then, as Cockburn closed in from the water, the right flank of Ross's army came up on the main road, fully expecting an American stand and battle. Recklessly, Ross led three or four of his officers in a mounted charge riding the few horses available to them. Monroe and his dragoons wisely wheeled about and galloped through the town streets and northward toward Upper Marlborough. The Battle of Nottingham, hoped for by the British, proved little more than a skirmish.[65]

That night, the British hunkered down at Nottingham with Cockburn's tenders, barges, and boats hovering at anchor where Barney's barges had lain only hours before. The army's right flank rested on the town and river. Its left flank extended westward beyond the town, secured from surprise by a liberal use of pickets. At dawn, August 22, the invaders resumed their march but with some trepidation. One officer recorded in his journal that there "seemed indeed to be something like hesitation as to the course to be pursued, whether to follow the gun-boats, or to return to the shipping."[66] They need not have worried. That afternoon, as the army entered Upper Marlborough, the reverberations of explosions were felt up and down the river, as the Chesapeake Flotilla self-destructed. Two days later, Washington itself was in flames.

Sixty-three-year-old Robert Bowie was furious as he consulted with Dr. William Beanes in Upper Marlborough on the afternoon of August 27 regarding the terrible state of affairs in Prince George's County. It was bad enough that the British Army had bested American arms at the Battle of Bladensburg, sacked and burned the nation's capital, and then returned entirely unimpeded toward Nottingham laden with plunder. But when a band of British deserters had taken to pillaging the neighborhood in the wake of the enemy's retirement toward Nottingham, adding further insult to injury, it was practically unbearable. Bowie and Beanes thus quickly resolved to organize a roundup of the scavengers before their depredations caused further injury to the inhabitants of the countryside. Within a short time, more than half a dozen enemy stragglers and deserters had been captured and dispatched to Queen Anne's Town for detention.[67] Except for one, who successfully bolted. His escape would prove to be most significant.

Even as Bowie and Beanes were organizing a posse, the vanguard of the British Army on its triumphant retirement from the capital had begun to enter Nottingham. Here, Ross and Cockburn decided, they would let their men rest and recuperate after the strenuous march. A Royal Navy gun brig and a number of longboats and other launches had already made their way from Benedict against the current and had come to anchor opposite the town. Soon, the walking wounded were being carried aboard the brig, while the spoils of war, including large quantities of flour and tobacco, were transferred to the smaller vessels and shipped downstream to the main fleet anchorage. Fearful that the defeated American Army might be regrouping in his rear to take up pursuit, Ross dispatched a body of soldiers on captured horses back toward Upper Marlborough to reconnoiter. Satisfied that there was no pursuit, the horsemen were about to turn around toward Nottingham when they encountered the escaped deserter, who informed them of the fate of his fellow stragglers. The horsemen promptly returned to the town and captured Dr. Beanes, identified as one of the instigators of the seizures, and carried him away as a prisoner.[68]

On August 29 the British Army broke camp at Nottingham and commenced its march to Benedict, taking with them the elderly Dr. Beanes. The following day, the first of a flurry of efforts to free the doctor began. Finally, on September 7, as the British fleet prepared for an all-out assault on the defenses of Baltimore City, John S. Skinner, acting as the American exchange officer for prisoners of war, and a lawyer named Francis Scott Key boarded the British flagship *Tonnant* in Chesapeake Bay and commenced negotiations with the invaders for the exchange of Beanes. Few would remember Skinner or Beanes, who was released on September 16, but Key would go down in history as the author of a stirring poem called the "Defence of Fort M'Henry." Weeks later, the poem, sung to the tune of the popular drinking song "To Anacreon in Heaven," would be dubbed "The Star-Spangled Banner."

The end of the war provided a return to normalcy as old ties and domestic tranquillity were resumed. Nottingham's most famous resident, Robert Bowie, returned to the political arena and in 1815 and 1816 stood unsuccessfully for the U.S. Senate. On January 8, 1817, attended by his cousin, the noted Dr. Beanes, Robert died of pneumonia at his home in Nottingham. Two days later, as a token of respect and esteem for the first citizen of Nottingham and four-time governor of the state, the Maryland House of Delegates resolved "that we wear crape on the left arm during the remainder of the session" and then adjourned to mourn its fallen leader. By his will, Robert Bowie left to his widow the house and farm at Nottingham. The family plantation at Mattoponi was bequeathed to his son Robert W. Bowie. Other lands and properties were given to his two daughters and to his grandson, William T. Wootton. His great stocks of horses and cattle were divided among his children. And his personal body servant, Will Watson, was freed. In 1899, Bowie family genealogist Walter Worthington Bowie would write of Watson: "This old darky lived to be more than one hundred and ten years of age, and is well remembered by the present generation. He was very proud of having been the 'ole Guvner's body sarvent,' of which he boasted to the end of his life, retaining among his treasures an old Continental uniform, which he claimed 'ole Marster' had given him."[69]

Though Nottingham's most famous resident was gone, life in town went on. A regular postal route was finally established by the U.S. government running once a week between Upper Marlborough to Nottingham, Aquasco, Benedict, and Charlotte Hall, a distance of forty-six miles. Business was booming, if the granting of licenses for ordinaries to sell liquor was any gauge. In 1818 alone, licenses were granted to Josias Young, Pilemon Chew, Jr., Henry Boswell, and Thomas N. Bladen. Boswell and William G. Jackson were also granted a license to operate an ordinary at Nottingham Ferry.[70] Yet, it was the town's role as an official American port of entry, replete with its own customs office, that clearly delineated Nottingham from the rest of the Patuxent towns.

In the spring of 1819 Nottingham was to bear witness to one of the most celebrated piracy captures of the era. The affair began half a hemisphere away at the remote island of Margarita on the coast of Venezuela, a region in revolt against Spanish dominance. The revolution, led by General Simon Bolivar, was seen by many Americans not only as an imitation of America's own successful campaign for independence but as a conflict that might bring profit. Not a few Marylanders had set off bearing letters of marque and reprisal from one side or the other, allowing them to join the fray as privateersmen. One such adventurer was Daniel Danels of Baltimore, who had set out from the Chesapeake in the armed brig *Irresistible* to seek his fortune in the revolution. Upon arriving in St. John The Greek Harbor, at Isla Margarita, Venezuela, Danels's ship was boarded by one of Bolivar's commanders, a naval officer named Arizmendi, captain of the warship *Nereyda*. He attempted to convince Danels to throw in with Bolivar's infant fleet. While the two men conferred, a third vessel, the Buenos Aires privateer *Creola,* manned largely by seamen from Baltimore, came to anchor nearby. Arizmendi did his best to convince *Creola*'s captain to join the revolutionaries also. *Creola*'s crew, however, had already had enough of South America and wanted nothing more than to return to Baltimore despite their commander's wishes, and they conspired on the best way to achieve their ends. Thus, in the dark of night, they boarded *Irresistible* by surprise and took over the ship. Many of the brig's Maryland crew were equally anxious to return home and joined them. After setting those seamen ashore who were unwilling to join the overthrow, the mutineers sailed for Baltimore. The following day, Danels, who had been conferring aboard *Nereyda,* learned of the mutiny and ordered one of his prizes, the ship *Venezuela* commanded by prizemaster Don Henriques Childs, to follow in hot pursuit.[71]

The crew aboard *Irresistible,* unaware of the chase, turned to piracy and frequently stopped along their route to plunder American, French, and English vessels. Among those robbed was the ship *Superior* of Baltimore, bound for New Orleans with passengers; her female passengers"were treated most rudely." Finally, about mid-April, either "glutted with plunder, or weary of piracy," the rovers entered the Chesapeake and anchored off New Point Comfort, Virginia, where many landed and made their escape. The pirates were still confident that word of their crimes had not preceded them. Unfortunately for them, on April 14, *Venezuela* had already arrived at Baltimore to spread the news and to search on its own for the freebooters.[72]

The U.S. revenue cutter *Active,* Captain John Marshall commanding, with a crew of six men was immediately dispatched down the Bay by the Baltimore customs officer. But *Venezuela* had not waited for the authorities and had already set off on its own accord. Childs soon found his quarry off the mouth of the Patuxent and captured her without difficulty. He immediately notified the Nottingham customs office surveyor, based at Town Creek on the lower river, who took formal possession of the brig. The inspector from Nottingham arrived soon afterwards and quarantined most of the pirate crew at the Nottingham Customs House. Others were left aboard the brig in chains or taken aboard *Venezuela.* The Nottingham Customs House was, without question, ill-equipped to incarcerate a large crew of tough, rowdy buccaneers, and within a short time after their arrival, all had escaped. About this same time, *Active* arrived on the river, seized the pirates still onboard the two ships, and rounded up all of those who had escaped into the countryside. Twenty-two pirates were placed in irons and carried to Baltimore by Marshall and Childs, accompanied by *Irresistible,* to stand trial.[73]

An immediate controversy exploded between the Nottingham and Baltimore customs district offices regarding jurisdiction over the pirates and *Irresistible,* which was deemed a valuable prize. For Daniel Danels, a long and costly admiralty case over ownership of his brig would haunt the courts for months. But for the port of Nottingham, the affair would only serve as a paradigm reflective of the stunning rise in importance and influence of the port of Baltimore and the commensurate diminution of the smaller riverports of the tidewater. Even as the Nottingham customs officer was fighting an unwinnable battle of jurisdiction against the more influential Baltimore district, the port itself had begun its gradual decline.

The decrease in port activity was at first imperceptible. In 1822, the state government was still optimistic enough to authorize an additional wharf to be erected on the town waterfront. In 1814, a British officer passing through on the way to Washington had described Nottingham as "a town, or large village, capable of containing from a thousand to 1,500 inhabitants." The officer's estimate, accepted as an accurate population count by some historians, suggested a size well beyond reality. In truth, the key words "capable of containing" indicated that the author might have been alluding to the overall spaciousness of the site or was including the population of the immediate countryside. Nevertheless, by 1828, the tax list for Prince George's County reported that there were only twenty-two owned lots in the town, four of which were unimproved. The total value of the town itself was assessed at only $9,186. Even when considering that the population of 1828 most certainly included nonresident shopkeepers and others who would not have been noted in the tax list, the decline had obviously been dramatic.[74]

Notwithstanding gradual stagnation, the core activities of the greatly diminished community persisted. Ferry operations, for one, continued to be maintained, ensuring the town's role as a crossroads on the river. In 1834 John Calvert and Robert M. Tomlin were authorized by the county court to manage the ferry. A state tobacco inspection warehouse was still maintained. But one of the former mainstays of commerce, the town's ordinaries, were another matter. In 1834 a statewide temperance movement dealt a deadly blow to liquor sales in Maryland with the adoption of chapter 244 of the Acts of 1834, passed on March 20,

1835. In Prince George's County the sale of liquor or cordials of any kind and any quantity was prohibited after May 1, 1835. The consequences for the hostelries of Nottingham were severe. Between 1845 and 1854, Prince George's County was authorized by an act of the state legislature to sell off its tobacco inspection warehouses, and that included the old facility at Nottingham.[75]

The occasional natural disasters and town fires added to the town's difficulties. On Monday, August 4, 1845, the *Marlboro Gazette* reported on one typical weather-related incident that was especially difficult for local farmers: "Hailstorm—A portion of Nottingham District, in this county, was visited by a severe hailstorm on Saturday evening last. It extended only about half a mile in width, and passed over into Calvert County. The hail was large enough to kill well grown fowls—and considerably injured the tobacco plants. "[76]

With the ascendancy of Baltimore and the redirection of trade, a new order was also emerging and its ambassador was the steamboat. By the 1840s steamship lines operating from Baltimore had already begun to service the river towns of the western and Eastern Shores, loading tobacco, farm products, and other goods as well as passengers at the riverport docks for transport to Baltimore. Necessary supplies, farm equipment, and dry goods would then be shipped back to the towns for sale and distribution through their own stores. Baltimore had, in effect, assumed the mantle worn during the colonial era by London.

By 1860, the entire Nottingham election district could boast of a population totalling only 2,476 people, while Baltimore counted 212,418.[77] The predominant occupation of the whites and free blacks in the district was farming, with a total of 120 planters and 57 free farm laborers and general laborers listed in the U.S. Census. The principal labor pool for the surrounding farms, of course, came from 1,360 slaves, who comprised more than half of the population of the district. Indeed, the district was anything but a melting pot, with only nine foreign-born residents (seven Irish, one German, and one Scot). In the agrarian slave economy that dominated everyday life in Nottingham, wages were low. In 1856 an average farmhand received $9 a month with board; a laborer 87 cents a day, or 62 cents a day with board; a carpenter $1.25 per day; and a female domestic $1.37 per week with board. The average pay for a day laborer was $2.00 a week. The citizens were a religious lot, for the district boasted thirty-one churches (twelve Episcopalian, fourteen Methodist, one Presbyterian, and four Roman Catholic), none of which were in Nottingham itself.[78] The town and its immediate environs could boast of only twenty-seven buildings, largely located around the block of streets that formed the town center. These included a town Temperance Hall, William Quinn's Hotel, several commercial emporiums such as Plater's Store and J. T. Stamp & Son's store (which also served as the post office), Robert Thompson's windmill (just outside of the town), and a number of residences and other shops.[79] Two roads entered the town from the west: one connected the town with Upper Marlboro and points north (becoming North Street as it entered the village), and the other connected the town with Magruder's Landing, Aquasco, and points south (Market Street). The western border of the town was Union Street, and its riverfront was bounded by Water Street.[80]

Although the Civil War came and went leaving nary a scar on Nottingham, by 1878 only a few improvements had been visited upon the town, and only a handful of newcomers had taken up residency, occupying dwellings or shops of others who had moved away or died off. Of the three wharves that lined the waterfront, one fronted the Weems Warehouse. To the north of North Street, a schoolhouse had been established, probably in the former residence of Doctor McCubbin. The ferry, described as being "an old scow with hinged gangways fore and aft and rails along the side . . . rowed by several stout black men," still ran. About 1910 a small commercial cannery called the Woodfield Canning Factory, said to have been operated by Bohemians, canned blackberries and tomatoes at the waterfront and shipped its products to Baltimore via steamboats of the Weems Line such as *Potomac* and *Anne Arundel.*[81]

By the end of World War I Nottingham had become a rural hamlet, little visited and less known. One rare visitor to the town in 1919 left a melancholy view of the place. While on a tour of the rural Maryland countryside, Wilfred M. Barton visited the run-down old port with his two young sons after a two-hour trip in an automobile over fifteen miles of rutted road from Benedict.

"We rode through the principal street," he later wrote, "Market Street, only a block long with three or four dilapidated houses on either side until we reached the old wharf, at the water's edge, with its wooden shed or warehouse. . . . Getting into the car we turned and rode back through Market Street, then to the right along Union Street, then sharply to the left into the road which led off in a straight course due northeast. For a distance of three-quarters of a mile this was perfectly straight."

"This used to be a race-course years ago," he told his boys as they rode along.

"How do you know?" asked the boys in unison.

"The steamboat captain on one of the Baltimore boats told me so last year when I took a trip with him on the *Anne Arundel.* He told me that he was born in Nottingham and his father before him had been also a captain on the river."[82]

Looking back as he rode away, Barton compared Nottingham to the hamlet described in Oliver Goldsmith's wistful poem *Deserted Village.*

"'Sunk are its bowers in shapeless ruin all. And the long grass o'ertops the mouldering wall.'"

By 1921, even the days of the colorful steamboats were numbered. The Patuxent River Line steamer no longer stopped at Nottingham on the weekday runs, and it visited only briefly on Saturday afternoons, "weather and tide permitting."[83] The town had lost its major link with the outside world, for when the steamship lines terminated service, all connections with Baltimore were severed. Farmers no longer came to town to ship their produce to Baltimore, having opted for rail service from Upper Marlboro or overland transportation that could utilize an improved network of state roads. On January 26, 1927, the post office was closed for good. By 1930, the Woodfield Canning Factory, located directly on the river but deprived of the means for cheap, convenient transportation for its canned goods, had closed down forever.[84]

In 1939 a reporter from the *Washington Times Herald* wrote of a visit to the all-but-forgotten town. "When you drive into Nottingham," he wrote,

you don't see anything but a couple of houses and a barn sitting in a tobacco field, with the blue waters of the Patuxent at the foot of the fields . . . It's difficult to picture in your mind colonial ladies dismounting from their coaches to stay overnight in the big Nottingham hotel on the way from the South to Philadelphia and New York . . . But they used to be there. Cotillions were danced in the hotel every night, ships laden with silks, satins, powdered wigs, and pipes of Madeira and port bobbed at anchor in the harbor and nearby in a mansion lived young and handsome [General] Robert Bowie, soldier statesman, with his

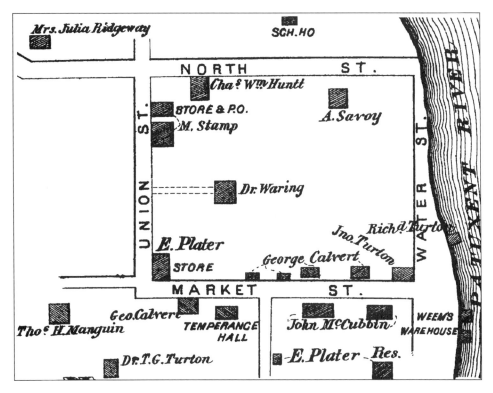

Top: Nottingham, Maryland, 1878. Detail from "Nottingham Dist. No. 4. Prince George County" by G. M. Hopkins, in the *Atlas of Fifteen Miles Around Washington Including Prince George County Maryland* (Philadelphia, 1878). Courtesy Library of Congress, Washington, D.C.

Bottom: Downtown Nottingham, 1919. At left is the Weems warehouse and at right is the old McCubbin house fronted by Market Street. Neither building is now extant. Photograph by Wilfred M. Barton in *The Road to Washington* (Boston, 1919).

bride, Priscilla Mackall with whom he [had] eloped when she was 15, he 19. . . . All that used to be there. But it's gone now. All that's left is the sepulchral, silver-grey ruin of Robert Bowie's house, gaunt, ravaged, tumbling down, haunted by courtly memories . . . We walked to the front door. It had been ripped out, wainscoting and all. Inside, crumbled plaster lay on the floor, a bed spring, a lawn mower, empty tin cans, cobwebs and dust. Wasps and flies buzzed. Weeds clutched at its foundations. It was a sad sight . . . Sloping away from the shaded house were fields in which I could see ruins of old houses, parts of which had been sold to antique collectors, parts burned by fires through the centuries, overgrown with bushes and weed.[85]

The reporter encountered an ancient Negro named Ambrose who "must've been a hundred if he was a day" and who had lived in the back rooms of the dilapidated old mansion. The place was known to locals as the Cedars, the Berry House, or simply Nottingham Farm. Not far away, another remnant of bygone days, by this time little more than a vine-covered chimney but once known as Harmony Hall, stood in dark ruination. Ambrose openly reminisced about his youth and the once vibrant town: "I can remember when there was a big town here, full of doctors and businessmens, and McCuppen's [McCubbin's] tavern was a-flourishin' and they wouldn't let the slaves drink out of the town spring 'cause the water was cold and give 'em cramps so they couldn't work in the fields."[86]

Yet even in its dissolution, the spectral ruins of Robert Bowie's stately home had its attraction. Visited by notable architectural historians and recordists such as H. Chandlee Foreman and James C. Wilfong, Jr., its historic allure was undeniable. Wilfong would later write that the dwelling "had been ruinous for a generation," yet even in its ebbing years it remained a point of interest for antiquarians and architects alike because of its noble lines and proportions. "It was," he wrote, "no doubt the oldest [then existing] building [of a half dozen somnolent residences] in Nottingham, and considering its historical background, it seems the more regrettable that disinterest finally brought about its end . . . with the destruction of this edifice one more bond between the 18th century and the 20th has been irretrievably lost." By 1952, the Cedars was no more.[87]

But the ghosts of Governor Robert Bowie and a forgotten town once known as Nottingham had already secured their small but important niche in history.

6 QUEEN ANNE'S TOWN

"Down yonder to this old bridge here"

June 20, 1999. The men who gathered on the old bridge ruins in the early morning hours were a cheerful lot. Most were black men from the surrounding area, bonded by a spirit of camaraderie and their love for fishing. They came to the bridge often—winter, spring, summer, and fall—to wage their skills, lines, and nets against the pike, perch, bass, herring, and catfish that dwelled in the shadows of the dilapidated structure, beneath the shallow, black waters of the upper Patuxent River. They laughed and exchanged stories and sometimes drank a little. A few brought folding chairs to sit upon while they snoozed. But mostly they just fished, as men have done at the bridge for as long as anyone could remember.

For nearly two and a half centuries, there has been a bridge of one type or another on this same spot, at the head of what had once been deepwater navigation on the river, joining Prince George's and Anne Arundel Counties together at their waists like Siamese twins. For those two and a half centuries, the crossing served as the focal point of the community, a geographic landmark defining political boundaries and a physical and symbolic crossroads of culture, time, and place. Its name was taken from the adjacent village whose citizens built it, used it, and profited from it—the uppermost seaport on any river in colonial Maryland, a port once known as Queen Anne's Town.

Demetrius Cartright is not a name that stands out in any history book, for his contributions were those of Everyman. On September 25, 1669, Cartwright secured title to a substantial tract of land on the Patuxent River which he dubbed Essington.[1] The new dominion was a splendid place for tobacco farming. The yellowish-brown sandy loam soil, which modern geologists classify as the Mattapex Series, lay on a moderately sloping littoral, terminated on its eastern border by steep hillsides and segmented by ravines descending into the valley of the Patuxent.[2] Within a little over ten years of Cartwright's acquisition of the land, no fewer than four more tracts surrounding Essington were secured by others. These included James Neale's Amptill Grange to the north, Robert Tyler's Brough and Thomas Bowdler's Bowdler's Choice to the west, and Ninian Geall's (or Beall's) Padworth Farme to the south. In 1699 a small strip of land to the northeast called the Angle was acquired by Thomas Larkin.[3]

Among the myriad tracts laid out in the region that would eventually form northeastern Prince George's County, Essington was in many ways unique. Its eastern border was located on a then-wide reach of the Patuxent, fifty miles above the mouth of the river at the head of tides and navigation. Situated on the eastern rim of the county's hinterland with then-deep water capable of hosting seagoing sailing ships of up to three hundred tons, its position as a potential inland shipping point was significant, and it was apparently employed as such early on.

Until the formation of Prince George's County, Essington had been part of Calvert County. In 1696, with the formal creation of the new county and its division into administrative areas, the tract became a part of Collington Hundred, which embraced a broad area between the Western Branch and Collington Branch, two tributaries draining into the Patuxent. For the next eight years, Essington was included in St. Paul's Parish. But in December 1704, a new parish called Queen Anne's, named in honor of the new queen of England, was created from the northern portion of St. Paul's. The act establishing the new parish specified that the dividing line extend from the Western Branch of the Patuxent as far north as Cabin Branch, westward to the head of the branch, and on the extreme west by a line drawn along the ridge between the Patuxent and the Potomac Rivers. Six of the most prominent men in the new county, Robert Tyler, Colonel Henry Ridgely, Thomas Odell, Philip Gittings, John Pottnger, and John Gerrard, were elected vestrymen. The Reverend Robert Owen was induced to conduct services every fortnight in a diminutive log cabin in Collington Hundred which had once served as a chapel for St. Paul's Parish.[4]

Sometime before 1706, a primitive marine facility had been established at the precise head of the Patuxent's deepwater navigation at Anderson's Landing on the old Essington tract. The county was growing rapidly, and it was thus no surprise when the site, "at the upper Landing in the Northwestern branch on the West side of the said branch" was named as a perfect place for one of the proposed new towns in Prince George's County in "An Act for the advancement of trade and erecting Ports & Towns in the Province of Maryland." On April 17, 1706, the act creating the town was read and assented to by the House of Delegates and the council and signed into law by Governor John Seymour two days later. On behalf of the secretary, the seal of secretary of the council Thomas Lawrence was affixed by Thomas Boardley, clerk of the secretary's office.[5] Lying within Queen Anne's Parish, the new port town would also come to be known as Queen Anne's, although not named as such in the act.

It was perhaps no coincidence that the town at Anderson's Landing was designated in the same year that plans for the parish's first brick church were submitted. The new house of worship was named Saint Barnabas Church and was erected on a two-acre tract of land called "Something," which had been donated by John and Mary Demall for the use of the parish. Within two years, taxables in the parish numbered 630 persons, and the Reverend Jonathan White was installed as its first rector. There were, at this time, hardly enough people to support a seaport of any size and like many of the new "paper" towns legislated into existence throughout the colony, Queen Anne's was slow in developing despite its superb location for inland shipping. But its purpose was soon obvious to all, even if the means to accomplish its construction wasn't.[6]

As with all sites designated by the 1706 act, Anderson's Landing, or Queen Anne's Town, was to be erected and developed on one hundred acres of land purchased and surveyed specifically for the purpose, with lots designated and streets and alleys laid out. Unfortunately, no original survey plat of the site has been located to date. That some development occurred early on is probable. Yet, by 1711, the designated townsite could boast of only a single ordinary, an establishment operated by Mary Belt. Two years later, Reuben Ross was also granted a license by the county court at Charlestown to run another ordinary in town, suggesting that visitation by travelers and locals alike was enough to support such establishments. Of significance is that at the same court where Ross had secured his license, an order was issued to repair the road running from Benjamin Hall's plantation to the town, indicating the site was already accessible by at least one byway.[7] In 1716, the infant town was finally awarded the trappings of municipal rectitude when the county justices ordered that stocks and a whipping post be erected.[8]

The importance of Queen Anne's Town's strategic shipping position on the upper Patuxent was obvious not only to the planters of Prince George's County, but to those of

Anne Arundel as well. Cognizant of the virtues of an inland port (which the delegates from Prince George's had so successfully pressed upon the General Assembly), the planters of western All Hallows Parish in Anne Arundel, who were obliged to ship their own tobacco from outlets on the South River, petitioned the Lower House on March 29, 1707, "praying a town to be erected on Patuxent River opposite Queen Ann's Town." The petition was read and granted.[9] The new Anne Arundel riverport, a sister to Queen Anne's, was named Kilkenny Town. Yet, its precise location and layout, as well as the course of its brief life, is even today conjectural owing to the lack of locational data or an actual survey plat. It is certain that its position was ill chosen. Unlike Queen Anne's, which was largely established on an elevation overlooking the river, Kilkenny Town was to be situated on the eastern shore of the river opposite Queen Anne's Town, quite probably on or adjacent to a marshy plain that was subject to periodic flooding. Despite that disadvantage, the new town was important in stirring further development at Queen Anne's, and it was instrumental in forwarding the improvement of the local road systems and communication between the two infant ports and the rest of the colony.

In 1712, the inhabitants of All Hallows Parish opposite Queen Anne's petitioned for a road to be built from South River to Kilkenny Town. This link, which was to be the last in a chain needed to connect Upper Marlborough and points south with Annapolis and points north, was critical to the overall betterment of the colony's traffic and commerce. The improvement did not go unnoticed, and the means to even better the linkage were not long in coming.[10] Perhaps even before the towns were formally established, highway traffic from Prince George's and the south had been obliged to employ the services of a ferry in order to cross to Anne Arundel. As overland travel increased in the colony, so did pressure to improve cross-river transportation. In 1719, Governor John Hart entreated the Assembly for the first time to provide for the construction of a bridge over the Patuxent at Queen Anne's Town and another over the Kent marshes on the Eastern Shore, "These two places being the great road, through the heart of this country, and also the usual and shortest passage for all travellers to, and from His Majesty's plantations on this continent." Such a structure over the Patuxent would also effectively connect Prince George's and Anne Arundel's principal towns while improving commerce and transportation throughout the colony.[11] The Assembly, not wishing the royal government to bear the burden of expense, placed responsibility for actually paying for construction squarely upon the two counties. With neither jurisdiction willing to foot the bill, the bridge-building initiative was stalled for the next quarter of a century.

Still, facilitated by an active ferry service, overland traffic was substantial enough that Queen Anne's and Kilkenny Town vied briefly for status as the principal crossroads of the upper Patuxent. Moreover, both sites had apparently already begun to serve as transshipment points for locally grown tobacco, albeit with the former having a slight edge over the latter. Eventually, Queen Anne's would take a substantial lead in the rivalry, all but dooming Kilkenny, first to the status of a minor landing and finally to extinction.

The earliest record of ferry operations between Queen Anne's and Kilkenny Town appears in 1721–1722, when the Anne Arundel County Court ordered that a new service be opened to cross the river between the two towns. The ferry was to be maintained by an annual levy upon Anne Arundel County taxables. However, every county-tax-paying man (or head of household), unless he was a nonresident with a working farm or plantation in the county, was entitled to free usage. His family, servants, and slaves were to be excepted, thereby limiting movement for most women and children, indentured workers, and black people.[12] The initial operation was not without its competitors or problems. There was already a privately maintained ferry somewhat to the south at Mount Pleasant Landing on the

Prince George's County side, and a few travelers were not happy with the county licensed service on the Queen Anne's–Kilkenny road. Some simply found the Mount Pleasant route more convenient. In 1722, one sojourner named Thomas White stated succinctly his reasons for using the Mount Pleasant ferry instead of the Queen Anne's–Kilkenny route. Traversing the Patuxent at Mount Pleasant, he noted, "is much the nearest way from the city of Annapolis to Marlborough Town as also the best & nearest way for all comers & goers from St. Marys & Charles County to & from Annapolis. I believe some of your worships is very sensible of the difficulty of passing & repassing over at Queen Anne Town, occasioned by the freshes of the river at some seasons, which is quite the contrary to Mount Pleasant."[13]

Conversely, at Mount Pleasant, travelers could not count upon the food and lodging facilities to be found at Queen Anne's, which was by now also beginning to serve as a minor hub of commerce. Competitive ferry operations on the Queen Anne's–Kilkenny route itself would be licensed by both Anne Arundel and Prince George's Counties. In 1726, the county court of Prince George's appointed John Boyd keeper of the ferry on the Prince George's side and the following year renewed his appointment, while also granting him a license to keep an ordinary or public house of entertainment in the town.[14]

Competition for the post of ferrymaster on both sides was often intense. In the period 1741–1743, the Anne Arundel court authorized annual salaries for the Queen Anne's ferryman ranging from £12 to £15. The work was tedious and often difficult. Monday through Saturday, free rides for county taxables were limited to the hours between sunup and sunset. On the Sabbath and after dark, Anne Arundel ferrymen charged six pence for a man and horse, a fee lowered in 1743 to two pence. There were numerous exemptions, including jurymen traveling after sunset, and sheriffs, justices, jurymen, and witnesses attending court. Although a ferryman was obliged to provide a good boat and hands, if he could also accommodate travelers with stables, lodging, and a place of entertainment, he stood to make a substantial profit from the spin-off enterprises.[15]

Of the men who operated the critical ferry service, little is known until the arrival of Isaac Hyde. Accompanied by his son Thomas, Hyde alighted in Maryland in 1716, while serving as a factor for a London merchant named Gilbert Higginson. He had traveled widely on behalf of Higginson, ranging from New England to Barbados until settling as a storekeeper in All Hallows Parish in Anne Arundel. His employment with Higginson had been good, for he had been paid travel expenses and a yearly stipend of £60, a portion of which was provided in goods that he was free to sell on his own. But working for another man was never Isaac Hyde's ambition. Independence was in his blood and he preferred to be his own boss. Without capital or sufficient credit, his horizons had been limited until he visited Queen Anne's Town. Liking the place and the opportunities for the autonomy it provided, he settled, rented a tavern, and successfully managed the ferry operation until his death in 1734.[16]

On August 22, 1727, the government again ordered that stocks—the symbol of civil authority and meted punishment for various transgressions of the law—be erected in Queen Anne's Town. It is thus suggested that the original stocks ordered eleven years earlier had either never been put up or had possibly worn out from use.[17] Whatever the reasoning, the order, perhaps, came none too soon, for in the fall of 1728 the town briefly served as the focal point for actions taken by a number of unnamed inhabitants of Prince George's in what the government deemed to be rebellious and illegal acts.

The government's concern was raised when "a seditious & scandalous paper," tacked up on trees at strategic ferry crossings in the county, came to the attention of Governor Benedict Leonard Calvert, brother of Lord Baltimore. The paper in question was circulated as a consequence of continued public dissatisfaction over the depressed state of the tobacco trade, a condition caused by the vast quantities of "trashy and Scentless tobacco" being sold and the government's seeming unwillingness and/or inability to remedy the situation. The poorer quality tobacco that glutted the market caused reduced prices and thereby injured the purchasing power of many large and small farmers alike, driving some into great debt and not a few into debtors' prison. The small independents and the tenant farmers, unlike the larger planters, had only limited acreage to grow tobacco upon and so were obliged to replant the same lands year after year, despoiling the soil and incrementally reducing the quality of each year's crop, thus driving prices down. It was a vicious cycle from which there appeared to be no escape. Many felt the only resolution was the enactment of legislation calling for stricter tobacco regulations.

Having plagued the colony for decades, the problem was not new and over the years had been the cause for frequent requests for governmental attention. As recently as May 1726, the inhabitants of several counties had petitioned the governor and council requesting that an Assembly be called "for the relief of tobacco the staple of this province." A special meeting of the legislature was soon convened to act. A letter was quickly sent to Virginia, which faced a similar crisis and was considering its own tobacco legislation, to inform that government of Maryland's intentions and to seek to coordinate the efforts of both colonies. The Virginia legislative initiative, unfortunately, had failed to pass on the grounds that it would give Maryland an unfair advantage in the market place. Soon afterwards in Maryland, though it was "agreed by a majority in both houses [that] the Tobacco Act is highly necessary," the Assembly was also unable to bring in legislation owing to "such a variety of opinions that we to our great dissatisfaction have not been able to reconcile them nor to enact any thing for the good of the staple tho very much wanted and earnestly pressed for by the people."[18]

The failure of the government to act had been deeply upsetting to many planters, particularly in Prince George's County. The passage of another growing season only proved to exacerbate the problem. Finally, by October 20, 1728, the situation had become so critical for many farmers that a circular was distributed to "Country-men & friends" calling for action. "Tis past doubt," read the flyer, "that the present state of the country might with facility be remedy'd (that is by suing for a Tobacco Law) 'tis miserably known how much 'tis wanting were honesty us'd as 'tis pretended now a sincere & hearty attachment to ourselves & posterity can't be better demonstrated then by pushing vigorously while the gap is open therefore as an expedient (my honest countrymen) let us meet at Queen Anne's Town on Monday the 28th of this instant to assert our rights, arm'd in a suitable manner to our good & honorable pretentions we desire may be publish'd."[19]

On October 26, the flyer having been brought to the attention of Governor Calvert and then laid by him before the council, it was deemed imperative that immediate government action be taken to nip the Queen Anne's assembly in the bud before outright rebellion erupted. After all, the flyer had used the phrase "assert our rights, arm'd in a suitable manner"! To the governor, that meant the threat of armed insurrection. The assembly, he felt, should not be dealt with lightly. The council recommended that a proclamation be issued calling on the civil and military officers of both Prince George's and Anne Arundel Counties "to have a faithful & watchful eye over the peace thereof" and to "discover & suppress all such riotous & unlawful meetings & assemblies." The council also ordered that a reward of £50 be offered to any person who disclosed the author or dispenser of the inflammatory circular which so "injuriously" reflected upon the legislature and sought to arouse "riotous disturbance" in Queen Anne's Town. The sheriffs of Prince George's and Anne Arundel Counties were then instructed to make the governor's proclamation public.[20]

The heavy-handed suppression of assembly at Queen Anne's was successful, and no meeting was convened. Unfortunately for the tobacco planters of Maryland, no viable tobacco inspection or quality control legislation would be forthcoming for almost two decades.

In the tobacco-based economy of Maryland, industries of other kinds were rare. But there were exceptions to the rule, one of which, the manufacture of iron, was to have a profound effect upon the town of Queen Anne's because of its special geographic position on the river.

In 1719 the General Assembly, seeking to encourage the production of iron mined from ore and bog iron deposits in the colony, passed an act offering one hundred acres of land to any individual or company that would erect a productive furnace. The recipient of the grant was to be permitted six months to complete construction and four years to commence actual production. To further encourage potential producers, the proprietor guaranteed rights-of-way to the plants, even if they should traverse the lands of others. And as a final sugar-coated incentive, companies employing eighty or more workers were to be given immunity from taxes for four years. Any person wishing to "set up [a] forging-mill, and other conveniencies for the carrying on of such iron-works" merely had to solicit from the Assembly a writ to purchase lands from private owners.[21]

One of those in Prince George's County who accepted the challenge was Richard Snowden, master of several extensive tracts on the Western Branch of the Patuxent, whose seat was at Birmingham Manor on the site of the modern town of Laurel. Hoping to capitalize upon the extensive iron deposits in the region, Snowden formed the Patuxent Iron Company. The Snowden Iron Works, as the company was commonly called, began to mine and smelt iron from company property at a location called Muirkirk today. The company was soon a successful and growing concern, and Snowden was accorded the nickname "the Ironmaster." The new enterprise faced many challenges, not the least of which was how to transport its products to markets. Overland hauling was an expensive proposition that taxed even Snowden's considerable capabilities. A man of both influence and political acuity, he readily observed that the Patuxent River offered the best hope for cheap and reliable transportation. Unfortunately, the river was navigable for seagoing ships only as far as Queen Anne's Town, approximately twenty miles below his plant, and the distance between was spotted with nasty shoals, sharp bends, snags, and occasionally swift flowing waters.

With characteristic panache, the Ironmaster surveyed the river and determined that with a well-engineered dredging project and the clearance of obstructions on the shores and in the water, the reach between the landing for his iron works and Queen Anne's Town could be made navigable for shallow-draft water carriage. Barges drawn by men or horses walking along the shores in difficult areas could be employed to carry his iron from the landing near the company furnaces to the town and transshipped from there to markets in America and Europe. In the March 1732 session of the General Assembly, undoubtedly after considerable lobbying by what might today be termed "a special interest group," a bill was introduced into the Lower House calling for "An Act to impower the Inhabitants of Anne Arundel and Prince George Counties, to make the main Branch of the River Patuxent Navigable, above Queen-Anne Town, in Prince George County" for a distance upwards of twenty miles. The bill was explicit in its parameters. It was to be unlawful for any person or persons "to make any hedge, ware [weir], or fence, in or a-cross the said Branch," or to repair any hedge, fence, or weir already extant, or "which shall be hereafter made" above Queen Anne's Town. It was also to be illegal to fell trees into the river "for the conveniency of fishing, or for any other matter or thing whatsoever" that might obstruct navigation. A fine of four hundred pounds of tobacco was to be levied for each offense. All money received from fines was to be applied toward the cost of clearance and maintenance of the upriver route. It was to be deemed lawful "for any person or persons, whatsoever, to clear and keep the river aforesaid open and navigable, at their own proper cost and charges, without being obstructed by any person or persons whatsoever." There was a stipulation. If the petitioners "shall not begin to clear the said river, or cause the same to be begun, within six months from the end of this session of Assembly . . . this Act shall cease, determine, and become null and void." If the clearance work was begun within the six-month-period but was not completed within six years, the act was also to be nullified. On April 12, 1733, the bill was presented to the proprietor for signing, and the following day it was passed into law.[22]

Snowden completed the clearance of more than twenty-five miles of waterway above Queen Anne's within four years. The Assembly belatedly noted that the work "will certainly prove very advantageous and convenient to every inhabitant and other person who may have occasion to convey any tobacco or other goods to any part of Patuxent River or to the counties bordering on the said river." But there were still some problems to be surmounted. Although navigation to Queen Anne's Town "is very practicable," there were still a number of shoals and rapids where it was necessary to portage the boats, either with horses or by man power. For most, the exercise proved "difficult and tedious" owing to a lack of cleared land at such strategic points. Thus, in April 1736, Snowden and company petitioned for a supplemental act empowering him to clear a road or roads "upon the banks of the Patuxent River above Queen Anne's Town in such and so many places on either side of the said river" as he saw necessary. The supplemental bill was handily approved. The Ironmaster was authorized to clear "such and so many roads, passages, paths or ways not exceeding ten foot wide on either or each side or sides bank or banks of the said Patuxent River above Queen Anne's Town" at his own expense. The roadways were to be employed specifically "for dragging or drawing any boat, vessel or other water carriage up or down the said River above Queen Anne's Town." When clearing the road, the company was not to be permitted either to make use of or to dispose of any of the cut timber that belonged to property owners whose lands were being traversed, but it was to be protected by law from molestation by anyone while engaged in the work.[23]

The success of the river clearance and towpath construction project was evident to all, although less than acceptable to some who owned property along the reach but were unable to utilize the waterfront because of the restraints of the acts. The restrictions, however, had little negative effect on Queen Anne's or Kilkenny Town, which were at the southern terminus of the towpath. Indeed, among the few benefits Kilkenny could boast of was a milling operation on the river, which would have been illegal just a few hundred yards to the north. The importance of the Snowden works to regional commerce was unquestionable. Within ten years, the Western Branch of the Patuxent, now navigable for barges as far as the plant landing, was commonly referred to as far west as Frederick County as Snowden's River.[24] With Queen Anne's occupying the closest transshipment point on the river, the opening of the upper waterway could not help but prove a commercial boon to the town.

Still, there were problems!

Despite the benefits of extended navigation and the town's central geographic location, the lack of an advantageously wide deepwater frontage, such as that enjoyed by Nottingham fourteen miles to the south or Lower Marlborough even further down, would prove difficult to surmount. Moreover, the increasing buildup of sediments in the waterway, a product of extensive deforestation and land clearance for tobacco farming, and the occasional obstruction of the narrow channel by floating trees and branches served to measurably impede access for shipping.[25] Some shippers were occasionally disinclined to employ the port at all. Others did so only grudgingly when absolutely necessary. Such attitudes were echoed by Dr. Charles Carroll of Annapolis in his instructions to Captain John Saterwhite, skipper of his schooner *Annapolis*, in May 1743. The captain had been ordered to proceed from Annapolis to Bridgetown, Barbados, to deliver his cargo. Then, he was to take on any freight "that offers for this river [Severn], Patapsco, South, West or Wye Rivers at three pounds sterling per ton." In the event that Thomas Wolford, Carroll's Barbadian agent, had any goods to ship to the Patuxent, Saterwhite was directed "to take in the same to be delivered at Queen Anne's to Mr. Wm. Murdock at three pounds ten shillings per ton" unless "it can not be done [because] the distance up the river is so great, [and] the landing difficult."[26]

Location was everything. The obstacles in getting shipping up to the town notwithstanding, it was soon apparent that Queen Anne's was becoming increasingly important and was eclipsing its sister village of Kilkenny on the Anne Arundel shore. The town was already a strategic crossroads linking Upper Marlborough and points south with Annapolis and points north. Traffic had for years severely taxed the capabilities of the ferry service. Finally, in August 1744, the Prince George's County Court contracted with John Fowler to build an arched bridge over the river at the site of the Queen Anne's ferry. The cost was set at £100 and was to be jointly paid by both Prince George's and Anne Arundel Counties.[27] This time, the two counties cooperated. The new bridge, the first to be erected over the navigable Patuxent, made the town ferry an instant and obsolete relic of the past. It also significantly increased the town's importance as a transit point on the highway system of the colony.

Accessibility was critical to the success of the town. And it was perhaps not a coincidence that the first horse races run in Prince George's County were held adjacent to Queen Anne's Town at a site central to many inhabitants of both Prince George's and Anne Arundel Counties. Announcements in the *Maryland Gazette* advertised that the races would be run at a fair held near the town on William Murdock's Old Fields. On the first day of the festivities, September 17, 1745, a race would be run on any horse, mare or gelding, with a purse of £30 "current money." Three heats of two miles each would be run, with every horse carrying a rider weighing 110 pounds. The following day, a second race would be run over the same course for a prize of £20. The winning horse on the first day was expected to also run on the second day. Entries were to be registered with William Beall at Queen Anne's Town on each day of racing. Every entrant was to pay an entry fee of thirty shillings for each horse for the first prize and twenty shillings for the second prize. All disputes and differences were to be settled by Thomas Harwood and Thomas Brooke, Jr.[28]

Horse racing was not the only recreation enjoyed by the local residents. In November 1754, the *Maryland Gazette* made note that a cricket match was held on Murdock's Old Fields between eleven men from Prince George's and eleven "South River Gentlemen" from Anne Arundel. The paper also reported that the latter had emerged victorious.[29]

Tippling in the town, a frequent pastime that was as common in the colonial era as it would be in the modern, was occasionally deadly. In mid-September 1755, it was reported that a group of revelers in Queen Anne's Town, "having drank too much, got to making Sport or running their Rig, (as it's term'd) with one of their Company, by tripping his Heels and throwing him down on a Floor, till they gave him a Fall which kill'd him." The unfortunate victim was a chap named Benjamin Jones, who left behind a wife and two small children.[30]

Not everyone, of course, tippled. Evidence of the intellectual interests of some of the local gentry is suggested by a notice advertising a sale in town of the library of the late Reverend Jacob Henderson. For thirty-three years Henderson had served as the second rector of Queen Anne's Parish. The sale of his library, which consisted of "a great many new books on divinity," was an event of some local importance and was to be held on May 12 at a public auction in town.[31]

Overall, daily events were not unlike those of any small port town in the tidewater. Not everyone, however, was delighted with their station in life in and about Queen Anne's Town, most especially indentured servants, slaves, and incarcerated criminals. Announcements of runaways being sought by their owners and reports on the sale of slaves in the neighborhood usually filled the pages of the colony's weekly newspaper. The descriptions of many who had run away from their owners provided a glimpse of the less attractive aspects of colonial society and of the unfortunate lower social castes locked within the system. In November 1748, town citizen Benjamin Lloyd reported the escape of an indentured servant belonging to him, John Key of Lancashire, England, and offered a £3 reward for his return. Lloyd described the servant, a weaver by trade, as "a likely smart fellow" with a cut under one of his eyes and an injury on one of his little fingers. He was attired in country-made linen and cotton, gray drugget breeches, gray worsted hose, a castor hat, brown wig, and linen caps. He also had a light-colored close-bodied great coat and a thin stuff coat with metal buttons and a velvet cape. He had taken with him a large bay stallion, branded with a double joined H on its rump and fitted with a plush hunting saddle.[32]

The Reverend William Brogden, curate and later rector of Queen Anne's Parish, also lived in the neighborhood and advertised a reward for the return of an indentured twenty-four-year-old Scotch servant named James Dandiss. From his description, it would probably have been difficult not to like the rougish Dandiss, even though he had escaped with substantial property pilfered from his master. Brogden reported him to be

of low stature, with short hair which he may probably cut off, or conceal with a coarse yarn cap; he speaks quick and coarse, but with little Scotch accent; has a struting gait, and a remarkable twinkling with his eyes when speaking to superiors; he writes tolerably, and may forge a pass; talks of having been a soldier and a sailor, pretends to understand navigation, and is supposed to have a nocturnal [precursor to a sextant] in his pocket. He had on, or with him, a grey half thick coat and breeches, with white metal buttons, not much worn; an old blue sailor's jacket, and wide trowsers, dark-color'd yarn stockings, turn'd up soal'd shoes half worn, brass buckles square and carv'd, a felt hat half worn, an osnabrigs and an old check'd shirt. He was intrusted in the morning with a twenty shilling bill, and took with him a pretty tall roan horse, low in flesh, branded ID and trots; and a new deep skirted Saddle, with iron swivel stirrups, but no housing.[33]

It is unknown if either Key or Dandiss made good their escapes or what became of them, but it is nice to think they would eventually find themselves freemen for they at least had the benefit of their skin color to help them blend in with white society. Not so fortunate were the Negro slaves.

The sale of slaves, though not a very common event in the town itself, was conducted in the neighborhood with some frequency and certainly without concern for the well-being of the human chattel being offered up. When Aaron Rawlings advertised the sale of "Several choice Negro slaves" at a public auction to be held at his plantation near the town, he lumped them along with "sundry cattle, horses, hogs, and sheep" that were also to be sold. Occasionally, the sale of a plantation, such as one on the Queen Anne's–Londontown Road belonging to absentee landlord Richard Hunt, a London merchant, would be preceded by the sale of all of the farm's slaves. Hunt's thirty-two blacks were advertised as "country born" and "well seasoned," most of which had "been brought up to plantation business." The "parcel" of slaves included a plowman, a house carpenter, a cooper, and a number of women who had been brought up in the plantation house and were adept at sewing, knitting, and spinning. Only two slave sales, however, are known to have actually been conducted within the town itself. Both were on behalf of men of wealth and importance in county and colony government: Philip Lee, Esq., who had served as a county court justice, commissary general of Maryland, and a member of the governor's council; and Thomas Bladen, a former governor of Maryland (1742–1751). The sales were administered on their behalf by Osborn Sprigg, one of the most influential politicians in Prince George's, and Benjamin Tasker, another former governor of Maryland (1752–1753).[34] The rank and social position of the slave owners or those who conducted the sales meant little to the black men, women, and children being sold. Yet, such events were then simply part of everyday life and society, and Queen Anne's Town was in that respect little different from anywhere else in colonial America.

Although Upper Marlborough, the administrative seat for Prince George's, was officially the locale where county justice and punishments were meted out, there were from time to time exceptions. Queen Anne's Town, of course, had its own stocks which were employed for minor offenses, but all persons incarcerated for more heinous crimes, such as murder, arson, or indebtedness, were confined to the prison in the county seat. In 1750, however, the jail burned down. It was believed that a Negro who had been imprisoned for murder set the fire to cover his escape. There was no other holding capacity for prisoners in the county; the situation was serious as the government wrangled over the procedures and expense of erecting a new jailhouse. In the meantime, the high sheriff of Prince George's County, Turner Wootton, who lived adjacent to Queen Anne's Town, was obliged to turn his own home into a temporary jail. For the sheriff, the situation proved to be anything but temporary. The substitute penitentiary would continue in service for nearly four years. Finally, on February 15, 1754, two of Wootton's dwellings and several outbuildings were burned to the ground. The fire began in the prison, reported the *Maryland Gazette* shortly afterwards, and was believed to have been set on purpose. It had then spread to the dwelling house, "which might have been saved, if they had had a ladder," presumably to facilitate a bucket brigade. Though Wootton suffered considerably, those who battled the fire managed to save the greatest part of his furniture, and, as an afterthought, all of the prisoners.[35]

In 1747, the central locations of both Queen Anne's Town and Kilkenny made them obvious candidates for tobacco inspection stations. The site named for the Queen Anne's warehouse was on the land of Thomas Lancaster, adjoining the town.[36] The Kilkenny warehouse was erected at Taylor's Landing somewhat to the south, situated near but not in the town, probably in the vicinity of modern Stockett's Creek. The inspectors at both stations were to be paid an annual salary of £50.[37]

Queen Anne's Town was now fitted with all of the attributes necessary for success within the Maryland tobacco trading system. Its location with respect to the road complex in the colony was excellent. The town was convenient not only for planters, but for travelers. One of the highways passing through extended from Oxon Hill (Addison's) on the Potomac to Annapolis on the Severn. The road from Annapolis branched off and ran through Upper

Marlborough, then ended at Piscataway Town, a port on the Potomac. Queen Anne's Town boasted that it was the most northerly tobacco inspection station and warehouse site in Prince George's and the most advantageously situated shipping center for the majority of planters in the upper county area. The advantages for those planters employing the town were plentiful. Since tobacco required careful handling in shipping, it was common wisdom that the shorter the distance to the inspection station, the better the chances that a hogshead of tobacco would arrive at the dock undamaged. As the next county inspection station and warehouse closest to Queen Anne's was Upper Marlborough, a good four to five miles to the south (a substantial distance when considering the difficulty of transporting the great hogsheads safely), many up-county farmers elected the more convenient port.[38] Moreover, unlike Queen Anne's, which lay directly on the Patuxent, Upper Marlborough's access to the river was via the Western Branch, a tributary that was silting up even faster than the main river trunk below Queen Anne's.

Nature, unhappily, created many inconveniences for Queen Anne's and Kilkenny, both of which were exposed to the occasional perturbations of the main river. The Patuxent, though generally a languorous, docile waterway, can become a vicious mistress, with flood-waters rampaging unhindered down the funnel of her ancient valley. In the spring of 1750, the river demonstrated its might by seriously breaching the main road in Queen Anne's Town. The impact upon traffic was so great that the General Assembly was obliged to pass an emergency act on June 2 empowering the justices of Prince George's County to levy a tax of £50 on the inhabitants of Queen Anne's Parish "to treat and agree with an undertaker or undertakers [contractors] to stop a breach now made from the North-West Branch of Patuxent River . . . across the main road in Queen Anne Town."[39]

As if to accentuate the river's power, the following year, after a particularly heavy period of rain, it was reported "a fine large bridge over Patuxent River was carried away by the freshes." It is uncertain whether or not the bridge in question was the 1744 structure at Queen Anne's or another span over the river. If the structure in question was the Queen Anne's Bridge, it was most certainly repaired quickly, for by November it was definitely again in use.[40] By 1754, however, it *had* become necessary to authorize the erection of a new bridge. The first structure had been deemed either unsafe or damaged, or else it had become simply incapable of handling the traffic. The new span was opened the following year. It lasted longer than the first, but by 1767, it again became necessary to replace the second with not one but two bridges, indicating that traffic traversing the river at Queen Anne's was by that time quite heavy. The structures were to be the first twin spans erected in Maryland.[41]

The establishment of commercial trading houses in midcentury in Queen Anne's Town but not in Kilkenny, even though both sites had the benefit of inspection station status, most assuredly signified that the days of the latter were over. The so-called town, which had simply failed to take hold, withered and died without record; all evidence of its existence was soon swept away in one of the many floods that periodically devastated the valley. Devoid of its closest competition, Queen Anne's blossomed despite all of its handicaps. That direct access by deep-draft merchant sailing ships was still possible to the Queen Anne's water-front until at least the last third of the century (siltation and obstructions notwithstanding) is indicated by the journal of the Reverend Andrew Burnaby, who passed through the town in the summer of 1760. Burnaby noted that he had been informed by the master of a schooner on which he had sailed that the Patuxent was indeed "navigable near fifty miles for vessels of three hundred tons burthen."[42]

Merchant trading houses were well established in the village by at least 1751, when John Moffatt, ensconced in his new store in town, advertised goods for sale, just imported from

London in the ship *Betsey,* Captain James Hall commanding.[43] Moffatt soon found himself in competition with other merchants such as William Hamilton, Stephen West, Jr., Richard Moore, and the Symmer brothers, Alexander and Andrew.

The town's boom days, it seemed, were finally at hand. Between the early 1750s and the onset of the Revolution, the pages of the *Maryland Gazette* regularly bore testament to the growth of international maritime trade at Queen Anne's Town. "Just imported," read one typical advertisement in May 1756, "in the Ships *Anne-Galley,* Capt. Hamilton, from London, and *Judith,* Capt. Sedgwick, from Glasgow, and to be sold at the subscriber's store in Queen-Anne-Town, at the most reasonable rates, for bills of exchange, current money, or tobacco, a choice assortment of European and East-India goods. William Hamilton."[44]

The merchants were a formidable and extremely competitive lot. One of the more successful ones to open in Queen Anne's Town was Stephen West, Jr., who may be credited with founding the first chain store operation in Maryland, with outlets in at least eleven ports and towns. West was the son and acolyte of Stephen West, Sr., a well-known merchant in London Town in Anne Arundel. In 1753 the young West married Hannah Williams, daughter of a wealthy Guinea slave trader, the late Captain Richard Williams, master of the Woodyard in Prince George's. He opened his first store in Upper Marlborough and soon expanded operations almost exponentially. He not only sold merchandise imported from Europe and the East and West Indies, but he purchased wheat, corn, pork, staves, and a variety of local commodities which were exported along with the usual shipments of tobacco.[45] In partnership with Richard Moore of Anne Arundel County, he opened an outlet at Queen Anne's Town in 1759. Their first advertisement read: "Just imported in the *Wilson,* Capt. Slator, from London, and to be sold by the subscribers at Queen Anne in Prince George's County, very cheap, for bills, cash, or tobacco, a large assortment of European and East-India goods. Likewise Barbadoes rum and Muscovado sugar. Stephen West, Richard Moore."[46]

By the following year, the Queen Anne's Town operation having passed into West's sole ownership, the Prince George's merchant found himself in stiff competition with the Symmer brothers, who opened stores in both Queen Anne's Town and Upper Marlborough and advertised their first shipment of goods from London brought in by the ship *Nelly,* Captain William Wilkinson commanding. The Symmer's operation was short lived. In 1761, unable to compete successfully with West and "having broke up their Store at Queen Anne's," the brothers called in all outstanding accounts and requested those indebted to them to pay their agent, William Turner Wootton.[47]

West was a survivor and a most innovative merchant to boot. In 1761, small coinage had become scarce in Maryland, threatening to stymie monetary transactions throughout the colony. To assuage the situation, at least as far as his own commerce was concerned, West ordered notes to be printed by William Rind and his partner Jonas Green, postmaster at Annapolis and also publisher of the *Maryland Gazette.* The bills were run off in small denominations of sixpence, one shilling, one shilling and sixpence, two shillings, and a half crown. At any given time, a sufficient quantity of these personal notes could be exchanged at any of his stores, including the one in Queen Anne's Town, at the rate of seven shillings sixpence per Spanish dollar, thereby guaranteeing the loyalty of his constituency and ensuring a continuation of business. The degree of acceptance of the scheme is indicated by the willingness of other Queen Anne's merchants, such as John Duvall, to accept the West bills as tender for their own business transactions.[48]

Walter Bowie was another Marylander who had an interest in large commercial enterprises in Queen Anne's Town. Bowie would eventually rise to prominence on the political front as a signer of the famous "Declaration of the Association of Freemen of Maryland." He also served as a member of the Committee of Correspondence and as an officer in the Maryland Militia. He became one of the framers of Maryland's first constitution and he served in the Maryland House of Delegates, in the State Senate and, in 1802, in the United States House of Representatives.[49]

As the town evolved into a trading port of importance as well as a strategic crossroads for travelers, it was not surprising to see frequent applications made in the county court for permission to establish ordinaries therein. In the years between 1761 and 1770, at least four new ordinaries were opened in town by John Elliott, Jeremiah Crabb, Thomas Rose, and Alexander Warren. The ordinaries served not only travelers seeking food and temporary shelter during breaks in their journeys, but also the business community, providing places where meetings and other transactions might take place. In July 1752, James Dick, a merchant from London Town, advertised the sale of a number of tracts of land throughout the colony, totaling 1,650 acres. The public sale was to be held in centrally located Queen Anne's Town, undoubtedly in one of the town's many ordinaries.[50]

The seeds of the end of Queen Anne's Town's all-too-brief heyday had already been planted, even as prosperity seemed a foregone conclusion. On the surface, all seemed well. In 1753, the General Assembly reconfirmed the warehousing and inspection status of the town, as well as that of the Anne Arundel station across the river at Taylor's Landing. The status was again confirmed by an act of the Assembly in 1763, in which it was ordered that the inspectors were to be paid an annual salary of 3,200 pounds of tobacco.[51] But now, as with other river towns in the Chesapeake tidewater, Mother Nature and the unwitting hand of man had already begun to collaborate on the slow but certain demise of Queen Anne's Town as a seaport. Land clearance for tobacco farming had dramatically increased the siltation rate of the Patuxent. Those who were dependent upon the upper river and its tributaries for navigation were finding it increasingly difficult to ply its waters. The long reach above the town, which had been cleared for water carriage by the act of 1733 and the supplementary act of 1736, was rapidly closing up. There were also political pressures to be considered. In April 1761, twenty-seven inhabitants submitted a petition to Governor Horatio Sharpe and the General Assembly requesting the repeal of the act of 1736. In the petitioners' succinct protest, it was claimed, "far from proving any advantage to Snowden and Company, for whose convenience it was passed, or to any inhabitants living on the river," the act had caused "a manifest injury" to many since construction of standing structures such as mills along the reach had been expressly forbidden. The scheme had simply been impracticable in the first place, as proven by the continued difficulties encountered in keeping the upriver open. The petition was read on April 21 before the Upper House, which ordered that notice of it be given to Richard Snowden for comment. Given the wealth and political clout of the Snowdens, it was not surprising that no further action was taken. The prohibitions established by the act remained in effect, and the diminishing capacity of the river to permit access to the town became evident to all.[52]

Not until 1770 would the next effort be undertaken to keep the river above Queen Anne's Town open to navigation, though this time it was not for the benefit of the Patuxent Iron Works. In May, it was briefly reported in the *Maryland Gazette* that work had been started to widen the channel specifically for the advantage of upriver inhabitants who traded with the town.[53] The effort was to produce only a short-lived reprieve. The grand experiment had, in fact, already failed, as barge traffic repeatedly ground to a halt. There would be no further efforts to keep the waterway above Queen Anne's open to water traffic. Snowden's river was simply no longer navigable. The boycott of British goods in the days leading to the rupture with England did not help matters in the least. Even though one of the largest merchant trading houses in the colony, Wallace, Davidson, and Johnson, opened a store in town, with Revolution heavy in the air, the town's decline had already been preordained.

The merchants and citizens of tiny Queen Anne's Town, like most of Prince George's County, were not immune to the growing discontent over the actions of the British government in the days following the close of the Seven Years War. The series of legislative endeavors of Parliament, such as the Revenue Act of 1764, the Stamp Act of 1765, the Declaratory Act of 1766, and the Townsend Act of 1767, had been met with many forms of protest, ranging from boycott to riot with varying degrees of success. By 1770, a nonimportation agreement among the merchant community in Prince George's County in response to the Townsend Act was strongly enforced. On April 12, when the *Maryland Gazette* reported that several ships from Great Britain were expected at any time in the Patuxent River with European goods, the inhabitants of the county "thought it necessary to meet in order to appoint proper committees" to support the nonimportation association. Accordingly, committees were designated to support the association for each major trading center in the county. Mordecai Jacob, William Wootton, Richard Duckett, Jr., Robert Tyler, James Mullikin, and Edward Hall were appointed for Queen Anne's Town.[54]

With conflict looming on the horizon, there seemed to be precious little to celebrate. But on April 18, news reached Queen Anne's that John Wilkes, a leader of the opposition in Parliament who had championed the American cause and been imprisoned for his trouble, had been ordered released, and there was widespread jubilation. On April 19, the *Maryland Gazette* reported on just how the town's citizens received the good news.

Yesterday being the day Mr. Wilkes was to be released from ministerial vengeance, great rejoicing was had on that occasion at Queen Anne, in said [Prince George's] County at the house of Mr. Jeremiah Crabb. The first table at dinner was decorated by forty-five ladies, who dined upon forty-five dishes: After them dined forty-five gentlemen, who after dinner drank forty-five glasses of wine, when the following loyal and patriotic toasts among others went round. The King—The Queen—The Prince of Wales and Royal Family—The Freeholders of Middlesex—John Wilkes, Esq;—Serjeant Glynn—The author of the last Junius—Sir George Saville—Lord Chatham—Lord Camden—Prosperity to Maryland—The Governor of Maryland—The Pennsylvania Farmer—The author of Considerations—The minority in the Case of Mr. Wilke's expulsion—The Glorious Ninety-two of Boston—Mr. Otis—Mr. Cushing—Col. Barre—Gen. Howard—Mr. Burke—Mr. Beckford—All friends to America—May Mr. Wilkes persevere in his patriotism—May English and American liberty never want a Wilkes, a Junius, and a Dickinson to patronize and defend them—The supporters of the Bill of Rights—May his Majesty ever make the interest and happiness of his subjects his first care—May the friends of liberty always have the management of public affairs—May all national animosity subside—May the subjects in every part of his Majesties dominions be united—May the succession to the British throne ever remain in the House of Hanover—May the Revenue-Acts be repealed on constitutional principles—May venality and corruption never exist in the British Senate, &c. &c. &c.[55]

There is no record regarding the condition of the celebrants after at least thirty-three individual toasts of wine were drunk by each, but there can be no doubting that mirth was universal—at least until the hangovers set in!

Within a month, it would be learned that Parliament had repealed the Townsend Revenue
Act but had maintained a symbolic tax on tea. For America, the repeal wasn't enough. The
tax on tea had to go. On June 9, the people of Prince George's County met, as in hundreds of
other jurisdictions throughout English America, and declared their determination not to import any goods from Britain. Revolution was guaranteed.[56]

The war years were, on the whole, kind to Queen Anne's Town. Travelers en route to business in Annapolis or Upper Marlborough still passed through, often stopping for food and
lodging. In 1774 Samuel Nichols and Thomas Rose were granted licenses to open yet two
more ordinaries in town. On September 1 of the same year, George Washington, en route
from the Potomac River port of Georgetown to attend the First Continental Congress meeting in Philadelphia, stopped briefly for breakfast before riding on to his next rendezvous
with destiny.[57] For the most part, the town appears only occasionally in the records of the
Revolution. But some of its inhabitants would be active in the achievement of American independence.

At a meeting of the Maryland Convention held in Annapolis between December 8 and 12,
1774, it was recommended that all gentlemen, freeholders, and other freemen between the
ages of sixteen and fifty organize themselves into companies of militia throughout the colony. Each volunteer was to be provided with a firelock, powder, and lead and was to hold
himself ready to act in the event of military emergencies. It was recommended that each
county, including Prince George's, raise the funds required for the purchase of arms and
munitions for the use of its own local militia. Prince George's was expected to raise ten
companies and £833. Two of the companies were to come from Queen Anne's Town and
the immediate neighborhood.[58] The town would contribute its share of men and money and
at least one noteworthy military leader.

Thomas Lancaster Lansdale was born November 10, 1748, into a family of wealth and
prominence. The Lansdale clan owned over a thousand acres of property ranging from
Calvert County to Collington Hundred in Prince George's. Married to Cornelia Van Horn
of Lothian, Anne Arundel County, Thomas Lansdale fathered two sons and three daughters. The site at which he elected to establish his plantation and raise his family was on a
scenic bluff overlooking the Patuxent River on the southern perimeter of Queen Anne's
Town, quite likely on the site of the lands of Thomas Lancaster. The Lansdale home was
built sometime prior to the Revolution, a simple one-and-a-half-story frame dwelling,
twenty-eight feet square, with a gambrel Jerkinhead hip roof in front and an interior brick
chimney.[59]

In 1774, Lansdale joined a group called the Baltimore Independent Cadets. On June 1,
1776, as the war began to heat up, he was appointed first lieutenant of a Baltimore company
under the command of Captain John Eager Howard, in the second battalion of the "Flying
Camp," which was composed of militia units from Pennsylvania, Delaware, and Maryland.
He participated in numerous engagements, including the Battles of Long Island, Harlem
Heights, and White Plains, as well as in the spirited defense of Fort Washington on the Hud-
son River, where he was taken prisoner at the surrender of the fort on November 16, 1776.
After being released in a prisoner exchange, he was promoted on December 10 to the rank of

captain in the Fourth Maryland Regiment of the Continental Army. On May 22, 1779, he was elevated to the rank of major in the Third Maryland Regiment and participated in most of the major northern campaigns of the war thereafter.[60]

Serving under General Washington was both a privilege and a task for Lansdale. In January 1783, after an inspection of his officers and men and their campsite by the commander in chief, the major received a scathing letter. "Sir," the general began, "I was hurt yesterday at the appearance of the detachment under your command." The general reprimanded Lansdale thoroughly for the disheveled appearance of his men and for the garbage strewn about the encampment. "I observed with concern that none of your officers had espontoons, that some were without side arms and those that had, some were remiss . . . as not to know they were to salute with them." The critique having been presented, he then demanded an immediate improvement. "It is my desire that you should inform the officers I shall expect to see a very great alteration in appearance of the men before the next inspection."[61]

The major did his duty. On February 7, after another review, Washington informed him: "Sir, it gave me . . . pleasure to observe . . . the very great alteration for the better in the appearance of the Maryland detachment."[62]

But Lansdale and the war were far from the snug village of Queen Anne's. In September 1777, the town would have its first and only chance to briefly witness the enemy firsthand, fortunately not under battlefield conditions. The foe in question, unhappily, was a group of fellow countrymen who had chosen to remain loyal to England, and as a consequence they were being sent to the town under guard of the county militia. From Queen Anne's, they were to proceed to Frederick, where they were to be incarcerated for the duration.[63]

As America baked in the furnace of revolution, life in and about Queen Anne's Town was physically unaffected, though the town's overseas trade had been severely injured by the war, almost from the very outset. At the end of 1775, as a result of the boycott and hostilities, debts in town owed to Wallace, Davidson, and Johnson totaled £3,114.12, and the prospects for improvement during the ensuing conflict were grim. Somehow, day-to-day existence continued. An increasing number of ordinaries in town provided travelers with food and lodging and attested to the strategic importance of the site on the overland road system. Not until the conclusion of major hostilities after the victory at Yorktown would a semblance of true normalcy return.[64] In September 1782, horse racing was finally resumed at Queen Anne's. A granary and tanyard, the first new major additions to the town in years, were erected soon afterwards.[65]

The signing of the Treaty of Paris, formally ending the war and ensuring independence, was greeted with joy by all of the inhabitants of the Patuxent Valley as elsewhere in the tidewater. Major Lansdale returned to his estate on the edge of town. He became a charter member of the Society of the Cincinnati (a patriotic organization of commissioned officers), formed a business in town with fellow townsmen Walter Claggett and Charles Hodges, and proceeded to expand his land holdings in a fit of optimism shared by the entire nation. Hopes for the rebirth of trade and a continuation of the town's growth, which had been truncated by the war, were understandably high. But it was not likely to be easy. By 1784, Queen Anne's ranked last among the Patuxent inspection warehouses in terms of the amount of tobacco shipped from the port. Although the postwar incarnation of WD&J, now known as Wallace, Davidson, and Muir (WD&M), reopened operations in the town with the firm of Tyler and Duckett serving as its agents, competition from downriver ports was fierce. Between 1785 and 1787, the port of Nottingham shipped 525,351 pounds of tobacco, more than any other location on the river, while Queen Anne's was able to ship only 310,563 pounds for the same period. Moreover, while shipping at Queen Anne's was primarily limited to the London trade, Nottingham was receiving ships not only from London but from Glasgow and other ports as well.[66]

Despite the postwar depression and the increasing out-migrations of planters prompted by the depletion of the soil, many of the tobacco towns along the Patuxent watershed, including Queen Anne's, endured. The river, of course, continued its relentless silting, but shippers adapted and began to rely on smaller, shallow-draft watercraft to move their products. In October 1790, the firm of John Petty and Company joined the small band of shippers already ensconced in the town, and the trade balance began to tip in the town's favor. Between 1793 and 1801, 11,952 hogsheads of tobacco were shipped from the inspection warehouse as opposed to only 9,375 shipped from Nottingham and 6,968 from Upper Marlborough. By March 1796, the population growth in the town was substantial enough to warrant the establishment of a post office.[67] The temporary supremacy was to be short lived, as nature and the city of Baltimore conspired to divest Queen Anne's of its commerce, the first by continuing the crippling degradation of navigational access and the second by usurping the bulk of all tidewater Maryland trade.

Throughout the decline, the usually placid but silting Patuxent waged its relentless and subtle war of erosion against the bridge. In early December 1796, an order was passed by the county court instructing Major Thomas Lansdale and Henderson Magruder, under bond, to supervise and maintain for a period of five years a smaller bridge over nearby Brooke Branch. The following year, with the two main bridges over the Patuxent at Queen Anne's Town having again fallen into disrepair, Colmar Bond, at the insistence of many local citizens, constructed a new one apparently without governmental involvement. But no provision had been made for maintenance and the new structure eventually required attention. Nearly nine years would pass before the state would address the problem.[68]

Like the sand in an hourglass, the silt continued to settle, and access to the upper Patuxent and the port of Queen Anne's Town was being squeezed off even to many shallow-draft vessel types. The peril, of course, did not go unnoticed, particularly by those most affected. Many leading citizens of Prince George's were again growing alarmed over the potential disastrous impact upon trade. Finally, on June 10, 1799, a number of prominent county residents concerned about the town's well-being, including Thomas Lansdale, Thomas Duckett, Samuel Hepburn, David Crauford, John Read Magruder, Samuel Tyler, Jr., Charles Claggett, John Hodges, and others, petitioned the state legislature for permission to act. Under the recent passage of a law authorizing the raising of "a sum of money to clear out the creeks leading to and from Upper Marlboro and Queen Anne in Prince Georges County," the petitioners proposed that a lottery be authorized for the purpose of raising $3,000 to clear the waterways.[69]

It is uncertain if actual efforts were launched at that time to counter the effects of siltation, but the impact of nature's slow but steady depredation was unrelenting. By 1800, only six lots in Queen Anne's appear on the Prince George's County tax lists, although between 1775 and 1800, at least twenty-three inhabitants in the town were mentioned by name in the pages of the *Maryland Gazette,* and there were undoubtedly many more who were not.[70]

The town's trade and actual physical size were without question on an irrevocable decline, though among the population that remained, a number of prominent Marylanders were still in residence. Major Lansdale continued to occupy his large estate overlooking the village, and in 1802, he supervised the addition of a north wing to his house, designed in the

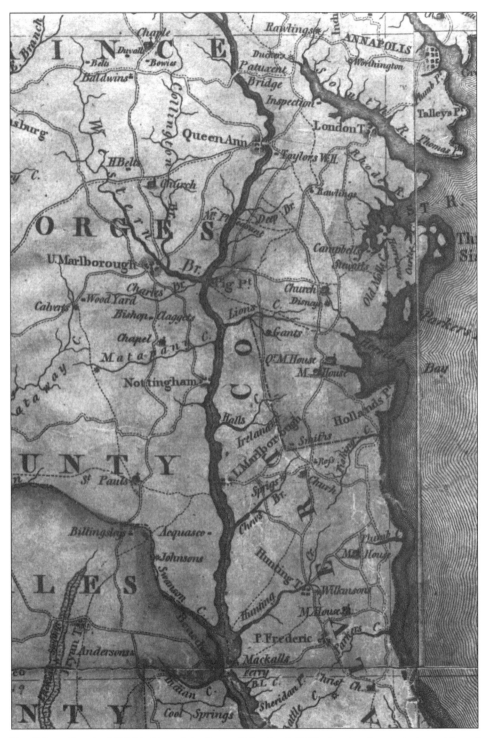

Detail from Dennis Griffith's *Map of the State of Maryland,* 1794, showing the strategic position of Queen Anne's Town, the southernmost bridge crossing on the Patuxent River. Courtesy Library of Congress, Washington, D.C.

new Federal style becoming popular throughout the region. The new addition was a two-story affair with an attic, a gabled roof, and an elegant new main entrance and foyer. A second fireplace was added with a cultivated mantelpiece over it. In keeping with the then-contemporary style, fragile interior moldings and ornaments, delicate and in low relief, were added. The addition was stylish and altogether befitting a family of wealth and status. Sadly, Lansdale would not live long enough to enjoy it, for on January 19, 1803, he passed away.[71]

Another notable resident was Richard J. Duckett, who was to play a significant role in the field of professional medicine in the state. In 1798, the General Assembly enacted legislation establishing and incorporating a surgical facility and a society of medical professionals. The avowed purpose of the act was to promote medical and surgical knowledge throughout Maryland, which "may in the future prevent the citizens thereof from risking their lives in the hands of ignorant practitioners or pretenders of the healing art." A board of medical review, the first in state history, was established, consisting of seven members from the western shore and five from the Eastern Shore. The board's mission was to grant licenses to those who could prove their qualifications to practice medicine and surgery in the state. Approval of practitioners was granted if the applicant passed a standardized state examination or presented a diploma or proof of graduation from a "respectable" college. Five of the boardmembers from the western shore were from Prince George's County and included the honorable Richard J. Duckett of Queen Anne's Town.[72]

By 1800, having fallen on hard times, the town was definitely less than a luxurious place to visit. That year, chapter 48 of the Acts of Assembly prohibited swine from running at large in Queen Anne's, suggesting that the rural nature of the surrounding environment was closing in upon the town at an accelerated rate. Even the ordinaries were in decline, and travelers passing through complained about the meager services provided them. Occasionally, there were a few independent efforts to improve the situation. In March 1804, Solomon Sparrow, a tavern keeper in town, advertised in the *Maryland Gazette* that because of many criticisms by stage passengers, he was going to begin serving breakfast to travelers at his tavern, an amenity which, since the days of George Washington's brief visit, had seemingly been dropped from the protocol of most town innkeepers.[73]

The same year that Sparrow improved his offerings, the Queen Anne's Bridge was again swept away by floodwaters. Colmore Duvall, who was contracted to repair or replace the bridge, apparently refused to work until funds were actually forthcoming to pay for the new construction. The state soon ordered Anne Arundel and Prince George's Counties to each pay Duvall $150 towards the repairs. The work was completed in 1805.[74]

By 1807, the river at Queen Anne's Town was navigable only by flat-bottomed boats. The abundant waterborne commerce enjoyed more than three decades earlier had all but died, although some light traffic continued for at least the next fifteen years. The town was still an important crossroads and as such continued to hang on. The maintenance of overland access was now imperative for its survival. At a May 16, 1808, meeting of the Prince George's Levy Court, several new roads were authorized for construction in the county. One of these started at Lansdale Branch, led from the much-used public road that connected Queen Anne's with Upper Marlborough, and ran along the Patuxent until it intersected with another road near Joseph W. Claggett's plantation. This road then continued to Oyster Shell Landing (later known as Claggett's Landing). The county supervisors of roads, who were in charge of actual roadbuilding, were to be paid ten shillings a day for every day they were on the roads with the construction crews.[75]

❖

The War of 1812, the arrival of the Chesapeake Flotilla, and the institution of a British blockade on the Patuxent in the summer of 1814 were destined to impose a lasting imprint on practically every town and landing in the river valley, including Queen Anne's Town. In June and July 1814, as the flotilla fought desperately for its survival, British raids on many sites along the waterway and its tributaries had tossed a blanket of panic over the entire watershed. In late June, enemy barges pressed as high as Hall's Creek in Calvert County, coming perilously close to the Prince George's county seat in Upper Marlboro. The court records were removed to Mount Lubentia, eight miles away. The move was not without cost, and the county was unable to pay for the effort. Thus, many outstanding debts owed the county were called in. On July 25, Truman Tyler, register of wills, and John Magruder, clerk of the court, ordered William Wells, the inspector at the Queen Anne's tobacco warehouse and one of those in arrears to the county, to pay up.[76]

By this time, the flotilla was at Nottingham, hopelessly blockaded by the superior enemy naval force downriver. The little American fleet consisted of thirteen armed barges, a row galley, a lookout boat, an ordnance schooner, and the flagship sloop *Scorpion.* The Navy Department began casting about for a means of escape in the event of an enemy thrust up the Patuxent. Secretary Jones soon fell upon a bold scheme: if Barney could get his fleet as far upriver as Queen Anne's Town, it just might be possible to haul the boats ashore, dismantle them, and convey them by horse-drawn carriage over the road to the South River, where they might be reassembled and redeployed. But it was now common knowledge that the river had been silted up and direct fleet access to the town was questionable.

On July 27, Barney dispatched his son, Major William B. Barney, commander of *Scorpion,* on a reconnaissance mission. He was to sound out the depth of water between Nottingham and Queen Anne's Town and then scout out the road from the latter to the South River to determine if such a feat were possible. Major Barney returned four days later and reported. He had not bothered to sound the depth between Nottingham and Pig Point, which was already well known. From Pig Point to Scotchman's Hole, four miles further north, there was sufficient water for the flagship *Scorpion* to traverse, but above that she could not proceed without being lightened. Even then, she might make only another mile as the depth was no more than five feet at best. The river itself varied in width, but above Pig Point to within a mile of Queen Anne's Town, it was quite narrow, in some places not exceeding eighty to one hundred yards. Moreover, the channel meandered from side to side. From a mile below Queen Anne's to the town bridge, "it is quite narrow and very winding, but no where wider than to admit more than one barge to row at a time." The shores at both the town and South River were firm and rose gently from the water. The eight-mile road from the town to South River, which traversed six to eight hills of gradual rises and descents, was generally good but required considerable repair at some points if the fleet was to be transported across it. Between Queen Anne's and South River, the route was also obstructed by twelve to fifteen gates with large gate posts that would have to be contended with. There were also two or three elbows in the road where trees would have to be cut to allow passage. There were only two very small marshy places. At several places along the way, the road passed between two banks; these would require a little cutting back in order to pass.[77] On the whole, though the young officer never stated it, the project actually seemed feasible.

Barney was cautiously optimistic in his August 1 report to Secretary of the Navy William Jones about the possibilities, but the project, if undertaken, would definitely not be easy. He determined that the whole fleet of barges and the row galley, which together weighed only

155 tons, might be moved. He calculated that he would need three horses to move every ton of shipping. Thus, 465 horses would be necessary for the barges alone, not to mention 64 wagons and 56 pairs of dray wheels to move the guns and stores. He did not include calculations for the heavier vessels such as *Scorpion* or the hired ordnance schooner *Islet*. Nor was there any mention of attempting to save the thirteen schooners of the merchant fleet that had sought protection in the river under the shield of the U.S. Navy. The whole move, he estimated, might be carried out in a day. However, the commodore was confident that unless the enemy was furnished with land troops, "I am led to believe we have little to apprehend at present."[78]

But the enemy did have land troops fresh from the Napoleonic Wars in Europe. On August 18, the British Army of invasion arrived at Benedict and the following morning began debarking from the largest hostile fleet to ever enter Maryland waters. Barney immediately reported the landing to the secretary of the navy in Washington. On August 20, Secretary Jones ordered the commodore to sail the flotilla to Queen Anne's Town, and in the event of an enemy advance against it, "to destroy the whole effectually" and to retire with his men to oppose the enemy's progress. By August 22, the flotilla had retreated as far north as possible and had come to anchor in a line above the bend of Pig Point, stymied in the rush to Queen Anne's by the shoals of the waterway above Mount Pleasant Landing. Only two second-class, fifty-foot-long barges, which drew less than twenty-one inches of water, were able to make it to the little town. Then, as ordered, Barney disembarked with approximately 400 of his flotillamen and joined the American Army assembling for the defense of Washington, leaving Lieutenant Solomon Frazier in command of 103 men to destroy the fleet. Shortly before 11:00 A.M., as Admiral Sir George Cockburn and a strong British barge force rounded the bend at Pig Point and the British Army marched into the environs of Upper Marlborough, the American fleet was "in quick succession blown to atoms." The invaders, of course, went on to defeat the American Army at the Battle of Bladensburg and to capture and destroy much of the city of Washington, D.C.[79]

Soon after the enemy had satiated himself and commenced the retrograde march back to his ships, stragglers and deserters from the British Army began to plunder individual homesteads along the way. At Upper Marlborough, Dr. William Beanes and former Governor Robert Bowie organized an effort to capture the looters. Six were readily apprehended and sent to Queen Anne's Town for temporary security. Unfortunately, one of the prisoners escaped and informed General Ross of the seizures. Ross immediately dispatched a troop of mounted soldiers to go back to Upper Marlborough and arrest Beanes. Thanks to the efforts of Francis Scott Key and John S. Skinner, of course, Dr. Beanes was eventually released, and a National Anthem was born. There is no record to show what became of the British deserters sent to Queen Anne's Town.[80]

Soon after the departure of the enemy, the flotilla wrecks became the subject of indiscriminate looting by local inhabitants. The government quickly contracted with a local salvor named John Weems of Richards, Maryland, to raise the fleet and to salvage the government property from it. Establishing a base of operations just below Mount Pleasant Landing, Weems salvaged twenty-two of thirty-two cannon, along with quantities of munitions, ships' anchors, and other items, which were all sent to Baltimore. The salvage mission proved far more difficult than had been anticipated, and only two vessels were recovered.[81]

In November, two of Barney's midshipmen and twenty-five seamen "went with pleasure to the Patuxent . . . and there saved from the bottom of the river all the guns, gun carriages, cambooses, anchors, cables, shot, &c. belonging to their late flotilla" which had been sunk. At Queen Anne's, the sailors managed to drag onto the shoreline one of the two barges that had reached the town, but they found it had been stove in by an explosion in the second, which lay nearby, and could not be salvaged. Goods recovered from the two barges were carried down the river to the schooner *Asp,* anchored off Mount Calvert, for transport to Baltimore. Lighterage was carried out by Christopher Lambert. On April 27, 1815, Secretary Jones ordered the salvaged goods sold at auction in Baltimore.[82]

Queen Anne's Town had been spared, but the two hulks—detritus of a war that had brought total ruination to the Patuxent Valley—would remain for the next century, first as visible reminders and later as simple curiosities of a conflict called by some America's Second War of Independence.

The quiet, mundane life of the little river town resumed its normal cadence as soon as the war was over. In May 1815, the county government arranged for Basil Duckett to make repairs to the abutments of the Queen Anne's Bridge, the cost of which was not to exceed $25. In 1818, Cephas W. Benson and John Clayton were granted licenses to operate retail liquor stores in town. And the following year, Isabella Nicholson applied for a license to operate a pool table in the town's first and only billiard parlor.[83]

As a postwar depression and its incumbent changes began to sweep the state, Queen Anne's Town, still an important crossroads village, took on added importance owing to the political influence of some of its leading citizens, who were active in the Republican Party. In 1820, when the party began the process to recommend a presidential elector and to choose candidates to stand for the Maryland House of Delegates and a U.S. Congressional seat, a committee from Queen Anne's Town was chosen to meet with a committee from Upper Marlborough to confer on the party's selections. On June 10, Republican leaders assembled for the first time in Queen Anne's in two separate meetings, the first of which was convened to appoint a committee to recommend a candidate for Congress. William Kilty was elected chairman and Robert W. Bowie (son of former Governor Robert Bowie) secretary. The committee endorsed Joseph Kent for Congress. The second meeting was held to select a presidential elector and a candidate for the House of Delegates. Walter W. Bowie served as chairman of the meeting and Edmund Duvall as secretary. Walter Bowie was endorsed for presidential elector, while Colonel Joseph Cross, Dr. Richard T. Hall, Thomas C. Lyles, and Julius Forrest were selected as the party candidates for the state House of Delegates.[84]

Two years later, on June 11, 1822, the Republican candidates for the House of Delegates were again selected at a convention held in Queen Anne's Town. Beall Duvall was called to the chair, and Dr. James Harper was selected as secretary. Dr. Benedict I. Semmes, Henry Culver, William Wootton, and Benjamin H. Marshall were chosen to be Republican candidates for the House of Delegates. All were subsequently elected.[85]

By the onset of the second decade of the nineteenth century, freight-hauling on the river as far north as Queen Anne's Town was possible only for a few small lighters and flats which serviced the tobacco inspection station. Yet, the traffic was substantial enough to warrant the General Assembly to pass an act on January 22, 1821, authorizing the purchase of land and the building of a wharf on the town's waterfront at a cost of $500 to accommodate the trade. But the struggle to keep the waterway open even to lighter traffic was an unending battle. On March 8, 1826, five years after construction of the wharf, the legislature was obliged to authorize yet another lottery to clear out both the Western Branch to Upper Marlborough and the reach of the main river leading to Queen Anne's.[86]

The tobacco industry had seen better days, and the state began to consider disposing of its tobacco inspection warehouses. In 1845, the tobacco inspection warehouse at Queen

Anne's was among the first to be sold off. Area planters no longer found it necessary to bring their tobacco to town for shipment. This, of course, meant that fewer people needed the town's services.[87]

Fortunately, other industries had finally begun to appear along the Patuxent watershed, the most prominent of which was logging. Sawmills opened in increasing numbers, and the need to regulate the lumber business followed suit. By an act of the Assembly in 1845, the governor was authorized to appoint lumber inspectors throughout the state. In Prince George's County, inspectors along the Patuxent were designated for Queen Anne's Town, Claggetts's Landing, Green Landing, and Mount Calvert, suggesting that the business along the upper waterway was substantial.[88] Even so, Queen Anne's Town as an urban commercial center was already near death.

By the start of the Civil War, only eleven buildings were in the town, ten of which were situated on the main street. Of these, three were stores. One was managed by James Davis and doubled as a post office. The other two stores were run by the Harwood and Evans families. Many years before, in 1823, the old Lansdale estate was sold by the colonel's widow to William Turner Wootton. Soon afterwards, Wootton sold it to Joseph E. Cowman, a planter and justice of the peace, who bequeathed it to his daughter Henrietta. Henrietta married a well-to-do physician named Archibald George in 1854, and the couple took up residence in the old house. In 1860, the Georges added a third section to the manse and probably moved the gambrel roof section southward to accommodate a new and loftier central section. The three-story-tall center was completed in the popular Victorian style of the day, with a large bay on the first floor and a lattice-work balcony on the second. The gable, porch, and eave trim was as ornate as the period demanded, and the two new heavy interior chimneys were also decoratively attired.[89] The house, by now known as Hazelwood, had become an elegant, albeit eclectic, hybrid of three eras, replete with the architectural embroidery of each tradition—Colonial, Federal, and Victorian.

By this time, a new bridge was needed across the Patuxent at Queen Anne's Town to keep the old road open from Upper Marlboro to South River and Annapolis. On June 21, 1861, the General Assembly passed an act authorizing the county commissioners of Prince George's and Anne Arundel Counties to levy an amount not to exceed $1000 to erect what was to become the sixth Queen Anne's bridge.[90] Although the bridge itself was apparently built, it would appear that the connectors linking it to the road on the Anne Arundel County side, a low flood plain subject to frequent inundations, were either inadequate or in need of replacement. Not until 1865 and the end of the Civil War would the state government be prepared to address the problem. Finally, the legislature appointed Richard Wootton of Queen Anne's and D. McCullough Brogden of Anne Arundel County as commissioners to oversee the construction of a causeway "connecting the bridge over the Patuxent River near the village of Queen Anne in Prince George's County to the main or firm land in Anne Arundel County opposite the said bridge."[91]

The end of the Civil War brought with it few changes to the diminutive village. The population of the town had diminished to such an extent that a post office could no longer be justified. The U.S. Post Office, which had been located at the corner of Queen Anne's Bridge Road and Queen Anne's Road and managed in its latter days by the Hardesty family, was moved to nearby Mitchellville.[92] Over the next dozen years, the hamlet saw little improvement. A small bypass on the main road leading to the bridge was built sometime before

1878, and several new buildings appeared. A few newcomers, including Dr. Joseph Duvall, J. D. Bowling, and Jonathan P. Hopkins, took up residence, but little else changed—that is, until 1879, when a highly educated man of mixed race, William Watkins, appeared on the scene.[93]

In many ways, William Lane Watkins was a pioneer. The son of a white man and a free light-skinned black woman, he was born in Baltimore on November 26, 1852, while his parents were en route from Maryland to New Bedford, Massachusetts. It is uncertain why they were traveling north, but one might assume it had something to do with their interracial marriage, as this would have been totally unacceptable in antebellum Maryland. The couple brought with them a maid and enough money to settle down and start a new life, passing all the while as a white family. According to the Watkins family history, young William, who was light skinned himself, had been taught to read and write by his father, and about 1872, accepted as a white man, he entered the Boston University Medical School, from which he graduated with a full medical degree. Soon after graduation, his mixed-blood origins were discovered, and he found it impossible to practice in Massachusetts. It was a stunning blow. For a short time he managed to make ends meet with a job hanging advertising posters in public places. But for a man with ambition and education, the pasting of broadsides on fence posts and barn sidings wasn't enough.[94]

In search of better employment, William Watkins migrated to Baltimore where he found a job in the U.S. Customs office. He was obviously a man of intelligence and learning and could not long go unnoticed, despite his mixed racial background. He was soon befriended by Jim Parker, a trustee of a new school for "colored" children only recently erected in Prince George's County in 1875, near the little village of Queen Anne's Town. Parker liked Watkins and invited him to Prince George's County. It was an offer the young doctor accepted with alacrity.

Upon arrival in the county, Watkins began searching for a room and soon found lodging near Queen Anne's Town with the family of Wilson and Jane Ellen Turner. Rent was $10 a month, a higher-than-average amount in those days, but the place did have its attractions, chiefly Wilson's winsome daughter. Within a short time, Wilson Turner's intellectual boarder had become a son-in-law and had begun to look for a home for his new wife and himself. About 1878–1879, Dr. Watkins decided to move into Queen Anne's Town proper, then an all-white community. It would not be easy, his son Harry Brooke Watkins later recalled, and he was repeatedly warned: "No niggers were going to live on Queen Anne Bridge Road." But Watkins proved as courageous as he was ambitious. "My father said he wasn't a 'nigger' and he *would* live here if he chose to."[95] And so he did, and many others followed in his steps.

William Lane Watkins, despite his mixed race, soon became active in Maryland Republican Party politics and was a fixture on the local political scene. His son Harry boasted that his father would eventually serve as the first nonwhite man to hold the post of recording clerk in the office of the Clerk of the Circuit Court in Upper Marlboro. He became a respected member of the Republican State Central Committee and remained a member until his death. When local politicians intended to run for a public office such as the county sheriff, Watkins became a part of the political equation. Even in Queen Anne's Town, where his acceptance had at first been difficult, his stature was considerable and his word carried enormous weight.

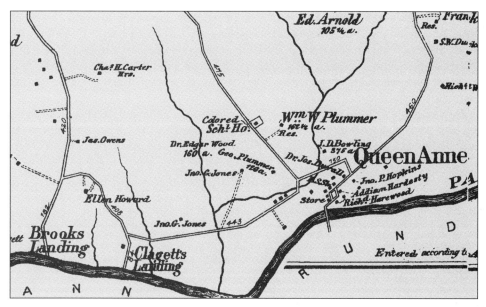

Queen Anne's Town and a portion of the Queen Anne District, Prince George's County, Maryland, 1878, from G. M. Hopkins, *Atlas of Fifteen Miles Around Washington Including Prince George County Maryland* (Philadelphia, 1878). Courtesy Library of Congress, Washington, D.C.

Watkins looked to the good of the community at large through his government and political service and later as a social worker. He soon bestowed the fruits of his own education upon his mother's race as well. Through the influence of Jim Parker, a trustee of the modest little school recently founded adjacent to Queen Anne's, Watkins gave up his post in government and took up teaching. The school was near a Methodist Episcopal church called Mt. Nebo, a small edifice which had been built by and for the local black community only two years after completion of the school itself. For some time, Parker had been looking for a teacher for the new Mt. Nebo School without success. No whites were willing to take on a teaching post in a black school in post–Civil War Maryland, a decidedly segregated state. Moreover, the school year for Negro children was shorter than that for whites, because black youngsters, considered an integral part of the farm labor pool, were expected to work in the fields during the spring planting and fall harvest, even while white children were still in classes. Thus a black teacher's income was noticeably reduced. The teaching job itself paid the princely sum of $17 a month. Yet, William Lane Watkins jumped at the chance. He soon became the first teacher and principal of Mt. Nebo School and, after a quarter century at the helm, was one of its most esteemed trustees.

In 1885, the first of many children was born in the Watkins household. There would be a total of five: three girls—Maude, Blanche, and Susie—and two boys—Wilson and Harry Brooke. Watkins's wife found employment with the post office in nearby Mitchellville, while William, to subsidize his teaching income, attempted to open a medical practice for the local population. In the polarized society of southern Maryland, he found it all but impossible. White patients went to white doctors, and black patients, if they had money, preferred white doctors as well. "They would come to him," his son later recalled, "only if they wanted credit." Slowly, his personal financial condition improved, thanks to shrewd real estate transactions. He purchased land and a house in the town from Jonathan P. Hopkins, and he bought farmland in the surrounding areas, which he later sold for a substantial profit.

Sometime between 1878 and the turn of the century, according to family tradition, Watkins suggested that the ancient name of Queen Anne's Town be changed. There was already a Queen Anne's on the Eastern Shore, he declared, and the nation no longer paid allegiance to the British monarchy. He opined that the hamlet should be renamed Hardesty in honor of his close neighbor and friend Addison "Ed" Hardesty—wheelwright and former postmaster and the town's oldest citizen.

Ever so gradually, old Queen Anne's Town, or Hardesty, as it was soon officially called on maps and tax records, became an integrated community, with whites and blacks living side by side in a land that was otherwise totally divided by skin color.

In 1889, the year of the famous Johnstown disaster, it was said the Patuxent River surged over its banks in one of the worst floods in memory. Many old-timers had seen the river inundate the bridge and completely flood the lowlands on the Anne Arundel side, but not since 1750 had it crept up the steep ravine walls and hillsides on the Prince George's side to cover the streets of the town itself. For some, the flood was more than a disaster. It caused a lifelong trauma. Harry Brooke Watkins recalled that the father of one of his sisters-in-law, a preacher who also owned a nearby sawmill, lost everything, including twenty mules. "It washed 'em away," he recollected, "and he lost his speech when they told him everything he owned had been lost. Thirty years afterwards, when my oldest brother and I were on a train with him, he suddenly says to my brother: 'Hello Wilson.' We were stunned. It was a miracle. After thirty years, his speech had come back."[96]

One of the major casualties of the flood was the Queen Anne's bridge. Efforts were soon underway to build a replacement. About 1890 the New York bridge engineering firm of Dean and Westbrook was contracted to design and construct a new span across the Patuxent at Hardesty, the seventh and last. Unlike the earlier wooden structures, the new bridge was to be a unique example of a durable "Pratt through truss bridge constructed of wrought iron Phoenix sections" with two spans. Each span featured four vertical members in compression braced by four diagonal members in tension. The lower chord members of the bridge were keyed into and supported by a concrete abutment on the Prince George's County side, but merely bedded in earth on the opposite shore. In later years, a macadam roadbed would be laid across the length of the bridge, and in 1931 the abutment would be rebuilt of poured concrete. It was said by some old-timers in town that the bridge was completed in 1891–1892, and that two beautiful bronze plaques were mounted on its eastern and western extremities by the county commissioners of both counties to commemorate the event.[97]

The sparkling new bridge soon became a community meeting ground, where the village folk would go to fish, gamble, or just pass the time. At the turn of the century, the river was wider and cleaner than it is today and filled with an endless variety of fish, including herring, pike, catfish, perch, and bass. For the local angler or net fisherman, there usually was, mercifully, a noticeable and welcome dearth of game wardens in the countryside. "I used to catch boatloads of fish down there," recalled Harry Brooke Watkins in a March 1998 interview shortly before his one-hundredth birthday. But the most exciting and daunting fish for Harry had been the occasional sturgeon, which are now extinct on the waterway. "When these things [were] coming up the river you could hear the water splashing." Sturgeon, never an abundant fish in the Patuxent, were not simply caught in the waterway at Hardesty—they had to be trapped. Fish traps, or weirs, twenty-five to thirty feet in length were built by the villagers by driving white oak stakes or slats into the bottom, lacing them with birch strapping, and attaching nets, each of which had a single inverted entry hole. The traps were not unlike the staked gill nets employed to harvest shad on the open waters of the Bay and larger rivers, though on some waterways, such as the York River, sturgeon were harvested in float seines or gill nets that floated with the tide. At Hardesty, the traps were frequently erected at the bridge itself, where everyone could watch the proceedings. Young Harry was not at all delighted by the prospect of netting sturgeon or the work of cleaning them. "Their scales," he stated with a grimace, "were like oyster shells, and double hard. You would have to build a fire and scald them out." As for cutting them up, he would have nothing to do with a fish so big that a small boy like him could put his head inside. But his uncle, John W. Turner, was an expert at trapping sturgeon and marketing the meat. "Oh, he would cut 'em up and carry 'em around and sell the steaks to everyone in town."[98]

Many of the locals preferred net fishing from the bridge and shores. To facilitate them, Mrs. Addison Hardesty made nets with quarter-inch mesh and sold them to piscatorial addicts. Occasionally, terrapins would be snagged, and some who liked turtle steaks would stalk the shell-backed creatures in the mud flats along the river's shores.[99]

In rare instances, Mother Nature did her part to provide the townsfolk with fish on a scale that was often unexpected and sometimes unwelcome. In the winter, when the river froze, there were special ways to fish. "We used to go down there and watch the pike fish, which we called 'suckers.' It wasn't much to catch 'em, though. When you see one under the ice, you take and you hit that ice hard. That jar would stun or kill 'em. Then you cut a hole in the ice [with] an ax and get 'em out."[100]

Occasionally, the waters of the river would recede rapidly, an event usually caused by a combination of extremely low tide and continuously high northwest wind. Many fish would be left stranded in holes and ditches of the swampy lands along the river banks. The fish trapped in the ponds and depressions in the mud flats were called "hinds" (derived from "left behind"). At first, the pickings of live "hinds" was easy and fun. But they soon died by the thousands from oxygen starvation, and their putrefying corpses became noxious. "All down in the swamp there was so many in them big holes," recalled Harry, "when they'd died they smelled so bad. Oh, the odor would run you away."[101]

The bridge also served as a strategic point between rival political and social jurisdictions. This proved convenient for the illegal gambling enjoyed by some of the townsfolk and visitors from the countryside. Craps was the preferred game. When the games were held on the bridge, escape from the local constabulary, when necessary, was easy. In later days, when Prince George's County constable Gus Davis showed up, the crapshooters would just walk over to the Anne Arundel County side, beyond his jurisdiction, and continue the game. When lawmen from both counties coordinated their raids, the gamblers would jump off the bridge into the river and make good their escape by swimming. "They couldn't catch 'em," remembered Harry with a wry smile. "No way."[102]

"Game chickens," or illicit cockfighting, was another popular form of gambling in Hardesty. The fights were usually held in a barn down by the river, and they drew spectators and bettors from all over Prince George's County. Wagers were made and after the bloody fights were over and the crowds had departed, the unfortunate contenders usually graced the dinner table of the William Lane Watkins household.[103]

As the years rolled by, Hardesty gradually changed its racial composition. The Watkins and Turner families proliferated, and the few remaining white residents died out or moved away. The racial equality hoped for as a byproduct of the Civil War failed to materialize, and stringent racial segregation became the social order of the times. The economic and social status of most blacks in white-controlled Prince George's County at the turn of the century was often abysmal, the achievements of men such as William Watkins notwithstanding. As a consequence, perhaps one of the most legendary but representative accounts of racial injustice in the county occurred in Hardesty on a harvest morning on the Hazelwood estate. The event was destined to become one of the more durable folk tales of the town.

Hazelwood was owned at the time by Dr. Edwin P. Gibbs, a white man who, it was rumored about town, had purchased the property with his brother Bradford L. Gibbs in 1899 for only $75 but had assumed a large mortgage. The property had, in fact, been acquired as part of a program called "homesteading" initiated by Governor Lloyd Lowndes (1896–1900) to encourage settlement of sparsely populated areas of the state. (The estate had once been owned by Dr. Archibald George. When he died in 1873, ownership passed to his son John. In 1891, John sold it, but the purchaser is unknown.) Gibbs's demeanor towards his black neighbors was anything but cordial. The overall estate, having expanded to include property on both sides of the river, was far larger than the doctor could work himself. Thus, as was common practice, he frequently employed young townspeople as farmhands. Occasionally he rented out the land to the farmers from the community, charging a specific cash fee and also taking a share of the crop. It was an ancient game and the property owner held all the cards, especially in Maryland when the owner was white and the tenants were black.[104]

On a hot morning in the summer of 1906, William Watkins's brother-in-law, Thomas H. Turner, a well-liked farmer who had leased some land on the Hazelwood estate to raise fodder, was haying in the fields he had been renting from Dr. Gibbs. His relationship with Gibbs had apparently been rocky for some time, and the doctor sought to have him vacate the land he rented. Turner resorted to a lawsuit to protect his contractual rights. The courts had found in his favor and possession of the land, at least for the term of the rental agreement, was decided against Gibbs "on the grounds that sufficient legal notice had not been given to Turner to vacate." Animosity between the two men exploded soon after the court's ruling. About 8:00 A.M. on July 3, Gibbs was informed by Clarence Hebron, a field hand from the town who worked for him, that Turner was haying in his rented field "without the doctor's knowledge." The master of Hazelwood resolved to end the dispute then and there. Marching into the field with a gun, the story goes, he engaged the black farmer, who was armed only with a pitchfork, in a heated argument. Then, in a fit of rage, Gibbs drew his pistol and shot forty-year-old Tom Turner to death.[105] Gibbs immediately surrendered himself to authorities in Upper Marlboro and was placed in the county jail.

Word of the murder spread instantly throughout Hardesty and the countryside. "It was nothing to kill a black man in Prince George's County back then," recalled Turner's nephew, Harry Brooke Watkins, especially if the murder was committed by a white landlord. The death of Tom Turner was to prove no exception, despite the black community's outrage. On the night of October 12, 1906, Edwin P. Gibbs was acquitted of all charges by the circuit court and freed. But Tom Turner, it was said, was well known and held in high esteem by a number of whites as well as blacks, including a wealthy and well-known physician from Upper Marlboro named Sasscer. "He was a white man," Harry recollected, "but he knew my uncle, and said he was a good man." With the law turning a blind eye, the tale goes, Sasscer attempted to assemble a party to lynch Gibbs, but the retribution never came because no other white men would join him. To kill a black man, a tenant farmer, was one thing. But to lynch a white man for the killing, and a doctor at that, was another! As a result of the murder, from that day forth, the Watkins family refused to set foot on the Hazelwood estate.[106] Edwin P. Gibbs would die of natural causes on December 13, 1915, mourned only by his wife Emma and his two daughters, thoroughly hated by the community around him.[107]

Despite such tragedies, the people of Hardesty were a simple, hardworking, churchgoing lot, always ready for a dance or a community picnic. The children attended classes at the Mt. Nebo School, and many of the families worshipped in the tiny Mt. Nebo A.M.E. Church next door. The church had been founded on June 8, 1877, two years after the erection of the school, under the pastorate of the Reverend N. Clay. Mt. Nebo Church was initially part of a circuit which included the Galilee A.M.E. Church in Anne Arundel County. It was built by its first trustees, Richard Wood, George Larkins, and Wilson Turner, on an acre of land, originally part of a tract called Poplar Ridge that had been purchased for the sum of $134.55 from William Plummer. The first structure was a simple affair, a one-story frame gable-roofed building built in several sections and popularly referred to as the "little old wooden church on the hill." It had no running water, electricity, or indoor plumbing. A pot-bellied stove provided heat in the winter. The Sunday offerings usually averaged about $4.00 from members who were able to offer only nickels and dimes from their meager earnings. But it was a House of God and a place where the black residents of Hardesty, mostly farmers, could commune in friendship and joy, regardless of the inequities of the outside world.[108]

On January 16, 1919, the Eighteenth Amendment to the Constitution of the United States was ratified. Better known as the Prohibition Amendment, it banned the sale of alcoholic beverages across the land and brought about the heyday of peephole speakeasies, bathtub gin, colorful bootleggers, and gangsterism. Hardesty was no exception to the rule when it came to an affinity for illegal booze. Even before Prohibition, Walter Nicholson's store in town had carried a large stock of liquor in barrels. The store was a place where the town rowdies frequently gathered, and mothers forbade their children to go there on weekends. Its strategic location in town on the main road from Annapolis to Upper Marlboro made it a much-visited spot for locals as well as for those from west Anne Arundel County who were eager to quench their thirst. Nicholson, by this time the sole white man in town and the father of an even dozen children, was a clever fellow, and it was said that he would "put the good stuff out until the Anne Arundel County boys would get drunk" and then quietly switch (at the same price) to an inferior brand which the locals called "kill-me-quick."[109]

Rivalries erupted between groups of men from the two county jurisdictions, and these sometimes turned into brawls. Eventually, gangs formed, and for a short time, Hardesty had its own home-grown brand that forcefully contended with interlopers from Anne Arundel. The village soon became known as a tough, hard-knuckled community—a reputation that was out of proportion to its actual size or condition. "I can remember I'd be scared to death when I was small," recalled Harry Watkins. "They'd gather at the liquor store. I could hear 'em up there at Nicholson's acussing and fighting and going on. Every Saturday night there'd be a fight there. And I'd be scared to death on those nights, because there'd always be a brawl between Anne Arundel and Prince George's County. And when they'd get drunk, then the Prince George's County boys would get on 'em and run 'em out. But my mother and father set tight on me and kept me out of it. After I grew up, I was glad that they did."[110]

When Prohibition came into force, it was said that illegal booze could be found in at least four major locales in west central Prince George's County—Hardesty, Mitchellville, Upper Marlboro, and Croom—but at only one principal location in central Anne Arundel—in Annapolis. Hardesty, old-timers remembered, soon boasted at least three speakeasies. The main outlet in town was managed by James King; he rented it out to a succession of tenants, said to be mostly Jews, who operated the illicit trade. At least four speakeasy operators, named Roane, Cohen, Wolf, and Cosden, managed the town watering holes.[111] But alcohol could be had in other ways as well. One was legally through a doctor's prescription. For the first time in his life, Dr. William Lane Watkins had a steady clientele, both black and white.[112]

Life went on, mixed with both tragedy and happiness. There were the wider events of the world, such as the arrival of the Spanish influenza that would claim hundreds of thousands of lives across the nation, including two of Harry Watkins's sisters. And there were smaller but still disastrous events to be absorbed, such as the day Walter Nicholson's store burned down. From time to time, new faces appeared in town, such as the Shorter family and later the Savoys, who came to settle.[113]

Of course, there were hard times. On December 31, 1929, William Lane Watkins died at seventy-seven years of age, a Republican Party stalwart and activist from 1887 until his death and the most respected and influential citizen of the village.[114] His loss was perhaps an omen of even sadder days to come. Only two months earlier, on October 24, 1929, known ever after as Black Thursday, the stock market crashed, ushering in the Great Depression and some of the meanest years ever experienced by the citizens of little Hardesty. Share-croppers and field hands living in the village could no longer find employment as many of the local farmers for whom they had worked lost their lands through foreclosures. Harry Watkins tried everything to make ends meet, from sharecropping to shoveling sawdust in a sawmill. He cut corn and hay from sunup to sundown for fifty cents a day, even as President Hoover was stating that a dollar a day was enough for any man. But the trough of depression was deep. Franklin Roosevelt's New Deal meant little to the tiny black village on the upper Patuxent. The community suffered degeneration beyond anything experienced in the past.[115]

Hazelwood, which had been in the hands of Emma Gibbs for twenty-one years since the death of her husband, had fallen into limbo. On March 3, 1936, Mrs. Gibbs died and the es-tate passed to her daughters and their spouses, Anna Maud Gibbs and her husband Chester Hyler and Mabelle Gibbs and her husband Andrew J. Lilburn, who divided the family hold-ings. Deeds filed in both Prince George's and Anne Arundel Counties stated the property was 195 acres on the east and south side of the Marlboro and Queen Anne's Roads and 60 acres in Anne Arundel County. The property had originally been conveyed in a partition of Edwin and Bradford L. Gibbs's land in both counties. On October 11, 1937, the estate was purchased by J. Paul Smith, an employee of the Internal Revenue Service, and his wife Maria, who utilized the land in the same way as all who had preceded them had.[116]

By 1940, Hardesty's population numbered only fifty-six people. Electricity had arrived only a few years earlier, and the telephone was still a rarity. Most people took their water from private wells. On February 12, J. Paul Smith gave right-of-way for power-line poles to be erected across his property by the Consolidated Gas Electric Light and Power Company of Baltimore.[117] Despite the arrival of the amenities of modern life, the long twilight of Hardesty was drawing to a close.

About 1960 the Queen Anne's Bridge collapsed under the weight of an overloaded truck. There were bold words about the importance of the bridge in some quarters. "Queen Anne Bridge," said the Maryland Historical Trust, "exemplifies the historical and industrial heri-tage of the County, and is a distinctive visual feature of the Patuxent River." But words were

Top: Dorothy Smith and Barbara Smith Fluharty, daughters of J. P. Smith and the last surviving private residents of the historic Lansdale House in Queen Anne's Town. The house has been termed by architectural historians as one of the most unique treasures of Maryland.

Bottom: The dilapidated Lansdale smokehouse, in need of urgent restoration, was once an important part of one of the more substantial estates in colonial Prince George's County.

The ruins of the last Queen Anne's Bridge, the antecedents of which provided a key link on one of the principal highways of colonial Maryland.

cheap, and unlike in earlier days, this time no one was prepared to actually pay for its salvation, or that of the once vital road that had assured the town's place in the sun. New roads and highways had long since supplanted the once strategic crossing at the bridge. When the State of Maryland decided not to repair the venerable old landmark, the last reason for Hardesty's existence as an independent town was gone, for it no longer held even a crossroads status. The "great road" (as Maryland's Governor Hart had called it in 1719) that once passed through the town was no longer relevant. And as if to provide a final parting insult, the beautiful bridge plaques commemorating the creation of the span itself were pried loose and carried away by vandals. The hamlet would survive, but just barely.[118]

On September 20, 1976, the Maryland National Capital Park and Planning Commission purchased 148 acres of land comprising the remains of J. Paul Smith's Hazelwood estate in Prince George's County for $306,508 as a major addition to Patuxent River Park. Smith was awarded a ten-year lease agreement at $1 per year with options to extend his occupancy in five-year terms until his death. Within a few years, the eclectic but elegant mansion that had been inhabited by heroes and murderers alike had fallen into almost irrevocable ruin. Hardesty, Maryland, once the most landlocked seaport in the state, was dead, its memory recalled by only a very few antiquarians.[119]

It was a cold, gray day on April 28, 1998, when Harry Brooke Watkins turned one hundred, a time for reflection as he told his children, grandchildren, and great-grandchildren about the good old days of Queen Anne's Town. He told them about the cannonballs he found in the garden, the Indian arrowheads he dug up, and the old white smoking pipes he found in profusion. He told them about the ruins across the street (the site of a tavern where George Washington himself ate breakfast) and about the two old shipwrecks down in the river where he swam when he was a boy. He told of the murder of Uncle Tom Turner, the brawling nights of the Prohibition era, his fishing days, and the trying times of the Great Depression. He would tell it all again and again and again, to the utter delight of everyone.

"I used to go out," he'd begin, "down yonder to this old bridge here . . ."

7 PORT TOBACCO

"The Court House movers are still on the rampage"

January 24, 1861. The public demonstration of military equestrian prowess presented in front of the Charles County Court House was unlike any ever witnessed there before or since. A majestic steed named Grey Medock, who belonged to Captain Samuel Cox, one of the most influential men in the county, went through paces that both amazed and inspired the local inhabitants. Then, while recently organized units of the Charles County Mounted Volunteers and Smallwood Rifles looked on in awe, the horse was put through its martial paces. As smartly dressed soldiers and troopers (who only days before had been next-door neighbors and local farmhands) mingled about the town square with their young ladies, there was an unquestionable mood of excitement and patriotic fervor not experienced here in Port Tobacco since the American Revolution. Everyone knew that a great national conflict was in the offing, and Charles County's finest were ready to do their part. The demonstration was perhaps as symbolic as it was festive, and the allegiance of those present was evident.

Only a month earlier, South Carolina had seceded from the Union. Then, on January 9, in the first act of outright rebellion, secessionists in Charleston Harbor, South Carolina, fired on the U.S. steamer *Star of the West* when it attempted to relieve Fort Sumter. The following day, Forts Jackson and St. Philip, Louisiana, had been seized by Louisiana Confederates. In Florida, Fort Barrancas and the Pensacola Navy Yard had been occupied by Florida and Alabama militia. The United States, it seemed, was rushing toward civil war. Charles County and the citizens of Port Tobacco, who were overwhelmingly sympathetic to the secessionist cause, had already picked sides. Maryland had yet to make its move, though everyone knew it would be for the South. Or so the revelers in the town square of Port Tobacco believed. In anticipation of their state's embracing the rebel cause, both the Mounted Volunteers and Smallwood Rifles had only recently pledged their allegiance to Maryland over the Union and were ready to march off at a moment's notice to join the Southern cause.

As they watched Grey Medoc lie down, stand up, and follow on command, the spectators were filled with military ardor. The crowd jumped and cheered as the horse showed no sign of fright, even when pistols were fired over his head. Then, as Grey Medock followed his rider, a chap named Emmons, through the courthouse doors, up the steps to the second floor, and "into one of the jury rooms . . . and down again," they cheered again.

Thus the American Civil War cast its long shadow across one of Maryland's oldest and most historic ports, the celebrated town of Port Tobacco. And so marked the beginning of its end.

❖

The Port Tobacco River is a beguiling stream in Charles County, a short but broad tributary of the Potomac River barely three and a half miles long and a fraction over a mile wide at its entrance. Some would call it little more than a creek. Its sides, once covered by verdant forests of red maple and slender poles of pine, are shouldered by gently sloping hills that form a valley as welcoming and snug as any in the tidewater. Its name is taken from the Potopaco Indians who occupied its banks at the moment of the first furtive contact with European civilization. The appellation was duly noted by Captain John Smith, who passed this way in 1608. Some said the name meant "land between the hills" or "the jutting of water inland," while others suggested it meant "tobacco leaves." Variants of the name were many, including Potu-bago, Portafaco, Portobag, Portobaco, Potobacke, and Potobac. Whatever the meaning, with its clear freshwater springs, its forests teeming with plentiful game and amply supplied with fruits and berries, and its deep waters bountifully filled with bluefish, clams, oysters, and crabs, the valley of the Port Tobacco was indeed an inviting place.[1]

When Captain Smith visited the region, he counted only twenty warriors at Potopaco. The tribe may have numbered between 100 and 120 men, women, and children in Smith's time. It was of the same Algonquian racial and linguistic stock as the mighty Powhatan Confederacy, to which it paid an allegiance of necessity to better protect it from Siouan and Susquehannock enemies to the west and north. Although the confederacy held general sway from coastal Virginia to the waters of the Great Falls of the Potomac and inland to the Piedmont, it was at best a feeble homage that the Potopacos paid to the great emperor to the south. From archaeological evidence, it is suggested that the tribe was comfortable in its element at the time of European contact and quite capable of constructing nets and weirs for fishing, domesticating corn to provide a nutritious cornmeal-based diet, and possibly even drying tobacco in special buildings erected for the purpose. All of that was soon to change.

The white man soon appeared more frequently on the river. In 1632 Captain Henry Fleet was the first European to call upon the village of Portobanos (undoubtedly the same site referred to by Smith nearly a quarter-century earlier) in his bark *Warwick* to secure provisions and information on the beaver trade. The natives, realizing that they might benefit from the trade in pelts, promised they would "take pains this winter in the killing of beavers and [would] preserve the furs" for him. Fleet departed with an agreement that the Potopacos would have at least five thousand furs for him by the following year.[2]

In 1639, the redoubtable Jesuit frontier pioneer and gatherer of souls, Father Andrew White, baptized the young "Queen of the Portobacco Indians" at St. Mary's City, and at the same time as many as 130 of her subjects at the Indian town of "Portobacco" also "received the faith with baptism." To assist in his missionary work while he lived among the Indians in their barrel-shaped longhouses, Father White composed a catechism and compiled a grammar and dictionary in the native language; these eventually found their way to the Vatican Archives in Rome. Joined in 1640 by Father Roger Rigbee, he deemed Portobacco a perfect base for his proselytizing work throughout the colony. In 1642 he reported to his superiors in Rome that the town "is situated on the river Pamac (the inhabitants call it Pamake) almost in the center of the Indians, and so more convenient for excursions in all directions, we have determined to make it our residence." With the village tucked away amidst the secluded folds of the little river valley, it was well protected from the depredations of the warring Susquehannocks and Senecas to the north.[3] The Jesuit mission lasted but two years, for by 1644, the Reformists seized power in England and the Maryland colony was immediately assailed by the Parliamentarian privateersman Captain Richard Ingle. The Jesuit headquarters at Portobacco was captured and Father White and another priest, Father Thomas Copley, were carried to England in chains, never to return.[4]

Ironically, within the next decade, the native peoples whom the Jesuits had come to save began to suffer directly from the encroachment of the civilization that had embraced them. Speaking for her people, the queen of the Portobacco Indians protested that "the stocks of cattle and hogs of the English yearly destroy their corn fields by which means they must of necessity come to famine, they not knowing the way and means to fence in their corn fields as the English do."[5] The peaceful natives maintained an amicable relationship with their white neighbors even though it was once charged that the Indians were planning "some mischief to the inhabitants of the province." Thomas Gerrard was sent by the government in St. Mary's to discover their plans and either disarm them or "secure the persons of any of the Indians," presumably to hold them hostage, but the allegation proved false. In 1663 the queen again appeared before Governor Charles Calvert and his council in St. Mary's to plead in behalf of her people. Without recognition of any native title, she complained, the lands surrounding the Port Tobacco River had been doled out at a heady rate from the Lord Proprietor himself directly to colonists. In the eleven-year period between 1649 and 1660, all of the lands around the river had been patented. Yet, the colonists were unsatisfied with their holdings and "do still take up land and seat themselves very high unto her Indians." Her tribe had "not only left their town standing by the water, but have removed themselves farther off, even to the utmost bounds of their land, leaving place to the English to seat on their ancient plantations by the river side." The governor, sympathetic to the natives' plight, ordered that all inhabitants cease and desist from taking up or settling upon any lands within at least three miles of any Portobacco village or settlement. Despite such edicts, within a decade the tribe had melted away entirely, presumably absorbed by the neighboring Piscataways. Within a quarter century, the last Native Americans in the entire valley of the Potomac had vanished.[6]

With the tentacles of white civilization snaking along the Potomac shores and into the hinterland, and the complex, crazy quilt of plats and patents proliferating, by 1650 much of the forest cover along the banks of Port Tobacco Creek was already stripped of its virgin timber. The fertile soil was turned over to the cultivation of tobacco for the marketplaces of Europe, an endeavor that quickly replaced the native subsistence-based economy of fishing, hunting, and hoe farming.[7]

Along Port Tobacco River, one of the earliest land patents had been taken up by Job Chandler, who with his brother-in-law, Simon Oversee, jointly held manorial rights to a vast but unnamed tract. Soon, a primitive little settlement called Chandler's Hope was established upon it. Though later altered to Chandler's Town (or Chandlee's Town), a name by which it would officially be known for decades, the settlement was locally referred to as Port Tobacco, a corruption of the native Potopaco. It wasn't much, but it was a start, and it was inextricably linked to the formation of Charles County. To understand the history and development of the town, it is necessary to first examine the origins and evolution of the county that it would serve for nearly two and a half centuries.[8]

Charles County may be said to possess two discrete periods of history: "old" Charles, embracing lands now largely occupied by modern Calvert and Prince George's Counties, and "new" Charles, erected on lands forming modern Charles County. In the winter of 1650, Robert Brooke of Whitechurch, Hampshire, England, a friend and loyal supporter of Lord Baltimore, arrived in Maryland accompanied by his wife Mary, ten children, and twenty-eight servants. He bore a commission from Lord Baltimore dated September 10, 1649, designating him as "commander" of a newly created county to be called Charles. As a member of the Council of Maryland, Brooke was one of the more formidable forces of his day and action to implement the formation of the new county was quickly initiated. Lands were surveyed and boundaries established. On November 2, 1650, old Charles County came into being. Brooke quickly moved, at his own expense, to bring settlers to Maryland to settle the land, and he commissioned his young son Baker as commander. But turmoil in Europe, the ascendancy of Oliver Cromwell in England, the subsequent loss of Lord Baltimore's authority over the colony, and the failure of the new county to meet the financial expectations of the governor and council soon resulted in the abolition of old Charles.[9]

In 1657 Maryland was restored to Lord Baltimore, and the influx of immigrants to his colony resumed. Many settlers began to occupy lands far distant from the St. Mary's courthouse, too far to permit many of the citizens to conduct business transactions in a timely fashion. On April 13, 1658, the governor's council finally addressed the problem by ordering the establishment of a new county to be carved from old Charles. Less than a month later, on May 10, Governor Josias Fendall proclaimed in the name of Cecil Calvert, Lord Baltimore, all of the lands in Maryland "bounded with West Wicomico River, up to the head thereof and South with Potomac River from the mouth of Wicomico up as high as any plantation under our government is now seated, and from thence with a right line drawn from such plantation as afores'd to the head of Wicomico River [to be erected] into a county" and to be named "in honor of our only son and heir apparent, Charles Calvert, Esquire."[10]

Small as it was, as the only settlement of note within the new county, Chandler's Town took on significant importance. Settlers in the county, who numbered approximately eight hundred souls in 1658, had nearly doubled to fifteen hundred by 1665. The county court, though not meeting in the settlement, was convened nearby. Court records for the period indicate that at least thirty or more households were clustered about this tiny outpost of civilization, and there were undoubtedly many more that were never mentioned. By 1668, the hamlet (for it could only by a stretch of the imagination be called a town) was one of only eleven sites designated as ports of entry in the entire colony. The ports were specifically "set aside for discharge & unlading of goods & mechandise out of ship, boat and other vessels."[11]

While the actual degree of prosperity and well-being of the denizens of Chandler's Town has been shaded by time, their spiritual needs were certainly not ignored. Two competing religions, Roman Catholic and Anglican, tended to the souls of the inhabitants. The first of these was centered at St. Thomas Manor on the east side of Port Tobacco River. The manor was administered by Jesuits who had been granted land there as early as 1649, only to have it seized (or "held in trust") during the Protestant Revolution and then returned to them in 1669.[12]

Sometime before 1683, Chandler's Town had also welcomed the erection of Christ Church, the Anglican house of worship established somewhat further up the creek, where the Reverend William Moore served as priest and rector. A third church is also referred to as lying somewhere at the head of the creek prior to 1684.[13] This may have been an Episcopal or Presbyterian church administered by the Reverend Francis Doughty, who had arrived in Massachusetts in 1637 and emigrated to Maryland two decades later. Doughty married the sister of Governor William Stone and is said to have gone around the country teaching and baptizing. He may have made his headquarters in the hamlet of Nanjemoy, not far from Port Tobacco.[14]

The precise location of early Chandler's Town has never been fully ascertained. Some have suggested that it was initially erected on the east bank of the Port Tobacco Creek at the head of the river and gradually migrated to the western bank owing to the invasive, erosive action of the water and other natural causes. Some substance is lent to this argument in that a graveyard, possibly related to old Christ Church, was visible as late at 1906 in a nearly inundated and eroding wetland west of the present town site.[15]

Life in seventeenth-century Chandler's Town was rigorous and almost totally dependent upon the tobacco commerce of the surrounding region. Yet, it had its benefits. The valley of the Port Tobacco was both beautiful and well endowed with nature's bounty. Its broad wa-

Detail from Augustine Herrman's manuscript draft map *Virginia and Maryland,* showing the site of the never-constructed Bristol Town in the vicinity later known as Chapel Point. Courtesy Library of Congress, Washington, D.C.

ters were buttressed by shores that gently sloped skyward, reaching a peak elevation of 120 feet at its Chapel Point entrance. The lands shouldering the tiny settlement were rich and productive, with soils ranging from loamy and clayish to swampy and sandy, the former being superbly suited for tobacco cultivation. The nearby forests continued to provide an abundance of wildlife, most of it gameworthy but some of it predatory. Indeed, bounties were occasionally set on wolves to successfully combat the loss of livestock.[16]

More importantly, the settlement's access to the wide and eminently navigable creek offered the pleasing prospect of profitability to be derived from serving as a transshipment point for the commerce of the entire county. If blessed with the privilege of serving as the official center for county government, it seemed that Chandler's Town could not fail to succeed. All that was needed was the establishment of a permanent seat for the county court. Pressure to that end was not at first overwhelming.

There is no record of where the first court of the newly erected county was held on May 25, 1658, but for the next two years, the record indicates, it was held at the home of Humpherie Atwikese. Thereafter, the court appears to have been somewhat mobile, convening at inns or private houses throughout the county. In 1671, court may have been convened in the settlement for the first time as 1,000 pounds of tobacco was paid to Edmund

Lindsey, a Chandler's Town innkeeper and planter, "for the trouble of his house for keeping court." The following year, county sheriff Benjamin Rozer received 450 pounds for permitting the court to meet in his house.[17]

In 1663 the Maryland Assembly ordered county commissioners of every county in the colony to build stocks and a pillory near each county courthouse and also a ducking stool at a convenient place. In addition, they were to provide irons suitable for burning brands onto malefactors who violated certain laws. The county sheriff was charged with administering the punishments and the specifics of the brands were set by the government. The letter H was to be seared into the flesh of a hog thief. Runaway slaves were branded with an R, murderers an M, and thieves a T. Counties that failed to comply with the direction were to be fined. The Charles County commissioners reacted swiftly, and although no site had been permanently set for a courthouse, the stocks and pillory were nevertheless ordered erected and a ducking stool was set up at Pope's Creek.[18]

In 1674 the Assembly finally passed an act requiring each county in Maryland to construct or provide for an appropriate courthouse and prison. Thus, in October, the Charles County commissioners directed that twenty thousand pounds of "good sound merchantable" tobacco "be raised in the said county by a public levy." The levy was to be used to purchase rights from John Allen to a one-acre tract called Moore's Lodge as well as a single dwelling placed upon it, located about four miles from the head of the river. As his part of the bargain, Allen was to build upon the property, to government specifications, both a courthouse and prison. Moreover, as part of the agreement, he was obliged to keep a "public ordinary or house of entertainment near unto the said court house & prison, for the convenient entertainment of his Lordship's Justice & all other persons." The precise location of Moore's Lodge is uncertain, although one authority suggested that it was probably situated at Clarke's Run on Zekiah Swamp. This site is approximately three miles south of modern La Plata and three miles east of Port Tobacco in the vicinity of a farm called Johnstown, near the site of the modern Charles County Fair Ground. Another historian has hazarded a guess that it was located on a branch flowing into Zekiah Swamp somewhere near modern Newtown.[19]

It was perhaps a bargain buy for the county, but for everyone else concerned, including the justices, the court would eventually prove to be far too remotely situated for convenience. There were other problems as well. Allen, by agreement, had been obligated to keep the courthouse, prison, and pillory in good repair, a task which he appears to have been disinclined to pursue with any ardor. In 1687 he sold the land and his obligations to Thomas Hussey. The new owner was soon crossing swords with the county commissioners over government regulated pricing of liquor. The commissioners ordered that the ordinary be handed over to another manager, Philip Lynes, and that Hussey turn over the court key and court lands to them. They also requested that the Provincial Court approve an order to finally lay out the lands for the public courthouse to the best advantage of the public and for the better accommodation of the court and that additional lands adjacent to the court lands be laid out as well.[20]

Angered by the commissioner's actions, Hussey retaliated by attempting to prohibit Lynes and his employees from supplying provisions for the courthouse.[21] Hussey was promptly arrested, and in April he was arraigned to answer charges of contempt. He was eventually cleared of all charges except for the harassment of Lynes, for which he was reprimanded with a slight fine. Although an additional two acres of property were later added to the court lands, it appears that they were not surveyed for nearly a decade. Finally, on September 16, 1697, surveyor Joseph Manning filed his report and a sketch of the tract.[22]

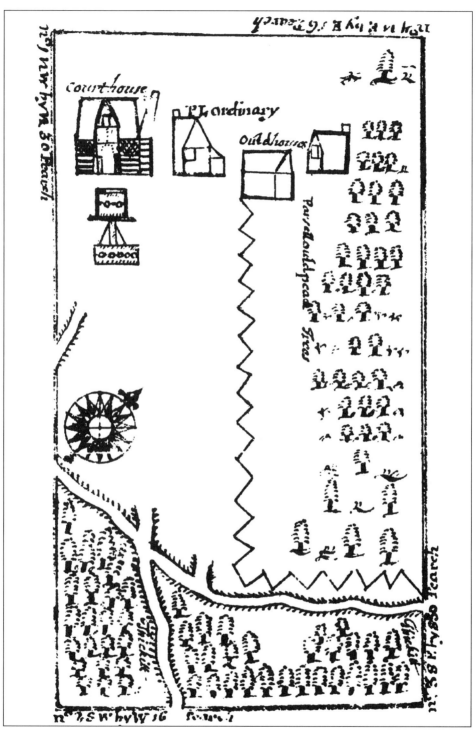

Surveyor's sketch of the Charles County Court lands in 1697. The courthouse was built on land then owned by Thomas Hussey. Charles County Court Records, courtesy Maryland Archives Hall of Records, Annapolis, Maryland.

❖

Even as the debate over the erection and management of the county court system simmered, the colony government was moving on another line that would lead to the permanent establishment of a number of new towns. On October 9, 1683, the sites for several new towns in the county were included in a list sent by the Lower House to Lord Baltimore. One of the proposed sites lay "In Port Tobacco Creek near the mouth." The revised wording for the site, to be formally erected by August 31, 1685, was "on the church land on the East side [of] Portobacco Creek near the mouth of the creek" at Chapel Point. Two dozen commissioners were selected to administer the formal erection of the town and to see to its laying out and the sale of town lots. The commissioners were less than dilatory: they did nothing at all![23] On April 21 the following year, little having been accomplished in the interim, another bill was proposed by a member of the Upper House "that a town be appointed at the head of Portobacco Creeke most commodious for the inhabitants of the forest in Charles County from whence comes yearly great quantities of tobacco." The proposed site near the river's mouth was abandoned, undoubtedly owing to objections by the Protestant General Assembly that the land belonged to Jesuits. The Lower House concurred the same day. Both houses voted that the new site was "necessary" and that it be included in "An Additional & Supplementary Act to the Act for Advancement of Trade." The selected site was now noted as "At the head of Potobacco Creek near the church there."[24]

The approach to the laying out of the new town on the Port Tobacco was anything but swift. Numerous excuses were offered up by the county commissioners, but the onus of blame was placed on the deputy surveyor of Charles County, Captain Randolph Brandt, who "was suspended before he could finish the same, much to the hinderance and prejudice of the inhabitants of the . . . county who were willing to build and promote so good a work for the advancement of trade in the county." Unwilling to accept any excuses, on March 5, 1684, the council ignored the commissioners' suspension and directed Brandt to "plot and finish the surveys of the several towns, ports and places of trade appointed" to the specifications outlined in the recent Act and to file his plans at St. Mary's City "with all convenient speed."[25]

The new towns program for Charles County barely sputtered along. Little, if any, work was completed on the sites, and the majority still had to be surveyed, the council warrant issued to Brandt notwithstanding. The deadline for construction of buildings on all lots taken up had come and gone, but few property owners had constructed anything at all. Finally, on October 3, 1685, Charles Calvert himself was obliged to issue a proclamation extending the deadline to December 31, 1686.[26]

In Charles County, the problem wasn't with construction but with the surveyor. For some undetermined reason, Captain Brandt failed to carry out his mission. Three days after the governor's proclamation, Robert Doyne, the high sheriff of Charles County, informed the council that some of the towns and ports appointed for development were "not fully finished" because the commissioners were of the opinion that because the new county deputy surveyor, Ninian Beall, lived in Calvert County beyond their jurisdiction, "they had no power to command his attendance there upon all occasions." Thus, the laying out of the towns in the county, "marking, loting and staking the same" had been effectually delayed, "and so was like still to continue unless some effectual care [be] taken to remedy the same." Irate over the obvious foot-dragging, the council ordered Beall to finish the job or face the consequences.[27]

The foundation for a permanent town was eventually laid, but unlike the primitive settlement at Chandler's Town, the new site immediately adjacent to it failed to take any substantial root, although it was provided with all of the official trappings of a port. At the September 1686 meeting of the governor and council, orders and instructions were given to Colonel Edward Pye, who had been appointed to superintend the transshipment of commodities brought into Chandler's Town, to register the arrival and departure of all ships that anchored before the town as well as the names of their masters. He was directed to inventory all goods and wares that were brought ashore and to provide certificates for all tobacco loaded aboard. He was duly authorized to clear all vessels for departure with the collector of the Potomac Naval District and to see that the various acts regarding trade were enforced.[28]

Old Chandler's Town was still little more than a few run-down dwellings. Though the county court continued to be held from time to time at the officially designated site, by 1704 the justices were finally meeting occasionally at the tiny hamlet on the Port Tobacco.[29] In April 1706, the town site designated by the 1683 act, having failed to develop, was given a second chance and submitted for reconfirmation as a port when the government considered an "An Act for the advancement of trade and erecting Ports & Towns in the Province of Maryland," in which it was written:

Be it enacted by the Queens most excellent Majesty by and with the advice and consent of her Majesty's Governor, Council and Assembly of this Province and the authority of the same that from and after the end of this present session of Assembly the towns, ports and places therein after mentioned shall be the ports and places where all ships and vessels trading into this province shall unlade and put on shoare all Negroes, wares, goods, merchandise and commodities whatsoever.[30]

The designated site was the place where the town had "formerly" been laid out, indicating that a plat had probably been produced already as directed by the 1683 act. On April 17, 1706, the act rededicating the site and declaring it as a port was read and approved by the council and the House of Delegates, and on April 19 it was signed into law by Governor John Seymour.[31]

The region was growing slowly but perceptibly. In 1696 Port Tobacco Parish, which had been partitioned from Durham Parish only four years earlier, could count on 250 taxable residents and an annual income of 10,320 pounds of tobacco. By 1712 the county population, including masters and taxable men, women, children, and slaves, numbered over 4,000. Although the county was still thinly peopled, the dynamics of civilization were dramatically changing what had only a few years before been a howling wilderness. By the mid-1720s it was generally acknowledged that since the official county courthouse, erected nearly four decades earlier, had fallen into such a state of decay, building a new one was imperative. Moreover, the distance of the existing court site from a landing and essential river transportation had proved increasingly inconvenient. In March 1725, the justices of Charles County themselves began to petition the Assembly "praying leave to purchase land and erect a court house at a certain town at the head of Port Tobacco Creek."[32] Chandler's Town, aside from the church, was little more than the shadow of a village, with little true substance to it. But it was still an official port and designated center for trade that could easily serve as the nucleus for county government.

Finally recognizing the need for the improvement of the county administration and justice system, the Assembly authorized in 1727 the abandonment of the old courthouse site and ordered the construction of a "Courthouse and prison on the East side of Port Tobacco Creek at a place called Chandler's Town." Three acres of land were to be purchased in the town; the site was to be laid out by a surveyor, and the court and prison were to be erected. On December 20 the survey work was completed at a cost of 2,000 pounds of tobacco. Contracts were let to John Hanson and Joshua Doyne for the construction of the courthouse, prison, stocks, and pillory for 122,000 pounds of tobacco. The courthouse was to be built to specifications filed by Colonel John Fendall.[33]

In 1729, realizing that the town site designated in the 1683 Act and redesignated in 1706 had failed to move forward, the Assembly reauthorized the site again. This time, the town site was specified to be sixty acres in extent and laid out where the courthouse was being built at Chandler's Town. The site was to be contiguous to that of the courthouse site, which was deemed "very convenient for a town, being near the center of the county, and commodious for trade . . . advantageous, as well to the inhabitants of the said county, as others trading or resorting thereto." Colonel John Fendall, Major Robert Hanson, John Courts, Samuel Hanson, Captain George Dent, Dr. Gustavus Brown, and Henry Holland Hawkins were appointed commissioners. They were to purchase the necessary land and have it surveyed and laid out "in the most convenient manner so as to adjoin to and encompass the lands belonging to Port-Tobacco Church, and the said court-house." One acre was to be devoted to a market place and the remaining land divided into one hundred equal lots, allowing for the usual streets, lanes, and alleys to be surveyed and staked out. As with all sites designated in the act, lots were to be numbered from 1 to 100. Out of the lots, the original owner of the land was to have the choice of any two he wished, provided he select them within fifteen days of the survey. The remainder were to be sold to any residents of the county, "provided such person or persons, shall not be allowed to take up more than one lot, during the first four months after laying out the same." Anyone who took up a lot, however, would be required to build a house no less than four hundred square feet in size exclusive of sheds and "regularly placed" upon it within eighteen months or lose the property. All houses were to be built fronting the edge of a street, lane, or alley. Upon completion of the survey, the surveyor was to turn over to the clerk of the county "a fair plat and certificate of the said town" which would then be entered into the county records. That an actual town plan was drawn up is suggested by the wording of the law, which stated that "nothing in this Act shall...prejudice any person or persons . . . who have comply'd with the requisites of the Act of Assembly, whereby part of the said land was actually survey'd and laid out into lots, and then call'd Chandler Town." In short order, the Assembly instructed that the town be renamed Charlestown, in honor of Charles Calvert.[34]

By April 26, 1731, when the first session was held within it, the county courthouse had been completed. As the county administrative center, where deeds were registered, wills were recorded, and justice was meted out in jail, at the whipping post, and beneath the gallows, it rapidly became the focal point of the region's judicial, political, and social life. Without question, it was the hub of commerce, the busiest port on the Potomac, and, small as it was, the only urban center of any importance in the county, the infant hamlets of nearby Nanjemoy and Newport notwithstanding. Situated in the heart of the colony's tobacco belt, the little village exported hogsheads of the golden leaf to England in exchange for manufactured goods and other commodities. On the creek near the town, on "Neal's land," a coastal protrusion commonly referred to as Warehouse Point was established as the official port of entry for the Potomac Naval District. Here, by the 1760s, more than a million pounds of tobacco (encased in at least a thousand hogsheads) and other export goods were annually inspected, weighed, and marked for shipment to Britain, the Netherlands, France, and Russia, while the necessities and luxuries of life were unloaded from incoming shipping and disbursed through Charlestown's commercial outlets.[35]

The rhythm of life focused on two primary activities: the spate of commerce involved in the annual shipments of tobacco and the regular sessions of the general court. These drew people from all over the county; they filled the town's inns and other available housing during court days and quenched their thirsts at town ordinaries operated by such entrepreneurs as Collin Mitchell.[36] There were, of course, weekly activities that revolved around the town's religious center, Christ Church (which, beginning in 1711, was served by the Reverend William McConchie), as well as recreational events, and on occasion, military related affairs.

War—especially the preparations for war—included regular military exercises and militia-related activities and provided a primary occupation and recreation for the men of the community. Indeed, service in the colony militia was considered a matter of public duty for most gentlemen, as a visible demonstration of both civic pride and social class. In 1740, Governor Samuel Ogle issued a call to arms to provide Maryland manpower for the British expedition against the great Spanish fortress city of Cartagena in South America. A recruiting officer replete with fife and drum arrived on the Port Tobacco to gather volunteers for the campaign. Although the record is generally silent on the role of the citizens of the county during the subsequent ill-fated expedition, a group of town volunteers and at least one officer, Captain William Chandler, are known to have participated. By 1748, the county militia counted 985 men, many of whom were citizens of Charlestown or Port Tobacco Parish.[37]

As the colony population slowly increased, better roads and transportation, both within Maryland and beyond, generated improved communications and a sense of closer kinship with other colonies throughout America. Local communication across the Potomac with neighboring Virginia was made possible by at least six ferry operations which served the Charles County shores, including one operated by George Dent, who boasted of having a marked road running directly from Charlestown to his ferry two miles above Thompson's Landing. The town, which by the 1740s included a handful of inns, a goldsmith's shop, a brewery, a kiln, and a sixty-foot-long two-story malthouse, was approximately a half-day's ride from the most popular crossing to Virginia, Laidler's Ferry. Travelers from Williamsburg and other points south would frequently stop for several days at Charlestown before continuing on their way to Annapolis, Philadelphia, or New England. Governor Horatio Sharpe, keenly aware of the need for better communication in the colony, sought to upgrade the rudimentary postal system. In 1764 he moved to establish "a route from Annapolis in Maryland to the several parts of that province where it might be proper to settle post offices," and specifically addressed opening a route from Upper Marlborough, the county seat of Prince George's County, to Charlestown, a distance of thirty miles.[38]

Improved communications and access brought growth, both physical and cultural, as well as wealth and consequence hitherto unknown in the county. Concern for public safety and health were evinced for the first time when town residents petitioned the General Assembly to pass a law to prohibit geese and swine from being raised within town limits and to prevent fires from being made in houses with wooden chimneys, specifically in those houses situated near storehouses and public buildings. In 1747, "An Act for amending the Staple of Tobacco, for preventing Frauds in his Majesty's Customs, and for the Limitation of Officers Fees" was passed into law by the General Assembly. This proved to be legislation that would directly benefit small urban centers such as Charlestown. Inspection stations were designated throughout the colony in each county. In Charles County, a total of six stations were established, one of which was "at the head of Port-Creek, on the Land of William Neale." Each government inspector at the station was to be paid £60 a year.[39]

As living standards inched upward, recreation and intellectual pursuits also improved. In October 1750, the *Maryland Gazette* advertised that Port Tobacco's first horse races would be held at the town, and all entries were to be registered with Henry Mitchell. In the summer of 1752, it was announced that the famous Company of Comedians, direct from Williamsburg, would perform at the major ports in the colony—Annapolis, Upper Marlborough, Piscataway, and Port Tobacco. The company was well known for its performances to colonial audiences and had included in its repertoire Shakespeare's *Richard III,* Dryden's *Spanish Fryer,* and Farquhar's *Sir Henry Wildair.* Although the presentation in Port Tobacco was not documented, it is likely that it duplicated that which was presented in Upper Marlborough and sponsored by the Ancient and Honorable Society of Free and Accepted Masons. The company first performed *The Beggar's Opera,* accompanied by instrumental music to each air "given by a set of private gentleman" and followed by a solo performance on the French horn. "A Mason's song by Mr. Wotaham" accompanied by a grand chorus followed. The performance was to be concluded with a farce called *The Lying Valet.*[40]

By 1753 the town's Anglican Christ Church was over seventy years old and had fallen into considerable disrepair. The parishioners, who had started fundraising and planning at least as early as 1751, erected a new edifice, "a very pretty church of free stone" and brick on the site of the original wooden structure.[41] The ability to provide musical accompaniment for services, however, was sorely lacking. The parishioners looked enviously at the Catholic chapel at nearby St. Thomas Manor on Chapel Point, which had an organ imported from Philadelphia and an organist who received an annual salary of £20. Thus, when Gustavus Brown, an immigrant from Scotland and a prominent member of the Christ Church congregation, offered to provide the church with an organ if Port Tobacco Parish would support an organist, a bill was passed by the colony's Protestant General Assembly empowering the justices of Charles County to levy a tax on the inhabitants of the town for the necessary funds. Church music was soon heard issuing forth from the new house of worship in Charlestown.[42]

Charlestown's growth was painfully slow, for fewer than an estimated seventy people actually lived in the little village. The domestic side of business was simple and straightforward. Manufacturing was very limited, and commerce was primarily devoted to service industries or production related to the necessities of the tobacco-based economy of the region. Tavern keepers such as John Gody provided food and refreshments to visitors. John Cranston sold staves for hogsheads to local tobacco farmers and merchant shippers. Factors and independent merchants such as Thomas Contee or Robert Mundell imported goods for sale from London and elsewhere, and they sent tobacco in return.[43]

Maritime business was regularly attended to, usually at the offices of the merchant factors of the big English trading houses that had established stores and residences in the town but occasionally in one of the village taverns. When Captain John True's ship *Nancy and Katy* of Glasgow was lost in 1759 on Smith Point at the mouth of the Potomac, the sale of the goods salvaged from the wreck for the benefit of the insurers was advertised in the *Maryland Gazette*. The wreck, along with its apparel and cargo, was to be sold by John Metcalf at John Duncastle's tavern in Port Tobacco, as the village was now generally called.[44]

Although most of the town residents were probably not epicurean, traditional fashions for the ladies were not ignored by village merchants. Benjamin Whitcomb, the town's staymaker, ensured that the distaff side was amply supplied with "stays, jumps, and sulteen stays" or with corsets already stiffened with whalebone. Somehow, the use of stays seemed to some a form of torture. In 1774, a young diarist in Virginia observed with disdain one such assemblage worn by a typical fashion-conscious woman of the tidewater: "Her stays are suited to come to the upper part of her shoulders, almost to her chin, and are swaithed around her as low as they possibly can be, allowing her hardly liberty to walk at all."[45]

Visitors to the town offered occasional tantalizing glimpses of Port Tobacco and its more "rustic" side. Philip Vickers Fithian, a teacher in the employ of the Carter family of Nomini Hall, Virginia, was passing through in April 1774 while en route to New Jersey, and he reported in his journal: "This is a small town of not more than twenty or thirty houses mostly of one story." On his return trip, he reported with disgust on his unpleasant stay one evening at an inn in the town, where throughout the night, he had for company in his room "Bugs in every part of my bed—& in the next room several noisy fellows playing at billiards." A disturbance brought about by drunkenness, however, was usually not condoned. According to another visitor, Nicholas Cresswell, there were perhaps a half dozen taverns or ordinaries in town, none of which were permitted to "suffer idle, loose or disorderly persons to tipple, game or commit other disorders or irregularities."[46]

Despite its somewhat unrefined appearance and diminutive size, by the third quarter of the eighteenth century, Port Tobacco had achieved a degree of importance and commerce that was eclipsed only by such ports as Annapolis, Oxford, Baltimore, and a handful of others. Yet, the little town's success was even then mutating, as the continued removal of forest cover, the clearing of land for tobacco cultivation, and the deep plowing in the surrounding countryside had altered the natural drainage of the region, producing enormous runoff, erosion, and silting up of the Port Tobacco River. No longer was the waterway deep enough to permit heavy-draft vessels direct access to the head of the creek. Loading and unloading of all but the lightest of shipping had to be carried out at Warehouse Point.[47] Increasingly, even without its own awareness, the town owed its survival to its role as a center for government rather than trade. Yet, the slowly changing environment failed to deter aggressive merchant houses from establishing themselves in a town whose prosperity was evident to all. Indeed, John Glassford and Company, the largest Scottish trading firm in the Chesapeake tidewater, had erected its Maryland headquarters in town, an example which other large firms, such as John Semple and Company, were quick to follow.[48]

Port Tobacco seemed comfortably confident of its role as Maryland's principal commercial entrepôt on the Potomac. In 1771, it would receive something of a shock from a scheme parented by Father George Hunter, a Jesuit priest ensconced at St. Thomas Manor. Hunter announced that he had been requested, "for the convenience of the inhabitants of Charles County," to draw up plans for yet another new town. The site, he tactfully proposed, would be named Edenburgh, in honor of the popular current governor of Maryland, Robert Eden. A survey was carried out, undoubtedly at private expense, and a plan of the proposed town was produced. The handsomely executed colored plat showed a town situated around a public square upon which sat a courthouse, with streets running to it and to the river. The town was to be located on St. Thomas Manor near the mouth of the Port Tobacco River. For the accommodation of trade and commerce, there was ample ground for wharves situated directly adjacent to waters deep enough to welcome vessels of the size that might call at any of the other towns on the river, such as Alexandria.[49] Approval of the concept did not hinge upon the potential siphoning off of Port Tobacco's commerce, which some historians suspected was the motivating factor, but whether or not Hunter might endanger continued Roman Catholic ownership of land in a now predominantly Protestant colony. It was a concern not to be scoffed at. The General Assembly ultimately refused the petition, but the rationale for its submission could not be denied.[50] Nearly half a century later, during demolition of the clerk's office near the center of the public square in Port Tobacco, Hunter's plan for "New Edinburgh," as it was later called, was rediscovered and erroneously believed to be a survey plat for the redevelopment of Port Tobacco itself. Though addressing the wrong town, the editor of the *Port Tobacco Times,* who was apparently familiar with the plat, correctly put his finger on the root cause for its instigation. "This shows," he wrote, "that the movement was seriously entertained in influential quarters, prompted, no doubt, by the rapid filling up of the creek and the fast growing destruction of the navigation at Port Tobacco. In my younger days I have heard many of our best men regret that the plan of removal did not succeed."[51]

Following the end of the French and Indian War, as colonial disenchantment with England and the policies of Parliament began to blossom, a local evolutionary change such as the erection of yet another new town was all but ignored. A military air was sweeping across southern Maryland, occupying the attentions of even the most civic minded of Port Tobacco's citizenry. As already noted, the passage by Parliament of the Stamp Act in 1765 and the subsequent levying of taxes on various trade goods, including tea, had led to virulent opposition in the form of boycotts of English imports. The residents of Port Tobacco, certainly not immune to the political turmoil brewing, began to cluster in groups to discuss and criticize Parliament's actions. Debate was hot as some of the region's leading merchants questioned their own willingness to undertake concerted efforts such as protests and boycotts while others vigorously demanded action.[52]

In 1768 nonimportation associations were formed throughout the American colonies to boycott British goods and to monitor and report violations of the boycott. These groups lent teeth to the protest. Although the boycott at first seemed to have the desired effect, the British government was not to be allayed in its efforts to assert its authority. Additional taxes were levied and were again met with unwavering opposition. By 1774, when the Boston Tea Party elicited strong measures from Britain in the form of a blockade of Boston Harbor, colonial indignation and anger reached fever pitch.

As throughout all of Maryland, many Charles County citizens reacted strongly to the so-called coercive acts. On June 14, 1774, a protest meeting was held at the courthouse in Port Tobacco and full agreement to support the boycott of English goods was reached. Seventeen deputies and a clerk, including among them many representatives from Port Tobacco Parish, were selected to attend a protest assembly in Annapolis. From this body was also appointed a Committee of Correspondence to receive and respond to all letters and to call emergency county meetings.[53]

One of the most significant early efforts of the Committee of Correspondence was to assemble a meeting at the courthouse in Port Tobacco on November 18 to vote for representatives to the Continental Congress. The meeting was chaired by Samuel Harrison, and although it was restricted to enfranchised voters, that is Protestant freemen whose net worth was £40 or more, the courthouse was crammed. The permanent Committee of Correspondence was formed of ninety of the most prominent men of the county, a veritable Who's Who of the leadership that would help guide Maryland and the emerging nation through the trying years of Revolution and the early years of independence, both on the battlefield and in the halls of state and national government. Among them were men destined for greatness: Thomas Stone of nearby Habre de Venture would become a signer of the Declaration of Independence; John Hoskins Stone would become Governor of Maryland; Major General William Smallwood would command the Maryland Line, which saved the Continental Army and the Revolution at the Battle of Long Island, and he would later serve as state governor; and Dr. James Craik of nearby La Grange, an early and intimate friend of George Washington, would become chief physician and surgeon of the Continental Army. There were also the merchants, planters, and shopkeepers of the county, many with names that would be associated with Port Tobacco for the next century—Marshall, Ware, and Muschett.[54] Other prominent citizens who could not be present but who would also serve the nation included Daniel St. Thomas Jenifer, a signer of the Constitution of the United States, and John Hanson of

Mulberry Grove, who would be selected to serve as the president of the United States in Congress Assembled under the Articles of Confederation. It was, indeed, a stunning array of leaders assembled in one place, equal to any that Virginia or Massachusetts or any other place would provide for the next century.

At the meeting, it was resolved that a dozen members of the Committee of Correspondence, including Francis Ware from Port Tobacco, would be sent to attend the next assembly of the Provincial Convention in Annapolis. Unless the coercive acts were repealed by Parliament, all importation from Great Britain would cease by December 1, 1774, and all exports to Britain, Ireland, and the British West Indies would be halted on September 10, 1775. In Annapolis, the convention authorized the raising of funds in each county to purchase arms and ammunition. Charles County's assessment was $800. On January 2, 1775, at another meeting in the Port Tobacco courthouse, the inhabitants of the county unanimously approved the proceedings of the Provincial Convention and resolved to raise the required funds in each of the county's five parishes. Robert T. Hooe was authorized to raise subscription moneys in the town and parish. An additional subscription was also to be made for the relief of Boston. A list of all who refused to subscribe was to be made "that their names and refusal may be recorded in perpetual memory of their principles." The actions, of course, were frightening to those of a more moderate inclination. Visitor Nicholas Creswell fretted with concern that there was "nothing talked of but war with England," and that the citizens "are all liberty mad."[55]

Creswell's anxieties were certainly warranted, as revolutionary fervor became all-pervasive in the county. There would be no middle ground. The first evidence of the "for us or against us" mentality was exhibited before Christmas when several members of the local Committee of Observation sought to shut down the county court, intimidating the judges into adjourning until February 1775. Although a full Committee of Observation had soon countered the actions of the few and reopened the court, the message was clear for fence-sitters. War was in the air. "We hear of nothing now," wrote William Fitzhugh, a prominent planter in nearby Calvert County, "but raising companys, military exercises, meetings of committees, siezing goods, advertising delinquents &c &c."[56]

Port Tobacco was clearly the geographic focal point of the patriotic movement in the county, even as town merchants, seeking to beat the clock, shipped more tobacco than had been sent out on consignment in nearly thirty years, and average citizens began to purchase and horde goods that might become scarce during an embargo.[57] Mars was on the rise.

On March 2, 1775, Dr. Robert Honeyman, a visitor, recorded in his journal an engaging view of the town and its environs on the eve of the War of Independence. His arrival, it seems, coincided with the onset of field exercises by a company of about sixty gentlemen learning military drills. The town itself, he noted, "is about as big as New Castle [Delaware] and is seated between hills at the top of Port Tobacco Creek which two miles below falls into the Potomac, and only carries small craft now. There are six stores in the place, four of them Scotch." He was even more impressed with the Jesuit establishment at Chapel Point. "Near the town is a Roman Catholic Chapel, very elegant with a fine house adjoining where live four or five Jesuit priests. They have a fine estate of 10,000 acres and two or three hundred negroes. There is also a very pretty church of freestone with an organ in it. There is also a warehouse for tobacco."[58]

Though generally supported in southern Maryland, the boycott was not universally accepted, and some town merchants even sought to evade it. In the spring of 1775, when the ship *Lady Margaret* arrived from England with town merchant John Baillie aboard, the effectiveness of the local association was tested for the first time. With the assistance of a village tailor, Patrick Graham, Baillie secretly unloaded banned goods, stored them at Graham's house, and then proceeded to sell them. Undoubtedly intimidated by the association, *Lady Margaret*'s captain revealed the scheme to the Charles County Committee of Observation, and a meeting was promptly assembled on June 3 at the courthouse to determine a course of action. With magistrate George Dent presiding, the assemblage resolved: "That the said John Baillie and Patrick Graham, for their infamous conduct, ought to be publicly known and held up as foes to the rights of British America, and universally condemned as the enemies of American liberty; and that every person ought henceforth to break off his dealings with the said John Baillie and Patrick Graham."[59]

The transgressors' only hope for redemption from public censure and commercial ostracism was to plead to the Provincial Convention for forgiveness and restoration of their rights as citizens. Armed with 120 signatures from Charles County citizens of all stations, they eventually evinced the mercy of the infant revolutionary government.[60]

On September 12, 1775, the freemen of the county again met at Port Tobacco to elect thirty-two men to the county Committee of Observation, which would then select five of their number to serve in the Provincial Convention. Almost simultaneously with the election, the Provincial Convention denied creditors access to the county courts to secure moneys owed them. This was a response to the current economic chaos, when so many personal and company debts had resulted from the disruption of trade. Creditors who had already won their cases in court, however, were free to seek "execution," that is the seizure of the property of debtors and the incarceration of insolvents.[61] In Port Tobacco, "riotous proceedings" erupted; the town jail was broken into, and a debtor was freed by friends. The resolves of the Provincial Convention and the Committee of Observation were totally ignored. On September 27 the Committee of Observation, which would serve as the only viable governing body in the county until the reorganization of local government under the Maryland Convention of 1776, unilaterally ordered that all "executions" be halted and that debts be collected "without repression."[62] The crisis temporarily abated.

On the first day of 1776, the Maryland Convention moved for the first time to improve the provincial defenses. Officers were selected to command the Maryland Line of the Continental Army, clothing and victuals were to be secured, and regulations for provincial troops were to be reported on. The province was divided into military districts, with Charles County forming part of the First District.[63]

Defense issues were paramount in everyone's mind, particularly the protection of the region's most likely avenue of invasion, the Potomac River. Indeed, Maryland and Virginia were both concerned about the exposure of the towns lying on that great watery highway. As early as 1775 Charles County's Committee of Observation had conducted a survey to ascertain the width of the Potomac channel and to sound the depths along county shores to determine the feasibility of sinking vessels to prohibit an enemy's passage. The project was deemed to be unfeasible. Early warning thus became the first line of defense. At the beginning of 1776, in the first cooperative venture of the war undertaken between the two provinces, Maryland and Virginia agreed to erect beacons on the Potomac shores—from its entrance at Point Lookout all the way up to Alexandria—to alert the region to waterborne invasion. On March 19, Brigadier General John Dent of Charles County, commander of the First Military District, and George Plater of St. Mary's County were instructed by the Maryland Council of Safety to confer with a committee from Virginia to "carry the necessary measures into execution." By March 25, the council had decided on a meeting place and time agreeable to both parties. The critical conference would be held at Port Tobacco on April 2.[64]

On April 30, Dent somewhat belatedly reported to the council that the committee had agreed to erect twenty stations, thirteen of which would be in Maryland: one in Prince George's County, nine in Charles, and three in St. Mary's "averaging about five miles from each other." The committee also agreed upon the design of each alarm post, which was "to be a kind of iron gate suspended by a chain on the end of a sweep fixed with a swivel so as to be agreeable to the wind." Although the committeemen had advanced funds for part of the project, specifically for a boat and men to begin work, it was necessary for the council to provide the rest.[65]

There is no further mention of the alarm posts in the record, and it is likely that for lack of funds, as with many other early defensive measures, the project was eventually dropped. That was unfortunate, for in midsummer a large British force under Lord Dunmore, the last royal governor of Virginia, conducted devastating raids up the Potomac and along the St. Mary's and Charles County coasts. Fortunately, Port Tobacco was spared the travails that other locations along the river suffered, primarily in 1776 and 1781, and emerged intact from the Revolution. Only once, on April 5, 1781, when Loyalist raiders in two armed barges landed at Port Tobacco Warehouse and then proceeded to Chapel Point and burned the property of Father Hunter, did enemy depredations even come close to threatening the port. Yet as a recruitment, marshaling, and logistics center, the town served both the state and nation throughout the war.[66]

Following the stunning Franco-American victory at Yorktown in 1781, Port Tobacco welcomed the coming of peace. An air of festivity swept over the town, although many of the men who had answered the call to arms were still in the field, much to the chagrin of the ladies. One native of the county, James Craik, Jr., reported in 1782 on the newfound exuberance elicited by the prospect of amity. "Since my last nothing but mirth and gaiety has attracted the attention of the polite circle of Port Tobacco," he began,

> having diverted themselves of their former ceremony now suffer friendship and familiarity to reign with proper energy which, I'll assure you, renders it the most agreeable circle I know, Philadelphia not excepted—we have had a great ball at the Widow Furry's about a fortnight ago, which consisted of thirty-two ladies and six gentlemen, a very disproportion. The mortification of the poor little girls exceeded anything I ever saw, they could scarcely reconcile dancing with each other, notwithstanding their propensity to that amusement. There was none of our family there except Miss Ewell. The old woman was greatly disappointed as she prepared a supper for twice the number . . . P.S. Dolly desires me not to forget to present her love to you & is impatient to see you once more at Port Tobacco.[67]

Predictably, when news came of the signing of the Treaty of Paris in 1783, the rebirth of prosperous commercial activity throughout Maryland was anticipated by all. Hitherto stagnant tobacco prices doubled, and a deluge of merchants, both domestic and foreign, were expected to flood the tidewater.[68] With its warehouses, stores, ordinaries, church, and courthouse intact (if a bit shabby from neglect and lack of funds and activity), Port Tobacco was expected to resume its earlier role as a center of local government and trade and as a strategic waypoint on the roads connecting the cities and towns of Virginia, Maryland, and points farther north and south. Thus, it came as a complete surprise in late August 1783 when a notice appeared in the *Maryland Gazette* stating that a number of county inhabitants, undoubtedly led by the redoubtable Father Hunter, intended to petition the General Assembly to transfer the county seat to Chapel Point.[69]

Chapel Point and its visual supremacy over the Port Tobacco Valley was imposing. One visitor, J. F. D. Smythe, published in London in 1784 an account of his impression of the region in *Tour in the United States of America*. "Port Tobacco is not larger than Piscataway, neither of them containing more than forty or fifty houses, but it carries on a much more considerable trade which consists of some wheat, but chiefly tobacco." But, like Honeyman before him, it was Chapel Point that had captured Smythe's fancy. "Near the town of Port Tobacco," he wrote, "upon a commanding eminence overlooking the Potomac is a seat belonging to the late society of the Jesuits in occupation of a Roman Catholic priest named Hunter in a situation the most majestic, grand and elegant in the whole world. The house itself is exceedingly handsome, executed in fine taste and of a very beautiful model; but imagination cannot form the idea of a perspective, more noble, rich and delightful than this charming villa in reality is. And as the best description I could give of it would come so far short as even to disgrace the place itself, I shall not hazard the attempt."[70]

The response by Port Tobacco's leading merchants to the petition was swift. Thomas Howe Ridgate, one of the merchants, rapidly organized a counterpetition drive among the citizenry to keep the court in town. The seat of county government, it was clear, simply could not be transferred to Catholic land. The Jesuit had tried a similar move before the war and failed, and such an action was still patently unthinkable to most, even with independence. Ridgate, however, mysteriously lost the signed petition before it could be dispatched to Annapolis. Then, amidst a flurry of complaints about the merchant's "mismanagement," Thomas Stone, a signer of the Declaration of Independence, took up the cudgel in the town's defense in the General Assembly.

Port Tobacco, he argued, must remain the county seat. With "a little repairing," the courthouse and church (a Protestant institution) could be made like new. The citizens, he pointed out, were already investing in and improving their own properties. It was, after all, still an established and profitable center for tobacco commerce. In stark comparison, he stated sharply, "because there is no reason to expect manufacturers to settle there," it was impossible to even conceive that a town could ever be successfully established at Chapel Point. Unless Port Tobacco burned to the ground, he could not foresee more than eight hundred hogsheads of tobacco a year—and no wheat at all for that matter—ever being shipped from Chapel Point "unless people from distant parts bring these commodities to the new town merely for the sake of incurring an expense." And most importantly, in the now democratized national context, not one public meeting had even been called to discuss the proposed relocation.[71]

The Assembly agreed and the county seat remained in Port Tobacco.

With the town's esteemed seat in the county and state hierarchy thus reassured, prosperity once again loomed on the horizon. Numerous trading firms such as Wallace, Johnson and Muir, John Glassford and Company, and John Jamieson and Company sought to establish or reestablish themselves in Port Tobacco. Some of the county's more notable personalities, such as John Hoskins Stone and Thomas Howe Ridgate, served as their agents.[72] Unfortunately, the nation, state, and county would be faced with a seemingly endless string of economic problems, not the least of which stemmed from the many British commercial houses seeking to secure payment of debts incurred before the war. The consequences of a veritable flood of lawsuits soon produced public upheavals that tested the mettle of the county court system and even the new constitution of the State of Maryland itself. On June 12, 1786, when attorney John Allen Thomas attempted to file suit in behalf of Piscataway factor Alexander Hamilton to secure payment of debts owed or to have the debtors consigned to jail, riots erupted in front of the Port Tobacco courthouse, and a mob of over one hundred men rushed the courtroom. Thomas was violently seized and, before an impotent court and at the peril of his own life, was forced to drop the case. Hamilton, who was not in the courthouse but in town, was saved from injury only because he could not be located by the so-called "Liberty Boys of Charles County." The magistrates of the court, despite their statements to the contrary, had done little to stem the mob or to ensure that normal court proceedings were carried out. Governor William Smallwood, one of Charles County's most famous sons, upon being informed of the affair, publicly admonished such actions and stated his determination to have the Port Tobacco riot thoroughly investigated. His intentions, however, were not matched by action. At an eventual inquiry convened on August 10, he declared that the Charles County magistrates were not guilty of violation of duty and provided some faint praise to Thomas. In the end, the perpetrators of the Port Tobacco court riot were exonerated. The affair was not without some positive results. At the courthouse shortly before the mob had assembled, Walter Hanson, one of the presiding justices who would sit quietly as the mob asserted its will, had stated that he "wish'd the wisdom of the legislature could fall upon some expedient to exempt the body of a free citizen from imprisonment for debt." In May 1787, his wishes were answered when the Assembly passed Maryland's first comprehensive bankruptcy act.[73]

Unhappily, prosperity, which had briefly flickered to life, proved elusive. The postwar economy of the town and nation alike stagnated. Hindered by undeclared wars with France and England, the European wars of the Napoleonic era, and by interstate trade barriers endured under the articles of Confederation, tobacco prices remained depressed and the future seemed clouded indeed. For Port Tobacco, the combination might have proved fatal, for maritime traffic was being forced almost yearly further from the town by the silting in of the creek. Tobacco culture in surrounding areas had used up the natural fertility of the soils, and the center of tobacco farming was rapidly migrating westward. Deep plowing for wheat caused topsoils to wash away. Yet, as the seat of county government, the town survived, and the air of a genteel, albeit somewhat tattered, society prevailed.

In 1788, the same year the United States adopted the Constitution, a debating society was organized in the town and counted among its first members Gerard B. Causin, Daniel Jenifer, Nicholas and Valentine Peers, Zephanian Turner, Michael Jenifer Stone, and Thomas Howe Ridgate. The numerous estates that surrounded the town, such as John Hanson's Mulberry Hill, the Neale family's Chandler's Hope, Rose Hill, Habre de Venture, and La Grange, were still occupied by some of the more formidable Maryland dynasties. And from time to time, a cosmopolitan atmosphere wafted across the scene when notables appeared: George Washington visited his friend and physician, Dr. Gustavus Richard Brown, at Rose Hill and feasted on baked sheepshead direct from the river; John Randolph of Virginia, replete with his entourage of hounds, hunted in the neighboring forest and attended the Port Tobacco races.[74]

In 1790 Father Charles Neale, S.J., returned to his homeland in Port Tobacco. A member of an old-line family that had arrived in Maryland in 1634, Father Neale had entered the priesthood and served for the previous ten years as chaplain of the Carmelite Monastery in Antwerp, Belgium. On the last leg of his voyage, Father Neale set out in a sloop from Norfolk, Virginia, bound for the Potomac River and his ancestral estate, Chandler's Hope at Port Tobacco. In his company were four Carmelite nuns who had come with the blessing and enthusiastic endorsement of America's first Roman Catholic bishop, John Carroll, to found a Carmelite Order in the United States. The Reverend Mother Bernadine Teresa Xavier (Ann Matthews), sister of Father Ignatius Matthews of St. Mary's County, had served for sixteen years as Prioress of the Carmel in Hoogsttraeten, Belgium. Her two nieces, Sister

Aloysia of the Blessed Trinity (Ann Teresa Matthews) and Sister Eleanora of St. Francis Xavier (Susanna Matthews), both of whom had served with her for the last five years, were sisters of Father William Matthews, Pastor of St. Patrick's Church in Washington, D.C. All three women were natives of Charles County. The fourth nun, Mother Clare Joseph of the Sacred Heart (Frances Dickenson) had joined the Antwerp Carmel from England but had also chosen to come to America to assist the order in its historic mission.[75]

Owing to English penal laws against Catholics in force in America until the end of the Revolution, Catholic churches had been forbidden in Maryland and Masses were usually confined to private homes and small chapels. In 1753, when a Roman Catholic priest from St. Thomas Manor was said to have publicly preached "to a mixed congregation in Port Tobacco Court House," and others had sought to teach Protestant children, the colony government had been called upon to impose strong punitive measures.[76] But with the new Constitution of the United States proclaiming religious freedom for all, a new era had begun. Mother Bernadine had been urged to return to Maryland by her brother, who told her: "Now is your time to found in this country." When the matter was placed before Bishop Carroll in 1789, he expressed his full confidence in the new recruits and assured them a cordial welcome. Father Neale and the four Carmelites departed Belgium on May 1 and suffered through violent tempests, a near shipwreck, and innumerable delays and detours, but arrived at Norfolk safely on July 9. The following day they disembarked in St. Mary's County and several days later proceeded to their new home, Chandler's Hope, situated on an eminence above Port Tobacco. Having felt obliged to travel incognito, upon their arrival, the nuns immediately resumed their Carmelite habits and on July 15, 1790, celebrated their first Mass in America. Although the Order would eventually be provided permanent quarters built by Father Neale two and a half miles north of the town, Chandler's Hope had become, for a short time, the first home of the Carmelite Order in the United States, the first religious community for women to be established in the new nation.[77]

As elsewhere in the tidewater, land clearance for tobacco cultivation and deep plowing for wheat exacerbated drainage problems. Runoff from the tilled fields and loss of forest cover continued to expedite the loss of once fertile topsoils and the further silting up of many streams that hitherto had provided deepwater navigation. The resultant economic malaise in Charles County, especially in Port Tobacco Parish, was unmistakable. In 1796, a traveler named Isaac Weld passed through Port Tobacco and reported that it "contains about eighty houses, most . . . are of wood, and very poor." He observed that the "large episcopalian church on the border of the town, built of stone, which formerly was an ornament to the place . . . is now entirely out of repair; the windows are all broken, and the road is carried through the church yard, over the graves, the pailing [fence] that surrounded it having been torn down."[78] The surrounding farmlands were being rapidly depleted, and farmers abandoned their fields for the richer soils of the Piedmont. From Port Tobacco to Hooe's Ferry on the Potomac River, the country was flat and sandy and "wears a most dreary aspects." Nothing was to be seen for miles but extensive plains worn out by the culture of tobacco. "In the midst of these plains," he wrote, "are the remains of several good houses, which shew that the country was once very different to what it is now. These . . . houses . . . have now been suffered to go to decay, as the land around them is worn out, and the people find it more to their interest to remove to another part of the country, and clear a piece of rich land, than to attempt to reclaim these exhausted plains. In consequence of this, the country in many of the lower parts of Maryland appears as if it had been deserted by one half of its inhabitants."[79]

By 1807 the town had been reduced to barely thirty houses, a tobacco inspection warehouse, the courthouse, church, and jail, the latter two structures being in exceedingly poor repair. The following year further degradation was imposed by Mother Nature when a severe gale nearly leveled both the courthouse and the church next to it. By 1811 the county jail was in such dismal shape that an act was passed by the state legislature to permit the Levy Court of Charles County to raise $2,000 for construction of a new "gaol" on the public grounds.[80]

Even this moderate improvement would have to await the passage of yet another conflict, this time the War of 1812. As during the Revolution, the strategic Potomac River was deemed extremely vulnerable. The towns and villages along its shores, not to mention the infant capital of the new nation erected near the head of navigation, were enticing targets for the Royal Navy, which methodically converted the Chesapeake into a British lake. Yet, at the outset, little concern was voiced regarding the vulnerability or utility of tiny, depressed Port Tobacco. Not until August 1813, when the port of Annapolis on the Severn River was threatened with enemy naval attack and all available American forces had been sent to its aid, did Brigadier General Joseph Bloomfield of the U.S. Army voice his concern that the enemy might make an end run by landing at Herring Bay and marching overland to attack defenseless Washington from the rear. After the destruction of the capital, the general warned, the foe might then march south to Port Tobacco and rendezvous with its fleet "without serious opposition."[81]

Port Tobacco and the Potomac were not without their defenses, limited though they were. Early in the war, when strong British naval forces menaced the mouth of the river, Secretary of the Navy William Jones ordered a force officially referred to as the Potomac Flotilla, hitherto based at the Washington Navy Yard, to reconnoiter and attack the foe if possible. Several gunboats were to be stationed at Port Tobacco as a reserve force. The commander of the flotilla, Lieutenant Alexander S. Wadsworth, was instructed to take special care to prevent all intercourse with the enemy and to block passage of any vessel which did not have a declared destination or which might fall within the enemy sphere. Communications with the Navy Department were to be sent through the post office at Port Tobacco.[82]

Throughout 1813, the defenses of the river, as well as its tendency to shoal, proved to be substantial enough deterrents that British depredations failed to penetrate higher than St. Mary's County. The following summer, however, Charles County would suffer heavily from both the enemy's fire and sword. British raiders devastated the shoreline; an army of invasion landed at Benedict on the Patuxent River and marched overland to destroy Washington. At the same time, a second force moved up the Potomac to attack Fort Warburton (later Fort Washington) and Alexandria as a diversionary feint, fortunately overlooking the dilapidated little town on Port Tobacco Creek. The nearest the enemy despoilers came to the town, in fact, was Cedar Point, where they destroyed a warehouse and then moved on.[83] Credit for the town's survival may well be given to the shallowness of the creek itself, which denied British naval access, rather than to enemy shortsightedness. Thus, like Alexandria, which surrendered to the invaders rather than be wiped out, Port Tobacco would live on.

After the war, state and local attentions began to refocus on the town's improvement. Finally, the village on Port Tobacco Creek was given a new lease on life with significant capital improvements. In 1815, the same special commissioners who had been appointed before the war to build the new jail were authorized to raise $3,000 in the same manner as before to build a new courthouse. But as in all public works, cost overruns rule, and the state legislature was obliged to authorize the levying of an additional sum not to exceed $15,000.

Although the building, which began construction in 1819, would not be ready for service until September 1821, it would stand for nearly three-quarters of a century as the symbol of a revivified town.[84]

The following year, the legislature authorized a lottery of $20,000 to be conducted in Port Tobacco Parish. From the proceeds the ancient, dilapidated Christ Church, which had been administered by the Reverend John Weems since 1787, would be fully repaired. On June 28, 1818, the restored building was officially consecrated by Bishop Kent. In 1822, the Reverend Lemuel Wilmer, a man of resolute convictions and personality, took over and served as minister until 1869. Ironically, the lottery to restore Christ Church was among the last lottery franchises specifically for religious purposes authorized by the state government. Yet the improvements to courthouse and church were but the first of many steps taken to improve the town as a whole. It is thus significant that these buildings—courthouse and church, along with the prison in the background—were deemed important enough to be commemorated nearly a century later on the sugar bowl of the silver service for the famed battleship *Maryland*, the only complete pictorial representation of the three structures known to exist.[85]

By 1818, the name Charlestown had all but faded from common usage, and the village was usually identified on maps of the period by the name most commonly employed—Port Tobacco. In 1820, after nearly a century, the town was officially renamed Port Tobacco.[86] Ever so slowly it began to savor a renaissance of sorts, despite the depressed economic visage of the surrounding countryside. The business of the county court ensured a steady stream of visitors, and the gentility of southern Maryland small-town grace was infused into the fabric of life. Writing more than a century after the official name change, historian Ethel Roby Hayden captured a glimpse of the measured pace of everyday life in the village. "Throughout the town stood homes solid and comfortable, their paneled rooms furnished with mahogany and black walnut. Lilies and roses from the gardens nodded in their Sevres vases, over the five o'clock tea tables." Afternoon tea was a traditional ceremony in the town, and when the lifestyles of the inhabitants grew more hectic after the Civil War, the practice was extended to early suppertime. Dinner was taken in the early afternoon, "and many New Orleans dishes were favorites on the Port Tobacco tables," including rolled French omelets and stuffed ham. Hayden asserted that these dishes were introduced by some Gullah cook from down the coast. "Stuffed ham," she noted, "an Easter treat, is ignored in Baltimore and nearly unknown farther north, but for the Charles Countian it is a sorry Easter table where the red and green dish is not."[87]

All genteel southern airs aside, there was no ignoring the dismal prospects for town and county that had gripped all of Maryland and much of the south. Runaway inflation consumed everyone's buying power. Soil exhaustion was universal. Landlords were forced to sell off property, and many small farmers were unable to survive. Between 1805 and 1830, more than four thousand people were forced to leave the county in search of livelihoods elsewhere.[88]

But there were some positive benefits for those who remained behind. When the county's first newspaper, an ephemeral temperance sheet called the *State Register,* made its appearance on May 16, 1842, it was printed in Port Tobacco. Two years later, in the spring of 1844, the town was given an influential public voice hitherto unknown when an enterprising pair of young newspapermen, Elijah Wells, Jr., and G. W. Hodges, issued the first edition of the *Port Tobacco Times and Charles County Advertiser.* The paper's beginnings were seemingly inauspicious, and not until December 1851 did it move to a prominent location on the town square "upon the main thoroughfare of our village and immediately in front of the Court House." Wells, who had learned his trade while on the staff of the *Maryland Republi-*

can, assumed full ownership of the new paper three years later and, until his death in 1877, served as Port Tobacco's most enthusiastic and vocal booster. Although born in Annapolis, he also assumed an increasingly persuasive position in the community's leadership, a role enhanced by an aggressive individualistic temperament which frequently bucked the traditional ties of family, property, and business relationships. His opinions on controversial issues such as temperance, religion, and secession often went against the grain of more popular or politically correct views and occasionally infuriated town advertisers. Wells was a man of stern stuff and earned the respect of one and all. Moreover, his paper's weekly circulation of only two to three hundred, small by today's standards, belied its enormous local influence, for its readers were among the most educated, elite, and prominent members of the business and social spectrum of the region. He served as an officer in countless societies and professional organizations, and he repeatedly advocated progressive moves beneficial to the town, county, and state. His professionalism and the quality of his newspaper were lauded throughout Maryland. Typical was the tribute paid by the *Maryland Journal,* which wrote: "No truer, purer heart ever beat in the bosom of a man than that of Mr. Wells. No newspaper today in the State of Maryland enjoys a higher reputation in all that makes a newspaper respected than that of the Port Tobacco Times. He made it the vehicle of truth and high purpose, and never in the heat of debate upon any subject did he use any but the most refined language."[89]

The establishment of a distinguished newspaper in town was perhaps symbolic of the sudden though limited surge in revivification that, by the mid-1840s, seemed to be taking hold. Among the most visible signs of growth were the hotels, which had taken over from the humble inns and ordinaries that served travelers in earlier times. No less than three grand hotels—the Union, the Indian King, and the Farmers' and Planters'—had sprung into existence by midcentury. Perhaps the noblest of the lot and the longest lived was the Union Hotel, originally founded as the Burroughs Hotel and in its later days renamed St. Charles. Occupying a plot on the northwest corner of town, the Union would eventually boast twenty-five large bedrooms, a basement, a dining room capable of seating two hundred people, a breakfast room, card room, double parlors, kitchen, proprietor's suite with living room, bedrooms, servants' quarters, ample stabling, and a spacious grassy lawn.[90]

Throughout their lives, all three hotels would serve multiple functions and welcome tens of thousands of guests. Political conventions were organized and held in them, politicians would make speeches on their steps, and annual social events celebrated in them "largely attended by the beauty and chivalry of the lower counties" would enliven the social scene of the entire town. On Independence Day, celebrants could be found at one or more of the hotels enjoying the gay festivities. Behind the hotels, the owners leased buildings for tradesmen, stalls for wheelwrights, carpenters, and blacksmiths, or stables for livery. For those seeking recreational activities, visitors could visit the "bowling saloon" attached to the Union Hotel. Storehouses situated directly on the town square could be leased from the owner of the Indian King. Salesmen would conduct business in their parlors, rent office spaces as needed, and after business hours enjoy savory meals prepared by the staff of black cooks. And, along a more sinister yet common side of commerce, the sale of slaves would frequently be carried out at all three establishments, occasionally by or under the administration of the proprietors themselves.[91]

In many ways, the rise and fall of the Port Tobacco hotels mirrored the latter-day fortunes of the town and its more important citizens.

Although the date of its founding is uncertain, the Union Hotel was operated as early as 1845 as the Burroughs Hotel by John H. Burroughs. By 1848, Burroughs had sold out to a

prominent town entrepreneur named David Middleton, who promptly renamed his enterprise the Union Hotel. Middleton, who also served as a county assessor, a trustee of the
county middle school in town, and a *pro tem* secretary of the town's literary and debating
society, was well known locally and was of some financial substance. He owned several
houses and lots in Port Tobacco and two farm tracts, known as Litchfield Enlarged and
Small Profits and totaling 204 acres, several miles from the town. In 1856, Middleton purchased a large and commodious two-story house adjoining his hotel on the north side of the
town square, which he proceeded to renovate and fit up in "neat and handsome" style as a
boardinghouse. In 1857, seeking to return to private life, he began to dispose of his holdings
and offered for sale the hotel, the bowling saloon, the boardinghouse, and a stable and carriage house. The following year he placed on the market several more houses and lots in the
town, as well as a slave woman who had served as the hotel cook and maid. He sought to replace her with hired help. Sale of the Union, however, did not proceed as planned, and in
1860 he again offered to sell his hotel, boardinghouse, and miscellaneous lots, resolving
that if the properties were not sold, he would rent them out individually. The immediate fate
of the hotel is uncertain, but Middleton continued to maintain an ordinary license until
1862, suggesting that the operation may have been sustained until at least that date. During
the Civil War, the establishment was known as the Brawner House when it was briefly operated by James Alexander Brawner, who had earlier managed an "oyster saloon" elsewhere
in town. By 1867, Samuel Hanson and A. H. Robertson, having secured ownership of the
complex in the interim, advertised the sale of the hotel as "the only house of the kind in town
and best in Lower Maryland, all in good repair." The property was soon thereafter acquired
by Benjamin F. Burch. By 1870, a number of artisans and tradesmen are known to have
been working in shops behind the old hotel itself, and Burch had also begun to look around
to dispose of his holdings. In April 1873, T. J. Moore, a handsome, young, successful hotel
entrepreneur from Leonardtown, acquired the hotel and proposed "to dispense hospitality"
which had made the Moore Hotel in St. Mary's County "famous." Burch remained in residence as the hotel "looker-on" and a "gentleman of elegant leisure and means." Moore rapidly proceeded to improve the property; he erected an elegant double piazza and renamed
the complex the St. Charles Hotel, under which title it continued in service until at least
1894. At the same time, George A. Huntt, a former constable, postmaster at Bryantown, circuit court clerk, court registrar, secretary of the Port Tobacco Democratic Conservative
Club, and clerk of the county commissioners, had purchased and moved into the "old
Middleton property." This was, presumably, the two-story boardinghouse adjoining the hotel, which Huntt promptly refitted and six months later reopened as a separate hotel named
the Centennial.[92]

The second of the triumvirate, the Indian King Hotel, was first owned by Peregrine Davis,
a saddle and harness maker, local justice of the peace, elections judge, and Democratic
Party functionary who, in 1861, would be elected to the Maryland House of Delegates. In
mid-December 1855, Davis purchased the Farmers' and Planters' Hotel for $4,065 and an-
nounced his intention to close down the Indian King and rent it as a private family dwelling.
Davis's political fortunes were on the ascendancy. In July he was appointed by the county
commissioners as elections judge and served for many years thereafter in various offices. In
1857, perhaps preoccupied with his many official duties, he readvertised the Indian King for
rent either as a hotel or for offices, and he boasted that good storehouses "eligibly situated
upon the public square" were also for rent. The property was soon occupied by Dr. Henry R.
Scott, formerly of Charlotte Hall, Maryland, who promptly began to advertise the hotel. In
February 1858 he announced with some fanfare that the hotel would be the scene of one of

many yearly balls, a "Grand Annual Party" corresponding with Valentine's Day to be attended by the "beauty and chivalry" of southern Maryland. Scott, who was soon serving on the Port Tobacco Board of Commissioners, hired a cook and in 1860 secured the necessary license to sell liquor. But with the decline in trade caused by the onset of the Civil War, the endeavor proved less than successful. By the second year of the war, the hotel and an adjoining house were being offered up for rent and an uncertain future.[93]

The third major hostelry was known as The Farmers' and Planters' Hotel and was owned by Lyne Shackelford, a town merchant. The establishment was considerable in extent. Aside from the main building, the complex included an icehouse, numerous outbuildings, a large and extensive stable, a garden, and a large lot suitable for the cultivation of hay. With two formidable establishments in competition with him, however, Shackelford found it difficult to compete. Worse, he fell behind in his tax payments to the state and struggled desperately to remain in business. In early 1851, believing that a change of management might reinvigorate the enterprise, he imported Mr. and Mrs. Howlett from Richmond to take over day-to-day management and soon afterward announced that he would sell off his mercantile trade to focus all of his attention on the hotel. Although the Howletts had thirty years of hotel management experience behind them, and Davis tried to cut down expenses, it wasn't enough. In 1853 the hotel and other Shackelford properties were seized by Samuel P. M. Hanson, the tax collector, and offered for sale. A broken man, Shackelford died in March the following year, and the hotel's future seemed uncertain. Within days of his funeral, his two sons, John and William B. Shackelford, reacquired the hotel in a bold effort "to sustain the reputation the house has always borne under the management of their father and its preceding proprietors." The siblings' partnership soon proved unmanageable and was dissolved the following year. John Shackelford struggled to continue operations for another year but was soon obliged to offer the hotel for sale. When Peregrine Davis purchased the establishment with the intention of closing down his own hotel, the Indian King, he could not have foreseen that the new acquisition would remain in his hands for only three years. By 1858, Davis himself was ready to retire from the hotel business, and the Farmers' and Planters' establishment was taken over by Zacharia V. Posey.[94]

The town was at last growing again. Professionals and tradesmen of all kinds could be found occupying an increasing number of shops, offices, and stores. Tailors, cobblers, blacksmiths, lawyers, doctors, milliners, dressmakers, hatters, saddle and harness makers, barbers, well diggers, fishermen, carriage makers, bakers, wheelwrights, undertakers, stencilers, mule sellers, house and sign painters, restaurateurs, grocers, dry-goods salesmen, and even a photographer carried on business daily at a brisk but comfortable tempo.

Port Tobacco boasted several large and prosperous clothing and dry-goods businesses, the likes of Boswell and Company, W. Meyenberger and Company, Lacey and Smith, and Day and Padgett, which provided customers with their every need. Tailors, such as C. W. Barnes, offered shoppers a wide variety of fabrics and clothing, such as fine "brown shirting, bleached shirting, domestic gingham, fancy prints, purple prints, black and white prints, plain black prints, plain English, Cashmeer prints, checkered prints, solid colored prints, satin jeans, flannels, ginghams, fancy mouslin delaine, Kentucky jeanes, satinett, woolen shawls, servants blankets, cotton yarn, pulled linsey, [and] quilt wadding."[95]

In 1839 mail service to Charles County was irregular at best, but Port Tobacco was among the five regular stops for the mail rider. Since the town's post office was responsible for more mail than any other post office in the county, its postmaster was reportedly the highest paid, though his hours were only from 9 A.M. to noon, and from 2 to 5 P.M. In 1848 mail usually arrived from Washington on Mondays and Thursdays between 3:00 and 4:00 P.M. and left on Wednesdays and Saturdays between 7:00 and 8:00 A.M. At any hour, however, the postal rider or any other visitor could secure a good meal at Captain James H. Norris's restaurant next door to the Union Hotel. In season, Norris advertised, patrons would find on his elegant menu oysters, fresh fish, wild duck, and terrapin. To pay homage to the growing temperance movement in town and to attract a greater number of women, he advertised that liquor would not be sold on the premises. Patronage for the restaurant was further increased through cooperative promotions with milliner M. A. Burroughs, who rented shop space from Norris and advertised that female patrons "will be furnished with dinners, oysters, cold snacks, coffee, etc., at moderate rates."[96]

One of the town's most colorful merchants, a lovable if feisty curmudgeon, was a German immigrant, Julius Quenzel, who had once made his living going from house to house and repairing clocks, watches, and jewelry. When he arrived in Port Tobacco in 1854, he elected to set up his first permanent shop. He was an industrious man whose work habits and talents soon paid off. Within two years, he rented a store front in the King House and advertised that he would repair clocks and watches and "warrant them to keep correct time for twelve months." His business prospered. Soon, he had augmented his enterprise to include the sale of jewelry and hired his own father, "a superior workman," to help with the repair business. Quenzel also dabbled in real estate, acquiring office and residential property in the town and leasing or renting it outright. He expanded his interests and opened a successful bakery. He was a crusty tradesman who often chose to ignore some of the local social conventions and legal restrictions such as the prohibitions regarding working on the Sabbath. On one occasion he was even hauled into court for working on Sunday but was found not guilty by a lenient jury. "Mr. Quenzel was at times an eccentric and irritable man," recalled publisher Wells in later years, "but withal had a kind and graceful heart, and nothing was too irksome or difficult for him to do for his friends." After the Civil War, as a "reconstructed Democrat," his diligence and public spirit would eventually lead to his election to office as town commissioner. In 1880, he became disconsolate when he ran for the town council and lost. Claiming that he would have won if all those who had promised to vote for him had done so, his acrimony knew no bounds. He called the people of Port Tobacco "an ungrateful set" that "had treated him shamefully, and that 'By ze Cots!' he intended to sell out and leave the place." But he would remain a devoted citizen until his death.[97]

Not everyone was delighted with the commerce of the town. Some residents complained of high prices. It was cheaper to send away to Alexandria for furniture paint than to buy it in town. A Baltimore visitor complained that a haircut in Port Tobacco was 40 percent higher than at home.[98] Still, retail trade was vigorous, and, unlike the agrarian economy that surrounded the town, it was only minimally dependent upon slave labor.

Life in antebellum Port Tobacco was perhaps typical of most small, southern tobacco towns. From time to time, its limited cultural life was intellectually stimulated, as exemplified by the rebirth of the Literary Debating Society in June 1847. The club, whose membership boasted some of the brightest of the youth and not a few of the leading elders of the town, organized regular debates and delivered patriotic public orations on occasions such as Independence Day and Washington's birthday. Esoteric and less than controversial topics prevailed in debates: "Which is the most essential to happiness, love or money?" "Is man happier in the civilized or uncivilized world?" "Ought capital punishment be abolished?"[99]

The organization of the Charles County Agricultural Society was an equally important event for Port Tobacco as quarterly meetings were usually convened there. On October 29, 30, and 31, 1848, the society's first annual agricultural fair was held in the town. The fair was destined to become the single yearly activity on which the entire population of the county would focus. By resolution of the committee managing the fair (comprised of most of the leading citizens of the county), only society members were permitted to compete for prizes, except for dealers exhibiting agricultural tools and equipment and entries in the ladies classes. Stalls for sheep, horses, mules, oxen, hogs, and cattle were erected on Mr. Hutton's lot west of the courthouse. Local farmers proudly exhibited their crops, vegetables, and fruits, while housewives displayed their butter, bread, quilts, spun cloth, and homemade soap. Monetary and silver plate awards were presented to the winners for the best entries in each category. A horse-powered thresher and other modern farm equipment were displayed by Charles H. Drury of Baltimore. A commemorative address was presented by the Honorable John G. Chapman, a Whig member of Congress for the district (and, perhaps fittingly for a politician, a member of the society's committee on the production, application, and relative value of manures). For the town it was unquestionably a most festive occasion. The Charles County Fair would become an annual county tradition which, although no longer held in the town, continues to this day.[100]

If Port Tobacco had a physical heart, it was the courthouse, the center of civic life and public activities. Court days usually saw an influx of visitors and consequently a surge in retail sales and social events. Visitors needed lodging, food and livery services, and frequently legal counsel. The dining rooms in the hotels and local restaurants were usually filled, and some enterprising citizens even set up trestle tables to sell farm dinners, fancy cakes, and buttermilk to street crowds in the town square on "Cote days." The town's offices were already flush with local attorneys who had wisely decided to hang their shingles near their main place of business. In 1852, of the nineteen members of the bar registered for Charles County, fourteen were in Port Tobacco. As long as the county court convened in town, Port Tobacco's existence was justified. Yet, the individual components comprising the social mosaic of the day were not to be overlooked. Often, the courthouse itself served as the setting for gatherings large and small—fund-raising efforts for charitable causes such as efforts for the relief of the poor, meetings of the Port Tobacco Temperance Society, and other social activities. Church fairs, tea parties, and charity dinners were also regularly held in town.[101]

Politics was another mainstay of social interaction. Whigs and Democrats frequently squared off for debates in the town. They also nominated candidates for state and national conventions and offices. Festive barbecues were held in the adjacent woods by both parties. In 1853 the Charles County Whig Convention was convened in Port Tobacco, and four years later, the local arm of the newly formed American Party assembled its first convention there as well.[102]

Perhaps the most festive annual occasion was the Fourth of July celebration. The commemoration was usually hosted by the town Literary Society. The president of the society would deliver a keynote address, and this would be followed by a reading of the Declaration of Independence by a prominent politician. A frolicsome party to which all citizens were invited would be thrown at one of the hotels in town. Such events were perfect for matchmaking. "We predict," wrote editor Wells of the merry prospects planned for the 1852 Independence Day party at the Indian King Hotel, "the presence on occasion of much of the grace and beauty for which the ladies of this section of our State are famous. There are many of our bachelor friends, old and young, who will doubtless also be present. We say to them, improve the opportunity, pop the question, in due time call in the minister, and let us announce the result. If you are patriotic men, as we believe you to be, take this advice, and let it appear that you have celebrated the Fourth to some purpose. Who are to celebrate our National Anniversaries when you are dead? Answer this question practically."[103]

Growth and prosperity required an increase of services, both secular and temporal. In March 1851, for the first time, cool water was conveyed to town hydrants by a new pipeline from the hills to the east, thereby reducing dependency on local wells, which were susceptible to tainting from sewage. New buildings were put up. In 1854, a second church, this one Methodist, was built in the town. The building was erected on a vacant lot north of Captain Day's property by a local contractor named Jeremiah Townsend. It was a substantial oak-framed structure, thirty-two feet wide by forty feet long, with dressed and painted weather boarding. The edifice was dedicated on the last day of the year with the Reverends R. L. Dashiell and B. N. Brooke officiating. Bids were also called for the construction of the town's first public schoolhouse, P.S. No. 8, which was to be a wooden framed structure twenty-four feet long, eighteen feet wide, and ten feet high with a pitched roof.[104]

By midcentury, Port Tobacco, the undisputed hub and soul of the county, was connected to all of the major and many of the minor towns and landings of the region by four major roads emanating north, south, east, and west. The maintenance of these arteries and their capillaries was an ongoing battle for the county government. Frequently, the county commissioners were petitioned to improve roads to connect the town with local landings and even out-of-county points such as Piscataway in Prince George's County. Local improvements for transportation were also addressed. In March 1853, James McCormick, clerk of the county commissioners, called for bids to build a new bridge over the head of Port Tobacco Creek north of town to replace the dilapidated structure that had stood there for years. Specifications were precise. The structure was to be twelve feet long and twelve feet wide. Its abutments were to be made of ten-foot lengths of locust. Handrails were to run the entire length of the bridge and were to be fastened with knees and braces. It was said that no bridge in the county was used more than the long bridge over Port Tobacco Run, which was within town limits adjacent to Day and Padgett's store and which stood in frequent need of repair owing to its almost continuous use. For travelers bound to more distant destinations such as Washington, access could be had directly overland by buggy or horseback or else by water via the Bumpy Oak Road to Marshall Hall, where a traveler could board one of the fast river steamers that regularly called there.[105]

As early as 1802 a mail stage line operated by Joseph Semmes and James Thompson connected the town with Washington and Georgetown to the northwest and Leonardtown to the east. Travelers were limited to twenty pounds of baggage each and were to board at Pyes's Tavern in town. By 1848 another overland mail stage and public transportation line advertised its schedule as follows: "Leave Washington Monday and Thursday 6 A.M. returning the following day. Leaving Newport in time to be at Port Tobacco at 8 A.M. Arriving in Washington before the [B&O Railroad] cars leave for Baltimore. Thus enabling persons from Newport and Port Tobacco going to Baltimore to get there the same day they leave home. Fare from Port Tobacco $2.00, Newport $2.50."[106]

Three years later, the firm of Reeside and Vanderwerken "placed upon the road from Port Tobacco to Marbury's Landing a beautiful and comfortable stage coach, for the convenience of passengers wishing to go the District cities [of Washington, Georgetown, and Alexandria] by steamboat."[107]

Although cut off from the luxury of direct waterfront commerce, Port Tobacco was ably served by the connection to nearby shorefront facilities at Wharf Point and by a new wharf erected in 1857 at Chapel Point. A small but regular packet operation owned by Captain Robert T. Herbert was thus made possible out of shallow Port Tobacco Creek, carrying travelers between the town and Baltimore or Washington. Upon Herbert's death in 1848, a new commercial line was established by James F. Stone who advertised that he would ply between Port Tobacco and Nanjemoy Creek, Alexandria, and Washington, and would go to Baltimore "on command" at any time.[108]

The maritime flavor of Port Tobacco, though no longer the dominant factor in the town's day-to-day life, was still present. Small freight haulers belonging to local merchants, such as the fast seventy-ton schooner *Fertile* owned by John T. Colton and Francis H. Digges, still carried grain and tobacco. Scows and yawls were common sights on the creek. Boat sales were regularly advertised in the pages of the *Port Tobacco Times,* and news reports of the occasional drowning of local mariners were received with all the proper solemnities. The activities of the various keepers of the nearby Upper Cedar Point Lightship, which had served as a permanent navigational aid on the Potomac at the entrance to the Port Tobacco River since 1821, were of continuing interest to the local citizens.[109]

The commercial concerns of Charles County and Port Tobacco were aware of the impact that the arrival of the steamboat age was having upon local business and agriculture. As Charles County historians Margaret Brown Klapthor and Paul Dennis Brown would later write for the tercentenary history of the county: "The invention of the steamboat opened an entirely new era of more rapid transportation for the whole country and especially for Charles County with its vast expanses of deep water."[110] Ever since the arrival of the first steamboat on the upper Potomac, the noble side-wheeler *Washington* in 1815, the river had welcomed the new titans of the steam age. But not until 1854 would a giant of Maryland steamship commerce, the Weems Line of Baltimore, aggressively seek to expand regularly scheduled service to many of the river ports and landings along the Charles County shore.

In September the Charles County Agricultural Society, concerned that the line might erect a monopoly over the region's commercial transportation, stepped forward to deal with the issue. The secretary appointed a committee to determine which points along the county shoreline were most suitable to construct depots to receive produce for shipment by steamboats. Two county men, General John Chapman and Port Tobacco's own William Boswell, were appointed chairman and secretary. Boswell and two other men, James H. Neale and H. A. Neale, all town residents, were appointed to ascertain the actual cost of building and operating a steamboat and the amount of stock that might be raised among county investors to forward the project.[111]

The committee sought the most knowledgeable informants possible to determine the most appropriate sites for steamboat landings in the county. They turned to Port Tobacco's Captain Joseph Lacey, who eagerly loaned his boat and shared information from his long experience on the water with the committee members to prepare their final report, entitled "Wharves, Depots and Steam Navigation." Two of the twelve sites selected were suitable for serving the town, but both had major drawbacks. Deep Point, more than three miles from town, was located on the east side of Port Tobacco Creek and about as high up the waterway as any steamboat could successfully ply. If the site was to be developed, lighters would have to be employed to transfer freight to and from the warehouse at Warehouse Point. Inbound cargo would have to be hauled by dray over the long road to town. It was thus decided that the site would be suitable for use only as a depot for conveyance of freight upstream by small craft and nothing more. The second site was Brent's Landing on the west side of the creek, but this site was even further away and in equally shallow water. Chapel Point was not even mentioned, possibly because of its history of competition with the town. Ironically, although both of the recommended sites would eventually see very limited service, the only landing on the creek that would regularly host steamboat traffic would be Chapel Point. And not until 1881 would a wharf facility suitable to receive steamers be erected at Brent's.

Upon further investigation of the expenses involved, the initiative toward building a steamboat was quietly shelved.[112] Port Tobacco, in its own assessment, had faced reality: it was formally and finally divorced from its maritime roots.

There were, of course, alternative prospects to be considered in lieu of waterborne carriage for improved overland transportation and communication, namely the railroad. But southern Maryland didn't have one. It was still considered by the only company capable of building one, the Baltimore and Ohio Railroad (B&O), as too rural, poor, and underpopulated to support one. And, for the town of Port Tobacco, transportation issues aside, there were more immediate problems that needed to be addressed on a daily basis.

Poor sanitation had become an open sore throughout the town. As early as June 1848 town meetings were held to discuss issues of public health and sanitation. A town board of health was appointed to conduct weekly inspections of homes and businesses to ensure that "impurities" were removed from the premises. It was, however, an agency without legal authority since the town was not incorporated, and compliance was only voluntary. Thus, the inspectors were authorized to "suggest improvements," upon which each citizen was to act, and to levy a sum of $5 upon each resident to pay for cleaning the streets. Fire was also a constant threat to the nearly all-wooden town. When a dry-goods store caught fire in January 1852, it was only by sheer luck that the fire was extinguished by an alert clerk and a possible conflagration of the entire village was narrowly averted. The town jail was a sieve, and prisoner escapes, though not exactly commonplace, became a nuisance that needed to be addressed. In late 1857 the county commissioners petitioned the state to build a new jail in town. Not only were jailbreaks a danger, but the sanitation and living conditions of the prisoners themselves were abysmal. Local crime, though minimal, was on the increase. There were occasional burglaries and a prank bombing in town was categorized as a "monstrous outrage."[113] It was time, many felt, that Port Tobacco be granted self-government through incorporation.

On January 28, 1858, the *Port Tobacco Times* reported that the residents of the town had finally submitted a petition to the legislature to incorporate, "having for its principal object the cleanliness and health of the place." Although incorporation would not be granted by the Maryland Assembly until 1860, the town had moved resolutely to institute a regular form of government and to address its primary problem—public health—well before recognition. By May 1858 the first Port Tobacco board of commissioners had been selected, with Elijah Day serving as president. The first act of business was to authorize a bailiff to give notice to owners or occupants of all houses in town to have privies and premises cleaned up and limed on or before May 20 or face a fine of $5 for each instance of neglect or omission.[114]

Despite the moves toward an improved public health environment, sickness and disease were occasionally pervasive, and epidemics were not uncommon. In October 1858, an outbreak of scarlet fever forced a postponement of the annual agricultural fair, but judging from the lack of increase in obituaries in the *Port Tobacco Times,* the preventative measure instigated by the town commissioners must have proved effective. Perhaps is was not surprising then that the newly formed Charles County Medical and Chirurgical Society chose Port Tobacco as the location for its first meeting and selected as its president Dr. F. R. Wills, one of the town's most prominent physicians and a leader in the cleanup movement.[115]

A wave of optimism regarding the future of Port Tobacco was at its peak by 1860, when incorporation was assured. No less than ten new business licenses were granted by spring; improvements in existing establishments or the opening of new businesses seemed to be occurring at an accelerating pace. There was even talk of draining the wetlands that lay to the southwest of town. Expansion was in the air. During the January 1858 session of the General Assembly, an act had finally been passed authorizing the construction of a new jail, and by May 1860 the new building, a two-story brick affair with a slate gable-ended roof surrounded by an imposing balustrade, had been constructed and inspected.[116]

Even as confidence began to build regarding Port Tobacco's fate, the undercurrents that would soon lead to civil war in America had already begun to sweep across Charles County. The close proximity of Maryland, a Southern slave state, to the nonslave states to the north created a geopolitically sensitive situation. The tobacco economy of the county was entirely dependent upon slave labor, placing it and its white citizens, particularly the landed gentry and planters, in direct opposition to the abolitionist sentiments which reigned to the northward. Moreover, the resident Negro population, consisting of both slaves and freemen, was readily susceptible to the infectious abolitionist rhetoric that filtered in from the bordering free states. As a consequence, a general unrest among the black population of Charles County in and around Port Tobacco was frequently experienced.

The institution of slavery was part of life in Port Tobacco. Since colonial times, slaves had been auctioned off in town, usually at one of the ordinaries and often at sales administered by some of the town's most respected merchants and public officials. In 1845, blacks were auctioned off to the highest bidders right on the steps of the Burroughs (Union) Hotel. When the importation of slaves from Africa was banned, entrepreneurs such as Lyne Shackelford negotiated contracts with sellers of locally born slaves from other counties to guarantee a ready supply of human chattel. Colonel William D. Merrick—one of the county's most noted politicians, a delegate to the Democratic National Convention in Cincinnati in 1856, and eventually a U.S. Congressman—advertised for public sale in Port Tobacco a passel of fifteen to twenty "valuable slaves of various ages and sexes." Young Negroes, of course, fetched the highest prices and were usually purchased for service by local planters.[117]

With the county court and jail ensconced in town, it was not unexpected to find punishments regularly meted out to slaves for misdeeds, perceived and real; mercy was only frugally extended. Indeed, three of the earliest public executions known to have taken place in the town were those carried out in 1755 on "Negro Jack" (for attempting to poison Francis Clements, his master) and on William Tratton and "Negro Toney" (for "poisoning the late Mr. Chase"). Lesser punishments such as public whippings (for various infractions of the white man's law) were commonplace for the next century. On a freezing cold day in December 1855, for example, two Negroes, father and son, owned by John L. Johnson, were publicly whipped in the town for the crime of simply being in the office of the Fergusson and Bateman lumber yard at Chapel Point—a place where they were not supposed to be.[118]

With the proximity of the free states serving as a burr, the fear of slave revolt was always present in Southern Maryland, and Charles County, with a black population equal to or greater than that of the white, was not immune to paranoia. The concerns of white slave owners were compounded by the fears of the general public concerning a sizable free black population of the county. During the summer of 1845, a reportedly failed "Negro insurrection" had resulted in the indictment of two men, Bill Wheeler and Mark Caesar, for serving as prime movers in the revolt. The crime was punishable by death, and the case was argued before Judges Dorsey and Magruder at Port Tobacco. John M. S. Causin argued for the defense, and George Brent, assisted by Thomas F. Bowie, argued for the prosecution. The case was singular in its importance to the local establishment, and, not unexpectedly, Wheeler was convicted and sentenced to death by hanging. A special act of legislation remitted him to a prison sentence in the state penitentiary, but before he could be transferred, he escaped from the county jail. Although a $100 reward was offered, Bill Wheeler was apparently never heard from again.[119]

As early as the 1840s, waves of insurrection scares began to paralyze the county and moves were soon afoot to organize a special police force. In early August 1845, a public meeting was convened in Bryantown for the purpose of raising money among slave owners to organize a paramilitary police force to keep freed slaves out of the district. The assembly also resolved that slaves were to be prohibited from holding any public meetings whatsoever, although they could still attend church services held by white ministers. A committee of twenty citizens was selected to solicit funds from the community. A few days later, a meeting was convened in Port Tobacco by Robert Digges, Jr., J. R. Robertson, and Colonel Merrick to organize a regular committee of vigilance. By February 1846 the organized effort, sans governmental approval but initiated with the tacit nods of county officials, was underway not only to police the district but to remove all black freemen from the county. It was feared they might foment rebellion among their less fortunate brothers and sisters.[120] Although the effort to purge the county of freed blacks failed, primarily because the poorer farmers could not endure the loss of cheap labor, the committee of vigilance patrols, as they became known, became fixtures on the scene for at least a decade.

By the 1850s it had become practice to enforce a curfew for slaves and to seek the separation of town blacks from those in the countryside to prevent the organization of groups that might cause trouble or assist in escapes through the Underground Railroad. As might be expected, ugly incidents in and around the town were not uncommon. One such event occurred on a hot August night in 1852, when the town constable, James Adams, Sr., was leading a patrol comprised of a few adults and "nearly every boy in the village" around Port Tobacco "to see that negroes from the country had left and those belonging in the village were at home." Between 9 and 10 P.M. the patrol spotted a lone black man and ordered him to halt. The startled Negro began to run and the patrol took up the chase. Adams's own son, John, Jr., was in the forefront of the pursuit and caught up with the fugitive as he was attempting to jump a fence. Then young Adams hit his quarry squarely in the forehead with a stick, felling him instantly. The dazed Negro, a townsman, wobbly but able to stand, was released and permitted to walk home, but soon afterwards, he was seized with spasms. Doctors were called in, but the case was termed hopeless. The only punishment meted out was by the editor of the *Port Tobacco Times* who chastised the practice of "allowing half grown boys and indiscreet persons on patrol" and calling for the prohibition of children being sent out on such missions.[121]

Efforts to prevent free blacks and slaves from roaming about at will, particularly at night, resulted in increasingly stringent measures and a more efficient patrol system. By 1854 it became necessary for blacks walking about in the evening to carry passes or face the consequences. All slave owners were instructed not to let their servants out unless a pass had been issued. To ensure compliance, regular patrol companies were formed in every section of the county, and the captain of each unit was instructed to deal rigidly with any Negro without a pass. By now, the action enjoyed official approval, as the overall operation was overseen by Elijah Day, justice of the peace, who approved of schedules and personnel employed and also selected the roads which were to be watched.[122]

Ironically, the most dramatic example deployed from the growing arsenal of abolitionist rhetoric had been provided by one of Charles County's own. Josiah Henson was a slave destined for international recognition. Born at Port Tobacco on June 15, 1787, to a slave who was the property of Dr. Josiah McPherson, he had been sold at the age of seven to a Montgomery County planter, Adam Robb. Two years later he was sold again to Isaac Riley and eventually moved with his master to Kentucky. In 1828 he became a preacher of the Methodist Episcopal Church, but throughout his life, he suffered considerably at the hands of his brutal master. In 1830 he finally escaped and made his way to Dawn, Ontario, Canada, where he became the leader of a community of escaped slaves. As the firestorm of controversy regarding the Fugitive Slave Act of 1850 was breaking, Henson related the details of his life to a New England abolitionist named Harriet Beecher Stowe, who employed him as the model for the brutalized slave in her book *Uncle Tom's Cabin*. The book, later described in Port Tobacco as a "sensational and untruthful fiction," sold over 300,000 copies in the northern states and inspired a ground swell of abolitionist fervor that would help sweep the entire nation towards Civil War.[123]

At the time of the publication of Stowe's work, the presence of paramilitary and officially endorsed groups organized to control the black population of the county inspired little concern among the white citizens of the Port Tobacco basin. Even before the Revolution, the town had grown used to the occasional presence of the military upon its streets. As recently as 1855, army recruiters had swept across the county in search of able-bodied young men between the ages of eighteen and thirty-five for the U.S. Cavalry. Port Tobacco was the authorized "cavalry rendezvous" for recruits. Military parades, particularly by local units such as Charles County's own Smallwood Rifles, became commonplace, organized as the storm clouds of war grew darker on the horizon. By the spring of 1860 the unit had begun to drill and parade in the town's public square every Saturday. On Independence Day 1860, Lieutenant Compton Barnes, on behalf of the ladies of Charles County, presented a flag to Lieutenant Philip H. Muschett in a ceremony that must have stirred townsfolk with mixed emotions.[124]

As the hotly contested national elections of 1860 neared and the prospects of a Republican president were considered, arguments and tempers flared in predominantly Democratic Charles County. The election of a Republican such as Abraham Lincoln was viewed by most county residents as nothing less than a national tragedy. In the election the county voted almost unanimously Democratic, either for John C. Breckenridge or Stephen A. Douglas. Following the election, anti-Lincoln sentiment reached such a pitch throughout the region that at one public meeting held in nearby Middletown, voters who had cast their ballots for the Lincoln-Hamlin ticket were censured and at least one Republican was forced to leave the county under threat of bodily harm.[125]

In January 1861, the *Port Tobacco Times* publicly opposed the right of the federal government to prohibit secession and heartily approved of a close association of common interests between the border states and Maryland.[126] Pro-Southern sentiments had, in fact, already been manifested in the organization of volunteer units whose allegiance would be offered not to the United States but to the State of Maryland. It was expected that, in the event of civil war, Maryland would side with the South. Within two months of the election, the Charles County Mounted Volunteers, sans arms and accoutrements (which were denied them by the state government), began to regularly drill in Port Tobacco. Subscriptions to provide the necessary equipment were initiated and, as during the Revolution, committees were formed to secure funds from the local election districts. Lieutenant Muschett of the Smallwood Rifles publicly offered a preamble and resolution sworn to by his unit: "That we hereby pledge our services to the State of Maryland for the protection of her honor and fair game under the Constitution of the United States, as given to us by our forefathers in its original purity." Allegiance, however, was to the state and not the nation.[127]

On April 15, the day President Lincoln declared seven states to be in open insurrection against the United States, the secessionist sympathies of Charles County and its principal urban center, Port Tobacco, were never in doubt. As a consequence, the people of the county soon found themselves as residents of an occupied territory. On June 17, acting upon information "of certain parties," a detachment of one hundred troopers of the Seventy-first Regiment, U.S. Army, under the command of Captain Ellis, departed Washington at 9:00 P.M. aboard the government chartered steamer *Mount Vernon* with the objective of seizing arms reportedly collected near Port Tobacco. On June 20, Ellis and his men landed at Chapel Point, marched directly to Captain Cox's home at Rich Hill near present-day Bel Alton, and demanded the immediate delivery of all state arms in his possession. Cox was well known as a leading supporter of secession and was deeply involved in forming and commanding several pro-Confederate paramilitary groups in the county before the outbreak of hostilities. He was destined to become one of the most active Confederate agents during the war and an agile survivor of it afterwards. And he most definitely was not about to be caught red-handed with a cache of weapons bound for the rebel army. "It so happened," wrote the editor of the *Port Tobacco Times* with some glee, "that the Captain had no arms of that description on his premises and the troops were thus obliged to return as they came." The disgruntled federals could only report that the mission failed "because the arms had been removed to Virginia" shortly before they arrived. Port Tobacco, however, cringed in expectation of a visit by troopers at any time, and everyone was on edge.[128]

On the same day as the surprise visit to Rich Hill, a strong Confederate battery was reported at or near Mathias Point, Virginia, directly opposite the mouth of the Port Tobacco River. In fact, rebel units had begun mustering at that place as early as June 4. On June 15, they had successfully boarded and burned a grounded schooner called *Christiana Keen* off Hooe's Ferry and then began to indiscriminately snipe at every passing ship. The rebel battery had been ordered erected but had yet to be put into operation. Soon it would be, with dire consequences. Within a short time, the defenses at Mathias Point and the land-sea engagements that would be fought over them would evince the first U.S. Navy casualty of the Civil War—the death of Commander James H. Ward of the USS *Thomas Freeborn.*[129]

Port Tobacco was only several miles from the scene of combat and the Virginia shore. It was thus with good reason that Union interest soon centered upon the town as a potential haven for Confederate spies and as an outlet for southbound supplies. In mid-July Federal troops descended in force upon Port Tobacco for the first time. They were set ashore, as on June 17, at Chapel Point, this time from the Potomac steamer *James Guy,* and marched quickly overland to the town. They commenced a search of one of the hotels with speed and efficiency and soon emerged with prey in hand. The prisoner was a former government clerk named Taliaferro, presumed by some to be a spy, who had been taken with a large bundle of letters addressed to secessionist leaders in the South. While in the town, the troopers had conducted themselves with appropriate civility, but upon their return to Chapel Point, they were accused by the townsmen of purloining yard goods and sundries and debasing themselves with foul language and whiskey.[130]

Union fears of a Confederate invasion of Southern Maryland ran high during the spring and summer of 1861 and seemingly had some basis in fact. Confederate troops were concentrating in massive numbers all along the Virginia shoreline. When an intercepted message was forwarded by Commander T. T. Craven of the Potomac Flotilla to Secretary of the Navy Welles, the ramifications for Washington were chilling. The message quoted a statement made on August 11 by Confederate President Jefferson Davis less than a month after the rebel victory at the First Battle of Bull Run; it recommended that Confederate agents restrain themselves from causing dissension in Maryland for the time being, for "in ten days I shall command the Potomac and cross between Mathias Point and Aquia Creek into Charles and St. Mary's counties (they are all friends there) and march upon Annapolis. Then, having two of the approaches to Washington in possession, let Baltimore rise and burn the bridges." Washington, thus cut off and surrounded by secessionist states, would then be captured. The intercepted message was, according to Craven, from an "unquestionable source" who had also revealed that a line of communication between Maryland and the Confederacy was being maintained by means of the St. Mary's steamer line up the Patuxent "and then in open boat from Port Tobacco to the Virginia shore after the police boat has passed."[131] For Port Tobacco, the consequence was nothing less than Union occupation, and for many of its pro-Confederate citizens, arrest and imprisonment.

About August 22, a third expedition into the heart of Southern Maryland, this time comprised of two hundred U.S. Marines under the command of Major Reynolds, was dispatched to investigate the activities of rebel sympathizers in the vicinity of Port Tobacco, Pope's Creek, and Leonardtown. The Marines were shipped aboard *Mount Vernon* and accompanied by the gunboat *Thomas Freeborn,* Lieutenant Abram D. Harrell commanding. And like the first expedition, it came up empty handed. Federal authorities were indeed perturbed, especially when reports flowed in informing them that many rebel sympathizers were crossing nightly from Maryland to Virginia with impunity, especially at Pope's Creek not far from Port Tobacco, which had become a prime staging area. "They use punts and low ducking boats," one intelligence report stated, "by which a person is enabled to pass within a short distance of a sentinel without being observed."[132]

Eight days later, when the schooner *Remittance* of Baltimore, bound from Port Tobacco ostensibly for the city on the Patapsco, was overhauled off lower Cedar Point by the USS *Yankee,* one of its crew, a black man named William Posey, told federal authorities that the vessel had been steadily employed hauling contraband to the Confederacy. Moreover, its owner, James H. M. Burroughs, was a rank secessionist. When other suspicious evidence was found, the schooner was quickly confiscated, and those aboard were sent for interrogation to the Washington Navy Yard.[133] These events, typical of many that occurred in the spring and summer of 1861, contributed to federal actions leading to the occupation of southern Charles County and eventually Port Tobacco itself.

Among the first troops to move into the county to stay was Smith's Excelsior Brigade, of Colonel Charles K. Graham's Seventy-fourth New York Infantry. They came not only to set up permanent bases but to begin to round up the most visible and vocal Southern sympathizers. In late September, Union officers visited Port Tobacco and arrested Elijah Wells, publisher of the *Port Tobacco Times,* for publishing or advocating the secessionist philosophy. A rumor quickly spread throughout the town that the newspaper office had been forcibly seized and its press and type carried off. Sometime before September 26, Wells, though seemingly perplexed by his "fiery ordeal," was released for lack of evidence and quickly assured his readers that his offices had been left intact and that he and his paper had emerged "without even a hair singed or the smell of fire about us." The *Port Tobacco Times* would continue to publish as before, though under the close scrutiny of the U.S. Army.[134]

The value of Wells's facilities was not lost on the Union occupiers. On September 27, soon after freeing the publisher, the army requested the use of his printing press and type to publish its own newspaper for the benefit of the soldiers encamped nearby. Given the events of the preceding week, Wells had little choice in the matter and wisely offered "no special objection." Printers from the regiment almost at once set to work, and within a short time, the first edition of the *Excelsior Edition of the Port Tobacco Times* was being circulated in nearby camps.[135]

Federal intentions were no laughing matter. Fear of a Confederate invasion across the Potomac prompted a Union Army of occupation, initially estimated at ten to twelve thousand strong under the command of General Joseph Hooker, to descend upon Charles County. Hooker's forces were ranged primarily from Mattawoman Creek to Budd's Ferry, but strong forces were also sent further south and east. On September 29, forward units of Hooker's army passed through the town en route to Camp Good Hope. "They kicked up a little dust," reported Wells, "but, in the language of stereotype newspaper correspondence, 'all is quiet in this portion of Charles.'" On October 31, the Fifth Regiment of General Daniel Sickles Brigade passed through Port Tobacco and encamped at Mulberry Grove, the residence of Dr. Robert Fergusson. A corps of artillery was soon occupying nearby Hill Top, near the Catholic Church. And finally, a guard was sent into Port Tobacco itself to ensure that civil tranquillity be maintained and looting by troops be prohibited.[136]

Within a short time, the difficulties of sustaining order were put to the test, as arrests of prominent and not-so-prominent citizens of the county accelerated. Judge William M. Merrick was among the most important men to be placed under military guard. Soon afterward, General Walter Mitchell, chairman of the infant Baltimore and Potomac Railroad, and John Hamilton, a prominent civic leader, Democratic Party functionary, and planter, found themselves under arrest. One preacher in the county, a Reverend Todd, was even arrested for omitting a prayer for the president during services. Thereafter, rarely a week passed that arrests were not made and local residents carted off to Washington for questioning and often imprisonment.[137]

Still, some of the residents managed to maintain a sense of humor about it all, albeit a black one. On October 24, the *Port Tobacco Times* playfully published a headline that could not fail to arouse Union ire: "The Enemy Approaches." Beneath the bold, provocative letters, in small print the text read: "The *Bed Bug Season* is now in hand and every family and owner of a bed should at once provide themselves with a bottle of *'Bed Bug Poison.'* It never fails as prepared, wholesale and retail by Apothecaries' Hall, Port Tobacco, Md., Corner fronting the Court House."[138]

The presence of the Union Army in Charles County, a force which by December had grown to twenty thousand men, had some notable impact upon the slave population. Runaways were soon making their way to Union bases such as Budd's Ferry or Camp Fenton near Port Tobacco, seeking and getting protection. Such defections soon grew from a mere trickle to a veritable flood. In a single week in June 1862, for instance, it was reported that forty Negroes had left their homes in Nanjemoy, thirty-seven had escaped from W. H. Mitchell's plantation, and five from Samuel Adams's.[139]

With the arrests of so many local citizens, the departure of innumerable sons to join the Confederate Army, the loss of so many slaves, and the resultant detriment to agricultural production, hostilities by an already pro-Southern population against the occupying forces were running dangerously high. On December 19, 1861, as Maryland officially declared neutrality (which was in effect a declaration for the Union), an editorial in the *Port Tobacco Times* vocalized the protest as diplomatically as possible under the circumstances. The State of Maryland, "has cast her vote for the Union and Government by the largest majority ever known to this State . . . Charles County then stands before the Government and the world this day a loyal county. Charles County has ever been loyal; we challenge a disloyal act to be laid at her door—and yet what is her condition? As a loyal county and State, obedient to the recognized law, faithful to the Constitution, the citizens of this State have a right, and undisputed right to protection in their person and property." The paper noted that there were still twenty thousand federal troops stationed upon the soil of Charles County, their camps extending from Mattawoman Creek to Liverpool Point. "These troops are here 'For our protection,' we are told; 'to protect us from the Rebels,' and yet, in fact, we are exposed to more danger, to more losses and damage or at least as much as if these very Rebels were here. Our farmers are deprived of their provender to such extent that their cattle must die. Our citizens are deprived of homes almost; and fences, farms, and fields fall prey to the ruthless hands of those very friends who come here to protect us." But the worst problem of all concerned the slaves. "Our negroes,—ah, this is the point,—our negroes—are taken from us time and again, with no remuneration and the threats of violence if we seek to recover them."[140]

Despite the publicly voiced attitude of the publisher's dismay as expressed in his paper, Union officials viewed the activities of the locals as anything but loyal. On November 27, 1861, General L. C. Baker reported to Secretary of State Seward that upon his arrival at Colonel Graham's headquarters in Port Tobacco, the inhabitants complained bitterly of their alleged ill treatment and the depredations committed under the colonel's command. "In justice to Colonel Graham," the general wrote, "I found on inquiring that the inhabitants had been the first aggressors. There are residing at this place but four or five union men, the balance either being sympathizers with secessionists or open and avowed aiders and abettors of treason. The postmaster at this place is secretly doing all in his power to further the interests of the Confederacy." At the nearby hamlet of Allen's Fresh some eight miles away, there were but two Union men to be found. In the Allen's Fresh post office, the general had found five letters addressed to fictitious names; upon opening them, he discovered that they contained sealed letters addressed to well-known secessionists in Virginia. Indeed, he had learned that the postmaster was one of those who assisted to organize and equip Confederate soldiers in Virginia. At the post office in the town of Newport, some two miles from Allen's Fresh, he found a package of thirty-four letters postmarked "Newport P.O., Maryland," all ready to be forwarded to different localities in the North. On examining the letters, he found they were all written in Virginia and had all been dropped into the office by one person.[141]

In point of fact, both sides had much to commend their grievances. When twenty or thirty soldiers "from the upper camps found their way to Port Tobacco," managed to obtain a "full supply of the 'juice,'" and became "rather boisterous and exceedingly annoying to the citizens," the matter was viewed with disgust by the townsfolk. Misconduct by Union troops, usually under the influence of alcohol, became common. When a band of drunken soldiers descended upon a lone house in Nanjemoy, burned it, and then beat the owner for attempting to save his bedding from the fire, the soldiers were merely arrested by a squad of cavalry and later released. A unit of the Sixth Regiment, New Jersey Brigade, under Colonel Vurling, was then stationed in Port Tobacco to prevent the sale of liquor to the troops.[142]

The citizens of the town and county were active in supporting the Confederacy. Communications with Virginia were surreptitiously maintained at Pope's Creek by Southern sympathizers, and boatloads of county men were carried across the Potomac on dark nights to swell the ranks of the Confederate Army. Signaling operations were maintained by a local rebel agent throughout the war, while mail and intelligence, despite the diligence of the U.S. Navy's Potomac Flotilla, were regularly delivered back and forth between the Maryland and Virginia shores. Dr. Stoughton W. Dent served as a courier under the guise of making professional calls and regularly delivered Confederate mail to Port Tobacco and other places in the county.[143]

Innumerable sons of Charles County, including citizens of Port Tobacco, served in the Confederate military. Many would never return, such as twenty-four-year-old Captain Michael Stone Robertson, who died in an engagement between Stonewall Jackson and John C. Freemont during the Shenandoah Campaign. Few answered the summons to arms from the federal government, as most eligible young men had gone South. The few who remained and were faced with the draft chose to pay substitutes to stand in for them, at prices ranging from three to seven hundred dollars. Fewer still were those who would boldly stand by the Union. One of those who did was the Reverend Lemuel Wilmer, rector of Christ Church in Port Tobacco, whose convictions never wavered despite the blatant and often intimidating sympathies of his congregation.[144]

Wilmer and his son, Dr. W. R. Wilmer, both ardent Union men, had been threatened with censure, ostracism, and worse by their neighbors, but remained steadfast in their loyalty. Reverend Wilmer even maintained an unfurled American flag in his church during services that were frequently attended by Union soldiers. The flag was to serve as a catalyst for one of the most emotional moments in his life. On April 30, 1863, a date proclaimed by President Lincoln as a "day of humiliation," Wilmer held a special service. The service was widely boycotted. Barely a dozen of his congregation were in attendance although "a goodly number of soldiers" had soon made up for the difference. As the soldiers entered the church at the back door, Wilmer suddenly noticed the flag had been furled, possibly in protest by someone in the civilian congregation. But when the soldiers were seated, he "observed the motion of the hand of the commanding officer, and the staff placed horizontally and a beautiful flag unfurled. I had nothing to do with it directly or indirectly. I knew then that bedlam would be let loose." For two minutes he was disconcerted, eyeing both civilians and occupiers facing off. But recovering his composure, the rector proceeded with the service and then with a sermon on the disastrous condition of the country, "that it was on account of sin that we were thus visited," concluding "that we should beseech the Lord to take the cause in his own hands." At the end of the sermon, his daughter Becky and son W. R. began to play the organ and were soon joined by the stirring voices of the soldiers which echoed through the church. The service ended peacefully. "My heart glowed," Wilmer later noted to Bishop Whittington. "I lost sight of flag, circumstances, everything."[145]

Port Tobacco's environs, notwithstanding the continued occupation of the area by Union troops, soon became a center for Confederate espionage thanks to its proximity to strategic Laidler's Ferry and other crossing points. In January 1865, Secretary of State Seward was apprised by the U.S. consular agent in Toronto, Canada, that a spy network was still actively employing the Port Tobacco River as a base for crossing into Virginia, despite regular Navy patrols on the river. The method of transporting secret correspondence and military data was innovative. The spies, the secretary learned, made their crossings in Indian rubber boats. The couriers wore metal buttons, on the inside of which were concealed "minutely photographed" dispatches that were imperceptible to the naked eye and could be read only with the aid of a powerful lens. Letters were written, but "closely interlined with imperceptible ink . . . to which when a certain chemical is applied, is easily deciphered."[146]

Other spies relied upon their personal wiles. At the nearby Rose Hill estate, then owned by the Floyd family (relatives of the original owners, the Browns), Union officers and troops were frequently billeted in the house and on the grounds although one of the family, Robert Semmes Floyd, was then serving in the Confederate Army under Robert E. Lee. Both Floyd's wife and his sister, an attractive socialite, Miss Olivia Floyd, were obliged to entertain the officers from time to time. Their propinquity to the Yankee army served as a perfect cover to mask their true allegiance. Directly under the noses of Union officers, Olivia was, in fact, serving as a rebel agent. Employing a wooden boat model made by Robert as a secret place for concealing money and papers, she became a critical link between Confederate agents in the North and the South. One trying episode involved saving a handful of rebels who had made a successful raid on St. Alban's, Vermont, and then had been captured by authorities after crossing into Canada. Extradited back to the United States, they were to be tried and hung as spies unless it could be proved that they were duly commissioned officers of the Confederate Army. An underground message started south requesting proof of their commissions. Olivia Floyd was the last link in the chain of rebel supporters who had hand-carried the information from the North to Virginia. No sooner had she received the message than a troop of Union soldiers arrived to search Rose Hill. Hiding the note in the ball of a pair of brass andirons right by the fire and at the foot of one of her unexpected visitors, she cleverly eluded detection. The message made it through, the commissions were produced, and the rebel raiders were saved from the gallows.[147]

As the war dragged toward its inevitable bloody conclusion, Port Tobacco remained an occupied town in an occupied country, sympathetic to the Confederacy but unable to wholly serve in its cause. Yet, it *was* to play an important role in one of the most tragic episodes of that grievous war: the events prior to, during, and following the assassination of President Abraham Lincoln.

On April 14, 1865, the City of Washington was basking in the glow of victory with the news of the capture of Richmond and the surrender of Robert E. Lee's Army of Northern Virginia at Appomattox Court House. The joy of success, however, was to be brief, for shortly after 10:00 P.M., while watching the play *Our American Cousins* at Ford's Theater, President Lincoln was shot and mortally wounded by John Wilkes Booth. At the same time, abortive assassination attempts were made upon Secretary of War Edwin Stanton and Vice President Andrew Johnson by Booth's co-conspirators, David E. Herold and George A. Atzerodt.

Herold, though not a citizen of Port Tobacco, professed a knowledge of the road system of Southern Maryland that had impressed Booth, for it was information vital to the formulation of an escape plan. Months before the assassination, during a period when only the abduction of the president was being considered, it had been Booth's intention to station a small boat in Port Tobacco River to facilitate escape. It is probable that the boat Booth planned to use was the one purchased from townsman Richard M. Smoot by Atzerodt, another townsman, some months before the murder.[148]

George Andrew Atzerodt was born in 1835 in Thuringen, Germany, and emigrated to the United States at the age of eight. In 1857 he had settled with his brother John in Port Tobacco and opened a carriage-making business, J. C. Atzerodt and Bro. The two brothers had advertised in the *Port Tobacco Times* that they would manufacture to order any description of carriage, wagon, or cart.[149] The business failed to prosper and the Atzerodts parted company, with John moving to Baltimore and George becoming a house painter. George remained in his adopted town and became known locally by the nickname "Port Tobacco" Atzerodt. During the war, he was an ardent Confederate sympathizer and frequently rowed friends back and forth across the Potomac. As his loyalty to the South intensified, his acquaintance with Confederate courier John Surratt also matured, and the Port Tobacco house painter inevitably found himself entwined in Booth's web of conspiracy.

Booth broke his leg when he leaped onto Ford's stage after shooting the president. It was an accident that foiled his carefully developed escape plan by forcing him to seek medical assistance. After a brief stop at the home of Mary Surratt in Surrattsville to pick up guns and ammunition stored there, he visited the home of Dr. Samuel A. Mudd, near present-day Waldorf, Maryland, to have his injury attended to. Mudd had an earlier passing acquaintance with Booth, and though it was never proved that he had a role in the actual conspiracy, he would later pay with prison time for the humane services rendered to the assassin. After the leg was set, Booth and Herold headed south into the perimeter of the Zekiah Swamp of Charles County and promptly became lost. While riding aimlessly through the bogs, they encountered a Negro, Oswald Swann, who guided them to the home of the well-known Confederate sympathizer Samuel Cox of Rich Hill. Cox hid the fugitives for nearly a week in a thicket near the town a mile west of his home while he made arrangements to ferry them across the Potomac.[150]

To help the assassins escape across the river, Cox sent for his foster brother, Thomas A. Jones, the chief mail agent for the secret line administered by the Signal Corps of the Confederate Army, who lived near Pope's Creek. Jones met Booth and Herold in the thicket, promised to help them, and later brought food and newspapers for them. Keeping the two fugitives hidden was no small task, for the countryside was swarming with fourteen hundred federal troops and detectives searching day and night for them. The swamps were scoured, and the entire country, from Cobb's Neck to Allens Fresh, was combed. Somehow, the assassins continued to evade capture.[151]

On April 18, Jones went to Port Tobacco to listen for gossip and to pick up whatever intelligence he could concerning the manhunt. Stopping for a drink at Brawner's Hotel, he encountered Captain William Williams, a detective, who informed him that a $100,000 reward was being offered for information leading to Booth's arrest. Jones did not betray the fugitives; he continued to provide them with necessities until the night of April 21, when he led them to a boat at Pope's Creek, aboard which they escaped to Virginia.[152] Both were unaware that far to the north, George Atzerodt had been arrested on April 20 while hiding at the home of a cousin, Hartman Richter.

Booth, of course, was soon afterward cornered and killed in Virginia in a gunfight with federal troops. Atzerodt and Herold were executed on July 7, 1865, along with Mary Surratt, who had provided the conspirators with food and shelter. Dr. Mudd was sent to prison at Fort Jefferson on the Dry Tortugas in the Florida Keys. Jones and Cox, far more fortunate than the others from the county, were arrested, held prisoner, and eventually released for lack of evidence.

The aftermath of the Booth escape through Charles County was dramatic. Between six and eight thousand U.S. Army troops were still garrisoned throughout Southern Maryland. Most were concentrated in quarters at Chapel Point and headquartered in Port Tobacco. Martial law prevailed, and woe be it to anyone who resisted swearing allegiance to the United States of America. For those who still had trepidations, Colonel H. H. Wells, the Union commander of the region, spelled out the consequences in a broadside from "Headquarters, Military District of Patuxent, Port Tobacco, Md. May 1st, 1865."

The wording began strongly enough: "A considerable portion of the inhabitants of this military district having heretofore rendered themselves notorious for their hostility to the government, many of them engaging in blockade running, supplying the enemy with goods, and in some cases with munitions of war, affording an asylum for the worst criminals, and more recently, giving the murderer of the President of the United States an uninterrupted passage through parts of three counties, feeding him and his confederate, and concealing their presence, it is necessary that this infamy should be blotted out and a new condition of things be inaugurated." Then followed a list of five regulations which were to be strictly adhered to and rigidly enforced: (1) No individual was to be allowed to engage in any occupation, trade, or profession without taking an unconditional oath of allegiance. The oath must state that it was taken voluntarily, without mental reservation, and acknowledged the right to require an authority to administer the same. Taking the oath was not be deemed conclusive evidence of loyalty; and, as none but loyal persons were to be permitted to carry on any business, the oath must be accompanied by consistent conduct and loyal acts. (2) The wearing of rebel uniforms or the display or possession of any rebel flags or insignias of rank was forbidden, as was the utterance of any disloyal sentiments or question by word or deed regarding the rightful authority of the government of the United States. (3) All officers, soldiers, and citizens who had been in Confederate service and had yet to take the oath of allegiance, and all persons who had engaged in running the blockade, aiding the enemy, concealing or aiding in the flight of Booth and his accomplices, or who had failed to give such information as they possessed of his intentions, his place of concealment, or of his orders and abettors, were to be arrested and sent to the headquarters at Port Tobacco. (4) All "truly loyal persons who sympathize with the government " were requested to furnish such information as they possess and "otherwise to cooperate in this effort to discover the guilty and vindicate the supremacy of the law and they are assured that the fullest protection will be afforded them." (5) All military commanders in the district were to be charged with the duty of enforcing the regulations and to "exercise the utmost vigilance to discover and arrest all guilty parties."[153]

Several days later the wording for the prescribed oath was published, and a dozen locations throughout the county, including Port Tobacco, were designated as stations where the oath was to be administered.[154] The gloom of defeat throughout town and county was all-pervasive and would linger for decades.

In Port Tobacco the reconstruction period following the Civil War was a microcosm of the economic and political transformation that was soon sweeping the South. Emancipation of the Negro had divested the county of its principal labor force, and economic collapse, facilitated by taxation and the invasion of Yankee "carpet-bagger" profiteers, loomed large. The change in the political environment, which saw the disintegration of the old Whig Party, the ousting of the Republican Party, and the rise of a new, reconstructed Democratic Party, caused a perplexing dilemma for the white population, for the county voting majority was decidedly black. In 1868 the state legislature authorized the redistricting of Charles County into nine districts. Port Tobacco was officially designated as the First District on July 2. The town's leading political champion was Dr. W. R. Wilmer, the hitherto hated Unionist, who formed a fusion coalition of Republicans and "Independent Democrats" which successfully captured and maintained political control of the county. Time and again anti-Wilmer forces rallied but failed to topple the fusion coalition. Interparty splintering was inevitable. In 1880, when the county Republican Convention met at the courthouse, the name of one of the first black candidates for office, Hillary Wade, was offered up as a potential anti-Wilmer delegate by Sydney E. Mudd, on the grounds that the majority of voters in the county were black and "they ought to have more of the emoluments of office."[155] But the coalition continued to maintain control.

Somehow, despite postwar depression and political realignments, Port Tobacco emerged whole, albeit a bit leaner and hungrier than in the golden days before the war. The town, which had long since lost its shipping owing to siltation, could boast of little industry. Prices for everyday commodities were higher than ever before and citizens suffered from the same defeatist malaise that had swept across the barren agricultural landscape of all of southern Maryland, a lethargy not seen since the agricultural depression of the 1790s. Industry and improved transportation were imperative for the county to again prosper. However, for Port Tobacco, the plum of survival was, as ever, its esteemed role as county seat—a role no one thought could be challenged.

Yet, the air reeked of change, and it carried the distinctive sooty aroma of the steam engine. Although the cornerstone of the first railroad in the state, the B&O, had been laid by Charles Carroll of Carrolton long before in 1826, southern Maryland had not benefited from the dynamic technological and social revolution it had rendered. The opening of the rail connection between Baltimore and Washington and the marvelous technical feat presented by the telegraph (first demonstrated along the B&O right-of-way by Samuel F. B. Morse) were all but foreign to Charles County.[156] That is not to say that the benefits of such innovations, plus the dynamic thirty-year-long railroad development program linking Baltimore with the wealth and resources of the middle west, were unappreciated by the county, for the planters had certainly made every effort to join the parade.

On May 6, 1853, the governor of Maryland had approved a charter authorizing the creation of a railroad company and the construction of what was intended to be the first complete rail system through southern Maryland. The line was supposed to run south from Baltimore, "through or near Upper Marlboro and Port Tobacco to the Potomac River between Liverpool Point and the mouth of St. Mary's River." The company, to be called the Baltimore and Potomac Railroad (B&P), would also have the right to construct lateral branches which were not to exceed twenty miles in length. The capital stock was fixed at $1 million, and actual construction was to begin no later than six years after passage of the act of incorporation. The effort had substantial support in Charles County. As early as 1854 many southern Maryland planters, merchants, and businessmen had begun efforts to secure railroad service for the county. None were more vocal in championing the cause than the *Port Tobacco Times*. After all, whatever was good medicine for Charles County could not help but improve conditions for everyone, including the conscientious townsfolk of Port Tobacco. Or so it was thought! Yet, without adequate capital, the project stood little chance of success.[157]

In 1860, the B&P managed to secure a ten-year extension of its charter. An immediate appeal for financial assistance to build the line was then presented to John W. Garrett, president of the B&O Railroad. Garrett was not impressed with the prospect. After all, the potential profits for passenger carriage through the thinly populated rural sectors of both Prince George's and Charles County were marginal at best, and the major freight commodity, tobacco, was already shipped by water from landings along the Potomac and Patuxent. The B&O declined to purchase any B&P stock.[158]

Although the B&P company charter had been given new life with the extension, without the B&O's support the project appeared to be halted. The war, of course, had put a hold on any motion at all, and the financial situation in southern Maryland had only grown worse afterwards. The directors of the B&P had one last option, an appeal to the B&O's archrival, the Pennsylvania Railroad. Immediately after the war, the Pennsy had mustered all its forces to make an aggressive bid to break the B&O's stranglehold on the lucrative Baltimore to Washington run. The monopoly had, in fact, been legally in place since 1833 by virtue of state aid legislation which forbade any other direct Baltimore-Washington line through Maryland. The Pennsy had managed, however, to acquire access to Baltimore through its subsidiary, the Northern Central Railway, but had been stymied in reaching its main objective, Washington, D.C. That is, until an appeal for assistance was submitted by the B&P.[159]

In August 1866, while reviewing the details of the B&P charter, the Pennsy's lawyers discovered a clause that would allow their company to circumvent the B&O Baltimore-

Washington route monopoly. Since permission had already been granted to run the proposed B&P line from Baltimore to Pope's Creek and also to build lateral branches up to twenty miles in length at any point and in any direction, it was possible to build a spur from the trunk to the District of Columbia. By routing the main line by way of present-day Bowie and Upper Marlboro, a branch less than twenty miles in length could easily reach Washington. Thus, reasoned the Pennsy's directors, by financially supporting the B&P and acquiring the lion's share of its stock, the Pennsy would not only control the line but would achieve the long sought access to Washington, effectively breaking the B&O's lucrative monopoly.[160]

The Pennsy officials promptly arranged for a surrogate—George Washington Cass, nephew of influential Democratic Party leader Lewis Cass and the former head of the Fort Wayne, Pittsburg, and Chicago Railroad—to enter into a contract to finance the B&P. Despite the best efforts of the B&O to abort the deal, in February 1867 the United States Congress agreed to let the B&P enter the District of Columbia. By September a financial agreement had been reached among the principal parties with the Pennsy quietly taking over the Cass contract and then investing $400,000 in the B&P, thereby taking control of the line. The B&O had been outmaneuvered and was powerless to respond. Construction of the new line was soon underway. In June 1868, one of Charles County's principal leaders, John G. Chapman, was appointed a commissioner for the infant rail line, and soon afterward the county itself subscribed to its stock by investing another $175,000.[161]

By the spring of 1870 the main line had reached Upper Marlboro, and on July 29, it was announced that grading had finally begun between that town and the Charles County line. The almost jubilant editor of the *Port Tobacco Times* reported weekly on the progress of the work, providing the most minute details on the project: the equipment employed, the materials purchased or needed, contracts that were sought or let, and the men who were boldly thrusting progress into southern Maryland. The work was good for the county economy, and local hands found steady if rigorous employment. Contractors, such as "Colonel" Samuel Cox (the same who had helped Booth escape), oversaw teams of hundreds of men, first doing the grading work, then laying down over 2,300 crossties for every mile of track, and finally placing the great iron rails themselves, each weighing over 666 pounds.[162]

The precise course for the main trunk line and the spurs that would radiate from it were hotly debated, for they would influence the structure of county commerce and development for years to come—as much or more than any system of roads that had ever been erected. The company executives of both the B&P and the paternalistic Pennsy had decided that the general route was to run straight from Baltimore to Bowie and then to Pope's Creek. From there, it was hoped, a bridge might be built to Virginia, and a linkup with a spur of the Richmond, Fredericksburg, and Potomac Railroad might be completed. However, the specific course, a distance run of forty-eight and one-half miles, was to be selected by the B&P's chief engineer, C. S. Emack. The route finally approved on July 5, 1870, was enthusiastically endorsed by most residents of Charles County, including Elijah Wells of the *Port Tobacco Times*.[163] Few paid any attention to the fact that the line ran no closer to Port Tobacco, the county seat, than three miles away.

Finally, on December 26, 1872, executives of the B&P and Pennsy made the first official trip on the completed line from Bowie to Cox's Station (modern Bel Alton) above Pope's Creek. It was an august and delightful affair as the train and its cargo of expensively clad executive elites "passed over." At Cox's Station, Colonel Cox greeted the party, and Eugene Digges enthusiastically delivered a specially prepared address. The visitors were then transported to Rich Hill where they partook "of more substantial comforts" and were entertained by rousing refrains from Professor A. C. Gray's "Brass Band and Musical Association of Cox's Station." On Wednesday, January 1, 1872, regular daily passenger service commenced with a typical run from Baltimore to Pope's Creek, taking only four and a half hours.[164]

Since Port Tobacco was not on the line of the shortest route between Upper Marlboro and Pope's Creek, the route had bypassed the town, but it was believed that the nearest completed station, located at the small hamlet of La Plata (once Chapmantown) only three and a half miles away, could provide service for the county seat. At first glance, La Plata was but one of many waypoints that sprang from the nourishing tendrils of the new rail line, but unlike others, it was destined to have a mortal impact upon Port Tobacco.

On February 21, 1873, the *Port Tobacco Times* announced that the B&P was going to erect a warehouse and a passenger room at La Plata, the first such facilities on the entire line. The following month it was reported that a storehouse was also to be built. "La Plata," applauded the paper, " is one of *the* Stations on our railroad and will prove [an] excellent place for business." Moreover, it was announced that Thomas R. Farrall, "one of our energetic and thriving young merchants, will occupy [the] station when finished and we heartily wish him success."[165] It would not be long before editor Wells was hurling editorial invectives at Farrall who, more than any single individual in the county or state, became the leading force in the commercial rise of La Plata. As such, he also bore the ultimate responsibility for initiating the decline and fall of old Port Tobacco. The town had seen its mortal enemy for the first time but had failed to recognize him.

The most convenient railroad depot for Port Tobacco was Salem Station, two miles from La Plata but situated directly on the road leading from the county seat to the small assemblage of houses known as Salem. Although the station was a half mile distant from the actual hamlet of Salem itself, it would directly service the loading of goods and passengers bound to and from Port Tobacco, and the significance of this was not lost on B&P company executives. In May 1873 the B&P renamed the station Port Tobacco Station, although the U.S. Postal Service preferred to call it Murdock's. The following month, a warehouse was erected from building materials taken from the deconstruction of the Townsend Street Station in Baltimore. Train schedules then dictated much of the daily life of Port Tobacco as well as the stunning growth of La Plata, which was rapidly emerging as its archrival. The weekly publication date for the *Port Tobacco Times* had to be changed, and mail was carried six times a week no further than Port Tobacco Station for transshipment by train rather than stagecoach or horseback.[166]

Southern Maryland finally had its own iron horse and a dazzling promise for the expansion of urban industrialism into the agrarian society of rural Charles County that would bring for the many wealth, power, and comforts hitherto available to only the few. Life would never be the same again. Yet, sacrifices would have to be made in the name of progress, and Port Tobacco was destined to be among the first. Many times in the past, the town had successfully staved off moves to siphon off its commercial prosperity or to dispute its right to serve as the seat of county government. But a new challenger was emerging as the complex equation of politics, commerce, and geography combined to produce the poison that eventually killed ancient Port Tobacco.

The first intimations of the coming contest appeared in an August 8, 1873, editorial of the *Port Tobacco Times,* when reference to Father Hunter's all-but-forgotten challenge to erect the new town of Edenburgh was made: "About 130 years ago [*sic*] or thereabouts Port Tobacco was very near being utterly extinguished by removal of the County Seat to Chapel Point and nothing but the then powerful influence of the Scotch merchants of the former place prevented it."[167] Within a short time, the same accusations would be leveled at the vigorous upstart La Plata. Port Tobacco had been weaned from the commerce of the sea, but it was in danger of being denied the means of commerce ashore. Soon, the battle for political and administrative control as county seat, the very core of its life, would be fought.

Still, the gathering storm went unnoticed by most. The town looked to its upkeep and sanitation as best it could. Laborers were hired to work on a small barge canal that had been dug between the town and Port Tobacco Creek to connect it with Port Tobacco River. New lightning rods were placed on the two wings of the courthouse, replacing the single rod on the main building, which was in more of a condition to invite destruction than to serve as a protection from the "subtle element." In the fall of 1876 Port Tobacco Parish sought to acquire three acres of land near the Christ Church rectory to be set aside for a cemetery, as the closest Episcopal burial ground was at St. Paul's Chapel ten miles distance, and the only one near the town was a private plot. Improvements were made. The first street lamps in town were privately erected in front of William W. Padgett's store in early 1880. Local pedestrian traffic in the town was enhanced with the construction of a causeway built from the St. Charles Hotel across the wetlands behind the town to the large bridge crossing the canal.[168]

In 1874 the town welcomed the establishment of a new publishing office, the *Maryland Independent,* on the east side of the village square, less than a few hundred feet away from the *Port Tobacco Times.* In the years to come, the two papers would become not only rivals, but key instruments in the life-and-death struggle for the town's survival.

Christ Church was in need of enormous repairs and the ladies of Port Tobacco Parish again dedicated themselves to raise money for the dilapidated edifice by sponsoring social soirées, suppers, fairs, bazaars, and "tableaux." In January 1876 they added to their fund-raising repertoire by importing the "highly amusing waxworks of the world-renowned Mrs. Jarley," which were to be exhibited in the St. Charles Hotel and could be enjoyed by the public for a small admission fee. Nor was the Young Ladies Society of the parish to be ignored in its own fund-raising efforts through festival auctions, "which, considering the hard times was doing very well." The ladies labored diligently to raise money "to renovate, remodel and generally improve their church . . . and have the present gloomy, jail-like structure transformed into a neat, handsome church." An architect named Cassell was hired to superintend the remodeling. By March 1883 it had become obvious to all that Christ Church was in need of more than remedial repairs—it needed an entire overhaul. Thus, the church rector, the Reverend Gilbert F. Williams, formed a building committee composed of the most influential members of his congregation, William Boswell, John G. Chapman, and Samuel Cox, to begin a funding campaign for the reconstruction project. Within a year construction of a new addition as well as general improvements were well underway. By December 1884 the stonework was finished, a new roof was on, and inside work and final plastering were nearing completion.[169] The new edifice was built of freestone hauled in from Aquia Creek in Stafford County, Virginia, from the same quarry that had supplied stone for the construction of the U.S. Capitol and the White House in Washington, D.C.[170]

By July 1874 a well-organized county baseball league was formed for the youth, and Port Tobacco was among the first to field a club. Called the Juvenile Base Ball Club of Port Tobacco, the team would take on other county squads such as the George Washington Club of Cox's Station, the Rough and Ready Club (later the Mutuals) of Pisgah, and the boys from Pomonkey among others.[171]

Jousting tournaments and elegant balls, usually held after the harvest in the late fall, continued to be enjoyed in town and provided a source of great gayety and mirth. The sport of jousting, based upon the tournaments of medieval days, had been brought to the new world by English colonists. In these competitions, riders were dubbed knights. Mounted on horseback and running at full gallop, the knights attempted to spear a series of increasingly smaller rings with their lances, all done for the privilege of selecting the queen of love and beauty. The festive events were usually presided over by the leading citizens of the county who served as chief marshal, aids, and heralds. A panel of arbitrators, also composed of the principal community leaders and merchants, served as judges. Orations were held during both the day and evening ceremonies. A grand ball "attended by the beauty and grace of old Charles" was then held in one of the town hotels. Prizes were awarded to the participants. The queen was crowned by the winning knight and her maids of honor by the runners-up.[172]

Local interest in the dramatic and literary arts, which had begun in Port Tobacco more than a century earlier, continued to grow with the county. In December 1880 the Charles County Dramatic and Literary Association, which had originally been formed as a debating society to provide the town with its first circulating library, formed a capital stock company to erect a "suitable Town Hall" for dramatic, literary, and other public entertainments and for a private reading room for the association.[173]

But, even as social life continued, the town itself began to slip gradually into decline. Port Tobacco's younger leaders were considered by some to be less than their predecessors. "One of our Town Commissioners," noted editor Wells in a scathingly cynical editorial on one of the new breed,

> is sojourning for a term at the "Canal Hotel [jail]," Sheriff Luke Martin proprietor. Domestic incompatibility on the one hand, and a too strong, spirit-compatibility on the other, brought about the change of the Town Commissioner's habitation. He had just re-opened bar and flung his flag to the breeze on Monday last, and, on Wednesday, under escort, goest to the "Canal Hotel." When he reached the hospitable hotel and after being duly registered, he asked that he might be allowed to occupy the parlor of the house, but Mr. Bateman, room clerk of the establishment, could not "see it," and assigned him to an apartment with pretty lattice work of iron about the doors and windows, and "the mother of Siscra looked out the windows, and cried through the lattice." He asked to have a keg of his lager brought to him for his use at the hotel, but Mr. Bateman, thinking that would be a reflection on the bars of the house, couldn't tolerate the proposition. Things were very much fermented without it.[174]

One by one, the town's older generation of guiding hands were passing away, moving on, or defecting to La Plata, leaving great gaps in the critical leadership which had sustained Port Tobacco in years past. On October 12, 1877, the town lost its voice with the passing of Elijah Wells. Although the newspaper he founded would continue, Port Tobacco's most ardent champion was gone. The courthouse, the symbol of the town itself, had again fallen into disrepair, a condition that had aroused civic ire. "Confound the old antiquated Court House!" wrote one critic. "What if it does leak! Pull the old thing down, and let us have in its place . . . a good temple . . . with its spire rising high up to the clouds!" The town schoolteacher complained that although the one-room schoolhouse was substantial, "its condition and furniture is a disgrace to our community." In June 1875 the President of the Prisoners Aid Society inspected the town jail and commented positively on its cleanliness, but could say little else favorable. He recommended a rearrangement of space so that prisoners would not be so crowded and sexes could be separated. The jail itself needed new bars, the want of which obliged the jailer to cruelly chain prisoners to prevent their escape. It seemed that for every step forward, there were two in reverse. Health hazards continued to plague the town.

The old and shallow private wells which continued to serve many of the residents were the cause of occasional outbreaks of typhoid fever. Malaria had been a recurring problem since midcentury, and time and again "bilious fever" swept through the population. Some blamed the fevers on an old pond behind Colonel J. S. Ammon's newly erected steam mill, into which sawdust was dumped. The site was generally deemed something of a foul-smelling cesspool quite suitable for producing yellow fever.[175]

As La Plata continued to grow, competition among the Port Tobacco service and merchant community for a share of the diminishing business pie became fierce. Nowhere was this more apparent than in the hotel trade of the town, which appears to have become something of a game of musical chairs. The old Indian King Hotel had long since closed, and one wing of the grand old building had been purchased by a cobbler named Wesley Bowie and fitted up as a residence. In 1879 George A. Huntt closed the Centennial Hotel to take charge of the St. Charles Hotel, which had been put up for rent by its owner, Benjamin F. Burch. Huntt's wife had soon opened a "millinery and fancy establishment" in the hotel parlor. Then, in 1881, under the direction of Huntt's wife, the Centennial underwent renovation and repainting, and Huntt returned to manage the new operation. Burch placed the St. Charles under the direction of David Smoot. In June 1882, the Centennial reopened for business, and by January of the following year Huntt, in an effort to draw clientele away from the St. Charles, had begun construction of a new bowling alley for the benefit of his patrons. The competition was too much for Burch, who offered the St. Charles for sale or rent in May 1884.[176]

With its many wooden buildings, the ancient town had other worries as well. One of the most sinister threats was the danger of fire. In March 1882, the town of Prince Frederick, county seat of Calvert County, had burned to the ground and many in Port Tobacco feared the same could happen to their own fair village. Over the years, numerous small fires had occurred, but with the total destruction of Prince Frederick and the Calvert County records, trepidations were born anew and not without justification.

On December 15, 1882, the *Port Tobacco Times* reported that the town's run-down schoolhouse had caught fire. The blaze had begun inside the building between the rafters and roof where the stovepipe had slipped from its position and sparks had escaped. The chimney supports had burned through and the chimney itself had collapsed, breaking the stove in the process. The fire obliged the schoolmaster to look for new quarters until repairs could be made.[177] The incident, though depriving Port Tobacco's children of their schoolhouse and causing a most serious problem, was but a foretaste of the disasters that were soon to be presented.

Two months after the school fire, on February 21, 1883, a major blaze very nearly incinerated the town. Sometime before 3:00 A.M., David Smoot's boardinghouse, known as the Carrolton and located behind the courthouse, burst into flames. A northwest gale was blowing hard and quickly carried the fire to the courthouse. Sparks went flying onto both the Centennial Hotel and the home of Mary Button, a town milliner. Through heroic efforts of the townsfolk, the courthouse, hotel, and the Button house were saved, but the Carrolton was razed to the ground. Suddenly, another fire broke out at Washington Burch's house on the extreme south side of town. That blaze, too, was fortunately quelled before it could successfully spread embers to other structures. Bucket brigades had fought throughout the early morning hours to prevent the total destruction of Port Tobacco, and as dawn broke, they congratulated themselves on the success of their valiant efforts. Yet, the near disaster renewed serious concerns that Prince Frederick's fate could well be Port Tobacco's if something wasn't done. Talk began to center upon the need for some type of fire-fighting apparatus. Within a short time, the town had settled for a central hydrant, surrounded by a neat plank fence that had been erected on the town square.[178]

The battle for Port Tobacco's survival, however, was destined to be fought at the ballot box. As an increasing number of local businesses emigrated towards La Plata, many county voters expressed a desire to move the seat of government to the vital new town growing up along the B&P Railroad. Both political parties in the county were split into violent partisan factions. The Democratic Party was divided; the faction that favored La Plata was led by J. Samuel Turner, clerk of the circuit court, while the Port Tobacco faction was headed up by Samuel Cox. In the Republican Party, the Port Tobacco side was led by Sydney E. Mudd, and the opposition was championed by State Senator Adrian Posey, publisher of the *Maryland Independent* and archrival to the *Port Tobacco Times.*

By the summer of 1881 the first great ground swell to move the county seat to La Plata was being felt throughout the region. "The Court House movers," warned the editor of the *Times,* "are still on the rampage." The focus of Port Tobacco's growing invective centered upon the first and most successful mover in the development of La Plata, T. R. Farrall, and the *Times* spared neither him nor his new town in its editorial comments. "It is said that T. R. Farrall removed two bricks from the Court House on Tuesday," noted the paper in August, after one particularly successful political coup had been administered. "When he gets four he intends to lay the cornerstone of a new Court House at La Plata. Our citizens must keep a close watch or those other two bricks will certainly go." The next week the *Times* gleefully followed up with a mock report: "Our sheriff says that if Mr. Farrall comes for those other two bricks he will put him in the little house around the corner [the jail], and there he can have just as fine a view of the Courthouse as if it was at La Plata."[179]

But humor could not delay what seemed to many to be the inevitable. In March 1882 a memorial was presented to the state House of Delegates requesting the right to vote on the removal of the county seat from Port Tobacco to La Plata. Believing that the county would vote in behalf of its ancient seat of government, Delegate Mudd introduced a bill to permit a referendum on the removal and the erection of a suitable new courthouse and jail. The La Plata faction was waiting and ready. A building committee including John G. Chapman, John B. Mitchell, B. G. Stonestreet, Pere Wilmer, and John Hoffman was appointed in the event of an affirmative vote authorizing a contract for the erection of the proposed courthouse and jail in La Plata. Yet, the game was new and it was anyone's call. "The Courthouse question comes in for a large share of discussion at this term at court," reported the *Port Tobacco Times* candidly. "Arguments for and against wax warm, and, as far as we can see, sentiment seems about equally divided."[180] The Maryland Assembly readily passed the bill and the referendum was scheduled for the congressional elections in November 1884.

Many La Plata supporters, certain that the referendum would go in their favor, began to buy up land surrounding the new town. Lemuel A. Wilmer, believing the verdict a foregone conclusion, purchased ten acres of land at $20 an acre, sure that after the referendum the property would be worth $200 an acre. Other more powerful men, such as John G. Chapman, were equally eager to put their money on a certain winner. In the spring of 1883 General Chapman became the chairman of a stock company to raise $2000 to build a town hall in La Plata when it became the county seat. Amazingly, when the referendum was held, the motion to remove was overwhelmingly defeated by a vote of 2,410 to 310.[181]

The political fight continued, and La Plata grew stronger with every passing month. Aware that the inevitable had only been delayed, the population and business base of Port Tobacco began to decline. The Ammon Mill, many of the town's stores, its leading shopkeepers, and not a few of its most elite citizens took their leave for better opportunities elsewhere, often into La Plata itself. In early December 1883, even the St. Colomba Lodge of Masons, a fraternal and organizational fixture in the town since about 1770, announced that it too would be selling the lodge and moving on.[182]

La Plata moved with sureness despite the referendum setback. On April 4, 1888, by an act of the state legislature, the new town was incorporated and the corporate limits officially established. The steamroller for transfer was moving again, but now the La Plata faction was testing its own voice in the *Maryland Independent,* which became the principal advocate for change under the leadership of its powerful owner, Senator Adrian Posey. In 1890 another bill for another referendum was introduced in the Assembly, and, as before, the La Plata side, championed by Posey, was bullish. An editorial in Posey's paper spared little sympathy for Port Tobacco. The county seat, it declared, must sooner or later be changed, and the real question was "has not the time arrived?"

"Why deter it? Port Tobacco, as a village, is going down more every year. Look at the changes that have taken place since the question was last agitated. Everybody who could has left the town and those remaining are watching the opportunity to get away. Why? Because the locality is unhealthy and unfit as a place of residence, and offers no business opportunities whatsoever . . . Everything is in a state of perfect dilapidation . . . The roof of the old courthouse building is worthless, the cupola all in pieces, the rafters rotten . . . and the plastering is falling down."[183]

But again, the La Plata faction was handed a defeat, this time by Governor Eliju E. Jackson, who vetoed the bill.[184]

A third try was soon underway. La Plata advocate Marshall Chapman sweetened the pot by announcing that if the election went in favor of the railroad town, he would provide land, without any charge whatsoever, anywhere in town that the building committee saw fit to erect a courthouse, jail, and other public buildings. The bill was passed and another special referendum was called for on May 2, 1892. The contest was split along clear factional lines between candidates specifically representing Port Tobacco and La Plata. As before, the citizens voted down the transfer proposal, though by a much smaller margin, 1,329 to 995.[185]

The controversy threatened to continue in a political purgatory until serendipity—or arson—swiftly set the contest on a new course. On August 23, 1892, the venerable seventy-three-year-old courthouse, the hub and heart of ancient Port Tobacco, succumbed to fire. The cause of the blaze, be it incendiary or accidental, was never determined although the circumstances were deemed by many as mysterious. The accepted tale, vigorously challenged by the Port Tobacco faction, was that there had been people in the courthouse on the night of the fire, reportedly engaged in a game of poker. When the blaze broke out, the poker players dropped their cards and, together with the townsfolk, attempted to save what they could of the court papers and records. Fortunately, and some would say suspiciously since certain members of the court were proponents of the move to La Plata, most of the bound records, principally for the period 1662–1786, and a book of deeds covering the period from 1785 to 1803 had been sent to the office of the land commissioner at Annapolis by an order of the Charles County court dated May 21, 1889. Still, the loss was a political calamity for the town. Accusations and charges of arson heated up the debates, and ill feelings between the two competing towns reached a fever pitch. Without a heart to rally around, even formerly stalwart Port Tobacco defenders in the Democratic Party began to break ranks in defense of a move to La Plata.[186]

Yet another referendum was called for, even as the citizens of Port Tobacco pressed for a new courthouse to be built in the town. Court business barely limped along in the old court's two surviving wings and in makeshift offices elsewhere in the town. The conditions for the courthouse staff in the cramped, uncomfortable rooms bordered on insufferable, especially during the sweltering heat of summer. The battle over transfer was filled with increasing acrimony. The La Plata faction was charged by the editors of the *Times* with bribing voters in the Allen's Fresh and Hill Top districts and elsewhere. The voices for removal were intensifying with the birth of yet another newspaper favoring La Plata, *The Crescent,* which was established in spanking new quarters in the new town. On January 19, 1894, the *Maryland Independent,* hitherto ensconced in the very heartland of the Philistines, announced that it was leaving Port Tobacco forever and "would go hereafter to subscribers from its printing office in La Plata where it is in touch with the outer world through the railroad and telegraph." The implication was clear that it could no longer survive in such a degenerating, isolated, backward hamlet as its former home.[187]

The La Plata supporters, taking a hard line now, argued effectively that Port Tobacco should not even be considered as one of the sites for a county seat in the final referendum. After all, with the old courthouse gone, why hold up progress? Chivalry had died, and this time, La Plata won hands down. Port Tobacco failed to even make the ballot. Two sites were selected for consideration, La Plata and Chapel Point, the latter of which could boast little more than a Catholic Church, a new recreational pavilion, and a steamboat landing. The outcome was almost a foregone conclusion. With the passage of the Court House Removal Act of 1894 and the selection of La Plata as the site of the new county seat, the future of Port Tobacco had been sealed in concrete. Diehard "croakers" (as the last resolute champions of the old town were dubbed by the *Independent*) attempted to fight a rearguard action when Francis P. Hamilton brought suit against the Charles County Commissioners to enjoin them from issuing bonds to finance the new courthouse in La Plata, but in vain.[188]

In 1894, Port Tobacco was still a sizable community with nearly twenty shops, several hotels and boardinghouses, and between sixty and seventy homes fanned out from the town center, but its heart had been cut out. Not long after the dedication of the new courthouse in La Plata in 1896, Christ Church was dismantled stone by stone and removed by ox cart to the new county seat, where it was finally reconstructed in 1904. The transfer of records from the offices of the clerk and the register of wills, which had been maintained until then in the fireproof wings of the old courthouse, was the last official act in the town. Port Tobacco's *raison d'être* was lost forever. The following year, its once lusty voice and conscience, the *Port Tobacco Times,* was purchased by Walter J. Mitchell and combined with *The Crescent* to become the *Times-Crescent,* which would henceforth be published in the new county seat. In the ensuing years entire buildings—homes and offices of both brick and wood— would be carefully dismantled and carted away to La Plata.[189] The death of the town was complete.

By the onset of the twentieth century, even the town's administrative capabilities had vanished. Police and fire protection, power, business, and economic concerns were managed from La Plata. In 1906 the recently formed Baptist Church of Port Tobacco moved into the south wing of the old courthouse, which had been left relatively intact after the fire, and converted it into a little chapel. Some years later, the north wing of the building would be torn down and its bricks recycled to build a steeple on the front of the chapel. On September 12, 1937, the last commercial steamboat called in the Port Tobacco River when the old steamer *Potomac* tied up at Chapel Point wharf. By the end of World War II, Port Tobacco proper consisted of little more than a handful of buildings.[190] The canal behind the town was filled in with sediment; a small depression and an eroding earthen berm on its shoulder provided the only evidence of its existence. The headwater of the river that had once given life to the town was little more than a wetland. By 1949 even the little Baptist chapel had disappeared.

Top: The reconstructed Charles County Courthouse at Port Tobacco, Maryland, now the headquarters for the Society for the Restoration of Port Tobacco.

Bottom: Stagg Hall, a restored Dutch colonial residence with gambrel roof, was originally built around 1723 and includes a detached former slave kitchen. Later known as the Padgett House.

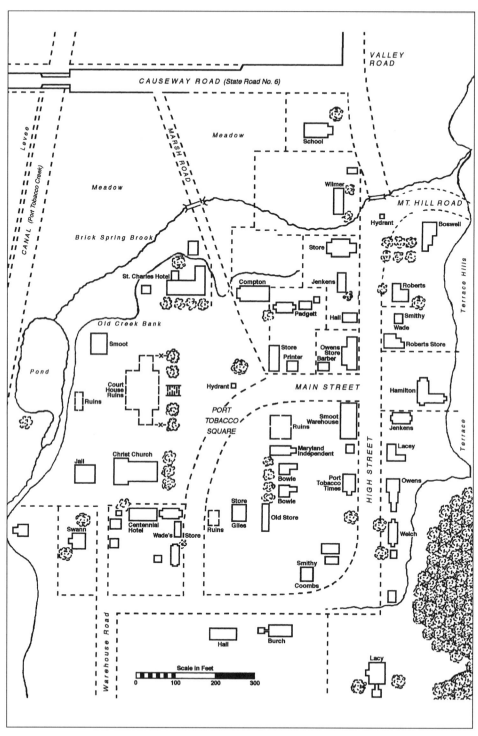

Plan of Port Tobacco, Maryland, ca. 1894. Based upon an unsigned and undated manuscript pencil-drawn map of the town by R. G. Barbour, from the original in the Maryland Historical Society, Baltimore, Maryland.

A Society for the Restoration of Port Tobacco was formed in 1947 by H. Holland Haekins, and by 1979 it boasted a membership of nearly two hundred individuals, only thirteen of whom were actual residents of the town. The accomplishments of the society were many. In 1958, to commemorate the three hundredth anniversary of the founding of the county, a replica of the spring house which provided the village with clean water was erected in the town square. The old 1819 courthouse lands were acquired, and some county residents projected grand visions of a genesis for the old town site. In 1965 the state legislature allocated a grant of $245,000 for the restoration of the courthouse, while Charles County provided an additional $25,000. Under the direction of noted architect and historian Frederick Tilp, the reconstruction was carried out, and on August 26, 1973, a wonderfully crafted replica of the courthouse was dedicated. As time went by, many of the remaining buildings were acquired and restored.[191]

Today, despite the valiant efforts of restorationists, it is the ghosts of the past that are all-pervasive, even as uncontrolled growth, strip malls, and cookie-cutter residential developments creep closer to the Port Tobacco Valley. Old St. Thomas Manor stands nearby on Chapel Point, attached to St. Ignatius Church with parts of the original seventeenth-century structure still extant, erected on the lands of a town that would never be. Nestled in the hills overlooking the site of old Port Tobacco are the great plantation homes of the town's historic elite: Dr. Gustavus Brown's Rose Hill, Thomas Stone's Habre de Venture, Dr. James Craik's La Grange, John Hanson's Mulberry Grove, William Smallwood's Retreat, and Daniel St. Thomas Jenifer's Retreat. In the town, around and near the old square itself, stand a few architectural relics of the past: Stagg Hall, also known as the Parham-Padgett house, attributed to merchant John Parham and built around 1732; the 1765 Chimney House, once the residence of merchant Thomas Ridgate; the Catslide House, built about 1700 and once the Burch homestead; the restored town schoolhouse; and the Quentzel Store, rebuilt in 1933 on the foundation of the old German clockmaker's original establishment. The square, the streets, the vacant lots—once filled with the commerce, politics, fortitude, and foibles that helped shape a nation—are for the most part empty, now governed only by specters of the past.

8 FRENCHTOWN

"Good God! Why didn't you stop the train?"

August 2, 1986. Our visit to Havre de Grace, one of Maryland's most wonderful undiscovered treasures, had been fruitful. My wife Carol and I had been invited by Dr. Ralph Eshelman, director of the Calvert Marine Museum and a longtime personal friend, to spend the day with him looking for antiques and more importantly, looking at some of the world-famous carved duck decoys on display in the town. After traipsing from one antique store to the next, a pursuit that rewarded us with ancient treasures and empty pockets, we ended up at the beautiful Concord Lighthouse park, overlooking the entrance to the scenic Susquehanna River. Stationed just beneath the squat white lighthouse, I leaned against a decrepit old carronade, its surface protected against the elements by uncounted layers of tar and paint, and our discussion turned to the War of 1812. This cannon had once been manned here by an Irishman named John O'Neill, who stood alone against the arrayed might of the Royal Navy. It had been an impressive if futile display of heroic patriotism by an immigrant citizen and it had become, over time, an integral part of the town's lore and heritage. Piqued by the marker outlining O'Neill's resolute stand in defense of his adopted country, our conversation quickly shifted to the towns and plantations of the upper Bay that had suffered most under the invader's heel: Havre de Grace, Spesutie Island, Principio, Georgetown, Fredericktown, and a little-known crossroads on the Elk River called Frenchtown.

Then and there, we resolved to pay our first visit to the least known of these sites. Within an hour, we were driving down the old Frenchtown Road. Ignoring the "no trespassing" and "mad dog" signs along the way, we finally arrived at a modest country house where we asked permission from the owners to walk about the grounds.

"What do you hope to find here?" asked the woman of the house politely, as a pair of large dogs snarled and barked at us from behind her skirt.

"Frenchtown, or whatever might be left of it," I replied.

"You ain't gonna find anything out there," she said, "but you're certainly welcome to try."

From the perspective of white colonists a quarter of a century after the establishment of Lord Baltimore's first permanent settlement in Maryland at St. Mary's City, the region around the headwaters of the Chesapeake Bay was still a wilderness frontier, occupied primarily by "sauvages" and wild beasts. Here and there, a few crudely fortified outposts of civilization had been erected, such as those on Watson's and Spesutie Islands and on Sassafras Neck near the juncture of the Great and Little Bohemia Rivers. Strong Indian towns and palisaded fortifications at places such as Iron Hill on the banks of the Susquehanna River reminded the white man that the natives were still in undisputed command of the hinterland. White expansionism, however, could not long be restrained. Though the danger of Indian attack was always present, the parceling out of the lands by the Lord Proprietor of Maryland had proceeded unimpeded even when actual surveys of the territory were impossible to accomplish.[1] It is thus not surprising that on the Elk River, in a region dominated by the powerful Susquehannock and Seneca Indians, the first stable settlement of any kind appears to have grown up around a humble trading post.

One of the earliest tracts of land patented in what is now Cecil County, on a site that would later become the village of Frenchtown, was a four-hundred-acre parcel on the Elk River taken up in 1659 under the name Thompsontown.[2] A few miles to the north, at the head of the Elk, another tract was patented by Nicholas Painter in 1681 under the name Friendship. It would be upon this tract that the town of Elkton, first referred to as Head of Elk, would rise to become the county seat in 1787.[3] Neither Frenchtown nor Elkton were part of the new town development program. Both sprang up as a result of strategic location and commerce rather than legislative edict. Only one was destined to survive.

October 1695. The Act for Naturalization as a citizen of the colony of Maryland was short and perfunctory. But for Captain John Hans Tilman and his son, John, Jr., the words were undoubtedly as sweet and golden as any an immigrant could have wished for, especially one filled with hopes and dreams for a new life in an untrammeled land. "Be it Enacted," read the law,

> by the Kings most Excellent Majesty by and with the advice and consent of this present General Assembly and the authority of the same that...John Hans Steelman and John his son of Cecil County be by this present Act naturalized and entitled to enjoy all rights and priviledges whatsoever within this province as any natural born subjects of this province might, could or ought to do and shall be capable to sue or be sued to defend or be defended and they and their heirs shall and may enjoy any lands, tenements, rents or hereditaments whatsoever to which they shall or may in any wise be intitled to as if they and every of them were or had been natural born subjects of this province any law, usage or custom to the contrary notwithstanding.[4]

Tilman and his son were Swedish immigrants, quite likely expatriates from the former Swede settlement at Christiana on the Delaware. They had adapted readily to the untamed environment of the Maryland tidewater and soon after their arrival had found themselves actively engaged in a profitable fur-trading operation with the Indians at the head of the Bay. Unfortunately, the senior Tilman's vita is unclear, partially because of the innumerable variations that his name takes in the documents of the era where, like many, it was phonetically anglicized and usually misspelled. In his naturalization papers, he was often referred to as Steelman, but he was also known as Stillman, Tilghman, Tilman, and occasionally simply as Captain John, John Hans, or Hance. Nevertheless, in the frontier environs of the upper Chesapeake, he was unquestionably a man of influence and prestige.[5]

Like most traders, Tilman was obliged to erect his trading stations at locations geographically convenient to the tribes he conducted business with. To be as close as possible to the substantial native population on the Susquehanna (who, in turn, had access to the fur trade as far west and north as the Great Lakes), he had erected a station at the mouth of that great river. It was an excellent choice of sites, for approximately thirty miles north of Octoraro Creek on the Susquehanna, near his depot but fifty miles distant from the Elk, lay the Susquehannock and Seneca towns of Caristauga and Chauhannauks. And to further facilitate his coverage, he had also established another post at or near the fork of the

Elk River and Little Elk Creek. From this base he enjoyed ready ingress to the Delaware Indian town of Minguannan, nine miles above the head of the river. It was around this site in the vicinity of Elk Landing, above which he owned land, that a small settlement soon sprang up.[6]

The first recorded mention of Tilman's trading post came in 1697 when two Swedish missionaries, while en route to settlements on the Delaware, had sailed up the Chesapeake Bay and into the Elk. At the head of the river they intended to disembark and hike overland across the narrows of the Delmarva Peninsula to Christiana Creek, Delaware. Near the headwaters of the Elk, they briefly landed at a small settlement which they later noted had been erected by one of their own countrymen. The place was called Transtown. That it was Captain Tilman's trading post is almost certain. Moreover, that the trading establishment and the captain who founded it were quite prosperous is suggested by Tilman's loan of £100 silver money (a rarity in the tidewater) to one of the missionaries, the Reverend Ericus Biork, for the use of the cleric's congregation in building a church on the Christiana.[7]

Tilman's friendly relations with the Indians as well as his facility as a translator earned him a certain esteem with the Maryland government, particularly when tensions between colonists and natives became frayed, as they frequently did. In the summer of 1697, at the direction of Governor Francis Nicholson and his council, Tilman was instructed to serve as an interpreter for four government envoys, Major John Thompson, Mathias Vanderheyden, Edward Boothby, and Lieutenant Colonel Thomas Richardson from Cecil and Baltimore Counties, who were being sent to powwow with the Indians. But it was Tilman himself whom the government entrusted to "bring the Indians at the head of the bay down to the Governor & Council" for an even more high-level conference.[8]

On June 1, Captain Tilman appeared before the Assembly and dutifully reported having met with the Susquehannock, Seneca, and other Indians at the head of the Bay. Unfortunately, although the chiefs of the Delaware and Chawhanan tribes had been willing to come down with him, three other important tribal leaders had been away hunting, "and because he understood the rest were willing to come down about a month hence, he did not bring them with him." He did, however, bring extensive and critical intelligence about the strength and disposition of the tribes, as well as a message for Governor Nicholson sent by the "King" of the Delawares.[9]

Tilman would continue to serve from time to time thereafter as a government go-between, trusted by both native and Englishman. But by the start of the eighteenth century, the Indian tribes with whom John Hans Tilman had traded in good faith and amity had all but vanished from the scene under the expanding pressures of white civilization. Transtown also disappeared from the record.

In 1700, either John, Sr., or his son dropped the name Tilman and began to bear only his surname and middle name, which was further anglicized to become John Hance. Eventually migrating south, Hance (or his son) was appointed as a justice of the peace in Calvert County and became the founder of a family that would grow to be one of the largest landowners in the region. His descendants would eventually acquire, among other holdings, the famous Taney Place plantation at Battle Creek.[10]

The precise location of early Transtown is perhaps conjectural. That its name was rather quickly supplanted by a new sobriquet—Frenchtown—is accepted by some but disputed by others. As one of the few towns *not* created by ordinance or act, the place was in many ways unique. The origins of the name Frenchtown are also only hypothetical. The French traveler and diarist Moreau de St. Mery, who passed through in 1794, claimed that the site was founded in 1715 as a settlement for French Acadians who had been exiled from Canada by the English, and it was then called La Ville Francaise. St. Mery's supposition is unlikely since Acadian settlement in Maryland did not begin until 1755. It is conceivable that the name could have been derived from French Labidists who may have settled in the area, but not, as often suggested, from French soldiers who passed through in 1781 on their way to Yorktown, or from those who remained in America following the Revolution.[11]

For a quarter of a century after the last mention of John Hans Tilman in the official records of Maryland, the site of Transtown was forgotten. At the onset of the eighteenth century, Cecil County was still sparsely populated by a melange of Quakers, English planters, Swedish refugees, Labadist separatists, African slaves, a handful of Indians, and even some Welsh miners. By 1720, four towns had been created in the county by proclamation or acts of legislation, but none had survived for long. Only at the head of the Elk and on or near the site of nearby Transtown had urbanization begun. By 1706, at the headwaters of the Elk, a mill supposedly erected by William Smith became the first commercial structure built on the site. Soon, an ordinary appeared, along with roads and bridges: the foundations for growth and the rise of Elkton had been laid. The first mention of Frenchtown, does not come until 1723, when a party of twenty influential county residents petitioned for a road "from the head of Elk to New Castle and Christine Bridge." In their petition, they stated that the road to those places had not been laid out despite an earlier court order to do so, and that the extant path was obstructed so "that carts were forced to go by the New Munster Road . . . and that strange travelers often went by Frenchtown instead of the head of Elk River, the Welsh having cleared and marked a road as far as their supposed bounds." The petition was approved and the road was ordered constructed.[12]

The rise of Frenchtown was arduously slow and totally dependent upon its strategic location on the narrow neck of land between the headwaters of the Chesapeake and the Delaware. Not until the assumption of supremacy by the Port of Baltimore on the Chesapeake and the Port of Philadelphia on the Delaware would the site achieve any significant place in regional history. During a visit in the month of May 1794, Moreau de St. Mery summed up the role assumed by Frenchtown as a simple commercial transshipment point between the two great cities.

"The Commerce which requires transportation between Baltimore and Philadelphia," he wrote, "would be too costly if carried by land; whereas if carried by way of the Chesapeake, it would be too long, too uncertain, and sometimes, during the winter, even perilous. A middle course, therefore, has been adopted. Goods are loaded on cargo boats bound for Frenchtown. From Frenchtown wagons and carts carry them to Newcastle. At that place other packets pick them up and take them to Philadelphia. It is by the same means, but employed in the contrary direction, that this latter city forwards goods to Baltimore."[13]

A voyage between Baltimore and Frenchtown aboard a charter packet boat was often an uncomfortable adventure even for the seasoned traveler. During the winter months, between Christmas and mid-March, the upper Bay was frequently clogged by ice, imposing a long period of inactivity for packet boat operations. And when operations were finally resumed, service and accommodations for the sojourner were often atrocious.[14]

When St. Mery left Virginia for Baltimore and points north, he had been amply warned that he should take precautions to reserve his berth on board any packet boat he might sail on and to mark his name upon it in chalk "because custom gave a sort of sacred right of possession to those who last engaged the places." The custom, he observed, had been respected upon his voyage from Norfolk to Baltimore, but in engaging passage aboard the thirty-five-ton packet schooner *Peggy* bound for Frenchtown, the captain himself provided the chalk with which the Frenchman was to mark the six berths to be reserved for St. Mery and his companions. Notwithstanding the captain's outward appearance of accommodation, securing a place to sleep was a trying affair. "When we arrived on board," St. Mery recorded with Gaelic indignation, "we found that the marks on two of them had been rubbed out, and when we wished to take possession of our quarter, some were occupied. Our complaints stirred up a lively quarrel and we only got the best of it by showing a grim determination not to let ourselves be robbed." The captain himself sided against St. Mery's party, which increased their irritation, primarily "because we were so indignant at his duplicity in favoring his compatriots above ourselves."[15]

The price for a passage to Frenchtown, including meals, was $1.25 plus 12½ cents for a drink. Dinner aboard *Peggy* was served at the captain's table about 12:30 P.M. and consisted of beef, potatoes, cabbage, and ham, each in separate dishes. The heavily salted meal, St. Mery determined, may have been designed to encourage drinking. "On the boat, as elsewhere, drink is a dominating idea. We wouldn't have known that any regulations of any sort existed aboard if we hadn't seen a little fly-bill which said that whoever gets into his berth with shoes or boots on must pay a fine of a bottle of porter." A glass of brandy or a bottle of porter "or heavy English beer" cost 31¼ cents. A bottle of Madeira wine cost $1.00. "Fortunately," the Frenchman concluded, "the prohibition did not speak of dirty feet, else the berths would have been almost entirely unoccupied, or would have been a rich source of fines."[16]

The voyage from Baltimore was anything but speedy. Delays were encountered once in stopping for additional passengers and once by unfavorable winds which obliged the ship to constantly tack. But the travelers consoled themselves that "the varied scenery of the Chesapeake, the ever-changing plantations of wheat, maize, tobacco and potatoes" more than made up for the slowness of the voyage. Aboard the boat, there were twenty-five passengers, for the most part strangers to one another, meeting perhaps only this once in their entire lives. But it was a rich mix savored by St. Mery, for whom "the diversified talk, the slumberers, the snorers, the tobacco chewers, the tipplers who packed this floating smoking-den made time pass rapidly for one who knew how to contemplate it with profit."

Although the boat touched bottom two or three times without damage or delay, by nightfall St. Mery and the rest of the passengers retired to their berths "in the hope of being in Frenchtown in a few hours." *Peggy* came to anchor off Frenchtown at 1 A.M. May 21, not long after all of her passengers had gone to bed. By 4:45 A.M., the sojourners had been roused and transferred to a "sort of ferryboat or scow" to transport them and their luggage to the landing.[17]

In 1794, Frenchtown was served by two stages, one with twelve seats drawn by four horses and the other a nine-seater drawn by two horses. There was also a wagon to carry travelers' luggage that could not be put in the trunks of the stage or behind the carriages. The fare between Frenchtown and New Castle was seventy-five cents. There was, unfortunately, little time for St. Mery or his fellow travelers to observe the town in any depth, for within forty-five minutes of his arrival ashore, the driver of the New Castle–bound stagecoach had cracked his whip as a signal for departure. Fifteen minutes later, the steeple and the thirty brick houses of Elkton came into view. By 6:30 A.M. the stage was already at Glasgow.[18]

For Moreau de St. Mery, the trip from Frenchtown to New Castle was most pleasurable and deserves retelling as it portrays a part of Maryland long since dead. "From Frenchtown," he wrote, "whose location is pleasant and whose surroundings are neat, up to Glascow [sic] both sides of the road as far as the eye can see are thickly planted with flax, wheat and corn. The trees are oaks and walnuts. Birds looking like large blackbirds, and turtle-doves brighten the scene. The soil is heavy, and a bit clayey. This section is said to be somewhat subject to destructive droughts. Glascow, where the stage stops for a scant fifteen minutes to water the horses, is made up of several houses. It is eight miles from Frenchtown. Beyond Glascow the road is as pleasing as before. One catches frequent glimpses of horses, cows, sheep, pigs, geese, fowl of all kinds. Two-horse plows turn up the fields; and young girls hoe them. Three miles outside Glascow one reaches the boundary between Maryland and Delaware. After another ten miles we arrived at a house where, according to the American custom, there was a fresh stop of a half quarter-hour to regale the stage horses with a huge bucket of cold water, after their bridles had been taken off. At this point, which is six miles from Newcastle, milestones begin to tell the distances from Newcastle and from Philadelphia. But what gives the eye the greatest pleasure in the eight or nine miles before reaching Newcastle are the living hedges peculiar to this section. They are formed of white thorn, whose flower is beautified at this moment by the charms which the month of May seems to give to all nature."[19]

An Englishman named John Davis was less effusive in his praise, particularly relating to Frenchtown itself. Landing at New Castle in the year 1800, Davis and fifteen other passengers boarded two coaches bound for Frenchtown, from whence they would embark the following morning aboard a packet for Baltimore. After a brief stop at the village of Glasgow, they arrived at their destination where they found "a surly landlord" and sorry accommodations. "It is not unworthy of remark," he noted in his diary, "that the landlord would not suffer cards to be played in his house; and that the negro-girl, who waited at supper, wearing a man's hat; a Quaker in company aspired to be witty by calling her Caesar." Their lodgings boasted only six beds, which had to be shared in twos and threes. Unwilling to be so cramped, Davis proposed they all sit up all night "and make an Indian file with our feet to the fender" of the fireplace, but eventually he succumbed and slipped into bed with several other passengers.[20]

Despite its name, by the beginning of the nineteenth century Frenchtown was anything but a town. In 1803 the "town" consisted of only nine buildings, a crib wharf, and a long wharf ensconced in a most bucolic setting.[21] Yet, its significance as a strategic crossroads between Baltimore, New Castle, and Philadelphia could not be denied.

In 1796 the first regularly scheduled sea-land packet service between Baltimore and Philadelphia was opened by William McDonald and Andrew Fisher Harrison. The McDonald-Harrison Line began operations with a fleet of four sloops running between Baltimore and Frenchtown. At Frenchtown, freight was transferred to wagons for carriage to New Castle and from there to packet boats for transport by water to Philadelphia.[22] Soon, a competing line was established running from Courthouse Point four miles south of Frenchtown to a point near Port Penn on the Delaware. Within a few years, the two competing lines would consolidate under a single name and focus the lens of history upon Frenchtown as never before.[23]

It has long been noted that the topography of the Delmarva Peninsula is generally flat, with but a slightly elevated watershed seldom exceeding one hundred feet above sea level. The peninsula itself is narrow and perforated on both sides by innumerable streams, the headwaters of which frequently come to within several thousand yards of each other. With the great estuary of the Chesapeake on its western side and the mighty Delaware on its northeast quarter, it was long considered a worthy endeavor to connect the two great avenues of commerce by a canal. In 1654, Governor John Rising, the last governor of New Sweden (now Delaware), was the first to express the need for a cross-peninsula canal. In 1661, Augustine Herrman echoed the concept, suggesting that a canal join the headwaters of the Elk in Maryland with the Christiana in Delaware.[24] The first true champion of the canal concept was a prosperous Philadelphia merchant and Quaker, Thomas Gilpin, who surveyed and explored the Chester and Duck Rivers and much of the Delmarva Peninsula for the most practicable route.[25] Though interest in the canal concept found many adherents, it was not until 1801 that the bill was passed in Delaware authorizing the actual formation of the Chesapeake and Delaware Canal Company. On May 3, 1803, the first company board of directors meeting was convened. The noted architect and engineer Benjamin H. Latrobe was engaged to conduct the surveying for the canal and assume the mantle of chief engineer.[26]

Latrobe launched into his work with gusto. Two general routes, usually designated as "upper" and "lower," were given immediate attention. The upper route was to extend from the upper Elk towards Christiana, emerging either at New Castle into the Delaware or else into the Christiana River and then to the Delaware. The suggested lower route was from Back Creek on the Elk to St. George's Creek on the Delaware. And one of the premier sites Latrobe would first visit in search of an appropriate upper western terminus for the canal was Frenchtown.[27]

In mid-1803 Latrobe surveyed Frenchtown itself and produced a delightful watercolor plan showing two "practicable" courses for the canal and an outlet just below the town wharves. Besides showing one of the many routes ultimately considered by the company managers, the plan provided a superb illustration of the diminutive site of the town itself, which could boast of only ten buildings and two wharves situated to the immediate north of the proposed canal outlet.[28] Unfortunately for Frenchtown, the lower and shorter route proved more feasible and was ultimately chosen for the course of the canal.

The proposed route between Frenchtown and New Castle, though not selected for the actual course of the canal (which, in any case, would not be completed until 1829), was not to be easily set aside. With an increasing packet trade running between Baltimore and Frenchtown, the difficulty of transporting freight and passengers across the peninsula on an often impassable road system, and the seemingly incessant delays in the actual construction of the canal, the value of an improved overland route was apparent. Moreover, the canal project itself was viewed with a jaundiced eye by many, and alternatives were readily sought. Thus, in 1809, the Frenchtown and New Castle Turnpike Company was formed under a charter by the Delaware state legislature, and the following year it received a charter in Maryland as well. Plans for the turnpike called for a bed one hundred feet in width, with a twenty-foot-wide artificial road constructed and bedded with wood, stone, and gravel clay sufficiently compacted to a depth to provide a solid foundation. For nearly three years the roadbuilding project progressed but with substantial difficulty owing to the discovery that the clay was unsuitable for road bedding material. By 1813, although the highway was already open to traffic, much of the work was still unfinished and the turnpike company was obliged to request an extension from the legislature to complete the work.[29] In his elegant history of Cecil County, George Johnston recorded many of the interesting provisions for the lengthy schedule of tolls that were introduced in 1809. For every conveyance, cart, or wagon with wheels that measured no less than seven inches and no more than ten inches in diameter, a toll of two cents per horse was charged. For carts or wagons with wheels greater than ten inches but not exceeding twelve inches in diameter, a toll of one and a half cents per draw horse was charged. And for carriages with wheels greater than a foot in breadth, one cent for each draw horse was charged.

Soon the onset of other events, namely the War of 1812, would considerably alter the outlook for the tiny crossroads settlement.

Frenchtown's first major contact with the war came about March 9 or 10, 1813, when 380 soldiers, composed of three companies of the Fourteenth U.S. Infantry Regiment under General William Henry Winder, embarked from Washington aboard a small flotilla of vessels. En route north to the Canadian theater of combat, they landed at the little town's wharf. The troops in Captains McKenzie, Barnard, and Flemming's companies had been recruited in Washington and all were described as "generally as firm a set of men as we have seen."[30] Unhappily, their fortunes and that of their commander, despite their firmness, were destined to be laced with defeat, death, and imprisonment.

American fortunes in the Chesapeake tidewater would prove to be equally distressing, especially after the arrival of a powerful Royal Navy squadron in the Chesapeake in February 1813. The Bay was quickly transformed into a British pond. By mid-April, having already conducted successful attacks and plundering raids against Sharps, Pooles, Tilghman, and Poplar Islands, the British commander on the upper Bay, Rear Admiral Sir George Cockburn, was instructed to penetrate the rivers at the head of the Chesapeake for the purpose of destroying American military supplies, foundries, stores, public works, and particularly depots of flour.

On April 28, 1813, a squadron of twelve barges, operating from a powerful naval task force in the Bay and manned with an estimated one hundred select seamen and three hundred marines commanded by Admiral Cockburn, landed upon Spesutie Island, where they secured supplies of vegetables, poultry, and other necessities. Soon afterwards, they descended upon Turkey Point at the confluence of the Elk River and Chesapeake Bay, where they endeavored to make friends with the inhabitants and purchase provisions as they had at Spesutie Island.[31]

The proximity of the enemy to the Elk River and the storehouses there filled with flour and other supplies needed by the military quickly gave rise to the handmaidens of war—alarms and rumors. Among the citizens of Elkton, one false alarm generated a wave of fear that trickled as far as the Pennsylvania line. Somehow, a rumor began to circulate that the enemy had captured Frenchtown. It soon spread north causing excitement and anxiety. It was said that the alarm had been started by a man named Ellis, who lived along Turner's Creek on the Sassafras River. He had two vessels engaged in carrying wheat from there to Elkton and, nervous about the nearness of enemy shipping to his own, he became anxious to know where his vessels were. Thinking they might be in the Elk, he went up in a large rowboat to look for them during the night. Some skittish persons at Frenchtown, hearing the sound of oars in the stillness of the evening and thinking they belonged to British barges, raised the alarm. By the time an Irishman at Turkeytown (present day Cowentown, a few miles north of Elkton) heard the tale, it had mutated substantially during the frequent retelling, and he personally began to spread the alarm from house to house. He first visited the home of an old lady whose husband was away on military duty and, while appearing half frightened to death, told her "there were fifteen hundred British and Indians at French-town and they spared neither women nor children." He then asked if she had any whiskey in the house. She gave him some, thereby reviving his faltering spirits, and he rode off to spread the alarm and terrify others even more. It was later reported that the man had been in partnership with a Britisher in a woolen factory on Big Elk Creek near the Pennsylvania border. Thinking that the machinery in the factory might face ruination at the hands of the enemy, the two partners hid it in a laurel bank along the creek. They hid it so well, in fact, they couldn't relocate it until after the war, by which time it had become rotten and useless.[32]

The rumors were prophetically close to the mark. On April 27, aided by information provided by some Americans, Cockburn turned his attention toward the vulnerable villages on the Elk. Taking with him a small squadron of warships and captured prizes, he decided to assail Frenchtown, which was reported to be a major depot for flour, military supplies, and other stores. The source of this intelligence may have been a "singularly ill-natured and quarrelsome man, named Zeb Furguson," who, it was later charged, had piloted the invaders from Turkey Point to Frenchtown.[33]

Lacking contemporary maps or soundings of the Elk but confident in the expertise of his American informant, Cockburn was correct in believing the little packet-boat port to be located "a considerable distance up the river." Without hesitation, about noon, April 28, he order his warships and the tenders *Fantome, Mohawk, Dolphin, Racer,* and *Highflyer* to be moored "as far within the entrance of this river as could be prudently effected after dark." Intent on taking his objective by surprise, about 11 P.M., he dispatched Lieutenant George Augustus Westphal, first lieutenant of HMS *Marlborough,* to ascend the waterway with a detachment of 150 marines under the commands of Captains Marmaduke Wybourn and Thomas Carter, accompanied by five artillerymen under First Lieutenant Robertson of the artillery corps, to take and destroy the stores at Frenchtown. *Highflyer,* a captured American privateer under the command of Lieutenant T. Lewis, was directed to follow behind "for the support and protection of the boats, as far and as closely as he might find it practicable." The barges upon which the invaders embarked were later described by those who witnessed the attack as being about thirty feet in length, with decks extending only a short distance from either side, leaving an opening in the middle which extended nearly from bow to stern, so that the oarsmen could stand on the bottom of the boat when rowing. Most were armed with a small swivel gun or two.[34]

The log of HMS *Mohawk,* Captain Henry D. Byng commanding, succinctly described what happened next. "Midnight . . . The boats of the fleet sent *to destroy* French Town." Even with the aid of a local pilot, conducting operations on a poorly charted waterway in the dark of night and in the heart of hostile territory almost proved too much for the seasoned British. The thirteen-barge expedition soon became disoriented and instead of keeping on the Elk, it proceeded some distance into the Bohemia River before discovering the error. Not until the onset of the first gray streaks of dawn, no doubt much to the chagrin of the tars manning the oars, was the mistake discovered.[35]

Rectifying the blunder, the expedition backtracked and by midmorning was once more bound up the Elk. But the alarm had already been sounded and the element of surprise had been lost. As the boats approached Welsh Point, a peninsula formed by the confluence of Back Creek and the main river, they encountered light arms fire from a small party of Cecil County militia commanded by Major William Boulden. The militiamen, reported one apologetic historian sixty-eight years after the event, "made a brave but ineffectual effort to intercept their advance, but having no artillery, it was useless." In truth, their firing had been so ineffectual the British failed to even report the event.[36]

The delay on the Bohemia and the loss of surprise might have proved fatal had the raiders been faced with an organized force. Frenchtown had received ample warning of the coming attack, and the local militia and inhabitants, had they moved quickly to mount a defense behind a small battery lately erected, might have had a chance. But they didn't.

When the British moved against Frenchtown, the town was physically trifling, consisting only of two warehouses, a tavern, two or three dwelling-houses, and a number of stables and outbuildings. The site was then almost entirely under the ownership of Cecil County justice of the peace Alexander Kinkead. "This place," noted the historian William M. Marine, was "of small importance being merely a point of relay for the stages between Baltimore and Philadelphia." The defenses for this small but strategic crossroads storage depot were equally insignificant. Some days prior to the landing, a battery intended for five or six guns had been erected on the wharf, but it was still in an unfinished state. The incomplete works consisted primarily of a log structure which, on the day of the attack, mounted only four small ancient 4-pounders that had seen service during the American Revolution and which had last been employed as ballast in a fishing vessel. The majority of Cecil County militiamen who manned the works, "thinking their number too small to successfully resist the enemy," had been removed upriver on the evening before the enemy attack to Fort Hollingsworth at Elk Landing for the defense of Elkton. All who remained to resist the invaders were a few stage drivers and a handful of more resolute militiamen, numbering no more than eight or ten men.[37]

In the river, nearly a half dozen hapless merchant vessels, including Captain Howell's *Susquehanna Packet,* swung at their moorings or were beached to await the denouement. One of the vessels was Captain Isaac Lort's schooner *Annon Ruth,* which had returned from a trip to Baltimore just before the British had entered the river. When Lort came in, he had discovered a vessel that was loaded with flour and aground near the mouth of Back Creek. The captain of the stranded ship, apprehensive that the British would destroy his valuable cargo as well as the vessel if they should ascend the river, begged the commander of *Annon Ruth* to at least carry the flour upriver to safety, which he did. But even the good Captain Lort was not immune to what happened next.[38]

Between 7 and 9 A.M., April 29 (the exact time varies with the source), the invaders, bone weary after seemingly endless rowing and not having eaten a thing in many hours, finally drew up their barges into the reach below Frenchtown. The few stolid defenders standing at their battery were ready and opened with a heavy fire. The accounts of the engagement which followed are skewed at best. The stage drivers, it was said by some, made a resolute stand, put up a spirited resistance, and repelled the enemy twice before being forced by overwhelming numbers to retire. Less favorable reports suggested that upon first sight of the enemy, the defenders expended all of their ammunition, consisting of about fifteen rounds, long before the foe was within range and "then quietly removed themselves to a place of safety." Casualties had been light, with but one defender killed by a rocket and none wounded.[39]

The official British report of the assault is perhaps more reliable, given the paucity of American data on the affair. "A heavy fire," Cockburn later reported, "was opened upon our boats the moment they approached within its [the battery's] reach; but they [the British marines] launched, with their carronades, under the orders of lieutenant Nicholas Alexander, first of the *Dragon,* pulling resolutely up to the work, keeping up at the same time a constant and well-directed fire on it; and the marines being in the act of disembarking on the right, the Americans judged it prudent to quit their battery, and to retreat precipitately into the country, abandoning to their fate French Town and its depots of stores."[40]

The British landed and immediately set fire to a new storehouse on the town wharf, which contained a large quantity of oats, the property of Alexander Kinkead. At the same time, another detachment put the torch to a fishery adjoining the wharf. Having completed their waterfront incendiarism, the invading force, which official American reports incorrectly inflated to 250 Royal Marines, marched from the wharf through Frenchtown, then up the river shore to Kinkead's house, where they demanded directions to Elkton. Upon learning that they would be obliged to cross the Elk to reach the town, "the whole force returned to Frenchtown, broke open the upper store house, which was at that time full of goods, some of which was the property of the United States, and the remainder belonging to different merchants of Baltimore, to the amount of $50,000 to $60,000, and plundered and carried off some of the goods." One of the village residents, Cora Penington, immediately rushed to the storehouse and begged the British officer in charge, Captain Wybourn, not to burn the building, which belonged to her brother. The officer informed her that he had come for the explicit purpose of burning the storehouses in the town as they were public property. Mistress Penington persisted, pleading with him to spare the storehouse. The officer was not swayed and proceeded to set fire to the building along with all of the stores therein.[41]

Out on the Elk, Captain Isaac Lort was unaware of the speed with which the invaders had ascended the river or of their occupancy of Frenchtown. Thus, when he came down again in *Annon Ruth* to determine the status of the flour schooner he had assisted the day before, he was dismayed to discover the schooner not only still aground but now in the possession of the enemy. The entire river seemed to be in enemy hands, and his own vessel was also a most inviting target. Having been able to run down as far as Cazier's Shore opposite Welsh Point without discovery or capture, he determined that eluding the big warships at the mouth of the river and the flotilla of barges filled with enemy marines would be next to impossible. Thus, in a desperate effort to save his boat from becoming a prize, he ran her aground at Cazier's and would have scuttled and sunk her so that she could be raised later had he not lost his axe. As quickly as possible, he took down her sails, carried them ashore to a place of safety, and then scurried off to his home.[42]

In the meanwhile at Frenchtown, as the upper storehouses burned, the marines began to form up in the road opposite the Penington home. Wybourn informed the frazzled Mistress Penington that it was his intention to burn the stage stable and to destroy all of the coaches. Again, he was beseeched not to destroy the property but replied in a most oblique manner by informing the townswoman that "the question they generally asked when they went to any place was, how they voted in the election, and inquired of this deponent if her uncle, meaning Mr. [Frisby] Henderson, voted for the war!"[43] Her response is not recorded.

After completing their nefarious work of destruction at Frenchtown, the invaders proceeded upriver to Elkton but were received there by a hail of gunfire from the shore and beat a rapid retreat. They next made a landing at White Hall, then owned by Frisby Henderson, who they tried to induce to show them the road to Elkton from the west shore of the river. Henderson, one of the largest landowners in this part of Cecil County, refused to cooperate. The raiders seized one of his terrified female slaves and attempted to bribe her into serving as their guide. The slave took them instead to Cedar Point, opposite a strong and well-manned military defense works called Fort Hollingsworth, then under the command of Captain Henry Bennett. Here too, the defender opened an unhealthy fire forcing the invaders to make another hurried retreat. The raid on the Head of Elk was almost at an end—but not quite.[44]

Despite the ineffectual attempts to capture Elkton (which he failed to comment upon in his report), Cockburn was delighted with the raid on Frenchtown and with the abundance of stores seized, "the whole . . . consisting of much flour, a large quantity of army-clothing, of saddles, bridles, and other equipments for cavalry, &c. &c., together with various articles of merchandize, were immediately set fire to, and entirely consumed, as were five vessels lying near the place." Deeming the guns of the battery too heavy to bring away, they were disabled "as effectually as possible" by Lieutenant Robertson and his artillerymen, after which the boats returned down the river without further molestation. Only one casualty had been sustained; a seaman of the *Maidstone* had been wounded in the arm by a grapeshot.[45]

The majority of inhabitants had watched the raiders from the safety of perhaps a mile's distance as their little port had been ravaged. But, as they had not taken part in the contest, they were allowed to remain unmolested, and not a single dwelling was destroyed. The invaders had too many other things to think about.[46]

While those ashore completed their business, at 9:30 A.M. part of the British squadron, including *Fantome, Mohawk, Dolphin, Racer, Highflyer,* the recently arrived *Hornet,* and a number of guard boats weighed anchor and stood for the Susquehanna, leaving *Maidstone* to pick up the marines. About 2:30 P.M., Cockburn and *Maidstone's* commander, Captain George Burdette, came aboard and informed the ship's officers of "having destroy'd a battery of 6 guns and burn't several vessels, 2 store houses," and then set off on another expedition. This time, their target would be an Elk River fishery belonging to Jacob Hyland, which was plundered without opposition. Hundreds of barrels of shad and herring stored in the fish house were carried away. Soon afterward, the invaders penetrated the Bohemia River and carried out similar foraging in several fish houses along its banks.[47]

As the barges filled with the plundered stores retired downriver, they left behind them not only a small town in ruins but five American merchantmen in flames, including Captain Lort's *Annon Ruth,* the flour ship she had sought to assist, and Captain Howell's *Susquehanna Packet.* They also brought with them a captured sloop called *Morning Star,* built at its home port of the village of North East on the Northeast River.[48]

The first to arrive at the ruins of Frenchtown after the British departure was Dr. Amos Alexander Evans, who only a short time before had served as a volunteer at the town battery but had gone to his home on Big Elk Creek when the militia was removed to Fort Hollingsworth. When he heard the firing at the battery, he mounted his horse and rushed to the fort, where he was joined by his friend H. D. Miller and several others. The group quickly procured a boat and rowed down to Frenchtown, arriving there almost in the wake of the departing Royal Navy barges. As a parting gesture, the retiring invaders fired a swivel gun at the men as they stood dumbfounded amidst the ruins of the town. "The ball," it was later noted, "struck the ground near them and scattered the gravel all over their persons." Fortunately, no one was injured.[49]

Little is known about the fortunes of Zeb Furguson, the singularly bad-tempered and surly man said to have piloted the British from Turkey Point to Frenchtown. Despite his claims that he had been captured by the invaders at Turkey Point and forced to guide them, those who knew him believed that he had joined the Brits voluntarily "in order to gratify his hatred towards all mankind." For a while, Furguson was imprisoned, but because the charges of treason against him could not be proved, he was eventually discharged.[50]

As for Frenchtown, its dissolution as a result of the enemy attack seemed all but accomplished. Yet, the hamlet's role as an important commercial transshipment point could not be denied, even though the town was in ruins. And, as the toll road between Frenchtown and New Castle was finally nearing completion, there seemed a dim hope that the village might again prosper.[51] Also two revolutionary forms of transportation were introduced that would reinforce the hamlet's strategic position and revivify its purpose for existence. Indeed, Frenchtown was to be closely associated with the advent of a new technology that would directly influence the course of tidewater history for the next century.

❖

Less than two months after British raiders had sacked the town, a strange looking watercraft, unlike any that had ever sliced through the waters of the Chesapeake tidewater, could be seen ascending the Elk and making directly for Frenchtown wharf. It was much larger than a normal packet boat: 137 feet in length, 21 feet abeam, and 7 feet deep in hold. There appeared to be no upper deck. A cabin was located at the stern and another forward. A single mast, fitted with a yard and sail, jutted from its foredeck. But behind the mast, a tall black pipe could be seen belching sooty black clouds into the bright summer sky. And behind the smokestack, a pair of giant A-frames supporting a crosshead betrayed the presence of an intricate machine hidden below. Two half-round wooden boxes, one on either side of the craft, concealed from view a pair of giant sidewheel paddles that the engines turned to propel the craft, even against wind and tide. On the sides of the paddle boxes could be seen in elegant, brightly painted letters the words *Union Line* and *Chesapeake*. The steamboat age had finally come to the tidewater.[52]

The diminutive steamboat *Chesapeake,* fielded by the recently formed Union Line packet boat company, was the ambassador of a new era of transportation and the herald of an era of renewed commerce for the innumerable little towns and landings that dotted the shores of tidewater Maryland. The ship itself had been built for the line by the William Flannigan shipyard in Baltimore Harbor at 55 St. Patrick's Row (the site of present-day Pratt Street near Market House) under the supervision of its first commander, Captain Edward Trippe. By June 13 the ship had already made her maiden run from Bowley's Wharf, Baltimore, to Annapolis and back and a second one a week later to Rock Hall on the Eastern Shore.[53]

But it was on Monday, June 21, that commercial history was made when *Chesapeake* made the first of her regular packet runs between Baltimore and Frenchtown, a round trip of 140 miles, in twenty-four hours. As with the prototype of any innovative technology, her navigational capabilities were relatively crude when compared to later refinements. Her wheels were ten feet in diameter and five feet in depth. Her engine was a crosshead, which revolved a cogwheel that worked upon a cast-iron shaft. The smokestack was amidships, behind the engine. The boiler was about twenty feet in length and was elevated two feet above the deck. There was no pilothouse or even a steering wheel. The pilot was obliged to stand at the bow and shout out the course to a man stationed amidships, who then relayed the directions to a helmsman. There were no bells to signal the engine room, and the captain was obliged to convey his commands by word-of-mouth relay or by simply stamping his heels on the woodwork over the engine room. Managing such a machine was a learning experience. Indeed, the ship had been in service for a full six months before the engineer accidentally discovered he could reverse the engine and back her up![54]

The regularity of the packet's schedule, no longer a slave to winds and tides, brought a vast improvement in efficiency, hence profitability. The Union Line had discontinued its Courthouse Point connection long before the war, having wisely focused its business on the Baltimore-Frenchtown run. Regular trips to Frenchtown were soon being made thrice weekly by *Chesapeake,* departing from Bowley's Wharf at 9 A.M. Mondays, Wednesdays, and Fridays. Upon arrival at Frenchtown, passengers transferred to a company stagecoach that carried them over the turnpike to New Castle, where they again transferred to the company steamboat *Delaware* for the trip to Philadelphia. *Chesapeake* was soon returning a 40 percent profit for investors.[55]

Within a short time, the Union Line's monopoly on steamboat commerce to the Elk had begun to severely cut into the business of its major rival, the firm of Briscoe and Partridge, which operated a sailing packet and stage line between Baltimore and Philadelphia via Elkton and Wilmington. Eager to accept the challenge, in 1815 Briscoe and Partridge chartered a Delaware River steamer named *Eagle,* brought her around to the Chesapeake, and on July 24 began making regular runs with her to Elkton. There, passengers would disembark, take the stage to Wilmington, and then board the company steamboat *Vesta* for Philadelphia. The new operation was called the Elkton Line.[56]

Competition stiffened even more in August 1816 when the Union Line fielded the newly built steamboat *Philadelphia* for deployment on the Frenchtown run and the steamboat *Baltimore* for service on the Delaware. Briscoe and Partridge escalated the contest on December 2, 1816, by announcing that yet another new steamboat named *New Jersey,* built only two years earlier, had arrived from Philadelphia via Norfolk and would commence operations running from the firm's Light Street Wharf in Baltimore. In 1818, the Union Line again upped the ante by acquiring the Baltimore-built steamer *United States.* By now, the rivalry had simply become too costly, and the Elkton Line could no longer compete. In 1819 Briscoe and Partridge succumbed and sold off *New Jersey* and *Eagle,* the first to their rival and the second to Captain George Weems, who opened his own line between Annapolis and the Patuxent.[57]

The Union Line now held a stranglehold on packet operations to the Elk, with Frenchtown reaping the benefits of the traffic. With competition gone, the line no longer needed four steamers, two of which were already worn out from hard service. In 1820, *Chesapeake* was abandoned, and a year later, *New Jersey* followed suit. But demand continued to increase. Thus in 1823, the Union Line added the speedy steamer *Constitution,* built at Baltimore. The company was obviously growing and would eventually evolve through at least three regimes: the Union Line, the Union Canal Line, and the Citizen's Union Line.[58]

By now Frenchtown had become a place of substantial importance, primarily from profits derived as a waypoint for both the shipping and stage operations. Farmers in the vicinity benefited from the sale of surplus horses, grains, and feed to the proprietors of the stage lines, and from the sale of food, supplies, and other goods to the hotel keepers in the village for the use of passengers. Occasionally, an illustrious notable of the day might pass through, leaving a fleeting reflection of notoriety or fame. In 1824, when General Lafayette arrived in America for his celebrated tour of his adopted country, he traveled to Frenchtown by stage and was there met by a committee aboard the steamer *United States,* commanded by Captain Trippe.

In October 1829 the 13.6-mile-long Chesapeake and Delaware Canal was finally opened, connecting two new landings optimistically named Chesapeake City on one end and Delaware City on the other and linked by a series of four locks. The new era of canalization in the Chesapeake tidewater had arrived, albeit not without competition. For many travelers and commercial interests, the C&D had yet to prove its value. Its strongest rival was to be the nascent railroad industry which had made its appearance in Maryland only three years earlier. Many visionaries believed that the railroad would readily unseat the canal as the most expeditious, inexpensive means of commercial transportation. As travel from Baltimore to Philadelphia on the Union Line had proved, a strong reliance by the public upon the already tried and true route across the peninsula via Frenchtown would soon point the way.

Moves were soon afoot to establish a railroad line between Frenchtown and New Castle. The initiative was launched by an enterprising group of Philadelphians led by John and Thomas Janvier of New Castle, founders of the Frenchtown and New Castle Turnpike Company. During the 1827–1828 session of the Maryland State legislature and later in the Delaware legislature, a new company was officially chartered with a capital stock of $200,000 as The New Castle and Frenchtown Turnpike and Railroad Company. The line was destined to become one of the first railroads to be built in the nation. Perhaps owing to doubts about the new transportation technology to be used in the enterprise, the charter contained a provision requiring the company to keep open a turnpike (presumably the one already extant) alongside the railroad.[59]

The contest between water, canal, and rail was on. The Union Line faced strong competition from yet another line, the new Pennsylvania-Delaware-Maryland Steam Navigation Company, which soon came to be known as the Citizens Line. The Citizens Line operated the Philadelphia-to-Maryland end of the canal and a stage running from Delaware City to Chesapeake City. On the Maryland side, the new company also fielded the steamer *Carroll of Carrollton* to run from Baltimore to Chesapeake City. The Union line responded in 1830 by putting on two new steamers, *George Washington* and *Robert Morris,* as well as a flotilla of its own canal barges in an effort to maintain its leadership.[60] The boom days for Frenchtown were at hand.

Despite early albeit cautious optimism, the Frenchtown and New Castle Railroad was not completed until 1831, and not alongside the highway as required, but a considerable distance to the south of the road on a more practicable terrain. From the outset of actual construction in July 1830, when ten thousand cedar rails and tons of blocks of graystone arrived in New Castle and a pair of passenger cars, each costing $510 and resembling stage coaches, came in from Baltimore, the project was undertaken with vigor.[61]

Johnston provides an interesting description of the manner of construction. "The rails were placed about the same distance apart as in modern roads, but instead of being laid upon wooden sleepers, as the rails of modern roads are, they were placed upon blocks of stone ten or twelve inches square. These stones had holes drilled in them, in which a wooden plug was inserted, and upon them were laid wooden rails about six inches square and ten or twelve feet long, which were fastened to the stones by means of a piece of flat iron shaped like the letter L, which was fastened to the stone by means of a spike driven into the wooden plug through a hole in one extremity of the iron, and another spike driven into a wooden rail through another hole at the other extremity." Placed about three feet apart, each stone had two of the iron attachments, one on each side of the rail. Flat iron bars were then spiked on top of the wooden rails to complete the structure. The great defect in the road was the lack of some means to restrain the rails from spreading apart. It was soon discovered that the only way to correct this deficiency was to use the ties extending from one rail to the other, to which both rails were fastened, as in later roads.[62]

Upon completion of the new railroad, which opened on July 4, 1831, the first cars were drawn by horses, perhaps owing to difficulty in securing locomotives. A single horse was attached to each car and fresh horses were changed at two stations on the road—Glasgow and Bear. For the next two years, traffic along the tracks would continue to be hauled by animal power rather than steam.[63]

Eminently aware of the challenge before them, the canal users sought permission to employ steam-propelled passenger barges in the canal, so that the canal barges "might rival in speed, as they would in comfort and conveniences, any other way of crossing the Delaware peninsula." Soon, the C&D faced an even more serious challenge when, in 1832, the Citizen's Line and the Union Line, both of which employed their own barges on the system, joined forces in a rate dispute with the canal company and refused to use the canal. When a temporary cessation of regular passenger travel through the canal ensued, most trans-peninsula traffic began to direct its business to the primitive, horse-drawn Frenchtown and New Castle Railroad. The F&NC line was now in the driver's seat, and in 1833 secured a monopoly on steam transportation from the Maryland legislature to protect it from rival up-starts in the area.[64]

The monopoly was broken the following year when yet another competitor entered the picture—the new Peoples Line, formed to run from Baltimore to Chesapeake City and from Delaware City to Philadelphia. The canal was soon back in use. The rigor of the competition between the new company and the Citizen's Union Line was evident from the outset. Highly touted races pitted the newer company's steamboats against the older vet-eran steamers of the Citizen's Union Line and were run on both the Delaware and the Chesapeake, rivaling in spirit and drama those colorful races that would later win eternal fame on the mighty Mississippi.[65] In 1833, when the Peoples Line steamer *Kentucky* bested the best of the Citizen's Union steamers in a sprint down the Elk and across to Bal-timore, it seemed for some a prognostication of the future. But for the canal supporters, the future seemed dark indeed.

In the same year as *Kentucky*'s victory, the first locomotive steam engine, built in Eng-land and called *Delaware,* was placed in service on the F&NC line. The introduction of a real steam-driven locomotive was not without its costs and difficulties, for railroading in its infancy was an era of trial and error. The entire track system soon had to be rebuilt with iron rails. Within a year's time, *Delaware* also had to be rebuilt and was then renamed *Phoenix.* The company soon realized that it had made no provision "to supply the screeching and panting monster with water, and had to serve it with this indispensable fluid, much after the manner of watering a horse, from the springs and wells along the road." Fuel for the fires, primarily pinewood, had to be chopped down along the shores of the Elk and shipped to Frenchtown by boat. The manner in which the train was brought to a full stop, at least in its early days, was archaic in the extreme. When the locomotive was nearing the point at which stopping was necessary, the engineer shut off the power and, by releasing steam from a safety valve, sent a message down the track that he was coming. Negro roustabouts at the station would then rush out, seize the train with their hands, lean backwards, and dig their heels into the ground, while the station agent shoved a fence rail through the spokes of the moving locomotive wheel. Such means for stopping occasionally resulted in serious acci-dents. Incredibly, the maiden voyage of *Delaware* took several days rather than several hours to complete. In August 1833, while attempting to "check" the company's new loco-motive *Virginia* too suddenly, the engineer, a chap named Raybow, succeeded in twice de-railing part of the train, two cars the first time and five cars the second. Although nobody was hurt, two cars were so badly crushed they had to be left on the side of the road.[66]

Despite such setbacks as the inexperience of the crews and the primitive nature of the cars and the locomotives that pulled them, the railroad eventually ran smoothly. It was a vast im-provement over the horse-drawn system. Soon, travelers disembarking at the wharf at Frenchtown could entrain aboard cars that comfortably carried ten to twelve passengers each and could be in New Castle in about an hour. The fare was fixed at 25 cents a passen-ger, 12½ cents for baggage not exceeding one hundred pounds. A rate of 3 cents per mile per ton was charged for freight. Two trains a day made the excursion. And business was good. The increase of traffic passing through Frenchtown resulting from use of the railroad soon obliged the Citizen's Union Line to make twice daily runs between Baltimore and

Frenchtown. In 1834, the steamer *George Washington* left Bowley's Wharf for Frenchtown Wharf daily at 6 A.M., and the *Constitution* left at 5 P.M. On any given day, as many as twenty-five to thirty small vessels employed in hauling fuel for the railroad could be found at the Frenchtown Wharf, which, together with the twice-daily arrival of the Citizen's Union Line steamers, made the place one of commercial importance.[67]

A train trip in these early days was an experience not to be forgotten and often required the traveler to have nerves of steel. Fortunately, the recollections of one bold sojourner, Thomas Colley Grattan, who traveled from Philadelphia to Baltimore via New Castle and Frenchtown, have preserved his adventures for posterity.

On quitting the steamboat at New Castle, he wrote in April 1840, he had embarked upon the railroad for the twenty-two-mile trip to Frenchtown. "We had made about two-thirds of our journey, when, at one of the 'crossings' a violent jolt, accompanied by a loud crash, made all the passengers start, and considerably alarmed some of them. The continued rapidity of our movement, however, satisfied all that no accident had occurred to the carriages; and in a quarter of an hour the train stopped close to the water-side at Frenchtown."

As the passengers stepped out, Grattan queried the conductor and engineer, who were standing together on the platform of the locomotive, regarding the cause of the sudden shock they had experienced.

"Well, it was in going over a chaise and horse," replied one of them, very coolly.

"There was no one in the chaise?" asked Grattan anxiously.

"Oh, yes there were two ladies," replied one of the railroad men.

"Were they thrown out?"

"I guess they were, and pretty well smashed, too."

"Good God! And why didn't you stop the train?" shrieked Grattan. "Can't you send back to know what state they're in?"

"Well, mister, I reckon they're in the State of Delaware; but you'd better jump into the steamer there, or you're like to lose your passage."

With these words the conductor turned his attentions toward some other inquirer, as Grattan glanced towards the steamboat, which was letting loose from the wharf. There was not a moment to spare as he rushed headlong down to the wharf to jump aboard.

"We were almost instantly cutting through the waters," recalled the traveler, "but, as may be supposed, absorbed for some time in the reflections which followed the shock our better feelings had received. Many of the passengers agreed with us, that it was inhuman of the conductor not to have stopped the train and looked after the injured persons. Others remarked that wouldn't have done any good, and that the train was obliged to be up to time, or have delayed the steamer for ten minutes or more. This was unanswerable: the subject dropped. But a few days afterwards I saw in a Baltimore paper a paragraph, stating that one of the ladies had been killed, the other badly wounded, the horse 'mashed,' and the chaise . . . broken to pieces. The miracle was that the train was not shaken off the track. But even that had no power to excite the phlegmatic conductor or go-a-head engineer."[68]

Frenchtown reached its peak in these boisterous, early days of steamboating and railroading. And although never officially designated as a town or port during the colonial period or for that matter any time thereafter, it had nevertheless achieved a certain historical pinnacle not to be denied. In the age of steam, it provided a strategic relay point that helped facilitate the rise of the young titan on the Patapsco and its commercial relationship with the older giant on the Delaware. It had successfully provided an alternative route across the Delmarva Peninsula at a time when the canal mindset reigned supreme in America. Yet physically it had never been anything more than a waterside crossroads.

On July 4, 1837, a new railroad was opened between Philadelphia and Wilmington. It was to be the first section of the Philadelphia, Wilmington, and Baltimore Railroad, and it was completed to Baltimore the following year to compete with and ultimately prevail over the Frenchtown and New Castle line. The two lines would soon merge, with the business of both being conducted under the name of the Philadelphia, Wilmington, and Baltimore Railroad. In 1844, yet another steamboat company, the Ericsson Line, secured permission to start a route from Baltimore via the C&D Canal direct to Philadelphia. Frenchtown and the land-sea route between Baltimore and Philadelphia that was its main reason for being could no longer hope to contend with the more direct connections of the competition. Finally, in 1853, the railroad between Frenchtown and New Castle was shut down and the last regular packets running between Frenchtown Wharf and Baltimore, the steamboats *Pioneer* and *Ohio,* ceased to call. The consequence was immediate decline and, finally, total abandonment.[69]

It was late afternoon as we lurched down to the river and walked along the shoreline of old Frenchtown. The tide was out, and some distance from our arrival point, I spotted the stubs of ancient wharf pilings barely peeking from below the surface. As I walked toward them to get a closer look, I stumbled over what I took to be a large stone. The beach was covered with them, all flat and round. And with square holes in their centers.

I was stunned, for spread out below for a distance of several hundred feet, I could see that the beach was covered with scores of millstones. Each was about three feet in diameter and heavily eroded by years of tidal action. It appeared that they had been deployed to counter erosion as ready-made riprap, and they had obviously been lying there undisturbed for many years. I immediately summoned my colleagues and set about to inventory what must certainly be one of the most unusual breakwaters in the Chesapeake tidewater. By the time the sun set and darkness wrapped us like a blanket, we had counted 156 millstones, one of which showed a most intriguing set of numbers chiseled into its face: "1776"!

The millstones were mysterious enough, but in the twilight of evening, as we made our way to the car tripping here and there over what I imagined were foundations of a long forgotten age, I wondered what history must still lie beneath us, hidden beneath the roots and soil of time.

There is little left today to recall the heyday of Frenchtown. On the road from Chesapeake City to Elkton, traces of the old railroad bed, which once connected the town with New Castle, may be discerned in the early spring when vegetation has yet to come in, or in early winter months after the plants have completely died back. Much of the bed was placed under cultivation after the demise of the railroad. Where the iron horse had once cut a bold swath, the lands were eventually covered in grasses and waving grain. Now, mundane asphalt and concrete highways, shopping malls, and tract housing dot the plain. At the Delaware terminus of the old rail line, in New Castle, stood the Frenchtown Monument, constructed of stone sleepers on which the wooden and iron rails once bore the rickety trains that served as the major instruments of commercial passenger transportation between Baltimore and Philadelphia. Not far from old Frenchtown Wharf lay the foundations of Frisby Henderson's house, which once served as a home and a hotel where travelers berthed three to a bed.

An unusual breakwater graces the waterfront at old Frenchtown on Elk River—scores of millstones.

Despite the ravages of war and decline, the old house had managed to survive until the midtwentieth century when it was finally burned down. And not far away, at Brantwood Farm, two ancient cannons still recall for the curiosity seeker the ignominious visit by British invaders nearly two centuries ago. But it is down on the Elk River in what was Frenchtown proper, where gray, eroded pilings project from the water at odd angles and weathered old millstones bulkhead the shores against the inevitable, that the true history of old Frenchtown lies.

Someday, perhaps, with the bite of the archaeologist's trowel and a little digging in the attic of the past, old Frenchtown's role in the making of tidewater history will at last be recognized.

9 GEORGETOWN & FREDERICKTOWN

"Tiger Banditti"

July 1608. There is no way to relate the elation that Captain John Smith and his daring band of adventurers, a dozen strong, must have felt when they discovered the mile-wide mouth of the Eastern Shore river known as Tockwough. It was certainly one of the most inviting and scenic maws of any of the scores of major and minor tributaries they had encountered so far on their historic voyage up Chesapeake Bay. But whatever exhilaration they may have experienced, it was most certainly short lived, for soon after entering the waterway, they found themselves surrounded in a most "barbarous manner" by a formidable fleet of canoes manned by scores of well-armed savages. Smith quickly discerned that the natives numbered about a hundred warriors and from the moment of their initial contact it was apparent that their language was different from the tribes of mainland Virginia. Fortunately, one among them was conversant in the dialect of the Powhatans, which the captain knew well. Through him, a friendly parley was soon opened.[1]

After several anxious moments brought on by the natives' discovery of weapons which the Englishmen had only the day before received from a party of Massawomekes (Iroquois), the mortal enemies to the Tockwoughs, the Indians conducted their visitors approximately seven miles up the river to a palisaded village. Here was a large fortified town "mantled with the barks of trees, with scaffolds like mounts, brested about with brests very formally." As the diminutive party of Englishmen pulled their little boat ashore, they were delighted to be welcomed by throngs of singing and dancing men, women, and children laden with fruits and furs and other possessions that were extended as gifts. Mats were quickly spread on the ground for the explorers to sit upon with their hosts who were "stretching to their best abilities to express their loves."[2]

Captain Smith was a diligent observer of detail and noted that his hosts were well armed with many hatchets and knives as well as pieces of iron and brass that had been acquired in trade with the mighty Susquehannocks to the north. The Susquehannocks, a mysterious people spoken of in awe and fear by other natives the Englishman had encountered, inhabited the region above the head of the Chesapeake, at least a two-day journey above the fall line of the Susquehanna River. The captain had for some time been anxious to make contact with this purported race of giants, and it seemed that this was his golden opportunity. After some negotiations, he was able to prevail upon the Tockwough interpreter to undertake a visit in company with an interpreter skilled in the Susquehannock language to arrange for a meeting with them. The interpreters agreed and for the next three or four days, the captain anxiously awaited their return. Finally, "sixty of those giant-like people came down, with presents of venison, tobacco pipes three foot in length, baskets, targets, bow and arrows." Despite high winds that made the Bay almost impassable, five of the chief werowances, or priests, boldly boarded Smith's barge to cross the Bay for the Tockwough village, leaving their comrades and their own canoes behind.[3]

Smith's party was in the habit of beginning each day with a solemn prayer, a Psalm, which filled the natives of both tribes with curiosity. When the prayers were done, the Indians busied themselves in planning their day and then engaged in their own form of worship. They "began in a most passionate manner," the captain later wrote in describing the proceedings (while referring to himself in the third party),

> to hold up their hands to the sun, with a most fearful song, then embracing our captain, they began to adore him in like manner . . . tho he rebuked them, yet they proceeded till their song was finished: which done with a most strange furious action, and a hellish voice, began an oration of their loves; that ended, with a great painted bearskin they covered him: then one ready with a great chain of white beads, weighing at least six or seven pounds, hung it around his neck, the others had 18 mantels, made of diverse sorts of skins sewed together: all these with many other toys they laid at his feet, stroking their ceremonious hands about his neck for his creation to be their governor and protector; promising their aids, victuals, or what they had to be his, if he would stay with them, to defend and revenge them of the Massawomecks.[4]

John Smith did not stay with the Susquehannocks as they requested, but he promised to visit them the following year. Nor did he tarry with his new friends at Tockwough. But his visit had been significant, for he had not only opened a correspondence with the mighty tribe on the Susquehanna, but had discovered a small but important tributary of the Chesapeake that might have gone unnoticed for many years thereafter. The little river upon which the village of Tockwough was ensconced and after which it had been named would soon come to be known to the white man as the Sassafras. And upon its steep banks, overlooking deep but placid waters, not far from where the English explorers had sat in conference with the noble looking Susquehannocks and the amicable Tockwoughs, would eventually be erected a pair of towns named after two most unfortunate sibling princes, George and Frederick.

The Sassafras River has been variously described by the esteemed tidewater historian Paul Wilstach as "a river of creeks" and as "one of the most beautiful bodies of water in Maryland." Another chronicler of Chesapeake lore called it "a fairyland river."[5] Even today it is all of these things and more. Geographically, the Sassafras is a short waterway, barely fifteen miles long, flowing in a comparatively straight line almost due west from Delaware and forming the border between Cecil and Kent Counties. Its waters, nourished by scores of meandering creeks and rivulets, drift lazily along an inordinately scenic terrain perforated here and there with deep inlets and coves.

European occupation of its shores, primarily around its entrance, came soon after the settlement of St. Mary's City many miles to the south, although little record has survived of these early pioneers. By some accounts, a ferry was in service perhaps by 1650 and certainly no later than 1679, running between what is now Ordinary Point on the river's central north shore and a peninsular projection upon which modern Kentmore Park is located on the south. Cost for a crossing was a shilling. By 1659, there was at least one large plantation on the creek owned by John Turner, who left his name to a major tributary which feeds the waterway from its southern midsection. But Turner was not alone in his efforts to settle the area, which had become a refuge for Swedes, Finns, Dutchmen, and other displaced émigrés from Delaware.[6]

The beauty and the teeming life that abounded along the Sassafras deeply impressed early travelers. In 1679, Jasper Danckers, traveling through Maryland to explore the possibility of establishing a Labadist colony on the Eastern Shore, recorded in his journal the wonders of the river's wildlife. "I have nowhere seen so many ducks together as were seen in this creek," he wrote. "The water was so black with them that it seemed, when you looked from the land upon the water, as if it were a mass of filth or turf; and when they flew up there was a rushing and vibration of the air like a great storm coming through the trees, and even like the rumbling of distant thunder, while the sky over the creek was filled with them like a cloud, or like the starlings fly at harvest time in the fatherland...They rose not in flocks of ten or twelve, or twenty or thirty, but continuously, wherever we pushed our way; and as they made room for us there was such an incessant clattering made with their wings upon the water where they rose, and such a noise of those flying higher up, that it was as if they were all the time surrounded by a whirlwind or storm. This proceeded . . . from ducks and other water fowl; and it is not peculiar to this place alone, but it occurred on all of the creeks and rivers we crossed, though they were the most numerous in the morning and evening, when they are most easily shot."[7]

The earliest effort to legislate into existence an urban center on the south bank of the Sassafras, then a part of Talbot County, came in 1669 with Lord Baltimore's proclamation decreeing that a town be erected "afore the town land in . . . Sassafrax River in Talbot County." The notation that the site was to be "afore the town land" strongly suggests that property had been purchased and was already set aside for such a purpose. The effort, like most of the other eleven sites so dedicated that year, failed miserably. Two years later Lord Baltimore tried again, this time declaring two sites on the river "at the land late of Mr. Hatton in Sassafrax River in Baltimore County" and "at the Land of Jonathan Sybery [Sibrey]" be selected for the erection of towns. Again the efforts failed, although both sites were noted on Augustine Herrman's map of Maryland. Considering that the map was compiled by a neighbor to both Hatton and Sibrey, who was a blatant proponent of early Maryland boosterism, the inclusion is not surprising even though the towns failed to take hold.[8]

In 1674, Lord Baltimore issued a proclamation creating Cecil County. The new county was to extend "from the mouth of the Susquehanna River and so down the eastern side of Chesapeake Bay to Swan Point and from thence to Hell Point and so up Chester River to the head thereof." Two of the new county's foremost citizens, Augustine Herrman, Lord of Bohemia Manor, and Jonathan Sibrey, were appointed to erect a courthouse and prison "in the most convenient place . . . upon a certain parcel of land lying on the north of Sassafras River." The tract they selected belonged to Jeffery Peterson and consisted of fifty acres of land called Young's Neck, "bounding on the creek of Burlies land on the one side & on Coofings Creek on the other side."[9] It was considered a strategically central location in the county, although perhaps as few as a dozen inhabitants of the county lived north of the Elk and these mostly along the Northeast River. The site itself was situated a short distance east of Ordinary Point and would eventually become known as Jamestown (in the nineteenth century, Oldtown), although little is known about either except that they were anything but towns. Very little is actually known about the court building except that it was built by Colonel Casparus Herrman. The specifications for the project, which had been delayed since 1692, were revised in 1695 to read: "That whereas the shingles were to be upon plank they shall be upon laths and whereas the house was to be all brick work it is to be of stone up to the water table for the building whereof he [Herrman] is to have two hundred thousand pounds of tobacco & two hundred and fifty pounds sterling."[10]

When completed, the building was quite small, for, as it was reported in evidence taken before a land commission a number of years later, jurors were often in the habit of removing themselves from the building during summer sessions and convening beneath a shady oak tree on the river bank to carry out their deliberations, a site which for many years thereafter was called the Jury Oak.[11]

While county growth sputtered along, in 1683, the legislature tried its own hand at new town development. This time one new site was selected on the Sassafras, located between the courthouse site and "that island" (presumably the Ordinary Point peninsula). The following year, the legislature authorized yet another site at a plantation called "John West in Sassafrax River." Although the location of the designated site is uncertain, is was probably situated on the south shore of the river at or just east of Turner's Creek in South Sassafras Parish and may have formed the fulcrum of what was later referred to as Shrewsbury Town. In any event, the site must have entertained some development, at least enough to warrant that a customs officer named William Nowell be sworn in to enforce the 1688 Acts of Trade there. By 1697, the town had failed to take hold, and the government was obliged to address customs duties in other ways. Thus, on December 24, William Wyvill was designated "Riding Surveyor for the two rivers of Bohemia & Sassafras in Cecil County, and on the heads of all other rivers on the Eastern Shore" as far as Susquehanna River. To prevent smuggling and illegal commerce, the "surveyor" (or roving customs inspector) was given full power and authority "to enter into any ship bottom, boat or other vessel, as also into any shop, house, warehouse, hostry or other place whatsoever to make diligent search into any wagon or cart, trunk, chest, pack, case, truss or any other parcel or package whatsoever for any goods, wares, merchandises to be imported or exported either by land or water."[12]

In 1706 the organization of Kent County required Cecil County to turn over all lands between the Sassafras and the Chester River to the new county. The effect was yet another round of new town petitions. In Kent County, a new county seat on the Chester River was authorized, but on the Sassafras, it appeared to be a new town redux. The old John West site, probably Shrewsbury Town had, of course, failed to mature, and the legislature reacted in a predictable manner: it reauthorized yet another town "at Sassafrax River where Shrewsberry Town was." The following year, the legislature thought better of the rededication and ordered "the place appointed for Shrewsberry Towne on Sassafrax River by the said Act appointed be also deserted and laid out where the Commissioners for Towns in Kent County aforesaid have purchased land for the same." The new site selected by the commissioners, a tract of fifty acres, was also on the Sassafras River "upon land purchased of Mr. Bennett," but it failed to survive.[13] Yet another town site had been ordered laid out in 1706 on "the land belonging to Isaac Calk" near the head of the Sassafras in Cecil County, but this site too failed to take hold and had to be renominated the following year, although with equally discouraging results. It would appear that after so many dismal failures, urban development on the Sassafras was unlikely to get off the ground soon, if ever.

By 1717, the demographic center shifted away from the Sassafras, and for the convenience of the inhabitants having business with the Cecil County Court, it was necessary to remove the court to a more central location. In June, a bill was introduced in the legislature to erect a courthouse on the Elk River at Long Point on the east side of Broad Creek in Bohemia Manor. Colonel Ephraim Augustine Herrman was allowed three hundred pounds of tobacco as payment for two acres of land for the building of the courthouse.[14]

For the inhabitants living along the Sassafras, the removal of the last social gathering place of any importance to them must have come as an unsettling shock. The potential for urban development on the river was not yet dead—but it seemed so.

❖

It is uncertain what motivation or political rivalries guided the citizens and freeholders of Cecil and Kent Counties when they petitioned the colonial government at nearly the same time for the erection of two new but separate towns directly opposite each other on the river. But one thing could not have been more clear: the sites eventually selected were among the most picturesque on the entire Eastern Shore and perhaps the most logical in commercial terms. At any rate, neither logic nor geography seemed to have served as paradigms for town site selection in colonial Maryland.

It is known that on March 21, 1732, the first petition was submitted by the freeholders of Cecil County, requesting that thirty acres of land overlooking the middle Sassafras on a site known as Pennington's Point or Prizing Point, straddling two tracts of land called Bunting-ton and Happy Harbour, be purchased for a town. After several days of massaging, a bill was finally produced in the Lower House of the General Assembly and sent for consider-ation by the Upper House, but after a week of negotiations (and for reasons unknown) it died aborning. Four years later, on March 24, 1736, another petition was submitted by "several freehoulders of Cecil County, praying leave to bring in a Bill to Erect a Town at Penning-tons Point," but because it was attached to two other unpopular bills, it was defeated by a vote of twenty-eight to seventeen. The following day, the petition was reintroduced on its own strength and moved forward. After considerable manipulation, the bill was finally pre-sented to the governor on May 6, 1736, and signed into law. The town was to be called Fred-erick Town after Prince Frederick, the ill-fated son of King George II who would die in early youth.[15]

It would seem that the inhabitants of Kent County were not to be outdone, and, perhaps in an effort to protect commercial interests, they submitted their own petition four days after the freeholders of Cecil County had posed theirs. One noted urban historian, John Reps, has suggested that the inhabitants of Kent may have been determined that they should not be in-convenienced by having to ship their goods through the town in the adjoining county. On March 27, 1736, the Upper House read the petition of Gideon Pearce and others requesting that a bill "to lay out eighty acres of land, part of a tract of land called Tolchester on Sassa-fras River in the possession of the said Pearce, into a town and that the town may be called George Town," after Prince Frederick's brother, Prince George (who would later become King George III, lose an American empire, and die a madman). They were successful in ob-taining their law, as Reps noted, "but not much of a town."[16]

To further the Cecil County town site development, the Assembly appointed Colonel John Ward, Joshua George, John Baldwin, Peregrine Frisby, and Alphonso Cosden, or a majority of any three among them, to serve as commissioners to purchase thirty acres of land "as lies most convenient to the said river" Sassafras for surveying and laying out sixty equal lots for Frederick Town. The commissioners were instructed to have completed the purchase and survey by December 31, 1736. The town lots were to be laid out in such a way as to allow sufficient space "for streets, lanes and alleys." The lots were to be numbered 1 through 60. As with many other new town initiatives, the owners of the land from whom the purchase was made had the first pick of any two lots, after which the remainder could be sold. During the first four months, no purchaser might acquire more than one lot, and addi-tional purchase restrictions were included to prevent speculators from profiteering. Special mechanisms were set in place to permit a jury decision in the event arbitration was required between the original property holders and the commissioners purchasing the land. The sur-veyor for Cecil County was to be paid £4 current money from the county levy and was re-quired to "return a plat thereof to the County Clerk to be by him kept among the county records." Any lot holder in the town who failed to build a house no less than four hundred

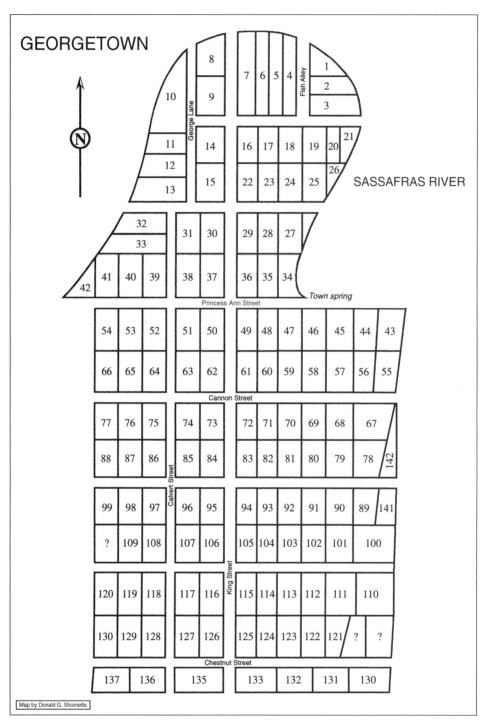

Plat of Georgetown, Maryland, 1787. From an unsigned and undated copy of a resurvey drawn by William Humphrey, now in the Maryland Historical Society, Baltimore, Maryland, entitled "Plat of Georgetown, Kent County, Maryland." The plan is typical of the simple grid pattern adopted for most new town plans throughout the Maryland tidewater.

feet square with a brick chimney upon his property within two years faced the loss of their property to anyone else who paid the commissioners for it following the designated time period. Finally, anyone taking up a lot in the new town was liable to pay an annual tax of one penny sterling to the Lord Proprietor and his heirs forever.[17]

The commissioners waited to the last minute to perform their appointed tasks, for not until December 11 was the town finally laid out. Unfortunately, the records relating to its actual design have been lost. According to Cecil County historian George Johnson, the only information available at that time was derived from a plat by Edward W. Lockwood taken from a copy of the original made by the well-known surveyor William Rumsey. This plat reportedly showed the designated thirty acres divided into sixty lots of about three-fifths of an acre each, separated by six streets which, with several small alleys, contained six and a half acres. At Frederick Town the Sassafras runs in a southwesterly direction, but the streets run due east and west or due north and south, crossing each other checkerboard fashion, "which causes the town to be very irregular and ill-shaped." Ogle Street, Frederick Street, and Orange Street extended north from the river, while Baltimore, Prince William, and George Streets extended west from the river.[18]

Interestingly, the act for erecting Frederick Town noted that the petitioners gave as their reasons for wanting a town only that "many benefits . . . may arise to themselves and others." Those in Kent County who had petitioned for the erection of a town on the Tolchester tract were equally hazy in noting "that many benefits and advantages may arise to themselves and others the Inhabitants of this province and the traders," suggesting that commerce was as important a consideration as simple convenience.[19]

The Tolchester tract in Kent County was owned by Gideon Pearce, a "Gentleman" and speculator who had already taken it upon himself to lay out and sell some lots even before passage of the act, primarily to several persons on the site where a ferry crossed the river. As with Frederick Town, the Assembly appointed a panel of commissioners to purchase the land, totaling sixty acres, "convenient to the ferry Landing" but not including the lots already sold. The commission consisted of Captain George Wilson, Philip Kennard, Christopher Hall, Jervis Spencer, and Thomas Hynson, or any three of them, and it was authorized to have a town consisting of one hundred lots laid out. Because the town size was to be nearly twice that of Frederick Town, the surveyor of Kent County was to be paid £8, twice the amount as his colleague in Cecil County. In every other way the legislation creating George Town duplicated the building requirements, rights of lot owners, taxation, and recordation that the Frederick Town act had, with the exception of extending protections and rights to the owners of lots which had already been purchased prior to passage. This may have been a legislative consideration prompted by Pearce's obvious speculation.[20] Unlike the commissioners of Cecil County, however, the Kent County commissioners failed to perform their appointed tasks in the allotted time. Thus, during the spring 1737 session of the General Assembly, a supplementary act was passed requiring the same commissioners "to do the several matters and things every way relating thereto in as full and ample manner as they might or could have done any time before the last day of December last" provided they complete their obligations by October 31.[21]

Although the original survey plat of George Town has never been found, a barely legible 1787 copy drawn by William Humphrey survives in the collections of the Maryland Historical Society and offers some insight into the 1737 design. The Humphrey plan may not be a totally accurate representation of the original since notes in the border indicate difficulty in reestablishing survey lines. It is also evident that at least forty-two lots were added at the time of the redraft, probably at the south end of the town, but the basic town design is apparent.

George Town, like Frederick Town, was laid out on a north-south grid. Its northern side, a substantial peninsula projecting into the river, contained forty-two lots, some of which were among those sold by Pearce and taken up prior to survey. The remainder were neatly situated in a rectangular checkerboard fashion on the hillside and plain to the south. Two main roads, named Calvert Street and King Street, ran north and south, the latter of which ran through the center of town to the ferry. Two shorter north-south roads, George Lane and Fish Alley, helped to subdivide the irregularly shaped northern end of the town. At least six avenues ran east to west in 1787 (later there would be seven), but the names of only three are known: Princess Ann Street, Cannon Street, and, after 1787, Chestnut Street.[22]

Despite the earnest efforts of the freeholders of both counties to have the new towns on the Sassafras founded, their proximity to each other appears to have offset the gains that either might have had if only one had been established. Nevertheless, with the principal north-south road of the Eastern Shore and the most direct route from the south to New Castle, Philadelphia, and New York passing through the centers of both sites, the two villages managed to sprout over the next decade and then to cling to at least a crossroads status. The main highway, though little more than a dirt track usually a foot deep in mud after a hard rain, was one of the major thoroughfares of colonial America. Another road bypassed the towns by running around the head of Sassafras; it was of equal distance, but it did not provide the conveniences so readily available at the two crossroads villages. At both Georgetown and Fredericktown (as their names were by this time generally given), travelers could find livery for their horses, a warm inn, a hot meal, and a tavern or two. Although commercial shipping appears to have been somewhat negligible in the early years, vessels did eventually begin to call, and water transportation was available for travelers and shippers alike. Indeed, many notables who traveled extensively are known to have passed through or spent a night. The most noteworthy, of course, was a Virginia gentleman named Washington.[23]

By 1747 both sites were considered suitably central enough to the tobacco trade that inspection stations were ordered erected at each. The inspector at Georgetown was to receive an annual salary of £50, and the officer at Fredericktown was to be paid £60. Yet the quantity of tobacco shipped from the two towns was far below the amount expected by the government. By 1753 the Georgetown inspector's salary was reduced to £40 and the Fredericktown inspector's to £35 annually, indicating that both stations were examining far fewer hogsheads per year than had been anticipated. It also appears that the Georgetown station was now somewhat more busy than the one across the river, which justified the reversal of salary supremacy.

There were, of course, underlying causes for the shift in agricultural production. When the Tobacco Inspection Act was passed in 1747, a considerable portion of both Kent and Cecil Counties had already begun their withdrawal from economic dependency upon the stinking weed, shifting in production to grains. Tobacco farming on the Eastern Shore entered into a period of serious decline, as demand for flour, corn, and wheat rose to feed the overpopulated islands of the West Indies, to replace the lost harvests of war-torn Europe, and to help satiate the ravenous appetite of New England. By 1763, the volume of tobacco inspected at both stations had fallen to such an extent that it was decided that both sites be merged under one inspection authority. The General Assembly was diplomatic enough to avoid contention by maintaining two inspectors, one from each county, to conduct the weekly inspections. The work would still be divided between the two sites. By terms of the 1763 Tobacco Inspection Act, it was finalized that every week between April 1 and July 31, inspectors would be obliged to attend at Georgetown on Mondays, Tuesdays, and Wednesdays and at Fredericktown on Thursdays, Fridays, and Saturdays.[24]

Everyday life in the two villages was simple and without much controversy. In 1752, the most notorious topic of discussion focused upon the failure of the General Assembly to pass "An Act to Prohibit of Swine and Geese in George Town in Kent County."[25] Indeed, few events of note occurred in the two villages during their early years of existence. Mentions in the colony newspaper, the *Maryland Gazette,* were rare.

Ironically, events far afield would play a significant role in the history of the two towns. With the outbreak of the French and Indian War in 1754, the English colonies of America, including Maryland, were placed on a wartime footing. Suddenly, an influx of military personnel from Europe, as well as the fielding of local militias on a scale hitherto not experienced in the tidewater, began to place demands upon Maryland that were difficult to cope with, not the least of which was finding adequate winter lodgings for many of His Majesty's troops.

In late 1756 Governor Horatio Sharpe was instructed by the British government to house seven companies of Royal Americans in the colony. The units were to be provided winter quarters in Charlestown, Fredericktown, Georgetown, and Chestertown in Cecil and Kent Counties "that they might be assembled at Philadelphia more readily" when the spring campaigns finally began. All of the towns were within a three or four day march to New Castle, which was considered suitable as a marshaling area.[26]

But difficulties abounded. "The Companies," Sharpe later informed Lord Baltimore, "instead of 100 do not exceed 50 men each but as the towns are very small even that number has been with great difficulty supplied with such necessaries and conveniences as soldiers expect to be furnished with in winter quarters." Smallpox had broken out in Annapolis, making it impossible for the capital to provide support. Thus, the residents in towns selected by the government, including those on the Sassafras, were obliged to provide the necessities of subsistence, namely shelter, beds, firewood, and the like for the troops. Although the soldiers were supposed to be provided supplies from contractors engaged for that purpose, the economic and physical burden upon the inhabitants of Fredericktown and Georgetown, as elsewhere, was inordinately heavy. Thus, by February 1757 a subscription had to be taken up "in hopes of being reimbursed by the Assembly." It is unclear if reimbursements were ever paid.[27]

In October 1757, the governor and legislature were again informed by London that twenty companies of British regulars were to be quartered in the province. And again, Charlestown, Fredericktown, Georgetown, and Chestertown, among others, were to receive a company each. Owing to difficulties experienced the year before, the colony government was obliged to pass and publish a lengthy list of rules and regulations known as the Supply Act, governing the quartering of the troops and the responsibilities that were to be borne by the public in such matters. Commissioners were appointed for each town to oversee that the government's measures were put into effect and the regulations regarding the feeding and quartering of troops were strictly adhered to. William Raisin and John Cooper were authorized to implement the law in Fredericktown and Georgetown.[28]

However, the inhabitants of two towns in Cecil County, Georgetown and Charlestown, were not content with bearing the expenses to be incurred and, together with some citizens of Kent County, petitioned the government for financial compensation from a rather unique source of revenue. To encourage Marylanders in their war against the French and Indians, the colony government had authorized an expenditure of £3,670 to reward the taking of enemy scalps and prisoners. Most of the money had gone unused, so the petitioners requested that £2,000 be appropriated from the fund to defray the cost of quartering His Majesty's forces during the coming winter. The government was not amused, and "resolved in the negative."[29]

For the most part, the citizens of Maryland reacted stoically to the burden placed upon them. The maintenance of their own militias was one thing but, as elsewhere in English America, the inhabitants of Georgetown and Fredericktown were less than happy about being forced to quarter and feed His Majesty's troops in their own homes. A few years later they would let the Crown know how they felt in no uncertain terms when they joined a revolution.

The war had unexpected repercussions for at least one of the Sassafras towns. In early August 1755, an organized effort was initiated by the British government to remove a potential French threat in Nova Scotia, which had been ceded to England by the Treaty of Utrecht in 1713. On September 4, the *Maryland Gazette* reprinted a dispatch from a Boston newspaper stating: "That it being determined to remove French inhabitants, seven thousand of them are to be disposed of among the British Governments between Nova Scotia and Georgia; for which purpose all the vessels in Halifax fit for that service are taken up, and orders are come to town to engage as many vessels as will carry two thousand persons." The goal was nothing less than the forced removal of the entire population of the peaceful French Acadians of Nova Scotia. The plan called for the expulsion of all French Catholic "neutrals" who were deemed a threat to British control over the island, although years before they had taken the oath of allegiance to his Britannic Majesty after being guaranteed that they would never have to bear arms against their former countrymen. The feeble excuse given by the Halifax government was that many had furnished arms and provisions to French cruisers and were in violation of the oaths of allegiance. The bloody defeat of Edward Braddock provided the moral imperative for the act. And the dispatch of a British fleet from Boston bound for Nova Scotia provided the means. The Acadians, who were in fact overwhelmingly loyal subjects, offered little resistance. The sudden descent of a force of British troops and the total disarmament of the civilian population took the Acadians by surprise. The stunned inhabitants were soon forced to swear another oath of allegiance, a Protestant oath which was so framed that as Catholics they could not take it. All who failed to swear against their church were deemed enemies of the King of England. A punitive and cruel example was then made when the unimposing settlement of Grand Pre, situated on the peaceful Acadian shore, was burned to the ground. In modern terms, the affair would have been called "ethnic cleansing." Ultimately, three thousand of the inoffensive artisans and farmers of Acadia were to be scattered throughout the thirteen English colonies. Maryland was assigned to receive a substantial proportion of these most unfortunate people.[30]

By November, the first six transport ships filled with Acadians had arrived at Boston, two of which, *Dolphin* and *Ranger,* were bound for Maryland. Conditions aboard the transports were terrible. The passengers aboard *Dolphin* were reported to be in a sickly state occasioned by severe overcrowding, with at least forty of them forced to lie at night on the open deck exposed to the inclemency of the season. Those aboard *Ranger* were "sickly & their water very bad." Provisions were short, with only a pound of beef, five pounds of flour, and two pounds of bread allotted per man a week. Nevertheless, by November 30, four ships bearing 903 Acadians had arrived at Annapolis. Many of these people had already been indiscriminately and forcefully separated from their families. The city was hard pressed to provide for them. It was readily apparent that it would be necessary to disperse the hapless victims throughout the various inhabited parts of the province. But what was to be done with them then? One proposal suggested that they be signed as indentured servants, slaves in effect, to Maryland planters and merchants, but the Acadians insisted on being treated as prisoners of war. Their insistence was heeded, for most Marylanders, including the governor himself, were sympathetic to their plight as hapless victims of war and did not consider them enemies to be dealt with.[31]

By early December, three of the four vessels carrying Acadians had been dispatched to the Patuxent, Choptank, and Wicomico Rivers, while the fourth was retained in Annapolis. A separate shipment was chartered by the governor to Baltimore County in early March 1756. By late March, the entire body of Acadians had been dispersed throughout every county of Maryland except Frederick. Most were obliged to subsist off the charity of private citizens. Although the new arrivals were French-speaking Catholics whose ancestral homeland was at war with England, the hearts of the citizens of Maryland went out to the destitute transplants. "Christian charity, nay common humanity," demanded the *Maryland Gazette,* "calls on every one, according to his ability, to lend their assistance and help to these objects of compassion." The nearly penniless colony government, however, despite the obvious thoughtfulness of Governor Sharpe, preferred to fix upon some expedient other than state aid and thus passed an act empowering the justices of each county court "to take care and provide for such of them as should be real objects of charity, and to bind out such of their children as they were unable to support; provided, the king did not order their removal to some other colony."[32]

Both Kent and Cecil Counties received a share of the unfortunates. Most of them, beggared, dispirited, and exiled in an unfamiliar climate, wished for nothing more than to return to their own people. Between thirty and forty Acadians are known to have been obliged to settle in Cecil County, most of them in tiny Fredericktown.[33]

The war raged for years, and the Acadians in Cecil and Kent, forced to live in a state of penury, grew increasingly desperate to return to their own homes. Finally, hostilities ended and many of the unfortunates petitioned the government for permission to return to French territory—any French territory. Among them were twenty-seven members of the Brassey, Auber [Huber], and Granger families living in Fredericktown. Their joint petition, submitted on March 24, 1767, more than a decade after their forced resettlement in Maryland, read:

> To the Worshipful, the Justices of the Peace for Cecil county: The humble petition of the French Neutrals in Fredericktown sheweth that, whereas, your petitioners have now an opportunity of removing to the French settlements on the river Mississippi, at their own expense & charge, which they, on account of their large number of small children and long captivity here, find themselves entirely unable to pay. They, therefore, humbly request your worships to grant such timely assistance and relief as may enable them to execute their purpose of removing. And the petitioners all ever pray.

The petition was signed by Issabel Brassey, head of a family of eight; Eneas Auber, head of a family of six; Eneas Granger, who managed the affairs of nine orphans of the late John Baptist Granger; and Joseph Auber.[34]

The ultimate fate of the Fredericktown Acadians is a mystery. But the travails of their lot would be forever memorialized by Henry Wadsworth Longfellow in his touching classic *Evangeline,* in which he wrote sadly of their "Exile without an end, and without an example in history."

After the war, the Sassafras drew its share of sojourners, mostly folks passing through en route from Annapolis or Philadelphia via New Castle, Delaware. By 1757 the business was brisk enough that a regular scheduled packet line employing both sea and land carriage was established by the Annapolis firm of John Hughes and Company. The route consisted of a weekly stagecoach run from Philadelphia to Fredericktown. There, travelers would embark for Annapolis upon a packet boat called the *Sassafras Stageboat,* commanded by Captain John Gray. The packet was not limited to passengers, carrying light freight as well.[35]

Surprisingly enough, except for the journals of a few travelers, there is little to provide any record regarding the situation of Georgetown and Fredericktown for many years. There were, of course, few amenities to attract attention in the two small towns aside from a tavern or two, such as Sarah Flynn's place down by the ferry landing in Fredericktown. And the daily cycle of commerce was of little interest to the majority of those passing through.[36] Yet, a few accounts provided by visitors are worthy of record.

On a warm June day in 1759, the well-traveled scholar and divine Andrew Burnaby, a graduate of Queen's College in Cambridge, England, in the midst of his second tour of the middle settlements of North America and in too much of a hurry to await the packet, hired a small schooner of about ten tons and set out from Annapolis for the head of the Bay. He made sail with a fresh breeze, "and after a pleasant passage of sixteen hours, in one of the most delightful days imaginable" arrived at Fredericktown about midnight. His description of the twin towns is suggestive of the crossroads status that they still maintained. "Frederictown [*sic*]," he wrote, "is a small village on the western side of Sassafras river, built for the accommodation of strangers and travelers; on the eastern side, exactly opposite to it, is another small village (George-town), erected for the same purpose." In the town, like most travelers, he found suitable accommodations and was even able to hire an Italian chaise with a servant and horse to attend him as far as Philadelphia. The following day he proceeded on his journey towards New Castle, thirty-two miles distant.[37]

In the spring of 1774 Philip Vickers Fithian, a young teacher en route from Virginia to New England via the Eastern Shore road from Rock Hall and Chestertown, provided another view of the towns on the Sassafras, describing the neighborhood and life along the river. Leaving Chestertown on the morning of April 14, he rode through a Kent countryside sick with "a malignant, putrid fever, & what is generally called spotted fever." The sixteen-mile ride to Georgetown was through a "land level, fertile, & vastly pleasant." Upon his arrival in town, he visited John Vorhees, "an eminent" tobacco merchant, who was partner with James Pearce in the firm of John Vorhees and Company. Vorhees, he wrote in his journal that evening, "seems to be a gentleman of peculiar smartness, industry & economy" and provided not only a favorable impression for the young traveler but also comfortable lodgings for the night. Fithian, like Burnaby, was not particularly impressed with the two towns and took more note of the fever that was raging throughout the village, along with a "general & very malignant" epidemic of whooping cough.[38]

While in Georgetown, the young traveler learned that several of his relatives had died and that a close friend was at that moment, far away, also dying of consumption. To curb his distress, he sought solace with an acquaintance named Rachel Stockton Ryley, who lived "in considerable grandeur" in an elegant brick house about a mile up the river but who was also suffering from either a bad cold or the onset of the fever. In what appears to have been an episode of gentle matchmaking, Fithian was introduced to Rachel's sister-in-law, who possessed "a small handsome fortune, & is perhaps agreeable." But the young teacher, en route home to see his own true love, was in no mood to tarry and, after returning to town and dining again with Vorhees, crossed the river on the ferry and pressed on.[39]

In the years before the coming revolution, the two sleepy Sassafras towns were in some ways like fabled Brigadoon—they emerged only occasionally to experience a bit of passing history. Trade had been good in the five years before the war, as tobacco wore out the soils and farmers turned increasingly to grains. Between 1770 and 1775, Georgetown alone was able to export fifty thousand bushels of wheat, three thousand barrels of flour, and ten thousand bushels of corn. It came as no shock then that when hostilities with the motherland commenced, the two towns would serve as important storage depots for both the Continental and the French Armies.[40]

That the citizens of the Sassafras towns served in defense of the new nation is probable. That some of them were less than patriotic is equally likely. On August 22, 1777, when an enormous British army aboard an invasion fleet two to three hundred ships strong cast anchor between the Sassafras and Elk, intent on a landing at the Head of Elk, it appeared that the war had been brought home, and many sunshine warriors altered their loyalties to suit the occasion. "Some people of Maryland, to the right of the fleet," recorded one mercenary Hessian officer aboard the fleet, "brought fowl, fruits, and milk to several of our ships, for which they were paid well." Fortunately for the Sassafras towns, the invaders had bigger fish to fry, and on August 25 landed on the left bank of the Elk for their overland push towards Philadelphia.[41] Not until October 23, 1781, would the war again come flashing by—ever so briefly but joyfully—for it was on that grand day that General Washington's aide-de-camp, Tench Tilghman, came thundering through en route to Philadelphia with news of the incredible allied victory on the plains of Yorktown.[42]

Between the end of that conflict and the beginning of the next, the War of 1812, neither of the towns appear to have grown appreciably. John Vorhees and Company of Georgetown resumed its trade with London through the Annapolis trading house of Wallace, Johnson and Muir.[43] Across the river, Captains John and James Allen, brothers, opened up a small shipping and packet boat operation. And scattered along the twin waterfronts could be found granaries, warehouses, and a few stores. On any given day, perhaps as many as three or four coasting schooners and freighters might be seen lying at anchor in the harbor. The ferry was maintained by a black ferrymaster who lived with his pigs by the river. By this time, Georgetown, with as many as two dozen homes had far outstripped its rival across the river in size. But it didn't seem to matter much. Indeed, the impression one draws through the mist of time is that they were good neighbors resigned to the fact that they would never become more than a bucolic crossroads joined at the waist by a simple ferry.

It seemed that nothing exciting was ever going to happen to the little towns on the Sassafras. That is, until Mr. Madison's War began.

Along the shores of the upper Chesapeake Bay, nearly thirty years of uninterrupted peace and tranquillity had effected a prosperity and growth that promoted the dramatic rise of such ports, towns, and crossroads as Baltimore, Havre de Grace, Charlestown, and Elkton. It also induced a lazy malaise that was dangerously inviting to any foe wishing to wreak havoc. The towns on the Sassafras, though without the stature of the aforementioned towns, were nonetheless as defenseless and exposed as any on the Chesapeake, and all were wholly unprepared to offer any resistance to a heavily armed invader.

By February 1813, the Chesapeake Bay had, of course, found itself under a strong British blockade. Without having to face serious naval contention, the enemy could go practically anywhere he wished, when he wished, and do as he wished. And it was only a matter of time before he would decide to strike at the towns at the headwaters of the Bay. That day arrived in April when an expedition under the overall charge of Admiral Sir George Cockburn commenced attacks on the towns and villages of the upper Chesapeake. On April 12, they captured Sharps Island and four days later threatened Baltimore itself. On April 20 they seized the Queenstown packet and three days afterward occupied Spesutie Island. On April 26 they again threatened Baltimore, menaced Annapolis, and then carried out landings on Pooles and Tilghman Islands.

The upper Chesapeake was in an uproar, but few believed the foe might actually devastate a major Maryland town. Then on April 29, Frenchtown was captured and pillaged; all of the shipping in the harbor was burned or carried off. Four days later, the bustling port of Havre de Grace was attacked, sacked, and partially leveled by fire and sword. The nearby Principio Iron Works and cannon foundry were totally destroyed. Few in Georgetown and Fredericktown could have doubted that their turn would soon come.

They did not have long to wait.

Admiral Cockburn was well aware of the commercial significance of the Sassafras River towns, small as they were. Both, he knew "were places of some trade and importance." Moreover, "the Sassafras being the only river or place of shelter for vessels at this upper extremity of the Chesapeake which I had not examined and cleared," his attentions could not help but be drawn to the plantations and towns on its banks.[44]

Thus, late in the afternoon of May 5, Cockburn arrived off the mouth of the river with a small squadron consisting of HMS *Maidstone,* of thirty-six guns, Captain George Burdette commanding; *Mohawk,* sixteen, Acting Captain Henry D. Byng; *Fantome,* eighteen, Captain John Lawrence; *Hornet,* sixteen; and the captured American privateers *Dolphin,* twelve, *Racer,* six, and *Highflyer,* five. Within hours he began to assemble a strong force of barges alongside *Mohawk* to attack and destroy the two towns. Although he later informed his superiors and warned the Americans that he intended no harm to the residents of either Fredericktown or Georgetown or to their property unless opposition was encountered (a tale British apologists have long supported), the captain's log of *Mohawk* clearly indicates otherwise. At 4 P.M., as the barges began to assemble but well before the departure of the expedition, it was recorded in the log that the boats and marines of the squadron were being specifically dispatched "to destroy George Town and Frederick Town." A 150-man landing party of Royal Marines under the command of Captains Marmaduke Wybourn and Thomas Carter and a small unit of Royal Artillery under Lieutenant Frederick Robertson—all aboard fifteen armed barges and three small boats, including a rocket boat—were soon underway up the river. The ascent and landing were to be commanded by Captain Byng, with the admiral himself going along, as he often did, to superintend the entire project. It was his intention that the landing party reach the towns, approximately ten miles distant from the fleet anchorage, by dawn to effectually surprise the Americans. At 12:30 A.M., May 6, the expeditionaries, many having been in their small boats waiting for over eight hours, finally departed. But even for the seasoned mariners of the Royal Navy, the effort was overflowing with difficulties; they were entirely unfamiliar with the river itself, "our total want of local knowledge in it, the darkness of the night, and the great distance the towns lay up it" all caused the invaders to become hopelessly lost.[45]

As the silver-gray of morning began to silhouette the shoreline ahead, it was obvious to the admiral that a surprise attack at dawn was out of the question. The British were in serious need of a guide. Thus, at the mouth of Turner's Creek, the invaders landed briefly and kidnapped a local resident named John Stavely at his house, placed him aboard Captain Byng's boat in the vanguard of the little armada, and forced him to serve as pilot. Soon afterwards, they encountered a small bateau with two mulattoes aboard. Their knowledge of the river and local terrain were readily recognized as an asset of value to the expedition. But their utility as messengers was perhaps even more significant.[46]

As the expedition passed Wicke's Farm, approximately a mile below the two towns, Captain Byng took a white handkerchief and fastened it to his espontoon. He was about to enter the bateau with the intention of personally informing the town that resistance should not be made when he was stopped by the admiral. Cockburn ordered that the two mulattoes be sent with the message instead, since "as they were known to the people in the fort above, he expected that they would believe what they told them." The two blacks, having informed their captors that there was no battery at either of the towns and wishing to be free of the enemy's clutches, willingly agreed to deliver the message, after expressing that they had no doubt that the inhabitants would be peaceably disposed.[47] Cockburn later informed his superiors that the two men were specifically instructed "to warn their countrymen against acting in the same rash manner the People of Havre-de-Grace had done, assuring them if they did that their town would inevitably meet with a similar Fate." If no resistance was offered, no injury would be done to them or their villages; only vessels and public property would be seized, and the strictest discipline would be maintained among the landing party. Whatever property or provisions might be found necessary for the squadron, it would "be instantly paid for in its fullest value."[48] Such claims, in light of the actual intent noted in *Mohawk*'s log, were merely employed to justify the subsequent event.

The approach of the enemy was not unexpected by the American defenders of the two towns. The alarm had gone out even as the British had begun to concentrate their forces off the mouth of the Sassafras. Recalling the recent destruction of Havre de Grace as the model, one participant in the contest that followed reported, "It was presumed their intention was also to destroy Frederick Town." A call was sent out for the Cecil County militia to form, but fewer than eighty men under the command of Colonel T. W. Veazey could be aroused, and not even a third of them were properly armed with muskets or ammunition. Most carried only their personal fowling pieces. Nevertheless, Veazey's command was under arms by 4 A.M., and a small breastwork, later referred to as Fort Duffy, was thrown up on the Fredericktown highland, overlooking the western approach to the town. The works, hastily erected by the colonel and his second in command, Captain James Allen, were pitifully armed, as only a single 6-pounder could be found to mount upon it, and only two rounds of cartridges were available to feed it. On the opposite shore, on Pearce's Point, a second small earthwork was erected by Kent County men, who were even fewer in number, less armed, and lacking artillery of any sort.[49]

At 5:40 A.M., from four miles down the river, scouts sent out by Veazey signaled that the enemy was approaching. Twenty minutes later, as the sun was on the rise, the oncoming invaders could be seen in all their fearsome splendor. One eyewitness, John E. Thomas of Elkton, later reported that it was the most beautiful sight he'd ever seen. The large British barges had formed a line four abreast and several hundred yards long, but in close and compact order. In each were the splendidly attired Royal Marines sitting ramrod erect, with their scarlet jackets afire in the new morning sun. A barge containing the admiral and bearing a colored flag was seen passing along one side of the line, then crossing ahead of the leading tier of boats. For a few minutes, the admiral waited patiently until the rear came up, bringing the entire squadron into view of the twin towns. For a few minutes more the barge force hove to. The defenders could see a single bateaux, manned by a pair of dark-skinned men, being sent forward.[50]

Colonel Veazey paid little attention to the two mulatto messengers or to the warning they carried—as Cockburn had undoubtedly hoped. Then, the admiral later reported, after "having allowed sufficient time for this message to be digested and their resolution taken thereon

I directed the boats to advance and I am sorry to say I soon found the more unwise alternative was adopted."[51] The British attack was on.

Shortly before 7 A.M., as the barges reached a position within a mile of the two elevated shoulders of the Sassafras upon which the towns were situated, the invaders gave three rousing cheers which were promptly answered by three more from the American side punctuated by a symbolic volley of muskets. Then, as the boats closed to within range, "a most heavy fire of musketry was opened" upon them from entrenched positions on both shores, accompanied by the cannonade of the lone 6-pounder in Fort Duffy. Judging from the hot fire directed against him, Cockburn incorrectly estimated that as many as four hundred men had been gathered to contest his landing. The invaders were inured to such opposition. "The launches and rocket boat smartly returned this fire with good effect," the admiral reported, "and with the other boats and the marines I pushed ashore immediately above the enemy's position."[52]

The sheer intensity of the assault was enough to daunt the stoutest of hearts. One anonymous eyewitness later recorded the British response and its consequences. "The fire was immediately returned by the enemy, by a general discharge of grape, cannister, slugs, rockets, and musketry, which made such a terrible noise that one-half of the men shamefully ran, and could not be rallied again. Whether it was from their political aversion to the present war, their dislike of shedding blood, or actually thro' fear, I cannot determine." Soon, only thirty-five men, less than half of those who had turned out, remained to contend against the whole force of the invader. "This gallant little band," the witness reported, "resisted for near half an hour, in spite of the incessant fire of the enemy, until they were in danger of being surrounded, when they retreated in safety with the loss of but one man wounded."

The British suffered five wounded, only one of whom was severely injured.[53]

During the firefight, the British rocket boat and artillery units were extremely active. Congreve rockets and 18-pound shot "flew over the towns and field in every direction," causing substantial damage and some later claimed reduced the towns to ashes "except two or three houses, saved by the entreaties of the women." Yet, it was the artillery rather than the rockets that had caused the most injury, primarily to Fredericktown. It was the subsequent acts of the British that were to result in incineration, not the initial bombardment. One participant, though at first frightened by the Congreves, stated later, "I think I saw and heard four rockets flying at once, and they were, to be sure, to ear and eye most terrific, but they all fell harmless, and are now objects of but little terror to many of our militiamen."[54] The heart of terror was not in rockets and bombs, but in the gleam of the Royal Marines' fixed bayonets as the landing was made above the fort. The few American defenders remaining, more fearful of cold steel than hot lead, fled terror stricken into the woods. American resistance "was neither seen nor heard of afterwards."[55]

Unaware of the total collapse of the militia, Cockburn sent several parties out to ascertain whether Veazey had fallen back to take up a new position and if not, then to find what had become of him. In his official report penned soon afterwards, he lightly brushed off the terrible incendiary actions that followed in short order. "I gave him [Veazey] . . . the mortification of seeing from wherever he had hid himself that I was keeping my word with respect to his towns," stated the admiral later, "which (excepting the houses of those who had continued peaceably in them and had taken no part in the attack made on us) were forthwith destroyed as were four vessels laying in the river, and some stores of sugar, of lumber, of leather, and other merchandise."[56]

The British depredations were first visited upon Fredericktown. The property of Captain John Allen and his brother James were to suffer the initial outrages. Personally led by Admiral Cockburn, the red-coated landing party was directly met in the Allen yard by the two brothers. Both had watched the enemy approach, James from the vantage point of the fort, which he had helped defend, and John presumably from the vantage of his own property.

The encounter was anything but civil. When the commander first saw James, he asked: "Sir, who are you?"

The militia officer replied haughtily, "A man sir, damn you."

"Did you suppose I took you for a woman?" retorted the admiral irately. "Take that fellow on board," he ordered. The guard immediately seized the brazen American and carried him off. The admiral was then all pompous feathers and feigned indignation as he turned his attention to John.

"Who the damnation," he demanded "are those that have kept such a damned firing upon me? Are they regulars?"

"No sir," replied Allen, "they are the militia."

"Where are they gone?"

"I don't know, sir."

"Where are all the men of your town?"

"Moving out, sir."

The admiral grimaced. "I sent you word, that if you would not fire upon me, I would not destroy any property." Looking round he saw a black youth, and demanded to know: "Are you the person I sent word by?" The boy replied in the negative.

"Had you not fired," he resumed, facing John, "and I had taken any thing away, I would have paid you for the same; but now, damn you, I will pay you with your own coin. Go on, my boys, knock down, burn, and destroy."[57]

The invaders immediately set to work on John Allen's estate, first plundering and then setting fire to his carriages, stable, dwelling house, kitchen, and furniture. Allen's own description bears witness to the methodical manner in which the British carried out their style of banditry in which nothing was overlooked. "The inside works of the clock [from the house] they took on board the barge," he later testified. "Then my meat house, small granary, boat and fish house, containing fifty barrels of salt-fish; all my bacon, and one year's provisions. . . . My family Bible and the life of Washington [a book] were taken away. Then the store was robbed of about $1200, in groceries; the heads of the liquor casks stove in, and mixed with molasses."[58]

Their looting, honed from repeated experience elsewhere, was total. The entire building complex was soon ablaze.

As John Allen helplessly watched the destruction of his home and property, Admiral Cockburn, sitting astride a stolen horse, shrugged with satisfaction and addressed his officers: "I think this looks pretty well, this will do."

Turning to John again, he asked stiffly: "How do you like the war now?"

Stifling his rage, the American replied defiantly: "Sir, I have not been the advocate for the war, but admit that if I was, it is not reasonable to suppose that I should like it now since all my property is destroyed; and which was got by many long years of hard labour, by the bay and coasting trade."[59]

But John Allen refused to give up. He begged the admiral to spare his storehouse, upon which his livelihood depended. Cockburn, always on the lookout for forage for his own men, replied with a demand that he be instantly provided with poultry. That would be the cost of salvation. Stunned, the captain responded that he had none. Soon, billows of black smoke were issuing from a large granary belonging to the Allen brothers' packet business and containing upwards of one hundred barrels of sugar, sundry casks of nails and boxes, ten to fifteen barrels of pear ash, four or five bales of hops, bolts of linens, four or five trunks of dry goods, two large casks of tobacco, suits of sails, and sundry other articles. All for the lack of a few chickens.[60]

John Allen did not relent as the destructors turned their attention next door; he began to plead with the admiral to spare his brother's house, as James's wife was in a very fragile condition and confined upstairs in bed after having given birth to a child only two days before.

"Damn ye," cursed Cockburn coldly. "Move her out."[61]

As the invaders prepared to lay torch to the building, however, Mrs. McDonough, James's mother-in-law, ran from the door with clasped hands, entreating the admiral to have mercy upon her daughter. To move her would kill her. Sir George finally condescended and ordered the building spared, although the adjoining houses were first looted of meat, clothing, and whatever other portable articles could be found, then set afire.

Still, Allen did not relent. When Cockburn, watching the destruction of the house with smug satisfaction, demanded food, the American was able to find several biscuits and some cheese for him which provided an opening for one final entreaty.

"Pray sir, discharge my brother you have [as] a prisoner in the barge, before you leave the waters of the Sassafras River, that we may be left together to try to get another small living, till peace is restored. He is the only support of his little family; [and] we are now made poor indeed! And if taken away his family must come to want. Only grant me this, and I shall feel a small relief in mind."

Allen must have watched with some incredulity as an officer was immediately dispatched to ride down to the barge where James was being held. The man jumped overboard to his waist, took the militia officer on his back, and landed him on the beach. He immediately returned. Cockburn then castigated the freed militiaman.

"Damn you, it is not for your sake I discharge you, but for your family."

Overjoyed, James Allen said, "Sir, I am obliged to you for that." But not much more. The total loss suffered by the Allen brothers was valued at over eight thousand dollars.[62]

And the invaders had only begun.

As an officer and two sailors entered the nearby home of Jonathan Greenwood, they swore that if they had found him in arms they would have "thrust him through with their bayonets." When a second and larger party entered the house, its hapless owner was robbed of everything that could conveniently be carried off, including his stock of food, amounting to two thousand dollars in value. The remainder of his goods were savagely hacked to pieces with cutlasses and dirks, an orgy of destruction in which the British officers appeared to be the most active of all. Greenwood's dwelling house, storehouse, and kitchen were then torched and completely destroyed.[63]

Many citizens were terrorized. Following the engagement, Richard Barnaby had escorted a number of women to a place of safety a short distance out of town and then returned only to run squarely into a score of Royal Marines and their officers. "Here is one of the damned rascals from the fort," one shouted after collaring the unfortunate man, who, in fact, had not been at the fort at all. Upon being questioned about where the militia had run off to, Barnaby claimed ignorance. Calling him a liar, the officer in charge drew his sword and intimated he would kill him, even as another soldier drew a bayonet and a third drew a cutlass. All threatened to run him through but finally released him. Barnaby, shaken by the intimidation, was reduced to scrambling for chickens for his captors to save his own home. Unlike Allen, he was able to come up with enough to placate the admiral. The house was saved but everything inside was plundered or destroyed.[64]

Anyone associated with the military was considered fair game by the British. Captain Francis B. Chandler, who had been among those who had fled from the fort early on during the fight, had made his way home without difficulty. Almost as soon as he arrived near his house, he observed a party of fifty Royal Marines and an officer, said to be a post captain (undoubtedly Captain Byng), running toward him. It was later learned that one of the enemy had heard someone address him as captain and immediately ordered him taken. Upon the arrival of the soldiers at his house, Chandler boldly stood upon the steps and requested that they not enter. The officer immediately "caught him by the breast," called him a damned rascal, threw him off the stairs, and entered the house with the entire party. The invaders gave three cheers and instantly began hacking up the staircase and window sashes and smashing the windows. Someone called for fire, and soon at least three small blazes had been started in different parts of the building. At that moment, Cockburn rode up and Chandler begged that the fires be extinguished, at least "until he could reason the case with him." The admiral demanded the American provide him with thirty bullocks in half an hour or the house would be incinerated. In desperation, Chandler agreed to try and find the ransom, and the fires were put out. Nearly in a frenzy, he mounted his horse, rode a half mile, fell in with Colonel Veazey, and told him what he was after. The colonel, whose own property was in no immediate danger, instructed the captain "to go back and tell the admiral he shall not have them." Despairing now, Chandler returned and informed Cockburn that he had come up empty-handed. Cockburn relented and gave him a second chance. Did the captain have a good deal of poultry anywhere? Chandler replied he had, whereupon the admiral set his own men and his captive to chasing chickens.[65]

It would have been an amusing sight if it wasn't in such deadly earnest, as the tough, scarlet-coated marines scrambled about Francis Chandler's chicken yard collecting their compensation. Even after the poultry had been rounded up, it still took the joint persuasions of the captain's wife and his sister to prevent the house from being burned. It wasn't enough to save the Chandler warehouse or the considerable quantity of goods therein from total destruction.[66] Nor was it possible to save the houses and property of other Fredericktown citizens, such as John Barnaby, Ann Moore, John Warmely, Betsy McClannon, Joseph Jarvis, John Mitchel, Barney O'Neill, Moses Wilson, and Perry Vollow, many of whom had fled in utter terror rather than face the invaders. Of the above, Wilson and Vollow were black, and only the latter's home was spared, although he was plundered of all of his tools and clothing as well as his life savings amounting to twenty dollars cash. Nor could such pleadings save four schooners in the harbor from confiscation as prizes of war. Three of the vessels were owned by Dorchester County men, while the fourth was a New England–built vessel.[67]

Having destroyed most of Fredericktown and fearing little from the local militia, Cockburn now boldly divided his landing force. The larger force was dispatched northward along the main road leading to Cecil Crossroads, ostensibly "to satiate their thirst for destruction upon the defenceless inhabitants of the neighboring farm houses." The smaller unit was sent across the Sassafras to capture and destroy Georgetown.

The first house the northbound force came to, less than a mile from Fredericktown, belonged to thirty-four-year-old Toilus Robertson, one of the militiamen who had stayed to fight at the fort until he was forced to flee. Like most of his comrades, he had gone home to defend his property rather than stay with Veazey and his unit. Shortly after his arrival home, upon the appearance of the invaders, he was again obliged to flee with his family in such haste that he left behind three black servants. The servants watched in silent terror as the British ransacked the house, piled all of Robertson's furniture in the yard in front of the doorway, and set it afire. The flames soon communicated to the building, which was totally destroyed. A barn, which stood about a hundred yards off from the house, was also set afire and consumed.[68]

The incendiaries next came upon the home of Moses Cannon, who had also fought at the breastworks until the very last and then, like Robertson, hastily retired to his home to save whatever he could. Cannon, knowing that the invader was at his heels and that he was likely to lose everything unless he acted quickly, occupied himself with turning his horses out into the wheat fields, where they could not be easily rounded up. While he was thus engaged, a party of soldiers approached his house, and he turned about on his horse to meet them and was immediately taken prisoner. The new captive was ordered to provide liquid refreshment for his captors but said he had none. The British taunted him with threats that his house would be burned unless food and drink were provided. They teased him, saying their captain was already inside preparing the blaze at that very moment. Cannon was sent to the house, where he found the captain and another person carrying off his bed cloths, a pair of boots, and a number of other articles to a party of soldiers in the yard. At that moment, an officer on horseback rode up and demanded to know "where the damned militia were." Pointing towards the nearby woods, Cannon informed them only that they had retreated. The officer was not amused, and declared that *he* must now burn the house. When Cannon expostulated and told him the difficulties he would labor under if it were burned, the officer changed the subject and demanded to known where the road to the mouth of Elk River was and if he could march his men there. The farmer replied that his government would not permit him to give up such critical information. The irate officer said that he knew that as well as Cannon did, "but that he might trust a British officer, and smiled, and turned his horse, and ordered his men to march, and they went off, without burning the house or asking any more questions." After the enemy's departure from his yard, Cannon went to a neighbor's house to check on the safety of his family. Then, when he returned to his own home, he was fired upon by a party of raiders stationed on the public road about 150 yards from the house. Instantly, he turned and retreated across a field, abandoning the house even as yet another party of soldiers marched toward it. Returning hours later, he found that the invaders had destroyed or taken away all his household goods and furniture and all but demolished his home.[69]

Joshua Ward was a militiaman who had resisted the British at the fort. He was one of the more prominent citizens of the area and the head of a large family, and he was the next to suffer. Ward had not reached his home by the time a party of between thirty to forty British soldiers, under the command of an officer said to be a post captain, arrived there. He was later informed that the invaders, having learned that Ward was with the militia, had placed an immediate guard around the building and had "inquired particularly" for him. Thinking that he may be hiding inside, they launched a thorough search of the property, swearing all the while that they would have him, dead or alive. Failure to locate their prey only incensed the raiders even more, and they promptly commenced looting what furniture they could and destroying that which could not be carried off. The officer in charge helped himself to "a pair of handsome looking glasses" while others of his party carted off bedding, clothing, plates, window curtains, and as much else as could be readily removed. Even the clothing belonging to Ward's children was stolen and carried away on the points of Royal Marine bayonets. Then, satiated by their pillaging, they placed charges of gunpowder in every room of the house and below the stairwell. A kitchen fire, which was always kept alight, was brought in and touched to kindling throughout the house. A bed in the cellar, broken chairs, tables, and the like were thrown in to feed the flames. Satisfied with their work, the invaders left the house and loitered about the yard to watch the fruits of their labors burst forth through the windows in billows of greasy smoke and fire. As the house was consumed, they swore that anyone who attempted to extinguish the flames would be immediately put to death. Observing one of Ward's sons in the distance driving off the family's flock of sheep, they fired at him for sport and declared loudly that they would later return and burn every- thing else on the farm that they had thus far ignored.[70]

As the raiders swept on into the surrounding environs of Fredericktown, they made good on their threats. They soon came upon a farmhouse owned by J. Robinson, but which they supposed to belong to Joshua Ward, for whom they were still searching. After conducting their usual destructive mischief, however, they resolved not to destroy the house. That is, until they discovered therein a hat with an eagle pinned to it. Swearing that the house "must belong to a damn'd Democrat" they promptly set the building afire.[71]

At the home of P. Ward, a relative of Joshua Ward, about a mile and a half from Fredericktown, the invaders again behaved "with great rudeness" giving "Mr. W. and his wife much abusive language." As the Wards pleaded with the soldiers to spare their house, the raiders occupied themselves with plundering the family larder of hams and the best ba- con before finally agreeing and departing. The pledge was more than likely prompted as much by a sudden alarm that the militia was coming as by any thoughts of mercy.[72] It is likely that the raiders were already overburdened with the fruits of their malicious labors in Cecil County and could physically proceed no further. The same, unfortunately, could not be said for the expedition sent over to the Kent County side of the Sassafras.

Cockburn had already turned his personal attentions upon Georgetown, which was the larger of the two villages but far more poorly defended. The admiral thought even less of the Kent County Militia than he did of the Cecil men, for he had dispatched no more than four boatloads of marines to totally incinerate the town. One observer reported in what might pass as an excuse that no defense was made because the Kent militia, although "a consider- able force was collected," was even worse off than their brethren across the Sassafras, "hav- ing no cannon, and badly armed with musketry, and not within reach of the enemy, at the point where the enemy passed, and where a small breast work was thrown up."[73]

Georgetown was taken without another shot being fired.

And as at Fredericktown, with most of the population fleeing or having already fled into the countryside, house after house was desecrated, plundered, and burned to the ground. One by one, at least twenty-four businesses, shops, homes, storehouses, and other buildings succumbed to Admiral Cockburn's incendiaries. Bagwell's cobbler's shop, Jackson's gra- nary, the widow Isabella Freeman's home, Hastleton's Tavern, and Negro Step's house were but a few of the many that were ignited by the invader's torch. It seemed that none would be spared. Even the hut of the black ferryman, who lived with his pigs at the water's edge, was plundered of its entire contents. By 7 A.M., the fires from what had once been the ports of Fredericktown and Georgetown could be seen from the decks of HMS *Maidstone* ten miles away and were so entered into the master's log.[74]

As in Fredericktown, any homes that had been abandoned were considered fair game for destruction. And almost everyone had fled in mortal fear, although some desperately at- tempted to save what portable valuables they could. Many years later, Mrs. William Ireland recalled that she, her small children, and their nurse had fled in a horse-drawn gig to a thick woods about two miles from the town. "From there, while they remained hidden, she made several trips back to her home, catching up her table silver, valuable papers and other small articles of clothing. She took everything she could in her small conveyance, thus saving a few of the possessions from the fire which afterwards consumed the town."[75]

As the raiders slowly worked their way up Georgetown Hill, devastating every house along the way, it seemed that nothing was to be spared. Nothing, that is, until the tough British Marines and Royal Navy tars encountered the indomitable Miss Kitty Knight.

Much has been written about Kitty Knight, both fiction and fact, usually in less than equal dollops. What is discernible from the historic record is that she was one of the most colorful women of the Eastern Shore. She was born Catherine Knight about 1775, the daughter of John Leach Knight, a prominent Cecil County justice and farmer, and Catherine Matthews, the sister of Dr. William Matthews, a state legislator and a Representative in the U.S. Congress in 1797–1799. Some say she was born in a splendid brick house at her father's Knight's Island farm on the Sassafras. And she adored her much older brother William, who had married a beautiful and very acceptable young woman from Chestertown who was close to her own age.[76]

Legend has it that Kitty Knight, even in her early teenage years, was vivacious, mature, temperamental, and extremely independent-minded. At the tender age of sixteen, perhaps jealous of her beloved brother's young wife, Kitty informed her mother that the big brick house on Knight's Island wasn't large enough for two women of the same age, and that she intended to live with her uncle, who had a penchant for spoiling her. She then hunted down her father who was at work in his fields, and she issued the same ultimatum. To reinforce her demand for liberation, she assured him that if they refused to permit her to go, she would strive to keep the household in utter tumult from then on. Knowing all too well their daughter wasn't bluffing, her parents soon decided it was time for her to be granted total independence, a most unusual move for the times. John Knight had only recently purchased two houses on top of Georgetown Hill and agreed to rent one to his fiery daughter. If such was truly the case, it is uncertain where Kitty, without trade or resources of her own, found the funds to pay rent, much less support the black "mammy" nurse, cook, maid, hostler, and the several servant boys she took with her.[77]

For several years, Kitty is said to have lived an unexceptional life, at least until she met a handsome and popular young bachelor, Colonel Perry Spencer, who lived several miles downriver from Georgetown. Beautiful, raven-haired Kitty and the dashing young colonel soon fell in love and speculations of marriage filled the vacant hours of the local gossipmongers. Then, according to legend, her fierce nature ruined it all. One afternoon Kitty and the colonel agreed to go horseback riding together. She dressed, but her beau was tardy, and to pass the time, she walked down to the stable to inspect her favorite riding horse. When she arrived, she observed that the horse appeared restless and soon discovered the reason: one of its back legs was torn and bleeding. She immediately accused the stable boy, a slave, of hitting the horse. The slave swore that he had not, saying that the animal had kicked at him but missed and hit the stall divider instead. Enraged over what she deemed to be a blatant lie, she dragged the boy from the building and commenced flaying him viciously with her riding crop, cursing him in the vilest manner with every stroke of her weapon.[78]

At that moment, Colonel Spencer rode into the front yard and observed the beating. He was immediately sickened by the sight of the woman he loved but had never seen this way. Without Kitty even knowing he was there, he turned his horse about and rode away. Soon afterwards, as Kitty worried about the whereabouts of the colonel, a slave appeared with a letter for her and then scurried off without awaiting a reply. The note was from Spencer and stated that he could never marry such "a profane and cruel women" even though he "loved her more than life itself and had hoped to marry her."[79]

The effect on Kitty was profound. She swore she would never love another man. She soon sank so low in spirit that her uncle William took her with him to Philadelphia, where Congress was then sitting, in an effort to revive her spirits. The city's society season was in full dominion, and soon the beautiful belle of backwater Georgetown was totally immersed in it. One evening Kitty was escorted to a theatrical performance which was to be followed by a ball. Her escort was handsome Benjamin Harrison of Virginia, later father of William Henry Harrison, the ninth president of the United States, and grandfather of Benjamin Harrison, the twenty-third president. The performance was also attended by none other than President and Mrs. George Washington.[80]

Philadelphia, then the largest city in North America with a population of nearly fifty thousand, was certainly no Georgetown, and its marvels excited Kitty. The presence of such an illustrious man as Washington was even more stimulating. Even the stage for the theatrical performance presented something of a wonder to her. Years later, in relating her experience, she told a relative: "I must explain the matter in which the theatre was built. The stage proper could be moved in sections, disclosing a circumference for giving performances in which horses and other animals could not jump in the space allotted to the audience. General Washington in moving around, speaking pleasantly to his personal friends, possibly noticing I was with Mr. Harrison, said to me, passing his hand down these iron bars, 'You are well guarded, Miss.' Then I said to him, 'I am, surely Sir, in your presence,' and curtsied."[81]

On that fateful morning in 1813, with the acrid smoke of Fredericktown and Georgetown heavy in the air and a party of Royal Marines making their way up Georgetown Hill at a rapid gait with fixed bayonets, memories of Colonel Spencer and George Washington were the last thing on Kitty's mind. She was now thirty-seven years old, unmarried but, it was said, still "tall and graceful, with clear courageous eyes, full of goodness and natural beauty. She could not be withstood."[82]

Although there are many versions of what transpired next, it seems best to rely on the account related by Kitty herself to her beloved brother William. At the top of Georgetown Hill were several brick houses, two of which stood close side by side on the west side of the avenue and had so far not been burned. In one of them was an old lady, possibly the Widow Pearce, sick and almost destitute, and to that building the British were proceeding. Kitty, whose brother's house had just been incinerated, ran after them, but before she could get to the top of the hill, they had already set fire to the building in which the old lady lay. In no uncertain terms, Kitty informed Admiral Cockburn that they were about to burn up a helpless human being and a woman at that. When her pleas were ignored, legend reports, she stood in the doorway directly in harm's way and shouted defiantly. "I shall not leave; if you burn this house, you burn me with it." Unfortunately, the legend may never be fully verified.

"I pleaded with him to make his men put the fire out," Kitty herself later reported. "This I succeeded in doing, when they immediately went next door, not forty feet distant, and fired the second of the brick houses. I told the commanding officer that as the wind was blowing toward the other house this old lady would be burned up anyhow. When apparently affected by my appeal, he called his men off. As they went off, [they] left the fire burning, saying, 'Come on, boys.' As they went out the door, one of them struck his boarding axe through the panel of the door."[83]

The British, perhaps set aback by the feisty Kitty Knight but more likely by the apprehension of being cut off from their ships by American dragoons sighted in the area, penetrated no further into the Kent County countryside. Cockburn, however, was pleased with his morning's work. "Well my lads," he was heard to say to his officers, as he viewed the smoking ruins of his handiwork from atop Georgetown Hill, "this looks well." As they marched back to the waterfront, they took time to stop and plunder another hapless resident, stealing his goods and several gowns belonging to his wife before proceeding on their merry way.[84]

At last the invaders boarded their plunder-laden barges and shoved off downriver, and John Stavely, their unwilling captive pilot, worried about his fate. A brief landing at a mill, where the raiders stayed long enough to pluck the earrings from the head of Mrs. Williamson, only added to the concern for his own safety. Stavely could not help but grimace when he heard Captain Byng declare that "if he could catch Colonel Veazey, who commanded at the fort below, he would quarter him, and give me part of his quarter for steaks, for that the fire he had received was one of Washington's rounds."

Several miles downriver from Fredericktown, probably in the vicinity of Ordinary Point, the invaders again landed to investigate a small hamlet about halfway up a little tributary of the river. Here, Cockburn observed, "I had the satisfaction to find that what had passed at Havre [de Grace], George Town, and Fredericktown had its effects, and led these people to understand that they have more to hope for from our generosity than from erecting batteries and opposing us by the means within their power. The inhabitants of this place having met me at [the] landing to say that they had not permitted either guns or militia to be stationed there, and that whilst there I should not meet with any opposition whatever, I therefore landed with the officers and a small guard only." After having ascertained that there were no military stores or public property of any kind, Cockburn's men purchased whatever articles they needed at market price and reembarked peacefully aboard their boats. Soon afterwards, or perhaps while ashore, the admiral also received a deputation from Charlestown in the Northeast River, which had been sent to assure him that that town was placing itself at the mercy of the British "and that neither guns nor militia men shall he suffered there." The admiral was elated and later assured his superiors "that all the places in the upper part of the Chesapeake have adopted similar resolutions . . . as there is now neither public property, vessels, nor warlike stores remaining in this neighborhood." Then, eight miles from the twin towns they again landed to pillage Colonel Veazey's home, but they failed to apprehend the elusive militiaman himself. At 4 P.M. the expedition barges, heavily laden with the plunder from two now-extinct towns, bumped aside their motherships. Two days later, apprehensive of the possible arrival of a French fleet in the Chesapeake (or so it was rumored), the British sailed for Lynnhaven Bay.[85]

Admiral Cockburn was literally gushing with praise for his officers and men and was eager to inform his superiors of their success at the destruction of the two towns.[86] Perhaps owing to the peaceable composure of the American delegation at Ordinary Point, John Stavely, who had worried incessantly about his fate, was finally released and put ashore "at Withered's shore," not far from his home.[87]

News of the attack spread rapidly. On May 9 Washington received the first details from the Sassafras. The first public announcement was published the following day in the *Washington Daily National Intelligencer,* which referred to the two ruined villages as "the small towns of Georgetown and Frederic."[88]

Newspaper headlines soon inflamed the public along the entire eastern seaboard. "WANTON BARBARITY," read one headline, which presented an eyewitness account dated from the smoldering ruins of Georgetown itself on May 7. "Yesterday morning I witnessed a scene that surpasses all description. It was the little villages of George and Frederick towns, nearly all in flames. It would have excited sympathy in any human heart, except a savage, or still more ferocious Englishmen; and they you know are so much inured to

Kitty Knight in her famous confrontation with Admiral Cockburn. Detail from *The Burning of Georgetown and Fredericktown,* mural by Marcy Dunn Ramsey, courtesy Louise and Terry Van Gilder.

villainy and destruction, that there is no mercy in their composition. It was Admiral Cockburn himself, who led on the morn that tiger banditti, who committed the devastation. In the afternoon I repaired to the smoking, burning ruins, and found only a few houses standing, that had been spared at the entreaties of the women and aged; and these few, with one or two exceptions, nearly plundered of their all. Desks, bureaus, clocks, looking-glasses, and such things as could not be carried off, were broken to pieces, and even beds cut open, the ticking taken off, and the feathers scattered to the winds. Even negroes cabins were reduced to ashes, or plundered of their scanty pittance of furniture and meat."[89]

While the invaders were demonized for their depredations, few castigated the militia for its failure to turn out. Colonel Veazey and his men were lionized for their short but spirited defense at the fort. The colonel, reported one eyewitness, perhaps embellishing a bit, "deserves much praise for the brave exertions he made, to encourage and support his little band, and Admiral Cockburn acknowledged it was the only opposition he had met with, and said they behaved more like regulars, than militia men." The exact numbers of the enemy that had participated in the firefight and the casualties they suffered, though unknown, were amplified in subsequent American reports in an effort to downplay the humiliation of the defeat. Though it was said the enemy acknowledged only four wounded (one badly), it was reported by some that there were as many as ten to fifteen killed and wounded, "as many bodies were seen wrapped up in blankets and sail cloth, in the bottom of their boats."[90] Even the artillery carried onboard the barges was increased in size from 18- to 24-pounder carronades in the press reports, and at least four men were reported to have deserted from the foe. The fight, it was suggested, had been so hot that the enemy had expended all but two or three shot of their ammunition and in desperation had used anything at hand for projectiles. Chain shot and pieces of iron of various shapes were reportedly picked up in the ruins of the fort and towns as well as several rockets and a great deal of other kinds of shot.[91]

Soon, a public dispute had erupted over whether or not the enemy had approached the towns with a white flag. Some people claimed that Admiral Cockburn complained that Colonel Veazey had fired upon his flag of truce, which caused the destruction of the towns. Such claims were challenged by others. "Can such a message," questioned one man, "sent by two negroes be constituted a flag of truce? Or can the noble Admiral imagine the people of Sassafras were so ignorant as not to discriminate his flag attached to the stern of his barge, which was in the center and rear of a formidable armed force, from a flag of truce?"[92] Still others questioned whether or not a flag of truce had even been flown. One British apologist for Cockburn, referring to the capture of the two mulattoes, even contended that a deputation had been sent to falsely inform him that the towns were not defended in an effort to trap him.[93]

John Stavely, later testifying before government officials, most positively declared "that there was no white flag ever hoisted in her or any of the other boats to my knowledge; nor did I ever hear any of the British officers or privates say they had ever hoisted a flag, or that one ever had been fired on." Although he couldn't say how many men were lost (since the British only acknowledged five wounded), he thought they sustained greater injury. One British deserter, it was even stated in a Washington paper, reported that as many as fifteen men had come away with him in a single barge, but such claims appeared to have been spurious at best.[94]

The after-the-fact disputes which followed in the wake of the invasion were of little interest to the bereft citizens of the two smoldering villages. Most had lost everything. A damage estimate for both towns was officially placed at $35,626.88½. A total of forty-five property owners reported destruction or losses, but the actual costs were far higher owing to the inability of some to travel to Annapolis to submit claims in person, as required by the state.

In Fredericktown damages were estimated by the fifteen property owners who later filed claims with the federal government at $15,871.07½. Ten estates suffered losses of dwellings, kitchens, meat houses, stables, carriage houses, and storehouses. Three granaries were destroyed. Eight more homeowners suffered the loss of furniture, clothing, and other property.[95]

The damage to Georgetown, a village of somewhat larger proportions and population than Fredericktown, was placed at $19,755.81 among thirty inhabitants. Thirteen dwellings, stables and other outbuildings, the shoemaker's shop, a tavern, a granary, and a storehouse were destroyed. Nine property holders were robbed of furniture, apparel, musical instruments, books, and provisions.[96] There were no tallies for the losses suffered by the inhabitants in the surrounding countryside.

The luckless residents of Fredericktown, Georgetown, and other sites suddenly found themselves in dire straits; efforts to address their problems were not particularly quick in coming. It had fallen to the residents themselves to travel to Annapolis to plead their case for assistance at a special session of the state legislature. On May 22, Robert C. Lusby, a Cecil County Militia sergeant who had fought at the fort, delivered a petition from sundry inhabitants of Fredericktown to the Maryland House of Delegates requesting relief. Kent County failed to follow suit, but Harford County, which had been hard hit at Havre de Grace, also submitted a request for assistance. The Cecil County petition was read and referred to Messrs. Lusby, Dorsey, Bayley, Bowles, and Belt. On May 25, both petitions were referred to committee and on the following day were reported upon. The hoped-for relief was limited at best. "While our committee regret that the exhausted state of our revenue, and the pressing calls which are made for defence against the enemy will not permit the state to indulge in that liberality which the character of the state for humanity and munificence would require," said the chairman, "they cannot but express their belief, that some legislative relief should be granted to the pressing and immediate distresses of the indigent," and promptly submitted the following resolution for action.

> Resolved, That the Treasurer of the Western Shore pay the sum of seven hundred dollars to the order of Messrs. James Scanlan, Lambert Baird, Richard Davis, Peregrine Biddle, and John Mercer, or a majority of them, out of any unappropriated money in the treasury, to be by them distributed among the needy and indigent of those who suffered by the burning of Fredericktown, in Cecil County; which was read the first and second time by special order, and the question put, that the house concur in the said report and assent to the resolution therein contained.

Havre de Grace received an appropriation of $1,000. The citizens of Georgetown received nothing.[97]

Despite the results of the raid that had so devastated Fredericktown and Georgetown, some wisdom was extracted from the tragedy. "I am now fully satisfied in my own mind," wrote one observer, "that they cannot take Baltimore, if your troops are only in tolerable subordination; and I believe 200 disciplined troops, commanded by experienced officers, would have saved us [at Fredericktown]. If you maintain your ground firmly in the onset, you will be in little danger; if you are driven back, it will be your ruin."[98]

Such arguments meant nothing to the residents of the two towns on the Sassafras, neither of which would ever return to their former state. True, a few inhabitants had been spared, and a handful of others would return to attempt to pick up the pieces. But Fredericktown and Georgetown would never again be anything more than crossroads hamlets or serve as anything other than the occasional terminal point for small mercantile operations.

In July 1828, the Baltimore shipping entrepreneur George Weems began test runs on the Sassafras with the steamboat *Patuxent,* which called at the two diminutive town sites and a few other landings on the river but "without leaving a permanent impression on the economic or social life along the banks of the short but picturesque river." Not long after the close of the Civil War, steamboats such as *Cyrus P. Smith* and *Van Corelear the Trumpeter* (affectionately known to most as simply *Trumpeter*) began making runs from Baltimore to the two villages.[99]

The few permanent residents of the old town sites would never forget that terrible day in 1813. Kitty Knight wouldn't let them. As the years tumbled by, Miss Kitty thrived and became a local celebrity, telling and retelling the tales of her meeting with General Washington and her confrontation with Admiral Cockburn. She had kept herself busy intellectually as well as physically, writing poems of unrequited love, compiling charts of weights and measures, studying mathematics, and conducting writing exercises and other disciplines. It is possible that she may have even served as a teacher in the great brick home across the street from the house she saved and now owned. Nor had Admiral Cockburn forgotten her, at least according to local legend. "Years later, a friend of hers told about the chance meeting on the Riviera of a Kent County gentleman and the same British officer who commanded the attack on Georgetown. The officer on learning the American came from Maryland, described his recollection of Miss Knight's courage in saving her home from the torch, and hearing that she was still alive, sent his sincere compliments."[100]

On December 7, 1852, Kitty made out her last will and testament to William Knight, Jr., her nephew, with whom she had spent the last years of her life at Essex Lodge. Nearly three years later in November 1855, having kept her vow to never marry, Miss Kitty passed away at the age of seventy-nine. Her obituary, which appeared in a local newspaper, read: "Died on Thursday the 22 ulto., at the residence of her nephew, William Knight, Esq., in Cecil County, Miss Catherine Knight, at an advanced age. This remarkable old lady possessed qualities of the head and heart which made her society interesting to all who sought it . . . She had a richly cultivated mind . . . by her heroism at the burning of Georgetown, she saved several families from being made homeless and friendless by the fire and sword of the British invaders."[101]

Although not a Roman Catholic, Kitty was interred in Old Bohemia Church Cemetery, north of Warwick, Maryland, beside her brother William. And on her stone, so that no one might ever accuse her of having married, she had engraved "Miss Kitty Knight."

By 1877 there were only twenty-one lots in Georgetown, the largest of which belonged to Dr. Charles C. H. Massey. There were, of course, a few commercial establishments: a store belonging to J. F. M. Woodall, who dealt in dry goods, notions, groceries, boots, hardware, hats, caps, ready-made clothing and the like; and another dry-goods store run by J. M. Armstrong. There was a burying ground, the Tresory Creek Cemetery. And there were a handful of homes belonging to T. W. Stewart, Captain James Scotten, John Jervis, J. G. Soloway, Captain Andrew A. Woodall, W. T. Belton, Miss S. L. Smith, Mrs. Wallis, and Jonathan Jerris. A single swing bridge, an unusual feature for tidewater landings dependent upon steamboat traffic, had long before replaced the old ferry operation down by the river. On both sides of the river, the bridge was shouldered by a few warehouses.[102] Many visitors

Top: Formerly belonging to the Sassafras River Steamboat Company and known as *Van Corlaer the Trumpeter,* the popular steamer *Kitty Knight* continued to frequent the Georgetown waterfront at the beginning of the twentieth century while under the ownership of the Tolchester Line. Courtesy The Mariners' Museum, Newport News, Virginia.

Bottom: The steamboat *Annapolis,* formerly *Sassafras,* at the Fredericktown wharf, ca. 1899. Courtesy The Mariners' Museum, Newport News, Virginia.

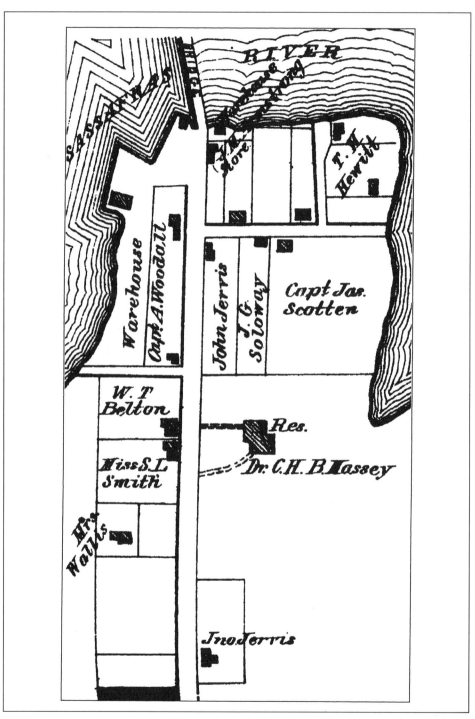

Plan of Georgetown, Maryland, 1877. Detail from "Fourth District Chestertown Kent Co." in G. M. Hopkins's *Atlas of Kent & Queen Anne's Maryland* (Philadelphia, 1877). The houses of W. T. Belton and Miss S. L. Smith were later joined to become the Kitty Knight House. Courtesy Library of Congress, Washington, D.C.

were taken with the idyllic setting and with "the beautiful Sassafras, with its low bluff banks and changing woods . . . agitated with leaping perch, which make the waters populous as the orchard, and the game-birds of autumn . . . twitter when the tide is low."[103]

Few are left to recall the last days of the steamboat age, when the harbor briefly emerged as a destination of note, albeit a minor one, the ruins of which are now hidden by stainless steel and fiberglass. Few recall that in 1899, *Van Corlear the Trumpeter* was renamed *Kitty Knight* in honor of Georgetown's most famous citizen, but unlike her namesake, the old steamer was destined for an ignoble end, abandoned by her owners and later dredged up and scrapped by the Maryland Derelict Boat Removal Program.

Today, the banks of the Sassafras River at Fredericktown and Georgetown are dotted with a few homes including a handful of buildings surviving from the days of Kitty Knight. The harbor below, which once played host to tobacco and grain ships, sailing packets, and majestic steamers now welcomes a vast but seasonal armada of as many as fifteen hundred recreational sailboats and power yachts docked at no less than five efficiently run marinas.

Looking down towards peaceful Georgetown Harbor from Kitty Knight's second-story room in the house that bears her name, it is hard to imagine the tramp of boots and the flames of destruction that were witnessed on May 6, 1813. The house still wears the indelible evidence of that terrible day, including the tear in the door from a Royal Navy boarding axe. Yet, there is a sort of harmony, a symbolism that is all-pervasive, even on Georgetown Hill. About 1900 the two houses saved by Miss Kitty were joined together to become one. In 1906, the building's ownership passed into the hands of Andrew and Alice Woodall. Then, during the ensuing years, the building devolved through innumerable owners, suffered through countless alterations, and served in myriad ways those who dwelled within. For some years one of its rooms was employed as a meeting place for a local Masonic Lodge and became known as the Masonic Room. Another, known as the Old School Room, is believed to be the place where Miss Kitty taught school. And the Washington Room was undoubtedly named after the only man she ever truly admired, besides her brother.[104]

On June 23, 1932, the London Bridge Chapter of the Daughters of the American Revolution formally dedicated the Kitty Knight House by placing a plaque on it that read:

In honor of Mistress Kitty Knight
Revolutionary Belle and Beauty
A Friend of General George Washington
When the British burned Georgetown in 1813
Her heroic efforts saved this house which
later became her home.

In May 1939, as World War II loomed on the horizon, the Kitty Knight House faced its darkest days since Cockburn's raid, when the building and all of its contents, presumably including many of the personal items that had once belonged to Miss Kitty herself, were sold at a sheriff's auction by Samuel T. Freeman and Company.[105] During World War II, the venerable old building, creaking with age and desperately in need of restoration and a new coat of paint, became a boardinghouse for young women who worked at the gunpowder factory in Elkton. During this period the first in a series of restaurants was opened on the premises. By the 1950s the Kitty Knight House was being operated as both a restaurant and an

The Kitty Knight House, Georgetown, Maryland.

inn, but it continued to pass from hand to hand. And through it all, it is said, the temperamental ghost of Miss Kitty herself superintended the proceedings.

Many tales are told regarding the specter of the famous Kitty Knight. Some of the most popular are eyewitness accounts from restaurant and hotel staff who have worked in the house for decades. There are, of course, the usual stories of doors opening on their own, furniture moving about when no one is there, a rocking chair that rocks of its own accord, and objects falling for no apparent reason. But one gets the distinct impression that there are also some antics more in keeping with Kitty's mischievous side. One waitress in the restaurant, which is partially situated below the room believed to be Miss Kitty's bedroom, noted that napkins would be taken and hidden, then would mysteriously reappear in place the following day. Others reported having seen the ghostly form of Miss Kitty herself, both in the house and in the adjacent parking lot, dressed in her pink satin gown with her raven hair draped over her shoulders. Some staffers have reported waiting on customers in the restaurant who said they felt very uneasy and complained that every time they ate in the house, strange little mishaps always occurred. One lady, reported a witness, claimed that "her croutons got tossed all over the floor, her tea ran out of the pot wrong, and went all over the table, and her dinner nearly ended up in her lap. Needless to say she didn't eat any dessert." Nor is it likely, a cynic might postulate, that she had anything else to drink![106]

As recently as 1994, Robert Garvine, the dining room manager, reported seeing Miss Kitty when he and a waitress walked through the house and passed a portrait purported to be of the heroine. "There was an image of a woman standing near the door . . . She looked identical to the woman in the picture. It sort of frightened us a little bit." Soon afterwards, Charles E. Metzger, general manager, noticed a light was on in one of the second-floor bedrooms and he heard someone walking around in the rooms, even though they were not booked.

When he checked, the lights were off and the rooms were empty.[107]

EPILOGUE

"Keep Calvert Country"

July 4, 2000. Dunkirk, Maryland, the little town where I live, is not a place of antiquity. It possesses no formal urban pedigree nor any industry of note. It was never subjected to the fire and sword of invaders as were some tidewater towns, nor did it suffer from the bitter commercial rivalry or political chicanery that doomed others. Located some distance from the water, it was not dependent upon a waterway's navigability, the loss of which through siltation condemned many more to oblivion. It is, by all outward appearances, a place of trivial interest to those who pass through, little more than a few buildings, a signpost, and a traffic light on a nondescript highway. Except for the din of the morning and evening commuter traffic that storms through, it is a quiet, rural place surrounded by farms, fields, and forest-covered countryside. The rustic, one-lane roads that spur off the main highway pass through delightful and welcoming terrain, where passers-by still wave to each other and crime is a foreign thing. In many ways my town has all the trappings of the idealized America that used to be: a market place, a firehouse that doubles as a voting center, nearby schools, a restaurant or two, churches of several denominations, banks, grocery stores, a pharmacy, a few gas stations, an active citizens organization, social clubs, ball fields, a handful of doctors, dentists, and lawyers, and a population of less than a thousand souls. Its citizens, mostly commuters who earn their livings elsewhere, are polite, patriotic, politically active, and usually well behaved. In short, my hometown is a perfect place to live.

Yet, like many of the tidewater towns created during the seventeenth and eighteenth centuries, with no clear economic base other than tobacco, Dunkirk's reason for being is ephemeral and ill defined. Like many similar sites throughout the state and nation, its future is clouded. Change is heavy in the air as my town, county, and state are forcefully weaned, for better or worse, from the centuries of tobacco culture that gave them birth and hindered the development of urban centers from the very beginning. In the process, the old order, with its sense of direction, time, and place, is vanishing, as is the individuality that once made the persona of tidewater society unique.

When the first settlers stepped ashore on the banks of the St. Mary's River, their objective had been clearly outlined by Cecil Calvert. They were English expatriates, many of whom were considered disposable labor in the old world, where freedom of choice and opportunity were not a part of the picture. But in the New World, amidst the vastness of the tidewater landscape, they could lay down roots and establish their own sense of purpose, community, and belonging. Their experiments in urban development boldly sought to fill the tidewater landscape with order and regularity.

As we have seen, the grand design at new town and port building, frequently interrupted by social upheavals, wars, and religious controversy, was generally doomed to failure. It was, ironically, not from lack of initiative, intelligence, or industry that these efforts proved ineffectual but from the innate desire to impose European concepts of centralization upon a single-crop economy entirely structured on decentralization. While laying out their scores of towns and ports to ensure greater control of revenue and taxation, the founding fathers repeatedly ignored the realities of the widely dispersed agrarian society whose commerce they sought to orchestrate. Amazingly, some towns actually took hold and thrived, only to be thwarted in the end by myriad causes, almost all of which were induced by human action. Wars took their toll on some, but the silting up of the waterways upon which most towns had been erected, a consequence of clearing the land for agriculture, doomed many more. The rise of Baltimore condemned the rest to a prolonged but certain collapse.

Now, on the cusp of the twenty-first century, the space presented to those early colonists has all but disappeared as eight million citizens shuffle about their daily business upon the Chesapeake's shores. Today we live in a society based on consumerism that thrives upon the newest and most attractive and systematically bulldozes the physical foundations on which the culture was built. In the process, the sites of innumerable ancient and historic towns, hamlets, and plantations have been torn apart in the name of urban renewal and progress. Former trading stations and crossroads have been paved over for parking lots. Onetime working ports on our rivers and bays have succumbed to armadas of plastic boats. In 1999 alone, fifty thousand acres of Maryland farmland were developed into subdivisions despite aggressive farmland preservation programs. We travel through what is left of the countryside in fast, gas-guzzling sport-utility vehicles, completely oblivious to the environment around us, seldom pausing to consider the land or its history as we speed by. We forget that our well-being as a people rests on a healthy connectedness to place—the unique mixture of property, nature, and community that is the focus of all society—which our forefathers struggled so hard to gain and maintain.

Have we failed to learn from our own history as we enter yet another era of experimentation in urban evolution? My home town is one of three designated by innovative local county government planners as "town centers" in a commendable effort to control rampant development and hold onto the concepts of space and individuality so cherished by our ancestors. The battle cry of bumper stickers plastered on the cars and trucks of many county residents, old and new, is "Keep Calvert Country." It is a plea not easily ignored by politicians in Annapolis who offer plans of "Smart Growth" that, in many ways, are little different from those offered by their predecessors several centuries earlier: centralize and contain commerce in urban centers through legislative fiat.

Lord Baltimore's primary directive to his colonists was "to settle the Plantation." The settlement was achieved thanks to that vast estuarine system upon which the colonists were ensconced, not through well-intentioned legislative efforts. Maryland grew and flourished despite the shortcomings of the colonial new towns programs. Sadly, the flawed but noble legacy of the early urban development initiatives is preserved now only in fragile artifacts of history, hidden beneath the soils of the land and its rivers and bays.

The archaeological record of urban growth and development in colonial Maryland, the physical link between who we were and who we are, is today besieged by the very success of the colony Lord Baltimore so carefully planned. The plantation, now the great State of Maryland, is indeed well settled and wealthy, and commerce thrives as never before. The state can proudly boast of its colonial patrimony and of its pioneering experiments in town planning. But therein lies the conundrum. As urban development, the goal of Maryland's founders, succeeds beyond their wildest dreams, it also destroys the physical evidence of its origins. As we enter this new century, it is up to us to focus upon the preservation of that all but forgotten legacy of our colonial heritage, our early towns and ports. Lord Baltimore would certainly smile upon that.

In the meantime, I'm glad I live in Dunkirk.

# APPENDIX

*Maryland Towns and Ports Authorized for Establishment,
Reestablishment, or Removal, 1668–1751*

Between 1668 and 1751, a total of 130 individual towns were designated for establishment in the colony of Maryland by means of three proclamations or edicts of the Lord Proprietor and forty-two subsequent individual acts passed by the General Assembly. These proclamations and acts produced 205 individual site listings in eighty-three years, 75 of which were redesignations of sites already authorized by earlier acts. A total of 6 sites were intentionally ordered to be removed or deserted, and 5 more were transferred to new locations. The names of many sites changed with each reestablishment. Some sites bore only the local property owner's name. Some names were abandoned only to be later reassigned to a newly designated site elsewhere. Duplications of a name in several counties was not uncommon.

The following tables list all of the towns authorized by official proclamation, edict, or act of legislation in Maryland from 1668 to 1751. Listings are presented by county. Counties appear in alphabetical order. Because many towns were designated for establishment in counties that were later subdivided to create new counties, all towns are given within the geographic boundaries of the counties as they exist today.

Column 1 provides a reference number for each site designated, redesignated, moved, or removed by the government of Maryland.

Column 2 indicates the year in which the specific town site was authorized to be established, although some acts stipulate actual survey and construction for later dates.

Column 3 notes the size of each town, if that information was provided in the proclamation, edict, or act.

Column 4 gives the precise wording in the official record designating the site either by town name, locale, or property owner. Whenever the site was authorized for creation in a former county, the earlier county is indicated in parentheses by its initials: Anne Arundel County (AAC); Baltimore County (BC); Calvert County (CAC); Cecil County (CLC); Frederick County (FC); Harford County (HC); Kent County (KC); Montgomery County (MC); Queen Anne's County (QAC); Somerset County (SC); and Talbot County (TC). The District of Columbia, though not a Maryland county, is also included since one port town was created on Maryland lands that later were incorporated within the district's boundaries.

Column 5 shows the common name or names by which the town was designated or came to be known. If a town was known by different names at different times, or was recreated under a new name at the same site as an earlier town, the multiple names appear in parentheses. Some names are only suppositional and are based upon circumstantial evidence such as a map designation or questionable locale description. Names that are unknown or uncertain are so noted.

Column 6 gives the approximate location of each designated town site. Whenever a town was redesignated, or a new town authorized for an existing site, the location is indicated by a reference to the appropriate earlier site number. Locations that are unknown or uncertain are marked.

A map has been included showing all known or presumed sites in the Maryland tidewater.

MARYLAND

NEW JERSEY

VIRGINIA

DELAWARE

Delaware Bay

Atlantic
Ocean

Chesapeake
Bay

Charlestown
Frenchtown*
Spesutie
Cecil Town 1
Cecil Town 2
Captain Johns Creek
Frederick
Town
Sassafras
Sassafrax ?
Joppa
"Old"
Baltimore
Gunpowder
Shrewsbury 1
George Town
Shrewsbury 2
Baltimore
Town
Middle Town
Worton
Jonestown
Pooles
Island
Whetstone Point
Morgan's Plantation ?
Elk Ridge Landing
Chestertown 2
Chestertown 1
Kings Town
Darington
Milford Town
Ogle Town
New Yarmouth
Coursey's Town/Talbot Town
Gloucester Town
Swetenham's ?
Magothy Town
Corsica Creek [Town Land]
Bridgetown
Annapolis
Broad
Creek ?
Queenstown
Quoon Anne's Town
Kilkonny
Town
Bladensburg
London
Town
York Town
Hillsboro
Georgetown**
Coxes
Creek
West
River
Town
Doncaster (Wye)
Pitt's Bridge*
Upper Marlborough
Herring Town
Kings Town
Charlestown
Pig
Point
Bogues Bay ?
Aire
Nottingham
Dover*
Piscataway
Bowlington ?
Lower Marlborough
Guy
Coxtown
Whites ?
Milltown
St. Joseph's Town
Oxford
Warrington
Dangyes Point
Hunting Town
Stumpneck Town
Prince Frederick
Cambridge
Port Tobacco
Morgans ?/Dorchester 2 ?
Islington
Benedict Leonard Town
Bristol
Hallowing Point
Calverton
Vienna
Westwood ?
Newport
St. Leonards Town 2
Nanjemoy ?
Nanjemoy 1
Dorchester 1/Little Yarmouth
St. Leonards Town 1
Choptico
Salisbury
St. Clement's
Pukewaxen ?
Town
Tipquin
Harrington
Bristol
Green Hill
Half Round Hill
[St. George?]
James Jones ?
Pile's Town
Brickhill?
Ballards ?
Leonardtown
Lott's Wife ?
Britton [New Town?]
Somerset
Newport ?
Town 2
Plymouth ?
Barrows
Snow Hill
St. Mary's City
White House
Princess Anne
St. Jerome's Town
Oyster
Somerset Town 1
Neck
Rehoboth
Annemessex Town
[St. George's Town]

LEGISLATED TOWNS OF TIDEWATER MARYLAND 1668-1751

0 5 10 15 20 25
Scale in Miles

Map by Donald G. Shomette, 1999

Map Key

● Conjectured location of town based upon best evidence available
■ Known location of town
? Conjectural name of town
★ Town not created by edict or legislation
★★ Later ceded to Federal Government

Town Locations Unknown

Cecil County—William Frisbeys
Cecil County—John West Plantation
Kent County—Canterbury Town
St. Mary's County—John Bayleys or Taunts
St. Mary's County—Baltimore Town

ANNE ARUNDEL COUNTY

No.	Year	Acres	Description	Name	Location
1	1668	—	"Att Richard Actons land in Arrundell County"	Arundelton (Annapolis)	Present site of Annapolis, on Severn River
2	1669	—	"afore the Town Land purchased of Richard Acton"	Arundelton (Annapolis)	See No. 1
3	1669	—	"afore Herrington in Herring Creek"	Herring Creek Town	On Herring Bay, vicinity Town Point and Tracy's Landing
4	1671	—	"At Richard Actons Land"	Arundelton (Annapolis)	See No. 1
5	1671	—	"at herring Creeke in Ann Arundell County"	Herring Creek Town	See No. 3
6	1683	100	"att the Towne Land at Proctors"	Annapolis	See No. 1
7	1683	100	"att South River on Coll Burges his Land"	London Town	On the south shore of South River, on the peninsula between Glebe Bay and Almshouse Creek
8	1683	100	"att Herring Creeke"	Herring Creek Town	See No. 3
9	1684	100	"Att West River Vpon the land of John Hillen deceased and the land Thervnto adjacent"	West River Town	On West River
10	1684	100	"Att pigg Pointe vpon Mount Colverte mannor in Patuxent River" (CAC)	Pig Point	On the east shore of Patuxent River at Pig Point, immediately south of Bristol
11	1706	100	*Designated port:* "The Town and Port of Annapolis"	Annapolis	See No. 1
12	1706	100	"London Towne on the south side of South river"	London Town	See No. 7
13	1706	100	"a Town in West river where the Town was formerly"	West River Town	See No. 9
14	1706	100	"att Hering Creek where the Town was formerly laid out"	Herring Town	See No. 3
15	1706	100	"in Maggotty river on the Plantation late in the Possession of Thomas Harrison On the south side of the said River"	Magothy Town	On south shore of Magothy River
16	1707	50	"at herring Creek"	Herring Town	See No. 3
17	1707	—	"Annapolis"	Annapolis	See No. 1
18	1707	—	"West river"	West River Town	See No. 9
19	1707	50	"at a place upon Petuxent River called Pigg Point"	Pig Point	See No. 10
20	1707	50	"upon the North branch of the said [Patuxent] River at a place opposite to Queen Ann's Towne in Prince George's County"	Kilkenny Town	On Patuxent River at Queen Anne's Bridge, opposite the village of Hardesty

BALTIMORE COUNTY

No.	Year	Acres	Description	Name	Location
21	1683	100	"in Patapsco River neere Humphryes Creek"	Darington (Darrington)	Vicinity of Bear Creek
22	1684	100	"att Mddle River on the land of Cornwallis or Leakins or both att the discretion of the Commissioners for the same County"	Middle Town	On Middle River
23	1686	100	"in Gunpowder River vpon the point comonly called Westburies Point"	Gunpowder	Within Gunpowder Falls State Park
—	1686	100	Removed: "the Towne in Baltemore County in Middle Riuer on the land of Cornowallis or Loakins"	Middle Town	See No. 22
24	1706	100	"at Whetstone neck in Patapsco river"	Whetstone Point	On Whetstone Neck, within Baltimore City
25	1706	100	"on Foster neck on Gun Powder river"	Gunpowder	Fosters Neck, in Gunpowder Falls Park
—	1707	—	Moved: "the place appointed for a Town on Gunpowder River on the Land Called Fosters Neck [BC] shall be deserted and in lieu thereof fifty acres of Land shall be Erected into a Town on a Tract of Land on the said River belonging to Ann Felks Called Taylors Choice [HC] and that the said Court House of the said County shall be built there"*	Gunpowder	See No. 25
26	1729	60	"on the North Side of Patapsco, in Baltemore County"	Baltimore Town	Within Baltimore City limits
27	1732	—	"on a Creek, divided on the East, from the Town lately laid out in Baltimore, called Baltimore Town, on the Land whereon Edward Fell keeps Store"	Jonestown	Fells Point, within Baltimore City limits
28	1745	—	"Baltimore" (joined with No. 29)	Baltimore Town	See Nos. 26 and 27
29	1747	—	"Enlargement of Baltimore Town, in Baltimore County"	Baltimore Town	See No. 28
30	1750	—	"Enlargement of Baltimore Town, in Baltimore County"	Baltimore Town	See No. 28

* The Taylors Choice site was eventually designated as Joppa. See No. 103.

CALVERT COUNTY

No.	Year	Acres	Description	Name	Location
31	1668	—	"at Hallowing point in Calvert Mannor in Patuxt riur"	Hallowing Point	At Hallowing Point on east bank of Patuxent River, opposite Benedict
32	1669	—	"afore Calverton in Battle Creek in the same [Patuxent] River"	Calverton (Battle Town)	On the north shore of Battle Creek, at the confluence of the creek and Patuxent River
33	1671	20	"at William berries Land in Battle Creeke in Patuxent River"	Calverton (Battle Town)	See No. 32
34	1683	100	"att St Leonards Creeke on Richard Smiths Land"	St. Leonards Town 1	On north side of St. Leonard's Creek, possibly on or near Peterson Point
35	1683	100	"on Hollowing point on his Ldspps Mannor"	Hallowing Point	See No. 31
36	1683	100	"at Warrington on the Clifts Towne Land"	Warrington	Vicinity of Dare's Beach, on Chesapeake Bay
37	1684	20	"att Colvert Towne in Batle Creeke"	Calverton (Battle Town)	See No. 32
38	1684	100	"Att the said Coxes Creek on the land Adjacent in the stead and place of John Bowlings land"**	Coxtown	On the north shore of Cox's Creek, at the confluence with the Patuxent River
39	1686	100	"att Harvey Towne and the land adjacent there"**	Harvey Town	Uncertain
40	1688	100	"on the south side of Petuxent River in Calvert County between Abington's Creeke & Joseph Edloes"	St. Joseph's Town	Probably south of Chews or Cox's Creek on east shore of Patuxent River
41	1695	100	"Bogues Bay"	Bogues Bay	Jug Bay, possibly below Halls Creek on Patuxent or vicinity of Lower Marlboro
42	1706	100	"at the head of Saint leonards Creek on both sides of the mill branch at the Mouth of the said Branch"	St. Leonards Town (St. Leonard's Creek Town) 2	Between Mill Branch and Quaker Swamp Branch, and on the opposite (west) bank of Mill Branch on St. Leonards Shores lands
43	1706	100	"at the head of Hunting creek on both sides of the said Creek"	Hunting Town	Headwaters of Hunting Creek, near Rt. 4
44	1706	100	"in the freshes of Petuxent river at the Plantation of George & Thomas Hardisty"	Lower Marlborough	At present site of Lower Marlboro
45	1725	—	"William's old Fields"	Prince Frederick	At present site of Prince Frederick

* Coxtown has often been confused with Lower Marlborough. Some historians claim that the two sites were erected on the same tract of land, which they clearly were not. Bowlings land was in what is now Prince George's County.

** This site may be confused with Warrington.

CAROLINE COUNTY

No.	Year	Acres	Description	Name	Location
46	1708	50	"at the mouth [head] of Tuckahoe Creek on or neare the Land of Collonall Nicholas Law" (QAC)	Hillsboro (Hillsborough)	At the head of Tuckahoe Creek at the corner where Queen Anne's, Talbot, and Caroline Counties converge

CECIL COUNTY

No.	Year	Acres	Description	Name	Location
47	1669	—	"[afore the Town Land in] Sassafrax River" (BC)	Unknown	Ordinary Point, north shore Sassafras River
48	1671	—	"at the Land of Mr Hatton in Sassafrax River" (BC)	Unknown	North shore of Sassafras River
49	1683	100	"att Capt Johns Creeke Willm Prices Plantacon in Elke River"	Unknown	On Cabin John Creek
50	1683	100	"in Sassafrax River at William ffrisbeys plantacon"	Unknown	Unknown
51	1684	100	"Att the plantation Called John West"	Unknown	Unknown
52	1686	100	"in Elk Riuer att a place called Caecill Towne at the mouth of Bohemia River"	Cecil Town 1	On Town Neck, north shore, mouth of Bohemia River
53	1706	100	"At Captaine Johns Creek where a Town was formerly laid out"	Unknown	See No. 49
54	1706	100	"in Elk river"	Cecil Town 1	See No. 52
55	1706	100	"the Land belonging to Isaac Calk in Sassafrax river"	Sassafras	At headwaters of the Sassafras River
56	1707	100	"on price Neck in Elk River where the Court house of the said [Cecil] County shall be built"	Cecil Town 1	See No. 52
57	1707	100	"on the plantation formerly belonging to Isaac Calk near the head of Sassafrax river"	Sassafras	See No. 55
58	1730	20	"at Broxen's Point"	Cecil Town 2	Broxen's Point, at the junction of Scotchman's Creek (Omealy) and Bohemia River
59	1736	30	"at Pennington's Point, or Happy Harbor"	Frederick Town	At present site of Fredericktown
60	1742	200	"at a Place called Long-Point, on the West Side of North-East River, in Caecil County"	Charlestown	At present site of Charlestown
61	1744	—	"at a Place called Long-Point, on the West Side of North-East River, in Caecil County"	Charlestown	See No. 60
62	1745	—	"at a Place called Long-Point, on the West Side of North-East River, in Caecil County"	Charlestown	See No. 60
63	1750	—	"at a Place called Long-Point, on the West Side of North-East River, in Caecil County"	Charlestown	See No. 60

CHARLES COUNTY

No.	Year	Acres	Description	Name	Location
64	1668	—	"Att Charles Towne in his lops fforrest nigh Humphrey Warrens plantacon in Wiccocomoco riur"	Charles Town	At the head of Port Tobacco River
65	1668	—	"at the land lately purchased by John England & Benjamin Rozer nigh Edmund lindseys"	Bristol (uncertain)	Vicinity of Chapel Point on the east side of Port Tobacco River (uncertain)
66	1668	—	"att Portobacco"	Chandlerstown (Charles Town)	See No. 64
67	1669	—	"in Charles County in Wicocomico River as near the Town lands as Ships and other Vessels can conveniently Ride"	Charles Town (uncertain)	See No. 64
68	1671	—	"at Charles Town in his Lordships Forest nigh Humphry Warrens in Wicocomico River"	Charles Town	See No. 64
69	1671	—	"at the Land lately purchased by Ino England and Benjamin Rozier nigh Edmund Lindseys in Port Tobacco"	Bristol (uncertain)	See No. 65
70	1683	100	"On diggs his purchase in Wiccomico River formerly ffendalls on the Creeke"	Wharton Town (uncertain) or Newport Town (uncertain)	On the Wicomico River
71	1683	100	"on the Church Land on the East side Portobacco Creeke neere the Mouth of the Creeke"	Bristol (uncertain)	See No. 65
72	1683	100	"on Stumpe necke neare Climyemuxen on Mr Reddish his Land"	Stumpneck Town	On the Stump Neck peninsula, between Potomac River and Chicamuxen Creek
73	1684	100	"Att the head of Portabacco Creeke neare the Church There"	Chandlerstown (Charles Town)	See Nos. 64 and 66
74	1684	100	"att westwood on the land of Mr Thomas Gerard"	Westwood (uncertain)	At head of Wicomico River, between Allens Fresh and Newport Run
75	1684	100	"att the Mouth of Nenjemy Creek Att or neare Lewises Neck"	Nanjemoy 1	At mouth of Nanjemoy Creek
76	1684	100	"Att the head of wickacomaca River"	Newport (uncertain)	Head of Wicomico River
77	1686	100	"at lower Cedar poynt in Pukewaxen hundred on or neere the land late of Mr James Tire deceased"	Pukewaxen (uncertain)	On Cobb Neck, at Lower Cedar Point, near Piccowaxen Creek
78	1686	100	"at dangyes point in Mattawomen or St. Thomas Creeke"	Dangyes Point (uncertain)	Possibly Deep Point on Cornwallis Neck, between Mattawoman Creek and the Potomac
	1686	—	Removed: "The Towne on stumpt neck neer Chingemuxen on the land late of Mr Reddishare"	Stumpneck Town	See No. 72
79	1706	100	"at Port Tobacco . . . where Towns were formerly laid out"	Port Tobacco	See Nos. 64 and 66
80	1706	100	"New Port . . . where Towns were formerly laid out"	Newport	At present site of Newport

Continued on next page

CHARLES COUNTY—Continued

No.	Year	Acres	Name	Description	Location
81	1706	100	Benedict Leonard Town	"at Benedict-Leonard Town in Petuxent river where the Town was formerly Erected"	At present site of Benedict
82	1707	100	Benedict Leonard Town	"Benedict Leonard Town"	See No. 81
83	1707	100	Nanjemoy 2	"on the upper Side of Nanjemy Creek on Potomack River upon part of the Land now or Late in the possession of Martin Campbell and the Land adjoining thereto"	Possibly on the west side of Nanjemoy Creek, on Taylor's Neck (uncertain)
84	1729	—	Charles Town (Port Tobacco)	"at the Head of Port-Tobacco Creek"	See Nos. 64 and 66
85	1732	15	Benedict Leonard Town (Benedict)	"Benedict-Leonard Town"	See No. 81

DORCHESTER COUNTY

No.	Year	Acres	Name	Description	Location
86	1683	100	Unknown	"on Morgans Land neare the head of ffishing Creeke in little Choptanke"	Vicinity of Pig Neck (uncertain)
87	1683	100	Dorchester 1 (uncertain)	"on Traverse his Land on the West side of the North West branch on Transquaquin River"	Northwest branch of Transquaking Creek
88	1684	100	Cambridge	"Att Daniell Joansis plantation on the south side of Great Choptancke"	At present site of Cambridge
89	1686	100	Islington	"in little Choptanck Riuer att Nicholas Maryes poynt, to be called Islington"	On Town Point, north shore of Fishing Creek, near mouth of creek (uncertain)
90	1686	100	Bristol	"in Hunger Riuer on the East side of the said Riuer on Andrew Fusleyes Neck to be called Bristoll"	On east side of Honga River (uncertain)
—	1686	—	Dorchester 1	*Removed:* "in Dorcester County now comonly called Dorchester"	See No. 87
—	1686	—	Unknown	*Removed:* "on Morgans land neere the head of ffishing creek in little Choptanck"	See No. 86
91	1688	—	Dorchester 2	"upon a Tract of Land called Morgan neare the head of ffishing creek in little Choptanck . . . to be called by the name of Dorchester"	See No. 86
92	1706	100	Cambridge	"at Cambridge in Great Choptank"	See No. 88
93	1706	100	Islington	"at Islington In little Choptank . . . where Towns were formerly laid out"	See No. 89
94	1706	100	Little Yarmouth	"Little Yarmouth in Transquaking River where Towns were formerly laid out"	See No. 87
95	1706	100	Vienna	"at the Emperours Landing in Nanticoke river"	Present site of Vienna
96	1707	100	Plymouth (uncertain)	"on a point Called Phillips his point on the north Side of Fishing Creek in Hunger River"	North side of Fishing Creek on Honga River
—	1707	—	Little Yarmouth	*Removed:* "Little Yarmouth on transquaking river shall be deserted"	See No. 94

HARFORD COUNTY

No.	Year	Acres	Description	Name	Location
97	1668	—	"Att Pooles Island" (BC)	Pooles Island	On Pooles Island in upper Chesapeake Bay, immediately south of the Aberdeen Proving Grounds, off Gunpowder Neck
98	1669	—	"afore the Town Land in Bush River" (BC)	"Old" Baltimore Town	On the Bush River side of Aberdeen Proving Grounds near Chilbury Point
99	1671	—	"at the Land of Thomas Samson in Bush River" (BC)	"Old" Baltimore Town	See No. 98
100	1683	100	"on Bush River on the Towne Land neere the Court House" (BC)	"Old" Baltimore Town	See No. 98
101	1686	100	"in Sposuty Creek on the land formerly Mr John Colletts now in possession of John Mould and the Land adjacent" (BC)	Spesutie	On Spesutie Narrows, on the Aberdeen Proving Grounds
102	1706	100	"Upon the Land called Chillberry in Brush river" (BC)	"Old" Baltimore Town	See No. 98
103	1707	50	"the place appointed for a Town on Gunpowder River on the Land Called Fosters Neck [BC] shall be deserted and in lieu thereof fifty acres of Land shall be Erected into a Town on a Tract of Land on the said River belonging to Ann Felks Called Taylors Choice and that the said Court House of the said County shall be built there" (BC)	Joppa	On the east side of Gunpowder River near present Joppa
104	1724	21	"at Joppa" (BC)	Joppa	See No. 103
105	1727	—	"at Joppa" (BC)	Joppa	See No. 103

HOWARD COUNTY

No.	Year	Acres	Description	Name	Location
106	1732	30	"at and about the Landing, called, The Elk-Ridge Landing, near the Head of Potapsco River, in Anne-Arundel County," (AAC)	Janssen Town (Elk Ridge Landing)	At the head of navigation on Patapsco River at Elk Ridge Landing
107	1734	30	"at and about the Landing, called Elk-Ridge Landing, near the Head of Potapsco River, in Ann-Arundel County," (AAC)	Elk Ridge Landing	Same as No. 106

KENT COUNTY

No.	Year	Acres	Description	Name	Location
108	1669	—	"in Kent County in the Creek afore Morgans Plantation"	Unknown	On Morgans Creek, three miles east of Chestertown
109	1671	—	"at the Land of Ionathan Sybery"	Shrewsbury 1 (uncertain)	Possibly on Turner's Creek, Shrewsbury Neck
110	1671	—	"at Morgans Plantation in Morgans Creek in Kent County"	Unknown	See No. 108
111	1683	100	"In Worton Creeke" (CLC)	Worton	Possibly on Handy Point near Worton Creek
112	1683	100	"att new Yarmouth in Grays Inn Creeke"	New Yarmouth	On Grays Inn Creek, off Chester River
113	1686	100	"at Swan Creeke on the plantacon & land of Wm Stanly To be called Milford Towne"	Milford Town	On Swan Point
114	1686	—	"Canterbury Town"*	Canterbury Town	Unknown
115	1688	—	"upon a certain point in the said [Langford] Bay called Cackaway point . . . formerly the Land of Toby Wells . . . to be called by the name of Glocester Towne"	Gloucester Town	On Cackaway Point on **Langford** Creek
116	1706	100	*Designated port:* "In Chester River on a plantation of Mr Joce's between Mr Willmores and Edward Walvins Plantation"	Chestertown 1	On Chester River
117	1706	100	"In Warton Creek on a Tract of Land where ffrancs Barne lives formerly laid out for a Town"	Worton	See No. 111
118	1706	100	"at Sassafrax river where Shrewsberry Town was"	Shrewsbury 1	See No. 109
—	1707	—	*Moved:* "the place for the Town and Port there by the said Act Erected upon Chester River shall be deserted and in Liew Thereof the said Port & Town with the Courthouse of the said County [Kent] shall be built upon the place where The Commissioners for Towns in the said County have purchased Land for the same"	Chestertown 1	See No. 116
119	1707	100	"where the Commissioners for Towns in the said [Kent] county have purchased Land for the Same"	Chestertown 2	Present site of Chestertown
—	1707	—	*Moved:* "the place appointed for Shrewsberry Towne on Sassafrax River by the said Act appointed be also deserted and Laid out where the Commissioners for Towns in Kent County aforesaid have purchased Land for the Same"	Shrewsbury 1	See No. 109
120	1707	100	"where the Commissioners for Towns in Kent County aforesaid have purchased Land for the Same"	Shrewsbury 2	Vicinity of Shrewsbury Church, near head of Turner's Creek
121	1708	50	"at Chester ferry at or near the place where the old Court-house stood"	Unknown	On Chester River, at site of Chestertown (I)
122	1730	100	"on Chester River, commonly called Chester Town"	Chestertown 2 (New Town)	See No. 119
123	1736	80	"part of a Tract of Land called Tolchester on Sassafras River in the Possession of [Gideon] Pearce"	George Town	Present site of Georgetown, on the Sassafras River

* An officer was designated for a town called Canterbury in Kent County in 1686, but the town's name is used only once and is not mentioned in any of the acts or proclamations creating towns and ports in the county.

PRINCE GEORGE'S COUNTY

No.	Year	Acres	Description	Name	Location
124	1671	—	"at Guy Whites Land"	Unknown	White's Landing on Patuxent River (uncertain)
125	1683	100	"att John Bowlings Land neere Gaunts Land" (CAC)	Unknown	Vicinity of White's Landing on Patuxent
126	1688	—	"at Bowlings Point in the ffreshes of Petuxent River to be called by the name of Bowlington" (CAC)	Bowlington	See No. 125
127	1706	100	"at the Land of William Mills in Petuxent river"	Milltown	At Milltown Landing, at the end of Milltown Landing Road, south of Magruders Landing
128	1706	100	"att Mattapany Landing on the Land of Thomas Brooke Esqr"	Nottingham	On a tract called Prospect, west side of Patuxent River at outlet of Kings Creek
129	1706	100	"at Mount Calvert where the Court house stands"	Charlestown (Mount Calvert)	On the peninsula formed by the confluence of the Western Branch and Patuxent River
130	1706	100	"at the upper Landing in the Western branch Comonly called Col Belts Landing"	Upper Marlborough	At present site of Upper Marlboro
131	1706	100	"at the upper Landing on the Northern branch [of Patuxent River] Comonly called Andersons Landing"	Queen Anne's Town	At present site of Hardesty* at the end of Queen Anne's Bridge Road
132	1706	100	"at broad Creek in Potomock river on the south side of the said Creek at Thomas Lewis's Landing"	Aire (Broad Creek)	South shore of Broad Creek off the Potomac River
133	1707	40/50	"on the South Side of Piscattaway Creek at or near the head thereof"	Piscataway Town	On lands of Piscataway Park
134	1707	3	"three acres of Land whereon George Harris of prince Georges County Merchant hath built Dwelling houses and Store houses shall from hence forth be adjudged accepted reputed and taken to be part of Nottingham Town within the said County whereunto it ajoyns"	Nottingham	See No. 128
135	1742	60	"on the South side of the Eastern Branch of Potomack River, in Prince George's County, near a Place called Garrison Landing"	Bladensburg	At present site of Bladensburg
136	1742	—	"Upper-Marlborough Town, in Prince George's County"	Upper Marlborough	See No. 130

* Resumed name of Queen Anne's in 1999.

QUEEN ANNE'S COUNTY

No.	Year	Acres	Description	Name	Location
137	1668	—	"Att Chester point in Chester riur" (KC)	Unknown	Old Chester Point
138	1669	—	"afore the Town Land in Chester River" (KC)	Unknown	See No. 137
139	1671	—	"at Corsica Creek in Chester River" (TC)	Corsica Creek (Town Land)	On Town Point, south shore Corsica Creek
140	1683	100	"at the Towne Land att the forke in Chester River" (TC)	Unknown	See No. 139
141	1683	100	"att Shipping als Coxes Creeke" (KC)	Unknown	On Batts Neck, Kent Island
142	1686	100	"Major Courseyes Fork" (TC)	Coursey's Town	On Spaniard Neck, north shore of Corsica Creek
143	1688	—	"on the North side of Corsica Creek at a place called Glevens point to be called by the name of Talbott Towne" (TC)	Talbot Town	On Spaniard Neck, on Corsica Creek
144	1706	100	"in Courseca Creek upon the Plantation where Robert Smith Esqr now lives"	Unknown	Corsica Creek
145	1706	100	"at Broad Creek on Kent Island where the Town was formerly laid out"	Unknown	On Broad Creek, west side of Kent Island, immediately south of Bay Bridge Airport in Stevensville
146	1707	100	"at the plantation of Master William Swetenham in Coursivall Creek in Chester River"	Swetenham's (uncertain)	North shore of Corsica Creek, vicinity of Centreville (uncertain)
—	1707	—	Moved: "on the Land of Robert Smith Esquire shall be deserted and in lieu thereof one hundred acres of Land upon the plantation of Major John Hawkins in Courseys Creek and the Convenient Lands adjoyning"	Unknown	See No. 144
147	1707	100	"upon the plantation of Major John Hawkins in Courseys Creek and the Convenient Lands adjoyning thereto shall be Erected into a Town where the Court house of the said [Queen Anne's] County shall be built"	Queen Anne's Town (Queenstown)	Present site of Queenstown
148	1732	60	"Part of a Tract of Land whereon John Hawkins now lives, and supposed to be the Right of John Hawkins, Junior . . . which said Tract is commonly known by the Name of Tully's Delight"	Ogle Town	On Prize House Point, Wilmer's Neck, at the mouth of South East Creek
149	1732	30	"South Side of Chester River, opposite to Chester Town, on a Tract now in Possession of John Dempster"	Kings Town (Kingston)	On Chester River, opposite Chestertown
150	1732	20	"near the Bridge near the Head of Great Choptank River, in Dorchester and Queen-Anne Counties"	Bridgetown	On Route 304 (Bridgetown Road) at Queen Anne's County–Caroline County line over Mason Branch of Tuckahoe Creek

ST. MARY'S COUNTY

No.	Year	Acres	Description	Name	Location
151	1668	—	"at East st Mary's in St Maries County"	St. Mary's City	Present site of St. Mary's City
152	1668	—	"All Brickhill point in Mattapany Manr"	Unknown	Uncertain
153	1669	—	"in St Mary's County in Saint Georges [St. Mary's] River afore the City of St Marys"	St. Mary's City	See No. 151
154	1669	—	"in Patuxent River afore Harrington"*	Harrington (Harrington, Harvey Town, uncertain)	On Patuxent River at or near Town Point
155	1671	—	"at East Saint Marys in St Marys County"	St. Mary's City	See No. 151
156	1683	100	"att the Citty of St Marys"	St. Mary's City	See No. 151
157	1683	100	"att Brittons bay"	Britton (Breton)	On Breton Neck or at its head
158	1683	100	"at John Bayleys or Taunts"	Unknown	Unknown
159	1683	100	"at the Indian Towne att Choptico his Lordshipps mannor"	Choptico (Chaptico)	At mouth of Chaptico Creek, on north shore
160	1684	100	"All Brittons neck between Britton bay and St Clements bay"	New Town	See No. 155
161	1686	—	"Baltemore Town"***	Baltimore Town	Unknown
162	1686	100	"at piles fresh on both sides of the said fresh on the Land of Mr Joseph Pile and Thomas Sympson"	Pile's Town (uncertain)	On the east side of the mouth of the Wicomico River
163	1688	—	"att the head of St Jeromes Creeke upon the Land of Mr William Gwyther to be called by the name of St. Jeromes Towne"	St. Jerome's Town	At head of St. Jerome's Creek, possibly near Dameron
164	1706	100	Designated port: "Saint Maries Towne"	St. Mary's City	See No. 151
165	1706	100	"Saint Clements Town"	St. Clement's Town	Head of St. Clement's Creek, possibly near Dynard
166	1706	100	Designated port: "on Beckwiths Island in Petuxent river"***	St. George	On Town Point in St. Mary's County or Solomons Island in Calvert County (uncertain)
167	1708	50	"at Shepherd's old feilds near the head of Brittains Bay . . . on the Land of Phillip Lynes"	Seymour Town	Present site of Leonardtown
168	1728	50	"in St. Mary's County, at a Place formerly called Seymour Town"	Leonardtown	See No. 167

* This site is reported as lying in Calvert County, although the 1670 Herrman map clearly indicates the site to lie on the west bank of the Patuxent in St. Mary's County.

** An officer was designated for a town named Baltimore in St. Mary's County in this year, but the town's name is used only once and is not mentioned as such in any town or port legislation. It may be an alternative name for either No. 159 or No. 160, both of which are unnamed in the legislative acts.

*** This site is mentioned in connection with its suitability for the construction of a fort, undoubtedly to defend the strategic narrows of the river opposite Point Patience than is Solomons Island, which commands a far wider reach—too wide for artillery or musket fire of the era to command adequately. A ferry managed by a man named Beckwith was known to have run between Town Point and Point Patience.

SOMERSET COUNTY

No.	Year	Acres	Description	Name	Location
169	1668	—	"Att Deepe point att Randall Revells in Somerset County"	Somerset Town 1 (Sommerton)	On Revells Neck, probably at Raccoon Point, in Manokin River
170	1671	—	"at deep point in Randal Revels in Somerset County"	Somerset Town 1	See No. 169
171	1683	100	"in Wiccomico River on the South side of the Land next above the Land of the Orphants of Charles Bollard [Ballard]"	Ballards	On Wicomico River
172	1683	100	"on the Land on the North side of Windford [Mudford] Creek (viz) Smiths & Glanmills [Glanvill] Land"	Somerset Town 2	On Kings Branch, south side of Manokin River, near site of Somerset Town
173	1683	100	"on Horseys Land formerly called Barrowes towards the head of Pokomoke in Annimessex"	Annemessex Town	On south side of Coulborne Creek, on the south side of Big Annemessex River
174	1683	100	"on the Land betweene Mr [Francis] Jenkins Plantacon & Mr [Edmund] Howards Plantacon on the North side Pokamoake"	Unidentified (Rehoboth)	West side of Pocomoke River, immediately south of Rehobeth
175	1684	—	Moved: "in Wicocomaca River . . . next Aboue the land of the orphans of Charles Ballards" to "att or neare A parcell of land in the said River Called Lotts wife on the land wch was formerly William Wrights land"	Unknown	On south side of Wicomico River opposite the town of Whitehaven
176	1686	100	"in Arnold Erzyes land & the land adjacent att Oyster Neck att the mouth of Monokin"	Oyster Neck	North side of Manokin River, west side of Goose Creek
177	1706	100	"At Rehoboth In Pocomoke river . . . were formerly Erected"	Rehoboth	See No. 174
178	1706	100	"on a point of Land lying in the fork of Monokin river where Captain henry Smith formerly lived sometime called the White house"	White House	South side of Manokin River and just southwest of Jones Creek, near Somerset Town 2
179	1706	100	"at Colebournes Creek in Annamessex"	St. George's Town (Annemessex Town)	See No. 173
180	1732	25	"at Head of Monokin River, on South Side thereof"	Princess Anne	At present site of Princess Anne
181	1745	—	"Princess Anne Town, in Somerset County"	Princess Anne	See No. 180

TALBOT COUNTY

No.	Year	Acres	Description	Name	Location
182	1668	—	"at Capt Robert Morrices land in Tredaven creeke" (KC)	Oxford	On Tred Avon River at present site of Oxford
183	1669	—	"afore the Town Land in Trudhaven in Choptank" (KC)	Oxford	See No. 182
184	1671	—	"at the Mouth of Wye River on the Eastern Side thereof"	Wye Town	On Bruffs Point at entrance to Wye River
185	1671	—	"at Tradaven Creeke in Choptank River in Talbot County" (KC)	Oxford	See No. 182
186	1683	100	"neere Tredhaven Creeke att the Towne Land"	Oxford	See No. 182
187	1683	100	"in Kingscreeke near the Towne Land"	Kings Town (Kings Creek Town)	At Kings Landing on Choptank River
188	1683	100	"in Wye River Towne Land there"	Wye Town	See No. 184
189	1686	100	"at or neer the Co[u]rt House vpon the land of James Downes & the land adjacent to be called Yorke"	York Town	On Skipton Creek, off Wye River, one mile west of Skipton Landing
190	1706	100	Designated port: "at Oxford formerly Erected into a port & Town"	Oxford	See No. 182
191	1706	100	"at Doncaster in Wye river"	Doncaster (Wye Town)	See No. 184
192	1706	100	"at Kings Town in Great Choptank"	Kings Town	See No. 187

WICOMICO COUNTY

No.	Year	Acres	Description	Name	Location
193	1669	—	"in Somerset County afore Iames Iones his plantation" (SC)	Uncertain	North side of Wicomico River opposite Wicomico Creek
194	1684	100	"att or neare Tipquin on the south side of Nanticoke River" (SC)	Tipquin	Probably Wetipquin or Tyaskin, on Wetipquin Creek
195	1706	100	Designated port: "on the Northwest side of Wicomoco river on the woo land Reach below Daniel Hast creek" (SC)	Green Hill	Northwest side of Wicomico River, below Daniel Hast Creek (formerly Jones Creek?)
196	1706	100	Designated port: "Green hill Town" (SC)	Green Hill Town	On Wicomico River at the terminus of Green Hill Road, near turnoff from Route 532
197	1707	100	"at a place Called half round hill on the South side of Wiccomoco River" (SC)	Half Round Hill (uncertain)	Possibly near confluence of Wicomico Creek and Wicomico River
198	1732	15	"at the head of Wiccomoco River, in Somerset County . . . and the Landing commonly called Handy's, or Carr's Landing" (SC)	Salisbury	At or near Pemberton Hall, at Handy's Landing, Salisbury

WORCESTER COUNTY

No.	Year	Acres	Description	Name	Location
199	1684	100	"at Sume Convenient place Between the Going into Selbyes bay & Cornelius Jones [also Innis] his land in Assateague bay on the Seabord side at the Discretion of the Commissioners for the said County" (SC)	Newport (uncertain)	On old Sinepuxent Neck, between Newport Bay and Sinepuxent Bay
200	1683	100	"on [Henry] Morgans Land formerly called Barrowes towards the head of Pokanoake" (SC)	Barrows	Near Snow Hill
—	1686	—	Removed: "The Towne on Morgans Land formerly called Barrows toward the head of Pocomoke" (SC)	Barrows	See No. 200
201	1686	100	"att Snow hill on the land formerly belonging to Henry Bishop and last to Ann Bishop his Widdow" (SC)	Snow Hill	At present site of Snow Hill
202	1706	100	"at Snow hill where the Towns were formerly Erected" (SC)	Snow Hill	See No. 201
203	1708	50	Land in Sinepuxent Neck . . . on the Land of John Walton"	Newport (uncertain)	See No. 199
204	1742	100	"Snowhill-Town" (SC)	Snow Hill	See No. 201

DISTRICT OF COLUMBIA

No.	Year	Acres	Description	Name	Location
205	1751	60	"on potowmack River, above the Mouth of Rock Creek in Frederick County" (FC, MC)	Georgetown	Northwest Washington, D.C.

NOTES

INTRODUCTION

1. Clayton C. Hall, *Narratives of Early Maryland 1633–1684* (New York: Barnes and Noble, 1910), 21.
2. Ibid., 21–2.
3. Andrew White, *Fund Publication, No. 1. Narrative of a Voyage to Maryland,* E. A. Dalrymple, ed. (Baltimore: John Murphy & Co., 1874), 31.
4. Ibid., 32–3.
5. Ibid., 36–7.
6. M. P. Andrews, *Tercentenary History of Maryland* (Chicago: S. J. Clarke Publishing Co., 1925), 32; John W. Reps, *Tidewater Towns: City Planning in Colonial Virginia and Maryland* (Williamsburg, Va.: Colonial Williamsburg Foundation, 1972), 56.
7. *Archives of Maryland,* hereafter cited as *Archives,* 73 vols. to date (Baltimore, 1883–), 5: 31.
8. Ibid., 32.
9. Ibid., 47–8.
10. Ibid., 92–4.
11. Ibid., 7: 278–80; Reps, 56.
12. Edward C. Papenfuse and Joseph M. Coale III, *The Hammond Harwood House Atlas of Historical Maps of Maryland, 1608–1908* (Baltimore: Johns Hopkins University Press, 1982), 11, 18.
13. J. Louis Kuethe, "A Gazetteer of Maryland, A.D. 1673," *Maryland Historical Magazine* 30, no. 4 (December 1935), 310–25; Reps, 94.
14. John Ogilby, *America: Being the Latest, and Most Accurate Description of the New World,* (London: 1671), 189.
15. John Speed, *The Theatre of the Empire of Great Britain,* 1676, William T. Snyder Collection, MdHR G 1213-368, in Papenfuse and Coale, 17.
16. John Thornton and Robert Greene, *A Mapp of Virginia, Maryland, New-Jersey, New-York & New-England,* [1678?], John Work Garrett Library, Johns Hopkins University, MdFR G 1213-250, in Papenfuse and Coale, 19.
17. Kit W. Wesler, "An Archaeologist's Perspective on the Ancient Town of Doncaster," *Maryland Historical Magazine* 80, no. 4 (Winter 1985), 383.
18. *Archives,* 7: 349.
19. Ibid., 350.
20. Ibid., 351.
21. Ibid., 351–2.
22. Ibid., 368–9, 379–80.
23. Ibid., 459.
24. Wesler, 384.
25. *Archives,* 7: 540–1.
26. Ibid., 612.
27. Ibid., 612–3.
28. Ibid., 613.
29. Ibid., 614.
30. Ibid., 615–6.
31. Ibid., 618.
32. Ibid., 617–8.
33. Ibid., 618.
34. Ibid., 13: 114.
35. Ibid., 17: 219–20.
36. Ibid., 13: 114.
37. Ibid., 113–5.
38. Ibid., 115, 116–7.
39. Ibid., 120.
40. Ibid., 17: 404–5.
41. Carville V. Earle, *The Evolution of a Tidewater Settlement System: All Hallow's Parish, Maryland, 1650–1783* (Chicago: University of Chicago Press, 1975), 143; Reps, 97.
42. *Archives,* 5: 497.
43. Ibid., 500–2.
44. Ibid., 13, 132–3. Reps incorrectly says four were removed, 98.
45. *Archives,* 8: 61.
46. Ibid., 13: 220.
47. Richard Walsh and William Lloyd Fox, eds., *Maryland: A History, 1632–1974* (Baltimore: Maryland Historical Society, 1974), 25–6.
48. *Archives,* 13: 560.
49. Ibid., 26: 332–3.
50. Evarts B. Greene and Virginia D. Harrington, *American Population Before the Federal Census of 1790.* (New York: Columbia University Press, 1932), 123–4.
51. Reps, 232.

52. Charles B. Clark, "The Career of John Seymour, Governor of Maryland, 1704–1709," *Maryland Historical Magazine,* 48, no. 2 (June 1953), 150–1.

53. Leonard Woods Larabee, ed., *Royal Instructions to British Colonial Governor 1670–1776* (New York: Appleton-Century, 1935), 2: 539–40.

54. *Archives,* 26: 636–7.

55. Ibid., 640–4.

56. Ibid., 643.

57. Ibid., 644–5.

58. Clark, 151; *Archives,* 27: 9, 10, 69, 70, 71, 73, 162.

59. *Archives,* 26: 636–7; 27: 162–3, 167.

60. Ibid., 27: 163–4; Lois Green Carr, "'The Metropolis of Maryland': A Comment on Town Development along the Tobacco Coast," *Maryland Historical Magazine* 69, no. 2 (Summer 1974): 124–45.

61. *Archives,* 27: 164.

62. Ibid., 167.

63. Ibid., 166.

64. Reps, 103.

65. Ibid., 104.

66. *Archives,* 25: 234; 27: 346–7.

67. Ibid., 27: 347, 348, 349.

68. Ibid., 44: 210.

69. Ibid., 42: 631–2.

70. Ibid., 26: 637; 27: 161. Taylor's Choice had been part of an original three-hundred-acre tract taken up on 28 July 1661 by John Taylor. Milton C. Wright, *Our Harford Heritage* (Havre de Grace, Md.: Privately printed, 1967), 48.

71. Wright, 48. Why the county would have undertaken such a measure on its own is suggested by Lois Green Carr's notion that Maryland gentry, having satisfied itself with building the model town of Annapolis as its capital, gradually reconciled itself to the lack of significant urban centers by extolling the virtues of county seats.

72. *Archives,* 29: 196; 35: 84; 36: 573.

73. Reps, 233. See John Thomas Scharf, *A History of Maryland: From the Earliest Period to the Present Day* (Detroit: Gale, 1967, reprint of 1879), 1: 413–5, and Walter W. Preston, *History of Harford County, Maryland* (Baltimore: Press of Sun Book Office, 1901), 44–7, for a historic overview of Joppa. Among those who purchased lots were Thomas White, surveyor and clerk of the town; Col. John Dorsey, for his son, Greenbury Dorsey; Joseph Calvert, merchant from Kent County; Aquila Paca, sheriff; Col. James Maxwell and Asaele Maxwell, his son; Joseph Ward, innkeeper; Catherine Hollingsworth, widow; Samuel Ward, carpenter; and John Higginson, innkeeper. Other lots were acquired by Roger Matthews, John Crockett, John Stokes, Richard Hewitt, William Lowe, John Roberts, John Hall, Jr., Captain Thomas Sheredine, Thomas Tolley, Daniel Hughes, Nicholas Day, William Hammond, Valentine Hollingsworth, Samuel Maccubins, James Isham, Benjamin Jones, Stephen Higgins, Hannah Ward, Abraham Johns, and Benjamin Rumsey. Preston, 50.

74. *Archives,* 26: 464–6; 37: 533–6.

75. Ibid., 35: 410; 37: 581–3; 36: 286–9, 456–9.

76. Ibid., 37: 549; 42: 409, 630; 44: 214–7, 463–4.

77. Ibid., 37: 172–7, 541–4; 544–6; 39: 490–3; 493–6.

78. Ibid., 46: 630–5.

CHAPTER 1: BATTLE TOWN

1. "Taney Place," *Centennial of Calvert County,* photocopy in Calvert County Historical Society, Prince Frederick, Md., 153.

2. Laurie Cameron Steponaitis, *A Survey of Artifact Collections from the Patuxent River Drainage, Maryland. Maryland Historical Trust Monograph Series No. 1* (Annapolis: 1980), 28.

3. Ibid., 29.

4. Ibid., 31–2. In 1936, the first significant archaeological explorations of the Patuxent were conducted by Richard E. Stearns, who reported on the Dukes Wharf and Parkers Wharf sites but failed to notice the Prison Point middens. Richard E. Stearns, *Some Indian Village Sites of Tidewater Maryland: Proceeding No. 9* (Baltimore: Natural History Society of Maryland, 1943), 24–8.

5. John Smith, *Virginia,* 1608 [1612], John Work Garrett Library, Johns Hopkins University; John Smith, *The Generall Historie of Virginia, New England, and the Summer Isles* (London: Printed by I. D. and I. H. for Michael Sparkes, 1624), 24.

6. Clayton C. Hall, *Narratives of Early Maryland 1633–1684* (New York: Barnes and Noble, 1910), 42–3.

7. Ibid., 43, 44.

8. Ibid., 124–5.

9. Ibid., 45.

10. Ibid., 88.

11. Walter R. Cosdon, "Battletown on the Patuxent," *Calvert Country Life* 1, no. 4 (September 1980): 10.

12. Charles Francis Stein, *A History of Calvert County, Maryland* (Baltimore: privately published, 1976), 18–9.

13. George F. Griffiths, *The Berrys of Maryland: An Old Prince George's County Family* (Chicago, Ill.: Adams Press, 1976), 5, 7. *Archives,* 47: 468–9, 502; Stein, 37, 236; Dennis J. Pogue, "Calverton, Calvert County, Maryland:

1668–1725," *Maryland Historical Magazine* 80, no. 4 (Winter 1985): 372; Patents Q:32, MSS, Hall of Records, Annapolis, Md.

14. Cosdon, 10.

15. Pogue, 372; Patents, 10: 203, MSS, Hall of Records, Annapolis, Md. In 1671 and again in 1674–1675 William Berry served in the Lower House. He owned watercraft, for the services of his boat were employed on government business in 1674–1675, for which he was paid 841 pounds of tobacco. *Archives,* 2: 355–6, 374, 422, 469, 492.

16. *Archives,* 5: 31, 47–8, 92, 94.

17. Griffiths, 10; Cosden, 10; *Archives,* 7: 279.

18. *Archives,* 7: 280; Stein, 239.

19. *Archives,* 7: 279–80, 289; Stein 19, 30; Pogue, 371.

20. Pogue, 371; Stein, 29–30, 222; Annie Leakin Sioussat, *Old Manors in the Colony of Maryland: Second Series, on the Patuxent* (Baltimore: Lord Baltimore Press, 1913), 6.

21. *Archives,* 7: 279; John Ogilby, *America: Being the Latest, and Most Accurate Description of the New World* (London: 1671), 189; Augustine Herrman, *Virginia and Maryland,* (1670 [1673]), Geographic and Map Division, Library of Congress, Washington, D.C. For details of place names on the Ogilby map, see J. Louis Kuethe, "A Gazetteer of Maryland, A.D. 1673," *Maryland Historical Magazine* 30, no. 4 (December 1935): 310–25.

22. Pogue, 373; Patents, 11:469, MSS, Hall of Records; Cosden, 12.

23. *Archives,* 15: 50, 52, 60

24. Henry Chandlee Forman, *Early Manor and Plantation Houses of Maryland* (Easton, Md.: privately printed for the author, 1934), 20; Cosden, 11.

25. *Archives,* 15: 52, 299–302; 57: 546–7; 67: 11.

26. Stein, 323.

27. Pogue, 372; Patents 7:639 MSS, Hall of Records.

28. Stein, 323; Pogue, 373; Patents 21:361 and Patents Q:362, MSS, Hall of Records.

29. Pogue, 373.

30. *Archives,* 7: 279.

31. Ibid.

32. Ibid., 280, 289–90.

33. Ibid., 280, 289.

34. Ibid., 289.

35. Ibid., 281.

36. Cosdon, 11.

37. Survey of Battle Town Area, 3 August 1682, Maps, 1682, Box 24, Folder 4, Hall of Records, Annapolis, Md., data reprinted in Cosdon, 11.

38. Ibid.

39. Clement Hill Papers, MS 446, Manuscripts Division, Maryland Historical Society, Baltimore, Md. This volume contains dozens of Jones's (and fellow surveyor Charles Boteler's) original survey notes and plats. This and a pair of accompanying volumes of seventeenth-century Calvert County land records have been readily accessible since the nineteenth century, though it appears that few researchers in early Calvert County history since H. J. Berkley in the 1930s recognized their significance or were aware of their existence. Berkley conducted extensive research on seventeenth-century Calvert County and produced an unpublished manuscript entitled "First Century of County of Calvert: 1634–1734." It is housed at the Maryland Historical Society, and a photocopy of the original is in the collections of the Calvert County Historical Society, Prince Frederick, Md. Berkley appears to have utilized the Clement Hill papers extensively in research for this work. A photograph of the Calverton plat was also included in Sioussat, *Old Manors.* Sioussat incorrectly dates the plat as that of Calverton in 1654. A loose redraft of the plat, undoubtedly based on the reproduction in Sioussat, was published by Stein in *Calvert County,* 222. Stein also labels the plat circa 1654, a misidentification probably originating with Sioussat. The redraft also is included with the same erroneous identification in Morris L. Radoff, Gust Skordas, and Phebe R. Jacobsen, *The County Courthouses and Records of Maryland. Part Two: The Records* (Annapolis, Md.: Hall of Records Commission, State of Maryland, 1963), 74. Radoff et al apparently considered Stein's redraft to be merely a credible attempt to depict the town and not an original map or accurate copy of one. Why Stein chose to redraw the plat is unknown. Pogue suggests that the decision may well have been derived from both Stein's and Sioussat's unsubstantiated assumptions that Robert Brooke had laid out a town in the area in 1654. Pogue, 371–2.

40. The plats were bound into the volume of Calvert County land surveys conducted by Jones (and several by Boteler) from 1682 to 1684. Taney's Landing was situated on the site of the present Prison Point farmhouse, and the Cosden wharf was located near the present site of the entrance to Prison Point Farm. Clement Hill Papers, MS 446; Pogue, 371; Cosden, 11.

41. Pogue, 374.

42. Ibid.

43. Ibid.; Cary Carson, Norman F. Barka, William M. Kelso, Garry W. Stone, and Dell Upton, "Impermanent Architecture in the Southern American Colonies," *Winterthur Portfolio* 16 (1981): 135–96.

44. Pogue, 374.

45. Ibid.

46. *Archives,* 7: 352.

47. Pogue, 372; Edward C. Papenfuse, Alan F. Day, David W. Jordan, and Gregory A. Stiverson, *A Biographical Dictionary of the Maryland Legislature, 1635–1789,* Edward C. Papenfuse, ed., (Baltimore: Johns Hopkins University Press, 1979), 132. Berry adjourned to a two-hundred-acre tract called Berry's Chance on the banks of the Little Choptank River for the rest of his days. *Archives,* 57: 550–1.

48. *Archives,* 7: 460, 465, 547.

49. Ibid., 17: 184, 186–218.

50. Ibid., 13: 22

51. Ibid., 13: 22, 26, 86, 91.

52. Ibid., 112.

53. Ibid., 5: 562.

54. Lois Green Carr and David William Jordan, *Maryland's Revolution of Government 1689–1692* (Ithaca: Cornell University Press, 1974), 34; See Tanner MSS, Bodleian Library, Oxford University, ff. 137, 138, 139 for quotations regarding the chapel.

55. *Archives,* 8: 118–21.

56. Ibid., 110; Stein, 323.

57. Pogue, 373; Inventories and Accounts, 10A: 3–15, MSS, Hall of Records, Annapolis, Md.

58. *Archives,* 19; 39–48, 68–73.

59. In 1693, the council was presided over by Colonel Nicholas Greenberry and attended by Thomas Tench, Thomas Brooke, and Captains John Addison and John Courts. In 1694 it was presided over by Sir Thomas Lawrence and attended by Colonels Nicholas Greenberry, Charles Hutchins, David Browne, Thomas Tench, Esq., and Captains John Addison and John Courts, *Archives,* 20: 39, 68.

60. Ibid., 19: 75; 23: 342–3, 344, 371.

61. Pogue, 373; *Archives,* 22: 102–3.

62. Pogue, 373; Radoff, Skordas, and Jacobsen, 73–5; Morris L. Radoff, *The County Courthouses and Records of Maryland. Part One: The Courthouses* (Annapolis, Md.: Hall of Records Commission, State of Maryland, 1960), 40; *Archives,* 25: 127.

63. *Archives,* 25: 165; J. J. Colledge, *Ships of the Royal Navy: An Historical Index,* 2 vols., (David Charles: Newton Abbot, Devon, 1969), 1: 402.

64. *Archives,* 25: 165.

65. *Archives,* 19: 119; 23: 342, 343, 344, 367, 371.

66. Ibid., 25: 165–7; David R. Owne and Michael C. Tolley, *Courts of Admiralty in Colonial America: The Maryland Experience, 1634–1776* (Durham, N.C.: Carolina Academic Press, 1995), 299.

67. Owne and Tolley, 299.

68. *Archives,* 27: 10, 69.

69. Richard H. Cohen, *Ebenezer Cooke The Sotweed Canon* (Athens, Ga.: University of Georgia Press, 1975), 16–8.

70. See Cohen, 18–9, for discussion on the motivation for Cooke's satiric assault on the law.

71. Lou Rose, "Ebenezer Cooke's The Sot Weed Factor and its Uses as a Social Document in the History of Colonial Maryland," *Maryland Historical Magazine,* 78, no. 4 (Winter 1983): 273.

72. Pogue, 373; *Archives,* 36: 581–3.

73. Stein, 323.

74. Stein, 324. Chief Justice Roger Brooke Taney was the second son of Michael Taney V. He was elected to the Lower House of the Maryland Assembly in 1799 but was defeated for reelection the following year. He was appointed attorney general of Maryland by Governor Joseph Kent in 1827. Five years later, President Andrew Jackson appointed him to his Cabinet as attorney general of the United States. In 1833 he became secretary of the treasury. In 1836, President Jackson appointed him chief justice of the Supreme Court of the United States. His famous opinion upholding the rights of a slave owner in the Dred Scott case aroused the wrath of the Abolitionist party against him. He married Anne Key, sister of Francis Scott Key, the author of "The Star-Spangled Banner." As chief justice he administered the oath of office to eight presidents of the United States, the first being Martin Van Buren and the last being Abraham Lincoln. Taney was a descendant of many prominent Calvert County ancestors, including Robert Brooke, the founder and first "commander" of the county, as well as the first Michael Taney, the high sheriff of Calvert County. Stein, 162, 324, 325.

75. Ibid., 324.

76. William M. Marine, *The British Invasion of Maryland 1812–1815* (Hatboro, Pa.: Tradition Press, 1965, reprint of 1913), 455; Stein, 163; Donald Shomette, *Flotilla: Battle for the Patuxent* (Solomons, Md.: Calvert Marine Museum Press, 1981), 64; Joshua Barney to William Jones, 8 July 1814, Secretary of the Navy Letters (hereafter Navy Letters), RG 45, M 124, R 64, National Archives, Washington, D.C.

77. George Cockburn to Joseph Nourse, 15 July 1814, Cockburn Papers, vol. 44, Manuscript Division, Library of Congress, Washington, D.C.

78. Ibid., Nourse to Cockburn, 23 July 1814, Cockburn Papers, vol. 38.

79. "A Personal Narrative of Events by Sea and Land," *Chronicles of St. Mary's* 8, no. 1 (January 1960): 9.

80. Walter Lord, *The Dawns Early Light* (New York: W.W. Norton & Company, 1972), 27.

Taney has been credited by Stein as having saved Huntingtown and Prince Frederick from British depredations. The record, however, indicates that both suffered heavily from British attack and captures. The tobacco warehouse at Huntingtown was destroyed, and the Court House and other buildings at Prince Frederick were burned down along with the county records. In both cases the militia under Taney proved totally useless. Stein, 163; Nourse to Cockburn, 23 July 1814, Cockburn Papers, vol. 38.

81. Stein, 163, 164; "Taney Place" *Centennial of Calvert County,* photocopy in Calvert County Historical Society, Prince Frederick, Md., 153; Swepson Earle, *Maryland's Colonial Eastern Shore* (New York: Weathervane Books [facsimile of 1916]), 166, erroneously calls Michael Taney V by the name of Miles.

82. "Taney Place," 153; Stein, 324. Colonel Taney's whereabouts were unknown until recently when a letter which he wrote in 1830 while living in St. Louis, Missouri, was discovered. This letter was written to Dr. James Gray of Calvert County to assist him in obtaining compensation for the destruction of his house at Sheridan's Point, which was burned by the British in 1814. Michael Taney VI sold Taney Place to Young Dorsey Hance. Stein, 324.

83. Stein, 165. The Hances are descended from John Hance, the son of John Hans Tilman, who settled in Calvert County. John Hance married Sarah Hall, daughter of Richard Hall, a wealthy Quaker residing on Hall's Creek. Two of the sons of John Hance married daughters of Richard Johns and were leaders of the Quaker community of the Cliffs. Benjamin Hance, a grandson of John Hance, owned Overton, a landed estate on the main highway between Huntingtown and Prince Frederick, and became one of the wealthiest men of his day in Calvert County. His daughter, Mary Hance, was the wife of General James John Mackall, the greatest land owner in the county. Stein, 164–5. There is an interesting gourd at Taney Place inscribed with the following names and dates upon it: 1800, Young Dorsey Hance; 1811, Young Duke Hance; 1855, Benjamin Hance; 1886, Young Duke Hance; 1917, Benjamin Hance; 1953, Young Duke Hance. The latter took over the property from his father the Hon. Benjamin Hance, a prominent lawyer and highly respected citizen of the county. In the gourd there are tobacco seeds supposedly started in Young Dorsey Hance's time. A little has been added each year from crops grown on the farm by each of the Hances in possession of this most delightful place. "Taney Place," 153–4.

84. Stein, 178.
85. Earle, 165, 166; Stein, 164; "Taney Place," 153.
86. Cosdon, 12.

CHAPTER 2: LONDON TOWN

1. For an account of the 1976 underwater archaeological survey at London Town see Donald G. Shomette, "London Town: The Reconnaissance of a 17th–18th Century Riverport Complex," *Beneath the Waters of Time: The Proceedings of the Ninth Conference on Underwater Archaeology,* J. Barto Arnold, ed., (Austin, Texas: Texas Antiquities Committee, 1978), 167–74.
2. Henry J. Berkley, "Extinct River Towns of the Chesapeake Bay Region," *Maryland Historical Magazine* 19, no. 2 (June 1924): 134–5.
3. Ibid.; All Hallows Church Tombstone of Colonel William Burgess; Anne Arundel County Patented Certificate of Survey, Q: 403.
4. Anne Arundel County Patented Certificate of Survey, Q:403.
5. Ibid.
6. Anne Arundel County Deeds, lB-l:270. William Burgess managed to expand his holdings during his lifetime throughout Maryland. These holdings included 480 acres of land in Baltimore County called Betty's Choice; 800 acres on Herring Creek, Anne Arundel County, referred to as Benjamin's Addition; West Puddington and Beard's Habitation, two tracts on the South River totaling 1,300 acres; 1,600 acres at the head of the Sassafras River, Cecil County; 500 acres on the Susquehanna River, Baltimore County; sundry small plots of land elsewhere throughout the colony; and, of course, the land from which London Town was carved. Anne Arundel County Wills, 4:242.
7. All Hallows Church Tombstone of Colonel William Burgess.
8. *Archives,* 17: 20–5, 74–7.
9. Ibid., 5: 31.
10. Ibid., 7: 343.
11. Ibid., 460, 465, 469, 547.
12. Ibid., 460.
13. Ibid., 609–16.
14. Ibid., 513.
15. Ibid., 17: 219–21.
16. Berkley, 135; *Archives,* 19: 122, 502; John W. Reps, *Tidewater Towns: City Planning in Colonial Virginia and Maryland* (Williamsburg, Virginia: Colonial Williamsburg Foundation, 1972), 121.
17. Anne Arundel County Deeds, WH-4: 168.
18. Ibid., WT-2: 56; All Hallows Church Tombstone of Colonel William Burgess; Berkley, 137.

19. All Hallows Church Tombstone of Colonel William Burgess; Berkley, 137; *Archives,* 19: 265.

20. *Archives,* 8: 196; Berkley, 137.

21. Berkley, 136–8.

22. *Archives,* 19: 265, 588; Berkley, 136.

23. Anne Arundel County Deeds, WH-4: 168; WT-2: 58; WT-2: 143.

24. *Archives,* 24: 341.

25. Anne Arundel County Judgments, G: 106; G: 115; Anne Arundel County Wills, Box H: 81.

26. Anne Arundel County Deeds, IB-2: 545.

27. "Vestry Proceedings, St. Ann's Parish, Annapolis, Md.," *Maryland Historical Magazine,* 7, no. 1 (March 1912): 59.

28. Anne Arundel County Deeds, WT-2: 43, 56, 57, 58; SY-1: 58; CW-1: 64; Anne Arundel County Wills, 13: 310; Anne Arundel County Judgments, TB-1: 688; TB-2: 231.

29. Anne Arundel County Wills, 13: 310.

30. *Archives,* 80: 61.

31. Leonard Woods Larabee, ed. *Royal Instructions to British Colonial Governor 1670–1776* (New York: Appleton-Century, 1935), 2: 539–40.

32. *Archives,* 26: 636–47; Reps, 100.

33. "Treaty of Utrecht," *The American People's Encyclopedia,* 18th edition.

34. Carville V. Earle, *The Evolution of a Tidewater Settlement System: All Hallow's Parish, Maryland, 1650–1783* (Chicago: University of Chicago Press, 1975), 221.

35. Anne Arundel County Deeds, IB-2: 290; IB-2: 471; IB-2: 473.

36. Higginson and Bird to Patrick Sympson, 2 December 1718. *Higginson and Bird Letterbook, 1718–1719,* no. 1727. Galloway-Maxey-Markoe Collection, Manuscript Division, Library of Congress, Washington, D.C.

37. Anne Arundel County Deeds, IB-2: 345, 401, 418; CW-1: 64, 74; SY-1: 251; RD-2: 314, 430, 465, 528; RB-1: 418.

38. Ibid., IB-2: 487.

39. Ibid., RCW-2: 223.

40. Ibid., SY-1: 58; WC-1: 33–6; Anne Arundel County Inventories, 79: 34–8.

41. Anne Arundel County Deeds, CW-1: 227; CW-1: 268; Louise Joyner Heinton, *Prince George's Heritage* (Baltimore: Prince George's County Historical Society, 1972), 110; Earle, 92.

42. Anne Arundel County Deeds, IB-2: 545; Anne Arundel County Judgments, G: 646.

43. Anne Arundel County Deeds, RB-1: 307.

44. Ibid., RD-2: 63, 65, 218, 340; RB-1: 85.

45. Ibid., RD-1: 16.

46. Ibid., RCW-1: 223; RCW-2: 223.

47. Ibid., RCW-2: 186, 219, 253; IH-2: 540; RD-2: 259; RD-3: 125; RB-2: 547.

48. Earle compares London Town in size and stature as equal to almost any colonial capital city in America of the seventeenth century, 91.

49. Anne Arundel County Deeds RD-3: 32, 125; RB-1: 85; RB-3: 91; BB-1: 74.

50. *Maryland Gazette,* 12 October 1752; 6 February 1751, 9 July 1752, 17 May 1753, 18 April 1754; *Archives,* 52: 480.

51. *Maryland Gazette,* 28 October 1756; *Archives,* 9: 22; 52: 609; *Maryland Gazette,* 25 October 1758.

52. *Archives,* 55: 723, 726. The agents were permitted to draw £300 in funds. The company that was to winter at London Town was a unit from a regiment under the command of the Earl of Louden.

53. Earle, 181; *Maryland Gazette,* 11 January 1749, 4 January 1753, 9 March 1758.

54. *Maryland Gazette,* 11 February 1746.

55. Ibid., 4 March 1748, 1 May 1751, 31 July 1751, 23 April 1752, 21 June 1753, 28 June 1753.

56. Ibid., 26 July 1759, 2 August 1759, 9 August 1759.

57. Ibid., 22 September 1747, 26 October 1748, 13 July 1754, 15 August 1754, 10 April 1755, 14 July 1755, 18 March 1756, 9 June 1757, 22 June 1758, 26 July 1759, 13 July 1760.

58. Higginson and Bird to Colonel Edward Lloyd, 27 September 1718, *Higginson and Bird Letterbook,* No. 1557; Ibid., 2 December 1718, No. 1727.

59. *Maryland Gazette,* 29 April, 13 May, and 17 June 1729.

60. Earle, 74.

61. Hofstadter, Richard, *America at 1750: A Social Portrait* (New York: Vintage Books, 1973), 85; Anne Arundel County Deeds, RB-2, f. 515. This deed, among other things, cites the inclusion of slaves in a business deal on 28 May 1737 between Dr. Richard Hill, a surgeon who lived in His Lordship's Manor at Scorton, a tract of land immediately adjoining London Town, and John Galloway. Galloway in turn executed a deed with Daniel Dulany and Charles Carroll, transferring the property to them. The sale included 200 acres in Puddington's Gift; 2 lots in London Town; 50 acres in the Scorton tract; 100 acres in Besson's Denn; 20 acres in Sutton's Addition; 200 acres in Harness; all land in South River Neck inherited from his uncle Joseph Hill; a lot in Chestertown, Kent County; two lots in Bealetown, Prince George's County; the ship *Frederick,* commanded by Alexander Scougall with all the salt on board; the snow *London Town,* Anthony

Beck, captain; the sloop *Benedict,* Francis Kipps, captain; the slaves Valentine, Bob, London, Argalus, Will, Batchelor, two named Tom, Larreas, Sam, Cudjo, Jack, Weber, York, Jimmy, Jenna, Salolpina and her child Mandy, Parthenia and her two children Charles and Sarah, Phillus and her child Diana, Jack, Dick, Polydone, Lucy, Rose, Barehus, Plato, and Sambo; the year's crop of tobacco grown by these slaves on all the above lands; 400 bushels of Indian corn on two plantations; 300 bushels of beans in a storehouse at Queen Anne's Town; 60 cows and heifers; 58 steers; 50 sheep; 100 hogs; 19 horses; 4 mares; the sloop *Swan;* the sloop *Swallow;* the sloop *Bachelor's Hall* with all the wine, salt, and other goods it was bringing from Madeira Island; one no. 12 hogshead flat; one no. 9 hogshead; 2 silver tankards, 2 silver half-pint cans, 1 silver teapot, 1 silver milk pot, 10 silver tablespoons, 6 silver teaspoons; 12 Rushia leather chairs, 6 cane chairs, 6 wrought bottom chairs, 7 finished rush bottom chairs; 1 silver strainer, 1 pair silver tongs; 10 feather beds and furniture; 4 flock beds and furniture; 18 iron pots, 2 brass kettles, 2 bell metal skillets; 4 large looking glasses; and 1 copper still and worm.

62. *Maryland Gazette,* 17 July 1760.

63. Ibid.

64. Ibid., 28 November 1750.

65. Ibid., 12 June 1753.

66. Reverend Andrew Burnaby, *Travels Through the Middle Settlements of North America, 1759 and 1760. With Observations on the State of the Colonies* (Ithaca: Cornell University Press, 1976, reprint of 1775), 56; Earle, 56. The distance noted by Burnaby is questioned by Earle, who feels the visitor probably meant the distance to the head of the estuary, eight and a half miles. Earle, 126.

67. Anne Arundel County Inventories and Accounts, 2, ff. 228–9; Ibid., 5, f. 280; Anne Arundel County Judgments, TB-1: 49, TB-2: 231.

68. *Maryland Gazette,* 12 July 1734, 23 December 1747.

69. Anne Arundel County Judgments, VD-1: 50; TB-3: 155a, 156a; ISB-1: 352, 629; TB-1: 49; IB-1: 326; EBY: 304; 1773: 59; Earle, 151–2.

70. Anne Arundel County Judgments, IB-1: 326; 1773: 59; Earle, 152; Anne Arundel County Mortgages, PK: 375. Rumney also owned lot 62 as a deed of gift from William Maccubbin to Elinor Maccubbin Rumney. Anne Arundel County Deeds, IB-2: 194.

71. Anne Arundel County Judgments, August 1773 Ct: 59.

72. Ibid., IB-1: 326; IB-4: 295; *London Town Ferry Accounts,* 1778–1779, Maryland Historical Society, Baltimore, Md.

73. *Maryland Gazette,* 23 December 1747.

74. Ibid., 26 October 1769.

75. Ibid., 18 October 1753; *London Town Ferry Accounts.*

76. Anne Arundel County Judgments, IB-1: 78; Earle, 154, 156.

77. Earle, 157.

78. Ibid., 162; Arthur Pierce Middleton, *Tobacco Coast: A Maritime History of Chesapeake Bay in the Colonial Era* (Newport News: Mariners' Museum, 1953), 158–87; John Hemphill, "Freight Rates in the Maryland Tobacco Trade, 1705–1762," *Maryland Historical Magazine* 54, no. 1 (March 1959): 54–5, Appendix, 158–87.

79. Earle, 165; Anne Arundel County Deeds, IB-3: 510; *Maryland Gazette,* 28 January 1746.

80. *Maryland Gazette,* 16 August 1745.

81. Ibid., 14 October 1747.

82. Ibid., 26 October 1748, 11 October 1749.

83. Ibid., 25 November 1747.

84. Anne Arundel County Deeds, RB-1: 418, RB-3: 326; *Maryland Gazette,* 25 October 1745, 7 July 1746, 7 July 1747, 16 September 1747, 26 April 1749, 11 July 1750, 26 April 1759, 20 December 1759, 15 May 1760. Scougall may have been associated with London Town as early as 1733, for he is noted as arriving in the colony on March 3 of that year in command of the Maryland snow *London-Town,* bound in from Madeira. The following year, he made a voyage to Barbados and back as commander of the ship *Frederick.* Ibid., 16 March 1733, 9 August 1734.

85. Anne Arundel County Deeds, SY-1: 12; *Maryland Gazette,* 24 March 1747, 28 June 1753.

86. *Maryland Gazette,* 11 May 1748.

87. Ibid., 24 March 1747.

88. Ibid., 11 May 1748.

89. The Dick-West relationship appears to have been an offshoot of Dick's affinity for the elder West. James Dick, in fact, seems to have acted in the capacity of business tutor to young West and was known to have even aided him in establishing his store in Annapolis. Though in apparent competition, both men ardently touted the products of the London Town Manufactory, giving the impression that some form of partnership may have been maintained beyond the public eye.

90. *Maryland Gazette,* 18 May 1748.

91. Ibid., 19 July 1749, 18 April 1754.

92. Ibid., 17 January 1750, 5 December 1750, 27 March 1751.

93. Ibid., 2 June 1757.

94. Ibid., 20 November 1760.

95. Earle, 96.

96. *Archives,* 46: 453–5. For extensive coverage, see Middleton, 120–6.

97. *Archives,* 46: 19.

98. *Maryland Gazette,* 23 November 1758; Proceedings of the Visitors of the Free School of Anne Arundel County, 17 March 1724, Gift Collection G610, Hall of Records, Annapolis, Md.

99. *Maryland Gazette,* 29 August 1750, 20 November 1751.

100. Ibid., 19 February 1756, 5 October 1752.

101. Anne Arundel County Deeds, RB-3: 101; BB-2: 69; BB-3: 219.

102. A typical account of the dangers to shipping caused by shoals in the South River appear in the 18 September 1760 issue of the *Maryland Gazette.* The account reads as follows: "Monday last as the ship *Betsey,* Capt. Strachan was going down the South River, she touch'd the Ground, and Five Hands in the Boat went to carry out an Anchor; but having put a Coil or two too much of the Cable in, at a few Yards Distance from the Ship, her Stern sunk, and she fell Bottom upwards upon the People, by which Accident Two of them, William Cunningham and one Johnson, a Foreigner, were unhappily Drowned. Their bodies are since taken up."

103. A French visitor noted in 1765, "This is a Very Small place not above a Doz'n houses." In that same year another referred to the town as a "pleasant village." After the Revolution travelers passing through failed to even take note of the site at all. Earle, 96.

104. Richard Walsh and William Lloyd Fox, eds., *Maryland: A History, 1632–1974* (Baltimore: Maryland Historical Society, 1974), 72. Stephen West, Jr., was one of the leaders of the Prince George's Association, a body of merchants organized to support the boycott of British goods in 1770. *Maryland Gazette,* 12 April 1770.

105. Walsh and Fox, 78.

106. Anne Arundel County IB-3: 457; IB-3: 510; DD-5: 431; IB-4: 26; IB-4: 297.

107. "Confiscated British Property," *Maryland Historical Magazine* 8, no. 4 (December 1913): 370.

108. Anne Arundel County Deeds, NH-6: 667.

109. John Thomas Scharf, *A History of Maryland: From the Earliest Period to the Present Day,* (Detroit: Gale, 1967, reprint of 1879), 1: 77.

110. Anne Arundel County Deeds, NH-13: 158.

111. Ibid.

112. Ibid., NH-10: 518; NH-13: 266; NH-14: 323, 344, 362; NH-15: 73, 75, 569.

113. Ibid., WSG-11: 288; WSG-13: 314.

114. Ibid., WSG-13: 314.

115. Minute Books of the Trustees of the Poor, 1820, 1871. Proceedings of the Levy Court, 1820–1828; Minutes of the County Commissioners, 1857–1866, 1878–1883.

116. Robert H. Burgess and H. Graham Wood, *Steamboats Out of Baltimore,* (Cambridge, Md.: Tidewater Publishers, 1968), 189.

117. *Baltimore Sun,* 30 May 1998.

CHAPTER 3: ST. LEONARDS

1. See Donald G. Shomette, *Flotilla: Battle for the Patuxent* (Solomons, Md.: Calvert Marine Museum Press, 1981), 42–97, for complete account of the first and second Battles of St. Leonard's Creek.

2. Official Report of the Transactions at the Battery on 25 and 26 June 1814, Navy Letters, RG 45, M 124, R 64, National Archives, Washington, D.C.

3. Ibid.

4. Solomon Rutter to Joshua Barney, 3 July 1814, Navy Letters, RG 45, M 124, R 64; Log of HMS *Loire,* 2 July 1814, *Chronicles of St. Mary's* 8, no. 10 (October 1960); Log of *St. Lawrence,* 2 July 1814, *Chronicles of St. Mary's* 13, no. 4 (April 1965).

5. Rutter to Barney, 3 July 1814.

6. Log of HMS *Loire,* 2 July 1814.

7. Rutter to Barney, 3 July 1814.

8. Joseph Nourse to George Cockburn, 4 July 1814, Cockburn Papers, vol. 38, Manuscript Division, Library of Congress, Washington, D.C.; Joshua Barney to William Jones, 8 July 1814, Navy Letters, RG 45, M 124, R 64; Rutter to Barney, 3 July 1814; Log of *St. Lawrence,* 2 July 1814.

9. John Smith, *Virginia,* (1608 [1612]), Geography and Map Division, Library of Congress, Washington, D.C.

10. Calvert County Wills, 1: 5. Among the early settlers in Calvert County was Captain John Thomas Clagett, great-grandfather of Bishop Clagett. Captain Clagett came from the parish of St. Leonard's in London and, according to Swepson Earle, gave the name to the place where he settled and to the creek upon it. Earle's account is clearly incorrect in that the creek had been called St. Leonard's for almost two decades before Clagett settled on its shores in the 1670s. The origin of the name for the creek is uncertain. It has been variously attributed to Leonard Calvert (who was not a saint) and to an obscure Catholic monk (who was). The original St. Leonard was believed to have been a Frankish courtier who was converted to the Catholic faith by St. Remigus and refused the offer of a see from his godfather, King Clovis I, to become a monk at Micy, France. He lived as a hermit at Limoges and was rewarded by the king with all the land he could see in one day while riding on a donkey. The land was in payment for the monk's prayers,

which were believed to have brought the queen through a difficult child delivery. He founded Noblac monastery on the lands thus granted to him, which grew into the town of Saint Leonard. He remained there evangelizing in the surrounding area until his death. His name is invoked by Catholic women in labor and by prisoners of war because of the legend that Clovis promised to release every captive Leonard visited. His feast day is November 6. Swepson Earle, *Maryland's Colonial Eastern Shore* (New York: Weathervane Books [facsimile of 1916]), 108; Charles Francis Stein, *A History of Calvert County, Maryland* (Baltimore: privately published, 1976), 250; Catholic Online Saints, 1997 (http://saints.catholic.org/saints/leonard.html).

11. *Archives,* 3: 258.
12. Ibid., 1, 4, 28; 4: 53.
13. *Archives,* 4: 53; That Bishop was an intimate of Leonardson, who was probably familiar with his estate, is suggested by the fact that in 1641 he had served as coexecutor with his housemate Denibiel Simon of Leonard Leonardson's estate. Ibid., 162.
14. Ibid., 1: 36.
15. Ibid., 146; 4: 162, 166.
16. Ibid., 1: 146; 4: 53.
17. Ibid. 1: 36; 3: 107.
18. Ibid., 1: 130; 4: 292; Stein, 5.
19. Patents, AB&H: 217. The tract was sold to Robert Blinkhorne in April 1657.
20. Patents, AB&H: 152.
21. *Archives,* 1: 244.
22. Patents, AB&A: 153.
23. *Archives,* 41: 65, 138, 200, 268.
24. Gust Skordas,*The Early Settlers of Maryland: An Index to Names of Immigrants Compiled from Records of Land Patents, 1633–1680, in the Hall of Records, Annapolis, Maryland* (Baltimore: Genealogical Publishing Company, 1968), 428; *Archives,* 10: 542; 41: 59.
25. *Archives,* 19: 466; 41: 285; 49: 356; Patents, AB&H: 153.
26. Augustine Herrman, *Virginia and Maryland,* (1670 [1673]), Geographic and Map Division, Library of Congress, Washington, D.C.
27. Hugh Jones letter, 23 January 1698, cited in *The Recorder* 27, no. 23 (20 March 1998): A-4.
28. Stein, 313.
29. *Archives,* 7: 609.
30. Stein, 57.
31. Ailene Hutchins, "St. Leonard Creek Town and Related Tracts," typescript MSS, Calvert County Historical Society, Prince Frederick, Md.; Wayne E. Clark and Michael A. Smolek, *An Archaeological Inventory of Point Farm, Calvert County, Maryland.* Monograph Series,

Number 1 (Annapolis, Md.: Maryland Historical Trust, 1981).
32. Hugh Jones letter, 23 January 1698.
33. Records Pertaining to Maryland Committee of Accounts, Port Records, Tobacco Taxes, etc. 1689–1702. Abstract: Ships Clearing from Port of Patuxent 28 August 1695–20 August 1701. CO5/749, Public Record Office, London. Photocopies in Calvert Marine Museum, Solomons, Md. A total of 115 vessels cleared for London, 30 for other English ports, 12 for Maryland ports, 26 for colonial ports, 8 for others, and 12 for unknown destinations.
34. *Archives,* 19: 178. The hogsheads shipped from the Patuxent District in the period 1689–1696 are as follows: 1689—2,678 hhds; 1690—19,330 hhds; 1691—5,109 hhds; 1692—27,377 hhds; 1693—20,003 hhds; 1694—12,355 hhds; 1695—21,619 hhds; 1696—6,571 hhds; 1697—21,022 hhds; 1698—14,423 hhds; 1699—16,729 hhds; 1700—12,391 hhds; 1701—13,367 hhds. The low numbers for the 1689 shipment from the Patuxent District, which accounted for 87 percent of all the tobacco shipped from the colony that year, was undoubtedly due to the military revolution that swept the land. Morriss explains that the great variance of shipments between 1690 and 1691 probably resulted from the recent political unrest in the colony and the Government of Association and other delays in shipment during the autumn of 1691. The figures may have included some of the 1690 crop held over for shipment until 1692 when an unusually large fleet was in the colony. By 1706 the combined Maryland and Virginia tobacco fleet sailing for England had grown to 300 vessels. Records Pertaining to Maryland Committee of Accounts, CO5/749; *Archives,* 8: 236; Margaret Shove Morris, *The Colonial Trade of Maryland 1689–1715,* Johns Hopkins University Studies in Historical and Political Science, Series 32: no. 3 (Baltimore: Johns Hopkins University Press, 1914), 31, 32, 33.
35. *Archives,* 26: 636, 638.
36. Patents, 8: 82.
37. Robert Blankenship's Will. Wills, 17:223; 14:83; St. Leonards Mill File, Pete Ferguson Collection, Lusby, Md. The actual mill site was rediscovered by Calvert County surveyor Pete Ferguson ca. 1965. The author and Ferguson revisited the site in the spring of 1999, and conducted a preliminary mapping of it on 1 April 1999. The site is believed to be one of the earliest mill complexes located to date in Maryland.
38. The first positive indication that a road was even opened by this period is suggested by a

1694 patent for "Smiths Hogpen" which refers to a "bounded hickory standing by the Road Side". Patents, B23: 151.

39. Michael A. Smolek, *A Survey of the History and Prehistory of St. Leonard Shores, Calvert County, Maryland*. Maryland Historical Trust Manuscript Series No. 10 (St. Mary's City, Md.: March 1980), 30; Robert J. Hurry, *An Archaeological Survey of a Portion of St. Leonards Town*. Jefferson Patterson Park and Museum Occasional Papers Number 5 (prepared for Bay Mills Constructing Inc., Owings, Maryland, and Friends of J. Patterson Park and Museum, Inc., St. Leonards, Maryland: June 1990), 13.

40. John W. Reps, *Tidewater Towns: City Planning in Colonial Virginia and Maryland* (Williamsburg, Virginia: Colonial Williamsburg Foundation, 1972), 103–5.

41. Smolek, 35, et seq.

42. Hurry, 14.

43. Ibid.

44. Among those plantations owned by Thomas Clagett were Croom and Weston in Prince George's County, and Greenland and Goodlington on the Eastern Shore. Stein, 70–1, 250. Stein, 250, incorrectly claims Clagett died in 1703, which is clearly impossible since he acquired the St. Leonards tract in 1706. See Will of Thomas Clagett in Gwynn Effie Bowie, *Across the Years in Prince George's County* (Richmond: Garrett and Massie, Inc., 1947), 118, et seq.

45. Records of Christ Church, Calvert County, Md. Thomas Johnson, son of John and Frances Johnson, is not to be confused with the subsequent governor of Maryland and Supreme Court Justice Thomas Johnson, son of Thomas Johnson II and Dorcas Sedwick, who was also born on the creek near its entrance. Stein, 67.

46. In 1710 Walter Smith inherited his father's house with all the lands that had been purchased of Governor Stone and others, including Robert Taylor. Will sealed 31 July 1710. Hall of Record Notes, Calvert County Wills, 14: 83, Richard Smith, Jr., 1714.

47. Patents, DD-5: 789.

48. Hutchins, 2.

49. *Archives*, 39: 170.

50. Ibid., 44: 608–10.

51. "Colonial Militia, 1740, 1748," *Maryland Historical Magazine* 6, no. 1 (March 1911): 53; *Archives*, 46: 218; Hurry, 10.

52. John Enys, *The American Journals of Lt. John Enys*, Elizabeth Cometti, ed. (Syracuse: Adirondack Museum and Syracuse University Press, 1976), 243.

53. Ibid., 349, n. 22.

54. *Calendar of Maryland State Papers: No. 1 The Black Book* (Annapolis, Md.: The Hall of Records Commission, 1943), 100, no. 677; *Archives*, 50: 318. That the Somervell family may have owned a lot in St. Leonards Town during this period is problematic, although Alexander Somervell most certainly did by 1782. Calvert County Tax List, 1782.

55. Calvert County Wills, 29:171; Will of Joseph Johnson, 1754, 29: 172; Will of John Johnson, 1754/1755, 29: 280.

56. *Maryland Calendar of Wills 1759–1764*, 12 (Westminster, Md.: Family Lee Publications, 1992), 44.

57. *Maryland Gazette*, 23 February 1758.

58. Ibid., 15 October 1759. In 1764 Mackall is listed as owning 87 acres of "The Angel or Angle" which was escheated by Aaron Williams. Rent Roll, no. 24, 3 September 1764.

59. That this land may have been situated on town lands is suggested by a codicil to the 1773 will of James Somervell, son of John Somervell, directing that "the moiety of my Lott in St. Leonard Creek Town" be sold to John Mackall, John Dare, and Richard Ireland. Wills, 39: 442.

60. *Archives*, 58: 451.

61. *Maryland Gazette*, 27 October 1783.

62. Debt Book, 1769.

63. *Archives*, 43: 271, 321.

64. Calvert County Tax List, 1782, 183; *1783 Tax List of Maryland, Part I. Cecil, Talbot, Harford & Calvert Counties*, Bettie Carothers, comp. (Lutherville, Md.: Privately printed 1977), 31–9.

65. Stein, 87.

66. Records of Christ Church.

67. *Archives*, 72: 80; Provincial Court Deeds JG-6: 156, 325. Only six landowners are listed in the 1783 tax list as owning lots "at Leonard Creek": Catherine Frazier (one lot); Dorcas Gray (two lots); Edward Hall of Frederick County (one lot); Samuel Johnson (one lot of one acre extent); Rebecca Somervell (one lot of one acre extent); and Brian Taylor (one lot). These lots were occupied by 19 individuals. *1783 Tax List of Maryland, Part I. Cecil, Talbot, Harford & Calvert Counties*, 191, 192, 193, 197, 198.

68. The lot holders included Brian Taylor (one lot in 1782); Edward Hall of Frederick, Md. (one lot in 1782); Alexander Somervell (one lot in 1782–1783); Dorcas Hall (two lots of an acre each in 1783); Catherine Frazier (one lot in 1783); Samuel Johnson (one acre lot from 1783 to 1793); Benjamin Mackall (lot no. 45, a ¾-acre plot, prior to 1786); John Turner (lot no. 45, from 1786 to 1810); Thomas Ireland (at least two lots prior to 1761); Richard Ireland (at least three lots between 1761 and 1802); John Griffiss (one lot

in 1793); William Somervell (one lot costing 5 shillings in 1802); George Gray (one lot, 1½ acres in extent, lying between John Griffiss's and John Turner's lots on the west side of Main Street prior to 1807); Bennett Sollers (one lot purchased from George Gray for $800 in 1807); John Ireland (one lot prior to 1810); James M. Sollers (one lot adjoining the lots of John Ireland and Bennett Sollers, purchased from John Turner in 1810 for $60); James and Margaret Heighe of Baltimore County (lot no. 40, a ¾-acre plot on the east side of Main Street prior to 1814); Hezekiah Coberth (lot no. 40, purchased from James and Margaret Heighe on 14 January 1814 for $50); Mary Frazier (a frame house in 1814 on one lot?). Calvert County Tax List, 1782; Tax List of Maryland, 1783, Part I; Wills of Maryland, DD-1: 235, Will of Thomas Ireland 1761; Calvert County Land Book No. 1: 16, Benjamin Mackall to John Turner 31 July 1786; Ibid., f. 104, Richard Ireland to John Griffiss, 15 November 1793; Ibid., f. 110, Samuel Johnson to Richard Ireland, 15 November 1793; Ibid., f. 283, Richard Ireland to William Somervell, 12 April 1802; Ibid., f. 314, George Gray to Bennett Sollers, 26 October 1807; Ibid., f. 395, John Turner to James M. Sollers, 1 March 1810; Ibid., f. 476, James and Margaret Heighe to Hezekiah Coberth, 13 January 1814; *American State Papers, Documents, Legislative and Executive, of the Congress of the United States,* 50 vols. (Washington, D.C.: Gales and Seaton, 1832–1861), *Claims,* 555.

69. Robert Barrie to George Cockburn, 11 June 1814, Cockburn Papers, vol. 38; Log of HMS *Loire,* 7 June 1814; Log of HMS *St. Lawrence,* 7 June 1814; Log of HMS *Jaseur,* 7 June 1814, ADM 51/2516, Public Record Office, London.

70. Mary Barney, ed., *A Biographical Memoir of the Late Commodore Joshua Barney: From Autobiographical Notes and Journals in Possession of His Family, and Other Authentic Sources* (Boston: Gray and Bowen, 1832), 256, 257; Hulbert Footner, *Sailor of Fortune: The Life and Adventures of Commodore Barney, U.S.N.* (New York: Harper & Brothers, 1940), 270; *American and Commercial Daily Advertiser,* 13 June 1814; Log of HMS *Loire,* 10 June 1814; Log of HMS *St. Lawrence,* 10 June 1814; Log of HMS *Jaseur,* 10 June 1814; Barrie to Cockburn, 11 June 1814.

71. Barrie to Cockburn, 19 June 1814, Cockburn Papers, vol. 48.

72. *American State Papers, Claims,* 552, 555.

73. The first campsite is now known as Fort Hill. A small fragmentary segment of the earthworks, upon which a private home was erected, remains on private property. The second site is believed to lie beneath or near the present White Sands Restaurant complex, north of the confluence of Johns Creek and St. Leonard's Creek.

74. Shomette, *Flotilla,* 66.

75. Footner, 272; Barney, 258.

76. Barney, 259; Official Report of the Transactions at the Battery on the June 25 and 26, 1814.

77. Ibid.

78. *American & Commercial Daily Advertiser,* 29 June 1814.

79. Hutchins, 9, suggests that the doctor referred to may have been Dr. James M. Taylor who assumed "Dorcas' part of the house rent in St. Leonard." It is my opinion that the house mentioned was merely occupied by Dr. Hamilton, surgeon for the flotilla, throughout the duration of the fleet's stay on the creek. The log of HMS *Loire* suggests that there was not a lot to destroy in the first place. "A.M. Fresh breezes and Cloudy Wr. Boats rowing Guard to observe the Enemy's motion. At 11 all the Boats of H.M. Ship Loire mann'd and armed went up St. Leonards Creek in Co. with the armed Schooners where finding two of the Enemy's Vessels dismantled destroy'd them with several others—loaded one Schooner with Tobacco. 8:30[P.M.] Boats returned after destroying several Vessels and storehouses—likewise houses belonging to Enemy's troops and flotilla. Midnight fresh breezes with rain." Log of HMS *Loire,* 2 July 1814, *Chronicles of St. Mary's* 8, no. 10 (October 1960).

80. Rutter to Barney, 3 July 1814.

81. Log of HMS *St. Lawrence,* 2 July 1814, *Chronicles of St. Mary's* 11, no. 12 (December 1963); George Cockburn to George Edward Watts, 9 July 1814, Cockburn Papers, vol. 25.

82. Barney to Jones, 8 July 1814.

83. *American State Papers, Claims,* 552, 555.

84. Ibid., 552–3.

85. Ibid., 555.

86. The postmasters of the St. Leonards Town Post Office and their dates of appointments were Dr. William Somerville (6 April 1796); John J. Hellen (19 June 1798); Thomas Dixon (18 September 1800); James Dixon (1 October 1801); Joseph Griffiss (22 February 1804); William C. Dawkins (ca. 1 October 1805); George Gray (ca. 13 January 1806); James M. Sollers (25 May 1807); William C. Dawkins (21 April 1823); Francis K. Parran (9 May 1826); discontinued 28 May 1828, reestablished 17 June 1828; Hezekiah Coberth (17 June 1828); Samuel S. Hodgkins (6 January 1832); Joseph Griffiss (30 January 1833); John Hooper (10 July 1835); Joseph S. Wilson (24 March 1837); James Sollers, Jr. (28 September 1838); Francis

K. Parran (7 June 1839); John A. Sangston (2 October 1842); Robert L. Clark (15 February 1843); James Humphreys (23 August 1847 [he may not have served]); Robert L. Clark (27 October 1847); B. H. Ireland (16 September 1853); William J. Parran (4 October 1856); James J. Blackburn (4 August 1865); discontinued 13 August 1866, reestablished 30 August 1866; James J. Blackburn (30 August 1866); James Dowell (1 May 1867); James H. Frazier (19 November 1869); name changed from St. Leonards to St. Leonard (21 March 1869); Dorcas D. Frazier (21 March 1894); John Thomas Bond (1 October 1898); James L. Johnson (2 December 1902); Katherine A. Long (1 April 1918). "St. Leonard Post Office, Calvert County, Maryland," USPS Historian, Corporate Information, Post Office Vertical File, Calvert County Historical Society, Prince Frederick, Md. For examples of the difficulties of mail carriage in the late nineteenth century in southern Calvert County, see *Calvert Journal,* 28 April and 27 December 1877.

87. The family burial ground and grave markers of the Hezekiah Coberth family are still extant on a plot of land lying near the intersection of U.S. Route 2-4 and Maryland Route 765. The town lot on which the graves are situated is conjectured by the author to be number 71. The gravestone of Hezekiah Coberth reads: "In Memory of HEZEKIAH COBERTH. Born March 1, 1773 and departed this life at St. Leonard, Calvert County, Md., October 28, 1841. In early life he embraced religion and united himself to the Methodist E. Church of which he continued to be an exemplary and useful member. This tribute is erected by his only son. It was his request that this yard never be disturbed."

88. Photocopy from unidentified geographic directory, 1882, St. Leonard Town Vertical File, Calvert County Historical Society, Prince Frederick, Md.

89. *Soil Map Calvert County Maryland,* 1928, Calvert County Soil Conservation District Office, Prince Frederick, Md.

CHAPTER 4: LOWER MARLBORO

1. *Evening Star,* 6 November 1965.
2. Ibid.
3. *Archives,* 7: 479, 609; Charles Francis Stein, *A History of Calvert County, Maryland* (Baltimore: privately published, 1976), 262.
4. Archives, 13: 26; John W. Reps, *Tidewater Towns: City Planning in Colonial Virginia and Maryland* (Williamsburg, Virginia: Colonial Williamsburg Foundation, 1972), 97.
5. Stein, 58, 59, 105, 252.

6. Richard E. Stearns, *Some Indian Village Sites of Tidewater Maryland: Proceeding No. 9* (Baltimore: Natural History Society of Maryland, 1943), 24–5; Donald G. Shomette, *Tidewater Time Capsule: History Beneath the Patuxent* (Centreville, Md.: Tidewater Publishers, 1995), 38.

7. *Archives,* 13: 112–3. In October 1685, fifty-eight inhabitants requested that the John Bowlings site be reconsidered as an appropriate town location, as they deemed the Cox site "altogether to us inconvenient." The council agreed, provided the petitioners "can get the land made over to them from the Owner soe as to be sure of his Title therewith," and promised to press the project the next Assembly. The project was not revived, however, and Bowling Town never got off the drawing board. *Archives,* 17: 408–9.

8. Reps, 103; *The Swampoodle Book* (Lower Marlboro, Md.: privately printed, 1983), 9. Stein, 252, states that the town was laid out by Thomas Cox himself, who had settled on Cox's Choice well before the designation of the site as a town. However, because Cox died ca. 1675, this assertion is undoubtedly in error.

9. Gloria L. Main, *Tobacco Colony: Life in Early Maryland 1650–1720* (Princeton, N.J.: Princeton University Press, 1982), 133.

10. *Archives,* 26: 636, 645.
11. *Swampoodle,* 9; Stein, 252.
12. Stein, 56; *Swampoodle,* 12.
13. *Swampoodle,* 13.

14. National Register of Historic Places Nomination Form. Grahame House, 13 December 1971. Lower Marlboro Vertical File, Calvert County Historical Society, Prince Frederick, Md.

15. *Swampoodle,* 14. Richard and Eleanor Smith had five children. Named in their father's will were Richard, who died young; Walter, who was called Captain Walter Smith and married Mrs. Christian Sim Lee, a widow; John Addison Smith; Rebecca Smith; and Rachel Smith. After Richard Smith died in 1732, his young widow married Captain Posthumous Thornton, sheriff of Calvert County. In 1744, not long after Thornton's demise, she married John Skinner, a Lower Marlboro merchant. Eleanor died two years later, at the age of forty-one. No record has been found to suggest that Eleanor Addison Smith Thornton Skinner had children by either Thornton or Skinner. Some sources claim that she also married Bennett Lowe of St. Mary's County before she married Smith. Several marriages were not uncommon for this time period. A wealthy young widow was never a widow for long. *Swampoodle,* 13.

16. Ibid., 10, 14; *Maryland Gazette,* 1 May 1747.

17. *Archives,* 44: 608, 610; 50: 318, 320; 58: 449, 451.

18. National Register of Historic Places Nomination Form. Grahame House, 3; *Swampoodle,* 16.

19. *Maryland Gazette,* 17 and 30 July 1760.

20. Stein, 118–9, 122–4, 128–9, 140, 265; *Swampoodle,* 16. It has been suggested by some that the Grahame House is not the original Patuxent Manor but may have been built upon the site of the first house since an iron plate in the back of the fireplace bears the date of 1741. Stein states that the Grahame House was built between 1740 and 1750. Stein, 119, 265.

21. *Maryland Gazette,* 1 August 1754; Will of Littleton Waters, 21 June 1750, Ailene Hutchins Collection, Lusby, Md. Waters's will, proved 1 August 1750, left to his daughters Sarah, Esther, and Dorothy his dwelling house and three lots in Lower Marlborough, as well as a "wharf and works standing on the river side and such part of the land called Terra in Aqua as front the lot and wharf aforesaid." He also left to John Wardrop, a merchant in town, part of Terra Aqua which fronted on Wardrop's lot. It has been surmised by Calvert County historian Ailene Hutchins that Wardrop may have been the proprietor of the old store that presently stands on the property. "Calvert County, Then and Now," newspaper clipping dated 9 December 1971, Lower Marlborough Vertical File, Calvert County Historical Society, Prince Frederick, Md.

22. *Maryland Gazette,* 13 May 1756, 26 August 1756, 21 July 1747. See 24 May 1749, 3 July 1751, and 24 May 1753 for additional examples. See also Marcus Rediker, *Between the Devil and the Deep Blue Sea: Merchant Seamen, Pirates, and the Anglo-American Maritime World 1700–1750* (Cambridge: Cambridge University Press, 1987), 101–4, for discussion on conditions encouraging desertions.

23. David Carcaud, card. Original Documents Section, Maryland Historical Society, Baltimore, Md.; *Swampoodle*, 15.

24. Allen Eustis Begnaud, "Hoofbeats in Colonial Maryland," *Maryland Historical Magazine,* 65, no. 3 (Fall 1970): 224.

25. Stein, 124.

26. M. P. Andrews, *Tercentenary History of Maryland* (Chicago: S. J. Clarke Publishing Co., 1925), 482; *Maryland Gazette,* 13 December 1959.

27. Walter Worthington Bowie, *The Bowies and Their Kindred: A Genealogical and Biographical History* (Cottonport, La.: Polyanthos, Inc., 1971, reprint of 1899), 408; Effie Gwynn Bowie, *Across the Years in Prince George's County: A Genealogical and Biographical History of Some Prince George's County Maryland and Allied Families* (Baltimore, Md.: Genealogical Publishing Co., Inc., 1975, reprint of 1947), 137; Stein, 250.

28. *Swampoodle,* 11; Stein, 135, 136, 138.

29. Henrietta Carcaud to House of Delegates, 18 December 1781, Original Documents Section, Maryland Historical Society, Baltimore, Md.; *Quebec Gazette,* 2 July 1778, 18 July 1778, Custom House Notices, RG 401, Reel N-27, Public Archives of Canada, Ottawa, Ontario.

30. *Calvert Journal,* 20 August 1887, transcript, Lower Marlboro Vertical File, Calvert County Historical Society, Prince Frederick, Md.; *Swampoodle,* 15; *Naval Documents of the American Revolution,* 10 vols. (Washington, D.C.: U.S. Navy, Naval Historical Center, 1964–1996), 5: 793.

31. *Naval Documents,* 5: 1311.

32. *Archives,* 12: 364; 16: 134, 153, 354–5.

33. *Calendar of Maryland State Papers: No. 1 The Red Book Part I* (Annapolis, Md.: The Hall of Records Commission, 1950), 68, no. 396.

34. Ernest McNeill Eller, ed. *Chesapeake Bay in the American Revolution* (Centreville, Md.: Tidewater Publishers, 1981), 229–30. See 248–51 for the career of *Conqueror* and 214 and 249 for the *Lydia* capture.

35. *Swampoodle,* 15.

36. *Archives,* 43: 270–1.

37. Donald G. Shomette, *Pirates on the Chesapeake: Being a True History of Pirates, Picaroons, and Raiders on Chesapeake Bay, 1610–1807* (Centreville, Md.: Tidewater Publishers, 1985), 261–3; *Archives,* 45: 37–8, 143; *Calendar of the General Otho Holland Williams Papers in the Maryland Historical Society* (Baltimore: Maryland Historical Records Survey Project, November 1940), 27, no. 65.

38. *Archives,* 45: 380.

39. Ibid., 47: 177, 343, 357.

40. Ibid. The fact that Fitzhugh and Allein were taken prisoner and later released suggests that they were of use only as hostages.

41. Ibid., 47: 177, 178, 200.

42. Ibid., 45: 585.

43. David Carcaud. Lower Marlboro Vertical File, Calvert County Historical Society, Prince Frederick, Md. The indictment against Carcaud continued in the general court of the State of Maryland to the June term of 1804 and again to the February 1817 term although on 10 April 1787 the convictions of Carcaud and others listed with him in the indictment were dropped. David Carcaud Memorial, Film from Public Record Office, London, Audit Office 13, Series II, MG 14, Bundle 97, Reel B-2201, Public Archives of

Canada, Ottawa; Ibid., File from Public Record Office, London, Audit Office 12, Series I, MG 14, Vol. 80, Pg. 17/2, Reel B-1172; Stein, 144; "List of Outlawries, Western Shore," *Maryland Historical Magazine* 4, no. 3 (September 1909), 287–8. William Molleson Carcaud's surname and middle name were taken from London tobacco merchant William Molleson suggesting that David Carcaud may have been engaged in some business or other activities with the merchant. See Edward C. Papenfuse, *In Pursuit of Profit: The Annapolis Merchants in the Era of the American Revolution 1763–1805* (Baltimore: Johns Hopkins University Press, 1975) for further details on the affairs of William Molleson.

44. Papenfuse, 115, 174.

45. Calvert County Tax Rolls for Lower Marlborough Hundred, 1782, reprinted in "Calvert County Then and Now" by Ailene Hutchins, *Calvert Independent,* 9 December 1971. The following year, in 1783, tax records indicate a total of twenty-four lots owned by thirteen owners. Owners were identified as: Samuel Chew (five lots); Cook Ham (one lot); Denmund Cramphin (one lot), Thomas John Clagett (one lot); John David (two lots); Colonel William Fitzhugh (three lots); Asenath Graham (two lots); Thomas Harwood (two lots); Dr. Edward Johnson (two lots); Richard Stallings (one lot); James Stone (two lots); James Weems (one lot); and Philemon Young's heirs (one lot). The tax list indicates, however, that only sixteen whites occupied these properties. *1783 Tax List of Maryland, Part I. Cecil, Talbot, Harford & Calvert Counties.* Bettie Carothers, comp. (Lutherville, Md.: privately printed, 1977), 177, 178, 179, 183, 184, 186, 187.

46. Papenfuse, 174.

47. Dennis Griffith, *Map of the State of Maryland,* 1794 [1795].

48. *Maryland Gazette,* 28 April 1791.

49. Stein, 161.

50. *Calvert Journal,* 20 August 1887.

51. Shomette, *Flotilla: Battle for the Patuxent* (Solomons, Md.: Calvert Marine Museum Press, 1981), 120; Joshua Barney to William Jones, 1 August 1814, Navy Letters, RG 45, M 124, R 64, National Archives, Washington, D.C.; Robert Barrie to George Cockburn, 19 June 1814, Cockburn Papers, vol. 38, Manuscript Division, Library of Congress, Washington, D.C.

52. Barrie to Cockburn, 19 June 1814.

53. Ibid.; Log of HMS *Jaseur,* 16 June 1814, *Chronicles of St. Mary's* 9, no. 1 (January 1961).

54. *American & Commercial Daily Advertiser,* 20 June 1814.

55. Barrie to Cockburn, 19 June 1814; Log of HMS *Jaseur,* 17 June 1814. The value of tobacco lost at Lower Marlborough is based on Barney's estimate of $50 per hogshead as of 1 August 1814. Barney to Jones, 1 August 1814, RG 45, M 124, R 64. The prisoner may have been Thomas Reynolds, a captain in the Calvert County Militia, or his father, Edward Reynolds, one of the wealthier landowners in the county. The British later attempted to conduct a prisoner exchange in which a British sergeant named Mahiou, who was thought to have been captured in a skirmish at Benedict (but had actually been killed), would be exchanged for a Mr. Reynold[s], who had been taken during the raid on Lower Marlborough. They attempted to negotiate the exchange at Sotterly Plantation on 23 June. Shomette, *Flotilla,* 225, n. 67. See Stein, 305–6, for coverage of the Reynolds family.

56. Shomette, *Flotilla,* 81, 104.

57. Cockburn to Cochrane, 22 August 1814, Cockburn Papers, vol. 24; George Robert Gleig, *A Narrative of the Campaigns of the British Army, at Washington, Baltimore, and New Orleans, under the Generals Ross, Packenham, & Lambert, in the Years 1814 and 1815 With Some Accounts of the Countries Visited* (Philadelphia: M. Carey & Sons, 1821), 99.

58. "New York Publication Reprints Article From Calvert Independent," photocopy, Lower Marlboro Vertical File, Calvert County Historical Society, Prince Frederick, Md.

59. Genevieve Frazier Cockey to Ralph E. Eshelman, 20 January 1976, photocopy, Donald G. Shomette Collection, Dunkirk, Md.; Ralph Hinman, "More Sidelights of Calvert County History," *Calvert Independent,* 23 September 1954, typewritten transcript of article, Lower Marlboro File, Calvert Marine Museum, Solomons, Md. It seems unlikely, folk traditions aside, that there were any British graves in the vicinity of the town. En route up the river, the British did not tarry for more than a few hours at White's Landing. En route down, they stopped briefly at Nottingham, where they transferred their wounded and dying to barges and brigs for transport to the fleet anchorage at Benedict. The purported wreck may have been one of the American merchantmen or a captured flotilla barge taken on 22 August 1814 when the American fleet was destroyed above Pig Point. A dive upon the site by the author and Dr. Fred Hopkins of the University of Baltimore in 1983 failed to produce any positive data regarding the date of the wreck. A second wreck site which was also investigated proved to be a private wooden fishing boat of modern construction.

60. *Swampoodle,* 11.
61. Eshelman & Associates, Calvert County Steamboat Wharves and Landings: Architectural Level Survey and Inventory (Report prepared for Calvert County, Maryland Planning Commission: December 1996), 52.
62. Stein, 178.
63. Beitzell, *Point Lookout Prison Camp for Confederates* (Abell, Md.: privately printed, 1972), 7–8.
64. *War of the Rebellion: Official Records of the Union and Confederate Armies,* Series I, (Washington, D.C.: Government Printing Office, 1880–1901), 5: 385–6.
65. *Calvert County, Maryland Tercentenary 1654–1954.* Maryland Tercentenary Edition, September 23, 1954. Duplicated courtesy of the Calvert County Public Schools. Photocopy book from *Calvert Independent,* Calvert County Historical Society, Prince Frederick, Md., 65; *Calvert Independent,* 28 March 1979.
66. Ailene Hutchins, "Calvert County Then and Now," 6 January 1972, Lower Marlboro Vertical File, Calvert County Historical Society, Prince Frederick, Md.; *Swampoodle,* inside cover.
67. *Calvert Journal,* 23 June 1877, 18 August 1877.
68. *Calvert County, Maryland Tercentenary 1654–1954,* 182.
69. *A Century of Methodism: Largents Chapel, 1869–1969.* (Privately printed, [1969]), 6; Hutchins, "Calvert County Then and Now," 6 January 1971. About 1889, civic-minded members of the town formed the Lower Marlboro Aid Society to provide charity to the less fortunate. *Calvert Gazette,* 9 February 1889.
70. U.S. Army, *Annual Report of the Chief of Engineers for the Fiscal Year Ending June 30, 1888* (Washington, D.C.: Government Printing Office, 1889), Part 2, 851; *Swampoodle,* 20; Stein, 92; *Calvert Journal,* 21 June 1888.
71. "For Gates or Against Gates," photocopy of transcript by Margaret W. Cook, October 1983. Lower Marlboro Vertical File, Calvert County Historical Society, Prince Frederick, Md.
72. *Swampoodle,* 19; Miss Susan Magruder was the schoolteacher in 1888. She was followed by James Frazier and Parker Duke, and, after the school was moved into the town, by Miss Addie Smith and Miss Betty Talbott. Hutchins, "Calvert County Then and Now," 6 January 1972.
73. *A Century of Methodism,* 7, 8.
74. Ibid., 7.
75. Ibid.
76. Ibid., 7, 8.
77. U.S. Congress. *U.S. Congress, House, 60th Congress, 1st session, Document no. 531* (1911),

5; *Maryland Delaware & Virginia Railway Company Annual Report, Statement of Freight and Passenger Revenue by Wharves for the Fiscal Year Ending December 31st, 1907.* Calvert Marine Museum, Solomons, Md.; Donald G. Shomette, *Tidewater Time Capsule: History Beneath the Patuxent* (Centreville, Md.: Tidewater Publishers, 1995), 111.
78. Leida Ruth King interview notes, Ailene Hutchins, comp., 1971, Lower Marlboro Vertical File, Calvert County Historical Society, Prince Frederick, Md.; miscellaneous notes on Lower Marlborough, Lower Marlboro Vertical File, Calvert County Historical Society.
79. *A Century of Methodism,* 8.
80. Leida Ruth King interview notes; *Swampoodle,* 21. Electric lighting had reached only a tiny section of the town by 1924, but electricity provided by an independent plant had been installed in the church by that time.
81. Robert H. Burgess and H. Graham Wood, *Steamboats Out of Baltimore* (Cambridge, Md.: Tidewater Publishers, 1968), 103.
82. Miscellaneous notes on Lower Marlborough.
83. *Calvert County, Maryland Tercentenary 1654–1954,* 71.
84. *Swampoodle,* 21; Shomette, *Tidewater Time Capsule,* 274; Burgess and Wood, 105.
85. *A Century of Methodism,* 8.
86. *Swampoodle,* 22.
87. Ibid., 19.
88. Newspaper clipping, 4 April 1936, Lower Marlboro Vertical File, Calvert County Historical Society, Prince Frederick, Md.; *Washington Post,* 4 April 1936.
89. Eshelman & Associates, 52.
90. *Swampoodle; Calvert County, Maryland Tercentenary 1654–1954,* 182.
91. *Baltimore Sun,* 1 May 1972; *News Leader,* 2 September 1971; James C. Wilfong, "The Van Vleck Operation," undated newspaper clipping, Lower Marlboro Vertical File, Calvert County Historical Society, Prince Frederick, Md.
92. *Washington Post,* 2 May 1985.
93. *Evening Star,* 6 November 1965.

CHAPTER 5: NOTTINGHAM

1. "Minutes of the Board of Patuxent Associators," *Maryland Historical Magazine* 6, no. 3 (September 1911): 305.
2. Walter Worthington Bowie, *The Bowies and Their Kindred: A Genealogical and Biographical History* (Cottonport, La.: Polyanthos, Inc., 1971, reprint of 1899), 76, 77; R. Lee Van Horn, *Out of the Past: Prince Georeans and Their Land* (Riverdale, Md.: Prince George's County Historical Society, 1976), 163.

3. *Maryland Gazette,* 12 April 1770; Van Horn, 141–2; *Maryland Gazette,* 10 May and 14 June 1770; Louise Joyner Hienton, *Prince George's Heritage* (Baltimore: Maryland Historical Society, 1972), 171–2.

4. *Maryland Gazette,* 6 August 1772; Prince George's County Court Record, CC-1: 312; Hienton, 47.

5. Van Horn, 124–5, 126, 140.

6. *Maryland Gazette,* 1 April and 3 June 1773, 14 April and 26 May 1774.

7. Bowie, 77.

8. *Maryland Gazette,* 29 December 1774; Bowie, 77; Van Horn, 152.

9. *Archives,* 18: 34, 36–7; Bowie, 77; Van Horn, 163.

10. Bowie, 78.

11. Van Horn, 172, 173; *Archives,* 43: 271, 302, 318.

12. *Archives,* 47: 151, 177, 203, 214.

13. A company of artillerymen were to erect a fort, "of not less than ten nine Pounders with one or two block Houses," but there is no indication it was ever completed. *Archives,* 45: 418, 419–20.

14. "Minutes of the Board of Patuxent Associators," 305–6.

15. *Archives,* 26: 636.

16. Ibid., 637; Heinton, 133, 645.

17. *Archives,* 27: 69, 160.

18. Prince George County Court Records, HH: 398.

19. *Maryland Gazette,* June 3–June 10, 1729.

20. *Archives,* 46: 159, 341, 501; *Calendar of Maryland State Papers: No. 1 The Black Book* (Annapolis, Md.: The Hall of Records Commission, 1943), 98–9, no. 662; *Archives,* 50: 319, 321; Heinton, 64. See *Archives,* 44: 595–638, for full text of "An Act for amending the Staple of Tobacco, for preventing Frauds in his Majesty's Customs, and for the Limitation of Officers Fees."

21. *Maryland Gazette,* 29 June 1748.

22. Mary Anne Tolzman, "Case Studies Of Decline In Southern Prince George's County, Maryland: The Quiet Death of Charlestown, Queen Anne, and Nottingham," typescript photocopy (29 April 1975), Calvert Marine Museum, Solomons, Md., 19.

23. *Maryland Gazette,* 23 June 1747; Van Horn, 100.

24. Tolzman, 20.

25. *Maryland Gazette,* 8 May 1751, 21 June 1752.

26. Ibid., 5 December 1754, 27 May 1756, 14 October 1756.

27. Ibid., 13 August 1752, 24 May 1753, 16 August 1753.

28. Van Horn, 89.

29. *Maryland Gazette,* 20 February 1752, 12 March 1752.

30. Van Horn, 90; *Maryland Gazette,* 20 February 1752; Van Horn, 115.

31. *Maryland Weather Service* (1899), 1: 348, 349.

32. "Minutes of the Board of Patuxent Associators," 306, 308.

33. Ibid., 307–8.

34. Ibid., 308, 309.

35. Ibid., 309–17.

36. Ibid., 314, 316–7.

37. *Archives,* 47: 184.

38. Ibid., 45: 472; 533, 597.

39. Ibid., 47: 288, 483.

40. The ultimate fate of *Nautilus* is unknown, but a little more than a century and a half later, a shipwreck was discovered off Nottingham by relic hunters. In 1979 the wreck was archaeologically investigated by Nautical Archaeological Associates and tentatively dated as a revolutionary era schooner. See Donald G. Shomette, *Tidewater Time Capsule: History Beneath the Patuxent* (Centreville, Md.: Tidewater Publishers, 1995), 158–64, for a further account of the archaeological survey.

41. Tolzman, 23. On 30 August 1780, Allen Bowie was appointed inspector. Bowie resigned soon afterwards and was replaced by John Eversfield on 30 September. On 7 October, Eversfield was replaced by John Warring. *Archives,* 43: 270–1, 302, 318; Basil H. Brune, "Tobacco Landings and the Tobacco Marketing System in the Patuxent River Basin, 1730's–1830's," (Unpublished master's thesis, University of Maryland, College Park, Md., 1972), 62.

42. William Johns applied for a license in November 1781, John Lawson Naylor in August 1783, and John Nevitt in June 1788. Van Horn, 184, 190, 204.

43. Ibid., 202, 205, 206; Hienton 198.

44. Hienton, 48; Van Horn, 219.

45. Van Horn, 206, 220, 221, 222, 228.

46. Ibid., 228.

47. Ibid., 229–30; Hienton, 208.

48. *Laws of the United States of America, from the 4th of March, 1789, to the 4th of March, 1815* (Washington: John Bioren and John Duane, 1815), 3: 143, 144.

49. *Daily National Intelligencer,* 2 March 1804.

50. Bowie, 80.

51. Van Horn, 255–6.

52. Shomette, *Flotilla,* 67; *Daily National Intelligencer,* 18 June and 20 June 1814; *American and Commercial Daily Advertiser,* 20 June 1814.

53. *American and Commercial Daily Advertiser,* 23 June 1814; *Calendar of the General Otho*

Holland Williams Papers in the Maryland Historical Society (Baltimore: Prepared by The Maryland Historical Records Survey Project, Division of Professional and Service Projects, Work Projects Administration, November 1940), 353, no. 1010.

54. *American and Commercial Daily Advertiser,* 23 June 1814; *Daily National Intelligencer,* 18 June and 24 June 1814.

55. Clement Hollyday to Urban Hollyday, 12 July 1814, Manuscript Division, Library of Congress, Washington, D.C.

56. *Daily National Intelligencer,* 19 July and 22 July 1814.

57. Ibid., 29 July 1814.

58. Barney to Jones, 1 August 1814, Navy Letters, RG 45, M 124, R 64, National Archives, Washington, D.C.

59. George Robert Gleig, *A Narrative of the Campaigns of the British Army, at Washington, Baltimore, and New Orleans, under the Generals Ross, Packenham, & Lambert, in the Years 1814 and 1815 With Some Accounts of the Countries Visited* (Philadelphia: M. Carey & Sons, 1821), 57.

60. Van Horn, 257.

61. "A Personal Narrative of Events by Sea and Land, from the Year 1800 to 1815 Concluding with a Narrative of Some of the Principal Events in The Chesapeake and South Carolina, in 1814 and 1815," *Chronicles of St. Mary's* 8, no. 1 (January 1960): 4; Shomette, *Flotilla,* 168.

62. Jones to Barney, 20 August 1814. Navy Letters, RG 45, M 124, R 64.

63. Stanislaus Murray Hamilton, ed. *The Writings of James Monroe* (New York: G. P. Putnam's Sons, 1901), 5: 289.

64. Walter Lord, *The Dawns Early Light* (New York: W.W. Norton & Company, 1972), 67.

65. Gleig, 107; Lord, 66–7.

66. Gleig, 109.

67. *Norfolk Herald,* 6 September 1814; Lord, 186.

68. Gleig 148–9; William M. Marine, *The British Invasion of Maryland 1812–1815.* (Hatboro, Pa.: Tradition Press, 1965, reprint of 1913), 183–4.

69. Buckholtz, 60; Bowie, 82–5.

70. Van Horn, 271, 273–4.

71. Fred Hopkins, "For Flag and Profit: The Life of Commodore John Daniel Danels of Baltimore," *Maryland Historical Magazine* 80, no. 4 (Winter 1985): 396.

72. *Record of Movements: Vessels of the United States Coast Guard 1790–December 31, 1933* (Washington: Treasury Department, 1989), 125, 126; *Niles' Weekly Register,* 15 May 1819.

73. *Record of Movements,* 126. There is conflicting testimony as to whether or not the ship was abandoned, for Marshall states that when he arrived, he placed in chains those pirates who were still onboard *Irresistible,* but the letter from the collector of Baltimore to the secretary of the treasury states she was found abandoned.

74. Van Horn, 281; Prince George's County Tax Assessment List, 1828; Tolzman, 27–8.

75. Van Horn, 306, 325; Maryland Acts of Assembly, Chapter 73, 1847.

76. *Alexandria Gazette* reprint from *Marlboro Gazette* account, 28 January 1847.

77. *New Topographical Atlas of the State of Maryland and District of Columbia,* (Baltimore: Stedman, Brown, and Lyon, 1873).

78. *Martenet's Map of Prince George's County Maryland* (Baltimore: Simon J. Martenet, 1861), Geography and Map Division, Library of Congress, Washington, D.C., 22. The 1860 census also listed 2 attorneys, 7 blacksmiths, 12 carpenters, 6 clerks, 1 ditcher, 1 hotel keeper, 23 managers, 7 mechanics, 7 merchants, 2 ministers, 3 millers, 7 physicians, 1 plasterer, 1 pump maker, 1 sailor, 1 schoolteacher, 5 servants, 1 sheriff, and 1 tailor. Ibid., 11, 20–1.

79. Residents of Nottingham included John R. Bladen, Mrs. Thomas Belt, Major George Calvert, Mrs. Gray, Thomas Gurley (Gourley?), Robert Humphrey, one Jones, Dr. John McCubbin, Mrs. Mills, E. Plater, Mrs. Julia Ridgeway, Mrs. Rollins, J. T. Stamp (and possibly his son), R. Thompson, Dr. John E. Turton, and Captain Weems. *Martenet,* 27.

80. David C. Holly, *Tidewater by Steamboat: A Saga of the Chesapeake* (Baltimore: Johns Hopkins University Press, 1991), 266; G. M. Hopkins, *Atlas of Fifteen Miles Around Washington Including the County of Prince George Maryland* (Philadelphia: G. M. Hopkins, 1878), 18. The town streets of Nottingham are not named in Martenet but are presumed to be the same as the names published in Hopkins twenty-eight years later.

81. Tolzman, 27.

82. Wilfred M. Barton, *The Road to Washington.* (Boston: Gorham Press, 1919), 135.

83. Robert H. Burgess and H. Graham Wood, *Steamboats Out of Baltimore* (Cambridge, Md.: Tidewater Publishers, 1968), 103.

84. Tolzman, 31.

85. H. Chandlee Forman, *Old Buildings, Gardens and Furniture in Tidewater Maryland* (Cambridge, Md.: Tidewater Publishers, 1967), 233.

86. Ibid., 233, 237.

87. Ibid., 237.

CHAPTER 6: QUEEN ANNE'S TOWN

1. Prince George's County, Patents, 12: 385. The tract is also referred to as Essenton.

2. *Soil Survey Prince George's County* (United States Department of Agriculture Soil Conservation Service in cooperation with Maryland Agricultural Experiment Station, April 1967), 49, and plate 24.

3. Prince George's County Court Records, James Neale, 16: 3, 28 May 1670, X-9; Robert Tyler, 12: 616, 30 August 1670, W-9; Thomas Bowdle, 22:19, 2 July 1670, X-10; Ninian Geall, assigned to George Yate, 21: 175, 1 July 1680, X-10; Thomas Larkin, B-23: 340, 14 July 1694, X-9.

4. Louise Joyner Hienton, *Prince George's Heritage* (Baltimore: Maryland Historical Society, 1972), 75, 76.

5. *Archives*, 26: 636, 637, 645.

6. Hienton, 76, 75.

7. R. Lee Van Horn, *Out of the Past: Prince Georgeans and Their Land* (Riverdale, Md.: Prince George's County Historical Society, 1976), 48, 51.

8. Prince George's County Court Records, H: 86.

9. *Archives*, 27: 69.

10. Anne Arundel County Judgments, TB-3:140.

11. *Archives*, 33: 370.

12. Anne Arundel County, 1720–21: 514; 1722–23: 32; Carville V. Earle, *The Evolution of a Tidewater Settlement System: All Hallow's Parish, Maryland, 1650–1783* (Chicago: University of Chicago Press, 1975), 150; Anne Arundel County, VD-1.

13. Anne Arundel County, 1722–23: 50; Earle, 150.

14. Van Horn, 59, 60.

15. Anne Arundel County, IB-1: 326; IB-4: 295; TB-3: 155a; ISB-1: 352, 629; IB-4: 295.

16. Edward C. Papenfuse. *In Pursuit of Profit: The Annapolis Merchants in the Era of the American Revolution 1763–1805* (Baltimore: Johns Hopkins University Press, 1975), 43.

17. Van Horn, 69.

18. *Archives*, 25: 453, 454–5, 458–60.

19. Ibid., 498–9.

20. Ibid., 499.

21. Ibid., 33: 467–9.

22. Ibid., 37: 393; Ibid., 39: 7, 8, 10, 21, 53, 60, 121–2, 408, 412, 413, 423, 436, 442, 444, 450, 454, 455, 460, 483; the first act was reprinted in the *Maryland Gazette,* 6–13 April 1733.

23. *Archives,* 39: 483–4.

24. Earle, 85; *Maryland Gazette,* 27 January 1747 and 19 September 1754. Archaeological evidence that Patuxent iron reached Europe was discovered during an underwater excavation of the French warship *Marchault,* sunk in Canadian waters during the Seven Years War. Iron ballast pigs bearing the imprint "Patuxent" were recovered in quantities. A similar sample was recovered from the river at Nottingham by a member of the Prince George's County Historical Society. A sample from the *Marchault* excavation is on display at the Calvert Marine Museum, Solomons, Maryland. The Nottingham sample is privately owned.

25. Mary Anne Tolzman, "Case Studies Of Decline In Southern Prince George's County, Maryland: The Quiet Death of Charlestown, Queen Anne, and Nottingham," typescript photocopy (29 April 1975), Calvert Marine Museum, Solomons, Md., 10; Arthur Pierce Middleton, *Tobacco Coast: A Maritime History of the Chesapeake Bay in the Colonial Era* (Newport News, Va.: The Mariners' Museum, 1953), 86.

26. "Extracts from Account and Letter Books of Dr. Charles Carroll of Annapolis," *Maryland Historical Magazine* 20, no. 3 (September 1925): 269. Satherwhite is identified as commander of *Annapolis* in *Maryland Historical Magazine* 20, no. 2 (June 1925): 174.

27. Anne Arundel County, 1B-5: 14; Earle, 153.

28. *Maryland Gazette,* 6 September 1745. William Murdock served his county and state often as both an elected official and as a citizen. "Old Fields" is believed to have been part of his Padworth estate in a section of the county called "the Forest." Murdock's home, also known as Padworth, survived as a derelict until at least 1912 but eventually became a total ruin. Part of the property is occupied by a 4-H Center and the land is now owned by the Maryland National Capital Park and Planning Commission. *Prince George's Enquirer,* 22 March 1912. See also Heinton for the contributions of William Murdock.

29. *Maryland Gazette,* 4 November 1754.

30. Ibid., 12 and 18 September 1755.

31. Ibid., 28 August 1751, 9 April 1752, 16 April 1752.

32. Ibid., 2 November 1748.

33. Ibid., 15 November 1749. Brogden died 1 November 1770 after a long illness. Ibid., 8 November 1750.

34. Ibid., 21 April 1747, 26 May 1747, 15 December 1751, 2 March 1758.

35. Ibid., 29 August 1750, 21 February 1754.

36. Hienton, 134.

37. *Archives,* 44: 608, 610.

38. Tolzman, 17.

39. *Archives,* 46: 470; *Maryland Gazette,* 6 June 1750.

40. *Maryland Gazette*, 23 January 1751. The Prince George's County Court record of 26 November 1751 mentions that Dr. John Hamilton presented a bill for the treatment of Mary Hall, it having been necessary for him to make one round trip via by Queen Anne's Bridge to do so. Van Horn, 92.

41. Anne Arundel County, 1SB-3: 44; Earle, 153; Hienton, 134; Anne Arundel County, IMB-2: 2–3, 240.

42. Reverend Andrew Burnaby, *Travels Through the Middle Settlements of North America, 1759 and 1760. With Observations on the State of the Colonies* (Ithaca: Cornell University Press, 1976: reprint of 1775), 46, 51.

43. *Maryland Gazette,* 26 June 1751.

44. Ibid., 24 May 1756. In June 1758 Hamilton imported goods from London aboard the ship *Russell,* commanded by Captain John Anderson. The following year Hamilton died. On 18 October 1759, his widow, Martha Hamilton, serving as administratrix of his estate, called for all those indebted to make payments to David Crauford at Queen Anne's Town. Ibid., 8 June 1758, 18 October 1759.

45. Ibid., 26 April 1764; Hienton, 126.

46. *Maryland Gazette,* 19 July 1759. West employed the *Wilson* the following year and advertised goods from the ship for sale at Upper Marlboro, Queen Anne's Town, Pig Point and St. Leonard's Creek on Patuxent River; Piscataway, Rock Creek, Broad Creek, Bladensburg, and Georgetown on Potomac River; Elk Ridge Landing on Potapsco River; and Frederick on the colony frontier. It is thus unclear if the vessel actually visited the Patuxent or precisely where she unloaded. In 1761 West advertised goods from London brought aboard the *Wilson Frigate* for sale at Queen Anne's Town, Captain Judson Coolidge. Ibid., 19 June 1760, 12 April 1761.

47. Ibid., 26 June 1760, 4 June 1761.

48. Hienton, 126–7; *Maryland Gazette,* 27 August 1761. In 1769 West would be appointed deputy postmaster in Upper Marlboro and would later play a significant role in organizing the county defenses during the Revolution.

49. Van Horn, 163–4.

50. Ibid., 113, 115, 126, 132; *Maryland Gazette,* 2 July 1752.

51. Van Horn, 100; *Archives,* 58: 450, 453.

52. *Archives,* 56: 410; *Calendar of Maryland State Papers: No. 1 The Black Book* (Annapolis, Md.: The Hall of Records Commission, 1943), 163, no. 1122.

53. *Maryland Gazette,* 31 May 1770.

54. Ibid., 12 April 1770.

55. Ibid., 26 April 1770.

56. Van Horn, 141–2.

57. Ibid., 140; John C. Fitzpatrick, ed., *Diaries of George Washington, 1748–1799,* 4 vols., (Published for the Mount Vernon Ladies' Association of the Union, Boston and New York: Houghton Mifflin, 1925), 2: 162.

58. *Maryland Gazette,* 15 and 29 December 1774.

59. *The Bowie Blade-News,* 3 July 1997; Hazelwood, Prince George's County, Maryland: Architectural Preservation Study (Prepared by the University of Maryland School of Architecture, Problems and Methods of Architectural Preservation, Spring 1986), 8; Prince George's County Historic Sites Summary Sheet, Prince George's County Survey, 74B-13, Hazelwood. File Copy. Maryland National Capital Park and Planning Commission, Riverdale, Md.

60. Hienton, 179, 181, 183; Rieman Steuart, *A History of the Maryland Line in the Revolutionary War 1775–1783* (Towson, Md.: Society of the Cincinnati of Maryland, 1969), 5, 7, 15, 17, 106.

61. *The Bowie Blade-News*, 3 July 1997.

62. Ibid.

63. *Archives,* 16: 368–9.

64. Papenfuse, 74. On 25 August 1778, Thomas Rose and Alexander Burrell petitioned to operate an ordinary in Queen Anne's Town. On 27 August 1782, Burrell again sought another license. In September 1782, he was again authorized to maintain an ordinary, Rose having dropped from the picture. The following year, in August 1783, the court authorized John Ijams and Burrell to operate ordinaries. On 25 September Maureen Duvall applied, as did John Reigall on 23 June 1788. In 1795 Benjamin Hodges received a license to operate a retail liquor business in town. Van Horn, 173, 175, 190, 200, 205, 222.

65. *Maryland Gazette,* 31 October 1782; *Prince George's Journal,* 11 August 1988.

66. *The Bowie Blade-News,* 3 July 1997; Basil H. Brune, "Tobacco Landings and the Tobacco Marketing System in the Patuxent River Basin, 1730's–1830's," (Unpublished master's thesis, University of Maryland, College Park, Md., 1972), 62, 66; Papenfuse, 170; Tolzman, 19.

67. *Maryland Gazette,* 7 October 1790; Papenfuse, 221; Tolzman, 10.

68. Van Horn, 224, 242.

69. *Aspects of the History of Maryland and Prince George's County,* (Upper Marlboro, Md.: Board of Education, Prince George's County, 1967, rev. ed.), 58–61.

70. Prince George's County Tax Assessment List, 1800; Tolzman, 12.

71. Hazelwood, 10–4; Lansdale was buried in the family cemetery at a location near modern Route 197 and Northview Avenue in Bowie. The site was rediscovered when real estate developer William Levitt bought the old Belaire estate, approximately 3,800 acres, in 1957. The grave was situated on a site destined to become part of Belair Village. A clipping from a 1968 article in the *Enquirer-Gazette* notes the hilltop site was guarded by a hundred-year-old oak tree and the writer worried that the future of the historical grave, enclosed in a rough wood and wire fence, was questionable. It was proposed that ITT, which had acquired Levitt Inc., developers of the land, make it into a park, but it was never done. Originally the grave site was part of an estate known as Enfield Chase and was to have remained a grave site in perpetuity. The original gravestone was smashed by vandals and is now kept in the Anderson House of the Society of the Cincinnati in Washington, D.C.

72. Van Horn, 230. Duckett, who had served on the county Committee of Observation in 1775, died in 1801. Other prominent citizens were William Wells and Thomas Hodges, the state inspectors charged with management of the tobacco inspection at the town warehouse. Wells had earlier served as a member of the county court. It was his duty to report yearly to the county Levy Court on the taxes produced by the inspection operation. Ibid., 245, 246, 247.

73. Ibid., 236; *Maryland Gazette,* 30 March 1804. In 1807, the two inspectors were ordered to pay £100.14 to the County Almshouse.

74. Acts of the General Assembly 1805, Chapter 91, in Van Horn, 242; Susan G. Pearl, "Early Towns in Prince George's County, 1637–1787," file photocopy, Maryland National Capital Park and Planning Commission, Riverdale, Md., 3.

75. Lewis C. Gottchalk, "Effects of Soil Erosion on Navigation in the Upper Chesapeake," *Geographical Review* 35, 1945; Van Horn, 246–7.

76. Van Horn, 257.

77. Joshua Barney to William Jones, 1 August 1814, Navy Letters, RG 45, M 124, R 64, National Archives, Washington, D.C.

78. Ibid.

79. George Robert Gleig, *A Narrative of the Campaigns of the British Army, at Washington, Baltimore, and New Orleans, under the Generals Ross, Packenham, & Lambert, in the Years 1814 and 1815 With Some Account of the Countries Visited* (Philadelphia: M. Carey & Sons, 1821), 104–5; William Jones to Captain Joshua Barney, 20 August 1814, Barney Papers, Dreer Collection, Pennsylvania Historical Society; Barney to Jones, 3 January 1815, Navy Let-

ters, RG 45, M 124, R 41), National Archives, Washington, D.C.; Admiral Sir George Cockburn to Admiral Alexander Cochrane, 22 August 1814, Cockburn Papers, Vol. 24, Manuscript Division, Library of Congress, Washington, D.C.; Barney to Jones, 24 March and 17 April 1815, Navy Letters, RG 45, M 124, R 41 and R 70; Donald Shomette, *Flotilla: Battle for the Patuxent* (Solomons, Maryland: Calvert Marine Museum Press, 1981), 166–86.

80. Undated and unannotated newspaper entry [ca. 26 August 1814], photocopy, Donald G. Shomette Collection, Dunkirk, Md.

81. John Weems to William Jones, 7 September and 10 October 1814, Navy Letters, RG 45, M 124, R 40.

82. Record of payment to Christopher Lambert, 11 March 1815, James Beatty Papers, Accounts of the Fourth Auditor of the United States, National Archives, Washington, D.C.

83. Van Horn, 267, 274, 275.

84. Ibid., 277.

85. Ibid., 282.

86. Ibid., 275, 286.

87. Maryland Acts of Assembly, 1847, Chapter 73; Tolzman, 21.

88. Van Horn, 327.

89. *Martenet's Map of Prince George's County Maryland;* (Baltimore: Simon J. Martenet, 1861), Library of Congress, Washington, D.C.; Hazelwood, 3–16.

90. Maryland Acts of General Assembly, Chapter 40, in Van Horn, 354.

91. Maryland Acts of General Assembly 1865, Chapter 121.

92. Tolzman, 21; *Prince George's Journal,* 11 August 1988.

93. "Queen Anne's District No. 7," G. M. Hopkins, *Atlas of Fifteen Miles Around Washington Including the County of Prince George Maryland* (Philadelphia: G. M. Hopkins, 1878).

94. Harry Brooke Watkins Interview, Hardesty, Md., 21 March 1998, audio tape, Fred Tutman Collection, Hardesty, Md.

95. *Prince George's Journal,* 11 August 1988. Harry Brooke Watkins indicated that his father assumed the post of teacher at Mt. Nebo before taking on the clerk's position, although the doctor's obituary in the *Enquirer-Gazette,* 10 January 1930, stated the opposite.

96. Watkins interview.

97. Maryland Historical Trust State Historic Sites Inventory Form. Survey No. P.G.#74B-12, 1–2; Watkins interview.

98. Watkins interview. Sturgeon were harvested commercially in the tidewater until the second decade of the twentieth century primarily for

their roe, which was transformed into caviar. In 1880, more than 108,000 sturgeon were caught on the James River, 288,000 on the Potomac, and 17,700 on the Rappahannock. There is no report of commercial sturgeon fisheries on the Patuxent. See Larry S. Chowning, *Harvesting the Chesapeake: Tools & Traditions* (Centreville, Md.: Tidewater Publishers, 1990), 3–4, for review of sturgeon fishing in the Chesapeake tidewater.

99. Watkins interview.
100. Ibid.
101. Ibid.
102. Ibid.
103. Ibid.
104. Ibid.
105. Ibid.; *Laurel Leader,* 6 July 1906.
106. *Laurel Leader,* 19 October 1906; Watkins interview.
107. The will of Edwin P. Gibbs was probated by the Orphans Court for Prince George's County and recorded in Wills Record W.A.M. Book 1, f. 727, Adm. 2666, Prince George's County Court, Upper Marlboro, Md.
108. "The History of Mt. Nebo A.M.E. Church," typescript photocopy, Fred Tutman Collection, Hardesty, Md.
109. Ibid.
110. Ibid.
111. Ibid.
112. Ibid.
113. *Prince George's Journal,* 11 August 1988.
114. *Enquirer-Gazette,* 10 January 1930.
115. Ibid.
116. Prince George's County Court Records, 37: 407; 468: 65, 67; 482: 445; Anne Arundel County, 154: 564. Smith, unfortunately, conducted gravel mining operations on large sections of his property, obliterating considerable evidence of the site's early inhabitants.
117. Maryland State Planning Commission, *Gazette of Maryland* (1941), 93; Watkins interview; Prince George's County, 560: 120.
118. Maryland Historical Trust State Historic Sites Inventory Form. Survey No. P.G.#74B-12, 1–2.
119. [Hazelwood] Lease Agreement 1 249-5006, photocopy, Maryland National Capital Park and Planning Commission, Riverdale, Maryland. In 1998, the Hazelwood Preservation Society, a nonprofit organization, was formed to raise funds to help in the preservation of the Hazelwood Estate, when funds from state and county agencies dried up. Headed by Dorothy Smith, daughter of J. Paul Smith and one of the last surviving private residents to live in the grand old manor house, the society seeks to stabi-

lize and preserve the venerable old building and its surrounding structures.

CHAPTER 7: PORT TOBACCO

1. Margaret Brown Klapthor and Paul Dennis Brown, *The History of Charles County, Maryland* (La Plata, Md.: Charles County Tercentenary, Inc., 1958), 3–5; Kim R. Kihl, *Port Tobacco: A Transformed Community* (Baltimore: Maclay & Associates, 1982), 17; John Smith, *The Generall Historie of Virginia, New-England, and the Summer Isles* (London: Printed I. D. and I. J. for Michael Sparkes, 1624), 49; Clayton C. Hall, *Narratives of Early Maryland 1633–1684* (New York: Barnes and Noble, 1910), 136, n.1; Frederick Tilp, *This Was Potomac River* (Alexandria, Va.: privately published, 1978), 314. For additional discussion on the evolution of the name Port Tobacco see Hamill Kenny, *The Placenames of Maryland: Their Origins and Meaning* (Baltimore: Museum and Library of Maryland History, Maryland Historical Society, 1984), 203.
2. Henry Fleet, "A Brief Journal of a Voyage made in the Bark Warwick to Virginia and other parts of America," *The Founders of Maryland,* Edward D. Neill, ed. (Albany: Joel Munsell, 1876), 29, 32, 35.
3. Andrew White, *Fund Publication, No. 1. Narrative of a Voyage to Maryland,* E. A. Dalrymple, ed. (Baltimore: John Murphy & Co., 1874), 82–3. The 1635 map *Nova Terrae-Mariae tabula* by Jerome Hawley and John Lewyn, in the John Work Garrett Library, Johns Hopkins University, places the village of the Potobacs on the west side of the creek.
4. Edwin M. Beitzell. *The Jesuit Missions of St. Mary's County, Maryland* (Abell, Md.; privately printed, 1960), 15.
5. *Archives,* 3: 489.
6. Ibid., 293, 489; Klapthor and Brown, 7; William J. Graham, *The Indians of Port Tobacco River, Maryland and Their Burial Places.* (Washington, D.C.: privately printed, 1935), 7.
7. Kihl, 21–2.
8. Ethel Roby Hayden, "Port Tobacco, Lost Town of Maryland," *Maryland Historical Magazine* 40, no. 4 (December, 1945): 262.
9. Charles Francis Stein, *A History of Calvert County, Maryland* (Baltimore: privately published, 1976), 18–9
10. *Archives,* 41: 87.
11. Ibid., 53: 67; Hayden, 263, 264; Kihl, 23; *Archives,* 5: 31.
12. Chapel Point and Cedar Neck were patents taken up by Thomas Matthews, a Charles County planter and lay trustee for the Jesuits, and Ralph

Crouch, a Jesuit lay brother. The entire patent was about 4,000 acres, on 500 acres of which St. Thomas was located. Klapthor and Brown, 34.

13. Ibid., 40.

14. "Port Tobacco Parish," *Maryland Historical Magazine* 22, no. 3 (September 1927): 303; Hayden, 263; Klapthor and Brown, 38.

15. It is possible that the grave of Daniel of St. Thomas Jenifer, a signer of the Constitution, which has thus far been lost to history, lies in the old Christ Church burying grounds. Lending circumstantial substance to the possibility is the fact that the Jenifer family plantation was but two miles distant from the town. The family was of the Episcopalian faith and most likely attended the town church, making it entirely possible that they would have been buried in the churchyard.

16. Hayden, 264.

17. *Archives*, 53: 1, et seq.; Klapthor and Brown, 16.

18. *Archives*, 53: 432; Klapthor and Brown, 16.

19. Klapthor and Brown, 17–21; Morris L. Radoff, *The County Courthouses and Records of Maryland. Part One: The Courthouses* (Annapolis, Md.: Hall of Records Commission, State of Maryland, 1960), 63, n. 11.

20. *Archives*, 8: 24–6; 60: 615–8; Radoff, *The County Courthouses and Records of Maryland. Part One*, 65, 67

21. See *Archives*, 17: 191, for Lynes's full petition for redress.

22. Charles County Records, vol. 5, no. 1, 1696–1698, A: 277.

23. *Archives*, 7: 460, 609. The commissioners selected for Charles County were Col. William Chandler, Edward Pye, Thomas Burford, Henry Adams, Ignatious Causeene, Capt. James Neall, Capt. Humphrey Warren, John Wheller, Capt. William Barton, Robert Henley, James Tyre, John Stone, James Smallwood, John Bayne, Joseph Cornall, William Smith, John Gouge, Henry Hawkins, John Reddish, Robert Pyne, John Munn, James Wheller, Edward Sanders, Edward Mings. Ibid., 611.

24. Ibid., 13: 29, 30, 89, 90; 5: 499–502.

25. Ibid., 17: 358.

26. Ibid., 403–7.

27. Ibid., 407.

28. Ibid., 5: 503.

29. *Calendar of Maryland State Papers: No. 1 The Black Book* (Annapolis, Md.: The Hall of Records Commission, 1943), 2, no. 6; Kihl, 24.

30. *Archives*, 26: p. 636–7, 645.

31. Ibid., 637.

32. Klapthor and Brown, 40, 43; *Archives*, 35: 436; 36: 92. For the first fifty years, Port Tobacco

Parish was under joint rectorship with Durham Parish. In 1729 the parish was redefined by an act and contained "all the remaining Part of the West Side of Port-Tobacco Hundred, that is not allotted to Durham, with the Hundred on the East Side of Port-Tobacco Creek; and such Part of the East and West Hundreds of Newport, as may be divided therefrom by a Line drawn from an Oak standing on Zachia Swamp, just below Henry Jameson's, to the Head of a Branch called the Hog-House Branch, including William Newman's Plantation; and from thence to the dividing Line between Charles and St. Mary's County." *Archives*, 36: 468.

33. *Archives*, 36: 92–4. Unfortunately the specifications for the courthouse building have been lost, but from the cost it is assumed to have been constructed of brick. Radoff, *The County Courthouses and Records of Maryland. Part One*, 69.

34. *Archives*, 38: 456–9; Kihl, 23; Klapthor and Brown, 46.

35. Jean B. Lee, *The Price of Nationhood: The American Revolution in Charles County* (New York: W.W. Norton & Company, 1994), 34; Hayden, 264–5.

36. *Maryland Gazette*, 29 June 1748.

37. Klapthor and Brown, 47; Hayden, 267; "Colonial Militia," *Maryland Historical Magazine* 6, no. 1 (March 1911): 54.

38. Klapthor and Brown, 49–50; *Maryland Gazette*, 2 June 1747; Lee, 34; Hayden, 268; "Correspondence of Governor Horatio Sharpe," *Maryland Historical Magazine* 12, no. 4 (December 1917): 371.

39. Lee, 34; *Archives*, 44: 608, 610.

40. *Maryland Gazette*, 10 October 1750, 18 June 1752, 27 August 1752. Hayden, 267, notes that there is disagreement as to whether the performance was carried out by the original company or was done under the notable direction of actor/manager Thomas Keane and drawn from the original Virginia group overseen by William Hallam. William Dunlap, in *A History of the American Theatre*, 2 vols., (London: Benther, 1833) states that it was Hallam's original company that played Port Tobacco, but Arthur Hornblow, in his own *History of the American Theatre from Its Beginning to the Present Time* (Philadelphia: J. B. Lippincott Company, 1919) states that this was a mistake and that the Keane Company played in the town.

41. *Maryland Gazette*, 26 June 1751, states William Hanson served as register. See reference to Honyman in Hayden, 268.

42. *Archives*, 65: index: *Organist*.; Ibid., 50: 527.

43. Lee, 34; *Maryland Gazette*, 1 July 1760, 25 June 1761, 1 October 1761.

44. *Maryland Gazette,* 18 January 1759. In 1757 the sale of various goods from the damaged ship *Industry,* Captain John Moore, was also held in the town for the benefit of the insurers. Ibid., 7 April 1757.

45. Ibid., 26 April 1754, 31 July 1760; Philip Vickers Fithian, *The Journal and Letters of Philip Vickers Fithian: A Plantation Tutor of The Old Dominion 1773–1774,* Hunter Dickinson Farish, ed., (Williamsburg, Va.: Colonial Williamsburg, Incorporated, 1965), 90.

46. Fithian, 97, 109; Nicholas Cresswell, *The Journal of Nicholas Cresswell, 1774–1777* (New York: Dial Press, 1924), 19–20.

47. For a block diagram showing the original and present conditions of Port Tobacco Creek as the result of erosion and silting see Ralph H. Brown, *Historical Geography of the United States* (New York: Harcourt Brace, 1948), 133.

48. Glassford and Company Papers, Box 21, 56–62, Manuscript Division, Library of Congress, Washington, D.C.; Lee, 35.

49. *Port Tobacco Times,* 8 August 1873.

50. Lee, 35; *Archives,* 63: 12.

51. *Port Tobacco Times,* 8 August 1873.

52. Lee, 110.

53. Klapthor and Brown, 51.

54. *Maryland Gazette,* 16 June 1774, 24 November 1774; Klapthor and Brown, 52–3.

55. Klapthor and Brown, 54–5; Cresswell, 42, 57.

56. William Fitzhugh to James Russell, January 6 [1775], Bundle 6, Russell Papers, Virginia Colonial Records Project, Williamsburg Foundation Library, Williamsburg, Va.

57. Lee, 117–8.

58. Hayden, 268; Klapthor and Brown, 55. For further account by Honyman, see Robert Honyman, *Colonial Panorama 1775: Dr. Robert Honyman's Journal for March and April,* Philip Padelford, ed. (San Marino, Calif.: Huntington Library, 1939).

59. *Maryland Gazette,* 15 June 1775.

60. *Archives,* 11: 5, 14, 35–7.

61. Lee, 127.

62. *Maryland Gazette,* 19 October 1775.

63. Klapthor and Brown, 56.

64. *Naval Documents of the American Revolution,* 10 vols., (Washington, D.C.: U.S. Navy, Naval Historical Center, 1964–1996), 4: 414, 512.

65. Ibid., 1344.

66. *Archives,* 45: 383; "Raid of British Barges," *Maryland Historical Magazine* 4, no. 4 (December 1909): 381. For examples of the town's role in providing troop and logistical support during the Revolution see *Archives,* 43: 155; and 45: 40, 89, 368–9.

67. Hayden, 269–70.

68. Lee, 224.

69. *Maryland Gazette,* 28 August 1783.

70. J. F. D. Smythe, *A Tour of the United States of America,* 2 vols. (London: G. Robinson, J. Robson, and J. Sewell, 1784) 2: 180.

71. Lee, 225; Thomas Stone to Daniel St. Thomas Jenifer, 9 December 1783, Louis Bamberger Autograph Collection, New Jersey Historical Society, Newark, N.J.

72. Edward C. Papenfuse, *In Pursuit of Profit: The Annapolis Merchants in the Era of the American Revolution 1763–1805* (Baltimore: Johns Hopkins University Press, 1975), 174, 198–9.

73. For a comprehensive review of the Port Tobacco riots, see Lee, 232–9.

74. Klapthor and Brown, 75–6; Kihl, 27. See also John T. Howard, "The Doctors Gustavus Brown," in *Annals of Medical History* 9 (September 1937), for a history of the surgeon who has been incorrectly blamed for bleeding Washington to death during his final illness.

75. Reverend Laurence J. Kelley, S.J., *A Carmelite Shrine in Maryland* (Privately printed: 1957), 1.

76. *Archives,* 50: 199.

77. Kelley, 1–4, 5.

78. Isaac Weld, Jr., *Travels through the States of America and the Provinces of Upper and Lower Canada, During the Years 1795, 1796 and 1797,* 2 vols. (New York: Augustus M. Kelley, 1970, reprint of 1799), 1: 138.

79. Ibid., 138–9.

80. Ibid.; Radoff, *County Courthouses, Part One,* 69.

81. *The Naval War of 1812: A Documentary History,* William S. Dudley, ed., 2 vols. (Washington, D.C.: Naval Historical Center, Department of the Navy, 1985–1992), 2: 383–4.

82. Ibid., 387.

83. In 1882 a bill was introduced in the U.S. House of Representatives by A. G. Chapman of Charles County seeking compensation for the heirs of the owner, John C. Jones, of Montgomery County. *Port Tobacco Times,* 7 April 1882.

84. Radoff, *County Courthouses, Part One,* 69, 71.

85. Klapthor and Brown, 105, 108; John S. Ezell, "The Church Took a Chance," *Maryland Historical Magazine* 43: no. 4 (December 1948): 276; *In a Place called Ivy Springs . . . Near the Pines: The History of St. Paul's Episcopal Church, Piney Parish.* (Waldorf, Md.: September 1992), 6. The silver service was prepared by Louis J. Feuchter in 1905 and was purchased on 31 May 1906. In 1960 it was presented to the State of

Maryland and placed on permanent display in the Maryland State House in Annapolis. Robert H. Burgess, *Louis J. Feuchter: Chesapeake Bay Artist* (Newport News, Va.: The Mariners' Museum, 1976), 9.

86. Klapthor and Brown, 105.

87. Hayden, 272.

88. [Edward P. O'Connell, S.J.], *A Forgotten Village: Bel Alton, Md.,* bound typescript, Calvert Marine Museum, Solomons, Md., 4.

89. *Port Tobacco Times,* 7 August 1845, 17 December 1851, 26 October 1877; Roberta J. Wearmouth, comp., *Abstracts from the Port Tobacco Times and Charles County Advertiser,* 5 vols. (Bowie: Md.: Heritage Books, 1990), 1: vii–viii.

90. Hayden, 272, refers to the hotel only in its 1894 incarnation; *Port Tobacco Times,* 13 August 1868.

91. *Port Tobacco Times,* 7 August 1845, 27 August 1851, 3 September 1851, 23 June 1852, 19 November 1857.

92. Ibid., 7 August 1845, 9 October 1845, 24 June 1847, 17 February 1848, 12 May 1852, 24 March 1853, 11 November 1853, 17 April 1856, 10 November 1857, 19 November 1857, 7 January 1858, 11 February 1858, 29 July 1858, 13 August 1858, 26 August 1858, 21 June 1860, 20 February 1862, 5 June 1862, 6 May 1870, 19 August 1870, 23 September 1870, 14 October 1870, 6 September 1872, 24 April 1873, 8 January 1875, 26 February 1875, 23 July 1875.

93. Ibid., 7 August 1845, 1 July 1847, 12 May 1853, 13 January 1855, 26 July 1855, 13 December 1855, 8 October 1857, 7 January 1858, 14 January 1858, 11 February 1858, 12 August 1858, 24 May 1860, 26 June 1862.

94. Ibid., 5 February 1851, 18 June 1851, 20 January 1853, 9 March 1854, 11 January 1855, 13 December 1855, 7 January 1858.

95. Ibid., 23 March 1848, 13 January 1853, 11 January 1855.

96. Klapthor and Brown, 116; *Port Tobacco Times,* 5 May 1852, 11 August 1853, 5 April 1855, 17 September 1868.

97. *Port Tobacco Times,* 12 October 1854, 1 May 1856, 10 December 1857, 26 July 1860, 7 May 1868, 12 February 1869, 20 May 1870, 24 April 1873, 3 November 1876, 28 April 1880, 20 January 1882.

98. Hayden, 273.

99. *Port Tobacco Times,* 10 June 1847, 8 June 1848, 22 June 1848, 6 July 1848, 29 May 1850, 3 July 1850, 23 June 1852, 2 December 1852, 17 February 1853, 12 May 1853, 1 April 1858, 7 June 1858.

100. Klapthor and Brown, 111; *Port Tobacco Times,* 15 June 1848, 26 October 1848, 16 November 1848; Hayden, 273.

101. Hayden, 276; Klapthor and Brown, 113; *Port Tobacco Times,* 17 June 1847, 11 May 1854.

102. *Port Tobacco Times,* 28 August 1845, 27 May 1847, 4 August 1852, 29 September 1852, 11 August 1853, 23 August 1855, 16 July 1857.

103. Ibid., 23 June 1852.

104. Klapthor and Brown, 115; *Port Tobacco Times,* 20 July 1854, 21 December 1854, 7 January 1858.

105. *A new Map of Maryland and Delaware, with their Canals, Roads & Distances* (Thomas Coperthwaite & Co., 1850), Maryland Hall of Records, Annapolis, Md.; *Port Tobacco Times,* 24 March 1853, 22 September 1853, 14 December 1854; Klapthor and Brown, 117.

106. *National Intelligencer and Washington Advertiser,* 12 April 1802; Klapthor and Brown, 117.

107. *Port Tobacco Times,* 22 January 1851.

108. Ibid., 10 June 1847, 18 May 1848, 24 September 1857.

109. Ibid., 15 January 1851, 7 January 1852, 21 January 1852, 12 May 1853, 24 August 1854, 12 October 1854, 2 November 1854.

110. Klapthor and Brown, 115.

111. *Port Tobacco Times,* 14 September 1854.

112. Ibid., 21 September 1854, 29 April 1881, 1 July 1881.

113. Ibid., 8 June 1848, 7 January 1852, 24 August 1854, 21 September 1854, 10 November 1857, 21 November 1861.

114. Ibid., 28 January 1858, 6 May 1858; Kihl, 30.

115. *Port Tobacco Times,* 28 October 1858, 24 May 1860.

116. Ibid., 28 January 1858, 24 May 1860, 12 July 1860.

117. Ibid., 7 August 1845, 3 January 1856, 12 March 1857.

118. *Maryland Gazette,* 10 July 1755; *Port Tobacco Times,* 13 December 1855.

119. *Port Tobacco Times,* 28 August 1845, 26 March 1846.

120. Ibid., 7 August 1845, 14 August 1845, 19 February 1846.

121. Ibid., 18 August 1852.

122. Ibid., 11 December 1856.

123. Ibid., 15 June 1883.

124. Ibid., 10 May 1855, 3 May 1860, 21 June 1860.

125. Ibid., 20 December 1860, 27 December 1860.

126. O'Connell, 7; Klapthor and Brown, 122.

127. *Port Tobacco Times,* 3 January 1861, 24 January 1861. Samuel Cox served on several grand and petit juries, and he was a county leader in the Whig Party. He headed citizens patrols that policed the county roads and was president of the Charles County Jockey Club. In 1854, he was captain of Company I of the First Militia Regiment and four years later was captain of a company of mounted volunteers. In April 1861, the mounted volunteers prepared to support the Confederacy but upon occupation of the county, they were disbanded. William A. Tidwell, "Charles County: Confederate Cauldron," *Maryland Historical Magazine* 91, no. 1 (Spring 1996): 19.

128. *War of the Rebellion: Official Records of the Union and Confederate Armies,* Series 1, (Washington, D.C.: Government Printing Office, 1880–1901), 4, 524; *Port Tobacco Times,* 20 June 1861.

129. *Port Tobacco Times,* 20 June 1861; Mary Alice Wills, *The Confederate Blockade of Washington, D.C. 1861–1862* (Parson, West Va.: McClain Printing Company, 1975), 33–45; *War of the Rebellion,* Series 1, vol. 4, 516–8.

130. *Port Tobacco Times,* 18 July 1861.

131. Eric Mills, *Chesapeake Bay in the Civil War* (Centreville, Md.: Tidewater Publishers, 1996), 79.

132. *War of the Rebellion,* Series 1, vol. 4, 662–3.

133. Ibid., 639–40.

134. *The Planters Advocate and Southern Maryland Advertiser,* Upper Marlboro, Md., 9 October 1861.

135. Ibid.

136. Ibid.; *Port Tobacco Times,* 31 October 1861.

137. *Port Tobacco Times,* 31 October 1861, 21 November 1861; *In a Place called Ivy Springs,* 9.

138. *Port Tobacco Times,* 24 October 1861.

139. Ibid., 28 November 1861, 19 December 1861, 19 June 1862.

140. Ibid., 19 December 1861.

141. General L. C. Baker, *The History of the Secret Service,* Philadelphia, 1867, excerpt reprinted in Klapthor and Brown, 124.

142. *Port Tobacco Times,* 5 December 1861, 23 January 1862.

143. Klapthor and Brown, 124–6.

144. *Port Tobacco Times,* 26 June 1862; Klapthor and Brown, 128.

145. *In a Place called Ivy Springs,* 8–9.

146. Mills, 265.

147. Klapthor and Brown, 128, 129; Kihl, 29–30.

148. Klapthor and Brown, 130.

149. *Port Tobacco Times,* 12 March 1857.

150. Klapthor and Brown, 130–1.

151. Ibid., 131–2. Thomas A. Jones was a farmer and fisherman who worked for Samuel Cox in the county Whig Party and served as constable of the second election district. He assisted Major William Norris in crossing the Potomac in the early months of the war. Norris became chief of the Signal and Secret Service Bureau of the Confederate War Department. Jones was once captured and imprisoned but released in 1862. Tidwell, 20, 21.

152. Klapthor and Brown, 132.

153. Ibid., 134–5; J. Thomas Scharf, *A History of Maryland: From the Earliest Period to the Present Day* (Detroit: Gale, 1967, reprint of 1879), 656–7.

154. Klapthor and Brown, 135. From 1861 through 1865 the Union Army occupied Chapel Point. C. J. Lancaster, the Jesuit farm manager, later presented the War Department with a list of damages incurred during the occupation, along with a bill totaling $31,416. The buildings had been occupied by 900 cavalrymen, then by Maulsby's Brigade, Colonel Greshams's Legion and, after the assassination of Lincoln, by Sheridan's Cavalry, which did the most damage. *A Forgotten Village: Bel Alton, Md.,* 8.

155. *Port Tobacco Times,* 17 September 1880.

156. Richard Walsh and William Lloyd Fox, eds., *Maryland: A History, 1632–1974* (Baltimore: Maryland Historical Society, 1974), 193, 217–8.

157. Wearmouth, 2: 1; John M. Wearmouth, *Baltimore and Potomac Railroad: The Pope's Creek Branch* (Baltimore, Md.: National Railways Historical Society, 1986), 1.

158. Herbert H. Harwood, Jr., *Impossible Challenge: The Baltimore and Ohio Railroad* (Baltimore, Md.: Barnard, Roberts and Company, Inc., 1979), 219–20.

159. Ibid., 228–9.

160. John F. Stover, *History of the Baltimore and Ohio Railroad* (West Lafayette, Ind.: Purdue University Press, 1987), 144.

161. Ibid.

162. *Port Tobacco Times,* 30 April 1869, 6 May 1870, 20 May 1870, 29 July 1870, 16 December 1870, 14 April 1871; Wearmouth, *Baltimore and Potomac Railroad,* 3.

163. *Abstracts from the Port Tobacco Times,* 1–2; Wearmouth, *Baltimore and Potomac Railroad,* 4.

164. *Port Tobacco Times,* 27 December 1872, 1 January 1873, 14 February 1873; Wearmouth, *Baltimore and Potomac Railroad,* 8; Harwood, 231.

165. *Port Tobacco Times,* 21 February 1873, 28 March 1873.

166. Ibid., 14 February 1873, 28 March 1873, 29 May 1873, 5 June 1873, 1 August 1873.
167. Ibid., 8 August 1873.
168. Ibid., 19 August 1870, 28 June 1872, 1 September 1876, 13 February 1880, 15 August 1884.
169. Ibid., 7 January 1876, 21 November 1879, 20 August 1880, 20 May 1881, 3 March 1883, 3 October 1884, 5 December 1884.
170. Arthur Pierce Middleton, *Tercentenery Essays Commemorating Anglican Maryland, 1692–1792* (Virginia Beach, Va.: The Donning Company Publishers, 1992), 74.
171. *Port Tobacco Times,* 31 July 1874, 15 August 1875, 20 August 1875, 17 August 1877, 14 September 1883.
172. Ibid., 29 October 1875, 12 November 1875, 23 September 1881; Klapthor and Brown, 112.
173. *Port Tobacco Times,* 13 August 1875, 3 December 1880.
174. Ibid., 1 August 1873.
175. Ibid., 10 April 1873, 4 June 1875, 6 October 1876, 26 October 1877, 20 September 1878; Wearmouth, *Baltimore and Potomac Railroad,* 16.
176. *Port Tobacco Times,* 20 June 1879, 23 November 1879, 11 March 1881, 16 December 1881, 23 December 1881, 2 June 1882, 26 January 1883, 23 May 1884.
177. Ibid., 15 December 1882.
178. Ibid., 23 February 1883, 23 May 1884.
179. Ibid., 1 July 1881, 5 August 1881, 12 August 1881.
180. Ibid., 3 March 1882, 17 March 1882, 19 May 1882.
181. Ibid., 14 July 1882, 2 March 1883; *The Baltimore Sun Almanac, 1883* (Baltimore, Md.: A. S. Abell Co., 1883), 43.
182. *Port Tobacco Times,* 19 September 1879, 1 April 1881, 17 March 1882, 7 December 1883, 25 July 1884.
183. John M. Wearmouth, *La Plata Maryland 1888–1988: 100 Years The Heart of Charles County* (La Plata, Md.: Town of La Plata, 1988), 5; *Maryland Independent,* 24 February 1890.
184. Morris L. Radoff, *The County Courthouses and Records of Maryland. Part One,* 71.
185. *Maryland Independent,* 21 April 1892; Wearmouth, *La Plata,* 6; *Baltimore Sun Almanac, 1893,* 42.
186. Morris L. Radoff, Gust Skordas, and Phebe R. Jacobsen, *The County Courthouses and Records of Maryland. Part Two: The Records* (Annapolis, Md.: Hall of Records Commission, State of Maryland, 1963), 97; Wearmouth, *La Plata,* 6–7; Klapthor and Brown, 42–3.
187. Wearmouth, *La Plata,* 8; *Port Tobacco Times,* 14 July 1893; *The Crescent,* 8 December 1893; *Maryland Independent,* 19 January 1894.

188. Wearmouth, *La Plata,* 7.
189. Klapthor and Brown, 142–3; Hayden, 276.
190. Kihl, 38; Frederick Tilp, *This Was Potomac River* (Alexandria, Va.: privately published, 1978), 224; *Historic Port Tobacco,* (Society for the Restoration of Port Tobacco: n.d.), 4
191. *Historic Port Tobacco,* 4; [John V. Hinkel], *Guide Book Port Tobacco, Charles County, Maryland: Home Tour Edition* (Washington, D.C.: Society for the Restoration of Port Tobacco, 1955), 7. See Kihl, 54–79, for the origins of and conceptual planning for the Society for the Restoration of Port Tobacco.

CHAPTER 8: FRENCHTOWN

1. George Johnston, *History of Cecil County, Maryland, and the Early Settlements Around the Head of Chesapeake Bay and on the Delaware River, with Sketches of Some of the Old Families of Cecil County* (Baltimore: Genealogical Publishing Co., Inc., 1989, reprint of 1881), 40–1.
2. Ibid., 40. The first Thompson Town is not to be confused with another of the same name which was a tract belonging to Walter Hanson, first mentioned in 1759 and located in Port Tobacco Parish, Charles County. *Maryland Gazette,* 8 March 1759.
3. Johnston, 224; *At the Head of the Bay: A Cultural and Architectural History of Cecil County, Maryland,* Pamela James Blumgart, comp. (Crownsville and Elkton, Md.: Maryland Historical Trust and Cecil Historical Trust, Inc., 1996), 62.
4. *Archives,* 19: 281.
5. Johnston, 225.
6. Ibid.; *Archives,* 19: 519, 520; 23: 444.
7. Johnston, 225, states that the church, later referred to as the "old Swedes church," was still standing in Wilmington in 1881.
8. *Archives,* 19: 527, 530.
9. Ibid., 520, 565–6.
10. Ibid., 25: 103, 104, 108; Charles Francis Stein, *A History of Calvert County, Maryland* (Baltimore: privately published, 1976), 453.
11. G[eorge] E. Gifford, *Cecil County Maryland 1608–1850 As Seen by Some Visitors* (Rising Sun, Md.: George E. Gifford Memorial Committee, Calvert School, 1974), 111. St. Mery's supposition that the town was of Acadian origin, a theory accepted by most historians, is either incorrect or St. Mery had his date wrong since the Acadians did not arrive in Maryland until the 1750s, well after the hamlet was already referred to as Frenchtown. The French Labidists, a more likely source for the name, were followers of Jean de Labadie, who treated the observance of the Sabbath as a matter of indifference and who

held that God can and does deceive men. The Labidists were present on the Maryland scene and in Cecil County in the late seventeenth century. See Bartlett B. James, *The Labidists Colony in Maryland* (Baltimore: Johns Hopkins Press, June 1899) for a thorough analysis of the Labidist efforts to colonize in Maryland. See also Me'de'ric-Louis-Elie-Moreau de Saint-Me'ry, *Moreau de St. Me're, American Journey (1739–1798)*, translated and edited by Kenneth Roberts and Anne M. Roberts, introduction by Stewart L. Minns (Garden City, N.Y.: Doubleday, 1947), 82–6; and *Voyage aux Etats-Unis de Unis de l'Amerique, 1793–1798*, Stewart L. Minns, ed. (New York: Yale University Press, 1913); and *Maryland Historical Magazine* 33 (September 1940): 221–40.

12. Johnston, 229.

13. Gifford, 109. Gifford's reprint of St. Mery's trip has been cited as it most readily places his visit in the context of passage through Cecil County.

14. Ibid., 110.

15. Ibid.

16. Ibid., 110–1.

17. Ibid.

18. Ibid. 112.

19. Ibid.

20. Davis, John. *Personal Adventures and Travels of Four Years and a Half in the United States of America during 1798, 1799, 1800, 1801 and 1802.* (London: 1817, reprint of 1803), 60, 77–8. For a biographical account of Davis, see *John Davis, The First Settlers of Virginia, an Historical Novel* (New York: I. Riley and Co., 1806), with "A Memoir of the Author," 275–84. See also Thelma Louise Kellogg, *The Life and Works of John Davis, 1774–1853* (Orono, Maine: University of Maine Studies, 1924) Series 2, no. 1.

21. "Rough Sketch of Frenchtown," 1806, in Benjamin Henry Latrobe Sketchbook IX-3, Maryland Historical Society, Baltimore, Md.; Benjamin Henry Latrobe, "Section of the Northern Course of the Canal from the Tide in the Elk at Frenchtown to the fork in Mr. Rudolph's Swamp," 1803, Geography and Map Division, Library of Congress, Washington, D.C.

22. David C. Holly, *Chesapeake Steamboats: Vanished Fleets* (Centreville, Md.: Tidewater Publishers, 1994), 12. Johnston, 405, states that the McDonald-Henderson Line commenced operations in 1806–1807.

23. Johnston, 405–6.

24. Albert Cook Myers, ed., *Narratives of Early Pennsylvania, West New Jersey, and Delaware* (New York: Barnes and Noble, 1912), 139–40;

Delaware: A Guide to the First State, compiled and written by the Federal Writers' Project of the Works Progress Administration for the State of Delaware (New York: Hastings House, 1955, rev. ed.), 335–6.

25. Joshua Gilpin, *A Memoir of the Rise, Progress, and Present State of the Chesapeake and Delaware Canal, Accompanied with original Documents and Maps* (Wilmington, 1821), Appendix, 1–16; Papers of the Chester River–Duck Creek Survey, Gilpin Papers, Historical Society of Pennsylvania, Philadelphia; Ralph D. Gray, *The National Waterway: A History of the Chesapeake and Delaware Canal 1769–1985* (Urbana, Ill.: University of Illinois Press, 1989), 3–6.

26. Gray, 14–5.

27. Ibid., 17.

28. Latrobe, 1803. "Section of the Northern Course."

29. Johnston, 405–6.

30. *Daily National Intelligencer,* 9 March 1813.

31. Johnston, 413.

32. Ibid., 416.

33. William M. Marine, *The British Invasion of Maryland 1812–1815.* (Hatboro, Pa.: Tradition Press, 1965, reprint of 1913), 41–2; Johnston, 414.

34. *Mohawk* Log, 28 April 1813, ADM 51/257, Public Record Office, London; Johnston, 414.

35. Ibid.; G. Auchinleck, *History of the War between Great Britain and the United States of America During the Years 1812, 1813 & 1814* (Redwood City, Calif.: Arms & Armour Press and Pendragon House Inc., 1972), 265.

36. William Milbourne James, *The Naval History of Great Britain* (London, 1837), 6: 82; Marine, 43; Johnston, 413; Auchinleck, 265.

37. *American State Papers. Documents, Legislative and Executive, of the Congress of the United States,* vol. 1, *Military Affairs* (Washington: D.C.: 1832–1861), 359; Johnston, 413, 493; Marine, 414. Cockburn reported the American battery was a six-gun affair. Auchinleck, 265.

38. Johnston, 415.

39. Auchinleck, 265; *American State Papers, Military Affairs,* 359; Johnston, 414; Marine, 41, 43; James, 82. Nearly seven decades later, George Johnston sought to conciliate the quick American defeat at Frenchtown by claiming the enemy attacked the town with a force of 400 men rather than the 150 marines noted in Admiral Cockburn's official report. Even when considering that each barge carried an average of up to a dozen marines, artillerymen, and officers as well as six to ten oarsmen, the number comes nowhere near the force size reported by the Cecil County historian.

40. Auchinleck, 265.

41. *American State Papers, Military Affairs,* 359. Johnston, 414, and Marine, 41, both state, without citing their sources, that the loss was valued at $20,000 to $30,000.

42. Johnston, 415.

43. *American State Papers, Military Affairs,* 359.

44. Marine, 41; Johnston, 414; Swepson Earle, *Maryland's Colonial Eastern Shore* (New York: Weathervane Books [facsimile of 1916]), 98.

45. Auchinleck, 265.

46. James, 82; Marine, 43. According to Marine, 41, the wharf was burned, but I have been unable to discover any record of this occurrence.

47. Master's Log, HMS *Maidstone,* 29 April 1813, ADM 52/4532, Public Record Office, London; Johnston, 415.

48. Johnston, 415, states that *Morning Star* was seen in Baltimore some years after the war, having been converted into a schooner hailing from Halifax, Nova Scotia.

49. Ibid., 493. Dr. Evans had served as a surgeon onboard the U.S. frigate *Constitution* and tended to Commodore Bainbridge, with whom he developed a lifelong friendship. He had participated in the battles with *Guerrier* and *Java* and was presented with two silver medals by Congress. He later served against the Algerians as fleet surgeon aboard *Independence.*

50. Johnston, 414.

51. Ibid., 406–7. For a comprehensive overview of the turnpike's history and development, see William F. Holmes, "The New Castle and Frenchtown Turnpike and Railroad Company, 1809–1838; Part III: From Horses to Locomotives," in *Delaware History* 10 (April, 1963).

52. Holly, 16–7.

53. *Baltimore Sun,* 12 June 1813; Robert H. Burgess and H. Graham Wood, *Steamboats Out of Baltimore* (Cambridge, Md.: Tidewater Publishers, 1968), xix.

54. Johnston, 424–5.

55. Burgess and Wood, xix; Holly, 159.

56. Burgess and Wood, xix.

57. Ibid., xix–xx.

58. Ibid., xx.

59. *Acts of Incorporation of the New Castle and Frenchtown Turnpike Company, Passed by the Legislatures of Maryland and Delaware* (Philadelphia, 1837); Johnston, 425–6; Alice E. Miller, *Cecil County, Maryland: A Study in Local History* (Port Deposit, Md.: Port Deposit Heritage, Inc., 1949), 48.

60. Gray, 71.

61. Miller, 48.

62. Johnston, 426.

63. Ibid., 427; Miller, 48.

64. Gray, 85, 87–8, 113.

65. Ibid., 88–9.

66. Johnston, 427–8; Miller, 49; Gray, 90.

67. Burgess and Wood, xx; Johnston, 426, 429.

68. Thomas Colley Grattan, *Civilized America* (London: Bradbury and Evans, 1859), 2: 161–2.

69. Burgess and Wood, xx, xxi.

CHAPTER 9: GEORGETOWN & FREDERICKTOWN

1. John Smith, *The Generall Historie of Virginia, New-England, and the Summer Isles* (London: Printed I. D. and I. J. for Michael Sparkes, 1624), 60. Kenny suggests Tockwough meant Sassafras. Hamill Kenny, *The Placenames of Maryland, Their Origin and Meaning* (Baltimore: Museum and Library of Maryland History, Maryland Historical Society, 1984), 232.

2. Smith, 60.

3. Ibid.

4. Ibid., 61.

5. Paul Wilstach, *Tidewater Maryland* (London: J. Stockdale, 1931), 117, 311; Hulbert Footner, *Maryland Main and the Eastern Shore,* (New York: D. Appleton-Century Company, 1942), 244.

6. Johnston, 28; Anne M. Hays and Harriet R. Hazleton, *Chesapeake Kaleidoscope* (Cambridge, Md.: Tidewater Publishers, 1975), 110; Johnston, 33, 88.

7. Johnston, 89.

8. *Archives,* 5: 47, 93; Augustine Herrman, *Virginia and Maryland,* (1670 [1673]), Geographic and Map Division, Library of Congress, Washington, D.C.

9. *Archives,* 16: 39; 51: 180–1, 479–80.

10. Ibid., 19: 159.

11. Johnston, 83.

12. *Archives,* 23: 356, 358–9.

13. Ibid., 27: 71, 160.

14. Ibid., 33: 39; Johnston, 247. The site is now known as Courthouse Point.

15. *Archives,* 39: 9, 14, 17, 62, 63, 67, 70, 342, 371–72, 373, 378, 381, 386, 392, 393, 413–14, 425, 436, 441, 446, 447, 456, 457, 460, 490–93.

16. Ibid., 324; John W. Reps, *Tidewater Towns: City Planning in Colonial Virginia and Maryland* (Williamsburg, Virginia: Colonial Williamsburg Foundation, 1972), 238–9.

17. *Archives,* 39: 490–3.

18. Johnston, 259.

19. *Archives,* 39: 490, 493.

20. Ibid., 493–6.

21. Ibid., 40: 98.

22. *Plat of Georgetown, Kent County, Maryland.* Unsigned and undated manuscript copy of a re-survey of Georgetown, Kent County, Maryland,

drawn by William Humphreys in 1787. Maryland Historical Society, Baltimore, Md.

23. *Routes Traveled by George Washington in Maryland, a Map Prepared for the Maryland Commission for the celebration of the Two Hundredth Anniversary of the Birth of George Washington, 1732–1932;* Alice E. Miller, *Cecil County, Maryland: A Study in Local History* (Port Deposit Md.: Port Deposit, Heritage, Inc., 1949), 33.

24. *At the Head of the Bay: A Cultural and Architectural History of Cecil County, Maryland,* Pamela James Blumgart, comp. (Crownsville and Elkton, Md.: Maryland Historical Trust and Cecil Historical Trust, Inc., 1996), 49; *Archives,* 44: 608, 609, 611; 50: 317, 319, 320, 321; 58: 329, 337, 449–50.

25. *Archives,* 50: 13.

26. Ibid., 1: 509, 521–2.

27. Ibid., 521–2.

28. Ibid., 55: 212, 307, 723.

29. Ibid., 212, 307.

30. *Maryland Gazette,* 4 September 1755; Basil Sollers, "The Acadians (French Neutrals) Transported to Maryland," *Maryland Historical Magazine* 3, no. 1 (March 1908): 5, 6; Johnston, 260–2.

31. Sollers, 9, 10, 11. See *Archives,* 1: 343, 345, 445, 471, for Sharpe's policies and support of the Acadians, and Sollers, 16–19, for support by the general population.

32. *Maryland Gazette,* 4 December 1755; Sollers, 11, 12, 13–4. See Sollers for a discussion of the Act, 13–6; Johnston, 262–3.

33. Johnson, 262–3.

34. Ibid., 263.

35. *Maryland Gazette,* 14 July 1757, 23 March 1758.

36. Ibid., 16 August 1759.

37. Reverend Andrew Burnaby, *Travels Through the Middle Settlements of North America, 1759 and 1760. With Observations on the State of the Colonies* (Ithaca: Cornell University Press, 1976, reprint of 1775), 51, 52.

38. Philip Vickers Fithian, *The Journal and Letters of Philip Vickers Fithian: A Plantation Tutor of The Old Dominion 1773–1774,* Hunter Dickinson Farish, ed., (Williamsburg, Va.: Colonial Williamsburg, Incorporated, 1965), 98.

39. Ibid.

40. Hays and Hazelton, 117; *Archives,* 43: 495.

41. *Revolution in America: Confidential Letters and Journals 1776–1784 of Adjutant General Major Baurmeister of the Hessian Forces,* translated and annotated by Bernard A. Uhlendorf (New Brunswick, N.J.: Rutgers University Press, 1957), 94–5.

42. L. G. Shreve, *Tench Tilghman: The Life and Times of Washington's Aide-de-Camp* (Centreville, Md.: Tidewater Publishers, 1982), 163.

43. Edward C. Papenfuse, *In Pursuit of Profit: The Annapolis Merchants in the Era of the American Revolution 1763–1805* (Baltimore: Johns Hopkins University Press, 1975), 179–80.

44. William S. Dudley, ed., *The Naval War of 1812: A Documentary History,* 2 vols. (Washington, D.C.: Naval Historical Center, Department of the Navy, 1985–1992), 2: 344.

45. Captain's Log of HMS *Mohawk,* 5 May 1813, PRO ADM. 51/2575, Public Record Office, London; *Narrative Respecting the Conduct of the British* [1814?], Library of Congress, Washington, D.C. (hereafter noted as *Narrative*), 32; Dudley, 2: 344; Master's Log of HMS *Maidstone,* 5 May 1813, PRO ADM. 52/4532, Public Record Office, London.

46. *American State Papers. Documents, Legislative and Executive, of the Congress of the United States:* vol. 1, *Military Affairs* (Washington, D.C.: 1832–1861), 359; *Narrative,* 30.

47. William M. Marine, *The British Invasion of Maryland 1812–1815.* (Hatboro, Pa.: Tradition Press, 1965, reprint of 1913), 46.

48. *American State Papers, Military Affairs,* 359; Dudley, 2: 344. Cockburn states that he ordered the boats to halt two miles below the towns, but according to the testimony of John Stavely, who was much more familiar with the river, they halted a mile from their targets.

49. *Narrative,* 28, 32. There is only one reference to the defense works on the Kent County side of the river on Pearce's Point, as its role was entirely negligible in the subsequent skirmish.

50. Ibid., 32; Johnston, 419–20; *American State Papers, Military Affairs,* 360.

51. Dudley, 2: 344.

52. Johnston, 420; *Narrative,* 32; Dudley, 2: 344.

53. Johnston, 420–1; Dudley, 2: 345.

54. *Narrative,* 33; *Daily National Intelligencer,* 14 May 1813.

55. Dudley, 2: 344–5.

56. Ibid., 345.

57. *Narrative,* 28, 29. The account of Captain John Allen in *Narrative,* 28, states that he observed the British approach from two and a half miles away. The list of the thirty-five defenders who stayed to fight includes James's name but not his brother John's.

58. Ibid., 28; *American State Papers, Military Affairs,* 361.

59. *Narrative,* 28.

60. Ibid., 29.

61. Ibid., 28.

62. Ibid., 29.

63. *American State Papers, Military Affairs,* 361.
64. Ibid., 360.
65. Ibid., 360–1.
66. Ibid.
67. *Narrative,* 30.
68. *American State Papers, Military Affairs,* 361.
69. Ibid., 362; *Narrative,* 31. Toilus Robertson is noted as Tylus Robinson in Johnston, 421.
70. *American State Papers, Military Affairs,* 361; *Narrative,* 31–2.
71. *Narrative,* 31, 33.
72. Ibid., 32, 33.
73. Ibid., 31.
74. Ibid., 30; Master's Log of HMS *Maidstone,* 6 May 1813.
75. "Miss Kitty Knight Defies the British," undated newspaper article, Kitty Knight House Collection, Georgetown, Md.
76. William H. Love, "Two Maryland Heroines," *Maryland Historical Magazine* 3, no. 1 (March 1908): 133; James F. Hurtt, Sr., "Kitty Knight 1776–1855 Georgetown, Maryland," undated typescript, Kitty Knight House Collection, 1; "History of the Brave Kitty Knight of Kent," undated newspaper clipping, Kitty Knight House Collection; Johnston, 359.
77. Hurtt, 1.
78. Ibid., 2.
79. Ibid., 1.
80. Love, 133. The visit to Philadelphia would have been in the 1797–1799 period when Matthew was serving in office, thus placing Kitty's age at between twenty-four and twenty-seven.
81. "History of the Brave Kitty Knight of Kent"; see Hulbert Footner, *Rivers of the Eastern Shore* (New York: Farrar & Rinehart Incorporated, 1944), 344–6, for popular account of Kitty Knight's life.
82. Love, 134; "History of the Brave Kitty Knight of Kent." Various accounts place her age at both thirty-five and thirty-six, but her tombstone notes she died on November 22, 1855, at the age of seventy-nine, which would place her birth at 1776–1777. Thus she would have been between thirty-six and thirty-seven years of age. Lane, 134; Hurtt, 3; George and Virginia Schaun, *Biographical Sketches of Maryland* (Annapolis: Greenberry Publications, 1969), 66; Kitty Knight tombstone, Old Bohemia Church.
83. Love, 135. The account was said to have been related by Kitty to her nephew, William A. Knight. "History of the Brave Kitty Knight of Kent"; Schaun, 66; Footner, 344–6, et seq. The identity of the Widow Pearce, or Persie, is only speculative, but as she is the only female resident on the Georgetown side whose house was listed as plundered of furniture and stores but spared

total destruction, it is likely. In *Narrative,* 30, she is identified by name as Pierce, and she may have resided in the home of the late James Pearce. In *Narrative,* 31, it is stated that the British pushed no further into the Kent County countryside than James Pearce's "about a short half mile down the river where they did no damage except pilfering a little, and bore off some spoons." Kitty's defiant demeanor, however, was certainly evident, but has been magnified to legendary proportions by the lens of time, even though others in the two towns also took bold individual stands against the invaders. Many unfounded stories erupted over the following years. One such tale related that after the town had suffered from the "hard day of burning and plundering," Kitty made a deal with the admiral and cooked a large meal for him and his officers, after which she read to him in her private sitting room and was obliged to stave off his amorous advances. Another account suggested that she shocked the hardened British veterans with her cursing, which held them at bay. Yet another had her "shooing them away with a pan of boiling water." Twice they attempted to start a fire and twice she put it out. An even more interesting account was that after the war "Commodore Cockburn" was raised in rank. He returned to the United States and visited Georgetown to offer his hand in marriage to her but was turned down. This is a pleasant story, but Cockburn was already married to Mary Cockburn, his cousin, who would survive him. He never returned to Maryland, although he visited the American station in 1833. "History of the Brave Kitty Knight of Kent"; typescript on Kitty Knight House; Kitty Knight House Collection, 5; "Miss Kitty Knight Defies the British"; Hurtt, 3. For Cockburn's subsequent career, see James Pack, *The man who Burned the White House: Admiral Sir George Cockburn 1772-1853* (Annapolis: Naval Institute Press, 1987), 179–276.
84. Love, 135; *Narrative,* 30, 31; *American State Papers, Military Affairs,* 361. The British left behind them no fewer than two dozen homes, shops, carriage houses, and a granary, all afire in Georgetown. Only three or four houses were spared destruction. Damage was reported to a small log house containing trifling property belonging to Philip Rasin; a house belonging to Miss Ann Pierce; Mr. Bagwell's shoemakers shop, tools, and stock; Francis O'Neill's dwelling house; Negro Step's house; Robert Elliot's house; Mary Henry's house; Mrs. Mary Evert's home and carriage house; Robert Elliot's home; Mary Henry's storehouse; Widow Persies's house, which was plundered and her furniture

destroyed but the building was saved; William Ireland's house; the home of Widow Down, a black lady; Widow Susan Wilson's house; the home of Jacob Road, a black man; Hastleton's Tavern, which was burned to the ground and part of the furniture destroyed; Mr. Dun Levy's (Donleavy's ?) house, where Colonel Spencer formerly resided, burnt with loss of furniture; tailor Arthur Nicholson's house; Widow Isabella Freeman's house; Mr. Jackson's storehouse, dwelling house, and granary; William Abbot's house; and William Knight's house. *Narrative,* 30.

85. *Narrative,* 30; *American State Papers, Military Affairs,* 359, 362; Dudley, 2: 345; Johnston, 422. Johnston states that the inhabitants actually requested to shake hands with the admiral, and that among those who greeted him were two inhabitants of Georgetown who had persuaded the local citizenry to adopt a peaceable demeanor. A deputation from Havre de Grace, recently burned, was also received aboard HMS *Maidstone* before Cockburn's return. Marine, 48; Master's Log of HMS *Maidstone,* 5 May 1813; Log of HMS *Mohawk,* 5 May 1813.

86. Dudley, 2: 345.

87. *American State Papers, Military Affairs,* 359.

88. *Daily National Intelligencer,* 10 May 1813.

89. Ibid., 14 May 1813.

90. It seems more likely that the blankets and cloth were used to cover stolen booty rather than citizens. With the exception of the temporary arrest of several residents, such as Captain James Allen, no account has been found to indicate the British carried out any kidnapping at this time.

91. *Narrative,* 33.

92. *Daily National Intelligencer,* 14 May 1813.

93. G. Auchinleck, *History of the War between Great Britain and the United States of America During the Years 1812, 1813 & 1814* (Redwood City, Calif.: Arms & Armour Press and Pendragon House Inc., 1972), 271.

94. *American State Papers, Military Affairs,* 1: 359; *Daily National Intelligencer,* 14 May 1813.

95. *American State Papers, Military Affairs,* 362.

96. Ibid., 363.

97. Marine, 51–2.

98. *Daily National Intelligencer,* 14 May 1813.

99. David C. Holly, *Tidewater by Steamboat: A Saga of the Chesapeake* (Baltimore: Johns Hopkins University Press, 1991), 36, 81, 231.

100. "Miss Kitty Knight Defies the British."

101. "History of the Brave Kitty Knight of Kent;" Register of Wills for Kent County, no. 1, f. 60; Schaun, 66.

102. *The 1877 Atlases and Other Early Maps of the Eastern Shore of Maryland* (Salisbury, Md.: Wicomico Bicentennial Commission, 1976), 115, 120.

103. *Rediscovery of the Eastern Shore: Delmarva Travelogues of the 1870's,* Harold D. Jopp, Jr., ed., (Wye Mills, Md.: Chesapeake College Press, 1986), 49.

104. *Kitty Knight House Catalogue,* Kitty Knight House Collection, Georgetown, Md.

105. Ibid.

106. Typescript on Kitty Knight House, 5–6.

107. Robin Warshaw, "Hosts to the Ghosts," *Mid-Atlantic Country,* October 1994, 53. The Hurtt story was recorded by James F. Hurtt, Sr., the oldest living resident in Georgetown as it was related to him when he was a child by the town elders, including his grandmother Mrs. J. T. M. Woodall and his great-uncle Andrew Woodall. The Woodalls owned the Kitty Knight House and were ten to twelve years old at the time Kitty died. Hurtt, 3.

INDEX

Ships by name are indexed under "Vessels"

Labidists, 249, 267
Lacey, Capt. Joseph, 221
Lacey and Smith, 217
Ladd, Capt. Richard, 45
Lafayette, Gen., 259
La Grange, 206, 211, 245
Laidler's Ferry, Md., 203, 230
Lambert, Christopher, 182
Lambeth, Anne, 63
Lancashire, Eng., 16
Lancaster, Thomas, 170
Lane, H. F., 131
Langley, Dr. Susan, 112
Lansdale, Maj. Thomas Lancaster, 175, 176, 177, 179, 183
Lansdale Branch, Md., 179
La Plata, Md., 198, 236, 237, 238, 240, 241, 242
Largent, J. J., 128
Largents Chapel, 113, 128, 129, 130
Larkin, John, 61, 62, 63
Larkin, Thomas, 161
Larkins, George, 189
Larkins, Thomas, 11
Larrimore, James, 84
Larrimore, Mary, 84
Latrobe, Benjamin H., 252
Laurel, Md., 166
La Ville Francaise, 249
Lawrence, John, 39
Lawrence, Capt. John, 278
Lawrence, Thomas, 162
Lax, Captain ____, 70
Leckie, Frank, 140
Lee, Hancock, 143
Lee, Philip, 170
Lee, Gen. Robert E., 55, 230, 231
Lee, Thomas Sim, 116, 144, 147
Leonardson, Leonard, 90, 91
Leonardtown, Md., 28, 216, 220, 227
Letchworth, Thomas, 38, 46
Letchworth's Chance, Calvert County, 38
Lewis, John, 78
Lewis, Lt. T., 254
Liberty Boys of Charles County, 211
Lilburn, Andrew J., 190
Lincoln, Abraham, 225, 230, 231; assassination, 127, 231; Lincoln-Hamlin ticket, 225
Lindsey, Edmund, 197–98
Lingan, George, 47
Linthicum, Thomas, 61
Literary Debating Society, 216, 218, 219
Little Bohemia River. See Bohemia River
Little Choptank River, 19
Little Elk Creek, 248
Liverpool, Eng., 66, 70
Liverpool Point, Md., 229, 234
Lloyd, Benjamin, 169

Lloyd, Edward, 17
Lloyd, Thomas, 68
Lockwood, Edward W., 271
London, Eng. 16, 38, 65, 66, 68, 69, 77, 78, 92, 95, 119, 134, 143, 157, 164, 170, 172, 176, 195, 204, 210, 273, 277
London Bridge Chapter of the Daughters of the American Revolution, 295
London Town, Md., 57, 60, 61, 62, 63, 64, 65, 55, 67, 68, 70, 71, 72, 73, 75, 76, 77, 78, 79, 80, 82, 83, 84, 85, 172; Catholic chapel, 62; courthouse, 61, 63; plat of, 60; streets: Back Street, 76; Church Street, 65, 66, 76; Cross Street, 65; Fish Street, 66, 76; Fleet Street, 65, 76; High Street, 75, 76; Lombard (Lumber) Street, 65, 76; Macklefresh Street, 76; Market Street, 67; Moore Street, 67, 76; Queen Street, 65, 76; Scott Street, 76; Small Street, 66; Watling Street, 67, 76; lots sold, 61, 63, 65, 66, 67, 75, 78, 83, 84
London Town Manufactury, 79, 81
London Town Publik House, 59, 73, 83, 84
London Town Publik House and Gardens, 87
London Town Publik House Commission, 57
Longfellow, Henry Wadsworth, 275
Long Point, Md., 268
Lort, Capt. Isaac, 255, 256, 257
Lost Towns of Anne Arundel County Project, 87
Lothian, Md., 175
Loudon County, Va., 54
Louisiana, 149, 193
Lowe, Col. Vincent, 11, 44
Lower Cedar Point, Md. 225
Lower Cliffs Hundred, 99, 101
Lower Marlborough (Lower Marlboro), Md. 101, 108, 114, 115, 116, 117, 118, 119, 120, 121, 122, 123, 124, 125, 126, 127, 128, 129, 130, 131, 133, 134, 135, 136, 139, 143, 146, 148, 149, 150, 167; academy, 118, 119, 123, 126, 129; buildings: Armiger House, 133; Cox House, 135, 136; David Carcaud House, 133; Grahame House, 117; Green Gable House, 133; Hinman's Store, 133; Mechanics Hall, 127; Methodist Church, 128; Millennia, 133; Sign of the Crown Inn, 117, 133; Spicknall House, 133; Windmill Hill, 127; post office, 113; streets: Goose Lane, 127; Varden Street, 127
Lower Marlborough Hundred, 122
Lowndes, Lloyd, 188
Lowndes, Richard J., 148
Luckenbach, Al, 87
Lusby, Jacob, 73
Lusby, Robert C., 291
Lyles, Thomas C., 182
Lynes, Philip 198
Lynnhaven Bay, Va., 288